HEALTH

A WELLNESS APPROACH

Linda Meeks-Mitchell, M.S.
Associate Professor of Health Education
College of Education
The Ohio State University
Columbus, Ohio

Philip Heit, Ed.D.
Professor and Chairman of Health Education
College of Education
Professor of Allied Medicine
College of Medicine
The Ohio State University
Columbus, Ohio

MERRILL
PUBLISHING COMPANY

A Bell & Howell Company
Columbus, Ohio
Toronto   London   Sydney

A Merrill Health Program

Health: A Wellness Approach, *Student Edition*
Health: A Wellness Approach, *Teacher Edition*
Health: A Wellness Approach, *Teacher Resource Book*
Sexuality: A Responsible Approach, *Student Edition*
Sexuality: A Responsible Approach, *Teacher Annotated Edition*

Linda Meeks-Mitchell and Philip Heit are the coauthors of *Health: Focus on You*, Merrill Publishing Company's K to 8 health program. Both authors conduct workshops in health science, curriculum design, and health methodology, in addition to the courses they teach at The Ohio State University. Both authors have taught health education in public schools. Mrs. Meeks-Mitchell and Dr. Heit have individually authored articles and texts. Mrs. Meeks-Mitchell is a coauthor of *Toward a Healthy Lifestyle Through Elementary Health Education*. Mrs. Meeks-Mitchell and Dr. Heit are the coauthors of *Teaching Health in Middle and Secondary Schools*.

Consultants

Robert T. Brown, M.D., Associate Professor of Clinical Pediatrics and Director, Division of Adolescent Medicine, The Ohio State University, Columbus, Ohio

Gus T. Dalis, Ed.D., Consultant, Health Education, Los Angeles County Office of Education, Downey, California

Florence M. Fenton, Ed.D., Supervisor of Health Education/Health Services, Prince George's County Public Schools, Upper Marlboro, Maryland

Todd F. Holzman, M.D., Child Psychiatrist, Harvard Community Health Plan, Wellesley, Massachusetts

Rick Kearns, M.S.Ed., Director: Center for Fitness/Wellness, Idaho State University, Pocatello, Idaho

Deborah C. Masters, R.N., B.S.N., M.A., Evanston, Illinois

Daniel P. Stanley, Ed.D., Department Chair HPER, Glassboro State College, Glassboro, New Jersey

Content Specialists

Safety
Wilbur M. Luce, Ed.D., Former District Coordinator of Health, Safety, and Physical Education, Waco Independent School District, Waco, Texas

Dental Health
John D. Mahilo, D.D.S., Gahanna, Ohio

Substance Abuse
Stuart Weibel, Ph.D., OCLC Office of Research, Dublin, Ohio

Nutrition
Barbara J. White, M.A., R.D., Public Health Nutritionist, St. Lukes-Roosevelt Hospital Center, New York, New York

Reviewers

Douglas J. Bunch, M.A., Teacher, Prescott High School, Prescott, Arizona

Charles A. DeCorsey, M.Ed., Teacher, Richfield Senior High School, Richfield, Minnesota

Charlene C. Gerak, M.Ed., Teacher, Parma Senior High School, Parma, Ohio

Lynne E. Kahn, Ph.D., District Coordinator, Health and Physical Education, White Plains Public Schools, White Plains, New York

Diane S. Scalise, R.N., M.S., Supervisor, Health Education, The School Board of Broward County, Fort Lauderdale, Florida

Ann Shelton, Ph. D., Health Curriculum Specialist, Portland Public Schools, Portland, Oregon

Project Editor: Mary Baker; *Editors:* Nerma C. Henderson, Debra L. Sommers; *Project Designer:* Patrick J. McCarthy; *Project Artist:* Dennis L. Smith; *Illustrator:* Nancy A. Heim; *Photo Editor:* Barbara Buchholz; *Production Editor:* Annette Hoffman; *Computer Charts:* Slidemasters, Inc. / Barb Cagley

Cover: A person's health status is a combination of healthful and risk behaviors. When you choose healthful behaviors, you move toward a higher level of wellness and optimum health. Cover photographs: Pictures Unlimited, Ted Rice, Edward Kumler

ISBN 0-675-07860-1

Published by
Merrill Publishing Company
A Bell & Howell Company
Columbus, Ohio 43216

PREFACE

Thomas Edison once said, "If we did all the things that we were capable of doing, we would literally astonish ourselves." You can apply Edison's statement to your health. A study by the Centers for Disease Control shows that you can reduce your risk of disease and possible premature death by making responsible decisions about your health. Approximately 53 percent of your ability to cope with disease is determined by your lifestyle. Another 21 percent is determined by your environment. Your physician can help you control another 10 percent. Only 16 percent is beyond your control or determined by heredity. Therefore, this study indicates that you can influence or control 84 percent of your ability to cope with disease.

Health: A Wellness Approach is designed to assist you in effective life management. By using this textbook, you will acquire knowledge about skills that are needed to become independent adults and to achieve optimum health. You will design health behavior contracts to practice these skills. You will be encouraged to set goals and use self-discipline to reach those goals.

Your first step is to focus attention on your attitudes and behaviors and how they affect your mental, social, and physical health. *Health: A Wellness Approach* will give you that opportunity. The textbook consists of an introductory chapter and eleven units. Chapter 1 discusses the process of achieving a healthful lifestyle and introduces the concept of wellness. Unit 1 contains three chapters that provide background information about the structure and function of your body systems. Units 2 through 11 contain information about ten important areas of your life: Mental Health, Family and Social Health, Growth and Development, Nutrition, Exercise and Fitness, Drugs, Diseases and Disorders, Consumer and Personal Health, Safety and First Aid, and Community and Environmental Health. In these units, you will discover how one behavior can have a holistic effect on your health. You will learn to differentiate between those behaviors that have healthful effects and those that have harmful effects. You will learn how to make responsible decisions in each of the ten areas of health.

Think again about Thomas Edison's statement. Astonish yourself by proving you can set and meet personal goals. Adopt the life management skills suggested in *Health: A Wellness Approach* for a rewarding, healthful lifestyle.

TABLE OF CONTENTS

Unit 1
UNDERSTANDING THE HUMAN BODY

Unit 2
MENTAL HEALTH

Unit 7
DRUGS

Unit 8
DISEASES AND DISORDERS

Chapter 19
COMMUNICABLE DISEASES

Chapter 20
CARDIOVASCULAR DISEASES AND CANCER

Chapter 21
CHRONIC HEALTH PROBLEMS

Unit 9
CONSUMER AND PERSONAL HEALTH

Unit 10
SAFETY AND FIRST AID

Unit 11
COMMUNITY AND ENVIRONMENTAL HEALTH

Chapter 26
COMMUNITY AND WORLD HEALTH

Chapter 27
ENVIRONMENTAL HEALTH

The day is beautiful. You have planned for this moment, and now you are here. You want to pause long enough to really see the beauty around you. You feel wonderful. You wonder what it will be like at the top of the mountain. You are ready.

Chapter 1

Self-Responsibility for Wellness

OBJECTIVES: You will be able to
- **set goals and make and follow plans for optimum health.**
- **describe the holistic effects of wellness and risk behaviors.**
- **design a health behavior contract and use a responsible decision-making model.**
- **demonstrate that a healthful lifestyle is a priority to you.**

What would it be like to climb to the top of a snow-covered mountain? The hikers in the photo have wanted to do this for a long time. They made many plans to accomplish this goal. If you were making such a trip, what would you do to get ready?

GOALS

First, you would set a goal. A **goal** is a desired achievement toward which you work. It is important to have goals to have purpose and meaning in life. A person who sets goals works with dedication and energy. What goals do you have? If you were the mountain climber in the photo, your goal would be to reach the top of the mountain.

1:1 Making Plans

After setting a goal, your next step is to make a plan. A **plan** is a detailed description of the steps you will take to reach your goal. If you were to climb this mountain, you would gather information about the trails leading to the top. You would list the supplies you would need. You might purchase special clothing to climb the mountain. What safety precautions will be necessary?

Goals and plans to reach the goals give meaning and purpose to life.

FIGURE 1–1. Making plans for a hike involves paying attention to many details. Some members of the group may plan the route to take; others may plan food for the group.

Who will go with you? What obstacles might you encounter? How will you deal with them? How long will it take you to get ready? How long will the actual trip take? A time frame is important when you make plans.

1:2 Striving to Reach Goals

Promote a healthful lifestyle by setting goals and following through with your plans.

You are finally ready to start your journey. You are confident and excited. You carefully follow each step of your plan. You overcome obstacles such as fatigue, unmarked trails, and heat. It takes many hours to climb this mountain. Finally, you reach your goal. What an exhilarating moment! You have completed what you set out to do. You feel good about yourself.

The same process you would use to prepare to climb the mountain can be used to achieve a healthful lifestyle. Your **lifestyle** is the way in which you live. To have a healthful lifestyle, you must set healthful goals, make plans, and follow them to reach your goals.

 Review and Reflect

1. How is a plan for healthful living similar to a plan for climbing a mountain?
2. What healthful goal do you have? What is your plan to reach this goal?

HEALTH PROMOTION

Every day you make many choices. How do these choices affect your lifestyle? Consider a lifestyle that focuses on health and health promotion.

1:3 Health and Wellness

Health is a quality of life that includes your physical, mental, and social well-being. Physical health is the condition of the body. Mental health is the condition of the mind and the emotions. Social health is the way you relate to others. Your health involves a continual state of adjustment of these areas to your heredity and environment.

Wellness is another way to describe quality of life. The wellness approach to good health includes all areas of your life and their relationship to and effect on one another. To obtain a high level of wellness, you take responsibility for your own health. This involves choosing behaviors that will promote good health for you and your environment and help prevent disease and poor health.

Behaviors that promote good health or wellness may be called healthful or wellness behaviors. A **healthful behavior** is an action that helps prevent illness and accidents, helps promote health for you and others, or improves the quality of the environment. Some examples of healthful or wellness behaviors are wearing a seat belt, exercising regularly, eating healthful foods, and getting sufficient rest and relaxation.

Behaviors that do not promote good health or wellness may be called harmful or risk behaviors. A **risk behavior** is an action that helps increase the likelihood of illness and accidents, threatens your health and the health of others, or helps destroy the environment. Some examples of harmful or risk behaviors are riding a motorcycle without a helmet, smoking cigarettes, and using illegal drugs. Your lifestyle is a major influence on your well-being. Your quality of life depends on whether you select healthful or risk behaviors.

1:4 Health Promotion

Health promotion is the informing and motivating of people to maintain or adopt healthful behaviors. Suppose you become interested in taking steps to prevent having heart disease. You learn that certain foods might affect your heart; you avoid those foods. You learn that exercise strengthens your heart; you exer-

The quality of your life is influenced by the behaviors you choose.

FIGURE 1–2. On a rafting trip, it is vital to choose behaviors that will promote safety. Everyone wears a life vest.

FIGURE 1–3. Risk behaviors cause a holistic effect. A behavior in any one of the ten components affects one or more of the other components.

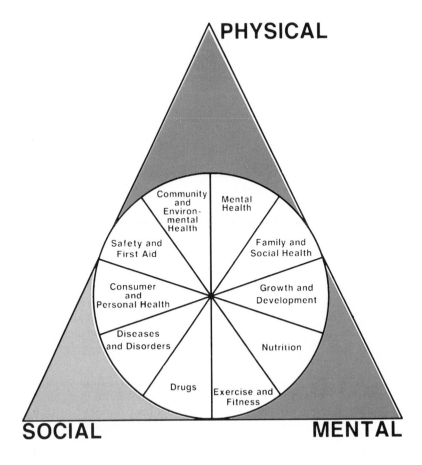

PHYSICAL

SOCIAL   MENTAL

Community and Environmental Health

Mental Health

Safety and First Aid

Family and Social Health

Consumer and Personal Health

Growth and Development

Diseases and Disorders

Drugs

Exercise and Fitness

Nutrition

cise on a regular basis. You eat nutritious foods and get sufficient sleep each night. Each of these behaviors would be a part of a health promotion program for a healthier heart.

The goal of health promotion is optimum health. **Optimum health** is the best condition of health possible for you. You can achieve optimum health by choosing healthful behaviors and making the most of your heredity and environment.

1:5   A Balanced Lifestyle

A health triangle (Figure 1–3) has three points—physical, mental, and social. These points of the triangle represent the three kinds of health that contribute to a balanced lifestyle.

Inside the triangle is a wheel. The wheel is composed of ten components, or parts, that relate to health and wellness: (1) Mental Health, (2) Family and Social Health, (3) Growth and Development, (4) Nutrition, (5) Exercise and Fitness, (6) Drugs, (7) Diseases and Disorders, (8) Consumer and Personal Health,

When you are informed and motivated to maintain and adopt healthful behaviors, you are more likely to achieve optimum health.

(9) Safety and First Aid, and (10) Community and Environmental Health. Every day you choose healthful or risk behaviors in each of these ten components. We can refer to the wheel as a Behavior Wheel.

Look at the center of the Behavior Wheel. A large black dot in the center connects the ten components. This black dot represents the holistic (or wholistic) effect that any behavior has on your health. Holistic means whole. The **holistic effect** means that a healthful or risk behavior in any one of the ten components may affect one or more of the other components.

Suppose you placed a single drop of dark ink into a glass of water. Within seconds the water would become dark. All the water in the glass would be affected by the one drop of ink. This represents a holistic effect.

A single behavior can affect your health in a similar way. Healthful and risk behaviors cause holistic effects. A healthful behavior has desirable effects on the whole person. A regular routine of running or walking is a healthful behavior that helps prevent illness and promotes optimum health. You may run or walk for 20 minutes three times a week to improve your fitness level. This healthful behavior represents the Exercise and Fitness component of the wheel. However, other components of the Behavior Wheel can also be affected (Table 1–1).

Your risk behaviors will also have a holistic effect on your health. Suppose you eat two donuts and drink a beverage containing caffeine for breakfast. This kind of breakfast represents a risk behavior. Why? It does not contain the kinds of nutrients your

A single healthful or risk behavior has a holistic effect on your lifestyle.

Table 1–1 Positive Holistic Effects

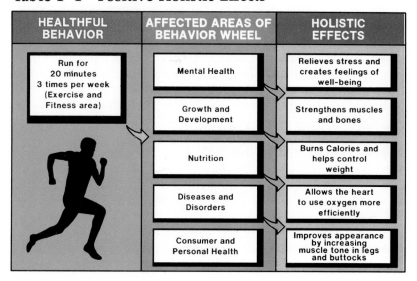

HEALTHFUL BEHAVIOR	AFFECTED AREAS OF BEHAVIOR WHEEL	HOLISTIC EFFECTS
Run for 20 minutes 3 times per week (Exercise and Fitness area)	Mental Health	Relieves stress and creates feelings of well-being
	Growth and Development	Strengthens muscles and bones
	Nutrition	Burns Calories and helps control weight
	Diseases and Disorders	Allows the heart to use oxygen more efficiently
	Consumer and Personal Health	Improves appearance by increasing muscle tone in legs and buttocks

Table 1–2 Negative Holistic Effects

RISK BEHAVIOR	AFFECTED AREAS OF BEHAVIOR WHEEL	HOLISTIC EFFECTS
Eat two donuts and drink a beverage containing level caffeine for breakfast (Nutrition area)	Mental Health	A high-sugar breakfast uses up Vitamin B necessary for a healthy nervous system
	Growth and Development	This breakfast lacks nutrients needed for proper growth
	Exercise and Fitness	This breakfast lacks nutrients needed to maintain energy throughout the morning
	Drugs	Caffeine is a drug that stimulates the central nervous system and increases heart rate
	Consumer and Personal Health	Sugar increases the likelihood of tooth decay; inadequate nutrition may cause weight-control problems

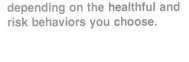

body needs to work efficiently. Your risk behavior represents the Nutrition component of the Behavior Wheel. Risk behaviors can also cause changes in other areas of your life (Table 1–2).

1:6   A Health Scale

Your health status fluctuates depending on the healthful and risk behaviors you choose.

Your health fluctuates daily depending upon the choices you make. Your **health status** is the combination of the healthful and risk behaviors you select. When you choose healthful behaviors, you move toward a higher level of wellness and optimum health. When you choose risk behaviors, you threaten your health and move toward illness and possible premature death. However, all healthful behaviors and all risk behaviors are not of equal importance. Some healthful behaviors are more beneficial to you than others. Some risk behaviors are more harmful to you than others. The ranges of health are illustrated (Figure 1–4).

  Review and Reflect

3. Why is there an emphasis on health promotion?
4. What is the difference between a healthful behavior and a risk behavior?
5. How can you control your health status?
6. What is one healthful behavior you chose today?
7. What is one risk behavior you chose today?

RESPONSIBLE HEALTH BEHAVIOR

There are four important steps in achieving optimum health.

- *Acquire health knowledge.* If you have health knowledge, you are better able to differentiate between healthful and risk behaviors.
- *Examine your behaviors to develop health awareness.* You must be aware of the behaviors you are choosing to promote your optimum health. At the same time, you must also be aware of the risk behaviors you are choosing that may increase the likelihood of disease or premature death.
- *Set personal health goals and design a specific plan to reach each goal.* After you examine your behaviors and identify the risk behaviors, assume the responsibility of changing these into healthful behaviors. You can do this by carefully stating your personal health goals. Then you can devise step-by-step plans to meet these goals.
- *Make responsible health decisions.* Whenever you have several behaviors from which you can choose, you must evaluate each. You must decide which behavior is the most healthful. This textbook will provide you with a strong foundation in each of the ten health components so that you can evaluate your own behaviors and make responsible decisions.

FIGURE 1–4. Your health status is a combination of the wellness and risk behaviors you choose.

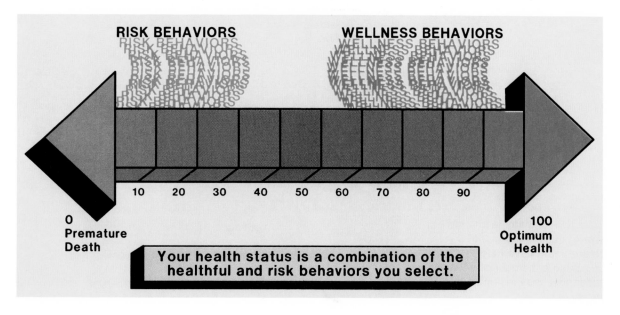

1:7 Health Awareness

Every day you are gaining knowledge about facts that affect your health. What magazines or newspapers do you read? What TV programs that feature health information do you watch? Are you aware that magazines, newspapers, and TV programs are sources of health information? **Health awareness** is the knowledge you gain about your own health behaviors. Using this knowledge, you can get a clear picture of your own health status. You learn that decisions you make result in healthful or risk behaviors.

Health appraisal is an evaluation of healthful behaviors and risk behaviors. One method of evaluation is a health behavior inventory. A health behavior inventory contains statements about health behaviors (Table 1–3). The directions for answering the inventory are simple; answer yes or no to each statement. A yes answer indicates you are promoting optimum health, and you are aware of behaviors you should continue. A no answer indicates that your behavior may lead to illness and/or possible premature death. A no answer should make you aware of behaviors you need to change. Although you should try to change all no answers, it is important to remember that some behaviors are more harmful than others.

Gain health awareness by completing a health appraisal (Table 1–3).

Some risk behaviors are more harmful and/or dangerous than others.

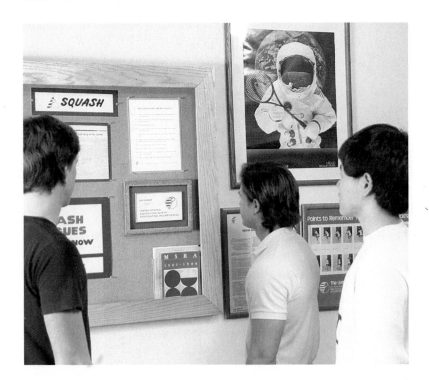

FIGURE 1–5. Many teams have lists of qualifications that a person must have before becoming a member of a team. These lists may resemble a health inventory.

Table 1–3   Sample Health Behavior Inventory

MENTAL HEALTH
1. I have a plan to relieve the effects of stress.
2. I like myself.

FAMILY AND SOCIAL HEALTH
3. I have at least one close friend.
4. I am able to share some of my feelings with my parents.

GROWTH AND DEVELOPMENT
5. I maintain my desirable weight.
6. I have correct sitting posture.

NUTRITION
7. I eat a well-balanced diet from the four healthful food groups.
8. I limit my intake of fatty foods.

EXERCISE AND FITNESS
9. I get at least six to eight hours of sleep each night.
10. I participate in a regular exercise program to strengthen my heart.

DRUGS
11. I refrain from drinking alcohol.
12. I avoid smoking.

DISEASES AND DISORDERS
13. I know the seven warning signals for cancer.
14. I avoid spreading germs when I have a cold.

CONSUMER AND PERSONAL HEALTH
15. I read labels on food cans and packages to determine the ingredients.
16. I select television shows that promote mental health and stimulate my mind.

SAFETY AND FIRST AID
17. I wear a seat belt when riding in an automobile.
18. I have smoke detectors in my home.

COMMUNITY AND ENVIRONMENTAL HEALTH
19. I buy returnable bottles whenever possible.
20. I properly dispose of trash.

1:8 A Health Behavior Contract

You show commitment to healthful behavior when you design and complete a health behavior contract.

Knowing facts and being aware of your health behavior are two important steps in working toward optimum health. Yet, these steps are futile if you do not choose healthful actions. To achieve optimum health, you must set goals and make plans to increase healthful behaviors and avoid risk behaviors. A **health behavior contract** is a specific plan that is followed to reach a desired health goal. A health behavior contract includes your signature and the date of your commitment to a healthful behavior; the name or topic of the health area upon which you are working; a specific goal that indicates a specific healthful behavior toward which you will work; a detailed description of how you plan to reach the goal and a time period for following the plan; a description or way of recording your progress in following your plan to reach the desired goal; and a statement that describes how this healthful behavior would improve your lifestyle.

A Health Behavior Contract on nutrition is included as a sample (Figure 1–6).

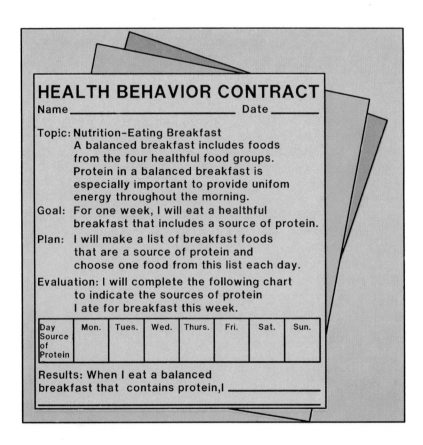

FIGURE 1–6. A Health Behavior Contract can be designed to help a person work toward optimum health in any of the health components.

1:9 Making Responsible Decisions About Health

You make many decisions every day about a variety of subjects. Think about some of the decisions you have already made today. Decisions that promote optimum health for you and others are **responsible decisions.** How can you know if you are making a responsible decision?

The **problem-solving approach** is a series of steps you apply to a situation to help you make a responsible decision. Consider each of the following steps in the problem-solving approach.

1. *Identify the problem.*
2. *Identify ways to deal with the problem.* There is usually more than one way to deal with a problem.
3. *Apply criteria for responsible decision making to each alternative.* There are five criteria that can be used to identify decisions that lead to responsible actions. The criteria are questions to ask yourself. For some decisions, all five criteria do not apply.
   - Would the results of my decision be healthful?
   - Would the results of my decision be safe?
   - Would the results of my decision be legal?
   - Would the results of my decision show respect for myself and others?
   - Would the results of my decision follow my parents' or guardian's guidelines?
4. *Make a responsible decision and act upon it.* After you have applied the five criteria to each possible alternative, make a responsible decision and act upon it. A responsible decision leads to behaviors that are healthful, safe, legal, show respect for self and others, and follow parents' guidelines (Figure 1–7). A responsible decision helps keep the environment healthful.
5. *Evaluate your actions.* To evaluate means to judge or rate. When you make a decision, you should evaluate the results. When you make responsible decisions, you feel good about yourself and your ability to make those decisions.

Healthful?
Safe?
Legal?
Respectful of self?
Follows parents' guidelines?

FIGURE 1–7. When you make responsible decisions, you feel good about yourself.

Responsible decisions result in actions that are healthful, safe, legal, respectful of self and others and follow parental guidelines.

 ## Review and Reflect

8. What are four steps in achieving optimum health?
9. How can completing a health behavior inventory benefit you?
10. How can you know if you are making a responsible decision?

PRIORITIES

Knowing what is important to your optimum health is only the beginning. Applying that knowledge by choosing responsible behaviors is necessary for reaching your goal of good health.

1:10   Commitment to a Healthful Lifestyle

Thomas Edison once said, "If we did all the things that we were capable of doing, we would literally astonish ourselves." Edison's statement can be applied to your level of wellness. A study by the Centers for Disease Control shows that you can reduce your risk of disease and possible premature death by making responsible decisions about your health. Consider these statistics. Approximately 53 percent of your ability to control disease is determined by your lifestyle. Another 21 percent is determined by the environment in which you live. Your physician can help you control 10 percent. Only 16 percent of your ability to handle disease is beyond your control or determined by your heredity. The study concluded that you can influence or control 84 percent of your ability to cope with disease. Figure 1–8 lists the leading causes of death for people your age. Relate this information to the above statistics.

To achieve optimum health, you must make it a priority (pri OR ut ee). A **priority** is something you consider to be of great importance. If optimum health is a priority for you, you will demonstrate that by your actions. You will assume responsibility for the areas of your health that are in your power to control. You will set health goals and choose healthful behaviors. You will make plans, follow them to completion, and have a strong commitment to good health.

It is important that you recognize the need for commitment, priority, and self-discipline. **Commitment** involves a promise to yourself that you will schedule your time so that your priorities can be realized. **Self-discipline** is the effort or energy with which you follow your plan to achieve optimum health. Suppose you have agreed to a health behavior contract similar to the one on

You can influence or control 84 percent of your ability to cope with disease.

When you make optimum health a priority, you assume responsibility to choose healthful behaviors.

FIGURE 1–8. The leading causes of teenage deaths

page 12. You make this commitment a priority by assigning some of your time to follow through with this plan. You plan to eat high-protein foods for breakfast. You get up early enough to eat breakfast. You exercise self-discipline to follow through with your plan.

It may be difficult to exercise the self-discipline needed to achieve your goals. If this is the case, you may need extra help in using self-discipline. Here are some suggestions you can use to motivate yourself.

- *Keep reminding yourself about your goal.* You are more likely to use self-discipline to complete a health behavior contract when the goal is foremost in your mind. One way to do this is to write your goal on five index cards. Put these cards in places where you will see them (1) a wallet or purse, (2) on a mirror in your bedroom, (3) on the refrigerator door, (4) next to your bed, and (5) on your desk at home or at school. Look at these cards several times each day.

- *Establish a reward system.* Perhaps you set a goal to be able to run five miles. You plan a running program in which you gradually increase your mileage. You decide to reward yourself with new running shorts when you are able to run three miles. A reward provides positive reinforcement to help you stick to your health behavior contract.

- *Select healthy role models.* The people with whom you associate influence you. Some of these people choose healthful behaviors while others choose risk behaviors. When you are working toward a goal, it is helpful to be with others who choose healthful behaviors. You may decide to quit smoking because it is a risk behavior. When you first stop, it may be very difficult. Suppose you have lunch with a friend who lights a cigarette and begins to smoke. Because you have a craving for a cigarette, you may find it difficult to maintain your self-discipline. On the other hand, you could eat lunch with a nonsmoker. You and your friend could sit in the nonsmoking section of the restaurant. Now, you have additional reinforcement to help you stick to your commitment to stop smoking.

You are more likely to engage in wellness behaviors when you select healthy role models.

Activity: Health Behavior Contract

Your lifestyle plays a major role in determining your ability to control disease. Evaluate your lifestyle and devise a health behavior contract that you will follow to reach a desired health goal. Follow the outline of the health behavior contract on page 12. The healthful behavior you choose may originate from any one of the ten components of the Health Behavior Wheel.

1:11   Rewards for You and Others

When you are committed to eliminating risk behaviors, you are making responsible decisions about your health. You are increasing your life potential and reducing your risk of disease and possible premature death. Each time you set and reach a goal that improves your health, you move toward optimum health.

When you eliminate a risk behavior, you affect not only your own health but also the health of others. For instance, if you are a smoker who decides to quit, you will improve the condition of your lungs and reduce your risk of getting lung cancer. You will no longer pollute the air with substances harmful to people around you. Your action may motivate others to quit; you will be a role model for others.

Suppose you are in a room with ten people. Each person takes a health behavior inventory and has 30 yes answers (healthful behaviors) and 10 no answers (risk behaviors). The sum total of the group's health behaviors can be summarized.

> 10 people × 30 healthful behaviors = 300 healthful behaviors
> 10 people × 10 risk behaviors   = 100 risk behaviors

Now suppose each person makes a commitment to change one risk behavior to a healthful behavior. Some might decide to use a seat belt regularly. Others might decide to eat breakfast every day. The summary of the healthful behaviors would change.

> 10 people × 31 healthful behaviors = 310 healthful behaviors
> 10 people × 9 risk behaviors   = 90 risk behaviors

Remember, all risk behaviors are not equally harmful to health. Reducing the group total of risk behaviors by even ten would be a significant change.

 Review and Reflect

11. Fifty-three percent of your ability to influence or control disease is determined by your lifestyle. Give examples of two of your risk behaviors that might influence your ability to control disease.

12. What are three ways to help motivate yourself to achieve your goals?

Choosing healthful behaviors influences your health, the health of others, and the quality of the environment.

Health
ADVANCES

The nation's first public health revolution was the struggle against infectious diseases. This revolution lasted from the late 19th century through the first half of the 20th century. The leading causes of death in 1900 were influenza, pneumonia, diphtheria, tuberculosis, and gastrointestinal infections. The death rate in 1900 for these diseases was 580 for every 100 000 people. Today, fewer than 30 people per 100 000 die each year from these diseases. This change was accomplished by major sanitation measures, the development of effective vaccines, and mass immunization.

1:12 *Healthy People: The Surgeon General's Report on Health Promotion and Disease Prevention*

Today, the major causes of death of all ages are different from those in 1900. Heart disease, strokes, and cancer account for 72 percent of all deaths. Accidents account for the next highest percentage. These facts have led to the nation's second public health revolution directed by the Surgeon General of the United States. The focus of the revolution is not on treating disease but on prevention. *Healthy People* is the title of the Surgeon General's Report.

The Surgeon General's report, *Healthy People*, identifies national goals for health promotion and disease prevention.

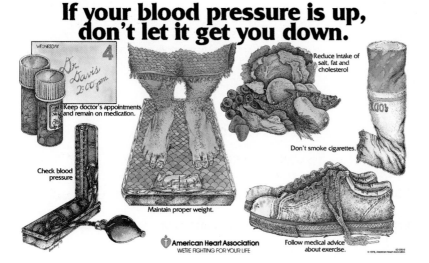

If your blood pressure is up, don't let it get you down.

WEDNESDAY
4
Dr. Davis 2:00 pm

Keep doctor's appointments and remain on medication.

Reduce intake of salt, fat and cholesterol

Check blood pressure

Maintain proper weight.

Don't smoke cigarettes.

♥ **American Heart Association**
WE'RE FIGHTING FOR YOUR LIFE

Follow medical advice about exercise.

FIGURE 1–9. Prevention of many kinds of health problems is a major concern of professional agencies such as the American Heart Association.

Healthy People identifies national goals for health promotion and disease prevention. These goals are concerned with the major health problems and the risks associated with them for the principal stages of life: (1) infancy, (2) childhood, (3) adolescence and young adulthood, (4) adulthood, and (5) older adulthood (Table 1–4). The Surgeon General has set the year 1990 as the target date to reach these goals.

After identifying these goals, the next step was to plan effective ways or strategies to meet the goals. Three major areas were the basis for the strategies: prevention, protection, and promotion. Five strategies in each area are identified (Table 1–5).

Table 1–4   The Nation's Health Goals

LIFE STAGE	GOAL
HEALTHY INFANTS AGE 0-1	To continue to improve infant health, and by 1990, to reduce infant mortality by at least 35 percent to fewer than nine deaths per 1000 live births.
HEALTHY CHILDREN AGE 1-14	To improve child health, foster optimum childhood development, and by 1990, to reduce deaths among children age one to 14 years by at least 20 percent to fewer than 34 per 100 000.
HEALTHY ADOLESCENTS AGE 15-24	To improve the health and health habits of adolescents and young adults, and by 1990, to reduce deaths among people age 15 to 24 by at least 20 percent to fewer than 93 per 100 000.
HEALTHY ADULTS AGE 25-64	To improve the health of adults, and by 1990, to reduce deaths among people age 25 to 64 by at least 25 percent to fewer than 400 per 100 000.
HEALTHY OLDER ADULTS AGE 65 AND OLDER	To improve the health and quality of life for older adults, and by 1990, to reduce the average annual number of days of restricted activity due to acute and chronic conditions by 20 percent to fewer than 30 days per year for people age 65 and older.

derstanding the
man Body

Table 1–5   Effective Strategies

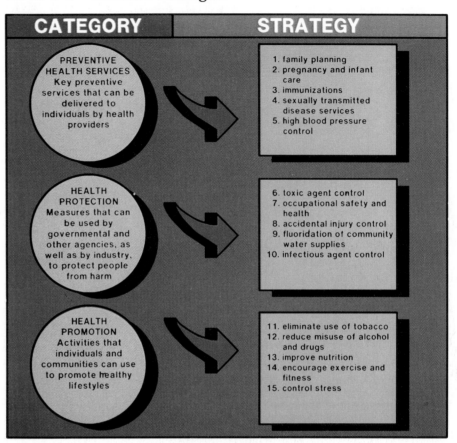

CATEGORY	STRATEGY
PREVENTIVE HEALTH SERVICES Key preventive services that can be delivered to individuals by health providers	1. family planning 2. pregnancy and infant care 3. immunizations 4. sexually transmitted disease services 5. high blood pressure control
HEALTH PROTECTION Measures that can be used by governmental and other agencies, as well as by industry, to protect people from harm	6. toxic agent control 7. occupational safety and health 8. accidental injury control 9. fluoridation of community water supplies 10. infectious agent control
HEALTH PROMOTION Activities that individuals and communities can use to promote healthy lifestyles	11. eliminate use of tobacco 12. reduce misuse of alcohol and drugs 13. improve nutrition 14. encourage exercise and fitness 15. control stress

Focus on
Life Management Skills

- Set health goals and make and follow plans to reach them.
- Be aware of current health information and regularly engage in health appraisal.
- Use the problem-solving approach to make responsible decisions that lead to actions that are healthful, safe, legal, and show respect for self and others, and follow parents' or guardian's guidelines.
- Use commitment and self-discipline in your lifestyle to engage in healthful behaviors and to avoid risk behaviors.

Summary

1. A goal identifies what you want to achieve. **Introduction**

2. A plan describes what you will do to reach your goals. **1:1**

3. If you want a healthful lifestyle, you must set healthful goals and make and follow plans to reach your goals. **1:2**

4. To obtain a high level of wellness, you take responsibility for your own health by choosing healthful behaviors. **1:3**

5. Optimum health is achieved by engaging in healthful behaviors and eliminating risk behaviors. **1:4**

6. A balanced lifestyle is achieved by choosing healthful behaviors in each of the ten components of health. **1:5**

7. Your choice of healthful behaviors or risk behaviors affects your health status. **1:6**

8. Health awareness gives you a clear picture of your own health behavior. **1:7**

9. A health behavior contract helps you achieve important health goals. **1:8**

10. Making responsible decisions about health involves choosing behaviors that are healthful, safe, legal, respectful of self and others, and in line with parents' or guardian's guidelines. **1:9**

11. When optimum health is a priority, you make a commitment to healthful behaviors and use self-discipline. **1:10**

12. Each time you set a health goal, make a plan, and reach your goal, you improve your health, the health of others, and the quality of the environment. **1:11**

13. *Healthy People* identifies health goals for the nation for the year 1990. **1:12**

Vocabulary

Below is a list of vocabulary words used in this chapter. Use each word only once to complete the sentences. Do not write in this book.

goal
health awareness
health behavior
contract
health promotion
holistic effect
optimum health
plan
priority
problem-solving
approach
risk behavior

1. Skipping breakfast will have a(n) ____ on the other areas of your health.

2. If you clearly state that you will run one mile each day, you have set a(n) ____.

3. Smoking is an example of a(n) ____.

4. A detailed description of how to meet a goal is a(n) ____.

5. The ____ is a series of steps that will help you make responsible decisions.

6. When you follow through on your goals and health plans, you show others that health is a(n) ____.

7. You gain ____ by completing a health appraisal checklist.

8. Motivating people to maintain or adopt healthful behaviors is ____.

9. A(n) ____ is a specific plan that is followed to reach a desired goal.

10. If you make the most of your heredity by engaging in wellness behaviors that promote your health and keep your environment healthful, you are working to achieve ____.

Review

1. How can you achieve a healthful lifestyle?

2. Identify and describe three kinds of health.

3. What are the ten health and wellness components that make up the Behavior Wheel?

4. What are the four steps in achieving optimum health?

5. What six items are included in a health behavior contract?

6. What are five questions to ask when you want to make a responsible decision?

7. What perce____ with disease____

8. What are th____ motivate you____ behavior con____

9. What inform____ *People*?

10. What are the____

Application

1. If you stay up late and get only four hours of sleep, how will that affect your health?

2. Examine Table 1–1. Suppose you eat a well-balanced breakfast each day. How will this behavior have a holistic effect?

3. Why is a decisi____ sible decision?

4. Examine the____ *Healthy Peopl*____ important to yo____

Individual Research

1. Copy the Sample Health Behavior Inventory (Table 1–3). Ask five persons to answer the questions. Total the number of healthful behaviors and risk behaviors. Suppose each person changed two risk behaviors to two healthful behaviors. Calculate these new totals. Describe the possible results.

2. Refer to Table 1–4. The nation's health goals identify reductions in death rates per

100 000 for thre____
of life. Make a ba____
stages of life and____
per 100 000 for t____

3. Visit the school____
that are classifi____
These books pert____
for a two-page re____

Readings

Ardell, Donald S., and Tager, Mark J., *Planning for Wellness*. Dubuque, IA: Kendall-Hunt, 1982.

Pryor, Karen, *Don't Sl*____
NY: Bantam Books,____

THE HUMAN BODY

You see an ad for a fantastic car. You imagine what it would be like to drive such a car. You set a goal to one day own a similar car. How much does a car like that cost? How long would it take you to save enough money to buy such a car?

Owning this car is a long-range goal. You must save your money and perhaps give up other desires you may have. However, you know that achieving this goal will be well worth the effort.

In this unit, you will learn the importance of setting a long-range goal of good health. One of the first steps in achieving this goal is knowing the importance of caring for your body systems.

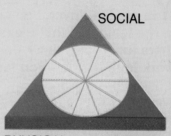

SOCIAL

PHYSICAL   MENTAL

You are the driver. You check every indicator on the console and put the key in the ignition. What messages do you get about the systems in the car? Is there fuel in the tank? Do the lights work? Your body has many systems that work together. Are you familiar with those systems? Do you know when your body is not functioning as it should?

Support and Control Systems

OBJECTIVES: You will be able to
- describe the functions of the skeletal and muscular systems and their relationships to health.
- identify ways to care for your skin.
- explain how care of the nervous system is important for good health.

Think about an automobile. An automobile is made of many different parts. The framework gives the car a definite style and also protects the engine and other inner structures. The car has an ignition system for starting the engine. Other systems work together to keep the engine running smoothly. Some mechanical parts in a car are capable of motion. These parts will move only if other factors are present and functioning properly. One of these factors is a source of energy, which is gasoline in most cars. Another factor is the engine. In the engine, the stored chemical energy in the gasoline is converted to mechanical energy. As a result, the car moves.

SKELETAL AND MUSCULAR SYSTEMS

Your body's mechanical parts are bones and muscles. Your body also has a source of energy. It is food. Food provides the energy necessary to move the mechanical parts in your body. Because of the functions of other body systems, the stored energy in food is converted to the kind of energy your body can use. As a result, your body moves and is flexible.

Food serves as a source of energy so that your muscles and bones can work together to help you move.

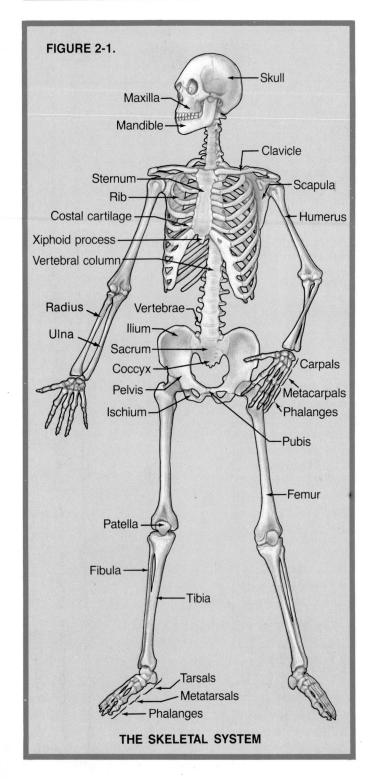

FIGURE 2-1.

Skull
Maxilla
Mandible
Clavicle
Sternum
Rib
Scapula
Costal cartilage
Humerus
Xiphoid process
Vertebral column
Radius
Vertebrae
Ulna
Ilium
Sacrum
Coccyx
Carpals
Pelvis
Metacarpals
Ischium
Phalanges
Pubis
Femur
Patella
Fibula
Tibia
Tarsals
Metatarsals
Phalanges

THE SKELETAL SYSTEM

2:1 Skeletal System

The skeletal system consists of bones, ligaments, and cartilages. Your body has over 200 bones, each serving many purposes. Bones serve as a framework for your body (Figure 2–1). Your bones work in harmony with your muscles. Bones also protect you. Your ribs and breastbone protect your heart and lungs. The bones of your skull protect your brain. Because of the muscles and many small bones in your hands and fingers, you can handle objects with ease and skill. **Bone marrow** is a special kind of tissue in the hollow center area of some bones. Red blood cells are produced in marrow.

When you were born, your skeletal system was not as strong as it is now. At birth, most of your skeletal system was composed of cartilage. **Cartilage** is connective tissue that is rigid but softer than bone. As you grew older, ossification took place. **Ossification** is a process by which bone cells and minerals replace cartilage. This process continues through childhood and into early adulthood. However, even after ossification is complete, some body parts remain as cartilage. The tip of your nose and the outside of your ears contain cartilage.

Cartilage is also present as a cushion in many joints. A **joint** is a place where two bones meet. Bones do not always touch at a joint. They are held together by tough bands of connective tissue called **ligaments.** Most joints are also lubricated so that the body moves freely.

2:2 The Skeletal System and Health

Certain conditions must be present for bones in the skeletal system to keep healthy. Bones must receive sufficient

Table 1–5   Effective Strategies

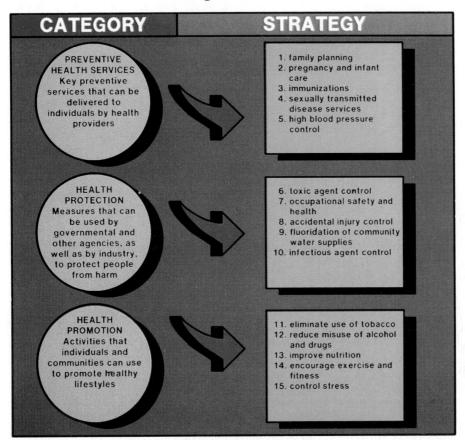

CATEGORY	STRATEGY
PREVENTIVE HEALTH SERVICES Key preventive services that can be delivered to individuals by health providers	1. family planning 2. pregnancy and infant care 3. immunizations 4. sexually transmitted disease services 5. high blood pressure control
HEALTH PROTECTION Measures that can be used by governmental and other agencies, as well as by industry, to protect people from harm	6. toxic agent control 7. occupational safety and health 8. accidental injury control 9. fluoridation of community water supplies 10. infectious agent control
HEALTH PROMOTION Activities that individuals and communities can use to promote healthy lifestyles	11. eliminate use of tobacco 12. reduce misuse of alcohol and drugs 13. improve nutrition 14. encourage exercise and fitness 15. control stress

Focus on
Life Management Skills

- Set health goals and make and follow plans to reach them.
- Be aware of current health information and regularly engage in health appraisal.
- Use the problem-solving approach to make responsible decisions that lead to actions that are healthful, safe, legal, and show respect for self and others, and follow parents' or guardian's guidelines.
- Use commitment and self-discipline in your lifestyle to engage in healthful behaviors and to avoid risk behaviors.

Summary

1. A goal identifies what you want to achieve. **Introduction**

2. A plan describes what you will do to reach your goals. **1:1**

3. If you want a healthful lifestyle, you must set healthful goals and make and follow plans to reach your goals. **1:2**

4. To obtain a high level of wellness, you take responsibility for your own health by choosing healthful behaviors. **1:3**

5. Optimum health is achieved by engaging in healthful behaviors and eliminating risk behaviors. **1:4**

6. A balanced lifestyle is achieved by choosing healthful behaviors in each of the ten components of health. **1:5**

7. Your choice of healthful behaviors or risk behaviors affects your health status. **1:6**

8. Health awareness gives you a clear picture of your own health behavior. **1:7**

9. A health behavior contract helps you achieve important health goals. **1:8**

10. Making responsible decisions about health involves choosing behaviors that are healthful, safe, legal, respectful of self and others, and in line with parents' or guardian's guidelines. **1:9**

11. When optimum health is a priority, you make a commitment to healthful behaviors and use self-discipline. **1:10**

12. Each time you set a health goal, make a plan, and reach your goal, you improve your health, the health of others, and the quality of the environment. **1:11**

13. *Healthy People* identifies health goals for the nation for the year 1990. **1:12**

Vocabulary

Below is a list of vocabulary words used in this chapter. Use each word only once to complete the sentences. Do not write in this book.

goal
health awareness
health behavior
  contract
health promotion
holistic effect

optimum health
plan
priority
problem-solving
  approach
risk behavior

1. Skipping breakfast will have a(n) _____ on the other areas of your health.

2. If you clearly state that you will run one mile each day, you have set a(n) _____.

3. Smoking is an example of a(n) _____.

4. A detailed description of how to meet a goal is a(n) _____.

5. The _____ is a series of steps that will help you make responsible decisions.

6. When you follow through on your goals and health plans, you show others that health is a(n) _____.

7. You gain _____ by completing a health appraisal checklist.

8. Motivating people to maintain or adopt healthful behaviors is _____.

9. A(n) _____ is a specific plan that is followed to reach a desired goal.

10. If you make the most of your heredity by engaging in wellness behaviors that promote your health and keep your environment healthful, you are working to achieve _____.

Review

1. How can you achieve a healthful lifestyle?
2. Identify and describe three kinds of health.
3. What are the ten health and wellness components that make up the Behavior Wheel?
4. What are the four steps in achieving optimum health?
5. What six items are included in a health behavior contract?
6. What are five questions to ask when you want to make a responsible decision?
7. What percentage of your ability to cope with disease can you influence or control?
8. What are three suggestions you can use to motivate yourself to complete your health behavior contracts?
9. What information is contained in *Healthy People?*
10. What are the five principal stages of life?

Application

1. If you stay up late and get only four hours of sleep, how will that affect your health?
2. Examine Table 1–1. Suppose you eat a well-balanced breakfast each day. How will this behavior have a holistic effect?
3. Why is a decision not to hitchhike a responsible decision?
4. Examine the Surgeon General's report, *Healthy People.* List three goals that are important to you. Explain.

Individual Research

1. Copy the Sample Health Behavior Inventory (Table 1–3). Ask five persons to answer the questions. Total the number of healthful behaviors and risk behaviors. Suppose each person changed two risk behaviors to two healthful behaviors. Calculate these new totals. Describe the possible results.
2. Refer to Table 1–4. The nation's health goals identify reductions in death rates per 100 000 for three of the five principal stages of life. Make a bar graph showing these three stages of life and the anticipated death rates per 100 000 for the year 1990.
3. Visit the school library. Examine the books that are classified in the 612 numbers. These books pertain to health. Select a book for a two-page report.

Readings

Ardell, Donald S., and Tager, Mark J., *Planning for Wellness.* Dubuque, IA: Kendall-Hunt, 1982.

Pryor, Karen, *Don't Shoot the Dog.* New York, NY: Bantam Books, Inc., 1985.

Understanding the Human Body

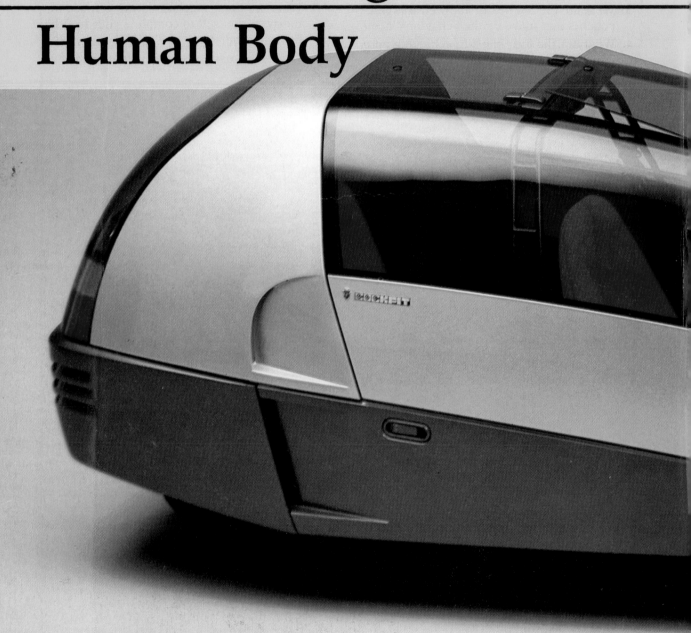

THE HUMAN BODY

You see an ad for a fantastic car. You imagine what it would be like to drive such a car. You set a goal to one day own a similar car. How much does a car like that cost? How long would it take you to save enough money to buy such a car?

Owning this car is a long-range goal. You must save your money and perhaps give up other desires you may have. However, you know that achieving this goal will be well worth the effort.

In this unit, you will learn the importance of setting a long-range goal of good health. One of the first steps in achieving this goal is knowing the importance of caring for your body systems.

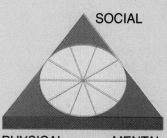

SOCIAL

PHYSICAL   MENTAL

You are the driver. You check every indicator on the console and put the key in the ignition. What messages do you get about the systems in the car? Is there fuel in the tank? Do the lights work? Your body has many systems that work together. Are you familiar with those systems? Do you know when your body is not functioning as it should?

Support and Control Systems

OBJECTIVES: You will be able to
- **describe the functions of the skeletal and muscular systems and their relationships to health.**
- **identify ways to care for your skin.**
- **explain how care of the nervous system is important for good health.**

Think about an automobile. An automobile is made of many different parts. The framework gives the car a definite style and also protects the engine and other inner structures. The car has an ignition system for starting the engine. Other systems work together to keep the engine running smoothly. Some mechanical parts in a car are capable of motion. These parts will move only if other factors are present and functioning properly. One of these factors is a source of energy, which is gasoline in most cars. Another factor is the engine. In the engine, the stored chemical energy in the gasoline is converted to mechanical energy. As a result, the car moves.

SKELETAL AND MUSCULAR SYSTEMS

Your body's mechanical parts are bones and muscles. Your body also has a source of energy. It is food. Food provides the energy necessary to move the mechanical parts in your body. Because of the functions of other body systems, the stored energy in food is converted to the kind of energy your body can use. As a result, your body moves and is flexible.

Food serves as a source of energy so that your muscles and bones can work together to help you move.

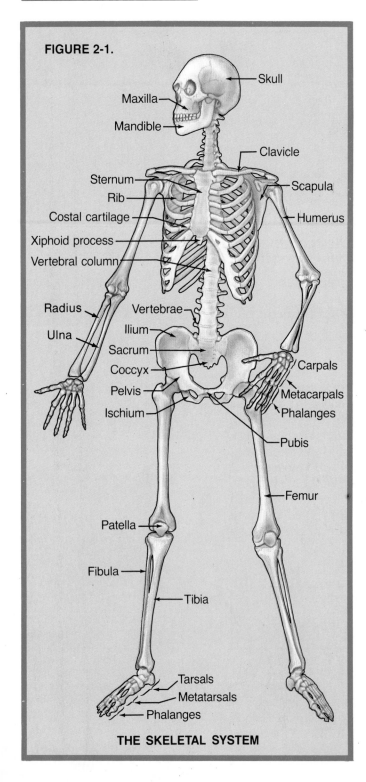

FIGURE 2-1.

Skull
Maxilla
Mandible
Clavicle
Sternum
Rib
Scapula
Costal cartilage
Humerus
Xiphoid process
Vertebral column
Radius
Vertebrae
Ulna
Ilium
Sacrum
Coccyx
Carpals
Pelvis
Metacarpals
Ischium
Phalanges
Pubis
Femur
Patella
Fibula
Tibia
Tarsals
Metatarsals
Phalanges

THE SKELETAL SYSTEM

2:1 Skeletal System

The skeletal system consists of bones, ligaments, and cartilages. Your body has over 200 bones, each serving many purposes. Bones serve as a framework for your body (Figure 2–1). Your bones work in harmony with your muscles. Bones also protect you. Your ribs and breastbone protect your heart and lungs. The bones of your skull protect your brain. Because of the muscles and many small bones in your hands and fingers, you can handle objects with ease and skill. **Bone marrow** is a special kind of tissue in the hollow center area of some bones. Red blood cells are produced in marrow.

When you were born, your skeletal system was not as strong as it is now. At birth, most of your skeletal system was composed of cartilage. **Cartilage** is connective tissue that is rigid but softer than bone. As you grew older, ossification took place. **Ossification** is a process by which bone cells and minerals replace cartilage. This process continues through childhood and into early adulthood. However, even after ossification is complete, some body parts remain as cartilage. The tip of your nose and the outside of your ears contain cartilage.

Cartilage is also present as a cushion in many joints. A **joint** is a place where two bones meet. Bones do not always touch at a joint. They are held together by tough bands of connective tissue called **ligaments.** Most joints are also lubricated so that the body moves freely.

2:2 The Skeletal System and Health

Certain conditions must be present for bones in the skeletal system to keep healthy. Bones must receive sufficient amounts of the minerals calcium and phosphorus to help bone formation. Milk and other dairy products are good sources of these minerals. Bones need vitamin D, which helps the bones make use of calcium and phosphorus. Fortified milk, sunlight, and fish liver oils are good sources of vitamin D. Hormones are important for bone growth. The pituitary gland produces a growth hormone that helps bones form and grow.

A balanced diet and regular exercise help keep your bones strong. A lack of calcium in a person's diet combined with a lack of exercise may cause osteoporosis (ahs tee oh puh ROH sus) in older people. **Osteoporosis** is a bone disease in which bone tissue becomes brittle and porous due to a loss of bone calcium. As a result, bone fractures are likely to occur, especially in older women. An adequate amount of calcium in the diet throughout life is an important factor in helping to prevent this disease in both men and women.

2:3   Muscular System

Movement in your body is controlled by a network of over 600 muscles (Figure 2–2). These muscles make up the muscular system. All muscle tissue does not have the same appearance. However, all muscles have one unique characteristic, the ability to shorten, or contract. This ability allows body movement.

There are three types of muscles in your body—skeletal, smooth, and cardiac. These muscles consist of bundles of fibers grouped together. Different muscle types have different functions in the body.

Skeletal muscles are the muscles that move the bones of the skeleton. Skeletal muscles are attached to bones by tough bands of tissues called **tendons.**

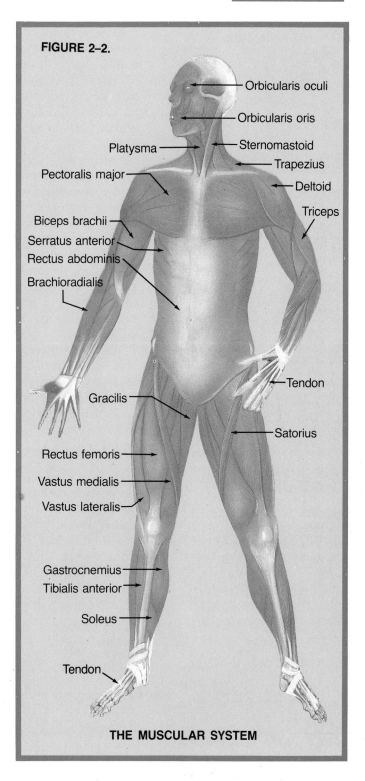

FIGURE 2–2.

Orbicularis oculi
Orbicularis oris
Sternomastoid
Trapezius
Deltoid
Triceps
Platysma
Pectoralis major
Biceps brachii
Serratus anterior
Rectus abdominis
Brachioradialis
Tendon
Gracilis
Satorius
Rectus femoris
Vastus medialis
Vastus lateralis
Gastrocnemius
Tibialis anterior
Soleus
Tendon

THE MUSCULAR SYSTEM

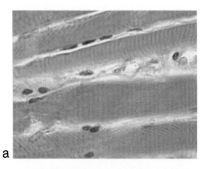

a

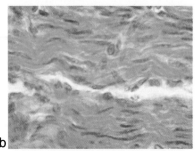

b

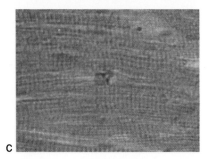

c

FIGURE 2–3. Three types of muscles: (a) skeletal, (b) smooth, (3) cardiac. All three types are shown magnified 450 times.

The heart is a special kind of muscle that pumps blood throughout the body.

Muscle fibers contain bands, or striations, that give skeletal muscle a striped appearance (Figure 2–3a). Because of these bands, skeletal muscles are sometimes called striated muscles. When a skeletal muscle contracts, the bone to which it is attached is pulled toward the muscle. Skeletal muscles are called voluntary muscles. **Voluntary muscles** are those muscles over which a person has control. Extend your fingers; move your foot. You are using your voluntary muscles when performing these activities.

Smooth muscles form the walls of many internal organs, such as the stomach. The action of some smooth muscles helps move food through your digestive tract. There are also smooth muscles in your eyes that help you focus clearly. Blood vessels also have a layer of smooth muscle. Smooth muscles are called involuntary muscles. **Involuntary muscles** are muscles over which you have no control (Figure 2–3b). You do not control how food moves through your digestive tract or how your blood circulates in your blood vessels. Some muscles, such as the tongue or those in the eyelids, are sometimes involuntary but can also be controlled voluntarily.

The heart is composed of **cardiac muscle.** Cardiac muscle has some characteristics of skeletal and smooth muscles, but it is regarded as a distinct kind of muscle (Figure 2–3c). Cardiac muscle is also an involuntary muscle. It pumps blood an average of 70 times each minute, 40 million times a year for a lifetime.

2:4 The Muscular System and Health

As long as you are alive, your muscles will be working to help keep you healthy. There are muscles that help you breathe and move. Your heart muscle pumps blood throughout your body. For your muscles to work at optimum level, you need to practice healthful habits. The more a muscle is used, the stronger it becomes. In Unit 6, you will learn about the importance of exercise in the development of strong, healthy muscles. The foods you eat also influence the health of your muscles. A sensible diet of foods helps sustain muscle strength and promotes growth.

 Review and Reflect

1. Why is the skeleton of a baby softer than the skeleton of an adult?
2. How do tendons differ from ligaments?
3. How is the heart muscle similar to an involuntary muscle?

INTEGUMENTARY SYSTEM

The system that covers and protects the body is the integumentary system. It is composed of skin and hair follicles, nails, and glands that are outgrowths of the skin layers.

2:5   Skin Function

The skin is the largest organ of the body. It consists of two main layers—the epidermis and the dermis (Figure 2–4). Notice the position of the hair follicles, oil glands, and sweat glands.

The skin has several important functions. It protects against injury and helps keep microorganisms from getting into your body. A skin pigment called melanin protects you from the ultraviolet rays of the sun. The amount of melanin present determines the color of the skin.

Skin helps in maintaining body temperature. For example, when your body produces excess heat during exercise, sweat glands produce perspiration. The water in perspiration evaporates from the surface of your skin and cools your body. Body heat also radiates through your skin from blood vessels near the surface of your skin when the air around you is cool.

The skin is the largest organ of the body consisting of the epidermis and dermis.

The skin protects by preventing harmful microorganisms from entering the body and by regulating body temperature.

THE SKIN

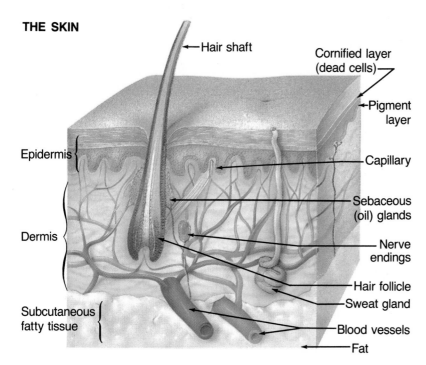

FIGURE 2–4. Cross section of the layers of the skin.

Skin contains nerve endings. Some nerve endings make you aware of changes in your environment. Other nerve endings are sensitive to pressure, pain, and temperature.

2:6   The Integumentary System and Health

Your skin needs constant care. Skin glands produce secretions that collect on the surface of the skin. Secretions of the sweat glands contain waste materials that must be rinsed from the skin's surface. **Sebum,** an oily secretion from the oil glands, may block the ducts and pores and cause pimples or blackheads.

Vitamin A, found in dairy products, is important for healthy skin.

Your diet is important to the health of your skin. Vitamin A is necessary for healthy eyes, skin, and hair. Good sources of vitamin A are dairy products, and leafy green and deep orange vegetables.

There are several skin conditions that may affect you. Being aware of these different conditions and how to handle them can help you be better prepared to keep your skin healthy.

Sunburn and acne are two skin conditions that most often affect adolescents.

Sunburn is a condition that results when the skin has been overexposed to the sun. Symptoms of sunburn include redness, pain, and inflammation. Sunburn occurs more often in light-skinned persons because of the small amount of melanin present. Being overexposed to the sun does not allow the skin ample time to produce the amount of melanin needed to protect itself. Overexposure to ultraviolet light is the major cause of skin cancer. Sunburn and skin cancer may also result from improper use of sunlamps. The best prevention is to avoid ultraviolet light. If you are exposed to ultraviolet light, use a sunscreen. A sunscreen is a chemical that is applied to the skin in the form of a lotion to protect the skin against ultraviolet light. There are many kinds of sunscreens available. The effectiveness of these sunscreens is determined by the amount of PABA in them. PABA is a substance that protects the skin from the sun's ultraviolet rays. The higher the PABA number, the more effective the sunscreen. If you become seriously sunburned, seek medical attention.

Acne is a skin infection that occurs when sebum blocks ducts and pores. This may produce blackheads, pimples, or lumps like boils. Most often, acne appears on the face, where it is also most visible. A person should not squeeze blackheads and pimples. The infection might be forced deeper and cause permanent damage to the skin. Acne can be treated by specific medications.

People with severe acne may be treated by a dermatologist. A **dermatologist** is a physician who specializes in diseases and disorders of the skin. Some medications have proven effective in treating acne by drying up the sebum and preventing its formation. Astringents can be used to help prevent acne. An **astringent** is a substance that contains alcohol and can dry the skin. Drying the skin helps prevent the buildup of sebum.

A **boil** is a skin infection that invades the layers of the skin. A boil often begins in a hair root. As it develops, skin tissue is destroyed. Swelling, redness, and pus may be seen on the skin's surface. A boil may require medical treatment. A doctor can drain the pus from the boil or prescribe medication.

Dandruff is dead cells on the scalp. Dandruff occurs when the scalp is too oily. The oil causes the dead cells to clump into flakes. In most cases, dandruff can be treated with regular shampooing. Sometimes special shampoos are needed to effectively treat dandruff.

Psoriasis (suh RI uh sus) is a skin disease characterized by red skin and raised white scales. Psoriasis is commonly found on the scalp, elbows, and knees. It appears and disappears in cycles. Both the cause and cure of psoriasis are not known. Medications are available to treat this condition.

Athlete's foot is a common skin infection. **Athlete's foot** is an itching, redness, and cracking of the skin between the toes that is caused by a fungus. A fungus is a plantlike organism that grows best in dark, warm, and moist areas. If left untreated, athlete's foot can spread. However, athlete's foot can be prevented and controlled by wearing slippers in locker rooms, pools, and public showers. It can be treated by keeping the feet dry and using a special powder. Athlete's foot may have to be treated by a physician.

Hives are small, itchy lumps on the skin. They can be caused by an allergic reaction to a food, medicine, or pollen. They are frequently a result of stress. It is best that a person know the cause of hives so that the agent causing them can be avoided.

Warts are raised skin growths caused by a virus. Warts can grow anywhere on the body and can be spread from person to person. A **plantar wart** is a wart that grows on the bottom of a person's foot. Warts can be treated with medication or removed by a physician (Figure 2–5).

Other skin conditions that may cause problems are boils, dandruff, psoriasis, athlete's foot, hives, and warts.

Athlete's foot can be prevented by wearing slippers in locker rooms, pools, and public showers.

FIGURE 2–5. A plantar wart

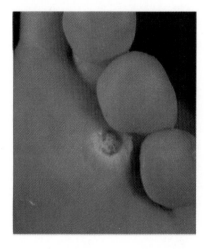

 Review and Reflect

4. State two functions of the skin.
5. Since your skin needs constant care, what are some ways you can keep your skin healthy?

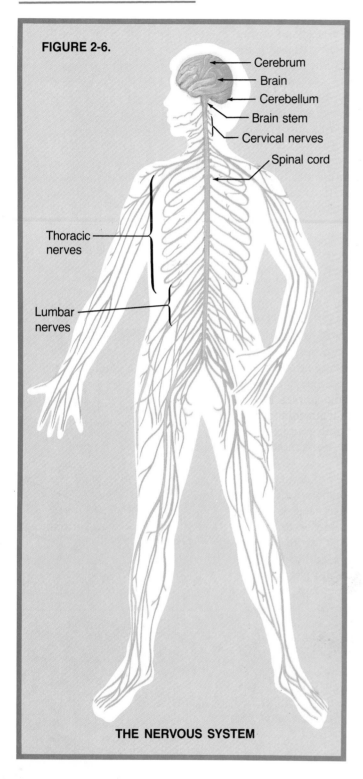

FIGURE 2-6.

Cerebrum
Brain
Cerebellum
Brain stem
Cervical nerves
Spinal cord
Thoracic nerves
Lumbar nerves

THE NERVOUS SYSTEM

NERVOUS SYSTEM

The central office at a telephone company and a control tower at an airport share similarities. Each is involved in communicating and coordinating many different activities and events. At the central office of a telephone company, messages are received and coordinated through a network of computers. This enables you to speak with a person who may be many miles away. At an airport control tower, air traffic controllers communicate important information to pilots and coordinate airport activities so that airplanes can take off and land safely.

Many activities in your body are controlled by different body systems. These activities are taking place each moment that you are alive. As you read this page, your eyes follow the words on the line. Your eyes move back and forth. You use your fingers to turn pages. These are two of the numerous activities that your body's control center coordinates.

2:7 Central Nervous System

Your body's control center is called the nervous system. The **nervous system** is the network of nerve cells that carries messages or impulses to and from the brain and spinal cord to all parts of the body (Figure 2–6).

The nervous system consists of the brain, the spinal cord, and branching nerves. Nerve tissue is composed of masses of nerve cells called **neurons.** Neurons may vary in size and shape, but they have common characteristics (Figure 2–7).

The nervous system is divided into two major parts, the central nervous system and the peripheral nervous system. The **central nervous system** is composed of the brain and spinal cord.

The brain is considered the most complex part of the central nervous system and is protected in many ways from injury. It has its own kind of helmet called the cranium. The brain is also protected and nourished by three cushions called meninges (muh NIHN jees). **Meninges** are membranes that surround the brain. Spaces between the meninges are filled with cerebrospinal fluid that further cushions the brain from blows. A concussion is a brain injury resulting from a severe blow to the head. Inner spaces of the brain, called ventricles, also hold fluid that helps protect the brain.

The **spinal cord** is like a thin cable that extends from the base of the brain about two-thirds of the way down the back. Like the brain, the spinal cord is well protected. It is surrounded by meninges and cerebrospinal fluid.

2:8 Peripheral Nervous System

The **peripheral** (puh RIHF rul) **nervous system** consists of many nerves that branch from the brain and spinal cord to the periphery, or outer edges, of the body. Twelve pairs of cranial nerves branch from the brain and transmit information to and from the eyes, ears, nose, and tongue. Cranial nerves also control muscles in the face and neck. Thirty-one pairs of spinal nerves branch from the spine. Spinal nerves transmit information to and from all other parts of the body. The peripheral nervous system can be further subdivided into two main divisions, the somatic nervous system and the autonomic nervous system.

The **somatic nervous system** is concerned with a person's external environment. This system consists of sensory and motor neurons. Sensory neurons transmit impulses from sense organs to the central nervous system for interpretation. Motor neurons transmit impulses from the central nervous system to activate muscles or glands. The result is a response to a stimulus. When touching a sharp or hot object, you move your hand away within fractions of a second. Within that time frame, an impulse had traveled along sensory neurons to the central nervous system and along motor neurons to muscles in your hand.

The **autonomic nervous system** involves a person's internal environment. This part of the peripheral system controls involuntary actions and regulates heart rate and body temperature. The autonomic system is a two-part system. One part, the sympathetic nervous system, prepares the body for emergencies. The other part, the parasympathetic system, counterbalances the sympathetic system. This system maintains the body's normal state and restores balance after an emergency.

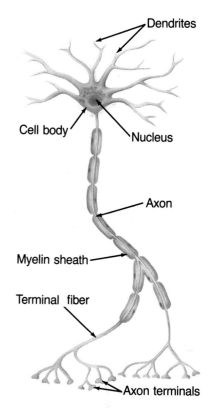

FIGURE 2–7. The basic structure of the nervous system is the neuron. Messages are transmitted from one neuron to another, moving from the dendrite to the cell body and along the axon to the terminals where the impulse is transferred to another neuron.

The brain is protected by the cranium and meninges.

The somatic and autonomic nervous systems are the two main divisions of the peripheral nervous system.

2:9 Sense Organs

Your body's senses play a role in everything you do. Suppose you are eating popcorn. You see the popcorn. You touch it as you place it in your mouth. As you taste the popcorn, you may also smell it. You hear it crunch as you chew. You experience all five senses as you eat popcorn.

You are able to experience each sense because of special neurons that act as receptors. **Receptor neurons** receive information and transmit it on sensory neurons to your spinal cord and brain. Your brain sends back impulses on motor neurons and you respond to the initial information.

Vision—You are able to see objects because you have special receptor neurons in the retina of your eyes. These receptors are sensitive to light and color. Receptors that are receptive to light are called **rods.** Receptors that register color in bright light are called **cones.** These receptors convert light rays to nerve impulses and send information along sensory nerves to your brain. Your brain interprets what you are seeing (Figure 2–8a).

A person's vision can be affected by the shape of the eyeball. If the eyeball is too long from front to back, the image does not form on the retina (Figure 2–8b). The person would not see the object clearly. This condition is called **myopia,** or nearsightedness. A person with myopia can clearly see objects that are near. Distant objects would not be as clear.

If the eyeball is too short from front to back, the image does not form on the retina (Figure 2–8c). In this case, the person has clear vision for objects that are far away. Objects that are close are not seen clearly. This condition is called **hyperopia,** or farsightedness. Both of these conditions can be helped by wearing prescribed corrective lenses.

Protect your vision by having eye examinations on a regular basis and by wearing safety goggles when appropriate. Some sports also require special safety glasses.

Rods and cones are two kinds of receptors in the eyes.

A person who has myopia cannot see distant objects clearly; a person who has hyperopia cannot see close objects clearly.

FIGURE 2–8. The shape of the eyeball determines where an image forms. In (a) the light rays converge on the retina and vision is clear.

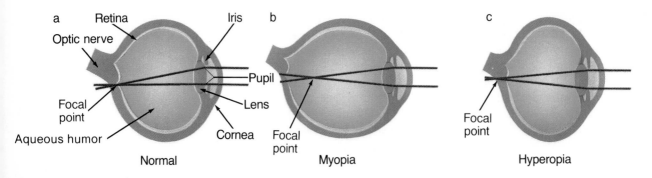

a   Retina   Iris   b   c
Optic nerve
Pupil
Focal point   Lens
Aqueous humor   Cornea   Focal point   Focal point
Normal   Myopia   Hyperopia

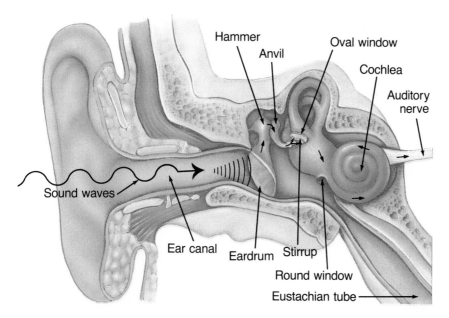

Hammer
Anvil
Oval window
Cochlea
Auditory nerve
Sound waves
Ear canal
Eardrum
Stirrup
Round window
Eustachian tube

FIGURE 2–9. The outer ear receives sound waves and conducts them through the ear canal to the eardrum. Vibrations from the sound waves move through the middle ear causing the three small bones to vibrate. Vibrations cause movement in the fluid in the inner ear, stimulating nerve endings.

Hearing—You are able to hear because of special receptor neurons in your ears. These receptors are sensitive to vibrations set in motion by sound waves. In the inner ear, sound waves are converted to nerve impulses. These are transmitted to your brain on sensory neurons. Your brain interprets what you are hearing (Figure 2–9).

Care of the ears is important. Wax is produced in the canal of the outer ear. This wax, along with tiny hairs in the canal, helps prevent foreign objects from getting into the ear. Objects of any size should never be put into the ear because these objects might puncture the eardrum. A puncture would allow dirt or microorganisms to get into the ear and cause infection.

The Eustachian tube leads from the middle ear to the back of the throat. This tube allows the pressure of the air inside the middle ear to be equalized with the outside air. It is possible for throat infections or cold germs to invade the middle ear through this tube.

An infection in the middle ear can affect hearing. Some kinds of deafness can be helped with hearing aids. However, nerve deafness resulting from damaged nerves in the ear cannot be corrected. Protect your hearing by avoiding exposure to loud noises and wearing ear protectors when appropriate.

Taste, Smell, and Touch—Special receptor neurons are also involved in your ability to taste, smell, and touch. Receptor neurons called **taste buds** respond to chemicals in foods. These taste buds are sensitive to substances that are sweet, salty, bitter, or sour.

Sound waves in the ear are converted to nerve impulses.

Protect your hearing by avoiding unnecessary exposure to loud noise.

Taste buds respond to chemicals in food; olfactory receptors respond to chemicals in vapor form.

Receptors in the nose are called **olfactory receptors.** These receptors are sensitive to chemicals in vapor form that enter the nose. The sense of smell is closely associated with taste. The enjoyment of most foods is a combination of smell and taste. This is especially noticeable when you have a cold and are not able to smell food odors.

Receptor neurons in the skin are sensitive to pressure, cold, heat, and pain. In many cases, you are protected from danger because of these special neurons. For example, a person whose hands have been severely burned may no longer be sensitive to pressure, cold, heat, and pain.

2:10 The Nervous System and Health

Your nervous system plays an important role in helping you keep well. Suppose you accidentally touch a hot stove. Your hand would jerk away from the stove. This action is called a reflex (Figure 2–10). A **reflex** is an involuntary response to changes inside or outside the body. The signal, initiated by your touching the stove, traveled along sensory neurons to your spinal cord. Motor neurons from your spinal cord signaled the muscles in your hand to pull away from the stove. The path of this impulse along sensory neurons to the spinal cord to motor neurons is called a **reflex arc.** Because of the reflex arc action, you pulled your hand away quickly in an involuntary, unconscious response. At the same time, impulses were transmitted to your brain, and you were conscious of having touched a hot stove. In actual seconds of time, however, it has been measured that you would have pulled your hand away before you realized that you had touched something hot.

Sometimes the nervous system needs special attention. Perhaps an injury or an illness has threatened the system. A **neurologist** is a physician with special training who diagnoses and treats diseases and disorders of the nervous system. A neurologist may request an EEG (Figure 2–11). An **EEG,** also known as an electroencephalogram, is a record of the electrical

Reflexes are involuntary responses that can protect you from injury.

An EEG is a record of electrical activity in the brain.

FIGURE 2–10. The reflex arc

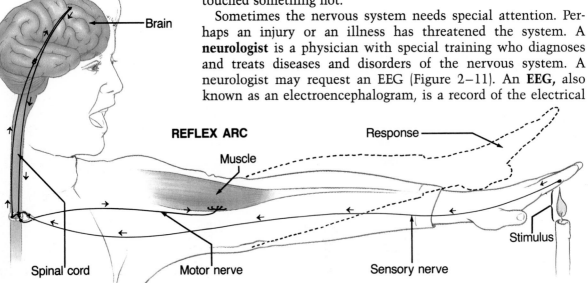

Brain

REFLEX ARC

Response

Muscle

Stimulus

Spinal cord

Motor nerve

Sensory nerve

activity in the brain. The EEG can provide a neurologist with information about the brain's condition. It can be used to diagnose disorders of the brain.

A neurologist can also diagnose nervous system disorders by performing a spinal tap. A **spinal tap** is the insertion of a needle into the fluid in the spinal column. Cerebrospinal fluid is removed and analyzed. This can help a physician identify and treat various disorders.

Perhaps one of the most effective methods of diagnosing diseases of the nervous system, as well as other parts of the body, is the use of a CAT scan. A **CAT scan** is a combination computer and X-ray machine that produces pictures of internal body parts. These pictures convey more information than ordinary X rays (Figure 2–12).

 # Activity: ### Being Impaired

Divide into two groups. Designate one group as visually impaired and the other group as hearing impaired. The visually impaired group will wear a cravat bandage to cover their eyes. The hearing impaired group will put cotton in their ears and wear a cravat bandage around their heads to further block out sound. You will be shown a movie or a filmstrip with auditory cues. Afterward, you and your classmates will remove your props and answer oral or written questions about the film.

Review and Reflect

6. How do the two divisions of the peripheral nervous system differ?
7. What is the difference between myopia and hyperopia?

FIGURE 2–11. Electrical activity in the brain is recorded by attaching electrodes to areas of the head. The electrical impulses moving through the wires are magnified and activate an electromagnetic pen to record the brain waves on paper.

CAT scans can be used to take pictures of internal body organs.

FIGURE 2–12. (a) An NMR scanner is a special kind of computer to analyze body parts. (b) Printout from an NMR scanner shows a slice of cranial anatomy.

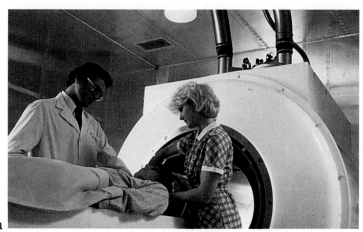

a

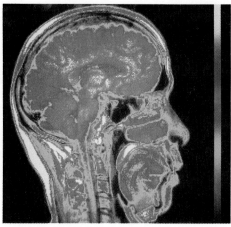

b

Health
ADVANCES

Millions of people who use wheelchairs are paralyzed because of injuries to the central nervous system. If spinal nerves or the spinal cord itself are injured, some functions are affected. If the injury is minor, the loss of a function may be temporary. If nerve fibers are severed, normal functions may be permanently lost. When nerve pathways are blocked or severed, impulses cannot be carried to and from the brain and spinal cord to body parts.

2:11   Computers That Stimulate Nerves

Nan Davis was a passenger in a car when she and a friend were coming home from a party. They had been celebrating graduation from high school. Nan's friend leaned over to put another tape into the tape deck. Just then Nan thought, "We're not going to make that curve." Nan was correct. The small car could not handle the sharp curve at 45 miles per hour. The car flipped over several times. Nan's friend escaped with just a scratch on the arm, but Nan was not so fortunate. She suffered injuries that left her a paraplegic. A **paraplegic** is a person who is paralyzed in the lower part of the body, including both legs.

This accident began the saga of Nan Davis. Eventually, Nan made medical history because she became the first person with paralyzed limbs to walk at will.

Nan's ability to walk was a result of the work of Professor Jerrold Petrofsky at Wright State University in Dayton. Professor Petrofsky designed a special computer that stimulated the damaged nerves in Nan's legs. As a result, Nan was able to take several jerky steps. These steps marked the first time a paraplegic was able to "walk." Television networks and newspapers around the world told about this historic event.

Those first steps taken by Nan marked the beginning of a new way to rehabilitate paraplegics in the future. Wright State's National Center for Rehabilitation Engineering has since developed a portable walking system that has enabled other individuals to walk long distances and negotiate steps and ramps.

While the walking system is still experimental, much progress has been made since Nan's first walk in 1982. The work continues at Wright State to bring the walking system to the point where it is ready to be commercialized, thereby making it available to anyone who may need it.

New technologies are being developed to treat people with nervous system disorders.

FIGURE 2–13. Gene Leber, Nan Davis, and Jennifer Smith, all paraplegics, take a walk using the new hybrid walking system at Wright State University.

Focus on
Life Management Skills

- Exercise regularly to help make your bones strong.
- Eat a balanced diet that contains calcium, phosphorus, and vitamin D to keep bones healthy.
- Select exercises that will enable the different muscles in the body to become strong.
- Eat sources of vitamin A to help keep your skin healthy.
- Keep your skin clean and avoid squeezing blackheads and pimples.
- Prevent athlete's foot by wearing slippers in locker rooms, pools, and public showers.
- Protect yourself from injury by wearing a seat belt in an automobile.
- Wear a safety helmet when riding a bicycle, moped, or motorcycle.
- Wear corrective lenses when prescribed.
- Wear safety goggles when required for class or sports.
- Never place objects in your ear.

CHAPTER REVIEW 2

Summary

1. The skeletal system serves as a framework of support, protects body organs, and is a source of new red blood cells. 2:1

2. Regular exercise and a balanced diet are important in maintaining a healthy and strong skeletal system. 2:2

3. The three types of muscles in the body are skeletal, smooth, and cardiac. 2:3

4. Exercise and a balanced diet influence the development of healthy muscles. 2:4

5. Skin protects against injury, helps maintain body temperature, and contains nerve endings that keep you in touch with your environment. 2:5

6. Some common skin problems are acne, boils, dandruff, psoriasis, athlete's foot, hives, warts, and plantar warts. 2:6

7. The central nervous system is composed of the brain and spinal cord. 2:7

8. The peripheral nervous system consists of branching nerves that extend to the outer edges of the body. 2:8

9. Sense organs are important in helping a person respond to the environment. 2:9

10. Reflex arc action helps protect you from injury. 2:10

11. Special computers are being developed experimentally as future possibilities to help people who are paralyzed to walk again. 2:11

Vocabulary

Below is a list of vocabulary words used in this chapter. Use each word only once to complete the sentences. Do not write in this book.

cardiac muscle	neurons
cartilage	osteoporosis
joint	smooth muscles
meninges	tendons
myopia	voluntary muscles

1. Muscles are attached to bones by ____.
2. Another name for nerve cells is ____.
3. Two bones meet at a(n) ____.
4. ____ are protective membranes that cover the brain.
5. At birth, the skeletal system contains connective tissue called ____.
6. Another name for nearsightedness is ____.
7. The internal organs contain ____.
8. Muscles over which people have control are ____.
9. Another name for heart muscle is ____.
10. A disease in which bones break easily is ____.

Review

1. Describe several functions of bone.
2. Why is bone marrow important?
3. Describe why calcium in the diet is important.
4. How do voluntary and involuntary muscles differ?
5. Describe the integumentary system.
6. Describe a reflex arc action.
7. How does the skin play a role in maintaining body temperature?
8. How can you avoid getting athlete's foot?
9. Identify the divisions of the nervous system and describe each.
10. Describe how the shape of the eyeball can affect vision.

Application

1. Why will drinking milk at your age be significant to you as an adult?
2. How does sweating help control your body temperature?
3. Describe why it is best not to squeeze blackheads and pimples.
4. Identify pieces of protective equipment used in any sport. Describe why each piece of equipment is used.

Individual Research

1. Osteoporosis is becoming recognized as a disease that is occurring in epidemic proportions to women over age 40. Write a report about this problem, including ways to prevent it.
2. Athletes are concerned about injuries to muscles. Identify two types of muscle injuries common to athletes and describe how they can be prevented.
3. Dermatologists use many procedures to relieve acne. Investigate one treatment for acne and discuss its advantages and disadvantages.

Readings

American Physical Fitness Research Institute, *Here's to Wellness: A Common Sense Guide to Health of Mind and Body.* New York, NY: Vanguard Press, Inc., 1984.

Fardon, David, *Osteoporosis.* New York, NY: Macmillan Publishing Co., Inc., 1985.

Ingram, Tere, and Hunter, Mack, *Healthy Skin, Beautiful Skin.* New York, NY: Walker & Company, 1985.

Classic cars are very valuable. Many people have a hobby of collecting old cars and restoring them to excellent condition. The collector studies the original design of the car so that the systems can be restored to function as originally planned. Your body systems need care. Do you have a plan to maintain your body in excellent condition?

Chapter 3

Energy and Transport Systems

OBJECTIVES: You will be able to
- name the digestive organs and their roles in health.
- describe why the circulatory system is important to one's health.
- describe the mechanics of breathing and identify why it is important to have a healthy respiratory system.
- describe the function of the urinary system and its relationship to health.

Think again about an automobile. Most cars are designed to use gasoline as a source of energy. However, it is not enough to have gasoline in the tank. If the car is to move, systems in the car have to work together. The gasoline must flow to the engine and mix with air before being ignited. As gasoline is burned, waste products are produced. These must be eliminated from the car through the exhaust system. In this chapter, you will learn that the human body has systems that are involved with the use of energy and the disposal of waste products in body cells.

DIGESTIVE SYSTEM

Regardless of where they are located in the body, all cells need energy in order to function. Energy comes from fuel. The fuel your body uses for energy is food.

Your body needs a constant supply of energy.

FIGURE 3-1.

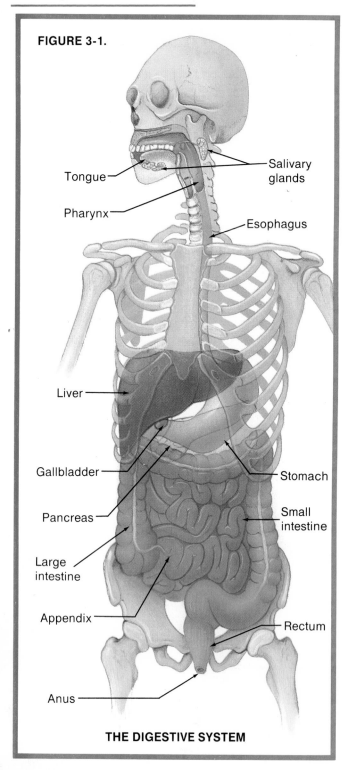

Tongue

Salivary glands

Pharynx

Esophagus

Liver

Gallbladder

Stomach

Pancreas

Small intestine

Large intestine

Appendix

Rectum

Anus

THE DIGESTIVE SYSTEM

3:1 Digestive Tract

Food must be processed in your body to provide nutrients. **Nutrients** are substances in food that provide energy and materials necessary for the growth, maintenance, and repair of cells. It is important to eat the kinds and amounts of foods that will provide the essential nutrients to your cells.

Digestion is the process in which food is chemically changed to a form that can pass through cell membranes. This process occurs in the organs of the digestive system. The main organs of this system form a continuous tube or tract through which food moves. Other organs release secretions that help break down the food (Figure 3–1).

When you chew solid food, the different kinds of teeth in your mouth help break the food into smaller pieces. As food is chewed, it is mixed with saliva. **Saliva** is a secretion of the salivary glands. Saliva not only moistens the food but also contains an enzyme called amylase. An **enzyme** is a chemical that speeds up a chemical reaction. Enzymes help break down food into simpler substances.

After food is chewed and swallowed, it moves through the esophagus by peristalsis. **Peristalsis** is a series of involuntary muscle contractions. Peristalsis is a powerful action. Even if you stood on your head and swallowed a piece of food, it would move through your esophagus. On occasion, peristalsis reverses. This occurs when you are sick and vomit.

From the esophagus, food moves into the stomach. The stomach is like an elastic pouch that acts as a temporary storage place for food. Food remains in the stomach about four hours.

Special glands in the lining of the stomach produce digestive juices that contain additional enzymes. The churning action of peristalsis and the digestive juices change the food into a thick paste called **chyme** (KIME). Food in this state moves into the small intestine.

Digestion is completed in the small intestine. The small intestine is a coiled tube measuring about 7 meters (23 feet) in length. Additional enzymes are produced in glands in the lining of the small intestine. The lining of the small intestine also contains millions of tiny, fingerlike projections called villi. The presence of the villi in the small intestine greatly increases the surface area of this part of the digestive system. When food is completely digested, it is absorbed into the bloodstream. The food is absorbed into the blood vessels of the villi.

Food that is not digested passes into the large intestine. The large intestine, or colon, absorbs water from the undigested material. This absorbing of water through the walls of the large intestine into body tissues is an important factor in maintaining the body's water balance. The remaining material forms a semi-solid mass called feces. **Feces** are waste materials that must be expelled regularly from the body. The expelling of feces from the rectum is called a bowel movement.

3:2 Other Organs Involved in Digestion

Other organs that are not part of the digestive tract are essential in the process of digestion. These organs are the liver, pancreas, and gallbladder (Figure 3–1).

The liver is the largest gland in the body. One important function of the liver is the production of a digestive secretion called bile. Bile is not an enzyme, but it is essential in the digestion of fatty foods. Fat in foods tends to clump together. Bile causes fat particles to break up into smaller droplets.

Bile produced in the liver moves through tubes called ducts to the gallbladder where it is stored. When food is present in the stomach, bile is released from the gallbladder. The bile moves through a duct and empties into the small intestine.

The pancreas is also a gland. It secretes enzymes necessary for the digestion of carbohydrates, fats, and proteins. More information about digestion and the action of enzymes will be discussed in Unit 5.

3:3 The Digestive System and Health

There are many common ailments that affect the organs of the digestive system. Many are minor conditions that can be treated. Some are more serious, especially if they keep occurring, and should be treated by a physician. Whether minor or serious,

Food moves from the esophagus to the stomach where special substances change the food into a paste called chyme.

Undigested food material is expelled from the rectum.

The liver produces bile, which aids in the digestion of fatty foods.

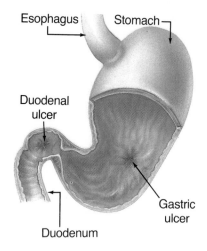

Esophagus | Stomach

Duodenal ulcer

Gastric ulcer

Duodenum

FIGURE 3–2. Ulcers

Some causes of indigestion can be controlled by changing eating habits and by learning to deal with stress.

Constipation may be caused by a lack of foods containing fiber as well as lack of exercise.

anything that upsets the body's ability to process food has a holistic effect (Chapter 1).

Indigestion is a term used to describe a variety of symptoms such as stomachache, nausea, vomiting, or mild pain in the abdomen. Symptoms of indigestion might indicate a minor problem. If they persist, the condition might be a serious one. Symptoms of indigestion can be caused by eating too fast, emotional stress, or food poisoning.

Some causes of indigestion can be controlled. The habit of eating too fast might be changed by learning to eat more slowly. Emotional stress may often be relieved by physical exercise such as walking or by talking over problems with a trusted friend.

Digestive juices produced in the stomach are called gastric juices. Gastric juices are acid in nature. Alcohol use, cigarette smoking, stress, or poor diet can cause an overproduction of acid. Ulcers are often a result of this excess acidic condition. Ulcers are open sores in the lining of the stomach and small intestine (Figure 3–2). They may bleed or penetrate the stomach tissue. Ulcers may be treated with medications and diet, but surgery is sometimes necessary. Ulcers are a serious medical condition that require treatment by a physician.

The appendix is a small sac attached to the end of the small intestine. It has no known function. Appendicitis is an infection and inflammation of the appendix. When this occurs, the appendix should be surgically removed to prevent it from rupturing. If the appendix ruptures, infected material may enter the abdominal cavity and cause a serious infection called peritonitis. A ruptured appendix can result in death.

Constipation is a condition that results when wastes move through the colon too slowly. Too much water is absorbed into body tissues, causing the feces to be hard and dry. This type of bowel movement becomes difficult and is often painful.

Constipation can be caused by a lack of foods containing fiber, such as bran, whole wheat, fruits, and leafy vegetables. Other causes are lack of exercise, lack of water in the diet, and postponing a bowel movement. Having regular bowel movements, usually once a day or once every other day, is important to a person's health.

If constipation persists or recurs often, a physician should be consulted. A physician may recommend a laxative to relieve constipation. A laxative is a medication that stimulates the digestive tract so that there is a bowel movement. Misuse of laxatives can cause the muscles of the intestine to work improperly and lose the ability to function on their own.

Diarrhea is a condition that occurs when intestinal wastes move through the colon too quickly. The feces remain watery and bowel movements are very frequent.

Diarrhea can be caused by emotional stress or by microorganisms in food or drink. If diarrhea is not treated, it can cause dehydration. **Dehydration** is loss of water. Dehydration is more likely to occur in infants. A person who has diarrhea often may lose a great deal of the mineral potassium from the body. Bananas often are recommended to be eaten in cases of diarrhea because they contain large amounts of potassium. Prolonged cases of diarrhea should be treated by a physician.

Emotional stress and harmful microorganisms can cause diarrhea.

Hemorrhoids are enlarged veins within the rectum, the lower part of the large intestine. The veins may bulge outside the anus or inside the rectum. Hemorrhoids can burst and bleed. They may be caused by sitting for long periods of time, by straining during bowel movements, or by straining during childbirth. Medications are available, but sometimes surgery is needed to correct extreme cases. Healthful behaviors for a healthy digestive system include the following.

Hemorrhoids can be controlled by the use of medications or by surgery.

- Eat a balanced diet.
- Chew food thoroughly and slowly.
- Exercise regularly.
- Drink water with each meal.
- Have regular bowel movements.

 Review and Reflect

1. What is the function of saliva in the process of digestion?
2. How is bile important to digestion?
3. Identify the organs of the digestive tract, starting with the mouth.
4. How is diet related to constipation?

FIGURE 3–3. Fruits and vegetables are essential for a healthy digestive system.

CIRCULATORY SYSTEM

Think of each body cell as an individual functioning unit. Each cell must continually receive needed materials and release waste products. The transport of these materials to and from each body cell is the function of the circulatory system.

3:4 Blood

Blood is the fluid by which essential substances are transported to cells throughout the body. Blood is also the means by which waste materials are removed from body cells and transported to specific organs for disposal.

The liquid part of blood is called **plasma.** Plasma is about 90 percent water and contains dissolved materials, including nutrients. Plasma also contains blood cells.

There are three kinds of blood cells, each with its own unique function (Figure 3–4). These are red cells, white cells, and platelets. The main function of **red blood cells** is to carry oxygen to body cells. Red blood cells are normally the most numerous in the human body. Red blood cells contain hemoglobin. **Hemoglobin** is a substance that combines with oxygen and gives blood its red color. As oxygen is delivered to body cells, the blood picks up carbon dioxide and carries it to the lungs where it is released from the body.

Red blood cells are continually being produced in bone marrow. These cells have a life span of one to four months after which time they are removed by the spleen. The **spleen** is an organ of the lymphatic system.

White blood cells destroy germs or substances that enter your body and might cause infection. They are manufactured in the bone marrow and lymph nodes. Normally, there is about one white cell for every 500 to 1000 red cells. However, when harmful microorganisms enter the body, more white cells are produced. The white cells surround these organisms, destroy them, and remove the remaining wastes. This is the reason the white cell count increases when you are sick or have an infection.

Platelets are the smallest type of blood cell. **Platelets** are blood cells that help form clots to prevent blood from leaking from injured vessels. However, some people are born with a condition called hemophilia. **Hemophilia** is a disease in which blood clots form too slowly or not at all. People with hemophilia can bleed to death from even a small cut or an internal injury. There is no cure for hemophilia. However, special treatment can help control bleeding.

Red blood cells contain hemoglobin, which carries oxygen to body cells.

FIGURE 3–4. Three kinds of blood cells.

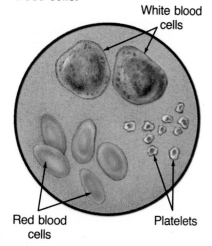

White blood cells

Red blood cells

Platelets

3:5 The Heart

The human heart is an incredible organ that beats between 70 and 80 times each minute, or about 100 000 times each day. The heart is about the size of a clenched fist. It weighs about 300 grams (10 to 11 ounces).

The heart is a strong muscle that lies under the sternum between the lungs. A fluid-filled sac called the **pericardium** encloses the heart. The fluid within the pericardium cushions the heart.

The **myocardium** is the muscular wall of the heart. Within the heart are four chambers, two atria and two ventricles. A wall called the **septum** separates the two sides (Figure 3–5).

The heart beats 70 to 80 times each minute or about 100 000 times each day.

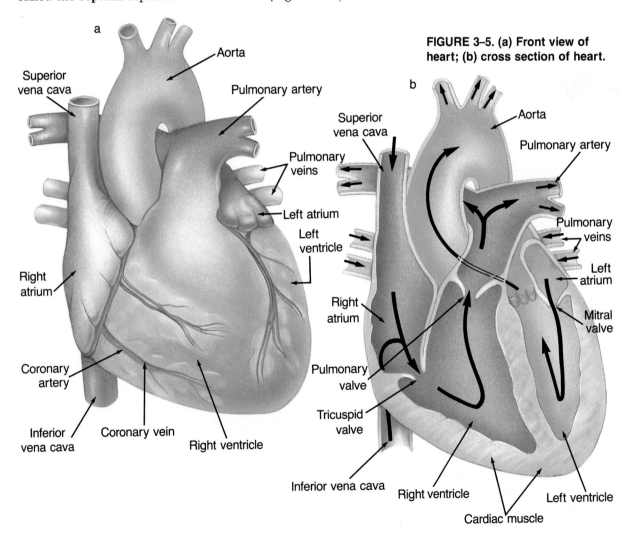

FIGURE 3–5. (a) Front view of heart; (b) cross section of heart.

FIGURE 3-6.

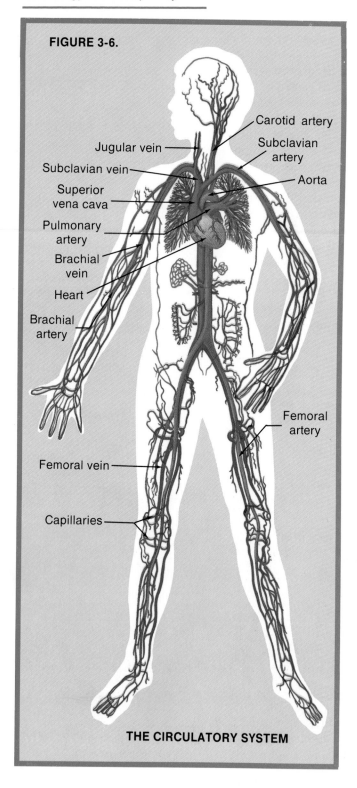

Carotid artery
Subclavian artery
Jugular vein
Subclavian vein
Aorta
Superior vena cava
Pulmonary artery
Brachial vein
Heart
Brachial artery
Femoral artery
Femoral vein
Capillaries

THE CIRCULATORY SYSTEM

3:6 Blood Vessels and Circulation

Blood is continually circulating in a series of closed tubes that carry it from the heart to all body cells and back to the heart again (Figure 3–6). These tubes are called blood vessels. There are three main types of vessels—arteries, capillaries, and veins. Arteries carry blood away from the heart to all parts of the body. Near the heart, arteries are large, elastic, and thick-walled. Away from the heart, the large arteries continually subdivide into smaller arteries called arterioles. Arterioles further subdivide to form capillaries. Capillaries are microscopic, thin-walled vessels that spread throughout body tissues. Capillaries connect arterioles to small veins called venules. Blood flowing through venules and veins is on its way back to the heart. The walls of veins are not as thick as artery walls.

As blood flows through capillaries, some liquid enters into spaces between the body cells. The clear liquid is **lymph.** Lymph belongs to a part of the circulatory system called the lymphatic system. The **lymphatic system** contains structures that serve to filter harmful organisms in the body. These structures are called **lymph nodes.** There are lymph nodes in various parts of the body. These lymph nodes filter and destroy harmful organisms in specific areas of the body. Suppose you had a sore throat. Most likely, the lymph nodes located on the side of the neck would be swollen. Lymph nodes in the side of the neck filter germs from the mouth, nose, and throat areas.

3:7 The Cardiac Cycle and Blood Pressure

Each heartbeat represents a sequence of events called the **cardiac cycle.** During the cardiac cycle, the heart muscle alternately relaxes and contracts. When the atria relax, both fill up with blood. While the atria are filling, the atrioventricular valves remain open to allow the blood to flow into the ventricles. As the atria contract, the valves close and the ventricles are filled with blood. The ventricles then contract, forcing blood out through the aorta and the pulmonary arteries.

Blood pressure is the force exerted by the flowing blood against the walls of the arteries. The pumping action of the heart creates the force. Every time the heart beats, the pressure increases. When the heart relaxes between beats, the pressure decreases. When a physician measures your blood pressure, a measurement is taken of both the "upper" and "lower" pressures. The upper pressure is greatest and occurs during a contraction. It is called systolic pressure. The lower pressure occurs when the heart rests between contractions. It is called diastolic pressure.

Think about the last time you had a physical examination. The physician checked your blood pressure using a sphygmomanometer (sfihg moh muh NAHM ut ur). A **sphygmomanometer** is an instrument that measures blood pressure. To determine a person's blood pressure, an inflatable cuff is placed around the person's arm just above the elbow. A pump is used to inflate the cuff. This action temporarily stops the flow of blood. The physician then places a stethoscope over a blood vessel below the cuff.

The force exerted by blood against the artery walls is called blood pressure.

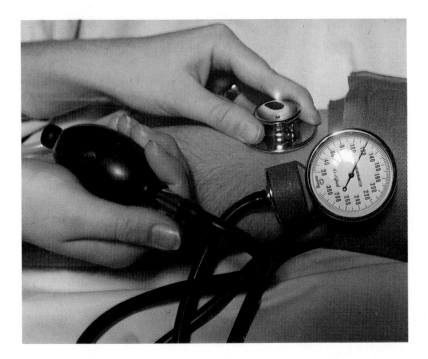

FIGURE 3–7. Pressure in the inflated cuff does not allow blood to circulate below the cuff. As the cuff is deflated, a measurement can be made to determine when the flow of blood begins to return.

A stethoscope is used to hear sounds inside a person's body.

For young adults, normal systolic blood pressure is 110–140; normal diastolic blood pressure is 65–90.

Blood pressure may rise under conditions such as anger or stress.

FIGURE 3–8. Exercise is an important factor in maintaining optimum health.

A **stethoscope** is an instrument that enables a physician to hear sounds inside a person's body. As air is released from the cuff, the cuff loosens and a point is reached when a pulse can be heard again. A **pulse** is the rhythmic expansion of an artery. Each contraction of the ventricles starts a new pulse that proceeds as a wave of contractions through muscles in the artery walls.

When the pulse is heard, the physician will check a gauge on the sphygmomanometer to record the measurement. This is the systolic pressure. The physician will continue to deflate the cuff until the sound of the pulse is no longer heard. This measurement is the diastolic pressure. Thus, blood pressure will be recorded as $\frac{\text{systolic blood pressure}}{\text{diastolic blood pressure}}$. The blood pressure measurement is read as two figures such as $\frac{120}{80}$.

These figures can vary. To help keep the circulatory system healthy, blood pressure should be kept within a normal range. The normal range for young adults, according to many sources, is 110 to 140 for the systolic pressure and 65 to 90 for the diastolic pressure.

3:8 Blood Pressure and Health

Blood pressure varies from one person to another and in the same person. It goes up when you are excited and goes down when you are asleep. It is possible to have sudden spurts of high blood pressure when you are angry or stressful or after vigorous exercise. You may have high blood pressure without knowing it. Continued high blood pressure is the most common disease affecting the heart and blood vessels and can lead to a serious heart condition. The only way to know for sure that your blood pressure is not high is to have it measured regularly. Healthful behaviors for a healthy heart and blood vessels include the following.
- Avoid smoking.
- Reduce the amount of fat and salt in your diet.
- Practice healthful ways to deal with stress.
- Get enough exercise and rest.

You will learn more about the effects of cigarette smoking, diet, stress, and exercise as you continue reading this book.

 Review and Reflect

5. Explain how the flow of blood through the heart is controlled.
6. Describe the two major paths through which blood is pumped.
7. What is the cardiac cycle?

RESPIRATORY SYSTEM

Just as all cells need a source of energy, which is food, all cells need a way to chemically release the energy from the nutrients. This release of energy in the cells is accomplished by the chemical action of oxygen. In this process, carbon dioxide is produced as a waste product. The respiratory system is involved in making oxygen available to cells and in ridding the body of carbon dioxide. This system and the circulatory system work together in this process.

3:9 Respiration

When you breathe, air enters and leaves your body through the organs of the respiratory system (Figure 3–9). Respiration refers to the exchange of gases between a living organism and its environment. In your body, respiration takes place in two stages, external and internal.

External respiration takes place as oxygen and carbon dioxide are exchanged between the blood and the air in the lungs. **Internal respiration** takes place as oxygen and carbon dioxide are exchanged between body cells and blood circulating near them.

3:10 Mechanics of Breathing

An adult inhales about 12 times each minute at rest. The lungs take in about one pint of air each time a person inhales. In one day, a person exhales and inhales about 21 600 times. If a person exercises, this number increases.

The process of taking air into the lungs is called inhaling or **inspiration.** During inspiration, the rib muscles contract,

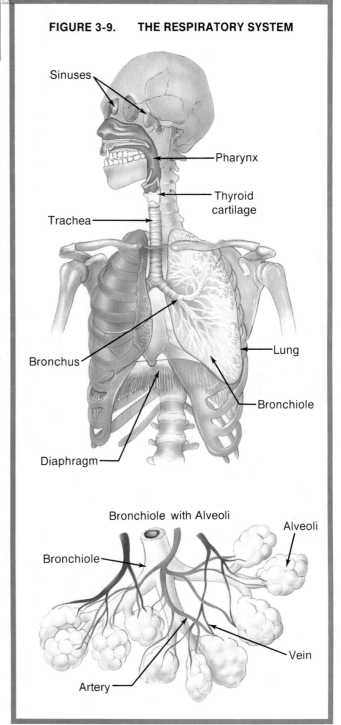

FIGURE 3-9.   THE RESPIRATORY SYSTEM

Sinuses

Pharynx

Thyroid cartilage

Trachea

Bronchus

Lung

Bronchiole

Diaphragm

Bronchiole with Alveoli

Alveoli

Bronchiole

Vein

Artery

causing them to be pulled up and out. As this happens, the diaphragm also contracts. As it does, it moves downward enlarging the chest cavity. This results in reduced air pressure within the chest cavity. The lungs fill with air. The pressure inside the lungs is equalized with the outside air pressure.

Inspiration is the taking of air into the body; expiration is the forcing of air out of the body.

The process of forcing air out of the lungs is called exhaling or **expiration.** The process of expiration works opposite to that of inspiration. During expiration, the rib muscles relax and move downward and inward. The diaphragm relaxes and moves upward increasing the pressure around the inflated lungs. Air is forced from the lungs (Figure 3–10).

Breathing is controlled by involuntary actions in the body.

For the most part, breathing is an involuntary action. The rate of breathing is controlled by two factors. One factor is chemical and involves the amount of carbon dioxide in the blood. The other factor involves the respiratory center in the brain and nerve pathways from that center.

Perhaps you have tried to hold your breath. After a short while, you could not hold your breath any longer, and you exhaled. While you were holding your breath, the amount of carbon dioxide in your blood was increasing. This increase stimulates the respiratory center and breathing resumes.

If you were to breathe deeply and quickly for several minutes, you would exhale an excessive amount of carbon dioxide. The carbon dioxide level in the blood would decrease because you would be exhaling carbon dioxide faster than it was being produced in your cells. This process is called hyperventilation. You

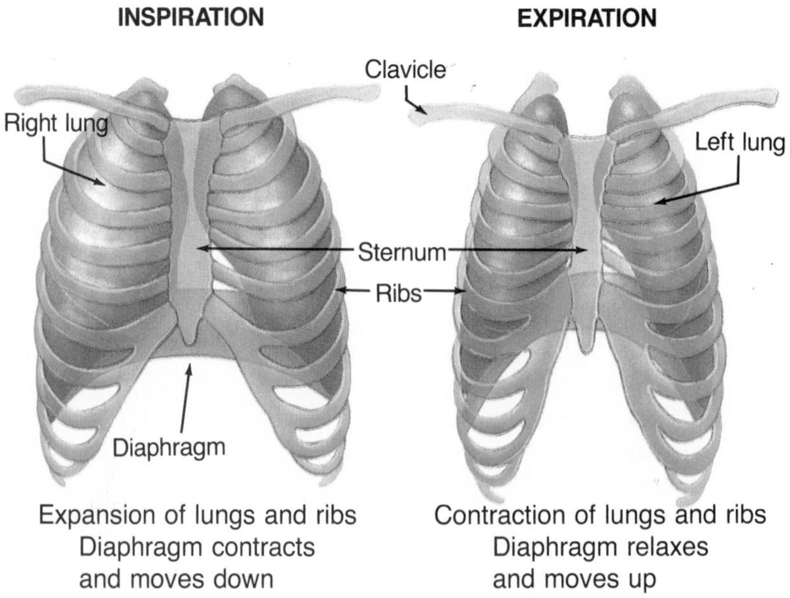

INSPIRATION   **EXPIRATION**

Clavicle

Right lung

Left lung

Sternum

Ribs

Diaphragm

Expansion of lungs and ribs
Diaphragm contracts
and moves down

Contraction of lungs and ribs
Diaphragm relaxes
and moves up

FIGURE 3–10. Expansion of the lungs and rib cage causes inhalation. Oxygen in the inhaled air is absorbed by the blood passing through the lungs. During expiration, waste carbon dioxide is expelled.

would become dizzy and might even faint. Breathing rate would decrease. Normal breathing rate will resume when the carbon dioxide level of the blood returns to a more normal level.

3:11   The Respiratory System and Health

Air that you inhale is cleaned, warmed, and moistened as it moves to your lungs. Sticky mucus and tiny hairs in the nose and throat moisten and clean the air. It is warmed by blood circulating in the area of the nose and throat.

Sometimes, the air you breathe contains dust and particles that could harm lung tissue. If you are exposed to heavily polluted air over a long period of time, lung tissue is affected. Breathing may become difficult. Emphysema is a serious lung disease that results from the destruction of lung tissue. The lungs lose their elasticity and do not function efficiently. This disease is common in people who smoke and who regularly inhale polluted air.

Lung cancer is a leading cause of cancer deaths in males in the United States. Among women, cases of lung cancer are increasing rapidly. The main cause of lung cancer is cigarette smoking. Heavy smokers are 20 times more likely to develop lung cancer than nonsmokers. Cigarette smoking is the greatest and yet most preventable cause of premature death. Smoking marijuana may also cause lung damage. Healthful behaviors for a healthy respiratory system include the following.

- Avoid smoking.
- Exercise regularly to strengthen the diaphragm muscle and to make breathing more efficient.
- Avoid heavily polluted air.

Inhaled air is cleaned, warmed, and moistened as it moves to the lungs.

Cigarette smoking is a main cause of lung cancer.

✔ Review and Reflect

8. How is inhaled air cleaned before it enters your lungs?

 ## Activity: Blood Pressure Differences

Using a sphygmomanometer, measure the blood pressure of two adults who smoke and two adults who do not smoke. Record the results. Have the adults who are smokers each smoke a cigarette and inhale deeply. Remeasure their blood pressure. What changes occur? How do the initial blood pressure readings of the smoking adults compare to the readings of the nonsmoking adults?

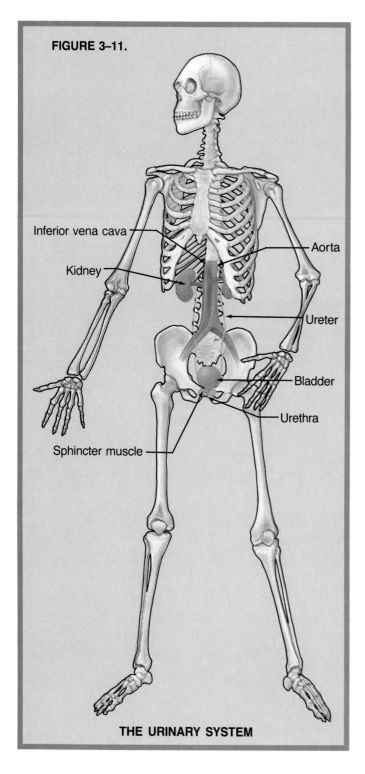

FIGURE 3–11.

Inferior vena cava

Kidney

Aorta

Ureter

Bladder

Urethra

Sphincter muscle

THE URINARY SYSTEM

URINARY SYSTEM

Another important system in the removal of wastes from the body is the urinary system. The organs of the urinary system are the kidneys, ureters, bladder, and urethra. These organs remove wastes from the blood and help control the amount of fluid in the body (Figure 3–11).

3:12 Kidneys and Bladder

The kidneys lie near the lowest ribs in the back. Connected to each kidney are an artery and a vein. As blood circulates through each kidney, the kidney acts as a filter. Waste materials that are filtered out form urine. Urine is about 95 percent water in which solid wastes are dissolved. Urine then flows into the ureters. The **ureters** are tubes that extend from the kidneys to the urinary bladder. The **urinary bladder** stores urine. When the urinary bladder becomes full, nerve impulses stimulate both voluntary and involuntary muscles to release urine from the urethra. The **urethra** is a narrow tube leading from the bladder through which urine passes out of the body.

3:13 The Urinary System and Health

To maintain healthy kidneys, it is important that you have the equivalent of at least six glasses of water in your diet each day. Many foods you eat contain water.

Sometimes, a kidney must be removed because of a disease. In such cases, one healthy kidney can perform the task of two. If both kidneys are removed, or fail to work properly, a person may be placed on a dialysis machine. **Dialysis** is a process in which a person's blood is filtered by a special machine. This machine takes the place of kidneys. The person's blood is circulated through tubes into a filtering machine. The blood is cleansed and then returned through a tube to the person's body.

An alternative to dialysis is a kidney transplant. A **kidney transplant** is the exchange of an unhealthy kidney that does not function for a healthy kidney. The healthy kidney often comes from a blood relative of the person who receives the transplant. This reduces the chances of the kidney being rejected by that person's body. The transplant is a surgical procedure. Normal kidney function is usually immediate after the surgery. Kidney transplants are the most successful of organ transplant operations. The life span of the kidney donor is usually not affected.

Urine can be used to diagnose problems in the body. This is done through a process called urinalysis. **Urinalysis** is the chemical examination of a person's urine. A urinalysis is a routine part of.most physical examinations to detect substances that normally are not in urine, or substances that are in larger than normal quantities. Through urinalysis, conditions such as diabetes can sometimes be detected. A urinalysis also detects problems in the urinary tract. The earlier a problem is detected, the sooner it can be treated.

Dialysis serves to filter wastes from a person's body.

Urinalysis can be used to detect diseases such as diabetes.

 ## Review and Reflect

9. What is the function of the urinary system?

Health
ADVANCES

Many people between the ages of 30 and 50 develop kidney stones. Kidney stones form from calcium salts and other substances. These stones can become lodged within the kidney itself or pass into the ureter. The stones may vary in size from one as tiny as a pinhead to one as large as a walnut. The danger of kidney stones is that they can obstruct the flow of urine into the bladder. If urine backs up into the kidneys, it can cause infection and destroy kidney tissue. If stones cause such an obstruction, they must be removed or the patient could die.

Calcium salts and other substances are responsible for formation of kidney stones.

FIGURE 3–12. Kidney stones

The lithotripter is a device that is used to crumble kidney stones.

3:14 The Kidney Stone Crusher

New advances in medicine now make it possible to remove stones more efficiently and safely than ever before. Currently, there are several methods used to treat kidney stones. Certain medications can help dissolve the stones. When this procedure is not successful, the stones may be surgically removed.

However, there is now a remarkable new device called a lithotripter. It was developed in West Germany and approved for use in the United States in 1985. The **lithotripter** is a machine that uses a focused shock wave to crumble kidney stones. No incision is needed because the shock wave passes through body tissues without harming them. The wave hits the stones causing them to crumble. The pieces can then be passed out of the person's body through the urine. The use of the lithotripter is less expensive, less painful, and requires less recovery time than kidney stone surgery.

Compared to surgery, the use of the lithotripter is a mild treatment. During the treatment, the patient sits in a tub of water. The shock waves are focused on the kidney stones. The lithotripter technique requires a three-day hospital stay and less than a week of recuperation. Although the lithotripter can be used with most patients, there is a small percentage of the population that cannot be helped. However, the success of this device on most kidney stone patients makes the lithotripter a major advance in medicine.

Focus on
Life Management Skills

- Eat slowly and avoid stress to prevent indigestion.
- Help prevent ulcers by avoiding the use of cigarettes and alcohol.
- Eat foods containing fiber, such as bran, whole wheat, fruits, and leafy vegetables to help prevent constipation.
- Use laxatives only when recommended by a physician.
- Eat bananas after having diarrhea to replace loss of potassium.
- Help control your blood pressure by avoiding smoking cigarettes, reducing fat and salt in your diet, managing your stress, and getting sufficient exercise and rest.
- Help prevent lung diseases by not smoking cigarettes and marijuana.
- Drink six glasses of water daily to help maintain healthy kidneys.

Health
CAREERS

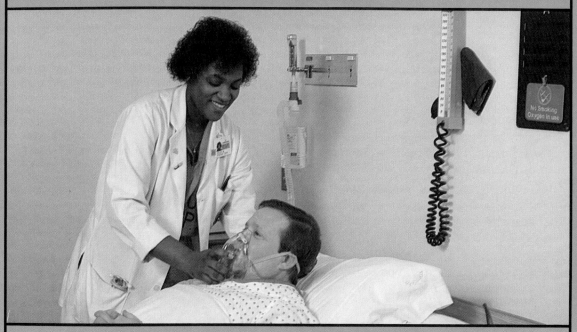

Respiratory Therapist

Zelee Porter usually has a busy day at the hospital. She may need to administer oxygen to a heart attack victim. She may treat an asthma victim who has difficulty breathing. Zelee is a respiratory therapist. A **respiratory therapist** is a person who has received special training in the treatment of patients with respiratory problems.

Respiratory therapists follow physicians' orders and use special equipment that helps patients breathe. They also show patients and their families how to use this equipment at home. Most respiratory therapists work in hospitals. Others may work for oxygen equipment rental companies, ambulance services, or nursing homes.

Respiratory therapists are trained in either a two-year or four-year college program. Areas of study include human anatomy and physiology, chemistry, physics, microbiology, and mathematics. Other areas of study focus on how to deal with procedures, equipment, and clinical tests.

Respiratory therapists can advance in their field. They can become an assistant chief or chief therapist. If they further their education through graduate studies, they can become an instructor of respiratory therapy at the college level.

People who want to become respiratory therapists should enjoy working with people and understand the physical and psychological needs of patients who have breathing problems. They must also be able to work with, and be a cooperative member of, the entire medical team.

Summary

1. The organs of the digestive tract form a continuous tube through which food moves during the digestive process. 3:1
2. The liver, pancreas, and gallbladder are organs involved in digestion. 3:2
3. Disorders of the digestive system such as indigestion, ulcers, constipation, and diarrhea can be prevented and treated. 3:3
4. The liquid part of blood, plasma, contains dissolved materials and cells. 3:4
5. The heart is an important muscle that pumps blood to all parts of the body. 3:5
6. The heart pumps blood through arteries, capillaries, and veins to all body cells and back to the heart again. 3:6
7. Blood pressure is the force exerted by blood flowing through arteries and is measured by the use of a sphygmomanometer. 3:7
8. Regular blood pressure checks will help prevent a serious heart problem from developing and motivate you to adopt more healthful behaviors. 3:8
9. The exchange of gases between your body and the environment takes place in internal and external respiration. 3:9
10. Breathing is an involuntary action that occurs approximately 12 times each minute at rest in an adult. 3:10
11. Polluted air that enters your lungs may cause respiratory diseases. 3:11
12. The kidneys filter wastes from the body. 3:12
13. It is important to include water in your diet each day in order to maintain healthy kidneys. 3:13
14. The lithotripter is a device that can crush kidney stones in some patients. 3:14

Vocabulary

Below is a list of vocabulary words used in this chapter. Use each word only once to complete the sentences. Do not write in this book.

chyme	lymph nodes
dehydration	myocardium
dialysis	peristalsis
hemoglobin	saliva
inspiration	urinary bladder

1. The muscular wall of the heart is the ＿＿.
2. Diarrhea often causes a loss of water, which is called ＿＿.
3. ＿＿ is a series of involuntary muscle contractions.
4. The process of breathing in or inhaling is also called ＿＿.
5. A mechanical process for filtering wastes from the blood is ＿＿.
6. A part of the circulatory system that contains structures that filter harmful organisms for the body is the ＿＿.
7. Partly digested food in the stomach is called ＿＿.
8. In the body, urine is stored in the ＿＿.
9. Food in the mouth is softened by ＿＿.
10. ＿＿ in red blood cells combines with oxygen.

Review

1. Identify three main organs of digestion.
2. Describe three common ailments of the digestive system.
3. Identify the major arteries that leave the heart.
4. How do arteries and veins differ in structure and function?
5. Describe the two major paths through which the heart pumps blood.
6. What is the main function of white blood cells?
7. Differentiate between systolic and diastolic blood pressure.
8. Name three healthful behaviors for a healthy heart.
9. Name three healthful behaviors for a healthy respiratory system.
10. How does a lithotripter work?

Application

1. What would happen to the food you eat if your mouth did not contain saliva?
2. Why might a person who has ulcers avoid eating spicy foods?
3. Why do people who smoke cigarettes increase their chances of having serious lung diseases?

Individual Research

1. Indigestion often is caused by stress. Identify five behaviors a person might practice to reduce stress.
2. Your local chapter of the American Heart Association has pamphlets about blood pressure. Obtain some of these pamphlets and study them. Write a report about blood pressure and the dangers of prolonged high blood pressure.

Readings

Friedman, Meyer, and Rosenman, Ray H., *Treating Type A Behavior and Your Heart.* New York, NY: Alfred A. Knopf, Inc., 1984.

Kahn, Ada P., *Help Yourself to Health: High Blood Pressure.* Chicago, IL: Contemporary Books, Inc., 1983.

Nugent, Nancy, *How to Get Along with Your Stomach.* Boston, MA: Little, Brown & Co., 1978.

The process of assembling the parts of an automobile is a continual process. At the end of the assembly line, the car will be complete and ready for use. Many cars will be similar, but very few are exactly alike. How are you similar to other people? How are you different?

Chapter 4

Endocrine and Reproductive Systems

OBJECTIVES: You will be able to
- **identify the endocrine system glands and their effects on health.**
- **describe the parts of the male and female reproductive systems, and identify how they can be kept healthy.**

In an auto assembly line, there is a definite and planned pattern of activity. Each assembled piece has a purpose and a custom fit. It becomes a part of the whole car and is vital to total performance. The assembly line starts with the frame. Next, the axles and wheels are added, then the engine and transmission. The addition of the body of the car, the exterior paint, and outside fixtures combine to give the characteristics of the car's make and model. Interior finishes complete the assembly. The assembled car parts work together to function as a unit.

Just as in an auto assembly, the human body also functions as a unit. Body systems normally work together in a definite and controlled pattern.

ENDOCRINE SYSTEM

You have learned that the nervous system regulates and controls body functions. Another body system, the endocrine system, works closely with the nervous system to maintain the body's normal state of balance. Because of your nervous system, you react quickly to changes in your environment. You pull your hand away from sharp objects. You blink if an object comes too close to your eyes and face. You run to catch a ball. The endocrine system works more slowly. It regulates internal activities such as growth, sexual development, and the way your body uses food.

The endocrine system works closely with the nervous system.

The endocrine system controls functions such as growth, sexual development, and the use of food.

4:1   Endocrine Glands

The **endocrine system** consists of glands that control many of
the body's activities by producing hormones (Figures 4–4 and
4–7). These hormones are secreted directly into the bloodstream.
Hormones are chemicals that act as messengers and regulate body
activities. Most glands continuously secrete hormones so that
they are always present in the blood. Hormones are usually
specific. This means certain glands produce specific hormones for
specific purposes (Table 4–1).

Perhaps the gland with the greatest influence on the body is the
pituitary gland. The pituitary gland is known as the master gland
because it produces hormones that control other endocrine
glands. The pituitary gland also produces a growth hormone that
influences the growth of bones.

The thyroid gland produces a hormone that controls metabolism. Metabolism refers to the body's use of food. This includes
all the changes involving the use of energy in foods by living cells.

A well-functioning thyroid gland is important to health. Some
people have thyroids that are overactive. An overactive thyroid
produces excess hormone, increases metabolism, and causes the
body to burn up food too rapidly. This may result in weight loss
and an increased appetite. Some people have thyroids that are
underactive. An underactive thyroid produces too little hormone,
decreases metabolism, and causes the body to burn up food too
slowly. This may result in weight gain and a feeling of sluggish-
ness. A person with an overactive or underactive thyroid may
develop a goiter. A **goiter** is an enlarged thyroid gland. A goiter
causes the front of the neck to be swollen.

There are four parathyroid glands under the surface of the
thyroid gland. The parathyroid glands control the amount of
calcium and phosphorus in the body. Calcium and phosphorus
are important minerals necessary for bone growth, muscle contraction, and teeth development. Underactive parathyroids cause
the calcium level in the blood to fall. Overactive parathyroids
cause calcium to be removed from the bones and enter the
bloodstream. This produces muscle weakness. Both underactive
and overactive parathyroids may be controlled by prescribed
medications or surgery.

Think about the last time you had to react suddenly. Perhaps
someone yelled at you to get out of the way of an oncoming car.
Maybe someone walked up quietly behind you and startled you.
These kinds of situations produce changes in your body. Your
heartbeat rate may have increased suddenly. Your muscles may
have felt tight. If so, this resulted from the action of your adrenal
glands.

Table 4–1   Endocrine Glands

Gland	Some Hormones Produced	Function of the Hormone
Pituitary anterior	Somatotropin	• promotes the growth of nearly all tissues
	Follicle-stimulating	• activates the ovaries
	Luteninizing	• causes the follicle to release an egg from the ovary
Thyroid	Thyroxine	• regulates the body's use of oxygen and nutrients
Parathyroid	Parathormone	• regulates levels of phosphorus and calcium
Adrenal medulla	Adrenaline	• affects the circulatory system in response to a stressful emergency situation
Thymus	Thymosin	• helps in the development of the body's immune system
Pancreas	Insulin	• regulates blood sugar level
Testes	Testosterone	• produces male secondary sex characteristics
Ovaries	Estrogen	• produces female secondary sex characteristics
	Progesterone	• maintains uterus during pregnancy

Each adrenal gland functions as two separate glands. The inner part is called the medulla; the outer part is called the cortex. The main hormone of the adrenal medulla is adrenaline, or epinephrine (ep uh NEF run). Adrenaline helps the body respond to a stressful situation or an emergency. As a result, heart rate and blood pressure increase, and blood sugar level rises. These changes help a person respond to critical situations.

Adrenaline can be produced in the laboratory for medical uses. It can help a failing heart function again. It can increase the circulation of the blood when a person is suffering from shock. It can also relax the tiny air passages in the lungs and help a person with asthma to breathe easier.

The function of the adrenal cortex is more complex. The cortex produces several hormones that are involved in regulating water balance in body tissues, and in increasing blood sugar level.

The thymus gland functions to help fight infection in young children. Before a baby is born, its thymus gland produces one type of white blood cell. After the baby is born, the thymus produces a hormone that is involved in helping protect against disease. The thymus gland is most active in the first few months after birth.

The endocrine glands are the pituitary, thyroid, parathyroid, adrenal medulla, thymus, pancreas, testes, and ovaries.

FIGURE 4–1. The red line indicates a person's blood sugar level after eating an apple. The blue line indicates blood sugar level after eating a candy bar.

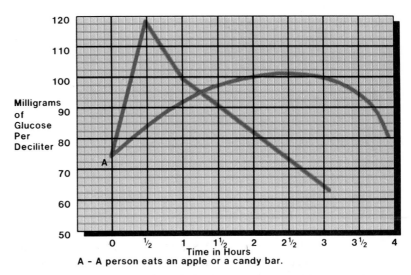

A - A person eats an apple or a candy bar.

The pancreas is called a mixed gland. It is mixed because one kind of cell produces the hormone insulin and another kind of cell produce digestive enzymes (Chapter 3). Insulin is produced in cells called **islets of Langerhans.** Insulin regulates the level of sugar in the blood (Figure 4–1).

If too little or no insulin is produced, or if insulin does not function as it should, diabetes mellitus results. **Diabetes mellitus** is a disorder in which the blood sugar level is abnormally high. This condition may be controlled by diet, but usually is treated by periodic shots of insulin. High blood sugar level is sometimes called **hyperglycemia.** High blood sugar level causes a person to experience constant thirst and frequent urination.

Sometimes too much insulin is produced. This results in a condition known as hypoglycemia. **Hypoglycemia** is an uncommon condition in which there is too little sugar in the blood. This results in a person feeling weak and nervous. Hypoglycemia can be treated by diet under the supervision of a physician.

Reproductive glands are called **gonads.** In the male, the testes are the reproductive glands; in the female, the ovaries are the reproductive glands. The testes and ovaries each have two main functions: the testes produce sperm and male sex hormones; the ovaries produce ova (egg cells) and female sex hormones.

The testes and ovaries function at a minimum level as endocrine glands until some time after the age of ten. Hormones produced by the pituitary gland affect the action of the gonads. Hormones produced by the testes and ovaries are sometimes called sex hormones. They are responsible for the changes that occur during puberty (PYEW burt ee). **Puberty** is the stage of sexual development during which males and females become

Diabetes mellitus usually is controlled by a program of rest, diet, and exercise. However, some people with diabetes need medications or insulin injections.

High blood sugar is called hyperglycemia; low blood sugar is called hypoglycemia.

The testes are male reproductive glands; ovaries are female reproductive glands.

physically able to produce offspring. The testes produce the hormone testosterone (teh STAHS tuh rohn). The ovaries produce hormones called estrogens (ES truh juns) and progesterone (pro JES tuh rohn).

Perhaps the most visible signs of puberty are the physical changes that occur. In a female, these changes are larger breasts, underarm hair, hair in the pubic area, and widened hips. In males, the changes include pubic and underarm hair, facial hair, broadened shoulders, and a deepened voice. These changes are often referred to as secondary sex characteristics. Sex hormones will be discussed in more detail later in this chapter.

4:2 The Endocrine System and Health

The glands of the endocrine system work together. When functioning properly, their production of hormones is in balance. Under certain conditions, a greater amount of a hormone may be secreted from a gland. For example, the adrenal glands will produce more adrenaline when a burst of energy is needed by an athlete to perform at his or her best. Likewise, the amount of hormone produced by the adrenal glands will return to normal after the athletic event is over.

Sometimes the endocrine system does not function as it should. This can result in a person feeling unusually tired, thirsty, or nervous. The person may experience sudden weight loss or weight gain. When this occurs, a checkup by a physician is needed. Through blood tests, a physician can detect a glandular problem in the thyroid or pituitary glands. Urine tests may help determine a problem in the functioning of the pancreas. Any suspected glandular problems should be treated by a physician.

FIGURE 4–2. An athlete experiences a burst of energy as a result of increased adrenaline in the blood.

The adrenal glands produce adrenaline, which is used when additional energy is needed by the body.

Being tired, thirsty, or nervous may indicate an endocrine problem.

 Review and Reflect

1. Describe the different results of an overactive thyroid gland and an underactive thyroid gland.
2. Why is the pancreas called a mixed gland?

REPRODUCTIVE SYSTEM

Reproduction is the process of producing offspring. Unlike other body systems, the reproductive system is not vital to an individual's survival. However, this system is vital to the continuation of the human race.

FIGURE 4–3. Parents and offspring resemble each other. Heredity influences every component of a person's life.

Female internal reproductive organs are the ovaries, Fallopian tubes, uterus, and vagina.

4:3 Heredity

Think about your family. How are you like other members of your family? How do you differ? Many of your features were determined by your biological parents. These features helped you become a total person. You developed into a mental, physical, and social individual.

Heredity is the transmission of features from one generation to the next. Parents and offspring have many features in common. Yet, no two people are alike. All living things are composed of cells. Each cell has a nucleus that contains chromosomes with genes. Genes are responsible for transmitting features from parents to offspring. The development of a new individual begins when two cells, a sperm and an ovum, unite. This union is called **fertilization,** or conception, and results in the formation of a single cell, or zygote. A **zygote** is a fertilized ovum. The zygote contains genes from each parent.

Activity: Inherited Traits Survey

Devise a survey to be distributed to all students in your grade level or school. List several possible inherited traits. Students will indicate which traits they possess. Traits may include hair color, eye color, the ability to roll the tongue, having diabetes, or dimples. Prepare a space for students participating in the survey to indicate their sex. Total the results of each category by sex, and compute your class' percentage in relation to all participants. How does your class compare in the number and types of inherited traits?

4:4 Female Reproductive Organs

The internal reproductive organs of the female include two ovaries, Fallopian tubes, uterus, and vagina (Figure 4–4). The ovaries are two almond-shaped glands. As stated earlier, the ovaries have two main functions. They produce egg cells and hormones. Each ovary contains clusters of cells called follicles. One egg cell matures from a follicle about every 28 days and is released from an ovary. This process is called ovulation.

A Fallopian tube, or oviduct, extends from each ovary to the uterus (YEWT uh rus). The Fallopian tube serves as a pathway for the egg cell as it is released from the ovary. It carries the egg cell from the ovary to the uterus. If fertilization of an egg cell by a sperm occurs, it usually takes place in the Fallopian tube. The two cells form a zygote.

The uterus is a hollow, muscular, pear-shaped organ in which a baby develops after an ovum is fertilized. The uterus is normally about two inches wide at the top and three inches long. The uterus expands greatly during a pregnancy. The cervix is the opening of the lower end of the uterus into the vagina.

The walls of the uterus are composed of three layers. The inner lining of the uterus is a soft, spongy tissue called the **endometrium.** The endometrium is supplied with glandular secretions and blood vessels. This layer thickens each month as part of the menstrual cycle. The middle layer is a muscular layer called the myometrium. The outer layer is called the perimetrium.

The vagina is a muscular tube that connects the uterus to the outside of the body. A baby moves through the vagina from the mother's uterus during birth.

4:5 Associated Reproductive Structures

The external parts of the female reproductive system are known as the genitalia, or genitals. The genitals include the mons veneris, labia, and clitoris. These parts together are known as the vulva.

The mons veneris is a rounded, fatty pad of tissue that lies over the pubic bone. The labia are liplike, fatty tissues that lie along both sides of the vagina. The labia cover the opening to the vagina. The labia also cover the opening of the urethra (yoo REE thruh). The urethra is the passageway through which urine leaves the body. The clitoris is a small knob of tissue in the front of the vaginal opening. It contains blood vessels and nerve endings.

The mammary glands of the breasts secrete milk that can be used to nourish a baby after birth. Milk drains through ducts to the openings in the nipples.

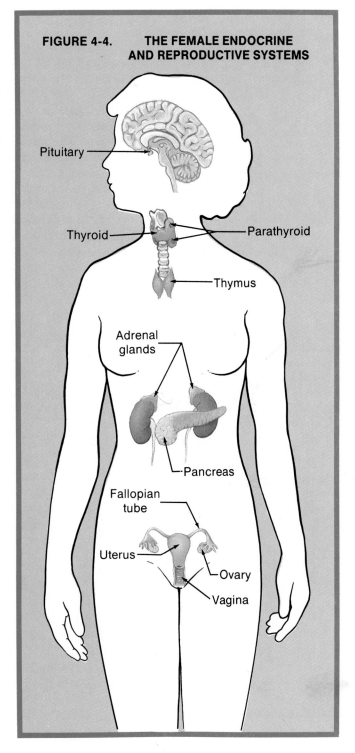

FIGURE 4-4.   THE FEMALE ENDOCRINE AND REPRODUCTIVE SYSTEMS

Pituitary

Thyroid

Parathyroid

Thymus

Adrenal glands

Pancreas

Fallopian tube

Uterus

Ovary

Vagina

4:6   The Menstrual Cycle

The menstrual cycle in the female begins during puberty.

Sometime between the ages of 8 and 13, a female begins the process of puberty. During puberty, the menstrual cycle begins. The **menstrual cycle** is a monthly series of changes that occur in a woman's body. During the menstrual cycle, the ovaries produce a mature egg cell, the lining of the uterus is prepared for a fertilized egg, and the lining breaks down if an egg is not fertilized. The first menstrual cycle is called menarche (MEN ar kee).

Usually, the menstrual cycle occurs in regular phases (Figure 4–5). During one phase, the pituitary gland secretes FSH. **FSH** (follicle-stimulating hormone) stimulates the growth and development of follicles in the ovaries. A maturing follicle produces and releases estrogen. This allows the uterus to prepare for the egg. One follicle will then produce a maturing egg cell. As the egg cell matures, it moves to the surface of the ovary. During this phase, the ovary produces estrogen.

Release of a mature egg from the ovary is called ovulation.

The next phase of the menstrual cycle is ovulation. **Ovulation** is the rupturing of a follicle and the release of the mature egg cell from the ovary. This occurs when there is an increase in the secretion of LH. **LH** (luteinizing hormone) is a hormone secreted by the pituitary gland. LH promotes ovulation. The mature egg moves through the Fallopian tube to the uterus.

Following ovulation, the part of the follicle left in the ovary changes and forms a temporary endocrine gland called the **corpus luteum.** The corpus luteum secretes the hormone progesterone. This hormone stimulates the lining of uterus and causes the endometrium to thicken. The result is that the uterus is prepared to support and feed a fertilized egg. If fertilization does not occur, the corpus luteum breaks down and hormone production ceases. If fertilization occurs, the corpus luteum continues to produce progesterone during pregnancy.

FIGURE 4–5.-The menstrual cycle, showing the developing egg and the changes in the uterine lining.

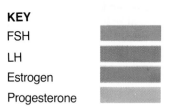

KEY

FSH

LH

Estrogen

Progesterone

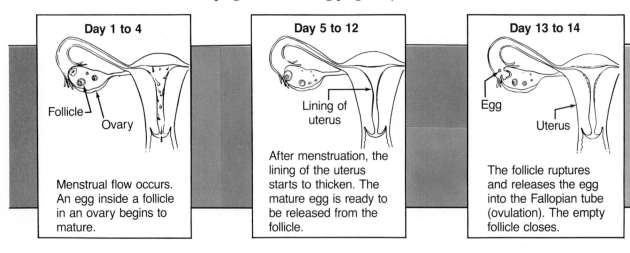

Day 1 to 4

Follicle
Ovary

Menstrual flow occurs. An egg inside a follicle in an ovary begins to mature.

Day 5 to 12

Lining of uterus

After menstruation, the lining of the uterus starts to thicken. The mature egg is ready to be released from the follicle.

Day 13 to 14

Egg
Uterus

The follicle ruptures and releases the egg into the Fallopian tube (ovulation). The empty follicle closes.

If fertilization does not take place, cells in the endometrium gradually die because the corpus luteum is no longer producing progesterone. Some bleeding occurs. This dead tissue passes out of the body through the vagina. The release of this tissue and blood is called the menstrual flow or menstruation. Menstrual flow occurs each month about two weeks after ovulation. The menstrual flow lasts from three to seven days. During this time, about two ounces (50-60 mL) of blood may be lost.

The menstrual cycle normally continues until a woman is 40 or 50 years old. As the function of the ovaries decreases with age, the menstrual cycles become irregular and eventually cease. This period in life is called menopause.

At times, menstruation may cause discomfort and pain. The term for painful menstruation is dysmenorrhea (dihs men uh REE uh). The amount of discomfort varies from one female to another. Cramping in the pelvic region is the most common type of discomfort. Other problems may be headaches, backaches, and a full feeling in the pelvic area.

About 70 percent of menstruating women experience some psychological and physiological changes the week before menstruation. These symptoms are referred to as premenstrual syndrome, or **PMS.** These symptoms may include severe headaches, depression, undue stress, and on rare occasions, violent behavior.

The exact causes of PMS are not known. However, mood changes seem to be related to fluid retention caused by premenstrual hormonal imbalances. Recent studies of PMS sufferers indicate a relationship between progesterone deficiency and tension and/or headache symptoms. Without sufficient progesterone, sugar metabolism slows and results in hypoglycemia, or low blood sugar. PMS can begin during the teenage years and last through menopause. Many forms of therapy, including vitamin therapy, are being researched.

Symptoms of
TOXIC SHOCK SYNDROME (TSS)

- sudden high fever (102°F or 38.9°C or higher)

- vomiting

- diarrhea

- dizziness, fainting, or near fainting when standing up

- a rash that looks like a sunburn

If you get TSS symptoms during your menstrual period, remove your tampon if you are using one. Seek immediate medical attention.

If you have had TSS, seek medical advice before using tampons.

FIGURE 4–6. Follow precautions to avoid the possibility of Toxic Shock Syndrome (TSS).

Symptoms of PMS may include headaches, depression, undue stress, and on rare occasions, violent behavior.

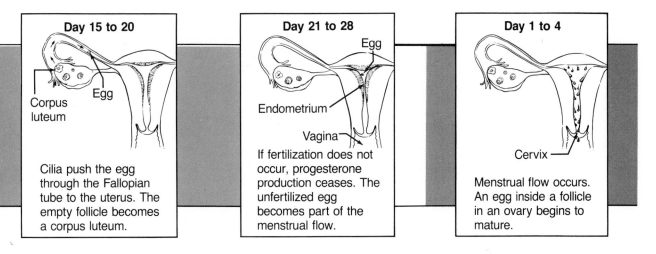

Day 15 to 20

Corpus luteum — Egg

Cilia push the egg through the Fallopian tube to the uterus. The empty follicle becomes a corpus luteum.

Day 21 to 28

Egg

Endometrium

Vagina

If fertilization does not occur, progesterone production ceases. The unfertilized egg becomes part of the menstrual flow.

Day 1 to 4

Cervix

Menstrual flow occurs. An egg inside a follicle in an ovary begins to mature.

4:7   Female Reproductive Health

To improve and maintain a healthy reproductive system, it is important for a woman to be aware of healthful behaviors and risk behaviors that affect this system. It is also important to plan for reproductive health.

Cancer of the breast is the most common form of cancer in women. Most cases of breast cancer occur after age 25, although some cases have been reported in younger women. Because breast cancer is a major risk to health, women are encouraged to perform breast self-examination. In breast self-examination, a woman checks her breasts to detect the presence of a lump. This examination should be done once a month after each menstrual period. Studies show that more than 80 percent of the lumps found in breast tissue are not cancerous. However, all lumps should be checked as soon as possible by a physician.

If breast cancer is suspected, a physician may order a mammogram. A **mammogram** is an X-ray examination of the breasts. Another procedure used is thermography. **Thermography** is a process used to detect heat in the body. Because cancer cells multiply rapidly, they produce heat. Thermography can detect cancer in a breast.

If cancer in a breast is detected, treatment and cure may include radiation therapy, chemotherapy, or surgery. A combination of the three may be used. If surgery is necessary, the severity of the cancer will determine the type of surgery recommended. Surgery can range from removal of the breast and its underlying muscle and the lymph nodes to just removal of the actual cancerous lump. The treatment recommended will vary with the patient.

A Pap smear is a simple test in which cells from the cervix are examined in a laboratory for cancer. Should cervical cancer be detected, options are available depending on the extent of the cancer. If surgery is necessary, a hysterectomy may be performed. A hysterectomy is the surgical removal of the uterus. Sometimes, surgical removal of the ovaries is necessary. Scheduling a Pap smear at least once a year is a wise, preventive measure.

It is important to remember that early detection of cancer is important. The earlier cancer is detected, the greater the success of treatment and cure.

Vaginitis is an inflammation or irritation in the vagina. It may result from changes in the chemical makeup of the lining of the vagina. These changes may be due to the prolonged use of medication or other factors that result in certain bacteria growing too rapidly. Some forms of vaginitis may result from sexual contact. Vaginitis can be treated and cured with medication. It can be prevented by practicing proper hygiene.

Women are encouraged to perform breast self-examination once a month after each menstrual period.

Early detection and treatment of cancer improve the chances of cure.

Sometimes, the tissue that is normally part of the menstrual flow is found growing outside the uterus. This condition is endometriosis (en doh mee tree OH sus) and is often associated with infertility. Infertility is the inability to produce offspring.

4:8 Male Reproductive Organs

The main organs of the male reproductive system are the testes. Testes are sometimes called testicles. The other organs of this system can be grouped as internal and external reproductive organs (Figure 4–7).

Testes are two glands that are contained in a sac called the scrotum. Sex hormones and reproductive cells called sperm are produced by the testes. Sperm are produced in the seminiferous (sem uh NIFH rus) tubules and stored in the epididymus (ep uh DIHD uh mus). Before leaving the body, sperm move through a series of small tubes. From the epididymus, sperm move through the vas deferens (VAS · DEF uh runz) to the prostate gland. The prostate is a gland that secretes a fluid to nourish the sperm.

Behind the prostate gland lies the seminal vesicles. The seminal vesicles are sac-like structures that secrete fluids that enable sperm to move through the reproductive system. Sperm also receive secretions from the Cowper's glands. Cowper's glands are two glands lying on either side of the urethra. Cowper's glands secrete a fluid that prepares the urethra for the passage of semen. **Semen** (SEE mun) is the mixture of sperm and fluids from the different glands.

As sperm travel through the prostate, they enter the ejaculatory duct. The ejaculatory duct is a tube that leads from the

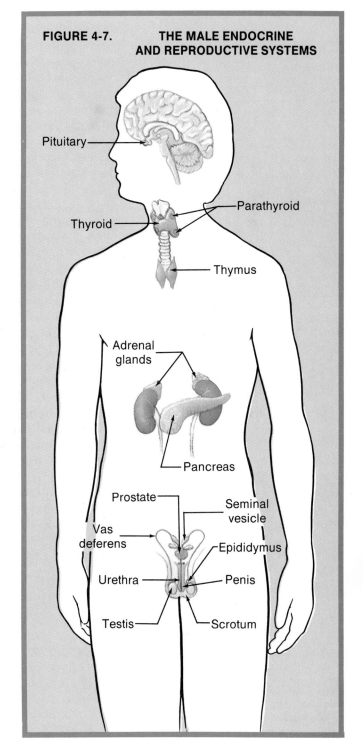

FIGURE 4-7.   THE MALE ENDOCRINE AND REPRODUCTIVE SYSTEMS

Pituitary

Parathyroid

Thyroid

Thymus

Adrenal glands

Pancreas

Prostate

Seminal vesicle

Vas deferens

Epididymus

Urethra

Penis

Testis

Scrotum

prostate to the urethra. The urethra in the male serves as a passageway through the penis for both urine and sperm. However, urine and sperm do not pass through the urethra at the same time. A special muscle allows only one to travel through at a time. The urethra extends through the penis to the outside of the body.

At birth, a male's penis has a foreskin. The foreskin is a fold of skin at the tip of the penis. Many parents choose to have the foreskin of the penis removed from their male children a few days after birth. This is done with a minor surgical procedure called circumcision.

The penis is composed of three layers of spongy tissue. These tissues are filled with many spaces, much like a sponge. Many blood vessels and nerves are supplied to these tissues. When these tissues become filled with blood, they cause an erection. An **erection** is an expanding and stiffening of the penis. An erection usually occurs when a male is sexually stimulated.

A male can have an erection without being sexually stimulated. For example, a male might wake up in the morning with an erect penis. This erection can be due to a full bladder. The full bladder can cause nerve cells to stimulate the penis. Also, the penis can become erect if a male wears tight clothes or puts pressure on his penis while sleeping on his stomach.

When a male does have an erection due to sexual stimulation, he may have muscular contractions in the genital area. This causes semen to be released from the urethra. The discharge of semen from the urethra is called an **ejaculation.** During an ejaculation, about a teaspoon of semen containing about 300 million sperm is released. After a male ejaculates, the penis returns to a limp state.

Dreams involving sexual feelings are common during puberty. A male may become excited when dreaming about sex. His penis will become erect and he may ejaculate. If he ejaculates while he is sleeping, it is called a nocturnal emission or wet dream. A male has no control over nocturnal emissions. They are a normal part of growing up.

4:9   Male Reproductive Health

Cases of cancer of the testes have been increasing in recent years. It is one of the most common cancers in men 15 to 34 years of age. Early signs of this kind of cancer may be an enlarged scrotum or a hard, painless lump in one of the testes.

A change in the testes may be found by doing a self-examination each month. Finding a change does not always indicate cancer, but any change should be checked immediately by a physician. Treatment and cure may include surgery and chemotherapy. If one testis has to be surgically removed, the other one will continue to function. Thus, a male's reproductive system can remain healthy. Early diagnosis and treatment of testicular cancer increase the rate of cure. When detected early, almost 100 percent of cancers of the testes can be prevented from spreading to other body parts.

There are many other diseases that can affect the male reproductive organs. These diseases may be transmitted through sexual contact and are called sexually transmitted diseases (STDs). STDs pose a major health concern since their incidence has been increasing at alarming rates. Through early diagnosis and treatment, most STDs can be cured. Unfortunately, there are many people who suffer lifelong consequences of untreated STDs.

For some STDs, there are no cures. Not only can they result in lifelong problems, but they can also be fatal. What can you do to prevent having an STD? What are the signs and symptoms of STDs that indicate the need for medical help? The answers to these questions and additional information about STDs are found in Chapter 19.

 ## Review and Reflect

3. Why is it important to have a lump in a breast checked immediately by a physician?
4. Why are nocturnal emissions considered involuntary actions?

Focus on
Life Management Skills

- Have regular medical checkups.
- Females should begin to develop the habit of doing a monthly breast self-examination and having a yearly Pap smear.
- Males should begin to develop the habit of doing testicular self-examinations each month.

CHAPTER REVIEW 4

Summary

1. The endocrine system consists of glands that control many of the body's activities and produce hormones to regulate body activities.   4:1

2. When the endocrine system functions properly, hormone production is in balance and body organs function normally.   4:2

3. Genes transmit features from parents to offspring.   4:3

4. The ovaries, Fallopian tubes, uterus, and vagina make up the female reproductive system.   4:4

5. The vulva and breasts are considered to be associated female reproductive structures.   4:5

6. The menstrual cycle occurs with the onset of puberty, usually between the ages of 8 and 13.   4:6

7. Healthful behaviors, such as breast self-examination and a yearly Pap smear, can help maintain a healthy female reproductive system.   4:7

8. In a male, the testes are the main reproductive organ and produce hormones and reproductive cells.   4:8

9. Males should examine their testes monthly for lumps, swelling, or pain and see a physician if any of these signs and symptoms appear.   4:9

Vocabulary

Below is a list of vocabulary words used in this chapter. Use each word only once to complete the sentences. Do not write in this book.

ejaculation
endometrium
gonads
hormones
LH

ovulation
puberty
semen
thermography
zygote

1. The testes and ovaries are known as _____.

2. Using _____, lumps in a female's breasts can be detected.

3. _____ is a pituitary hormone that promotes ovulation.

4. _____ occurs when an ovary releases a mature egg cell.

5. When an ovum becomes fertilized, it is called a(n) _____.

6. The mixture of sperm and fluids leaving the male body during ejaculation is _____.

7. Chemical messengers in the body that regulate body functions are _____.

8. The _____ is the inner lining of the uterus.

9. Males and females reach _____ when they are physically capable of reproducing.

10. During a nocturnal emission, _____ will occur.

Review

1. What can happen to a person with a malfunctioning thyroid gland?
2. In what way do the endocrine glands function somewhat like a scale of justice?
3. Identify some traits that may be passed through heredity.
4. What is the role of the Fallopian tubes in reproduction?
5. What is the endometrium?
6. What may cause dysmenorrhea?
7. How does a thermography differ from a mammogram?
8. Describe why Cowper's glands in a male are important in reproduction.
9. Why is it important for males to perform testicular self-examination?
10. Why are mammary glands considered associated reproductive structures?

Application

1. What may cause a person to lose weight while eating more than usual?
2. Why might a person with malfunctioning adrenal glands have difficulty performing an important physical task such as lifting something heavy?
3. What physical change during a female's menstrual cycle might indicate she is pregnant?
4. Why should a woman who finds a lump in her breast see a physician immediately even though she may be convinced the lump is a minor problem?

Individual Research

1. Make a chart listing each of the endocrine glands named in Section 4:1. For each gland, describe one disease or disorder that affects it and describe the required treatment.
2. Identify five diseases that can be transmitted through heredity. Describe the signs and symptoms of each disease.

Readings

Ewy, Rodger, and Ewy, Donna, *Teen Pregnancy.* New York, NY: Signet Books, 1984.

Norris, Ronald V., *Premenstrual Syndrome.* New York, NY: Berkley Publishing Corp., 1984.

Seiden, Othniel, *Coping With Diabetes.* Blue Ridge Summit, PA: TAB Books, Inc., 1985.

Mental Health

MENTAL HEALTH

Every day you make decisions resulting in actions that influence the quality of your lifestyle. Are you able to think clearly? Are you able to examine problems and identify alternatives? Do you seek assistance when necessary to make responsible decisions? When life situations cause tension and stress, do you know what to do? This unit focuses on achieving optimum mental health. It describes persons who are mentally healthy and those with mental disorders. Mentally healthy persons use the skills described in this unit.

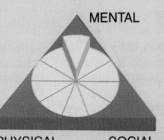

MENTAL

PHYSICAL   SOCIAL

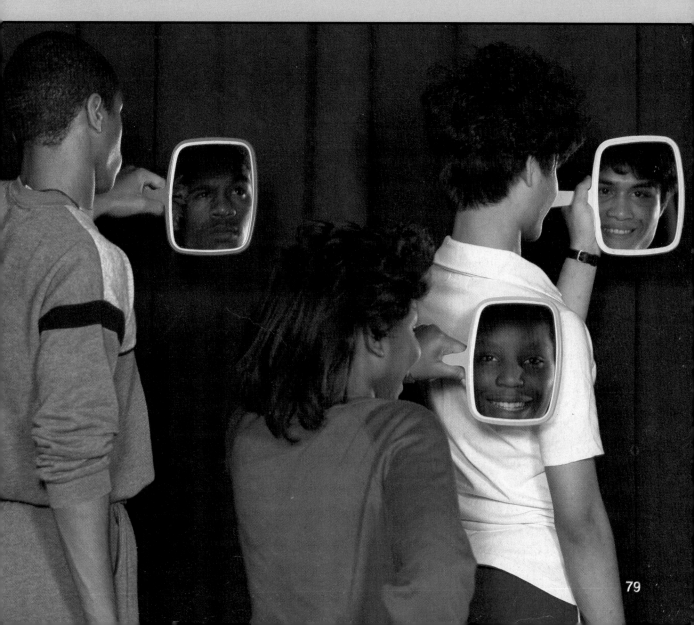

79

The girls are facing a challenge. They knew about the race ahead of time, and they are ready. Some challenges are unexpected. There is no time to get ready for them. What challenges do you face each day? Are you mentally ready to face everyday situations?

Chapter 5

Promoting Mental Health

OBJECTIVES: You will be able to
- identify the characteristics of persons who are mentally healthy.
- describe the ingredients of a healthful personality and philosophy of life.
- express emotions and use defense mechanisms in healthful ways.

Imagine that you are at the starting line of a race. You anticipate the challenge ahead of you. You have trained for this race and you are ready. You are excited and anxious. You glance around at the other runners. The excitement is contagious.

There are other kinds of challenges you face each day. One challenge is to use each day wisely and to live life fully. This involves
- being satisfied with the way you spent your day.
- doing your best and helping others to do the same.
- facing problems with a positive attitude.
- completing daily tasks in order to achieve personal goals.
- achieving and maintaining positive mental health.

UNDERSTANDING MENTAL HEALTH

Think of a few persons whom you consider to be well adjusted. On a sheet of paper, list five characteristics that describe these persons. Examine your list. Which of these characteristics do you possess? What constitutes positive mental health?

5:1 What Is Mental Health?

Mentally healthy persons like themselves and relate well with others.

The National Association for Mental Health defines **mental health** as (1) being comfortable with yourself, (2) feeling good about your relationships with others, and (3) being able to meet the demands of life. This definition might also include being able to express emotions in healthful ways and being able to cope successfully with circumstances in your daily life.

The association also has a list of 27 characteristics that describe a person who has positive mental health (Table 5–1).

Table 5–1 Characteristics of Positive Mental Health

1. I feel comfortable with myself.
2. I am not overwhelmed by my emotions—fear, anger, love, jealousy, guilt, or worry.
3. I can take life's disappointments.
4. I have a tolerant, easygoing attitude toward myself and others; I can laugh at myself.
5. I neither underestimate nor overestimate my abilities.
6. I can accept my shortcomings.
7. I have self-respect.
8. I feel able to deal with most situations that come my way.
9. I get satisfaction from simple, everyday pleasures.
10. I feel good about my relationships with other people.
11. I am able to give love and to consider the interests of others.
12. I have personal relationships that are satisfying and lasting.
13. I like and trust others and expect that others will like and trust me.
14. I respect differences I find in people.
15. I do not push people around, or allow myself to be pushed around.
16. I feel that I am part of a group.
17. I feel a sense of responsibility to my neighbors and other persons with whom I come in contact.
18. I am able to meet the demands of my life.
19. I do something about my problems as they arise.
20. I accept my responsibilities.
21. I shape my environment whenever possible; I adjust to it whenever necessary.
22. I plan ahead but do not fear the future.
23. I welcome new experiences and new ideas.
24. I make use of my natural capacities.
25. I set realistic goals for myself.
26. I am able to think for myself and make my own decisions.
27. I put my best effort into what I do and get satisfaction out of doing it.

Reprinted from the National Association for Mental Health publication, *Mental Health Is 1, 2, 3*. Washington, D.C.

FIGURE 5–1. Problems should be solved as promptly as possible.

According to Table 5–1, positive mental health does not mean the absence of problems. Everyone has problems. Throughout your life, you will have many problems both large and small. You will struggle with yourself, with your relationships, and with demands placed upon you by others. Some problems will be easy to resolve; others may be more difficult. In some cases, you may need to seek the assistance of a counselor or therapist. You will be able to resolve most problems yourself if you learn how to confront them and deal with them. How you develop your problem-solving skills is the challenge of achieving positive mental health.

Mentally healthy people struggle to solve problems as they arise.

5:2 What Is Mental Illness?

Refer again to the list of characteristics describing a person who has positive mental health (Table 5–1). How would the characteristics of a person suffering from a mental disorder differ from these?

A mental disorder does not mean that a person is insane. **Mental illness** is characterized by (1) having a low self-esteem and self-concept, (2) being unable to relate to others, (3) being incapable of coping with personal problems, such as extreme nervousness or shyness, and (4) having difficulty distinguishing among fantasy, imagination, and reality. Persons who suffer from mental illnesses are not able to meet the challenges of day-to-day living.

A person with mental illness has low self-esteem and poor relationships with others.

A person with mental illness is not able to cope with problems.

Optimum health cannot be achieved without having positive mental health. The sections that follow focus on the information and skills you need in order to promote positive mental health.

 ## Review and Reflect

1. What are some ways mentally healthy persons differ from those who are mentally ill?
2. How do mentally healthy persons deal with problems?

EXPLORING THE SELF

The Greek philosopher Socrates said "know thyself." Self-knowledge is a key ingredient in learning to be comfortable with yourself and accepting of yourself.

5:3 Personality and Self-Concept

If you wrote a paragraph describing yourself, you would probably include descriptions of your personality. **Personality** is an individual's unique pattern of characteristics. These characteristics are a blend of physical, mental, and emotional traits. Personality is influenced by four factors—heredity, environment, culture, and self-concept.

Heredity is the transmission of traits from one generation to the next. What traits did you inherit? Are you tall, short, brown-eyed, or blue-eyed? You may have also inherited the potential for the way you think, feel, act, reason, or learn.

Your **environment** includes everything that is around you and its influence upon you. It includes your family, your friends, the people around you, the air you breathe, and the water you drink. Your physical environment may include mountains, an ocean, rivers, or desert. Your environment may be one of poverty, wealth, or urban or country living.

Your **culture** is a blend of the influence of the people in your home, city, state, and nation. In many ways, you learn to act like the people with whom you spend most of your time. You may speak or use sayings unique to your family. You may have noticed different accents, attitudes, or mannerisms of someone who has just moved to your school from a different part of the country or from outside the country.

Your **self-concept** includes all the beliefs you have about yourself including a self-evaluation of your strengths and limita-

Personality is a blend of physical, mental, and social traits.

Heredity, environment, culture, and self-concept influence personality.

Beliefs about your strengths and weaknesses determine your self-concept.

FIGURE 5–2. Identical twins are like mirror images of each other. They inherited the same genes from their parents. As a result, their personalities are usually very similar.

tions. You may think of yourself as ambitious, talented, and intelligent or lazy, unskilled, and dull. You may think of yourself as friendly and kind or as shy and critical of others. Each of these beliefs helps determine your self-concept. Some people are unduly hard on themselves while others have a realistic view of themselves.

The opinions that you feel others have about you also help determine your self-concept. If your parents believe you to be a worthwhile person, most likely you will share their belief that you are worthwhile. The opinions that other persons significant to you portray, like your coaches, teachers, and friends, also influence your self-concept. As you become older and more mature, you may become less dependent on the opinions of others.

5:4 Ideal Self, Public Self, and Private Self

You are a complex person. You are a blend of many selves— your ideal self, public self, and private self. Let us look at each self and learn why the three selves must blend in order for you to have a healthy personality and self-concept.

The **ideal self** is your conscience, which tells you (1) how you ought to be or (2) how you would like to be. Much of your ideal self is influenced by your parents and their values. If your parents expect you to be thoughtful and to achieve in school, you may begin to see yourself as being thoughtful and as being an achiever.

Your ideal self, public self, and private self influence your personality and self-concept.

Your ideal self is your conscience.

Your public self is the reputation for which you strive.

The actual you is your private self.

When you act in thoughtless ways, your conscience may bother you and make you aware of your actions. This small voice may remind you when it is time to do your homework.

Your **public self** is the view or opinion you would like others to have of you. In other words, your public self is the reputation you want to have. You choose actions and words to influence others in forming certain opinions of you. For example, you may want others to think you are associated with a popular group at school. You spend time with this group and join their activities. You want others to think you are popular.

It is possible for your public self and your ideal self to be the same as your private self. Your **private self** is the actual you. Your private self may be kind, generous, thoughtful, serious, lazy, or pessimistic. Your private self may or may not be what you think you ought to be (ideal self) or what you want others to think of you (public self). A similar ideal self, public self, and private self contribute to a healthy personality.

5:5 Maslow's Hierarchy of Needs

Your health and happiness depend on your ability to fulfill your basic needs. **Basic needs** are requirements for sustaining life and promoting physical and mental growth.

Abraham Maslow identified a hierarchy of five basic needs all persons have.

Abraham Maslow, a famous psychologist, identified a hierarchy (HI rar kee) of needs (Figure 5–3). A hierarchy is similar to a pyramid. You begin at the lowest level and progress to the highest level. Maslow believed that the needs at the lower levels of the hierarchy must be met before the needs at the higher levels can be attained.

Maslow listed physiological needs as the most basic or first level. Physiological needs are those that you require for life— food, water, and sleep. Your parents or others satisfied these needs for you when you were an infant and young child.

The second level of needs are those involving safety and security. For example, it is important to feel protected from bodily harm. Your parents also satisfied these kinds of needs.

The third need on the hierarchy is your need for love and affection. Again, this need is first satisfied in your family. Your family teaches you many lessons about love and affection. When you learn to give and receive love in your family, you can then form healthful relationships with others.

The fourth level of the hierarchy focuses on your need for self-esteem. **Self-esteem** is the feeling of respect or worth you have about yourself. How do you gain self-esteem? As you develop skills and talents, you build on these to try new and

FIGURE 5–3. Maslow's hierarchy

MASLOW'S HIERARCHY OF NEEDS

different skills. For example, when you were a baby, you began to feel confident as you learned to crawl. Once you mastered the ability to crawl, you began to learn to walk, another achievement for you. With each success you experience now, you continue to build self-esteem. You are learning skills that will help you assume responsibilities and become independent.

Your self-esteem is strengthened by gaining skills that make you independent.

The highest level on Maslow's hierarchy is the need for self-actualization. When people reach the point of making full use of their abilities, they have attained **self-actualization.** The process of striving for self-actualization can be compared to learning to play the piano. You learn by mastering steps that become increasingly more difficult. You begin to play the piano by playing tunes that use just a few keys on the keyboard. As you continue your lessons, you learn to use more and more keys. A skilled piano player is able to master all the keys on the keyboard. The music becomes more and more harmonious and free-flowing.

Self-actualization is the highest level in Maslow's hierarchy.

Self-actualization also includes realizing your talents and developing your capabilities. This can be accomplished through personal growth, achievement, or vocational fulfillment. When you are self-actualized, you are like a skilled pianist. You are able to blend your talents and skills and values into harmonious behavior. There is a natural, harmonious, and orderly flow to your life.

Self-actualization is a process that continues for a lifetime.

Abraham Maslow estimated that fewer than one out of one hundred persons achieve self-actualization. Two of the people Maslow listed as having achieved this state were Abraham Lincoln and Eleanor Roosevelt. Although both of these persons are well know, it is not necessary to be famous to become self-actualized. Everyone has the potential. The most important characteristic is a desire to develop all one's talents to their fullest.

You work toward self-actualization by always doing your best.

5:6 Developing a Philosophy of Life

Another important aspect in knowing yourself is examining your philosophy of life. A **philosophy of life** is an overall vision of life or an attitude toward life and the purpose of life. A philosophy of life reflects a person's values. A **value** is anything that is desirable or important to you, such as honesty, loyalty, and optimum health. Your values influence everything about you— your thoughts, your goals, your decisions, and your actions. If a value is important to you, your actions will be consistent with your values. For example, if optimum health is a value, you will live your life choosing healthful behaviors. If your actions are inconsistent with a value, it is not truly a value.

Your philosophy of life reflects your values.

Your parents' or guardians'
values influence your philosophy
of life.

Your philosophy of life
influences your thoughts,
emotions, and performance.

How does a philosophy of life develop? Like self-concept, your parents have had a major influence. Their attitudes about life and the purpose of life affected most of their decisions. Their decisions have had an effect on you. Their values have also influenced your family life. For many families, religion helps establish a philosophy of life. It is important to talk with your parents about their philosophy of life. In what ways do you share their philosophy?

It is also important to examine ways your philosophy of life affects your thoughts, your emotions, and your body (Figure 5–4). Consider this example. You have a test in school tomorrow. You think about the test. Your philosophy is to always do your best and accept the results from this effort. You are relaxed and feel ready for the test. In this kind of situation, your philosophy of life is a healthful influence on your thoughts, your emotions, and your performance.

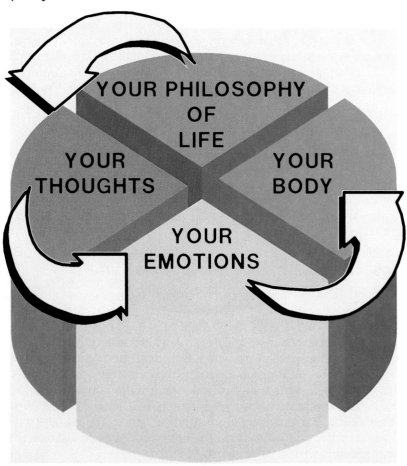

FIGURE 5–4. Your philosophy of life affects your thoughts. Your thoughts generate emotions or feelings. Emotions affect performance.

Suppose your philosophy is to do just well enough to get by in life. However, you do not want to fail. Your thoughts about failing a test cause a different emotion—worry. This emotion results in different body changes. You get a headache, your muscles feel tense and you may even perspire. You seem to have no energy. Your philosophy of life has a harmful influence on your thoughts, your emotions, and your performance.

What is your philosophy of life? What is your attitude toward life and the purpose of life? When you are faced with decisions, how does your philosophy of life affect your thoughts, your emotions, and your body?

It is important to examine how your philosophy of life influences your decisions.

 Review and Reflect

3. How might your health behaviors be related to your self-concept?
4. Why might a teenager smoke in public when he or she would not consider smoking when alone?
5. Why might a teenager smoke alone and not smoke in public?
6. Why may the process of self-actualization take a lifetime to achieve?
7. How might your philosophy of life influence your success in school?

EXPRESSING EMOTIONS

Think about the many feelings you experience. You may feel excited, disappointed, happy, or angry. You may feel guilty or depressed. Each of these feelings is an emotion. Learning to cope with emotions is important to a person's mental health.

5:7 Emotions and Mental Health

Emotions are the feelings you have inside you in response to events and life situations. Because your life situations vary, you experience many kinds of emotions. Your emotions and how you cope with them tell a lot about your mental health.

Probably no other emotion affects mental health as much as love. Erich Fromm, author of the book *The Art of Loving*, states "Love is the only satisfactory answer to the problem of human existence."

FIGURE 5–5. Emotions are reactions to situations.

Your ability to give and receive love influences your mental health.

What exactly is love, and why is love so important? **Love** is a strong affection or liking for someone or something. When you were born, your parents began to teach you about love. They allowed you to experience loving feelings in many different ways. As you have become older, you have learned to love others, and you have been loved by others. What you learn and experience in your early years about love is critical to your mental health. The following poem exemplifies this.

What you learned as a child often affects how you behave as an adolescent.

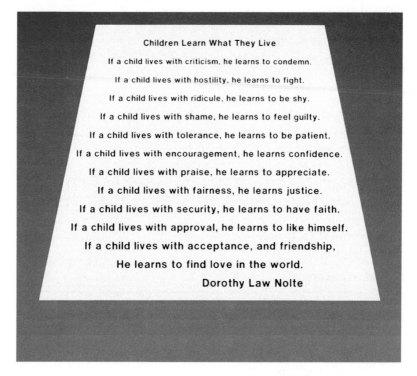

Children Learn What They Live

If a child lives with criticism, he learns to condemn.

If a child lives with hostility, he learns to fight.

If a child lives with ridicule, he learns to be shy.

If a child lives with shame, he learns to feel guilty.

If a child lives with tolerance, he learns to be patient.

If a child lives with encouragement, he learns confidence.

If a child lives with praise, he learns to appreciate.

If a child lives with fairness, he learns justice.

If a child lives with security, he learns to have faith.

If a child lives with approval, he learns to like himself.

If a child lives with acceptance, and friendship,

He learns to find love in the world.

Dorothy Law Nolte

There are ways to gather information about your mental health. The answers to certain questions give information about your mental health (Table 5–1). As you might expect, an important question would be "Do you feel loved?" Other questions might be "Are you happy? Do you have close friends?"

A person who is happy has feelings of great pleasure and of being a fortunate person. However, no one is happy all the time. But, if your happy times outweigh the unhappy ones, you are more likely to have positive mental health. Being happy has a holistic effect (Chapter 1). It affects your family life, your grades in school, and your likelihood of staying healthy. The effects of emotions on physical health will be discussed in more detail in Chapter 7.

Happy feelings have a holistic effect on your lifestyle.

5:8 Experiencing Loss or Rejection

Some experiences in life may prevent a person from feeling loved or happy. For a variety of reasons, some people have to learn to do without someone or something that is very important to them. Other people never have had the opportunity to know someone or have something that is important to them. In his book, *The Language of Feelings,* Dr. David Viscott identifies three types of losses that affect a person's mental health.

Loss of Love As you might expect, the loss of love in a person's life is very important. For example, some teenagers have experienced the death of a person whom they loved and who loved them. Other teenagers may feel the threat of a loss. They may think that if their parents get a divorce, one or both of the parents may stop loving them. Another example of loss of love might be when someone you love stops caring for you as he or she once did. People often become attached to a pet and experience a sense of loss when the pet dies.

A person who experiences a real or imagined loss of love may feel unloved or rejected. To feel **rejection** means to feel abandoned and unloved and no longer of any worth. During such a time, family or friends are a good source of emotional support. Some people who feel rejected may have to seek professional help. They may need to discuss their real or imagined losses with a trained counselor or therapist.

Loss of Control Some persons believe they are worthy of love only if they have power, money, position, title, or influence. Their self-loving feelings are dependent on achieving and gaining importance. They fear losing control in their lives so they try to be in control at all times. These persons live by rules and details. They are usually perfectionists, that is, they are unhappy or angry with anything less than perfect. Often they set and reach goals without being able to enjoy them. They may set unrealistic goals. These persons can learn through counseling that they are worthwhile as individuals with or without achievements or possessions.

Loss of Self-Confidence Everyone experiences failure. Some people learn and grow as they survive this kind of experience. Others lose self-confidence when they fail. People who have lost their self-confidence worry what others will think of them should they fail again. Because of this fear of failing, they may not try new or different experiences. This limits their chances for mental and social growth.

A loss of love may influence mental health.

Adolescents may feel a loss of love when parents divorce.

Adolescents may feel a loss of control when they set unrealistic goals.

Fear of failure may limit mental and social growth.

FIGURE 5–6. Learning to share feelings and ideas is important to a person's mental health.

5:9 Expressing Emotions in Healthful Ways

Situations that result in feelings of being loved and happy contribute to optimum health. Some situations may result in feelings of loss or rejection. In these situations, other powerful emotions such as hurt, anxiety, anger, guilt, and depression are felt or experienced. To achieve optimum health, a person must learn healthful ways to deal with and express these emotions.

Feeling **hurt** can be defined as feeling distressed and harmed. If you pretend that nothing hurts you, you are falsely telling yourself and others that you do not care about what is happening to you. If you succeed in keeping your feelings inside you, the effect will be holistic. You may experience stomach pains or feel tense. You may become irritable in a social situation or angry with a friend. A healthful way to deal with being hurt is to identify the source of your hurt and then to express your feelings. Perhaps a friend has betrayed you. It is best to be open with your friend and share your hurt feelings.

Anxiety relates to an anticipated or imagined situation. Fear relates to an actual situation. When you feel anxious or fearful, your heart may beat faster, or you may get cold feet, a nervous stomach, or sweaty hands. You may experience difficulty in sleeping and relaxing.

FIGURE 5–7. Many people experience anxiety on rides at an amusement park.

It is important to acknowledge anxiety. Pretending you are not anxious is a risky behavior. Anxiety alerts you to possible danger. If you do not deal with the anxiety, it usually will not go away. A healthful approach involves asking "What is causing my anxiety? Does it remind me of other troubling situations? How can I deal with this situation?" The better you feel about yourself, the less anxiety you may experience. You will feel confident that you can handle most situations. One way to cope with anxiety is to exercise. You will learn more about exercise and mental health in Chapter 7.

> It is healthful to identify and deal with the sources of anxiety.

Anger is the feeling of being irritated, annoyed, and furious. Anger usually follows a hurt. When anger is not expressed, it can harm you mentally, physically, and socially. You may be unable to concentrate on other things or anything. Harmful changes may occur in your body, such as increased heart rate and blood pressure, upset stomach, asthma, and headaches. You must learn to cope with your anger.

> When anger is not expressed in a healthful way, harmful mental and physiological changes occur.

Usually the most effective way to deal with anger is to talk about your hurt feelings. Talk with the person who has caused you to become angry. This should be done privately as soon as you are calm.

If it is not appropriate to share your angry feelings, it is still important to express your feelings. You might confide in others such as your family or close friends. You might pretend to talk to the person involved. You might write a letter expressing your anger and not mail it. Remember, anger that is not outwardly expressed will be directed inward. As a result, your health and well-being may suffer.

Guilt is the feeling of having done wrong, or of being at fault. One type of guilt comes from being angry at someone you love. Many people your age feel they are bad or evil if they become angry with their parents or with friends. These teenagers may try to hide their angry feelings and guilt. It is normal to feel angry at times with persons you love.

> Adolescents often feel guilty when they are angry with parents.

The most common cause of guilt is doing something that hurts another person. When you deny that you have hurt that person, you may intensify your feelings of guilt. When you admit that you have done something wrong, guilt is usually relieved by accepting the responsibility for your actions and apologizing for your actions. Admitting that you have done something wrong also strengthens your relationship with the other person.

> Admitting that you are wrong helps relieve guilt.

Depression is the feeling of being sad, unhappy, discouraged, and "down in the dumps." Depression is the leading mental health problem in teenagers. For this reason, depression will be discussed in detail in Chapter 6.

> Depression is the most common mental health problem among adolescents.

FIGURE 5–8. Daydreaming is a means of escaping from reality.

5:10 Defense Mechanisms

Sometimes you delay expressing how you really feel. **Suppression** involves delaying or postponing emotional responses to allow yourself time to reason, plan, and think. During this time of delay, you may find yourself using one or more defense mechanisms. A **defense mechanism** is a behavior that you use to cope with uncomfortable situations or emotions. One may purposely try to use a defense mechanism or one might use one unconsciously or automatically without knowing it. Typical defense mechanisms are described in Table 5–2.

Defense mechanisms may help you solve a problem, or avoid solving a problem. In this way, they may lead to harmful habits. Usually, you are unaware of defense mechanisms. An awareness of these defense mechanisms may help you develop more effective behavior.

Defense mechanisms are sometimes used to solve problems or to avoid solving problems.

It is helpful to evaluate your use of defense mechanisms.

Activity: Defense Mechanisms

Working in groups of three to five students, select a defense mechanism from Table 5–2. Develop a skit that demonstrates the use of the defense mechanism your group selected. Perform your skit for classmates. Have the class members guess what defense mechanism is being portrayed and their criteria for the choice. Discuss the skit. What are some healthful behaviors that could replace the defense mechanism that was used?

Table 5-2 Defense Mechanisms

TYPE OF DEFENSE	EXAMPLE	POSSIBLE RISK BEHAVIOR
Compensation is trying to make up for your weaknesses by using a strength in another area.	You try out for the cross-country team and do not make it. You compensate by singing in the glee club.	You may not work hard enough to overcome your weaknesses.
Daydreaming is a simple escape from unpleasant, boring, or frustrating situations.	You are disappointed that you do not have a date for the school dance. Rather than finding a date, you daydream about being the most popular person at school.	Daydreaming will not change your boredom or frustration and only provides momentary relief from anxiety.
Displacement is transferring the emotions you feel from the original source to another object.	You have an argument with your best friend and instead of talking it out, you go home, kick the chair leg, and yell at your brother or sister.	You do not resolve conflicts and take your feelings out on others, thus, alienating other people.
Idealization is placing great value on someone or something in an exaggerated manner.	You admire someone so much that you cannot admit that they have any faults at all, even when you discover it.	You view a person unrealistically and deny any flaws the person might have.
Identification is the process in which you assume the qualities of someone you admire.	You admire a professional athlete or movie star. You begin to dress the same way and to eat the same food.	You begin to see yourself as similar to someone else rather than focusing on your own uniqueness.
Projection is the shifting of blame and responsibility for your actions or thoughts to someone else.	You do not study enough. You fail the test and blame the teacher saying she or he made the test too hard.	You do not take responsibility for your behavior.
Rationalization is giving acceptable reasons for your behavior that are not the real reasons.	You have a test tomorrow but decide to go biking instead of studying. You rationalize by saying you have been working hard and need a break.	A rationalization keeps you from feeling guilty rather than taking the appropriate action.
Reaction formation is behavior that shows opposite characteristics than you truly possess.	Suppose you are selfish. You act very generous because you feel selfishness is socially unacceptable.	Your ideal self, public self, and private self are inconsistent.
Regression is reverting behavior to childish ways.	Suppose you are playing a board game with family members and sense that you will not win. You turn the board over and say you will not play.	Your behavior will be emotionally immature, and you will revert to the way you handled problems as a child.
Repression is attempting to bury conscious thoughts into the unconscious part of the mind.	You witness a terrible accident but don't remember a thing about it.	The memory always exists in the subconscious and may emerge at a later time.
Sublimation is the channeling of unacceptable impulses into socially acceptable goals.	You like to be the center of attention. It is not possible to be the center of attention at all times and have good relationships. You get the lead in the school play or become class president.	You still need to recognize and change your unacceptable impulses.
Substitution is replacing one goal for another attainable goal.	You want to make good grades at school but you have difficulty. You substitute by becoming a good skier.	Substitution is not healthful when the two goals are not closely related. You may need to deal with the results of not attaining your goal.

Health
ADVANCES

We have been discussing individual responsibility in achieving positive mental health. Let us also consider time perspective as a means to this end.

5:11 Time Perspectives

Some research focuses on time perspectives. A **time perspective** is the way you usually view time. Do you spend most of your time thinking about the past? Do you ever think about the future? Or, is your life at present all that matters to you? The following chart allows you to examine your choices in time and the relationship of these choices to your mental health (Figure 5–9). As you read the chart, try to decide your own time perspective.

How might feeling happy in the present relate to positive mental health? How might worrying about yesterday's mistakes promote poor mental health? How does your view of time relate to your philosophy of life?

You can see that a variety of factors determine time perspective. Some people have a time perspective in which they feel that the past does not make a difference—only what is to come will make a difference. Others feel that the present is a waste of time—living in the present may interfere with future accomplishments. Others have never developed a sense of the future. They are unable to give up present pleasures to work toward future goals.

There may be risks in the frequent use of defense mechanisms.

A balanced time perspective contributes to optimum health.

FIGURE 5–9.

The Effect of Time Perspectives on Mental Health

Past	Present	Future
• learning from yesterday's mistakes	• living one day at a time • feeling happy • working toward meeting deadlines	• meeting deadlines early • setting goals for each day • completing projects
OR	**OR**	**OR**
• worrying about yesterday's mistakes, allowing them to hinder performance	• seeking thrills through dangerous actions • needlessly delaying important decisions • making spur-of-the-moment decisions • not thinking through my actions	• seeking only pleasures for myself • ignoring responsibility to myself and others

FIGURE 5-10. How do you view time?

What is your time perspective? How does your time perspective influence your mental health? A balanced time perspective may be healthful for these reasons.

1. A past-time perspective is valuable when you learn from your mistakes.

2. A present-time perspective is necessary to enjoy the pleasures of day-to-day living and work on accomplishing goals.

3. A future-time perspective is needed to set goals and to become self-actualized.

Focus on
Life Management Skills

- Develop a positive self-concept by developing strengths, recognizing limitations, and understanding your feelings.
- Make your ideal self, public self, and private self consistent with each other.
- Take steps to satisfy your basic needs.
- Be aware when you are using defense mechanisms; try to identify what you are attempting to avoid.
- Develop a philosophy of life that influences your thoughts, emotions, and body's performance in healthful ways.
- Express love, hurt, anxiety, anger, guilt, and depression in healthful ways.
- Balance your time perspective to include your past, present, and future.

Summary

1. The National Mental Health Association describes a mentally healthy person as someone who is comfortable with himself or herself, feels good about relationships with others, and is able to meet the demands of life. **5:1**

2. Persons who suffer from mental illness are not able to meet the demands of day-to-day living. **5:2**

3. Personality is influenced by four factors—heredity, environment, culture, and self-concept. **5:3**

4. To achieve a healthy personality, the ideal self, public self, and private self should be consistent with one another. **5:4**

5. Maslow's Hierarchy of Needs includes the following: (a) physiological, (b) safety and security, (c) love and affection, (d) self-esteem, and (e) self-actualization. **5:5**

6. A philosophy of life affects your thoughts, your emotions, and your actions. **5:6**

7. Being happy promotes positive mental health and has a holistic effect. **5:7**

8. A loss of love, a loss of control, and/or a loss of self-esteem may affect mental health and optimum well-being. **5:8**

9. There are healthful ways to express hurt, anxiety, anger, guilt, and depression. **5:9**

10. Defense mechanisms are behaviors used to cope with uncomfortable situations. **5:10**

11. A balanced time perspective is one way to help you achieve positive mental health. **5:11**

Vocabulary

Below is a list of vocabulary words used in this chapter. Use each word only once to complete the sentences. Do not write in this book.

anxiety	public self
basic needs	self-actualization
environment	self-concept
personality	self-esteem
philosophy of life	suppression

1. Your school, your friends, and your home life are each a part of your _____.

2. Your _____ is influenced by your heredity, environment, culture, and self-concept.

3. Your _____ represents the view or opinion you want others to have of you.

4. The feeling of worth that you have about yourself is _____.

5. You experience _____ when you fear what might happen.

6. Delaying or postponing the expression of how you really feel is _____.

7. Your beliefs about yourself and your strengths and limitations is your _____.

8. Physiological needs are examples of _____ that are needed to sustain life and promote growth.

9. A(n) _____ is an overall vision or attitude that influences your thoughts, emotions, and body reactions.

10. You have achieved _____ when you make full use of your abilities.

Review

1. Identify ten characteristics of a person with positive mental health.
2. What are four factors that influence personality?
3. Identify the five levels of Maslow's Hierarchy of Needs in proper order beginning with the most basic need.
4. In what ways do parents influence one's development of a philosophy of life?
5. What are three types of losses that might affect your mental health status?
6. What is a healthful approach to sharing your hurt feelings?
7. Why is it not healthful to pretend that you are not afraid?
8. What is the leading mental health problem among teenagers?
9. Differentiate between projection and rationalization.
10. What are three reasons to have a balanced time perspective?

Application

1. How does a person who is mentally ill differ from a person who has positive mental health?
2. Why are you more likely to have a healthful personality when your parents, friends, and teachers emphasize your strengths?
3. Explain why being clothed and fed is a more basic need than achieving high self-esteem.
4. Why might a person with a positive philosophy of life live longer than someone with a negative philosophy of life?

Individual Research

1. Interview five persons. Ask each one to define the term mental health. Compare their definitions with those in Table 5–1. Write a report on your findings.
2. Identify someone (living or deceased) whom you would add to Maslow's list of self-actualized persons. Write a one-page report giving your reasons for this person's selection.
3. Discuss philosophy of life with your parents. Have them share three of their important values with you. How are they similar or dissimilar to your own?
4. Identify two experiences from your past that had an effect on your present and future. Identify two aspects of your present life that are important to you. Identify two future goals toward which you are working.

Readings

Anthony, Dr. Robert, *Total Self Confidence*. New York, NY: Berkley Publishing Corp., 1985.

Harris, Amy, and Harris, Thomas, *Staying OK*. New York, NY: Harper & Row Publishers, 1985.

Mental health is an important part of a person's health status. If you are mentally healthy, you can learn new skills and feel good about your relationships with other people. What skills are you developing? Are you learning skills that will help you become an autonomous adult?

Mental Disorders

OBJECTIVES: You will be able to
- **draw, label, and describe the mental health status continuum.**
- **identify and reduce the causes of mental disorders.**
- **identify and describe types of mental disorders.**
- **describe actions to take to prevent suicide for you and others.**
- **identify types of treatment, facilities, and personnel who assist with mental health.**

The traditional view of health focused on regular medical evaluations of one's physical health. People were said to have optimum health if their physical bodies were free of malfunction or disease. This concept has changed with advances in research and in the practice of medicine. A modern view of health also focuses on regular mental health evaluations.

MENTAL HEALTH

In Chapter 1, you learned that health status is not just the absence or presence of disease or illness. Rather, health status is the combination of healthful and risk behaviors. Relate health status to a scale that ranges from 0 (death) to 100 (optimum health). During one's lifetime, the level of health fluctuates between these two extremes.

6:1 Levels of Mental Health

Mental health status can be viewed in the same way as one's physical health status. **Mental health status** involves the combination of your healthful and risk behaviors with regard to being comfortable with yourself, feeling good about your relationships with others, and being able to meet the demands of your life. Of

Your mental health status depends on the risk and healthful behaviors you choose.

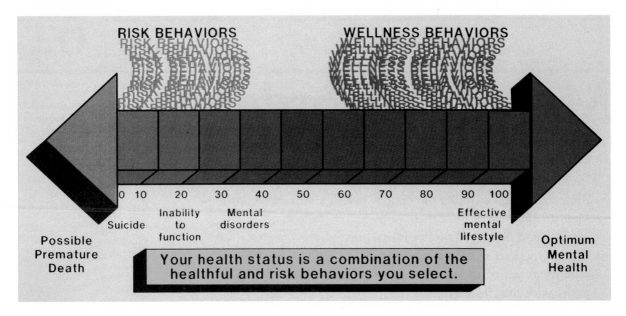

RISK BEHAVIORS   WELLNESS BEHAVIORS

0 10 20 30 40 50 60 70 80 90 100

Suicide   Inability to function   Mental disorders   Effective mental lifestyle

Possible Premature Death   Optimum Mental Health

Your health status is a combination of the healthful and risk behaviors you select.

FIGURE 6–1.

Your mental health status may fluctuate from day to day.

course, not all behaviors are equal. Some risk behaviors are more threatening to mental health status than others. Some healthful behaviors contribute to optimum mental health more than others.

Mental health status could also be related to a scale ranging from 0 (death) to 100 (optimum mental health) (Figure 6–1). The top of the scale (100) describes persons with optimum mental health. These persons function extremely well on a day-to-day basis. They relate well with others and express emotions in healthful ways. Persons who usually handle problems effectively would also be close to this end of the scale. Most of the time their relationships are healthful, and they express emotions in healthful ways.

Persons with poor mental health would be closer to the opposite end of the scale. Some may suffer from mental disorders but are able to function in society. Others close to the zero end might be persons who are hospitalized because of their inability to function in society. Persons at the very extreme end (0) might consider suicide if coping with life is overwhelming to them. You have learned that persons with mental disorders do not feel comfortable with themselves and do not have satisfactory relationships. They are unable to express emotions or meet the demands of life. These persons score in the lower ranges of the mental health scale. In this chapter, you will examine types of mental disorders. You will study harmful behaviors associated with these disorders.

6:2 Causes of Mental Disorders

Every day, many people experience situations that might be described as a life crisis. A **life crisis** is a shocking experience that causes a high level of mental stress. Some people are able to make adjustments to a life crisis while others despair and become unable to function. Why do individuals respond in such different ways to a life crisis? There is no simple answer. Several factors have a holistic effect on a person's response to a given situation.

People respond to a life crisis in different ways.

Environmental Factors **Environmental stress** refers to the physical or mental demands associated with your surroundings. Several factors in your environment may influence your mental health status. The most influential factor is your family. Parents influence mental health status in the way they teach their children to express emotions and cope with problems. The way a family interacts influences self-concept and helps determine behavioral patterns.

Your family interactions influence your self-concept and the behavioral patterns you use.

Other factors in the environment, such as high levels of noise and air pollution, poor lighting, or uncomfortable temperatures may affect mental health. For instance, on a hot, humid night, you may not be able to rest or get an adequate amount of sleep. This might affect your performance the next day.

Hereditary Factors It is difficult to distinguish between the influences of heredity and environment. Certain types of mental disorders tend to run in families. Are behavioral patterns learned in the family or is there a genetic cause for a particular disorder? Researchers are gathering evidence to support the theory that a tendency toward mental disorders might be inherited. Even if such a theory is proved to be true, other nonhereditary factors could influence whether or not a disorder might actually occur.

There may be an inherited tendency for some mental disorders.

FIGURE 6–2. Parents influence their children when they teach skills and ways to solve problems.

Factors That Affect the Brain The brain is like a vast computer that controls the performance of all mental and physical functions of the body. Thoughts, emotions, memory, personality, and actions are all part of this complex human computer. Anything that temporarily or permanently affects the brain can influence a person's mental health status.

An **organic mental disorder** is a change in mental health status caused by a physical condition that affects the brain. Physical illnesses, such as brain tumors, strokes, brain injuries, or syphilis, can also affect brain function. A lack of oxygen caused by a near-drowning or choking can destroy some brain cells. Other factors that affect brain function are chemicals such as alcohol and marijuana. Chemicals can be taken orally, by injection, or by inhalation.

Chemical abuse and certain physical illnesses may cause organic mental disorders.

 Review and Reflect

1. Why might two teenagers in the same family respond differently to their parents' divorce?
2. What is the most stressful part of your environment? Why?
3. How is the family an important influence in healthful and/or harmful environmental stress?
4. In your opinion, does heredity or environment influence mental health the most? Why?
5. Why do many chemically dependent persons have mental problems?

TYPES OF MENTAL DISORDERS

Mental disorders are classified by the American Psychiatric Association according to their common patterns of behavior.

6:3 Anxiety Disorders

Anxiety disorders are disorders in which real or imagined fears occur so often that they prevent a person from enjoying life. Three types of anxiety disorders are phobias, obsessive-compulsive behaviors, and general anxiety disorders. We all exhibit some symptoms of one type or another at some time. Unless these symptoms are persistent or recur frequently, there should be no need for concern.

Everyone experiences some anxiety in day-to-day living.

Table 6–1 Phobic Reactions

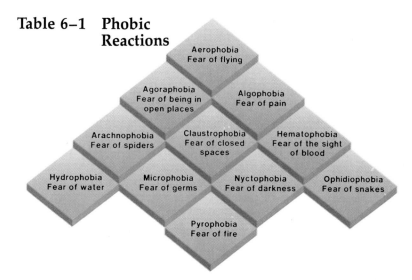

Aerophobia
Fear of flying

Agoraphobia
Fear of being in
open places

Algophobia
Fear of pain

Arachnophobia
Fear of spiders

Claustrophobia
Fear of closed
spaces

Hematophobia
Fear of the sight
of blood

Hydrophobia
Fear of water

Microphobia
Fear of germs

Nyctophobia
Fear of darkness

Ophidiophobia
Fear of snakes

Pyrophobia
Fear of fire

A **phobia** is the excess fear of a situation, object, or person. However, the source of the fear does not actually present a real danger. Usually a phobia is related to some past experience that was very upsetting to the individual. Suppose you accidentally locked yourself in a small closet when you were a child and no one found you for several hours. You were terrified. As a result, you may have developed claustrophobia, a fear of closed places. Now you may become terrified in elevators or other places where you might feel closed in. Another person experiencing a similar situation as a child may not develop claustrophobia.

It is hard to explain the cause of phobias. Counselors may help persons examine their phobias and overcome their fears. Some examples of other phobias are listed in Table 6–1.

Obsessive–compulsive behavior is behavior that is characterized by unreasonable thoughts and actions that are rigid, inflexible, and repetitive. Suppose you want to be a marathon runner. Every day you plan your activities around your training schedule. Eventually, your running interferes with studying and other school activities. You have no time for family and friends. Your behavior is obsessive. You become so obsessed with running that other commitments are overlooked.

Compulsive behavior involves repeating a behavior when it is unnecessary. For example, you may read in the newspaper about a burglary in your neighborhood. You check to see that the doors in your home are locked. This is a healthful response. However, if you check your doors ten times, your behavior is compulsive.

When a person suffers from a **general anxiety disorder**, he or she may feel anxious, tense, fearful, and upset most of the time. There is no specific object or situation that produces the fear.

A phobia is usually an excess fear that results from a past experience.

Your behavior is obsessive when you do one thing so often that you ignore other commitments.

Your behavior is compulsive if you unnecessarily repeat the same thing over and over.

6:4 Dissociative Disorders

Dissociative disorders involve behaviors in which persons separate themselves and their memories from their real personality. The most common dissociative disorder is amnesia. **Amnesia** is the inability to recall past experiences. Amnesia is not an intentional forgetting, but is the result of aging, illness, or injury. A person might not recall who he or she is and assume a different identity. Usually, amnesia lasts a short time and is not as dramatic as portrayed in movies or on television.

Amnesia may result from aging, illness or injury.

Some people have a multiple personality. A **multiple personality** is a rare mental disorder in which two or more personalities coexist within the same person. Depending on the circumstances, the person may shift from one personality to another. Each personality is unaware of the other personality's thoughts and actions.

6:5 Mood Disorders

In Chapter 5, you learned that it is normal to have different emotions or moods—loving moods, happy moods, hurt moods, anxious moods. **Mood disorders** involve moods that are extreme and interfere with daily living.

It is normal to experience different emotions or moods.

Depression is a feeling of hopelessness, sadness, or helplessness. Everyone experiences these feelings at one time or another. Short periods of depression are normal during adolescence. However, prolonged, persistent depression is not normal. Symptoms

Prolonged periods of depression are not normal for adolescents.

FIGURE 6–3. Everyone needs a friend who will listen and help.

of teenage depression include loss of sleep, loss of interest, loss of appetite, loss of energy, and loss of ability to concentrate. People who are severely depressed may not have a neat and clean appearance. They may complain about physical ailments such as muscle aches, dizziness, headaches, constipation, and heartburn. They may feel a tightening of the chest or have difficulty breathing.

Depressed people begin to withdraw from others. They may cease to show affection or enthusiasm about people for whom they care. Depressed people are sad. They do not respond to humor; they may cry frequently. Depressed people are often irritable and anxious. They may display angry, hostile behavior.

What causes depression in teenagers? There are at least five causes.

- *Disappointment.* Teenagers may become depressed when they expected something that did not happen, when they feel someone has let them down, or when they feel they have let someone else down. For example, teenagers who experience parental divorce may feel that their parents let them down because their original family structure is broken.

  Depression may result from a disappointment.

- *Loss of self-esteem.* Some teens expect too much of themselves. They are never satisfied with themselves. This is especially true of teens who are perfectionists or high achievers in school. Since it is hard to meet their unrealistic personal standards, they cannot find many sources of happiness.

  Perfectionists and high achievers may become depressed when they have unrealistic standards.

- *Unfair comparisons.* Frequently teens compare themselves to others. The media presents teenagers in movies and on TV as beautiful, handsome, slender, bright, and successful. Often these comparisons leave teens feeling that they do not measure up to others. Realistically, very few people measure up to these idealized portrayals of teenagers.

  Few people are as successful and attractive as teens portrayed on TV.

- *A sense of hopelessness.* The teenage years are an in-between time. Teens are no longer children, and yet, they do not have the authority and privileges of adults. Because of this, they may feel trapped during this period of their lives. Teens who feel this way often demonstrate risk behaviors. They may be hostile to their parents or teachers.

  Teens may struggle during the years when they are trying to achieve independence.

- *Illness.* Teens who are frequently ill or who have a long-term illness often become depressed. They may not be able to spend time with friends or participate in the activities they once enjoyed. Infectious mononucleosis, or mono, is an example of a common viral disease that can last several weeks or months. Teens who have mono are frequently depressed.

The diagram below illustrates what might take place when someone is depressed. Usually one of the five causes of depression occurs first. Any of these causes can produce anger. A teenager may become angry when his or her parents divorce. A teenager who cannot get a job feels trapped and angry. A teenager with cancer may be angry about having the disease. If the anger resulting from each of these causes is not expressed, it may turn inward. Persons who are angry with themselves become depressed. Inward anger is multiplied when the person begins to experience self-pity. Why did this happen to me? Why is everything hopeless? There is a feeling of losing control and nothing seems to help. Depression increases.

Inward anger and feelings of self-pity increase depression.

CAUSE OF DEPRESSION + ANGER X SELF-PITY = DEPRESSION

Expressing anger outwardly is better than directing it inwardly.

There are many ways to relieve the feelings of depression.

What should a teenager do who feels depressed? Table 6–2 offers some guidelines. For optimum health, a person needs to learn to deal with each of the five potential causes of depression. The anger that accompanies each cause must be outwardly expressed rather than directed to oneself.

For example, when you experience a cause of depression, you might examine your thoughts with a fresh outlook. You might have inaccurate perceptions about what has really happened. Your thoughts about a situation can help control your feelings. When a situation cannot be changed, a change in outlook can help. However, if you ever experience continual depression, you may need professional help. Various forms of treatment are discussed later in this chapter.

Table 6–2   What to Do When You Feel Depressed

- Talk with someone – a parent, coach, school counselor, or mental health specialist.
- Examine your thoughts about what bothers you with a fresh outlook.
- Plan your day.
- Make a list of the things you must do and check them off as you finish.
- Make a list of your strengths and review them.
- Plan something fun to do.
- Engage in vigorous exercise (Chapters 14, 15).
- Dress neatly to feel good about yourself and your appearance.
- Eat balanced, healthful meals (Chapter 12).
- Get plenty of rest and sleep (Chapter 15).

A **bipolar disorder** or **manic-depressive disorder** is a mood disorder in which a person's moods vary from being very high to being very depressed. The manic phase is the high mood. During the manic phase, a person experiences great joy for no reason. The person may laugh, sing, or talk all the time. The manic phase may also be a restless stage with outbursts of intense anger. This anger may turn into violence making the person dangerous to him or herself or to others.

During the depressive phase, the person experiences a passive mood and has very little energy. At this stage, the person may be suicidal and must be observed. The depressive phase ends when behavior swings back in the other direction—the manic phase. With professional help, psychotherapy, and/or drug therapy, persons should be able to learn to balance their feelings rather than experience these two opposite or bipolar behaviors.

In manic depressive disorder, a person's moods swing from excitement to depression.

6:6 Personality Disorders

In Chapter 5, you learned that personality is a combination of mental, physical, and emotional traits. As you become mature, your personality undergoes changes. Your ways of thinking, feeling, and acting should become more consistent and predictable.

Some adults have unusual patterns of thinking, feeling, and acting. When a person's personality is so unusual that it interferes with happiness and daily living, that person is said to have a **personality disorder**. Someone with a personality disorder is not comfortable with him or herself, does not have satisfying interpersonal relationships, and is unable to cope with the demands of daily living. There are several types of personality disorders. A person with a(n)

Adults who have unusual patterns of thinking, feeling, and acting have a personality disorder.

- **avoidant personality** prefers to avoid all social contact because of low self-esteem and fear of rejection. This intense fear is usually the result of an earlier painful experience.

- **dependent personality** is very insecure and leans on others for advice and support. This person is afraid of making decisions or doing things without help because others may not be accepting of his or her choice.

- **histrionic personality** has emotional outbursts and constantly behaves in ways to draw attention to him or herself. Although enthusiastic, this person is easily bored with the people and situations with whom he or she acts excited.

- **narcissistic personality** is vain, boastful, conceited, and inconsiderate of others. This person believes he or she is better than others and turns them off.
- **passive–aggressive personality** switches back and forth between being forceful and frightened with people and events. The person's daily performance changes drastically.
- **schizoid personality** has disturbing thought patterns, prefers social isolation, and does not enjoy life.

6:7 Schizophrenia

A schizophrenic experiences a breakdown in logical thought processes.

Schizophrenia is a mental disorder in which there is a split or breakdown in logical thought processes. The split results in unusual behaviors. Actions, words, and emotions are confused and inappropriate for the situation. A person who is schizophrenic may appear desperate and withdraw into an inner world of fantasy. Research indicates that schizophrenia may have physical as well as mental causes. Professional help is always recommended for recovery. Schizophrenia from physical causes may be treated with medication. Hospitalization is usually required during treatment.

A paranoid schizophrenic has delusions of persecution or grandeur.

Paranoid schizophrenia is a disorder in which a person has delusions of either persecution or grandeur. Delusions of persecution are feelings that others are trying to harm you. For example, paranoid schizophrenics may think someone is following them and trying to kill them. These delusions are real to the person. Delusions of grandeur are feelings of being unusually great. Persons with this type of paranoid schizophrenia may believe they are president of a country, a famous athlete, or a television star. These delusions prevent a normal healthful lifestyle.

6:8 Somatoform Disorders

A **somatoform disorder** includes a group of disorders in which there are physical symptoms of illness from emotional causes but no physical explanation of illness. **Hypochondria** is a somatoform disorder in which there is constant anxiety about illness. A person who experiences constant anxiety about illness is called a **hypochondriac.** A hypochondriac constantly feels aches and pains and worries about developing heart disease, cancer, or some other serious problem.

A hypochondriac has a somatoform disorder.

A **conversion disorder** involves sudden changes in a person's body that, to some extent, provide a solution to a problem. Some physical changes that might occur include sudden loss of vision or hearing, loss of sensation in the skin, or paralysis of a body

A conversion disorder is a somatoform disorder.

part. For example, a teenage girl may decide to try out for the drill team. She may begin to worry that she is not skilled or attractive enough to be selected. Suddenly, she becomes ill and loses the use of her legs. A physician examines her to discover a reason for her paralysis. Several weeks after the tryouts are over, the girl regains the use of her legs. The paralysis temporarily solved the girl's problem—she did not have to try out for the drill team and risk failure. However, the source of her fears has not changed.

 ## Review and Reflect

6. Why are some people afraid to ride a Ferris wheel?
7. Why is it important to express anger in healthful ways?
8. Why might someone lose his or her voice the night before giving a speech in front of 1000 people?

SUICIDE

Suicide is the second leading cause of death in teenagers and young adults. Each year, thousands of teenagers and young adults attempt suicide. More than 5000 teens commit suicide annually. The suicide rate among young people in the 1980s has more than doubled since 1960, and it has tripled since 1950.

Suicide is a leading cause of adolescent death.

6:9 Causes of Suicide

Suicide is the intended taking of one's own life. Teenage suicide is not necessarily a result of having a mental disorder. Most teen suicides might have been prevented if those teens had developed life management skills. Why would a teenager attempt or commit suicide? The causes of suicide are closely related to the experiences of loss or rejection discussed in Chapter 5. The loss of love may leave a teen with a feeling of hopelessness or that "no one cares about me." The loss of control may result in a feeling of being helpless. The loss of self-confidence may result from years of low self-esteem followed by competition at school or poor peer relationships. This loss may lead to an attempt to gain attention. Teenagers may view suicide as a way to get even with those who have rejected them.

Teens who attempt suicide often feel loss or rejection.

Two other losses are related to suicide and to suicide attempts. The loss of health, particularly with a serious illness like cancer, may leave a teen feeling there is no hope for the future. And finally, the feeling of confusion that often is part of growing from childhood to adolescence to adulthood can be very disturbing to some individuals. This may result in a loss of stability.

6:10   Signs of Suicide

There are signs that indicate someone may have suicidal thoughts.

Some teens who experience one or more of these losses may show signs of severe depression. If they are thinking about suicide, the following changes in behaviors might provide a clue to those around them. A person who is contemplating suicide might
- exhibit a drastic change in personality.
- withdraw from family and other people.
- lose interest in personal appearance.
- lose interest in schoolwork.
- have difficulty getting along with others.
- increase the use of chemicals, such as alcohol or marijuana.
- change sleeping and eating habits drastically.
- give away valued possessions.
- talk about getting even with parents.
- talk about suicide.
- ask questions about death.

6:11   Suicide Prevention

When you suspect someone is suicidal, there are steps you should take to prevent the occurrence.

Francine Klagsbrun in her book *Too Young To Die: Youth and Suicide* identifies ways that you can help when you suspect that someone is thinking about suicide.

1. Recognize the signs of suicide (Section 6:12).
2. Trust your own judgment. If you believe someone is in danger of suicide, act on your beliefs. Do not let others mislead you into ignoring suicidal signals.
3. Tell others. As quickly as possible, share your knowledge with parents, friends, teachers, or other people who might help in a suicidal crisis. Do not worry about breaking a confidence if someone reveals suicidal plans to you. You may have to betray a secret to save a life.
4. Stay with a suicidal person until help arrives or the crisis passes.

5. Listen intelligently. Encourage a suicidal person to talk to you. Do not give false reassurances that everything will be OK. Listen and sympathize with what the person says.

6. Urge professional help. Put pressure on a suicidal person to seek help from a psychiatrist, psychologist, social worker, or other professional person during a suicidal crisis or after a suicide attempt. Encourage the person to continue with therapy treatments.

7. Be supportive. Show the person that you care. Help the person feel worthwhile and wanted again.

 Review and Reflect

9. If you had a friend who confided in you that he or she was contemplating suicide, what steps could you take to prevent such a thing from happening?

 Activity: _____ **The Will to Live**

It is unfortunate that some teenagers would choose suicide or another destructive behavior when there are so many ways to enjoy life. Think about the many activities you like to do. Make a list titled "The Will to Live." Identify the things that you find pleasure in doing now and look forward to enjoying in the future.

You should always take threats of suicide seriously.

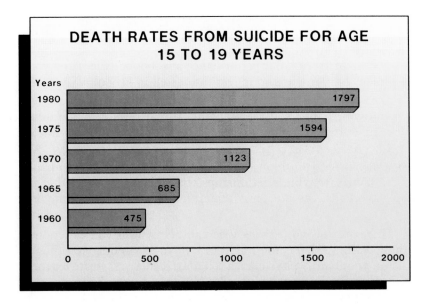

DEATH RATES FROM SUICIDE FOR AGE 15 TO 19 YEARS

Years
- 1980: 1797
- 1975: 1594
- 1970: 1123
- 1965: 685
- 1960: 475

(0, 500, 1000, 1500, 2000)

FIGURE 6–4.

TREATMENT AND SERVICES

There is an important health saying, "Good health adds years to your life and life to your years!" How do you add life to your years? The key is to strive for and maintain optimum physical, mental, and social health. It involves

- recognizing harmful behaviors that are symptoms of poor health.
- changing harmful behaviors or seeking treatment to modify harmful behaviors.
- utilizing mental health services when necessary.

6:12 Recognizing Mental Health Problems

To stay mentally healthy throughout life, it is important to assess your health behavior often. Learn to recognize risk behaviors and know when and how to change them to healthful behaviors. In his book, *Healthy Personality*, Sidney Jourard identifies six warning signs that indicate it may be time for you to change a risk behavior.

- *Boredom.* Daily activities that used to satisfy you no longer satisfy you.
- *Illness.* You are not healthy, or you are experiencing mental distress.
- *Chronic Anxiety and Guilt.* You are anxious, unable to sleep, and cannot concentrate on schoolwork. You feel guilty about your behavior.
- *Failure at Work.* Your performance at school changes and your grades fall. You are no longer interested in school activities.
- *Fear of Being Unmasked.* You are aware that your private self and your public self are different. You are afraid that if other people find out what you are really like, they will no longer like you.
- *Unexpected Failure in Personal Relationships.* You are unable to have satisfying relationships with others. You feel that no one really loves you. It is difficult for you to care about anyone else.

There are several persons who can help you if you experience these warning signs. You might talk to your parents, a brother or sister, your family physician, a religious leader, a favorite teacher, school nurse, or school counselor. You might also choose to see a mental health specialist.

To stay mentally healthy, it is important to assess your behavior regularly.

Recognize risk behaviors in your life that you should change.

FIGURE 6-5. There are many sources of help available to a person who needs it.

6:13 Mental Health Specialists and Types of Therapy

Mental health specialists are persons who are trained to help you examine and change behaviors that are harmful to mental health. Mental health specialists include psychiatrists, psychologists, psychiatric social workers, psychiatric nurses, and school psychologists.

A **psychiatrist** is a medical doctor who specializes in the treatment of mental disorders. The person has a medical degree and at least three years experience in evaluating and treating mental disorders. A psychiatrist must pass an examination to be licensed. With the medical degree and license, a psychiatrist can prescribe medications for treatment.

A **psychologist** does not have a medical degree but is trained to administer psychological tests and diagnose and treat human behavioral disorders. A psychologist is required to have a master's degree and, in most states, must pass requirements for certification. Many psychologists have a Ph.D. degree.

A **clinical psychologist** has a Ph.D. degree and has had an internship in a psychiatric setting. He or she must also pass a test to be licensed. Clinical psychologists often use tests to help diagnose and treat mental disorders.

A **psychiatric social worker** concentrates on mental health casework. He or she usually has an M.A. degree with field work at a family service agency, hospital, or clinic. Standards for this work are set by the National Association for Social Workers.

Many mental health professionals are available to help people.

A psychiatrist has a medical degree; a psychologist does not.

The **psychiatric nurse** has training in the care of persons with mental disorders. This specialized nurse often works in a hospital setting.

6:14   Therapeutic Approaches

If you meet with a mental health specialist, you will discuss your problem in more detail. The goal of counseling or therapy is to help people work toward (1) being comfortable with themselves, (2) feeling good about their relationships with others, and (3) being able to meet the demands of life.

The psychiatrist Sigmund Freud believed that repression is the cause of many disturbances that come up later in one's life. **Repression** means removing an anxiety-producing thought or event from the consciousness. The individual becomes unaware of the thought or event and has no control over this action.

Freud founded the process of psychoanalysis as a way of helping people resolve repressed conflicts. **Psychoanalysis** is a form of therapy in which a patient examines past experiences in order to understand how those experiences might affect his or her present thoughts, emotions, and actions.

Carl Rogers, founder of client-centered therapy, believed that the goal of therapy was to help a client examine present choices and make decisions about his or her behavior. **Client-centered therapy** or **nondirective therapy** is a form of treatment in which the client understands his or her present behavior and choices and decides what the goal of the treatment should be. The person is called a client rather than a patient because he or she is not viewed as being sick but rather as desiring change. The therapist provides a comfortable, supportive environment during this changing process. The therapist helps the client develop a positive self-concept. The client tries to learn how to function better in the present.

Behavior modification is a form of therapy in which the therapist teaches the patient new behavioral patterns to use when responding to difficult life situations. The focus is not on understanding why situations are difficult but what to do when they occur. The techniques used to teach new behavioral patterns include controlling reinforcements, desensitization, and modeling.

- **Controlling reinforcements** is a technique in which a patient is given a reward for desirable behavior and a punishment or lack of attention for undesirable behavior. For example, people may have emotional outbursts when they do not get their way. This behavior may cause others to give in to their desires or to give

---

The goal of therapy is to help people work toward positive mental health.

Sigmund Freud used psychoanalysis to help patients examine repressed conflicts.

Carl Rogers used client-centered therapy to help persons examine and make choices about behavior.

Behavior modification includes controlling reinforcements, desensitization, and modeling.

them attention. By withdrawing attention and ignoring the behavior, these people learn that this action is not acceptable. When they act in a mature way, they receive a reward.

- **Desensitization** is a technique used to help patients overcome fear and anxiety by gradually learning to cope with increasingly stressful situations. Consider a person who may not be able to express anger appropriately. At first, the person learns to express anger to the therapist then to a friend. Gradually, the person can express anger to those persons who mistreat him or her.
- **Modeling** is a technique in which the patient learns to handle a given situation by observing how someone else would respond to a similar situation. Frequently, the therapist is the model. In this way, the patient learns new patterns of behavior.

During **group therapy**, a number of individuals meet together with a therapist to react to one another as they discuss new ways of behaving. While in group therapy, persons are able to practice social and communicative skills. Group therapy can also involve other forms of expression. Sometimes groups use music, art, or dance as part of therapy.

Group therapy could involve persons who are focusing on a specific life crisis. Alcoholics Anonymous involves group sessions for persons who are alcoholic. Weight Watchers involves group meetings for persons needing support for weight control. Cancer patients may also belong to a group that offers peer support.

Group therapy enables persons to practice social and communicative skills.

FIGURE 6–6. Group therapy is usually conducted in a relaxed atmosphere. The individual participant can share and benefit from the experiences of others.

Family therapy is a form of group therapy. In these sessions, the patient and family members meet with a therapist to interact with one another and discuss new ways of behavior. Sometimes, family therapy focuses on how each person influences the other's behavior. At other times, the family may meet because one family member has mental problems and needs their support.

Psychopharmacology is the use of drugs in treating mental disorders. Psychopharmacology is usually used in combination with one or more of the other treatments discussed. The drugs used may help persons to function well enough to benefit from therapy or to maintain a regular lifestyle while learning to adopt healthful behaviors. However, there are precautions in the use of drug therapy. The drugs may change a person's mood, but the source of the problem still exists. A person may abuse the drug or experience side effects. A psychiatrist considers many factors before selecting drug therapy as a means of therapy.

Drug therapy is usually combined with other forms of therapy to alter behavior.

6:15 Mental Health Services

Where are these various forms of treatment for mental disorders available? In the past, most treatment was done at a hospital with the patient staying for the duration of treatment. Today, most persons receive treatment as an outpatient. Being an outpatient means that a person is able to live at home while receiving mental health care on a regular schedule at a hospital, clinic, or private office. Some outpatients may also continue to work at a workplace or maintain their regular lifestyle. The following mental health services are available.

Crisis intervention services consist of a 24-hour service to help persons who experience a crisis such as a suicide attempt, abuse of a child, or an overdose of a drug. Usually, there is a hotline or special phone number to call to seek immediate help. Trained persons are available to assist the person through the crisis and to help identify other resources that might help alleviate the problem. The crisis intervention service may be at a hospital or at a community mental health center.

FIGURE 6-7. This sign appeared on a bridge where there has been a history of suicides.

DESPERATE?
LIFE IS WORTH LIVING!
PICK UP
HELPLINE
24 HRS. A DAY

DUTCHESS COUNTY MENTAL HEALTH CENTER

To Use: Hold door open
Talk into Box

THIS PHONE IS HERE
TO SAVE LIVES
PLEASE DO NOT TAMPER!

Community mental health centers provide a variety of services such as crisis intervention, emergency services, and short-term inpatient or outpatient services. Patients are able to maintain their lifestyles while having the benefit of these services near their homes. Usually the charges for the services are based on one's ability to pay for them.

Sometimes, a brief hospital stay of two-to-six weeks is needed for treatment of severe mental disorders. Sometimes a stay of two months or longer is necessary. Inpatient hospital care combines psychotherapy, drug therapy, and group therapy. After the hospital stay, the patient may receive outpatient services.

 Review and Reflect

10. Why would a normally healthy person seek help from a mental health specialist?
11. How does modeling by a therapist help a client change harmful behavior?
12. Why do mental health specialists often include family members of clients in therapy?
13. Why do many cities have a hotline phone number to call for crisis intervention?

Focus on
Life Management Skills

- Assess your mental health status regularly.
- Avoid environmental stresses such as high levels of noise, air pollution, poor lighting, and uncomfortable temperatures.
- Avoid the use of alcohol, marijuana, and other drugs that might harm the brain.
- Learn to express anger in healthful ways in order to avoid depression.
- Develop a philosophy of life that focuses on living life to the fullest.
- Recognize the signs of suicide and assist others in suicidal prevention.
- Recognize warning signs that indicate it may be time to change risk behaviors to healthful behaviors.
- Be aware of the mental health services and treatment facilities available in your community.

CAREERS

School Psychologist

Carole Peters enjoys the challenge of working with teenagers in her dual career as a licensed psychologist in private practice and as a certified school psychologist. To prepare for her career, Carole obtained both a master's degree and a doctoral degree in Guidance and Counseling. She studied courses in counseling techniques, human emotions, human behavior, behavioral change, and testing and measurement. To become a licensed psychologist, Carole passed a licensing examination given by the state Psychology Board. She completed an additional one-year internship in school psychology to become a certified school psychologist.

As a school psychologist, Carole's work involves administering psychological tests, evaluating the results, and helping students determine what choices they should make based on their test results. In her private practice, Carole works with adolescents and helps them explore behaviors that promote healthful living.

"Adolescents are challenging," says Carole. "They are making important decisions in their lives. They are curious and exploring. They spend time with me engaging in the decision-making process and exploring their commitment to change. Many adolescents come to see me because they are concerned about their friends and want to know how they can help. It is encouraging to see this concern for others." Carole finds her career both challenging and rewarding.

CHAPTER 6

Summary

1. Mental health status is a combination of healthful and harmful behaviors and can be measured on a scale ranging from 0 (death) to 100 (optimum health). 6:1

2. Factors that have a holistic effect on a person's response to a given situation include environmental factors, hereditary factors, and factors that affect the brain. 6:2

3. Anxiety disorders such as phobias, obsessive–compulsive behaviors, and general anxiety disorders prevent a person from enjoying life. 6:3

4. Dissociative disorders such as amnesia and multiple personality cause a person to separate themselves from their real personalities. 6:4

5. Two types of mood disorders are depression—the leading mental problem of teens—and manic-depressive disorder. 6:5

6. Six types of personality disorders are avoidant, dependent, histrionic, narcissistic, passive–aggressive, and schizoid. 6:6

7. Persons who suffer from schizophrenia have a breakdown in their logical thought processes and exhibit unusual and inappropriate behaviors. 6:7

8. A somatoform disorder, hypochondria, and a conversion disorder result in physical symptoms from emotional causes. 6:8

9. Some teenagers commit suicide because they are unable to cope with loss of love, loss of control, loss of confidence, loss of health, or loss of stability. 6:9

10. Teenagers who are thinking about suicide often display one or more risk behaviors that indicate they need help. These signs should always be taken seriously. 6:10

11. When a suicidal crisis is suspected, stay with the suicidal person and ask another person to get help as quickly as possible. 6:11

12. Warning signs that may indicate time to change a risk behavior include boredom, illness, chronic anxiety and guilt, failure at work, fear of being unmasked, and unexpected failure in personal relationships. 6:12

13. Mental health specialists include psychiatrists, psychologists, clinical psychologists, psychiatric social workers, and psychiatric nurses. 6:13

14. Mental health specialists help persons change risk behaviors using a variety of approaches: psychoanalyses, client-centered therapy, behavior modification, group therapy, family therapy, and drug therapy. 6:14

15. Mental health services and therapy are available at crisis intervention centers, community mental health centers, private offices, and hospitals. 6:15

Vocabulary

Below is a list of vocabulary words used in this chapter. Use each word only once to complete the sentences. Do not write in this book.

amnesia   phobia
anxiety disorder   psychiatrist
hypochondriac   schizophrenia
life crisis   somatoform
mood disorder   suicide

1. A medical doctor who specializes in the treatment of mental disorders is called a(n) _____.

2. Someone who experiences symptoms of illness with no physical cause has a(n) _____ disorder.

3. A(n) _____ is a person who experiences constant anxiety about illness.

4. Depression is an example of a(n) _____.

5. A person who forgets his or her name or assumes a different identity suffers from _____.

6. An excessive fear of heights or a fear of closed places is a(n) _____.

7. A(n) _____ is a disorder in which real or imagined fears occur so often that they prevent a person from enjoying life.

8. A shocking experience that causes a high level of mental stress is a(n) _____.

9. _____ is a mental disorder in which there is a split or breakdown in logical thought processes.

10. _____ is the second leading cause of death in adolescents.

Review

1. What is mental health status, and how is it measured?

2. What are six factors in the environment that might affect your level of stress?

3. What does research say about the role of heredity in mental disorders?

4. What might influence the development of organic mental disorders?

5. What are four types of phobias?

6. What behaviors are characteristic of a multiple personality?

7. What are five causes of teenage depression? What happens when someone is depressed?

8. Identify and describe six types of personality disorders.

9. What behaviors are characteristic of a person with schizophrenia?

10. What behaviors are characteristic of a hypochondriac?

11. What are five causes of teenage suicide?

12. What are ten behaviors that indicate someone might be thinking about suicide?

13. How might you help in a suicidal crisis?

14. What six behaviors indicate that a person might have poor mental health?

15. Identify five mental health specialists.

16. Describe four ways to treat mental health problems.

17. Describe places that provide mental health services.

Application

1. Suppose a friend asks you to stop by his or her home after school. Your friend talks about suicide and asks questions about death. Your friend's parents are not at home. What would you do?

2. Your friend's parents have recently divorced. Your friend was depressed, talked with his parents, and then decided to go to a counselor. Some other friends are very critical. They believe that anyone who seeks counseling is weak in character. What would you say to your friends?

Individual Research

1. Interview a mental health specialist who works with persons your age. Write a paper discussing the background and training of the specialist, and the kinds of problems his or her teenage clients often experience.

2. Review the six symptoms that indicate it might be necessary to change some risk behaviors to healthful behaviors. Describe how these changes might have a holistic effect and influence one or more of the ten areas in the Health Behavior Wheel. Give specific examples.

Readings

Klagsbrun, Francine, *Too Young To Die*. New York, NY: Pocket Books, 1984.

McCoy, Kathyleen, *Coping With Teenage Depression*. New York, NY: Signet Books, 1982.

Myers, Irma, and Myers, Arthur, *Why You Feel Down and What You Can Do About It*. New York, NY: Atheneum Publishers, 1982.

Powell, John, *Why Am I Afraid to Tell You Who I Am?* Niles, IL: Argus Communications, 1979.

If you were the gymnast, would you be feeling any stress? Imagine the preparation necessary to be ready for a performance like this. How do you cope with stress? There are skills you can learn to cope with stressful situations in ways that will not harm your health.

Chapter **7**

Stress Management

OBJECTIVES: You will be able to

- **explain the stages of the general adaptation syndrome when stress occurs.**
- **describe the holistic effects of stress.**
- **utilize stress management skills.**

An Olympic gymnast demonstrates perfect balance during her routine on the balance beam. What an incredible performer! Imagine the training schedule she endured to prepare to compete in the Olympics. This gymnast met the challenge of many mental, physical, and social demands in her quest for a gold medal as an all-around gymnast.

WHAT IS STRESS?

Each day of your life, you also will be challenged by many mental, physical, and social demands. How are you able to meet the challenge of these demands? How do you demonstrate a balanced, healthful lifestyle?

7:1 Types of Stress—Eustress and Distress

Stress is the nonspecific response of the body to any demand made upon it. A **stressor** is a demand made upon the body. A stressor may be physical (running in a race), mental (taking a test), or social (calling on the phone to ask for a date). A stressor may be from any of the ten areas of health (Chapter 1). Your response to a stressor may be healthful or harmful.

A stressor may be physical, mental, or social.

125

Eustress is positive and
healthful.

When you respond to a stressor in a way that produces positive results, you have coped well and experienced the feeling of success. **Eustress** is a healthful response to a stressor. The gymnastic competition was a stressor for the gymnast. The gymnast's response was positive and, therefore, it was healthful. This stress helped her perform at her best. The approaching competition motivated her to eat a balanced diet and get enough sleep. She practiced her routine over and over. She had to think like a winner.

Harmful responses to a stressor
results in distress.

Distress is unsuccessful coping or a harmful response to a stressor. What if the preparation for competition was overwhelming to the gymnast? She may have skipped meals so she could practice longer; it may have been difficult for her to relax and get to sleep. She may have been so overwhelmed by the competition that she panicked and could hardly perform her routine. In this case, the response to the stressor was harmful.

The same stressor can produce
either eustress or distress.

The same stressor can produce either distress or eustress depending on a person's response. To understand how this can happen, you will need to know about the changes that occur in your body when you experience stress.

7:2   General Adaptation Syndrome

Your body responds to stress in three different stages. Hans Selye, a pioneer in the study of stress, referred to this response as the general adaptation syndrome, or GAS. The **general adaptation syndrome,** or **GAS,** can be defined as the body's response to stress. The three stages of GAS are the alarm stage, the resistance stage, and the exhaustion stage.

The general adaptation
syndrome is divided into three
stages.

The alarm stage of GAS
prepares the body for action.

The **alarm stage** is the body's initial response to a physical, mental, or social stressor. During this stage, the body's defenses prepare for sudden action and quick movement. The alarm stage is sometimes called the fight or flight response. The adrenal glands secrete adrenaline into the bloodstream. Adrenaline causes many changes to occur in the body (Table 7-1).

The alarm stage of GAS is also
called the fight or flight
response.

Study the changes that occur during the alarm stage. These changes may be healthful or harmful depending on what happens when they occur, how long they last, and whether you are overwhelmed or successful in your reaction. Here are two examples.

The gymnast responded positively to the stressor and experienced eustress. She vaulted into the air during her gymnastic routine. She made use of the extra sugar in her bloodstream and the oxygen gained from increased respiration. Added strength and

Table 7–1   The Alarm Stage

- The adrenal glands release adrenaline into the bloodstream.
- Heart rate and blood pressure increase.
- The rate of digestion slows.
- Blood flow increases to muscles.
- The liver releases sugar into the bloodstream making more energy available for muscles.
- Muscle tension increases and results in increased strength and endurance.
- Respiration increases providing more oxygen to body cells.
- The pupils dilate allowing more acute vision.
- Hearing becomes more acute.
- Thrombin (a blood clotting hormone) is released into the bloodstream in preparation for quick clotting if there is a cut.

endurance from increased muscle tension improved her performance. These physiological changes combined to act as eustress; she coped successfully.

Suppose the gymnast had reacted to the stressor in negative ways. She may have been overwhelmed and dominated by anxiety. The extra energy made her fidgety. She felt a tightness in her stomach. Her muscles may have become so tense that she fell from the balance beam. After the competition, she felt so anxious that she did not sleep or eat. The physiological changes combined to produce distress; she did not cope well.

The second stage of GAS is called the resistance stage. During the **resistance stage,** the body attempts to regain a state of internal balance, or homeostasis (hoh mee oh STAY sus). **Homeostasis** is the usual state in which the body maintains a balance of internal functions regardless of external changes. Homeostasis is also described as the state where the body has balance. During the resistance stage, the pulse, breathing rate, and blood pressure return to normal levels. The pupils of the eyes return to normal size. Tensed muscles relax. Extra blood that was diverted from the digestive system now returns and normal digestion occurs. Examine how the resistance stage differs in the two examples of the gymnast.

In the first example, the gymnast experienced anxiety but coped successfully. She felt a wonderful sense of mastery and the competition was a eustress. During the competition, she used the changes in her body to her advantage. When the competition was over, or shortly after, the resistance stage began. Her body regained homeostasis in a short period of time.

The alarm stage of GAS may be healthful or harmful depending on the individual.

The body attempts to regain homeostasis during the resistance stage of GAS.

In the second example, the gymnast experienced distress. The body changes resulting from overwhelming anxiety and the alarm stage were not healthful. These changes continued for a few days. The resistance stage was delayed. It was several days before the gymnast's body regained homeostasis. During such a time period, the body does not function at its best.

When the resistance stage of GAS is prolonged, the body does not function well.

To remain healthy, it is important that you experience stressors as eustress or that you regain homeostasis very quickly after experiencing distress. Suppose that distress continues for several days, months, or years. The body's balance remains disturbed. A new stage of stress begins. The **exhaustion stage** of GAS results in wear and tear on the body, lowered resistance to disease, and/or death. The results depend on the person's physical and hereditary makeup and his or her abilities for coping, and the amount and duration of the distress. The exhaustion stage is experienced only after prolonged periods of distress.

Harmful body changes may occur during the exhaustion stage of GAS.

Activity: The Pain of Distress

Dr. Kenneth Sehnert, in his book *Stress/Unstress,* describes a procedure to demonstrate the muscle pain that may occur from prolonged muscle contractions during distress.

1. Raise your arm high over your head.
2. Open and close your fist rapidly while counting to 20 slowly.
3. Now, tightly clench your fist for another 20 seconds.
4. Lower your hand.
5. Look at the skin color of the palm of your hand.

Muscle pain may result from prolonged muscle contractions during stress.

According to Dr. Sehnert, you will feel stiffness, numbness, and perhaps some pain. "The pain is from the decreased blood flow and essential oxygen to the tissues involved. When you look at your hand, you will notice that it had a pale look for a few seconds before it turned pink when normal blood flow was restored. The major cause of musculoskeletal pain is the same for any part of the body: head, neck, upper back, lower back, shoulder. Once you have acquired a habit of tenseness for any group of muscles, when you overreact to stressful situations, there is lessened blood to the muscles and this can lead to chronic pain."

Review and Reflect

1. Why might the alarm stage of GAS also be called the "fight or flight" response?
2. Why is giving a speech either a eustress or a distress?

Kenneth Sehnert, M.D., *Stress/Unstress.* Minneapolis: Augsburg Publishing House, 1981, p.76.

HOLISTIC EFFECTS OF STRESS

Stress has a holistic effect. This means a stressor in any one of the ten areas of health may affect one or more of the other areas. Suppose a teenager's parents get a divorce. The divorce may become a stressor. The teenager may find it difficult to study (Mental Health), to eat (Nutrition), and to sleep (Growth and Development). In this way, one stressor can create other stressors affecting all areas of life.

In the sections that follow, you will learn about the effects of stress in each of the ten areas of health. Remember, the intensity of a stressor is critical in determining the effect on a person's health status. An individual's temperament, social support, socioeconomic status, and ability to cope are also factors.

A stressor in one area of health affects all other areas.

7:3   Stress and Mental Health

A research group studied the effects of personality types on the incidence of heart disease. The study concluded that persons having certain excessive personality traits tend to react to stress as distress. Typical behaviors of each personality type are identified.

The Type A personality is characterized by an intense sense of time urgency and the need to accomplish as much as possible in the shortest possible time. The Type A personality is very competitive and achievement-oriented. Persons who are Type A are likely to accomplish a great deal and have high self-esteem. However, too much Type A behavior can result in excessive competitiveness, too much pressure, unnecessary frustration, and low self-esteem. The result can be distress produced by anxiety.

The Type B personality usually takes things in stride and does not place as much emphasis on doing things quickly. For this reason, the Type B personality may be more calm and more relaxed than a Type A personality. However, too much of a good thing may also cause distress. Suppose a Type B person relaxed to the point of not taking on meaningful and interesting goals. The result might be boredom. Frequent and prolonged times of boredom usually produce distress.

In summary, you may be a Type A personality, a Type B personality, or a combination of the two. The way you cope with life events will determine your level of eustress and/or distress.

Too much Type A behavior produces anxiety that creates distress.

Too much Type B behavior may produce boredom that creates distress.

FIGURE 7–1. In every group of people, there are both Personality A and B types represented.

FIGURE 7–2. Stress affects everyone. It is important to recognize the source of the stress and to learn how to deal with it.

Possible teenage stressors include parental death or divorce, loneliness, inability to communicate, new environment, and poor peer relationships.

7:4 Stress and Family and Social Health

Teenagers were surveyed to learn what stressors occurred in their families and in their social lives. The stressors identified most often were divorce of parents, death of a loved one, loneliness, lack of communicative skills, moving to a new neighborhood, and having difficulty in peer relationships. There are ways to help a person cope with stressors in this area of health. These include discussing problems with family members and friends, having someone to love, developing good communicative skills, and becoming interested in a variety of social activities. In Chapters 8 and 9, you will learn more about developing these skills and forming healthful relationships.

7:5 Stress and Growth and Development

Early or late growth and development during adolescence may create distress.

During puberty, hormones cause many body changes. Some of the changes may cause a teenager to experience distress. It is not uncommon for an adolescent to grow four inches in one year. Growth rates vary among individuals. Adolescents who grow and develop sooner or later than their friends may experience distress. Teenagers may also experience distress for other reasons, such as acne or obesity.

7:6 Stress and Nutrition

Your diet can affect you during periods when you are having difficulty coping. The following suggestions may help keep you in better health.

• Limit the amount of caffeine you eat or drink.

When you consume 250 to 300 mg of caffeine within a two-hour period, the alarm stage of GAS may begin. A 12-ounce cola contains about 50 mg of caffeine; a 1-ounce chocolate bar contains 20 mg; a cup of coffee contains about 100 mg.

• Limit the amount of salt you use.

When you eat salty foods, such as pretzels, or add salt to foods frequently, your body retains fluids. This could increase your blood pressure. High blood pressure is a contributing factor to heart disease.

• Limit the amount of refined sugar you consume.

High concentrations of refined sugar may cause your body to increase the production of insulin. This may result in hypoglycemia (Chapter 4).

• Limit the amount of cholesterol you eat.

Cholesterol is a fatlike substance found in animal tissue. Cholesterol has been identified as a major risk factor in heart disease. Too much cholesterol in the blood may cause fat deposits to accumulate on artery walls. The interior of the artery becomes clogged. As a result, blood flow diminishes and blood pressure increases. Too much cholesterol, along with increased heart rate and blood pressure, multiplies the risk factors in heart disease.

FIGURE 7–3. Some factors that influence growth and development are not within a person's control. This can be a source of stress.

Too much salt in the diet may increase blood pressure.

Too much dietary cholesterol combined with distress multiplies the risk of heart disease.

7:7 Stress and Exercise and Fitness

Exercise can be a eustress or a distress depending on the amount and the intensity of the exercise. Exercise as eustress will be discussed with stress management skills. The focus here will be on exercise and distress.

Lack of exercise is a stressor because the heart muscle and other body muscles do not get sufficient exercise. The muscles become flabby and weak. They are unable to do the work they should. Cardiovascular diseases and disorders may result from too little exercise. Lack of regular exercise is also a major contributing factor to weight gain. Weight gain is an additional stressor. For each additional pound of fat, the heart has to work harder to supply blood to all parts of the body.

Too little exercise may result in weight gain and a flabby heart muscle.

7:8 Stress and Drugs

Some drugs may increase distress by increasing the GAS effects.

The use of drugs such as tobacco, marijuana, cocaine, alcohol, and tranquilizers may decrease your ability to cope successfully. Tobacco, marijuana, and cocaine increase GAS effects. Alcohol and tranquilizers depress body functions, including the parts of the brain responsible for reasoning and judgment.

7:9 Stress and Diseases and Disorders

Prolonged distress suppresses the immune system, increasing the likelihood of disease.

Stress also affects the body's immune system. The immune system is made up of the white blood cells and other substances in the blood that destroy germs and other foreign substances. Periods of being overwhelmed and anxious may cause the immune system to be suppressed. This results in lowered resistance to disease. Communicable diseases such as the cold and flu are more likely to occur.

The relationship between stress and disease is clear. Many health authorities agree that stress, not heart disease or cancer, is the leading cause of death and disability.

7:10 Stress and Consumer and Personal Health

Each day you make many choices. How will you spend your time? How will you spend your money? A consumer is someone who spends time and money. Failure to learn how to handle time and money may make you feel anxious or frustrated.

Having either too little or too much to do can create distress.

Persons often feel anxious and frustrated when they have too little or too much to do. Boredom results from the lack of challenge. Relieve the effects of boredom by learning a new skill or spending time with friends.

People with too much to do rush from one activity to another. Their hectic schedules often result in such disorders as high blood pressure, heart disease, and allergic reactions. These effects of stress can be relieved by establishing new priorities and by setting limits on time and energy. Then you feel more confident and in control of your life.

Poor money management can create distress.

Another source of stress involves money. People without a budget are anxious and worried that their spending is greater than their earnings. Time and money management can be important in planning to achieve optimum health. One survey found that people who had a budget and lived within their means were more calm about money matters than those without a budget.

FIGURE 7–4. Learning how to drive safely is an important skill for everyone to master.

7:11 Stress and Safety and First Aid

An accident is an unpredictable, uncontrollable, and possibly unavoidable event that may produce injury, death, or property damage. Accidents are the end result of a series of behaviors and events. The occurrence of an accident, or a near-miss accident, no matter how small, may be a sign that someone is not functioning properly. Something might be bothering the person so that concentration is not as it should be. Stress is a major contributing factor in almost all types of accidents.

Many accidents occur during periods of stress.

Motor vehicle accidents are the leading cause of death in the 15-to-24 age group. In his book *Psychology and the Road*, David Shinar describes why some drivers are more likely to have accidents than others. He states that there is truth to the saying "People drive as they live." Research shows that people whose lifestyles are filled with caution, tolerance, thrift, loyalty, foresight, and consideration of others usually have safe driving records. People who are usually frustrated, aggressive, and emotionally unstable may not be able to concentrate on safe driving habits. These people may have much higher accident rates.

The way a person drives an automobile may indicate how that person manages other areas of life.

It is believed that many young people use driving as a way of acting out their feelings about personal problems. When teenagers are under stress, they are likely to demonstrate dangerous driving habits. Dangerous driving habits may be responsible for an increase in accidents.

Many automobile deaths are actually suicides.

Many highway deaths may not be accidents but actually attempts at self-destruction. One study involving persons hospitalized for suicide attempts showed that these same persons have an 81 percent higher accident rate and a 146 percent higher traffic violation rate than the total population. They also are more likely to have been drinking or using drugs at the time of the accident or traffic violation.

Chapter 24 includes more about accidents and safety. You will learn that motorcycle accidents, bicycle mishaps, drowning, and homicide are all potentially related to coping skills. There is a critical point for you to remember as you finish reading this section. Avoid driving an automobile when you are experiencing distress. Avoid riding with someone who is anxious, worried, and unable to concentrate. Also, remember that the use of alcohol intensifies the inability to concentrate and to act in safe ways.

It is responsible to avoid driving an automobile when you are experiencing distress.

7:12 Stress and Community and Environmental Health

In Chapter 1, you learned that health status is the combination of your healthful and risk behaviors. Expand your view of your community and environment by applying this definition to it. The community or environment in which you live is filled with healthful and harmful factors. Many of these factors increase the likelihood of producing the alarm stage of the general adaptation syndrome.

FIGURE 7–5. There are many evidences of conditions in a community that might be sources of stress.

Pollutants are harmful substances in the environment. Pollutants may be in the air you breathe, the water you drink, or the food you eat. These harmful substances activate your immune system causing the stress response. The federal government has established a standard for air quality called the Pollutant Standard Index (PSI). Harmful substances in the air, such as smog and smoke, raise the PSI. When the PSI is high, the alarm stage of GAS is triggered for many people. Because there is less oxygen in polluted air, you breathe more rapidly to obtain sufficient oxygen and your heart rate increases.

Pollutants in the air and water can create distress in persons.

Loud noise from rock music and concerts, heavy traffic, and airports also initiates the alarm stage of GAS. Persons around loud noise are more likely to make mistakes or have accidents. Typists often make more typing errors when loud music is playing in an office. You are more likely to have an automobile accident if music is blaring loudly while you drive.

Loud noises create distress for most persons.

The personality and health status of your family and other persons in your environment also influence your stress level. When you associate closely with persons who demonstrate several risk behaviors, you increase the likelihood of the alarm stage of GAS in your own body. Suppose your three closest friends could be described as follows.

The persons with whom you associate can reduce or increase your level of distress.

- Friend one is a chain smoker and drives recklessly.

- Friend two plays loud music even when you try to discuss a problem.

- Friend three argues with you to prove a point.

Your friends' behaviors change the quality of your environment. You breathe polluted air and are at risk in the automobile. You cannot concentrate while the loud music plays. You may be anxious during the argument. It has been said that the persons with whom you associate are the most important part of your environment.

 Review and Reflect

3. How might amount of sleep be a eustress or a distress to an individual?

4. Describe the Type A personality and the Type B personality and explain the stress that each type might experience.

5. Why are depressant drugs dangerous during periods of distress?

6. Why might you make more mistakes on homework if you listen to loud rock music while you study?

STRESS MANAGEMENT SKILLS

The problem-solving approach can be applied to alleviate situations that produce distress. Learning skills to cope with stress can be very helpful.

7:13   Problem Solving

Stress management skills are techniques used to help you cope and to prevent or lessen the harmful effects produced by the stress response.

Problem solving is a series of steps you apply to a difficult situation to help you make a responsible decision. (1) Identify the cause of your stress and anxiety. (2) Identify ways to cope with the situation. (3) Evaluate each way you could cope with what is happening. Will your way of coping result in actions that are healthful, safe, and legal? Will your way of coping show respect for yourself and others and follow your parents' guidelines? (4) Choose a responsible action to cope with the source of stress. (5) Evaluate the choice. Does it relieve your stress?

At times, you may be unable to identify the source of your distress or know appropriate ways to relieve it. Rely on parents, teachers, friends, clergy, and counselors to assist you.

7:14   Diet and Exercise

Two of the most healthful ways to cope when you are faced with difficult problems involve selecting a healthful diet and engaging in a regular program of exercise. Maintaining ideal weight is also beneficial in keeping your body healthful during periods of distress. You will study the importance of diet in more detail in Chapters 12 and 13.

In Chapters 14 and 15, you will learn how to plan an exercise and fitness program. The effects of distress on body organs can be reduced with regular exercise. Regular exercise uses up adrenaline and sugar in the blood and helps homeostasis to return sooner. It is best to exercise as soon as distress occurs. However, exercise up to 24 hours after the onset of distress will be beneficial in reducing harmful effects.

Persons who regularly exercise for at least 25 minutes three times a week for seven to ten weeks are thought to release beta-endorphins for 90 minutes after exercise. **Beta-endorphins**

You can use the problem-solving approach to alleviate stressful situations.

Knowing and using stress management skills helps keep you healthy.

FIGURE 7–6. Regular exercise is one of the most important ways of learning to cope.

are substances produced in the brain that relieve pain and create a feeling of well-being. A regular exercise program will help you have a positive attitude while you face stressful situations.

7:15 The Relaxation Response

In your earlier study of GAS, you learned that the alarm stage is accompanied by a fight or flight response. The body's reaction is one of excitement triggered by the sympathetic nervous system (Chapter 2). The role of the parasympathetic system in the resistance stage is to restore homeostasis (Table 7–2). The actions of these two branches of the autonomic nervous system usually occur involuntarily. However, there are self-induced techniques

Table 7–2 General Adaptation Syndrome

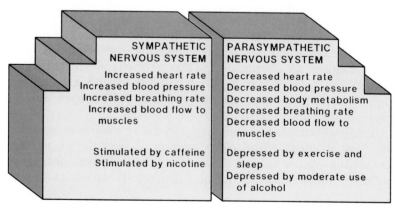

SYMPATHETIC NERVOUS SYSTEM	PARASYMPATHETIC NERVOUS SYSTEM
Increased heart rate	Decreased heart rate
Increased blood pressure	Decreased blood pressure
Increased breathing rate	Decreased body metabolism
Increased blood flow to muscles	Decreased breathing rate
	Decreased blood flow to muscles
Stimulated by caffeine	Depressed by exercise and sleep
Stimulated by nicotine	Depressed by moderate use of alcohol

that can be used to help restore homeostasis. The **relaxation response** is the body's return to homeostasis as a result of self-induced techniques.

Herb Benson is a pioneer in relaxation response research. He suggests in his book, *Beyond the Relaxation Response*, that to bring about the relaxation response four conditions are needed.

There are ways that you can self-induce the relaxation response.

1. A quiet environment with as few distractions as possible.
2. A mental device upon which to focus. (Usually a person repeats a single-syllable sound or word silently or in a low tone. This frees the person from thinking about other things.)
3. A passive attitude that does not try to judge performance.
4. A comfortable position to remain restful, such as in a high-back chair with support for the head and back. (Arms can be on the armrest or in the lap. Tight clothing should be loosened. Shoes may be removed and feet propped up.)

A quiet environment, a mental device, a positive attitude, and a comfortable position induce the relaxation response.

Several techniques trigger the relaxation response. Some of these techniques are meditation, progressive relaxation, autogenic training, and biofeedback.

Meditation is a technique used to alter the state of consciousness and trigger the relaxation response. It is a time for relaxed concentration. Try the simple meditation technique that is described below.

Several types of meditation techniques trigger the relaxation response.

1. Choose a quiet environment with few distractions.
2. Assume a comfortable position.
3. Shut your eyes. Inhale slowly and deeply through your nose.
4. Exhale slowly by blowing the air out of your mouth. As you exhale, say the number "one" to yourself.
5. Repeat for five minutes.

Progressive relaxation involves tensing and relaxing different muscle groups.

Progressive relaxation is a technique used to induce nerve-muscle relaxation. Developed by Edmond Jacobsen, the technique relaxes the mind by first relaxing the body. Different muscle groups are contracted and then relaxed until no tension is felt. For example, you might clinch your fist. Clinch it tighter and tighter, feeling the tension. Now relax. Let the fingers become loose. Notice the difference.

Autogenic training is a technique in which a series of exercises are used to increase muscle relaxation. Autogenic means self-generating. As you do the exercises, you focus on heaviness, warmth, and relaxation of muscles. You are able to relax yourself.

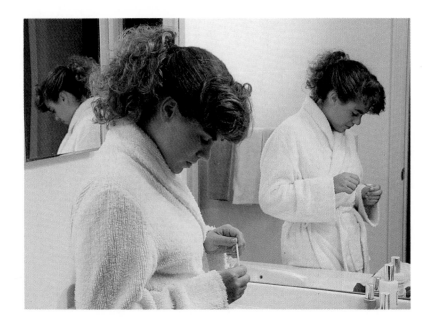

FIGURE 7–7. Taking your temperature is a method of biofeedback.

Biofeedback is a technique in which you are fed back information about what is occurring in your body at a particular time so that you can alter physiological function. Biofeedback instruments include any tools that are used to obtain physiological measurements. A basal body thermometer is a biofeedback instrument because it gives you information about your basal body temperature. Skin calipers used to measure body fat are also biofeedback instruments.

You can alter many physiological functions by using biofeedback.

Research has demonstrated that responses previously believed to be involuntary can be brought under voluntary control using biofeedback. Many physiological functions can be altered: heart rate, dilation of blood vessels, brain waves, muscle tension, blood pressure, and secretion of hydrochloric acid in the stomach. Obviously, biofeedback is helpful in altering the physiological patterns that accompany the alarm stage of the general adaptation syndrome.

Review and Reflect

7. How does regular exercise reduce the effects of distress on body organs?
8. How does progressive relaxation relieve distress?
9. What physiological functions can be altered by using biofeedback?

Health
ADVANCES

Stress-related and lifestyle-related illnesses and accidents are the leading causes of premature death and disability today. You have learned about several stress management techniques—problem solving, dietary changes, regular exercise, meditation, progressive relaxation, autogenic training, and biofeedback. Researchers continue to examine new stress management techniques and their impact on lifestyle.

7:16 Pets and Stress Management

Pets are effective in helping people of all ages cope with stress. An elderly woman talks to her parakeet and feels less lonely. A teenage boy grooms a horse and learns to be caring and gentle in relationships. A teenage girl suffering from depression begins to smile and respond as she watches an aquarium full of colorful fish. A middle-aged man recovering from a heart attack relaxes while playing with a puppy and may increase his chances of recovery. A woman with high blood pressure feels less tense while she strokes her cat.

FIGURE 7–8. A pet can be a source of comfort, enjoyment, and relaxation.

Why do these desirable changes occur when humans of all ages interact with pets? Several reasons have been given.

- Animals do not talk back. Blood pressure rises slightly during normal conversation and rises more so in stressful conversations. When under stress, talking to a pet relieves tension.
- Animals provide a constant relationship. Human relationships go through ups and downs. Animals remain faithful and loyal.
- Animals provide an opportunity to touch. It is not always appropriate or convenient to hug or kiss someone at the moment you want to give or receive affection.

The future of using pets for stress management seems unlimited. Pets can be used during therapy to help persons who are otherwise unresponsive. They can be used with teenagers who lack loving and caring skills. Petmobiles transport animals to nursing homes to help residents combat feelings of loneliness and isolation. Children can relate to pets while recovering in a hospital. Pets seem to have many advantages. The disadvantages —allergies, infections, and injuries—can be minimized.

Pets may help you manage stress by providing a constant, affectionate relationship.

Teenagers may learn loving and caring skills by interacting with pets.

 Review and Reflect

10. How are pets useful in stress management?

Focus on
Life Management Skills

- Make a plan to manage your time with a balance between work and play.
- Talk over your problems with family members or friends when you experience distress.
- Take part in a variety of social activities.
- Limit the amounts of caffeine, salt, refined sugar, and cholesterol in your diet.
- Avoid tobacco, marijuana, cocaine, alcohol, and tranquilizers.
- Follow a carefully planned budget.
- Avoid driving when experiencing distress.
- Check the PSI before participating in vigorous outdoor exercise.
- Avoid loud noises and/or wear ear protectors.
- Select friends who have healthful habits.
- Engage in a regular exercise program.
- Learn to use meditation, progressive relaxation, autogenic training, or biofeedback to initiate the relaxation response.

CHAPTER 7

REVIEW

Summary

1. Any kind of stressor can result in eustress or distress. **7:1**

2. The three stages of the general adaptation syndrome (GAS) are the alarm, resistance, and exhaustion stages. **7:2**

3. Types A and B personality traits can be stressors and affect mental health. **7:3**

4. Distress from social experiences can be relieved by talking to family and friends, having someone to love, developing good communicative skills, and engaging in a variety of social activities. **7:4**

5. Growth rates can be stressors during adolescence. **7:5**

6. Reducing the amounts of caffeine, salt, refined sugar, and cholesterol in your diet helps keep your body healthful, especially during periods of stress. **7:6**

7. Lack of exercise can produce stress. **7:7**

8. Tobacco, marijuana, cocaine, alcohol, and tranquilizers may decrease your likelihood of coping in a healthful way. **7:8**

9. Stress affects the immune system. **7:9**

10. Time and money management can give you confidence and decrease feelings of frustration and anxiety. **7:10**

11. Being anxious and unable to concentrate is a major contributing factor in many types of accidents. **7:11**

12. Pollutants, loud noises, and conflicts with acquaintances are possible environmental sources of stress. **7:12**

13. When a stressful situation occurs, apply problem-solving techniques to help relieve the situation. **7:13**

14. A balanced diet and regular exercise help keep your body strong and make you better able to cope with distress. **7:14**

15. Self-induced techniques that trigger the relaxation response include meditation, autogenic training, progressive relaxation, and biofeedback. **7:15**

16. In many cases, pets have proved effective in helping people of all ages cope with stress. **7:16**

Vocabulary

Below is a list of vocabulary words used in this chapter. Use each word only once to complete the sentences. Do not write in this book.

beta-endorphins
biofeedback
distress
eustress
general adaptation
   syndrome

homeostasis
progressive relaxation
relaxation response
stress
management skills
stressor

1. A(n) _____ is any mental, physical, or social demand on the body.

2. People who exercise regularly are thought to have high levels of _____ after exercising.

3. Hans Selye used the term _____ to describe the three stages that may result from stress.

4. After the alarm stage of stress, the body attempts to regain _____.

5. The _____ occurs when the parasympathetic nervous system slows body metabolism, blood pressure, and breathing rate.

6. A healthful response to a physical demand on the body is an example of _____.

7. When _____ is used, it is hoped that physiological function can be altered.

8. When distress occurs, it is important to use _____ to reduce harmful effects.

9. People often use the technique of _____ to induce nerve–muscle relaxation.

10. Persons with harmful habits may cause you to experience _____.

Review

1. What is the difference between eustress and distress?

2. What physiological changes occur during each of the three stages of the general adaptation syndrome?

3. Describe the Type A personality and the Type B personality and explain the stress that each type might experience.

4. Identify six social stressors identified by teenagers; list four ways to relieve them.

5. Explain growth changes that may produce anxiety during adolesence.

6. Identify six dietary tips that can help keep your body strong while coping with stressors.

7. Identify and explain how drugs can reduce your ability to cope successfully during periods of distress.

8. Identify diseases that may result when the immune system is depressed.

9. Describe four techniques that initiate the relaxation response.

10. List at least three benefits that pets provide in stress management.

Application

1. Your family will be moving to another city. You know the change will have many benefits for your family. However, you experience anxiety as you think about the adjustments you will need to make in a new school. Design a plan to manage your stress for the next few months. Why is it important to learn to manage stress?

Individual Research

1. Record all the foods you eat for two days. Refer to Section 7:6. Evaluate your diet. Do your eating habits produce or limit distress? Write a summary that describes what plan you should follow for healthful eating during periods of distress.

Readings

Benson, Herbert M.D., *Beyond the Relaxation Response*. New York, NY: Berkley Publishing Corp., 1985.

Friedman, Meyer M.D., and Rosenman, Ray H. M.D., *Type A Behavior and Your Heart*. New York, NY: Ballantine Books, Inc., 1985.

Family and Social Health

FAMILY AND SOCIAL HEALTH

In Chapter 1, you considered the Health Behavior Wheel. Family and Social Health is one of the components of the wheel. This component focuses on your relationships and how these relationships affect the other nine components of the wheel. The relationships you have greatly influence your health status. When you have positive, healthful, satisfying relationships, your life is more meaningful. In this unit, you will examine different types of relationships and the skills you need to make each relationship in your life one of high quality.

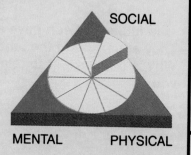

SOCIAL

MENTAL   PHYSICAL

The father and son have a relationship that goes beyond their family ties. They are enjoying the time together and hoping they can get the kite to fly. Why is it important to relate well with other people? What relationships do you enjoy the most?

Chapter 8

Healthful and Responsible Relationships

OBJECTIVES: You will be able to
- **identify and choose behaviors that promote healthful relationships.**
- **demonstrate effective communicative skills.**
- **make responsible decisions about dating and sexual behavior.**

This chapter is about the people in your life. It discusses your relationships. Your relationships are the associations you have with people. You will learn about skills needed to build healthful, responsible, loving relationships. Effective communicative skills will be described.

YOUR RELATIONSHIPS

There are many persons with whom you have a relationship. You have relationships with family members and friends. You also have relationships with persons at school, at work, and in your community. The quality of your relationships may positively or negatively affects your health status.

According to Maslow, self-esteem is one of the levels of your hierarchy of needs (Chapter 1). Good relationships can help promote your self-esteem. Feeling respect and worth from others reinforces positive feelings about yourself. As with other levels of the hierarchy, we first develop self-esteem from our family relationships.

The quality of your relationships influence self-esteem and health status.

147

FIGURE 8–1. Family relationships are strengthened when families enjoy recreation together.

You can focus on building positive family memories.

Your parents teach you values to assist you in responsible decision making.

8:1 Relationships with Family

Your **family** includes the persons with whom you are related by blood, marriage, or other legal action. Experts who study family relationships identify three factors that may affect your health status and the quality of your family relationships. These three factors are family communication, family memories, and family values. **Communication** is the verbal and nonverbal sharing of ideas, information, and feelings. Families that communicate well with each other tend to build strong family relationships.

When you share feelings with your family, they are able to know your concerns and can better respond to what is happening in your life. Take time to listen to other members of your family. Your actions will show that you care about what is happening in their lives.

Your family is the source of many of your memories. Some of the memories may be shared feelings of joy or sadness. You may have happy memories of birthdays or holidays. You may have sad memories if there has been a death in your family. If some kinds of memories trouble you, you should discuss them with your parents, a trusted adult, or a counselor.

Every day you are building memories. What do you remember from yesterday? from last week? from last year? Circumstances that happen to you today may be a part of your memory in the future. Every individual remembers different things from his or her past. You might ask yourself how you are building positive memories with different persons in your family.

Your philosophy of life is an overall attitude about life and the purpose of life. Your philosophy helps determine your values. Everyone in your family has a philosophy of life that is influenced by the other members. Your parents' philosophy and values especially influence you. Their values determine the standards they set for you. For example, because your parents value education, they may set high standards concerning your educational goals. They may encourage you to study hard so you may be admitted into college or technical school. As you make decisions in your life, you may often refer to the values and standards your parents have established.

Family communication, memories, and values affect your health status by promoting your self-esteem. A positive self-esteem enables you to express yourself, build meaningful memories, and respect your family's values. When you have positive self-esteem and healthful family relationships, you are more likely to have positive relationships with your peers. You have the foundation for satisfying relationships.

8:2   Separation, Dissolution, Divorce, and Remarriage

Family relationships may change because parents decide to separate either temporarily or permanently. A **separation** is an agreement between a married couple to live apart but remain married. Some happily married couples may live apart because of change in a job or health. This is not considered a separation, although it may cause a change in a family's lifestyle.

A separation occurs when a married couple agrees to live apart because they are having marital problems. During a period of separation, the couple may try to resolve their differences. In a small percentage of cases, couples reunite after a separation. However, in most cases, separation leads to the ending of marriage. A **dissolution** is a legal way to end a marriage in which the marriage partners decide the conditions for the settlement. A **divorce** is a legal way to end a marriage in which a judge decides the conditions for the settlement.

Separation, divorce, and dissolution create stress within a family. Each family member is affected in some way. Although many people believe that younger children are affected the most, research now shows that this is not necessarily true. Adolescents whose parents were divorced were studied to examine the impact on their lives. Most had guilt feelings and wondered what they might have done to prevent the break up of the family. Some felt depressed and withdrew from social activities. Others began to demonstrate angry, hostile behavior and to perform poorly in school. In each of these cases, adolescents were reacting to changes they felt were beyond their control. Teenagers who can communicate their thoughts and feelings with their parents usually learn to understand the problems involved. A school counselor or teacher may be a source of support. Usually, the children in a family are not the cause of a separation or divorce.

A **remarriage** is the marriage of two persons in which at least one has been married before. When persons remarry, there are new family relationships. Parents may attempt to combine two sets of values and behavior guidelines for the new family. Communicating feelings and ideas is very important in strengthening the new family. Many adjustments will be necessary.

8:3   Relationships with Friends

Acquaintances are persons whom you meet but with whom you share very little about yourself. Friends share ideas and feelings. They support each other through happy as well as

Family relationships may change when there is a separation or a divorce.

Family members usually need support and time to adjust after divorce or dissolution.

Teenagers may need to have counseling when angry, hostile behavior follows family change.

Cooperation and communication facilitate healthful family relationships after remarriage.

The quality of your relationships is more important than the quantity.

difficult times. Meaningful friendships contribute to your optimum health because you feel accepted. The number of friendships you have is not as important as the quality of the friendships.

People who maintain lasting and meaningful friendships have learned skills that increase their ability to be a good friend. Skills to be a good friend include

Frequent evaluation of your friendship skills is helpful.

- listening carefully and keeping confidences.
- offering suggestions on how to reach goals.
- offering expressions of affection.
- sharing new activities and new friends.
- providing good companionship.
- sharing joys and sorrows.

8:4 Relationships at School, Work, and in Your Community

You have many different responsibilities within relationships.

Other persons besides family and friends provide important relationships. You interact with people at school, at work, and in your community. These relationships can be healthful when you take time to understand your responsibilities in each of them.

- Find out what is expected of you.
- Follow through with your obligations.
- Be cooperative.
- Do your best.

School relationships include school authorities and teachers as well as classmates and friends. What is your role in these relationships? School authorities and teachers have the responsibility to educate students. In order to accomplish this goal, they must provide an environment that leads to learning. Standards have been established in the best interest of the individual and the entire student body. Know what is expected of you in your school relationships and abide by school rules. Complete your schoolwork to the best of your ability. Make an effort to get along with those with whom you come in contact. Respecting school rules, completing schoolwork, and making an effort in relationships provide a feeling of accomplishment and promote self-esteem.

FIGURE 8–2. You have special relationships with friends.

Do you have a part-time job? Unless you work for yourself, your job is a part of a larger operation. You will be under the guidance of a supervisor. Your relationship with this person is very important. Your ability to cooperate, follow guidelines, and do your assigned work results in financial compensation. If you are able to handle such a situation, you will begin to experience

FIGURE 8–3. What are some of your relationships in your community?

personal and financial independence. You will learn skills and gain experience that may help you qualify for better jobs in the future.

Whether you realize it or not, you are also building a network of relationships within your community. Do you shop at a particular grocery store? Who knows you in that store? When you go to the bank, do you go to a certain teller? Whether you go to a particular person or not tells you about the quality of your relationship in that situation. Having relationships within your community allows you to practice communicative and business-like skills. You will also make friends and contacts that may be of help in the future.

Your performance in school, on the job, and in the community often depends on the priority you give to these areas. Understand the value of these relationships for now and in the future. Work on building good relationships to promote positive feelings about yourself.

Your work relationships are healthful when you are cooperative and helpful.

You can practice communication skills with the network of persons in your community.

 Review and Reflect

1. How do healthful relationships help you meet Maslow's level of self-esteem?
2. Why is it important to share your feelings with your family?
3. What is the difference between dissolution and divorce?
4. Why is it important to have a positive relationship with an employer?

COMMUNICATION IN RELATIONSHIPS

Different levels of communication are appropriate in different situations.

Communication is important in all kinds of relationships. Different relationships require different levels of communication. Try to strengthen your relationships with communicative skills.

8:5 Levels of Communication

Think about the conversations you have had today. You may have had some casual conversations with persons you do not know well. You may have discussed something very important with your parents or a close friend. Your conversations most likely differed in their depth and intensity. The closer the relationship, the more you shared.

The amount of self disclosure that is healthful depends on the depth of the relationship.

Self-disclosure is the act of making yourself known to others. There are four different levels of self-disclosure used in conversations.

Cliché conversation helps you avoid silence.

- *Cliché* Cliché is the use of small talk that is sometimes used to avoid silence. Examples: "How are you?" "Great weather!" There is very little self-disclosure in this kind of conversation. Some people do not want to go beyond this stage. They do not want to reveal anything about themselves.

FIGURE 8–4. Levels of conversation may vary depending on the circumstances.

- *Reporting Facts* When you report facts or gossip, you talk about what someone else has said or done. Examples: "Mary's mother will not let her drive until she improves her grades." "I heard that John went to Florida." If you do not offer any personal comments, there is no genuine self-disclosure.
- *Sharing Ideas* You begin to disclose or share some of your ideas, judgments, and decisions. Examples: "I am not voting for anyone for class president." "I don't want to continue my friendship with Alicia." If you do not feel that your ideas, judgments, and decisions are accepted, you probably will stop sharing your ideas.

  > When you share ideas, you usually are interested in the reactions of others.

- *Expressing Feelings* When you are comfortable in a relationship, you may express the feelings behind your ideas, judgments, and decisions. Examples: "I am embarrassed when I have to speak in front of the class." "When you are late, I become angry because I feel taken for granted." Usually to have this level of communication, the person with whom you are relating must also be comfortable sharing feelings with you. This is the highest level of self-disclosure.

  > The highest level of communication involves the mutual sharing of feelings.

Communication at the highest level involves some risk. Some of your ideas and decisions may be rejected. However, the benefits are more rewarding than the risks. Communicating at this level promotes optimum health in several ways. One of these has to do with the possible prevention of psychosomatic diseases and disorders. When you keep feelings bottled up inside you, you can develop such problems as headaches, ulcers, or stomachaches. When you are able to express feelings in your relationships, you are healthier and your relationships are healthier. You are closer to others because you are sharing on a more intimate level.

> When you are unable to express feelings, psychosomatic diseases and disorders can develop.

8:6 I Messages and Active Listening

Communicating feelings can be established by using I messages. **I messages** are statements that tell about you, your feelings, and your needs. To have the greatest impact, I messages must have three parts: (1) a specific behavior, (2) an effect of that behavior, and (3) a feeling.

> I messages can be used to share your feelings.

> I messages contain a behavior, an effect, and a feeling.

Here are some examples of I Messages:

1. When you were late picking me up for the football game (behavior), I knew I would miss the kickoff (effect), and I was angry (feeling).
2. When you forgot to call me (behavior), it was too late to make other plans (effect), and I was furious staying home (feeling).
3. When I studied two extra hours for the test (behavior), I received an A (effect), and I felt proud (feeling).

Dr. Thomas Gordon, *Teacher Effectiveness Training*. New York: David McKay Co., Inc., 1974.

When you use I messages, you are trying to communicate more clearly with others. I messages are also called responsibility messages. When you use I messages, you are assuming the responsibility of sharing your feelings.

You also feel good about your communicative skills when you carefully listen to what others say. Table 8–1 includes a list of ways to encourage others to talk about important subjects with you. One way to be an effective listener on the feelings level is to use active listening. **Active listening** is a process in which you reassure the other person that you heard both the facts and the feelings behind them. Here are two examples.

Listening communicates to others your interest in what they are saying.

Activing listening helps you clarify what someone has said to you.

I Message:	When you picked me up late for the game, we were late and I was annoyed with you.
Active Listening:	I really understand why you are annoyed.
I Message:	When I studied an extra two hours for the test, I received an A, and I felt proud.
Active Listening:	Extra studying is paying off for you!!

Being a careful listener is important. Listening conveys the fact that you care. Active listening helps clarify what has been said (Table 8–1).

FIGURE 8–5. Telephone conversations often involve active listening.

Table 8–1   Tips for an Effective Conversationalist

- Look at the person to whom you are speaking.
- Ask questions and encourage others to express their opinions.
- Wait for a response before speaking again.
- Have some strategies to use if silence occurs.
- Do not interrupt while someone is speaking.
- Respond to what was said after someone has spoken.
- Offer positive comments whenever possible.
- Avoid critical comments and sarcastic remarks.
- Do not talk too much.
- Be considerate of the other person's feelings.

A frequent assessment of your listening skills helps you communicate effectively.

8:7   Nonverbal Communication

Another way of speaking and listening involves the use of nonverbal communication. **Nonverbal communication** is the use of behavior rather than words to show feelings.

Some nonverbal communication expresses a negative response. Frowning, pressing your lips tightly together, and shaking your head in disapproval are all behaviors that indicate a negative response. Crossing your arms and looking away are also ways to show rejection without the use of words. Tapping your foot may indicate a lack of patience.

Nonverbal communication allows you to express yourself without speaking.

Other behaviors indicate a positive response. Maintaining eye contact tells someone you are listening. A beaming smile express-es joy, acceptance, or excitement. A hug for a sad friend expresses understanding.

When you combine verbal and nonverbal communication, they should match. Suppose a friend asks you to go for ice cream when you need to study. If you frown and say OK, you have given your friend a mixed message. You have communicated NO and YES. If you shake your head NO and say, "I'd like to go but I have to study instead," your nonverbal and verbal behavior match. You have told your friend that you wanted to go and have been sensitive to your friend's feelings.

Your verbal and nonverbal behavior should communicate the same message.

8:8   Aggressive, Passive, and Assertive Behavior

There is another important way that your behavior is used to communicate with others. Your behavior may be aggressive, passive, and/or assertive.

You respond to situations with either aggressive, passive, or assertive behavior.

Aggressive behaviors communicate disrespect toward others.

Aggressive behavior is the use of words and/or actions that communicate disrespect toward others. Aggressive verbal behaviors include name calling, loud and sarcastic remarks, and statements of blame. Interrupting others and monopolizing the conversation are also aggressive verbal behaviors. Aggressive nonverbal behaviors include glaring at someone, using threatening hand gestures, and/or a stiff or rigid posture.

Passive behaviors indicate a lack of confidence.

Passive behavior is the holding back of ideas, opinions, and feelings. Persons who demonstrate passive behaviors have difficulty expressing their concern. Passive verbal behaviors include self-criticism, unnecessary apologies, and making excuses. Passive nonverbal behaviors might include looking away or laughing when discussing or expressing serious feelings.

Assertive behaviors include I messages and active listening.

Assertive behavior is the honest expression of thoughts and feelings without experiencing anxiety or threatening others. Assertive behavior is healthier than either aggressive or passive behavior. Assertive behavior promotes high-quality relationships. Persons who demonstrate assertive behavior use I messages and active listening. Nonverbal assertive behavior includes a confident body posture, hand gestures that compliment what is being said, and comfortable eye contact.

 Review and Reflect

5. Why is an I message also called a responsibility message?
6. Why is a mixed message confusing?
7. How do most people react to persons who are aggressive?
8. How might the frequent use of passive behavior be related to feelings of inferiority or insecurity?

FIGURE 8-6. Team captains must be assertive in order to communicate effectively.

YOU IN YOUR RELATIONSHIPS

In addition to your relationship with others, your relationship with yourself is a key one.

8:9 Sexuality

Your sexuality includes your sex role, your sexual orientation, and your feelings about yourself. Your **sex role** is the way you act as a result of your attitude about being male or female. Your early sex role is influenced by role models such as your father or mother or other adults you love or admire.

Your sex role should not limit your interests. You can be masculine or feminine and participate in activities and occupations that were traditionally chosen by persons of only one sex. Healthful sexuality is being comfortable with your attitudes about your sex role.

As adolescents relate with friends, they sometimes confuse their sex role with their sexual orientation. **Sexual orientation** is a preference that involves sexual activity with someone of the same or opposite sex. A **heterosexual** is a person who has a sexual preference for someone of the opposite sex. A **homosexual** is a person who has a sexual preference for someone of the same sex.

Suppose you have a warm, caring friendship with someone of the same sex. You may greet this friend with a hug. Does this display of affection indicate you are homosexual? This kind of action does not indicate a desire for sexual activity. You are not homosexual simply because you express concern or show affection toward someone of the same sex. You will probably have warm friendships with persons of the same sex throughout your life.

You are also not homosexual just because you enjoy activities that have been traditionally linked to the opposite sex. Cooking was traditionally a female role. However, a male who chooses to become proficient in cooking may be doing so because of need or because he enjoys it. Sexual preference is not a factor. One's style of dress is also not an indication of sexual orientation.

8:10 Responsible Dating

Dating is the sharing of social activities and time with members of the opposite sex. You may date a person because you like him or her and enjoy similar activities. You can enjoy being with this person without the involvement of sexual activity.

FIGURE 8–7. Knowing how to cook is an important skill in becoming an autonomous adult.

Your sex role, sexual orientation, and feelings about yourself influence your sexuality.

Your sex role and sexual orientation are not synonymous.

You are not homosexual because you have a warm, caring friendship for someone of the same sex.

Style of dress and interests or hobbies do not indicate sexual orientation.

You may date persons for whom you have different levels of feeling.

FIGURE 8–8. Dating is an opportunity to develop meaningful relationships.

Sexual involvement is illegal when a female has not reached legal age of consent.

Sexual involvement may damage feelings of self-respect.

Most parents discourage sexual involvement for their teenagers.

You are responsible for saying no to sexual activity.

You may also date someone to whom you are sexually attracted. Sexual feelings are normal and natural. These feelings will be easier to handle if you have set guidelines about sexual involvement. You need to decide what limits you will set for expressing affection when on a date. Your guidelines need to be determined before you are in an emotional situation and someone pressures you to become sexually involved.

Apply the criteria of the problem-solving approach to help you make a responsible decision about your sexual involvement. Your decision will affect many of the components that relate to health.

- Would the results of my decisions be healthful and safe? Before becoming sexually involved, consider the following possible consequences in light of their physical, mental, and social implications: the risk of pregnancy, sexually transmitted diseases (Chapter 19), and guilt-related stress. In Chapter 10, we will discuss many risk factors involved in teenage pregnancy regarding the health of both the mother and baby. A pregnant teenager must also consider parental responsibilities and a disruption of schooling and social activities. Most teenage relationships do not last forever, and they often break off after sexual involvement.

- Would the results of my decision be legal? Sexual involvement with a female before legal age of consent can be legally considered as corruption of a minor. Legal age of consent is when a female is considered responsible for her sexual actions.

- Would the results of my decision show respect for myself and others? If you were to become sexually involved, how would you feel about yourself? How would your friends react? Would this change your reputation? Are there certain people you would not want to know about your sexual activity? How would you feel about your sexual partner afterward?

- Would the result of my decision follow my parents' guidelines? Most parents have guidelines that prefer that their teenagers refrain from sexual activity. Disregarding your parents' guidelines will cause stress in your relationship with them. Would your actions hurt them?

Saying no to sexual activity can be difficult. You may want to experience a sexual relationship for many reasons: your own needs, pressure from your boyfriend or girlfriend, or the desire to fit in with friends who already have experienced sexual activity. However, you are responsible for your actions and any consequences. Consider the effects of your decision on future relationships. Would it bother you if your boyfriend or girlfriend had engaged in a sexual relationship with someone else? Make decisions that you can live with and enable you to feel good about yourself.

✔ Review and Reflect

9. Who was the most influential person in forming your sex role?
10. How does someone who has a homosexual orientation differ from someone with a heterosexual orientation?
11. Why is it important to establish guidelines for sexual behavior before someone pressures you to become sexually involved?
12. Why is it best to refrain from teenage sexual activity?

 ## Activity: The Perfect Date

Write a want ad for a perfect date. Describe the qualities that you enjoy most in a person. Describe what type of event you would like to attend. Include guidelines for responsible dating. Divide into groups of four, preferably with two males and two females in each group. Discuss each want ad. Are the want ads realistic? Discuss guidelines for responsible dating.

Focus on
Life Management Skills

- Spend time sharing ideas and listening to family members.
- Make the effort to build positive family memories.
- Know and follow the values of your parents.
- Develop satisfying, meaningful relationships with friends of both sexes.
- Know what is expected of you at school and follow school rules.
- Be cooperative and follow guidelines at work.
- Use I messages and active listening to communicate effectively with others.
- Communicate clearly using nonverbal behavior that matches what you are saying.
- Use assertive behavior instead of passive or aggressive behavior.

CHAPTER REVIEW 8

Summary

1. Family communication, memories, and values are important factors in family relationships. 8:1
2. Stress that may accompany separation, dissolution, divorce, and remarriage may be alleviated by discussions with parents and/or a counselor. 8:2
3. Satisfying friendships contribute to optimum health. 8:3
4. Relationships at school, work, and in the community are best when you find out what is expected of you, follow through with your obligations, are cooperative, and do your best. 8:4
5. A conversation has the most self-disclosure when you express your feelings about your ideas, judgments, and decisions. 8:5
6. I messages and active listening are effective ways to express and share feelings. 8:6
7. Communication is often clarified by using nonverbal behaviors to support what you have said. 8:7
8. Assertive behavior uses I messages and active listening and is healthier than either aggressive or passive behavior. 8:8
9. Your sexuality includes your sex role, your sexual orientation, and your feelings about yourself. 8:9
10. Saying no to sexual activity requires self-discipline. 8:10

Vocabulary

Below is a list of vocabulary words used in this chapter. Use each word only once to complete the sentences. Do not write in this book.

aggressive	I messages
behavior	nonverbal
communication	communication
divorce	self-disclosure
heterosexual	sex role
homosexual	sexual orientation

1. A preference that involves sexual activity with someone of the same or opposite sex is _____.
2. The use of behavior rather than words to show feelings is _____.
3. _____ is the sharing of ideas and information.
4. Statements that tell about you, your feelings, and needs are _____.
5. A person is not a(n) _____ just because he or she enjoys activities traditionally enjoyed by the opposite sex.
6. You are practicing _____ when you make yourself known to others.
7. When you display _____, you use words and/or actions that communicate disrespect toward others.
8. A(n) _____ has a sexual preference for persons of the opposite sex.
9. You learn your _____ from your mother, father, or some other adult you love and admire.
10. When a judge determines the terms for the legal end of marriage, a married couple obtains a(n) _____.

Review

1. Identify three factors that are helpful in identifying healthful and responsible family relationships.
2. What are some feelings that adolescents might have when parents divorce?
3. What are six skills that help develop healthful and responsible relationships with friends?
4. What are four guidelines for healthful and responsible relationships at school, work, and in the community?
5. What are four different levels of self-disclosure? List them beginning with the level that shows the least self-disclosure.
6. What are three parts of an I message?
7. What are five different nonverbal behaviors?
8. What is the difference between aggressive, passive, and assertive behavior?
9. What does your sexuality include?
10. When and why should you set guidelines for your sexual behavior on dates?

Application

1. One day your friend tells you some gossip about someone else with whom you are close. Write an I message that describes the feelings you have about the effects of your friend's behavior.
2. Someone cuts in the line ahead of you. You are angry. Describe the behaviors you might demonstrate that would be examples of aggressive, passive, and assertive behaviors.
3. Normally, you work after school on Tuesdays, but today you have the day off. Your employer calls and tells you that another worker is sick. She wants you to rush over to help out. What would you do? Why?

Individual Research

1. Refer to the list of six skills that build healthful and responsible friendships (Section 8:3). With a friend, discuss these and add four other skills that you both believe to be important.
2. Write an example of each of the four levels of self-disclosure identified in Section 8:5.
3. Write three examples of I messages that describe some recent experiences.
4. Research a career that can be selected after getting a college degree in communication. What responsibilities are expected? What appeals to you about the career? What does not appeal to you?

Readings

Buscaglia, Leo, *Living, Loving, and Learning.* New York, NY: Ballantine Books, Inc., 1982.

Fromm, Eric, *The Art of Loving.* Gainesville, GA: Perennial Publications, 1974.

Swinging is fun. Parents and children all enjoy having fun. However, there is more to being a parent than having fun. Parents must assume many responsibilities. How will you know when you are ready to be a parent? How can you prepare to be a responsible parent?

Adulthood, Marriage, and Parenthood

OBJECTIVES: You will be able to
- **make a plan to develop skills to become an autonomous adult.**
- **describe factors that contribute to a successful marriage.**
- **identify skills needed for responsible parenthood.**
- **outline procedures used to prevent or stop family violence.**

Suppose you could look into a crystal ball and get a clear picture of yourself ten years from today. You would no longer be an adolescent. Instead, you would be an adult. What are the challenges you might expect? Will you have planned an exciting career? Will you have healthful and responsible relationships? Will there be someone special in your life? Will you marry? Will you have children?

ADULTHOOD

During your adolescent years, you are developing skills needed for adulthood. You are learning skills you will need to think for yourself and to be on your own.

9:1 Developing Autonomous Adulthood

What are the skills needed to become autonomous? To be **autonomous** is to be independent. The first set of skills involves developing a responsible attitude toward your family and your home life. In your family life, there are certain demands placed upon you. You are expected to follow family guidelines and to help with household chores. These are the same chores that you will have when you live on your own and have your own family.

Assuming responsibility in your family is the first step in becoming autonomous.

FIGURE 9–1. Be aware of what job opportunities are available to you in your community.

EMPLOYMENT OPPORTUNITIES

You learn responsibility by doing what is expected of you with a cheerful, cooperative attitude. Other family members learn that they can count on you to do your share to make your home comfortable and your family life positive.

A second set of skills needed for autonomous adulthood involves planning your career. There are short-term and long-term goals upon which you must focus. Your short-term goals are to manage your time, study hard, and obtain the best grades you can. Another short-term goal is to finish high school in order to qualify for a job. Your career choice is a long-term goal. Will you enter the work force immediately? Will your career choice require on-the-job training, technical school, or college? You will need a plan to reach your long-term career goals.

A third set of skills needed for autonomous adulthood involves your ability to be able to support yourself financially. Your parents have been your means of financial support in the past. However, this responsibility will gradually shift to you. Perhaps you already have a part-time job that enables you to pay some of your own expenses. You are learning to manage money. You should be thinking about your career goals and making plans that will enable you to become antonomous.

A fourth set of skills needed for autonomous adulthood involves your ability to make decisions. Through your childhood and adolescent years, your parents help you form values and make responsible decisions. As an adult, it will be your responsibility to make decisions and to choose behaviors that are consistent with your values.

Short-term and long-term career goals are needed for autonomous adulthood.

Financial independence is a factor in gaining autonomous adulthood.

An autonomous adult makes responsible decisions.

In becoming autonomous, you accept responsibility for your family life. You complete your education, plan a career, learn to take care of yourself financially, and act in ways consistent with your values. You develop the skills needed to be independent. You have positive self-esteem when you are confident that you have learned to take care of yourself.

MARRIAGE

Ninety-five percent of Americans marry at least once. If something happens to the marriage relationship—death of a spouse or divorce—eighty percent remarry. Traditionally, marriage provides a framework in which to have and rear children. Marriage also serves to meet the need for intimacy, a special closeness shared between two persons. Marriage is one of the most important commitments a person can make. It is important to learn about the marriage relationship and to learn ways to increase the likelihood of a successful, satisfying marriage.

Knowing about the marriage relationship can increase the likelihood of a successful marriage.

9:2 Selecting a Marriage Partner

Marriage is a relationship in which two people make a legal commitment or pledge to love and care for each other. You are more likely to have a successful marriage if you select a marriage partner with whom you are compatible and can grow close to over the years. To be compatible means to be able to get along together

It is important to have a compatible marriage partner.

FIGURE 9–2. Marriage is a commitment.

well. During the adolescent and early adulthood years, your dating opportunities help you learn more about yourself and your interactions with others. You may take marriage and family living classes to gain greater understanding of yourself, others, and relationships.

Persons who are similar are more likely to have a successful marriage.

Although opposites may attract, research clearly indicates that persons who are similar are more likely to have a successful marriage. There are certain common factors that are important. These are listed in Table 9–1.

9:3   Making a Marriage Commitment

There are stages that are a natural progression to marriage. Usually, after a period of dating, you become especially fond of one particular person. You may decide to date only this person. This affords an opportunity for both of you to examine how compatible you are. It is important to discuss the factors in Table 9–1. What are your friend's values? hobbies? educational experiences? family patterns? future goals? It is also a time to examine the degree of autonomy each person has achieved. Have you both learned to take care of yourselves? Do you know how to manage a home? plan a budget? Remember, these skills are needed to manage an adult lifestyle.

Before making a marriage commitment, both people need to be autonomous.

Couples who are preparing to marry one another often choose a period of engagement. An **engagement** is the time period between announcing marriage plans and making the marriage commit-

Several factors increase the likelihood of a successful marriage.

Table 9–1   Factors That Increase the Likelihood of a Compatible Marriage

1. Similar values
2. Clearly-defined goals
3. Similar intelligence and educational experience
4. Families that have similar philosophies
5. Ability to communicate with each other
6. Physical attraction to one another
7. Healthful attitudes about marriage and sex
8. Equal sense of commitment to the importance of marriage
9. Similar views about having and rearing children
10. Compatible personality traits
11. Adequate financial resources
12. Similar age
13. Compatible hobbies and interests
14. Independence from parents
15. Premarriage counseling and/or premarriage classes

ment. Research indicates that a courtship and engagement of at least one year increase the likelihood of a successful marriage.

In a recent poll, married couples of thirty years or more were asked to identify the most important ingredient in their marriages. Almost all of these couples identified friendship as the most important ingredient. They felt that their friendship had become even more meaningful the longer they were married.

A courtship and engagement of one year increase the likelihood of a successful marriage

Friendship is a key ingredient in a successful marriage.

9:4 Teenage Marriage

When couples marry, they usually intend to have a successful marriage. The odds of this happening are increased when the partners have developed skills for autonomous adulthood and have closely examined the factors needed for a compatible marriage. Unfortunately, the statistics for a lasting, successful teenage marriage are very low. Three out of four teenage marriages fail.

Three out of four teenage marriages fail.

Most teenagers do not realize the responsibilities of marriage. They have not had enough time or opportunity to develop the skills for autonomous adulthood or family living. Teenagers who marry have not had adequate time to complete their education or to gain work experience at a trade. They may not have time to make career plans. They usually do not have much money because they have less education and qualify only for low-paying jobs. Because they must spend money on necessities, they are unable to spend money for recreation as their unmarried friends are doing.

Married teenagers have financial and educational stressors.

Teenagers who marry are suddenly in the role of making many decisions. If their values have not been clearly formed, there can be much confusion and conflict between partners. The additional years to mature emotionally and to learn by dating several persons have been cut short.

Teenagers who marry because the girl is pregnant or to get away from an unhappy home situation are at an even higher risk of having an unhappy marriage. In these circumstances, emotional and financial problems are even greater.

When married teenagers are expecting a baby, there are additional financial and emotional demands.

 ## Review and Reflect

1. What is the relationship between finishing your high school education and becoming financially independent?
2. Why do adolescents who set a goal to become autonomous develop higher self-esteem than those who do not?
3. What are some reasons that three out of four teenage marriages usually fail?

FIGURE 9–3. It is necessary to develop skills to be a responsible parent.

PARENTHOOD

Suppose you want to be a medical doctor. How would you prepare for this important profession? You would first complete college and then apply to a medical school. If accepted, you would take courses that would give you detailed medical information. Then you would complete an internship in which you would practice your skills under supervision. You would then take a comprehensive examination to obtain a license to practice medicine. You would be prepared for your profession.

Parenthood is the most important profession.

Think about parenthood. It is an important profession. How will you prepare for parenthood? Who will train you for this important task? How will you know that you are ready for parenthood and that you have skills necessary to be a good parent?

9:5 The Responsibilities of Parenthood

Unfortunately, there is no license that says Mary Smith or Tom Jones has completed the necessary training to be a responsible parent. In fact, there has been a lack of formal training to help persons be successful, satisfied, and responsible parents. Most of what people have learned about parenting has been learned by observing and imitating their parents. Thus, if a person's parents felt they made mistakes in their parenting, their children were likely to repeat the same mistakes.

Today, the trend is changing. Perhaps your parents are sharing with you their thoughts about parenthood. They are probably encouraging you to examine your values and to learn to be autonomous before marrying and becoming a parent. They may suggest that you take a course in parenthood. Many high schools are offering classes to teach skills needed for successful marriage and parenthood. Experts who teach about family living have identified a list of priorities that responsible parents have.*

Responsible parents
- set aside a quantity of time as well as quality time to spend with their children.
- learn about the way children develop at different ages.
- teach their children rules for health and safety.
- give their children love and affection.
- teach their children with a positive attitude, avoiding condemnation and criticism.
- teach their children values.
- teach their children self-discipline and self-control by example and by using effective disciplinary techniques rather than child abuse.
- provide economic security for their children.
- recognize that their children have rights and respect those rights.
- rear their children in a stable, secure family that is free from substance abuse (alcohol, marijuana, amphetamines, or barbiturates).

Parents who demonstrate certain priorities are more successful than other parents.

9:6 Teenage Parenthood

After examining the responsibilities you would assume if you became a parent, you might ask yourself, "At what age would I be mentally, physically, and emotionally ready for parenthood?" You have probably realized that during your adolescent years you are still maturing. You are still changing emotionally and physically. You are still gaining skills you need to become an autonomous adult. These are only a few of the reasons that you are more likely to feel successful and satisfied in marriage and parenting if you wait until you are in your twenties. There are other reasons to delay parenthood.

Consider these facts. About 40 percent of adolescent girls will become pregnant at least once before they are 20 years old. About

Parents who are in their twenties are usually more successful and satisfied than teenage parents.

*Adapted from: John Burt and Linda Meeks *Education for Sexuality: Concepts and Programs for Teaching*. CBS: Saunders Publishing Company, Philadelphia, 1985.

The number of teenage pregnancies is extremely high.

Babies born to teenage mothers are often malnourished.

Teenage mothers usually obtain less education than their peers.

Teenage fathers usually have less education and earn less money than their peers.

10 percent of adolescent girls become pregnant each year. These pregnancies result in one-half-million births to teenage mothers. One-fifth of all births in the United States are to teenagers.

There are some serious health consequences involved. Only three out of ten pregnant teenagers are checked by a physician in the first three months of pregnancy. Therefore, pregnant teenage girls usually do not receive prenatal counseling. They are likely to be malnourished. Their babies often have a low birth weight. **Low birth weight** refers to a baby's weight when it is under five and one-half pounds at birth. Body organs may not be fully developed in a newborn baby with a low birth weight. These babies may have difficulty maintaining a body temperature that is healthful. They are more likely to be mentally retarded and to die during infancy.

Besides caring for a new baby, teenage mothers have additional stressors. Two out of three teenage mothers drop out of school. Without an education, their potential income is only half of those women who finish high school before having a baby.

Teenage fathers experience similar stressors. They are also more likely to drop out of school and to earn less money than males who complete their education. These stressors can affect teenage marriages. Teenagers with children are more likely to separate and divorce than married teenagers without children.

 ## Review and Reflect

4. Why is raising children an important task?
5. Why are persons in their 20s better equipped to become parents than are teenagers?
6. Why are teenage mothers more likely to have babies with health problems than babies born to women in their 20s?

 ## Activity: Taking Care of a "Baby"

When you have children, you assume many responsibilities. To simulate these responsibilities, you and your classmates will participate in an egg activity. Bring a fresh egg from home. The egg will represent your newborn baby. Give your egg a name. Decorate your egg in any way you desire. Decide how you will handle your egg for the next two days to keep it safe from breaking (remember, a newborn baby is fragile). Your egg is your responsibility. You must have it with you at all times or arrange to have a babysitter. At the end of two days, write a one-page report describing what you have experienced.

There are many rewards and responsibilities for parenthood.

FAMILY VIOLENCE

In this chapter, you have studied facts that will help you prepare for marriage and parenthood. You have also examined some of the risks that accompany teenage marriage and teenage parenthood. There is another topic about which you need information.

Family violence is an unpleasant topic. Some polls have estimated that 50 percent of married couples in the United States resort to physical violence at least once in their marriage. Police officers are called to a home for domestic violence more often than for any other reason. A married person is more likely to be murdered by a spouse than by any other person. Also, there are more than ten million abused children.

Family violence harms the health of many family members.

Although these statistics are grim, there is a positive outlook. By educating adolescents like yourself about family violence, the problem may be solved. More people will recognize abuse, and help can be provided for the victim and the abuser.

9:7 Battered Spouses

A **battered spouse** is a person who is physically and emotionally abused by a marriage partner. Although some abusers are women, the most common abusers are men. The man usually has poor self-esteem, a high level of frustration, and a need to control others. In many cases, he was physically abused as a child. The most common victim is a woman who has low self-esteem and feels that leaving her husband would pose financial difficulties. She also may feel that she wants to maintain the marital relationship for the benefit of the children. The incidence of battered spouses is greater among couples who marry in their teenage years. Perhaps this is because of increased levels of frustration due to lack of job opportunities, lack of emotional maturity, and limited financial resources.

The incidence of battered spouses is highest in teenage marriages.

There are a variety of services available to help battered spouses. There are 24-hour crisis hotline services in many cities and volunteer shelters that provide a temporary home for the victim in most cities. There are also support groups for women. The legal system can issue a restraining order to keep the husband away from the home until he has had counseling or other professional help.

Counseling is available for both husbands and wives. The husband is taught to handle his anger and frustration in nonviolent ways. The wife learns that she is a person of worth and does not deserve to be abused.

Counseling may help family members interact in healthful, nonviolent ways.

9:8   Child Abuse

Child abuse is the maltreatment of children. Eighty-five to ninety percent of child abuse is by family members. Unfortunately, most child abuse is from a child's parents. Teenage parents are the most likely abusers. Perhaps they had not planned to have a baby. Perhaps they have financial pressures or are poorly trained in parenting skills. Parents who were abused as children are also much more likely to abuse their own children. Parents who are involved in substance abuse are less stable and more likely to abuse children.

There are four types of child abuse. **Physical abuse** involves harming the body in some way. Signs of physical abuse include bruises, burns, cuts, missing teeth, broken bones, and head and internal injuries.

Neglect involves inadequate or dangerous child-rearing practices. The signs of neglect may not be immediately obvious. These signs include abandoning the child, failing to supervise the child, improperly clothing the child for the weather, not feeding or providing shelter, and not providing needed medical attention.

Emotional maltreatment involves mistreating the child by relating to the child in a destructive way. Emotional maltreatment might involve withholding love or constantly criticizing or ridiculing a child. Consequently, the child may suffer from low self-esteem.

Sexual abuse involves inappropriate sexual behavior between an adult and a child. The signs of sexual abuse may be physical but are usually behavioral. A sexually abused child usually has poor peer relationships. He or she has difficulty behaving in sexually appropriate ways.

Children, including teenagers, who have experienced one or more of these four types of child abuse need help. It is important to discuss abusive acts with a trusted adult. The trusted adult might be a friend, teacher, physician, rabbi, minister, or priest.

Every state has laws that require physicians or other health professionals and teachers to report child abuse to child welfare authorities. Special child abuse teams then assist the family. Children who have been abused usually need professional help to build self-esteem. Often they believe they are at fault for their parents' actions. They must learn that they are worthwhile and should be treated with respect.

Abusive parents need counseling to change their low self-esteem, frustration levels, and often habits of substance abuse. In counseling, these parents may learn new coping skills and strategies. Abusive parents may join a Parents' Anonymous group. They may also use a 24-hour crisis intervention hotline.

Teenage parents are more likely to abuse their children.

Child abuse includes physical abuse, emotional maltreatment, and sexual abuse.

Abused children should talk about abusive acts with a trusted adult.

Abusive parents and their children usually benefit from counseling.

FIGURE 9-4.

Another form of sexual abuse is incest. Incest is any form of sexual activity that occurs between blood relatives as well as stepparents and stepchildren. Most cases of incest begin early in a child's life and continue for many years. Incest may consist of anything from unnecessary fondling to sexual intercourse. Most cases of incest occur between natural fathers or stepfathers and their daughters. Although less frequent, other cases of incest occur between parents or stepparents and their sons.

The father or stepfather may use his parental authority to force his daughter into unwanted sexual activity. A daughter may not refuse because she has been taught to respect parental authority. She might not tell anyone because she is afraid to hurt her mother or destroy the family's reputation.

Incest victims usually feel confused and guilty. They may believe they are at fault. Incest victims need to understand that they are not at fault for what has happened.

Incest victims should not blame themselves for what has happened.

Incest victims need to take action. They need to know that everyone has the right to remain healthy and safe and to be respected by others. They also need to know that incest is against the law. Here are some actions an incest victim can take.

- Speak to another family member, school counselor, or trusted adult.
- Call local child welfare authorities.
- Call local hotlines for information.
- Refuse unwanted sexual activity with family members.

Incest is a crime.

- Attempt not to be alone with the adult who is the aggressor.

 Review and Reflect

7. How is education about family violence helpful?
8. Why do many battered wives have difficulty leaving an abusive husband?
9. Why are teenage parents more likely to abuse children than parents who are older?

Focus on
Life Management Skills

- Develop a responsible attitude toward your family and home life.
- Complete your high school education and begin to plan for your future education and/or career.
- Consider part-time jobs and other ways to save and budget money to move toward financial independence.
- Take responsibility for making decisions and choosing actions consistent with your values.
- Participate in marriage and family living classes to prepare for future relationships.
- Examine the factors that increase the likelihood of a compatible marriage.
- Develop friendships with persons of the opposite sex as well as with persons of your sex.
- Recognize the responsibilities that accompany parenthood.
- Avoid teenage marriage and teenage parenthood.
- Recognize the symptoms of family violence, and take measures to prevent or stop it.

Health
CAREERS

Administrator of Special Adoptions

Kojo-Mbogba Odo works with families in his meaningful health career. Kojo is an Administrator of Special Adoptions. He finds families who will love and raise children who have special needs. These children may have a physical disability. They may have a mental disability and have difficulty learning. They may be unable to speak English. Kojo writes a story about each child and uses the stories to help place the children in homes.

Persons like Kojo who work in family services usually complete a college degree and then continue their education to get a Master of Social Work (MSW) degree. They then complete an internship in a social service agency.

Kojo feels that his career is rewarding. He himself has legally adopted 35 children with special needs. The children he chose were all classified as impossible to place in homes. One of his children was three and one half years old when he was adopted. He had a spinal birth defect and Kojo was told that his new son, Kosoko, would be in a wheelchair for life. Kojo worked with the child for six months and taught him to walk with crutches. Kojo believes Kosoko will be able to walk with braces some day. The love a child can receive in an adopted home can make the difference in the child's life. Kojo enjoys working with his own children and with other families who want this challenge.

CHAPTER 9

REVIEW

Summary

1. Skills needed to become an autonomous adult include developing a responsible attitude toward home and family life, completing your education, gaining financial independence, and using responsible decision-making skills. 9:1
2. Persons who have similar values, goals, education, family background, hobbies, attitudes toward children, and who are close in age are more likely to have a successful, satisfying marriage. 9:2
3. The marriage commitment with the greatest likelihood for success is one in which a couple has a close friendship. 9:3
4. Three out of four teenage marriages end in divorce. 9:4
5. Responsible parents set aside time for their children, teach them rules for health and safety; give them affection and love; teach them moral and ethical values, self-discipline and self-control; provide economic security; respect children's rights; and provide an environment that is free of criticism and substance abuse. 9:5
6. Teenage mothers are more likely to have low birth weight babies with health problems and are less likely to be satisfied with parenting than mothers in their 20s. 9:6
7. The incidence of battered spouses is greater among teenagers perhaps because teenagers are not as emotionally mature as those who wait to marry. 9:7
8. Teenage parents are more likely to abuse their children than parents who are older. 9:8

Vocabulary

Below is a list of vocabulary words used in this chapter. Use each word only once to complete the sentences. Do not write in this book.

autonomous	low birth weight
battered spouse	marriage
child abuse	neglect
emotional	physical abuse
maltreatment	sexual abuse
engagement	

1. Parents who engage in inadequate or dangerous child-rearing practices are guilty of ____.

2. A(n) ____ baby is more likely to have a poorly formed digestive system.

3. The maltreatment of children is known as ____.

4. Before marrying, it is important to learn to be ____.

5. Inappropriate sexual behavior between an adult and a child is ____.

6. ____ is an important commitment because it involves making decisions that are in the best interest of another person.

7. A time period of ____ increases the likelihood of having a successful marriage.

8. A(n) ____ usually suffers from low self-esteem and may need counseling.

9. Parents who criticize and ridicule their children and destroy their self-esteem are guilty of ____.

10. Parents who strike their children causing bodily injury are guilty of ____.

Review

1. What are four sets of skills needed to develop autonomous adulthood?
2. What are at least two purposes marriage serves?
3. List 14 factors that increase the likelihood of a compatible marriage.
4. Identify three reasons why teenage marriages are less likely to succeed than marriages between persons in their 20s.
5. Identify 10 priorities that responsible parents have.
6. What are four reasons that teenage parenthood is difficult?
7. How prevalent is domestic violence?
8. What services are available for battered spouses?
9. What are three reasons teenage parents are more likely to abuse their children than older parents?
10. What are four types of child abuse?

Application

1. Identify the four sets of skills needed to become an autonomous adult. Describe what you are doing to demonstrate each of these skills.
2. Pretend you are a parent. You have a teenage son and a teenage daughter. List at least five rules for health and safety that you would want your teenagers to follow. Explain your reasons for each rule.
3. A friend of yours is thinking about dropping out of high school to get married. Your friend asks you if his or her decision is responsible. Explain how you would answer your friend.

Individual Research

1. Find out the procedures for investigating child abuse in your community. What services are available to assist families?
2. Refer to Table 9–1 on page 166. Rank the factors from 1 to 14 beginning with the one you feel is the most important. In groups of four with your classmates, discuss the reasons for your rankings.
3. You are going to take a class on parenting. The class will meet once a week for 10 weeks. Identify 10 topics you would expect to be covered. Visit the library and local bookstores. List five books you might read on those topics. Identify three persons in your community who might be guest speakers for such a class.

Readings

Buscaglia, Leo, *Loving Each Other.* Thorofare, NJ: Slack, Inc., 1984.

Eyseneck, Hans J., and Kelley, Betty Nichols, *"I Do!"* New York, NY: World Almanac, 1985.

Growth and Development

GROWTH AND DEVELOPMENT

The human body is extremely complex and constantly changing. Changes have taken place since your conception and will continue throughout your life cycle. How have these changes contributed to your physical, mental, and social development? What behaviors should you be choosing now that would contribute to your optimum health in the future? In this unit, you will be considering the life stages that are a part of every person's development.

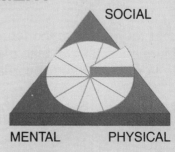

At four months, the fetus is developed so that you can recognize features. More changes will take place before birth. What does the term life cycle mean to you? How have you changed since you were born?

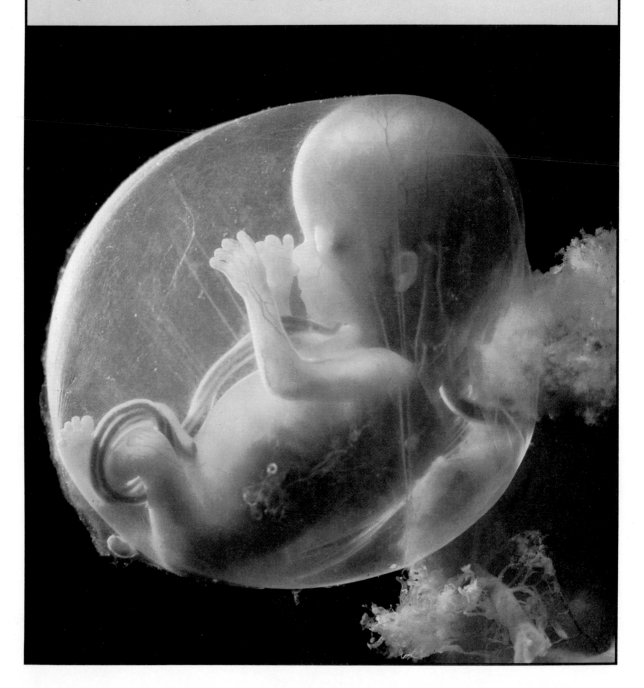

Chapter 10

From Conception to Adulthood

OBJECTIVES: You will be able to
- **explain the physical changes that occur in the body from conception through birth.**
- **describe characteristics of the different life stages.**

Humans, like many other organisms, have a life cycle. They originate from cells, develop, mature, grow older, and eventually die.

Think about your life. How have you changed since you were born? What future changes can you expect? This chapter describes growth and development from conception to adulthood.

CONCEPTION THROUGH BIRTH

Look around the classroom. Notice that no two people in the room look alike. However, all of you have one thing in common. You each began as two tiny cells in a remarkable process called conception.

10:1 Conception

The union of an egg and sperm is called fertilization. Another name for fertilization is **conception.** Conception usually occurs in the Fallopian tube when a sperm penetrates an egg and forms a zygote. A zygote is a single cell that contains the chromosomes from each parent.

Conception occurs when a sperm penetrates an egg.

As the zygote moves through the Fallopian tube, cell division continues to occur. This results in a cluster of cells that reach the uterus. These cells begin to attach themselves to the endometrium, the lining of the uterus. By the end of the first week of development, these cells have become fully attached or implanted. This marks the beginning of an embryo. An **embryo** is a developing cluster of cells.

The outer cells of the embryo and cells of the endometrium form the placenta. The placenta is an organ that anchors the embryo to the uterus. Other cells form the umbilical cord. The **umbilical cord** is the structure that connects the embryo to the placenta. Blood from the mother carries nutrients and oxygen to the embryo through the cord. Waste products from the embryo move to the mother to be excreted from her body.

Occasionally, the zygote does not move to the uterus. An ectopic pregnancy results. An **ectopic pregnancy** is the growth of a fertilized egg in a part of the body other than the uterus. The most common site of an ectopic pregnancy is in the Fallopian tube. One cause of an ectopic pregnancy can be a blocked Fallopian tube. Infection is the most common cause of such a blockage.

An ectopic pregnancy can end in one of two ways. The embryo may enter the abdominal cavity and disintegrate. Or, the embryo may expand and stretch the tube causing it to tear or rupture. This would cause pain, bleeding, and infection. If this occurs, a woman's life can be in danger. Medical attention is needed immediately.

An embryo receives nutrients and oxygen through the umbilical cord.

A blocked Fallopian tube can result in an ectopic pregnancy.

FIGURE 10–1. If an egg released from an ovary is fertilized in the Fallopian tube, cell division occurs as the zygote moves through to the uterus.

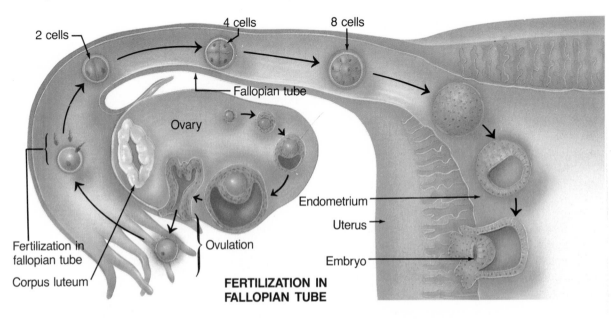

2 cells

4 cells

8 cells

Fallopian tube

Ovary

Endometrium

Uterus

Fertilization in fallopian tube

Ovulation

Corpus luteum

Embryo

FERTILIZATION IN FALLOPIAN TUBE

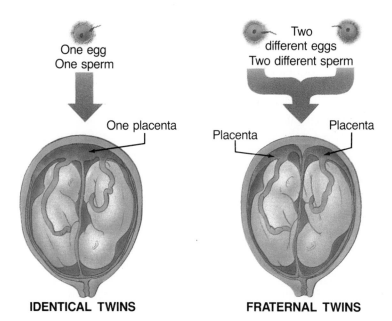

FIGURE 10–2. Identical twins share fetal membranes; fraternal twins do not.

Occasionally, a zygote splits in half and each half forms an embryo. **Identical twins** are two babies that develop from the same egg and sperm. Identical twins have identical chromosomes so they are always the same sex and always look exactly alike.

Twins may be either identical or fraternal.

One egg cell may be released from each ovary at the same time. If each egg is fertilized by a different sperm, **fraternal twins** will develop. Fraternal twins have different combinations of chromosomes because they developed from separate eggs and sperm. Fraternal twins are not necessarily the same sex and may not look alike.

10:2 Determining Pregnancy

The implantation of an embryo interrupts a woman's menstrual cycle. Ovarian hormones stimulate the tissues of the uterus to support and feed the developing embryo. The uterus will not shed its lining.

One of the first signs of possible pregnancy is a missed menstrual period. However, a missed period is not a definite sign of pregnancy. Poor nutrition, a change in hormone production, and stress are three conditions that may also cause a missed period. Other early signs of pregnancy may be frequent urination, enlarged breasts, and fatigue. The pregnant woman may experience nausea and vomiting. Nausea and vomiting are called morning sickness although these symptoms can occur anytime during the day.

A missed menstrual period may result from any of several conditions.

A definite diagnosis of pregnancy can be made by a physician. Using one type of pregnancy test, a physician checks for a special substance in urine. This substance is called HCG. **HCG** is a hormone produced by the placenta. The physician determines pregnancy by mixing certain chemicals with urine. The pregnancy test is positive (the woman is pregnant) when the reaction indicates that HCG is present in the urine. HCG can be detected in urine as early as one week after the missed menstrual period. However, the urine test for HCG is not reliable until the sixth to eighth week of pregnancy.

Another method for detecting pregnancy is a blood test called an RIA test. The **RIA test** detects the presence of HCG in the blood. This test has an advantage over the urine test because it can detect HCG five days before the missed menstrual period. This early detection of pregnancy is highly accurate. It enables the woman to seek care for herself and her baby as early as possible. This is especially important for a teenager who is pregnant. The health risks of teenage pregnancy can be life-threatening when proper care is not sought early.

10:3   Prenatal Development

Prenatal development is the growth of a baby in the uterus from conception to birth . This development is usually divided into three trimesters. A trimester is a three-month period.

The First Trimester At the end of one month, the embryo has a circulatory system. The head and nervous system are becoming evident. Hands and feet form during the second month. By the end of the second month, the embryo is recognizable as a human and is called a **fetus**. By the end of the third month, the fetus is about 10 cm (4 inches) long and weighs about 19 grams (⅔ ounce).

The Second Trimester As muscles develop, the fetus begins to move. This movement can be felt by the mother. Quickening is a term often associated with feeling the baby move for the first time. During the second trimester, the fetus will develop hair and fingernails. Growth is rapid in this trimester. At the end of the second trimester, the fetus is about 35 cm (14 inches) long and weighs about 900 grams (2 pounds).

The Third Trimester In the third and final trimester, the fetus may grow to a length of about 51 cm (20 inches) and weigh about 3 kilograms (7 pounds). At this stage, the development of the digestive and respiratory systems is completed. During this time,

DEVELOPMENT OF A FETUS

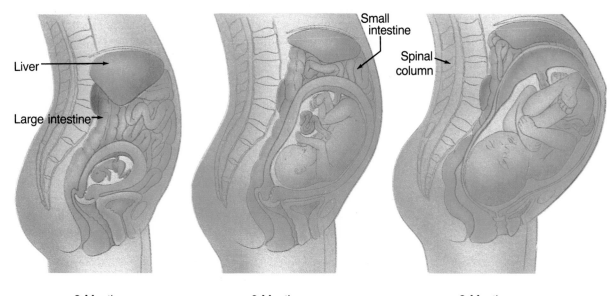

3 Months   6 Months   9 Months

FIGURE 10–3.

the fetus continues to acquire substances from the mother's blood through the placenta. These substances nourish and give protection from infections. The fetus also draws heavily on the mother's supply of calcium. Calcium is used for bone and tooth development. By the end of the ninth month, or fortieth week, the fetus is ready to be born.

10:4 Factors That Influence Prenatal Development

It is important for a woman to receive medical care early in a pregnancy. The health practices a woman follows during her pregnancy are referred to as **prenatal care.** The first step to good prenatal care is a complete medical examination to determine the health status of the pregnant woman. Blood pressure, weight, and other factors tell the physician how the pregnant woman is adjusting to pregnancy.

Medical histories of the parents provide the physician with important information. This information can be used to identify possible risks to the developing baby. Usually a pregnant woman will be treated by an obstetrician. An **obstetrician** is a physician who specializes in the care and treatment of a pregnant woman and her developing baby. The obstetrician also delivers the baby. The pregnant woman should have monthly checkups. These

Early medical care is important during pregnancy.

A pregnant woman can receive medical care from an obstetrician.

checkups become more frequent as the pregnancy develops. Several procedures are included in the obstetrician's examination. The condition of the internal and external reproductive organs are checked. Blood and urine will be tested regularly. The physician will also check the position and growth of the baby and will listen for the baby's heartbeat.

The physician will review special kinds of information a pregnant woman should know. Some of the information focuses on expected physical changes, prediction of delivery date, and medical costs. The physician will also stress how the woman's personal health care will affect the developing baby.

Good nutrition promotes a healthy pregnancy.

Good nutrition is an essential part of prenatal care. Poor nutrition practices by the woman can lead to slower fetal growth, premature delivery, and low birth weight of the baby. Prematurity and low birth weight result in higher infant death rates. Malnourished babies with low birth weights may be born with brain damage.

Adequate amounts of protein, calcium, iron, and vitamins A, B, C, and D are important for the pregnant woman.

Pregnant women need about 300 extra Calories daily. These Calories should represent extra amounts of protein, calcium, iron, and vitamins A, B, C, and D. Protein is important for the growth of the placenta and uterus. Calcium is necessary for the growth of the fetal skeleton. Iron is needed for the manufacture of red blood cells that prevent anemia in the mother.

Nutritional aspects of prenatal care pose a great problem for pregnant teenagers. Teenagers generally have different nutritional needs than adults. Added to this, teenagers often eat nutritionally poor diets compared to diets of more mature women. A poor diet contributes to low birth weight and increases risk to the baby. Thus, it is important for pregnant teenagers to confirm pregnancy early and receive proper medical care.

Low birth weight and birth defects have been linked to a pregnant woman's use of alcohol. The greater the amount of alcohol consumed during pregnancy, the greater the risks. A pregnant woman who drinks more than two servings of alcoholic beverages a day risks having a baby with FAS. **FAS,** or **fetal alcohol syndrome,** is a condition usually accompanied by birth defects caused by the mother's use of alcohol. Some of these birth defects include nervous system disorders, deformities of the face, and growth disorders. Health professionals currently recommend that a pregnant woman avoid all alcoholic beverages.

Smoking during pregnancy doubles the baby's risk of developing problems. The ingredients of inhaled cigarette smoke are carried in the mother's blood and reach the developing baby through the placenta. This can result in reduced birth weight. A woman who stops smoking early during pregnancy reduces the chance of delivering a low birth weight baby.

FIGURE 10-4.

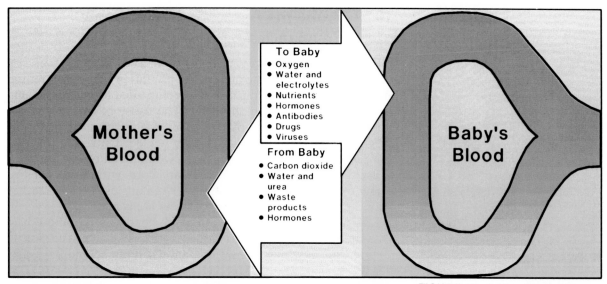

FIGURE 10-5. The developing
fetus receives its nourishment
from the mother's blood.

The use of drugs during pregnancy should be avoided. Only those drugs prescribed by a physician should be taken. Ingredients in drugs can pass from the mother's bloodstream to the baby's bloodstream. When not taken under a physician's care, drugs increase risks to the developing baby. Deformities and mental retardation in the unborn baby may result.

Some research indicates caffeine may be linked to birth defects. Caffeine is found in coffee, chocolate, cola drinks, and tea. It is important to follow a physician's advice concerning the use of these products during pregnancy.

Drugs can pass from the mother's bloodstream to her developing baby.

Activity: Pregnancy Proclamation

You have been asked to list the ten most important steps a woman can follow toward having a healthful pregnancy. Write a list of ten statements that would fulfill this objective. After your list is complete, work with another person to make a combination list by negotiating what you believe are the ten most important items from the two lists. Next, you and your partner are to combine lists with another pair, and again, negotiate the ten most important items. Continue to combine—a group of four will negotiate with another group of four, then a group of eight will negotiate with another group of eight. Eventually, the class as a whole will arrive at a consensus about the ten most important steps a woman can follow to achieve a healthful pregnancy.

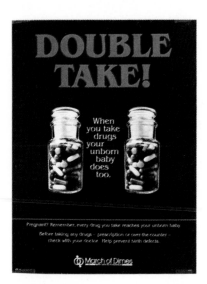

FIGURE 10–6.

Ultrasound and amniocentesis can be used to detect birth defects.

Pregnancies can be ended by either miscarriage or spontaneous abortion.

10:5 Problems Associated With Some Pregnancies

Toxemia of pregnancy is a condition marked by the sudden rise of blood pressure and the presence of protein in the urine after the twentieth week. Toxemia also is accompanied by edema. **Edema** is a buildup of fluid in the body. The cause of toxemia is not known, but it can be treated. Toxemia is most frequent in pregnant teenagers and women over age 35. Untreated toxemia can result in death for the pregnant woman and/or her fetus.

Each year, thousands of babies are born with birth defects. Many of these defects result from a woman's use of drugs or her poor dietary habits. Some birth defects are genetic.

Fetal defects can also be caused by abnormal chromosomes. One such defect is known as Down syndrome. **Down syndrome** is a condition in which a child is mentally retarded and has other disorders.

People who think they might be carriers of a genetic disorder and might give birth to a child with a birth defect can receive genetic counseling. In **genetic counseling,** a couple is advised about their chances of producing offspring with birth defects. Genetic counseling should be received before pregnancy occurs.

Some parents will seek testing about possible birth defects after pregnancy occurs. Using ultrasound, a physician can determine the position of the fetus in the uterus. An **ultrasound** examination uses high-frequency sound waves to produce an image of the fetus. After determining the position of the fetus, the physician can insert a needle into the amniotic sac and remove a sample of amniotic fluid to be analyzed. This technique is called amniocentesis. **Amniocentesis** is a technique that can detect fetal disorders. It is performed after the sixteenth week of pregnancy.

The **Rh factor** is a harmless substance in blood. If it is present, a person is Rh positive. If it is absent, a person is Rh negative. Problems may arise when an Rh negative woman is pregnant with an Rh positive fetus. During the pregnancy, there is little mixing between the blood of the mother and fetus. But if mixing does occur during pregnancy, there will be changes in the mother's blood. This will cause the Rh negative mother's body to create substances in her blood that are anti-Rh. If the mother becomes pregnant again with another Rh positive child, these anti-Rh substances may destroy this baby's red blood cells. A special vaccine given after the birth of the first baby can prevent the anti-Rh substances from harming future babies.

A **miscarriage** or **spontaneous abortion** is the ending of a pregnancy by natural causes. Miscarriages most often occur during the first trimester and account for 10 to 15 percent of all

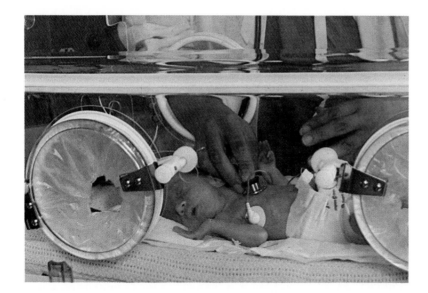

FIGURE 10–7. Premature babies need very special care.

pregnancy terminations. In about half of all miscarriages, the fetus has a defect. About 15 percent of miscarriages result from some condition of the mother, such as an illness or malnutrition.

A **premature birth** is the birth of a child before it is fully developed. Since the date of conception cannot always be accurately estimated, prematurity is often defined by weight rather than age. Thus, an infant who weighs less than 2.5 kg (5½ pounds) at birth is often considered premature.

Premature babies weigh less than 2.5 kg (5½ pounds) at birth.

About seven percent of births in the United States are premature. The smaller the weight of the premature infant at birth, the lower the chance of survival. New technologies have been developed that can help prevent a baby from being born prematurely. Certain mothers at risk may be given a special monitoring device that is worn around the waist. If slight signs of early labor occur, the mother is warned and goes to see her physician. Special medications will be given so that labor will stop, and the baby will have more time to continue to develop.

Advances in medicine can help prevent premature births.

10:6 Birth

The delivery of a baby from the mother's uterus is a complicated process called labor that may take several hours. During labor, the muscular walls of the uterus contract rhythmically. The contractions become more intense as they become more rapid. The cervix dilates or widens to allow the baby to move through the birth canal.

Labor may last for several hours.

Each contraction helps push the baby from the uterus into the birth canal. When the baby is out of the mother's body, mucus is suctioned from the baby's mouth. By this time, the baby has usually started to cry and breathe.

When the physician determines that the baby is breathing on its own, the umbilical cord is clamped and cut off. A stub on the baby's navel remains. It will dry up and fall off in a few days.

After the baby is born, the physician gives the baby an Apgar score. The **Apgar score** is a rating of physical characteristics of an infant one to five minutes after birth. Characteristics such as heart rate, color, respiratory effort, and reaction to sucking are scored to predict the health of the baby.

A cesarean section is performed when a baby cannot pass through the vagina.

Not all women can give birth by having the baby pass through the vagina. Perhaps the unborn baby is too large for the mother's pelvis. Maybe the baby is not positioned correctly. These are some reasons for a physician to perform a cesarean section. A **cesarean section** is the surgical removal of the baby through the mother's abdomen. The physician makes a surgical incision through the mother's abdomen and uterus. The baby then is removed. Modern surgery has made cesarean deliveries fairly safe. However, delivery by cesarean section is major surgery. The time of recovery from this type of delivery is longer than from a vaginal delivery.

10:7   The Postpartum Period

The postpartum period is marked by hormonal changes in the mother's body.

The **postpartum period** is the span of time that begins after the baby is born. It may last several weeks. During the postpartum period, hormones produce changes in the mother's body. For the first few days after birth, the breasts secrete colostrum. **Colostrum** is a watery substance that is believed to provide the baby with immunity to certain diseases. At the same time, a hormone called **prolactin** stimulates the breasts to produce milk. Some studies show that breast-fed babies have fewer cases of respiratory illnesses, skin disorders, constipation, and diarrhea. Breast-fed infants are less likely to gain excess weight in later life.

 Review and Reflect

1. Why do fraternal twins look different?
2. What might happen to a fertilized egg if the endometrium is not developed properly?
3. Why should a pregnant woman avoid using drugs?
4. Why is prenatal care important?
5. What foods would you recommend a pregnant woman eat?
6. Why does a physician suction mucus from a newborn baby?

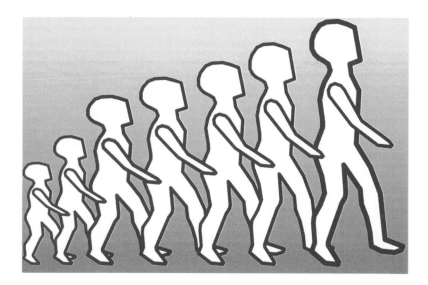

FIGURE 10–8.

INFANCY THROUGH ADULTHOOD

Think for a moment about how you have developed specific skills as you have been educated. You learned certain math skills in grade three. These skills enabled you to manage concepts that were required in grade four. In grade four, you learned math skills that prepared you for grade five, and so on. Your ability to progress through math at each grade level was developmental. Educators who developed the math program from which you learned were able to predict what you should be able to understand at each grade level.

You develop specific skills as you pass through the life cycle.

10:8 Stages of Development

Growth and development are fairly predictable. At each stage of life, there are experiences that prepare a child for the next stage. Erik Erikson, a well-known psychologist, developed a model widely used today that describes the development of the individual. This model is an eight-stage theory of psychosocial development. The term psycho is related to one's thoughts and emotions; social is related to one's interactions with others. The eight stages are infancy (birth to 1 year), early childhood (ages 1 to 3), preschool (ages 3 to 6), elementary (ages 7 to 11), adolescence (ages 12 to 19), early adulthood, middle adulthood, and late

Erik Erikson developed an eight-stage model of psychosocial development.

adulthood. Erikson's stages are psychosocial because they indicate the relationships between personality and a person's expanding social world. The stages are based upon the concept that knowledge and experience build from one stage to the next. Thus, different needs and challenges of early stages must be met before a child can constructively deal with problems at a later stage.

You grow physically as well as psychosocially.

In addition to growing psychosocially, you also grow physically. Changes occur both to the inside and outside of your body throughout your life cycle.

10:9 Infancy

The time period from birth to one year is called infancy.

Infancy is the period of development from birth to one year. During this time, an infant may grow rapidly and triple his or her birth weight. Teeth erupt and the muscular and nervous systems develop and become coordinated. The ability to sit, stand, and reach for objects is a normal part of an infant's development.

During this period, infants learn about themselves and their environment. They recognize familiar sights and sounds and begin to make associations. They play with objects in their cribs and follow movements of color.

Crawling enables infants to explore their world.

Infants explore their world more fully when they begin to crawl. Being allowed to crawl, infants discover new ways of being self-gratified. They receive a sense of accomplishment by seeing an object and grabbing it. Of course, parental supervision is always important when a baby crawls in areas that might have potential hazards. In addition to the emotional rewards, crawling allows the baby to receive physical benefits since the muscles are being used and developed.

FIGURE 10–9. Infancy

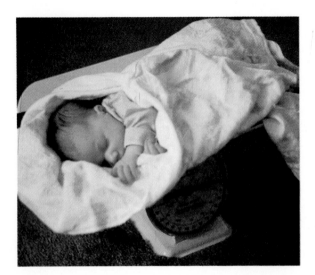 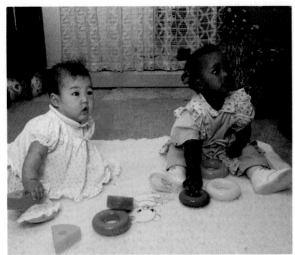

FIGURE 10–10. Childhood

10:10 Childhood

Childhood is the period of time between the end of infancy and the beginning of puberty. Childhood is marked by a steady growth rate. Permanent teeth replace primary teeth. Voluntary muscular control is further developed. Bladder and bowel control and habits are established. Communicative skills of writing and speaking become more refined.

Many abilities that affect self-esteem are developed during childhood. This is important within a family unit. All children want to feel that they not only belong to a family but also are contributing members of that family. Many children have responsibilities that show they can care for themselves as well as for other family members. They are given tasks such as putting away their toys or making their beds when they are able. They enjoy being shown that these behaviors are appreciated. This helps develop the feeling of contributing to the family. As children get older, they may need greater responsibilities, such as helping prepare a special dish for dinner, setting or clearing the table, and washing dishes.

Decision making is another concept developed during childhood. Children learn how to make responsible decisions by themselves. "What will I wear today?" "What will I have for lunch?" Parents need to understand that some decisions children make may not be responsible ones. At these times, parents need to guide their children toward appropriate alternatives.

The end of infancy to the beginning of puberty is called childhood.

Childhood is a period during which self-esteem is developed.

Work enables a child to develop competence.

Children also develop feelings of competence through work. This is evident when children begin school. They enjoy the opportunity to read to their parents or have their parents read to them. Children who read can also be encouraged to read by themselves or with parents or other family members. Children who are given the opportunity to develop verbal and reading abilities begin to understand a few of the many complexities in the world. This in turn leads to a feeling of competence.

It is important for children to be exposed to caring and loving people.

The total environment of the child plays a significant role in healthful development. When children are exposed to caring and loving family members, teachers, friends, and neighbors, a sense of acceptance, worth, confidence, and self-esteem is promoted.

10:11 Adolescence

The period of time from childhood to adulthood is adolescence.

Adolescence is the period of time between childhood and adulthood. It generally falls between the ages of 12 to 19. During puberty, anatomical and physiological changes make adolescents capable of reproduction. For the most part, these changes are controlled by hormones. They include the appearance of secondary sex characteristics and growth spurts in the muscular and skeletal systems. Growth spurts occur during adolescence. In females, these spurts usually occur between ages 11 to 13 and in males between the ages of 13 to 15.

Females usually undergo these changes earlier than males. Females may be taller and stronger than males in early adolescence. However, by late adolescence, the average male is usually taller and stronger than the average female.

During adolescence, many questions are raised. "Who am I?" "What do I want to be?" "Where am I going?" "What do I believe in?" Adolescence is the time in life during which many of these kinds of questions arise. Fortunately, most adolescents who have these questions are able to resolve them.

FIGURE 10–11. Adolescence

The influence of a peer group can have significant impact upon adolescent behavior. During this period, adolescents may seek more independence from their parents and place an increased importance on the decisions of their peer group. Parental advice may not be sought as frequently as in the past. Often adolescents may ask themselves, "Should I do what my friends want, or should I go along with my parents' choices for me?" Parents often wonder, "Will my child make the appropriate decision?" Numerous studies have been conducted over the years to analyze parent-adolescent relationships. In these studies, the overwhelming conclusion is that adolescents agree with their parents' ideas and share their values.

FIGURE 10–12. Adolescence

The key to a happy and healthy adolescence depends on the past and present. If a young child has been given the freedom to develop independently, feel secure, and practice self-discipline early in life, these attitudes will continue into adolescence. Parents and children need to maintain contact with each other. Parents can do this by developing an interest in their children's activities, scheduling events that can be done as a family, showing affection by expressing approval, and demonstrating trust and concern. As a result, children will find they have more self-confidence. They will be more willing to seek their parents' help and advice during adolescence.

It is important for parents and children to develop and share interests.

10:12 Adulthood

Adulthood is the period of time from adolescence through old age. Generally, adults change physically very little over the years. Depending on environmental and hereditary factors, and life-styles, chronic diseases and illness may occur. After age 30, skeletal muscles may lose some of their strength. The circulatory system may become less efficient. In later adulthood, skin may become wrinkled and hair turn gray. These physical changes should not be associated with an ability to be productive. Adults of today are more aware of the need to be physically fit than ever before. Some people become more physically fit as adults than when they were younger because they have adopted lifestyles that promote healthful behaviors. They may exercise regularly, eat more healthful meals, and rest better than when they were young.

The period of time from adolescence through old age is adulthood.

FIGURE 10–13. Adulthood

Many psychosocial changes begin to occur when people reach their 20s.

Middle adulthood is marked by the seeking of life goals and standards.

Late adulthood is often considered the most stable period of the life cycle.

Psychosocial changes also occur during adulthood. Early adulthood occurs for people in their 20s. This stage is characterized by independence and being responsible for themselves. How a person adjusts during this period is a measure of emotional maturity. During this period, friends often replace family members as a source of help. Intimate relationships are sought. These relationships may be short-lived. Many adults in this age group marry; some may become dedicated to a career.

Middle adulthood occurs for people in their 30s. In this period, one may seek to adjust life goals and standards. For example, a person who works on a job that is not satisfying may look for a new job. Energies may become focused on more attainable goals.

Late adulthood for some people may be characterized by an awareness that life does have an ending. This stage can be a depressing time for those who have not achieved a sense of closeness with others and who feel they have no control over their own destinies. On the other hand, this is a period of contentment for most. People look back at their accomplishments and value those accomplishments that have made them happy as adults. In this stage, some people often become advisors and teachers. They place emphasis on more simple aspects of life. In some respects, late adulthood is the most stable period of the life cycle. Men and women begin to pursue new interests. They may take up new hobbies or register for courses in a local college or university. Many people in this stage find freedom they have never had before.

Review and Reflect

7. How does school help improve a child's feeling of competence?
8. What can a parent do to promote a healthful parent–child relationship?

Health
ADVANCES

One in six married couples is unable to produce children of their own. The reasons are many. In some cases, conception does not occur because a woman's Fallopian tubes are blocked or otherwise not functioning.

10:13 In-Vitro Fertilization

In-vitro fertilization, or **IVF,** is conception that occurs in a laboratory environment rather than in a woman's body. Through this process, many women have been able to conceive and have healthy children.

In-vitro fertilization may enable many women to conceive.

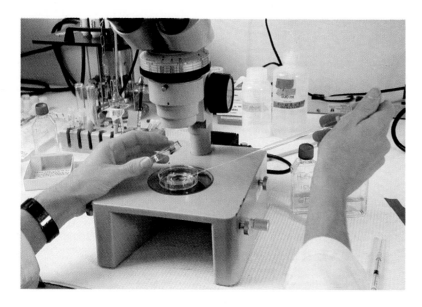

FIGURE 10–14. Egg cells are transferred to a dish containing nutrients.

In IVF, a woman's egg cell may be fertilized by her husband's sperm or the sperm of a donor, or a donor's egg cell may be fertilized by the husband's sperm or the sperm of a donor. The process of IVF may take place in a special clinic. When blood tests indicate that an egg cell is maturing, egg cells are extracted from an ovary in a delicate operation.

The surgeon inserts a special instrument called a laparoscope into the abdomen. The laparoscope enables the surgeon to see into the ovary. A long, hollow needle is then inserted through another incision, and the egg cells and surrounding fluid are suctioned into the needle and extracted.

Once extracted, the egg cells are washed, placed in dishes that contain special nutrients, and deposited in an incubator for four-to-eight hours. After this time, sperm are added to the dishes that contain the eggs. If all goes well, several eggs will be fertilized. When an embryo is two-to-eight cells in size, it is placed in a woman's uterus. Sometimes, more than one embryo is placed in the uterus to increase the chances of a successful pregnancy. When this occurs, there is often the possibility of a multiple birth. Generally, this procedure is delicate, and in most cases, pregnancy does not occur.

In-vitro fertilization is a delicate process that is not always successful.

For many couples, IVF has been successful. However, for most, it has not been successful. This procedure costs thousands of dollars. Future research into improved procedures for IVF holds promise for the one of every six couples affected by infertility.

Focus on
Life Management Skills

- It is important for you or someone with whom you are close to receive an early diagnosis of pregnancy so that healthful habits will be followed as early as possible.
- Support a pregnant woman's decision to avoid smoking cigarettes and drinking alcohol.
- A pregnant woman should receive regular medical treatment throughout her pregnancy.
- A woman who is pregnant should increase her daily intake of protein, calcium, iron, and vitamins A, B, C, and D.
- Help prepare yourself for responsible parenthood by understanding the physical, social, and emotional characteristics of children.

Health
CAREERS

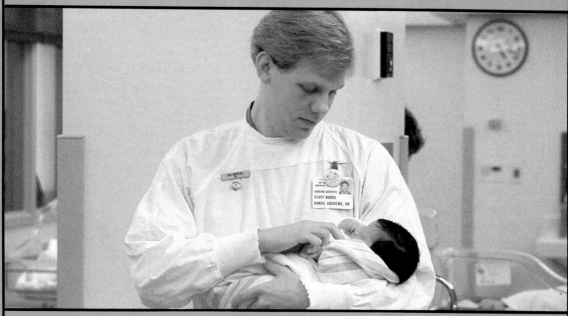

Registered Nurse

Daniel Andrews enjoys his career as a nurse in the maternity ward of a major hospital. During his shift, Dan regularly checks the newborn babies to monitor their growth and development. Babies with special problems are constantly watched. Dan also works with the mother of the newborn by providing her with information on child care.

Like most nurses today, Dan graduated from a four-year college that offers a Bachelor of Science degree in nursing. However, in some states, a person can become a registered nurse in two years with an associate degree in nursing. Dan completed courses in biology, chemistry, nutrition, sociology, psychology, and anatomy and physiology. Dan also completed many clinical courses that help him develop technical skills such as drawing blood from patients, giving shots, and taking blood pressure.

Nurses are involved in many areas of patient care. They administer prescribed medicines, set up IVs, assist the physician during an examination, maintain patient records, and help in surgery.

There are many opportunities for graduates of nursing programs. Nurses may find employment in a hospital, physician's office, nursing home, a private corporation, social service agency, or in home health care. A nurse may choose to specialize in an area within a hospital. These areas could include maternity, surgery, pedriatrics, the emergency room, or cardiology.

Summary

1. Conception occurs when an egg and sperm unite. 10:1
2. One way to confirm pregnancy is to test for the presence of HCG in blood. 10:2
3. Prenatal development occurs in three stages; each is called a trimester. 10:3
4. Factors that influence prenatal development are the mother's health status, diet, lifestyle, and prenatal care. 10:4
5. Genetic factors may cause problem pregnancies. 10:5
6. The birth process begins with muscular contractions of the uterus and dilation of the cervix. 10:6
7. During the postpartum period the mother's body experiences hormonal changes. 10:7

8. Growth and development involves both psychosocial and physical changes. 10:8
9. During infancy, children begin to learn about themselves and their environment. 10:9
10. Childhood is marked by a steady growth rate and the development of skills. 10:10
11. During adolescence, most teenagers seek greater independence and experience a growth spurt. 10:11
12. Adulthood is characterized by a minimum amount of physical growth and by accomplishments and new freedoms. 10:12
13. In-vitro fertilization is conception that takes place ouside a woman's body. 10:13

Vocabulary

Below is a list of vocabulary words used in this chapter. Use each word only once to complete the sentences. Do not write in this book.

amniocentesis	miscarriage
Apgar score	obstetrician
conception	prolactin
ectopic pregnancy	toxemia
HCG	umbilical cord

1. A(n) _____ is the growth of a zygote somewhere other than in a woman's uterus.
2. _____ is a technique used to detect fetal disorders.
3. The embryo and placenta are connected by the _____.
4. The rating of the physical characteristics of an infant soon after birth is called the _____.
5. _____ is produced by the placenta and can be detected in urine.
6. A(n) _____, ending pregnancy, occurs most often during the first trimester.
7. A physician who delivers babies and cares for the pregnant woman is a(n) _____.
8. A hormone that stimulates the breasts to produce milk is _____.
9. Another name for fertilization is _____.
10. A sudden rise in blood pressure during pregnancy may indicate _____.

Review

1. Describe the function of the umbilical cord.
2. What are some signs that may indicate pregnancy?
3. Describe how a fetus may develop and change from the second to the third trimester.
4. Why is a general examination by an obstetrician important to a pregnant woman?
5. How might a woman know she has toxemia?
6. What is a cesarean section?
7. How does a woman's body change during the postpartum period?
8. What physical growth occurs during infancy?
9. How is competence developed during childhood?
10. What is the role of the peer group during adolescence?

Application

1. Why is following a healthful diet important for a pregnant woman?
2. Why is genetic counseling important?
3. How can self-esteem be improved during childhood?

Individual Research

1. Review material from your library that discusses the latest research about drugs and pregnancy. Write a one-page summary about your findings.
2. The use of midwives in the birth process has received widespread attention. Research the role of midwives and related issues about their roles.
3. Observe the development of an infant. Describe the physical, mental, and social characteristics that this infant shows.

Readings

Editors of Time-Life, *The Commonsense Guide to Birth and Babies*. New York, NY: Holt, Rinehart and Winston, Publishers, 1983.

Scher, Jonathan, and Dix, Carol, *Will My Baby Be Normal?: How to Make Sure*. New York, NY: The Dial Press, 1983.

White, Burton L., *The First Three Years of Life*. New York, NY: Avon Books, 1978.

Good health can be a lifetime goal. You can promote your health and well-being by giving your body quality care during your lifetime. Will you be able to ride a bicycle when you are in your sixties? Are you choosing behaviors now that promote your optimum health?

Chapter 11

Toward Completion of the Life Cycle

OBJECTIVES: You will be able to
- **identify the physical, mental, and social characteristics associated with aging.**
- **define death and discuss issues related to dying.**
- **explain how death can be handled in a healthful way.**

From the time of birth, you have been undergoing physical, mental, and social changes that affect the quality of your life. These changes, and your ability to cope with them, are natural occurrences that continue throughout your life cycle.

Have you ever thought what life will be like for you as you move through the life cycle? According to research, life expectancy, or the number of years a person is predicted to live, is increasing. Data in 1985 indicated that Americans born in 1982 can expect an average life expectancy of 74.6 years. Females are expected to outlive males by about seven years. What can you do to increase your chances of living healthfully through the life cycle? What changes can you expect as you advance toward old age? What age is considered old? These and other questions are discussed in this chapter.

Throughout your life cycle, you undergo many physical, mental, and social changes.

Life expectancy is increasing.

THE AGING PROCESS

Have you ever seen an old car that looks better than one that may be many years newer? The old car was probably provided with quality care from the time it was first purchased. It was probably washed and waxed frequently. The oil and oil filter were changed according to manufacturer's specifications. Problems were corrected as soon as they were noticed. Years later, the

FIGURE 11–1. Square dancing is a good way to exercise as well as have fun.

quality care given to this car has paid off. It runs well and looks great. It most likely is worth more money now than when it was manufactured. The value of the car increased because of the quality of care it received. Even after many years, the car is considered a showpiece.

It is important to maintain good health now.

Your health status is also determined by the quality of care received throughout life. As you continue to follow healthful practices, you take steps to promote your health and well-being. Choosing healthful behaviors increases the quality of your life throughout your life cycle.

11:1 What Causes Aging?

There are many theories about when aging begins.

A person begins to age after physical maturity.

There are many theories about when aging begins. **Gerontology** (jer un TAHL uh jy) is the study of aging. **Gerontologists** are people who study aging. Some gerontologists believe aging begins the day a person is born. Others believe aging begins when a person's growth stops. This happens around age 25 when cells die faster than they reproduce. The latter theory of aging is most widely accepted. Aging occurs after a person's body matures, or stops growing.

Old is a term often used to describe aging. At what age would you consider a person to be old? At age 25? 40? 65? 80? According to many researchers, old is a state of mind and not a specific period of life. Thus, if you were age 75, jogged one mile each day, kept up to date on current events, and had a strong heart, you might consider yourself young. On the other hand, if you were age 45, did not exercise, were overweight, and had heart disease, you might consider yourself old. Perhaps the saying, "You are as old as you feel," is the most practical way to define the word old.

As a person ages, it becomes obvious that changes are occurring to the body. These changes may easily be recognized. Yet, the reasons for these changes may not be so easy to identify. Gerontologists have developed theories about the causes of aging.

- The wear-and-tear theory maintains that, like any machine, the human body simply wears out.
- The waste-product theory is based on the belief that waste products accumulate in body cells. These waste products damage body cells and cause them to lose their normal ability to function.
- The anti-immune theory proposes that the body's immune system attacks healthy cells instead of foreign substances that enter the body. Consequently, the body loses its ability to distinguish between healthy cells and foreign material.
- The cell-error theory maintains that as body cells divide, errors are introduced into the genetic material. As cells divide, the errors are reproduced. More and more cells accumulate errors, resulting in aging.
- The brain theory suggests that the brain initiates and controls the aging process by a mechanism not completely understood.

11:2 Physical Aspects of Aging

Physical changes occur to everyone at different times in the life cycle. Some people look and act old at age 30 or 40. On the contrary, many people who are age 60 and 70 look and act young. As a person ages, many physical changes become observable.

Many researchers believe that being old is a state of mind.

There are many theories about why people age.

Many physical changes occur as a person ages.

FIGURE 11-2. Young people can learn by sharing time with people who are older.

a

b

c

FIGURE 11–3. Many physical changes occur with age: (a) the young girl is about 15 years old; (b) the young man is about 40 years old, and (c) the older man is about 75 years old.

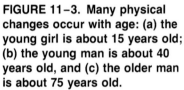

Body systems may begin to work less efficiently as a person ages.

Selecting healthful behaviors when you are young will help you maintain your health as you grow older.

Some of these changes may occur when people are in their 20s. For example, a male's hair may become thinner. Baldness may begin. Wrinkled skin may appear on people who are in their 30s. However, signs of aging, like baldness and wrinkled skin, may not appear on some people until they approach their 50s or 60s.

Internal changes also occur within the body as one ages. The circulatory system may no longer carry blood as effectively as it once did. The lungs may not be able to hold the same volume of air as in earlier years. Reaction to stimuli will be slowed since nerve impulses may not travel as fast as was once possible. The digestive and excretory systems will not be able to process nutrients and remove wastes as efficiently as those of a young person. The body's sense organs will become less sensitive with age. Even though the physical aspects of aging cannot be reversed, there are ways to help keep our bodies physically fit and healthy as we age (Section 11:5).

Many health problems of the elderly are considered chronic diseases. A **chronic disease** is an illness that develops and lasts over a long period of time, recurs frequently, and is often disabling. Some chronic diseases that affect older people more often than younger people are heart disease, cancer, arthritis, and high blood pressure. Many times the occurrence of these diseases can be traced to the effects of a person's lifestyle rather than the aging process. Research shows that a healthy young person who selects behaviors that promote health will most likely become a healthy older person.

11:3 Mental Aspects of Aging

Research has been conducted to determine the causes and cures of the mental aspects of aging. One area of research has focused upon a condition called dementia. **Dementia** is a condition in which the thinking processes are impaired. It is a general term used to describe the gradual development of mental impairment. Among the characteristics of dementia are a short attention span, memory loss, inability to handle simple math problems, and loss of concept of time and place. Dementia may cause personality changes. A person may become irritated easily and experience a decreased sense of humor. Sometimes, a person suffering from dementia may also become confused.

One form of dementia is Alzheimer's disease. **Alzheimer's disease** is a condition in which there is progressive deterioration of memory and other mental functions. It is associated with advanced age and can lead to death within five to ten years. The exact causes of Alzheimer's disease are not known. However, it is believed to have a gradual onset. Some researchers believe this disease may be related to a person's genetic background. No cure exists for this condition.

Another form of dementia is multi-infarct dementia. **Multi-infarct dementia** is a disorder in which a person suffers many small strokes. These small strokes, or broken blood vessels in the brain, destroy areas of brain tissue. This results in the characteristics associated with dementia. Medicine can control the causes of multi-infarct dementia, but the condition resulting from the small strokes cannot be cured.

Dementia is characterized by changes in one's mental health.

Alzheimer's disease is a condition that primarily affects people who are older.

FIGURE 11-4. The first signs of Alzheimer's disease are personality changes and memory lapses. Names of friends are forgotten, dates are tangled, and the hour of the day and even the season of the year are confused.

Inappropriate drug use can cause dementia.

Dementia may be a result of many physical diseases.

Most people over age 65 are healthy and can care for themselves.

There are many ways you can help a person who is elderly.

FIGURE 11–5. Many older people remain healthy and contribute their abilities and experiences in many ways.

Causes and cures are known for about 10 to 20 percent of the people who suffer from dementia. Two major causes of dementia are identified.

Inappropriate Drug Use   Older people may take medicines in the wrong amounts or at the wrong times. Perhaps a physician may have prescribed a medication when another was already in use. The combined use of the medicines may cause dementia. Fortunately, dementia caused by inappropriate drug use may be corrected. People suffering from dementia should have all medicines regularly reviewed by a physician. In some cases, it may be necessary to have someone check the patient's medicine cabinet at home rather than rely on a verbal report. Any change in the use of a medication should be supervised by a physician.

Underlying Physical Disease   According to the National Institute of Aging, there are at least 50 reversible causes of mental impairment. Among these are malnutrition, medication, infection, and misuse of drugs, including alcohol. Accurate diagnosis and treatment of the causes may cure mental impairment.

The aging process does not always have negative mental effects. Personality and intellectual capacity do not necessarily deteriorate as one ages. A person who practices a healthful lifestyle and remains mentally and socially active will most likely remain mentally healthy throughout his or her life.

The population of persons over 65 is becoming more and more healthy. Statistics show that fewer than five percent of all people over age 65 need constant care. However, suppose you have an older family member who is suffering from a mental disorder and needs special care. There are certain steps your family can take that will be helpful to both you and the elderly person.

- Find a qualified medical program in a hospital or other institution that specializes in evaluating the elderly. Special physical examinations as well as health histories can be conducted to identify the possible causes of a mental disorder.
- Contact a counselor, either one in private practice or in a mental health agency, who can guide you toward the care of the elderly person. Various agencies have programs that are free or minimal in charge. These programs can help you assist the elderly family member.
- Join support groups that can help you deal with your concerns. For example, some communities have support groups for those who have a family member with Alzheimer's disease.

Cases of severe depression may look like dementia. If depression is not diagnosed and treated, symptoms of dementia may continue. Proper treatment from a mental health professional may successfully cure both the depression and the symptoms of dementia that results.

11:4   Social Aspects of Aging

The population of persons ages 65 and older is increasing. The reasons for this increase are many. New drugs help treat illnesses that once were often fatal. Research about the relationships of risk factors to premature illness and death are encouraging people to change their health practices. Health promotion activities in schools and communities are encouraging people to take responsibility for their own health.

However, despite positive lifestyle changes, other social aspects of aging must be addressed. One concern related to growing older is ageism. **Ageism** is discrimination against a person based on age. Ageism is often a result of stereotyping. A **stereotype** is an assumption that people in a particular group will think or act in a certain way. Stereotyping is a socially harmful behavior because it ignores individual differences. There are many stereotypes about older people. Some of these focus on the physical and mental abilities of older people. Below are some myths and facts related to aging.

- Myth   Intellectual failure will occur.
- Fact   People who are intelligent during their early and middle years will probably be intelligent until they die.
- Myth   Retirement causes people to get sick and die early.
- Fact   A major reason people retire is ill health. Retirement does not cause ill health.
- Myth   Older people do not understand what is happening in the real world.
- Fact   Many company presidents, educators, and world leaders are over age 65. They are well-respected, and their wisdom will be sought until they die. Older people may have qualities that younger people do not have. They may have had certain experiences that have given them wisdom or a different perspective on life.

Loneliness is another social concern affecting some older people. Older people may find themselves isolated when their aging friends and/or spouse dies. In this situation, they need to develop new friends and social relationships. Unfortunately, this is especially difficult if transportation is not available. Social isolation thus becomes a problem for some people.

Young people often are not aware of the social needs of older people. They may think that older people have needs different than their own. Think about the needs you have. You may identify some of the following: friends with whom to talk; someone to give you love; someone to listen to you; someone with whom to do things; someone with whom to go places; time to be alone; opportunities to make your own decisions.

Ageism is discrimination of a person based on age.

There are many myths about aging.

Loneliness is a major concern for some older people.

FIGURE 11-6. As people age, they may develop new interests and hobbies.

FIGURE 11–7. A game of chess matches wits no matter the age of the players.

If one or more of these needs are not met, you may not be able to achieve optimum health. Think about the needs of an older person. This person's needs are very similar to yours.

You can help older persons meet their needs. You might choose to participate in an "Adopt a Grandparent" program by spending time each week with an elderly person. You can encourage this person to join in functions sponsored by agencies in your community. You might help arrange for transportation so that an elderly person can meet new friends and participate in new activities.

You can help older people meet their needs.

11:5 Planning for Good Health in Old Age

If you establish healthful behaviors at your present age, you will most likely continue them as you grow older. This lifestyle increases your chances of a longer, more healthful life. On the other hand, if you engage in harmful habits, you will probably continue these as you grow older. This increases your chances of poor health as you age and may cause premature death.

Establish healthful behaviors now to promote your health in the future.

Here are some healthful behaviors you can follow now that will promote a healthier lifestyle as you age.

- Be active both physically and intellectually. Engage in a program of exercise. Read and become involved in cultural or social events of your choosing.
- Plan for leisure in your life. Taking time to relax is one way to handle stress. A balance of work and play contributes to a satisfying life.

- Eat healthful foods. Many researchers believe that eating healthful foods is a key to good health.
- Learn new skills. Learning new skills, such as crafts or music, increases one's interest in life.
- Do things for others. Volunteering in community services brings gratification for you and others.
- Refrain from smoking. The U.S. Surgeon General says that cigarette smoking is the greatest preventable cause of death.

To refrain from smoking is an important behavior you can follow now.

 # Activity: ### Aging Healthfully

Fold a sheet of paper down the center and write a + (plus) on the left side and a − (minus) on the right side. On the plus side, list five behaviors you practice that will help you age healthfully. On the minus side, list up to five behaviors you practice that might interfere with your ability to age healthfully. Select one of these behaviors. Design a health behavior contract to follow that will improve your chances of aging healthfully.

A health behavior contract can be used to promote your health.

 ## Review and Reflect

1. Explain the statement "You are as old as you feel."
2. Why is it important for an older person with a mental impairment to receive medical attention?
3. How are your needs similar to those of a person who is older?

FIGURE 11–8. Being physically active is one way to plan for optimum health as you grow older.

UNDERSTANDING DEATH

Death is a biological fact.

Regardless of the number of healthful behaviors a person follows or how healthy he or she may be, death is inevitable. For most people, death comes during old age. However, death can occur at any age.

Even though death is a biological fact, talking about death is often avoided. The purpose of discussing death in this text is not to make you feel uncomfortable or insecure. Rather, it is just the opposite. People most often experience these feelings when they are not aware of the many factors concerned with death. Knowledge and understanding about death and dying may help you become more comfortable in the discussion of death.

Four criteria are used in many states to define death.

11:6 Defining Death

When does death occur? This question does not have a simple answer. At one time, it was thought that death occurred when the lungs and the heart ceased to function. By this definition, people who had heart attacks and were later revived would have been considered dead. Now, life-support machines can keep people alive if they cannot breathe or their hearts will not beat. **Thanatologists,** scientists concerned with the study of death, have been striving to develop a medical and legal definition of death.

In 1968, a Harvard Medical School Ad Hoc Committee developed a definition of death that is widely used today. According to this definition, a person is declared dead when the following four criteria are met.

Unreceptiveness and unresponsiveness—The person shows no response to painful stimulation applied to the body. For example, a person will not say anything or show any signs of reflexes.

No movements or breathing—When observed for over an hour, the person shows no spontaneous muscle movement or evidence of breathing.

No reflexes—The person does not swallow, yawn, or show a knee-jerk reflex. The pupils of the eyes do not respond to direct sources of light.

Flat EEG—An EEG, a record of the electrical activity in the brain, shows no electrical brain impulses for at least ten to twenty minutes.

FIGURE 11–9. (a) normal EEG, (b) flat EEG

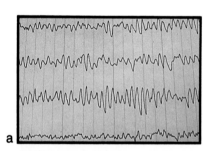
a

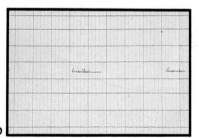
b

11:7   Stages of Dying

Many people die unexpectedly and have no advance notice of death. However, some people do have time to prepare for their death. They may have a terminal illness. **A terminal illness** is an illness that is incurable and will eventually cause death.

People who have a terminal illness experience psychological stages of dying. These stages describe emotional feelings most dying people experience. Dr. Elisabeth Kübler-Ross, a psychiatrist well known for her work with dying patients, identified five stages of dying. They include denial, anger, bargaining, depression, and acceptance. Dying persons do not necessarily go through the stages in the same order. Some may skip a stage, go back to a previous stage, or remain in one stage for an extended period of time.

Denial is called the "It can't be me" stage. People in this stage feel they are not terminally ill. They believe a cure will be found for their disease or that they will be the exception who lives. Dying persons can be helped by discussing with family members what medical options are available. Family or friends can encourage the person to get a second opinion from a physician to verify a condition.

Anger is called the "Why me" stage. Persons in this stage realize that they are going to die. This results in anger directed at family, medical staff, or friends. Often, anger is expressed in frequent arguing. During this stage, it is important for families to let the person know that they have a right to be angry. It is helpful to have an outlet for the anger.

The bargaining stage is a person's attempt to avoid death. Persons in this stage may make deals with God, their doctors, or family members. They may ask God to let them live long enough to witness an event such as a wedding. They may promise to change their ways if they recover. Families can help dying persons in this stage by assuring them that they are receiving the best care possible.

Depression occurs when bargaining does not produce desired results. Hope for recovery dims. Persons begin to feel the loss of family and friends. They become sad and begin to grieve. During this stage, persons need to be encouraged to discuss their depression. Family members can be most helpful if they do not deny the person's depression.

Acceptance of death is the goal of terminally ill persons. Not every person will reach this stage. Those who do need support from family members. Personal matters may be reviewed. Financial matters and funeral arrangements may be planned.

Elisabeth Kübler-Ross has identified five stages of dying.

The anger stage of death is also known as the "Why me" stage.

The final stage of death is acceptance.

There are many ways to help a dying person.

Understanding the stages of dying can help both the dying person and the family realistically cope with death. Often people are afraid to visit a friend or relative who is dying because they fear they may not know what to say or do. The following suggestions may be helpful.

Listen to the dying person. At times this person may want visitors and be talkative. Discuss what the person is interested in. At other times, the person may feel like being left alone.

Express your feelings. Understand that a dying person may cry in front of you. If you also feel like crying, do so. Do not be ashamed to cry; this can show concern. On the other hand, it is important to laugh and joke if the dying person does so. Continue to share good times.

Do what is natural for both of you. If you have always greeted each other with a kiss or hug, do not stop. If kissing and hugging were unnatural for both of you in the past, it may become more natural as you communicate and share more openly.

Reaffirm your feelings. Showing love, concern, and affection will help both of you cope more healthfully. If you desire, offer to help the dying person in some way.

11:8   Death with Dignity

Most terminally ill people want to be informed about their health status.

Like anyone, a basic need of a dying person is the need for communication. Research indicates that at least 80 percent of all people would like to be informed if they have a terminal illness. Research also indicates that most terminally ill persons who are not told they are dying already know or suspect their condition. They become aware of attitudes displayed toward them by family members and medical professionals. They may overhear discussions about their health or try to interpret the meaning of different treatments for their condition. Everyone, including the dying, wants to feel some control over decisions that affect them. Honest answers to their questions are important. Dying persons have the need to

Dying persons have many needs.

- feel valued and accepted.
- maintain confidence and self-esteem.
- have their feelings known.
- be assured of being remembered.
- participate in decision-making activities.
- participate in planning for death, such as helping to make arrangements for a funeral.

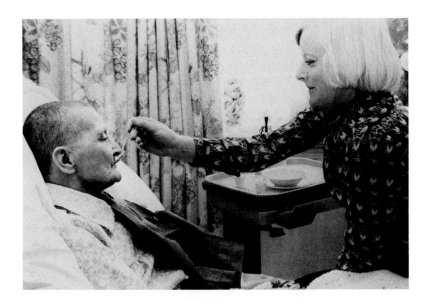

FIGURE 11–10. Many terminally ill patients choose a hospice because of the kind of care hospices offer.

One method used to promote the idea of death with dignity is hospice. The **hospice** is a facility or program of caring for terminally ill persons and of counseling their families. This concept is carried out in a homelike atmosphere for the terminally ill. The setting can be in the person's home or another location. Regardless of the setting, the hospice has certain unique features.

Care for the dying person—The hospice tries to make dying persons feel as comfortable as possible. Special medicines will be given to relieve pain. Persons are given as much control as possible over their treatments. A person's final days are made to be as meaningful and pleasant as possible.

Family support—Family members suffer along with dying persons. Recognizing this, the hospice concept tries to help family members in several ways. Families are taught how to participate in the person's care. Counseling services are available to families to work through their grief as well as care for business matters. Counseling is also available to a family after a death. Families are allowed to be with dying persons as long as they desire. Children are also permitted to visit with dying persons. This helps children understand the process of dying and death.

Team approach—Many different people are involved with dying persons and families in the hospice concept. These include nurses, physicians, physical therapists, social workers, educators, and pharmacists. These people are encouraged to develop an individual relationship with a dying person. This helps the person feel important and maintain dignity.

Terminally ill people can be helped at a hospice.

A team approach may be used in a hospice.

Other services provided by a hospice program include

- Medical control of physical symptoms, including pain management and control of nausea and vomiting.
- Home nursing care.
- Nutritional evaluation and counseling.
- Occupational therapy, physical therapy, and speech therapy.
- Emotional and psychological counseling and support.
- Spiritual support and guidance.
- Legal and financial counseling and advice.
- Continuing support and follow-up bereavement care for family members.
- Home support services (shopping, transportation, companionship, etc., by volunteers).
- Respite care (hospice volunteers temporarily staying with the patient to relieve family members).

Courtesy of American Cancer Society

11:9 Euthanasia

In many cases, dying may be prolonged and painful. Recovery may appear impossible, and the issue of euthanasia may arise. **Euthanasia** (from the Greek words for "good death") is the intentional ending of life for reasons of mercy. Sometimes, the term euthanasia is used as a synonym for "mercy killing."

Euthanasia is a controversial topic. Supporters of euthanasia argue that quality of life is more important than quantity of years lived. They feel that if staying alive means high medical bills, life-support machines, inability to care for oneself, and removal from family and friends, then persons should be allowed to die, especially if there is no hope for recovery. Those against euthanasia argue that cases of living and dying are not clear. Many people hold religious beliefs that do not include euthanasia. They feel others should not decide death for the dying person, especially if that person is in a coma.

Who is to say what level of pain and discomfort indicates the taking of a life? What happens if there is disagreement among family members? What if a diagnosis is wrong? How can physicians practice euthanasia when they are pledged to preserve life? It is likely that these and other arguments will be discussed in courts and other forums for years to come.

Euthanasia is a controversial topic.

Religious beliefs play a role in euthanasia.

Review and Reflect

4. Why is the denial stage also called the "It can't be me" stage?
5. Why is it important to understand the stages of dying?
6. Why is it important to communicate with a dying person?

DEALING WITH DEATH HEALTHFULLY

Death takes on special meaning in all societies. When a person dies, some kind of ceremony usually takes place. The type of ceremony is determined by local customs and religious beliefs.

There are many beliefs about death.

Regardless of its form, a ceremony marking death has several values. It is an occasion to remember the life of the deceased. It is a time to share personal accomplishments and joyous times spent with the deceased. It allows the opportunity for friends and relatives to come together and support each other. A ceremony also allows individuals to observe the death in a spiritual manner and seek comfort through their personal beliefs.

FIGURE 11–11. Arlington National Cemetery.

FIGURE 11-12. Many mausole-ums are large buildings with many available compartments.

11:10 Burial

If a dead person's body is not buried within 48 hours of death, many states require that the body be embalmed. **Embalming** is the replacing of a dead person's blood with a special fluid that helps preserve the body.

Most people in the United States who die have a funeral. A **funeral** is a ceremony in which family and friends pay respect to a person who has died. In a traditional funeral, a person's body may be on display in an open casket or kept in a closed casket. The funeral service may include music, religious observances, and a eulogy. A **eulogy** is a speech given in which the deceased is praised. Funeral services may take place in a chapel, a funeral home, or other setting.

A funeral allows the living to pay respects to the person who has died as well as to the family.

The body may be buried in the ground or, in some cases, be placed aboveground in a mausoleum. A **mausoleum** is a building with a compartment for the deceased. In a mausoleum, the deceased can be placed alone or alongside other family members who have died. Each space in a mausoleum has a place for an inscribed plaque.

Some families choose cremation rather than burial.

Some people choose to be cremated after death. **Cremation** is the complete reduction of the deceased's body to ashes by intense heat. In cremation, the deceased's body is placed in a special container and placed in a crematory. A **crematory** (or crematori-um) is the place in which a person's body is cremated. After cremation, the ashes of the deceased may be scattered or deposited in an urn. The urn may be buried or placed in a columbarium. A **columbarium** is a compartment in a special building that holds the ashes of the deceased. Services generally are held where the ashes are to reside or be scattered. It should be noted that cremation is discouraged by many faiths.

Sometimes, a memorial service is held instead of an actual funeral. A memorial service for the deceased may be held at a house of worship or other location. The body of the deceased is not present. The body may have already been buried, cremated, or lost, such as in a plane crash.

Memorial services can be held when the body of the dead person is not present.

11:11 Arrangements Before Death

Besides funeral arrangements, there are matters that must be handled by family members of the deceased. One major issue often centers around the distribution of valuables and other possessions of the person who died. It is important for everyone to have a written will. A **will** is a legal document that describes how a person's possessions are to be distributed. A will may also include directions for the care of surviving family members.

A will is a legal document.

Advice from a lawyer can be helpful in drawing up a will. If a person dies without a will, the courts will decide how possessions are to be divided. Sometimes the survivors of the deceased are not happy with the court's recommendations, even if the possessions are divided equally.

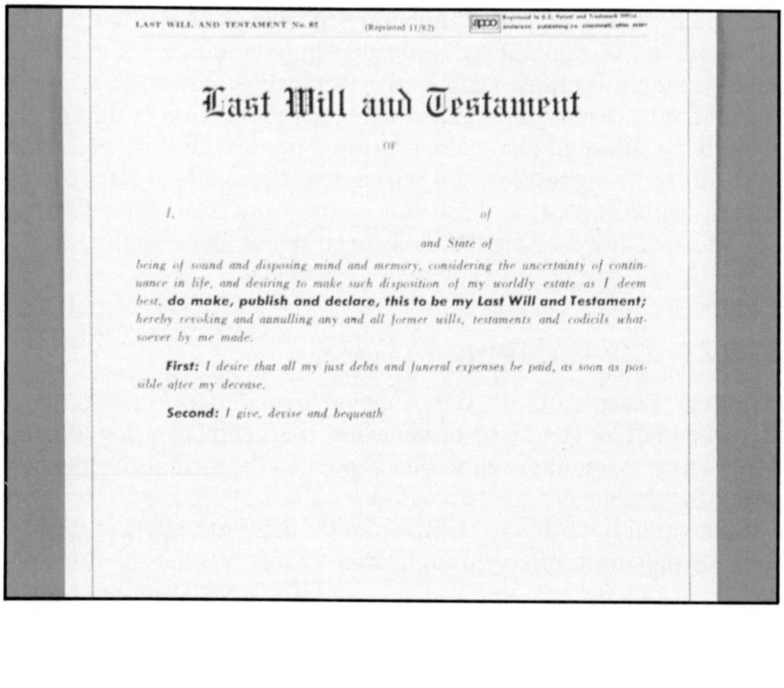

LAST WILL AND TESTAMENT No. 82 (Reprinted 11/82)

Last Will and Testament

OF

I, *of*

and State of

being of sound and disposing mind and memory, considering the uncertainty of continuance in life, and desiring to make such disposition of my worldly estate as I deem best, **do make, publish and declare, this to be my Last Will and Testament;** *hereby revoking and annulling any and all former wills, testaments and codicils whatsoever by me made.*

First: *I desire that all my just debts and funeral expenses be paid, as soon as possible after my decease.*

Second: *I give, devise and bequeath*

FIGURE 11–13. Standard forms are available for making out a will. Many people write their own statement about the distribution of their possessions.

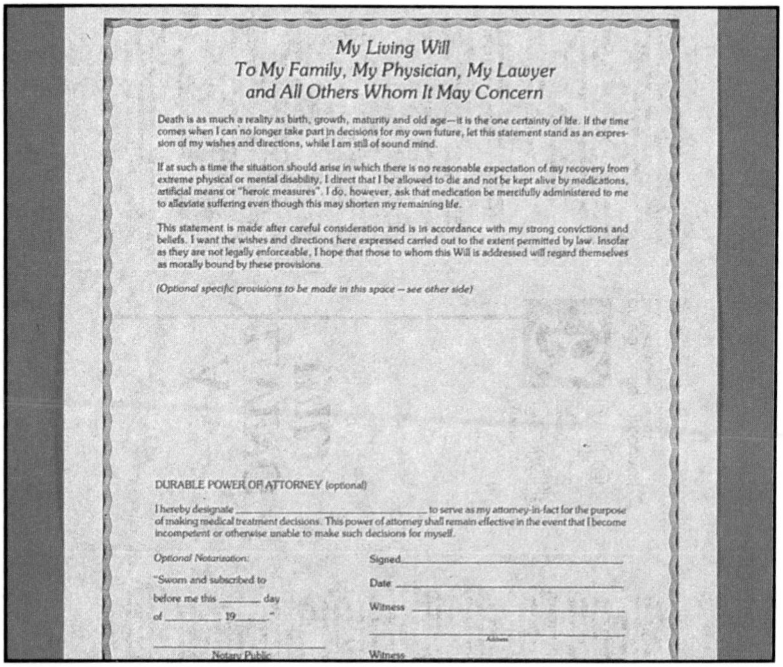

FIGURE 11–14. Living wills are statements about the person, not possessions.

My Living Will
To My Family, My Physician, My Lawyer
and All Others Whom It May Concern

Death is as much a reality as birth, growth, maturity and old age—it is the one certainty of life. If the time comes when I can no longer take part in decisions for my own future, let this statement stand as an expression of my wishes and directions, while I am still of sound mind.

If at such a time the situation should arise in which there is no reasonable expectation of my recovery from extreme physical or mental disability, I direct that I be allowed to die and not be kept alive by medications, artificial means or "heroic measures". I do, however, ask that medication be mercifully administered to me to alleviate suffering even though this may shorten my remaining life.

This statement is made after careful consideration and is in accordance with my strong convictions and beliefs. I want the wishes and directions here expressed carried out to the extent permitted by law. Insofar as they are not legally enforceable, I hope that those to whom this Will is addressed will regard themselves as morally bound by these provisions.

(Optional specific provisions to be made in this space — see other side)

DURABLE POWER OF ATTORNEY (optional)

I hereby designate _____ to serve as my attorney-in-fact for the purpose of making medical treatment decisions. This power of attorney shall remain effective in the event that I become incompetent or otherwise unable to make such decisions for myself.

Optional Notarization: Signed _____
"Sworn and subscribed to   Date _____
before me this _____ day   Witness _____
of _____ 19 ____ "   _____
Notary Public   Witness

Another kind of will that has received much attention recently is a Living Will. A **Living Will** is a written document of a preference for medical treatment in the event of severe illness or injury. The Living Will may include information that requests the withholding or withdrawing of life-support equipment or treatment if there is no hope of recovery. The Living Will removes the responsibility about decisions related to death from family and physicians. People who think they may want a Living Will should discuss it with family members. Family members need to be aware of and agree to follow the Living Will. A Living Will must be signed by two witnesses. Although not all courts accept a Living Will as legally binding, some states are passing laws to recognize Living Wills as legal documents.

Some states are passing laws that recognize Living Wills as legal documents.

11:12 The Grieving Process

When someone close dies, people experience bereavement. **Bereavement** is the state of suffering the death of a loved one. **Grief** is the open expression of sorrow. It is a normal reaction to bereavement.

There are physical and mental symptoms that may accompany grief. A person may go through three stages of grief. In the first

There are three stages of grief.

stage, a person will feel shock, denial, and disbelief at the loss of someone close. A feeling of numbness and crying may last for several days. In the second stage of grief, the person may long to see the deceased. Numerous memories will be recalled. Depression, sleeplessness, and sadness are common during this stage, which may last for many months after the death. The third stage of grief is acceptance. Survivors of the deceased often reach this stage within a year. Hopefully, a person can look back to the deceased and feel less pain about the loss. Survivors learn to live with their loss. As with the stages of dying, not everyone passes through all the stages of grief.

If you have lost a close family member or friend, you may experience behavioral changes. You may eat or sleep poorly. To help cope during this period, it is important for you to express your concerns to a family member or friend. Speaking with a trained adult, such as a school counselor, may help you adjust during this difficult period. Talk about the deceased and the good times you shared. Do not be afraid to show emotion. Continue to engage in your daily routine. Channel your grief into healthful and helpful activities.

There are sources for help for a grieving person.

Suppose you know a person who is grieving the loss of someone close. What can you do to help this person? Here are some suggestions.

Communicate—Do not avoid a grieving person. This person needs expressions of friendship. Saying, "I'm here if you need me" helps communicate your concern.

There are several ways to help a grieving person.

Be sincere—Show you care. It may mean giving the grieving person a hug or sharing another form of comforting. Crying is a healthful way to release feelings of grief. Avoid saying comments such as "Don't cry. You'll get over it."

Help the grieving person adjust—Offer to help with schoolwork. Encourage the person to continue in normal activities.

Show you care—You can show you care about a grieving person by sending a card with a meaningful note. You can invite the grieving person to share activities with you and your family.

It is important to show concern to a grieving person.

 Review and Reflect

7. How do funerals serve to help the living?
8. Why might some people avoid a grieving person?
9. What can you do to show you care about a grieving person?

Health
ADVANCES

Today, more and more people are choosing to donate all or parts of their bodies to medical science. The body or its parts can be used for research or for organ transplants. People choose this option because they believe they will help others lead more healthful lives. Hearts, livers, lungs, and kidneys are only some of the organs that are being transplanted regularly to increase life expectancy.

11:13   Organ Transplants

In 1967, the first heart transplant was performed. However, within several years, the number of surgeons performing this operation decreased. This decrease occurred because 80 percent of heart transplant patients were dying within one year after surgery. They died because they were given huge doses of drugs to suppress the immune system so that the transplanted heart (a foreign body) could survive. Unfortunately, suppression of the immune system to prevent rejection of the heart also caused the body to be unable to fight disease-causing substances in the body. This resulted in heart transplant patients dying from infections that ordinarily would be prevented in people with normally functioning immune systems.

Today, the medical profession is working to combat this problem with a drug called cyclosporine. **Cyclosporine** is a fungal compound that blocks the production of white blood cells that fight organ rejection but not those that fight infection. According to some reports, patients treated with conventional drugs to suppress the immune system had a 50-50 chance of surviving the first year of a kidney transplant. With cyclosporine, there is more than an 80 percent chance of survival. The success rate for liver transplants has doubled since the use of this drug. However, the effects of cyclosporine are still being researched.

People interested in donating their body parts can carry a Uniform Donor Card. This card explains their wishes to their families and physicians. However, a person must be at least 18 years of age to donate body parts.

Some states have a space on the driver's license that indicates a person's willingness to become a donor in case of accidental

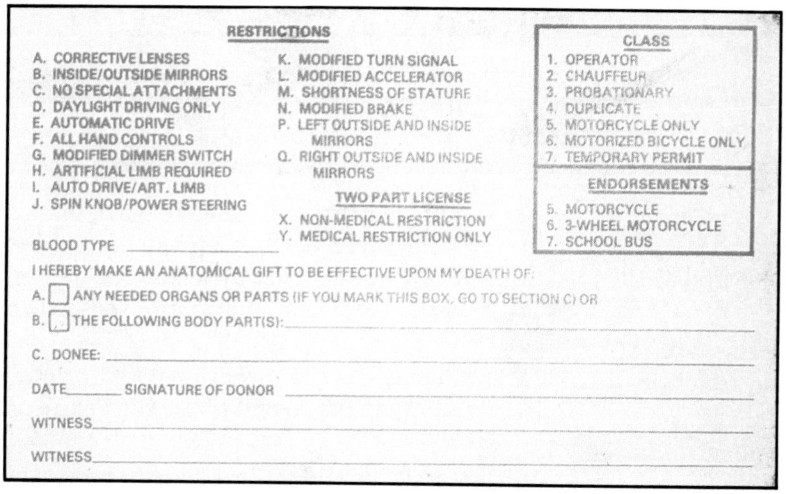

RESTRICTIONS		CLASS

RESTRICTIONS

A. CORRECTIVE LENSES
B. INSIDE/OUTSIDE MIRRORS
C. NO SPECIAL ATTACHMENTS
D. DAYLIGHT DRIVING ONLY
E. AUTOMATIC DRIVE
F. ALL HAND CONTROLS
G. MODIFIED DIMMER SWITCH
H. ARTIFICIAL LIMB REQUIRED
I. AUTO DRIVE/ART. LIMB
J. SPIN KNOB/POWER STEERING

K. MODIFIED TURN SIGNAL
L. MODIFIED ACCELERATOR
M. SHORTNESS OF STATURE
N. MODIFIED BRAKE
P. LEFT OUTSIDE AND INSIDE
   MIRRORS
Q. RIGHT OUTSIDE AND INSIDE
   MIRRORS

TWO PART LICENSE

X. NON-MEDICAL RESTRICTION
Y. MEDICAL RESTRICTION ONLY

CLASS

1. OPERATOR
2. CHAUFFEUR
3. PROBATIONARY
4. DUPLICATE
5. MOTORCYCLE ONLY
6. MOTORIZED BICYCLE ONLY
7. TEMPORARY PERMIT

ENDORSEMENTS

5. MOTORCYCLE
6. 3-WHEEL MOTORCYCLE
7. SCHOOL BUS

BLOOD TYPE _____

I HEREBY MAKE AN ANATOMICAL GIFT TO BE EFFECTIVE UPON MY DEATH OF:

A. ☐ ANY NEEDED ORGANS OR PARTS (IF YOU MARK THIS BOX, GO TO SECTION C) OR

B. ☐ THE FOLLOWING BODY PART(S): _____

C. DONEE: _____

DATE_____ SIGNATURE OF DONOR _____

WITNESS_____

WITNESS_____

FIGURE 11–15. Your signature will indicate that you are willing to donate your organs in the event that you die unexpectedly.

death. People who plan ahead what to do with their bodies in case of accidental death help others.

Several states have recently passed laws to encourage organ donation. These laws enable hospital personnel to ask families of patients who die for consent to use the patients' organs for transplants. Families are reminded that transplanted organs allow another person's life to be extended. It is expected that this new approach will increase organ donations.

Laws have been passed in several states to encourage organ donation.

Focus on
Life Management Skills

- Avoid stereotyping older people.
- Help older people by understanding that they have needs similar to your own.
- Plan activities with older persons.
- Plan to be healthy in old age by following healthful habits now: keep physically and intellectually active, eat healthful foods, learn new skills, and refrain from smoking.
- Understand the needs of dying people so that you can comfort them as well as learn how to cope with death.
- If you have contact with a dying person, listen to his or her needs, show that you care, and express your feelings.
- Help a grieving person by communicating your friendship, being sincere, and showing that you care.

Summary

1. Gerontologists have developed several theories about the causes of aging.   11:1

2. Physical changes occur in the normal process of aging.   11:2

3. Dementia can produce a deterioration of memory and other mental functions. 11:3

4. Ageism is a term that indicates discrimination against older people.   11:4

5. Ways to promote healthful aging include accepting leisure, eating healthful foods, learning new skills, and refraining from smoking.   11:5

6. Standards for determining death were established by a Harvard Medical School committee in 1968.   11:6

7. The five stages of dying are denial, anger, bargaining, depression, and acceptance. 11:7

8. A dying person has a need to participate, to be remembered, to feel valued, to have feelings known, to participate in decision making, and to maintain self-esteem. 11:8

9. Euthanasia is the intentional ending of life or allowing life to end for reasons of mercy. 11:9

10. Funerals provide the opportunity to pay respect for someone who has died and to comfort the grieving family.   11:10

11. Many people have a Living Will so that decisions about their death can be carried out according to their wishes.   11:11

12. To help a grieving person, it is important to communicate friendship, to be sincere, and to show you care.   11:12

13. Cyclosporine is a drug that helps prevent rejection of transplanted organs.   11:13

Vocabulary

Below is a list of vocabulary words used in this chapter. Use each word only once to complete the sentences. Do not write in this book.

Alzheimer's disease	gerontology
bereavement	mausoleum
cyclosporine	terminal illness
eulogy	thanatologist
euthanasia	will

1. A person with a(n) ____ has a condition that is not curable and will result in death.

2. Removing a person from a life-support machine can be a form of ____.

3. A legal document that describes how a person's possessions are to be divided is called a(n) ____.

4. The study of aging is called ____.

5. A building in which there are compartments for the deceased is a(n) ____.

6. A person with ____ may suffer from a loss of memory.

7. A(n) ____ is a speech given in memory of the deceased.

8. A drug that helps a person survive an organ transplant is ____.

9. A(n) ____ is a scientist who is concerned with the study of death.

10. The state of suffering the death of a loved one is called ____.

Review

1. Describe two theories about the beginning of aging.
2. What is one way to account for the fact that older people have more chronic illnesses than younger people?
3. Describe the characteristics related to multi-infarct dementia.
4. Identify three myths related to aging.
5. Identify healthful behaviors you can follow now that will promote healthful aging.
6. List the four criteria for determining death as established by a Harvard Medical School committee.
7. List and give a characteristic of each stage of dying.
8. What are three needs of a dying person?
9. Describe the unique features of a hospice.
10. Explain why euthanasia is a controversial topic.

Application

1. Why is the average life expectancy of Americans increasing?
2. What can you do to help an older person take medicines correctly?
3. How can you determine the needs of an older person?
4. What is the relationship between following healthful habits now and as you age?

Individual Research

1. Most states are passing laws favoring Living Wills. Write a report about why a Living Will is becoming more acceptable.
2. Use your school or public library to do research about cultural perspectives and death.
3. Read a book about death and funerals and write a list of important facts one should know about funeral arrangements.
4. Many legislators are interested in changing state laws about euthanasia. Write a report about some of the issues concerning euthanasia.

Readings

Alzheimer's Disease and Related Disorders Association, *Understanding Alzheimer's Disease.* New York, NY: Charles Scribner's and Sons, 1985.

Kübler-Ross, Elisabeth, *On Children and Death.* New York, NY: Macmillan Publishing Co., Inc., 1983.

Nutrition

NUTRITION

Imagine that you are at a picnic standing in front of a long table filled with food. The choice is yours! What kinds of foods will you choose? How much of these foods will you take?

Your health is greatly affected by what you eat. In this unit, you will study proper nutrition. You will study ways to maintain your ideal weight and prevent diseases. You will also learn how to shop to get the best nutritional value for your money.

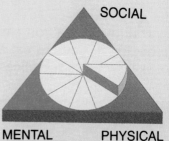

SOCIAL

MENTAL PHYSICAL

227

All the foods you eat have an effect on your health. Do you choose healthful foods to eat each day? Your choices affect your energy level and even your appearance.

Healthful Eating

OBJECTIVES: You will be able to
- **identify the nutrients needed for optimum health.**
- **plan a healthful diet based on the seven diet goals.**
- **make changes in your diet to reduce your risk of cancer.**

The nutrition component of the Behavior Wheel examines diet and the effects of diet on health, development, and performance. The popular saying, "You are what you eat" is verified by medical research. Diet, or the kinds of foods you regularly eat, has a holistic effect on your health. A healthful diet helps you perform well in school. It provides the energy you need for your favorite sports activities. A healthful diet is essential for normal growth and development, normal function of body organs and systems, repair of body tissue, and resistance to infection and disease.

Your diet has a holistic effect upon your health.

NUTRITION

You make many daily choices about eating. Will you eat a snack after school? What will your snack be? Will you eat before going to bed at night? Your choices play a part in how you function physically, mentally, and socially. To make wise decisions, you need to know about nutrition, diet, and nutrients.

12:1 The Importance of Nutrients

Nutrition is the relationship of the food you eat to your health and well-being. Nutrition involves the study of foods and the major nutrients. A healthful diet gives you energy to enjoy your favorite activities. It enables you to grow and develop and have a healthful appearance. A healthful diet and regular exercise help you maintain your ideal weight. Your physical health improves and you feel good about yourself.

A healthful diet reduces your chances of having many diseases.

A healthful diet promotes optimum health for your future. You can help prevent premature disease by being careful about your diet today. According to government studies, diet is linked to six of the ten leading causes of death: heart disease, stroke, atherosclerosis, cancer, cirrhosis of the liver, and diabetes. A healthful diet means good nutrition.

12:2   Nutrients in Foods

You need certain amounts of nutrients.

Suppose you could choose between a candy bar, a donut, or a carrot for a snack. Which would be the best nutritional choice? Why? Each of these foods contains nutrients. Knowing that you need certain minimum amounts of nutrients is the first step in making wise decisions about food. You also need to know which nutrients and how much of each are in foods. You will learn about nutrients and healthful eating habits in this chapter.

Nutrients include proteins, carbohydrates, fats, vitamins, minerals, and water.

Nutrients are chemical substances in foods that furnish body fuel for energy, provide materials needed for bulding and maintenance of tissues, and supply substances that function in the regulation of body processes. Each day you need a combination of fifty nutrients for good health. There are six main kinds of nutrients in foods. These are proteins, carbohydrates, fats, vitamins, minerals, and water.

FIGURE 12–1. A cheeseburger contains about 500 Calories. It would supply the average adult's daily requirement for protein and vitamin A, plus about one-third of the recommended amounts of phosphorus and calcium.

What amounts of each of these nutrients should you consume? A group of nutritionists and scientists (on behalf of the United States government) lists a Recommended Dietary Allowance (U.S. RDA). This list suggests daily amounts of nutrients that should be included for a healthful diet. These are suggested amounts and not minimum requirements. These recommendations are for healthy people; having an illness may change nutritional needs. This list is revised every four to six years.

The U.S. RDA list suggests daily amounts of nutrients.

12:3   Proteins

Proteins are chemical substances that are essential for the growth, development, and repair of all body tissues. Proteins are major components of all living cells. They are a major source of building material for muscles, blood, hair, skin, nails, and internal organs. Some hormones are proteins that control growth, sexual development, and metabolism. Enzymes and antibodies are also proteins. Proteins help regulate the body's fluid balance. When the diet does not contain enough protein, growth stops and muscles weaken.

Proteins are needed for growth, development, and repair of body tissues.

Proteins are made of small units or building blocks called **amino acids.** Your body needs twenty-two amino acids. Fourteen of these amino acids can be produced in your body. The other eight are called **essential amino acids** and must be obtained from the foods you eat. The proteins in foods of animal origin are known as complete proteins. **Complete proteins** contain all eight of the essential amino acids. Examples of animal-origin foods containing complete proteins are meat, cheese, eggs, milk, fish, and poultry. The proteins in foods of vegetable origin are known as incomplete proteins. **Incomplete proteins** lack one or more essential amino acids. Examples of vegetable-origin foods containing incomplete proteins are nuts, seeds, legumes, breads, and cereals.

Proteins are present in foods of animal and vegetable origin.

To meet daily requirements, the eight essential amino acids must be eaten together. **Complementary proteins** are proteins that are combined to provide the eight essential amino acids. Proteins of vegetable origin can be made complete by adding a small amount of animal protein. Certain combinations of plant proteins can be eaten at the same time to obtain the eight essential amino acids. If you are a vegetarian, you may want to eat complementary protein combinations. You may also select complementary protein combinations if you want to reduce your intake of animal fat. In addition, your family may begin to plan using complementary proteins to reduce food costs. Examples of complementary protein combinations are shown in Table 12–1.

The eight essential amino acids should be eaten together.

Table 12–1   Some Examples of Complementary Protein Combinations

PLANT–ANIMAL COMBINATIONS		
1. macaroni and cheese	macaroni	milk and cheese
	BREAD AND CEREALS	+ MILK AND MILK PRODUCTS
2. bran flakes and milk	bran flakes	milk
	BREAD AND CEREALS	+ MILK AND MILK PRODUCTS
3. split pea soup and	dried peas (legumes)	milk
a glass of milk	MEAT AND ALTERNATIVES	+ MILK AND MILK PRODUCTS
PLANT–PLANT COMBINATIONS		
4. peanut butter sandwich	peanut butter	bread
	MEAT AND ALTERNATIVES	+ BREAD AND CEREALS
5. baked beans and bread	dried beans (legumes)	bread
	MEAT AND ALTERNATIVES	+ BREAD AND CEREALS
6. rice-bean casserole	dried beans (legumes)	rice
	MEAT AND ALTERNATIVES	+ BREAD AND CEREALS

A protein-deficient diet affects growth and development.

A protein-deficient diet may affect you in several ways. Growth and tissue development of the hair, nails, and skin will be affected. Muscle tone may be lacking. During childhood, protein deficiency may stunt growth and retard mental development. During adulthood, protein deficiency may result in fatigue and mental depression. It may be accompanied by lowered resistance to infection and slower recovery from diseases and wounds.

12:4   Carbohydrates

Carbohydrates are chemical substances that are the main source of energy for your body. There are two main types of carbohydrates—starches and sugars. Because of their chemical structures, starches are called complex carbohydrates. For the same reason, sugars are called simple carbohydrates.

Starches and sugars are carbohydrates.

Complex carbohydrates in plant sources consist of starch and cellulose. Starch is essential in your diet as a source of energy. Grains and vegetables, such as potatoes, are main sources of starch. Cellulose cannot be digested by humans, but it is also essential. Cellulose is fiber that provides the bulk necessary to exercise the muscles of the digestive tract.

Sugars are found naturally in fruits, honey, milk, sugarcane, and sugar beets. A diet that includes a variety of plant material will provide both simple and complex carbohydrates. Simple carbohydrates are also called simple sugars.

Simple sugars rapidly enter the bloodstream and provide quick energy. Many fruits contain natural sugars of this type. Processed sugar is refined sugar or table sugar. Many foods that you eat are made with processed sugar—cookies, candy, cakes, and pies. Other foods that you purchase contain processed sugars—ketchup, spaghetti sauce, and sugar-coated cereal. Later in this chapter, you will learn that a diet high in sugar may be harmful to your health.

Carbohydrates are changed to a simple sugar called glucose in the process of digestion. Some glucose is transported to body cells by the blood. Glucose is the body's prime source of energy. If there is an excess of glucose, the liver and muscles are able to convert glucose into a storage form of starch called glycogen. Glycogen can be converted back to glucose in the body when blood glucose is low.

Carbohydrates are converted to glucose, the body's main source of energy.

FIGURE 12–2. A balanced diet should include both complex and simple carbohydrates.

12:5   Fats

Fats are chemical substances that provide additional energy and help your body store vitamins A, D, E, and K. Fats help the body absorb Vitamin D, which is needed for calcium to be used in the formation of bones, teeth, and other tissue. Fats are stored as fat tissue. They surround and cushion the internal organs, such as the liver, heart, and kidneys.

There are two kinds of fats. **Saturated fats** are fats from foods of animal origin and are usually in solid form at room temperature. Steak, pork, liver, and ham contain saturated fats. Dairy products such as whole milk, cream, cheese, and butter also contain saturated fats.

Saturated fats are the starting materials for the body's production of cholesterol. **Cholesterol** is a substance that is normally found in the brain, nerves, and skin. Even if there is no cholesterol in the diet, some is manufactured by the liver. A certain amount of cholesterol is needed for good health. However, it is believed that too much cholesterol may be harmful to health. The reasons will be explained later in this chapter.

Fats may be either saturated or unsaturated.

Unsaturated fats are obtained from foods of vegetable, nut, or seed origin and are usually liquid at room temperature. Olive oil, corn oil, peanut oil, and sesame oil are fats that are unsaturated. Unsaturated fats are also found in animals that fly or swim. Fish, chicken, duck, and turkey are foods that contain unsaturated fats. Later in this chapter, you will learn the importance of substituting unsaturated fats for saturated fats.

12:6   Vitamins

Vitamins are substances in foods that help chemical reactions take place in the body. Vitamins are divided into two types: water-soluble vitamins and fat-soluble vitamins. **Water-soluble vitamins** are easily dissolved and cannot be stored in the body. When there is an excess, these vitamins are excreted in the urine. Vitamin B complex and vitamin C are water-soluble vitamins. Your body needs a fresh supply of these vitamins each day. Water-soluble vitamins are measured in milligrams.

Vitamins are either water-soluble or fat-soluble.

Fat-soluble vitamins are vitamins that can be stored in the body. The liver is the main storage organ for the fat-soluble vitamins. Because your body stores fat-soluble vitamins, you do not need to consume large quantities. An excess of these vitamins is associated with headache, stomach upset, and fatigue. Fat-soluble vitamins are measured in International Units (I.U.).

The Vitamin Chart (Table 12–2) lists the U.S. RDA sources, functions, effects of a deficiency, and recent developments for

Table 12–2 Vitamin Chart

VITAMIN	U.S. RDA	SOURCES	FUNCTIONS	DEFICIENCY	NEW DEVELOPMENTS
A Retinol	Infants 1500 I.U. Children 2500 I.U. Adults 5000 I.U.	Carrots, sweet potatoes, yams, liver, deep yellow vegetables, green leafy vegetables	Aids in formation of skin and mucous membranes that line body cavities Needed for good night vision Aids in bone formation	Rough skin and drying of mucous membranes Night blindness Bone growth failure	There is increasing evidence that greater consumption of A may decrease cancers of the lung, breast, bladder, and skin.
B_1 Thiamin	Infants 0.5 mg Children 0.7 mg Adults 1.5 mg	Lean pork, nuts, fortified cereal, peas, dried beans, enriched rice or pasta	Aids the body's use of carbohydrates Necessary for normal appetite and digestion Promotes healthful nervous system and heart	Muscle weakness Leg cramps and swelling Mental confusion, irritability, poor memory	A B_1 deficiency occurs with many alcohol-related nervous system disorders. B_1 has been a treatment for children with frequent fever and swollen glands that do not respond to usual medications.
B_2 Riboflavin	Infants 0.6 mg Children 0.8 mg Adults 1.7 mg	Liver, whole milk, yogurt, cottage cheese, eggs	Aids in protein, fat, and carbohydrate metabolism Aids energy production in cells Promotes healthy skin and eyes	Visual disturbances Skin problems Cracks at the corners of the mouth Sore, red tongue	A study at Cornell University showed that women who exercise vigorously need twice the B_2. This may be due to the role B_2 plays in the production of energy.
B_3 Niacin	Infants 8 mg Children 9 mg Adults 20 mg	Liver, meat, poultry, fish, peanuts, fortified cereal products	Aids in normal digestion and appetite Aids in the body's use of carbohydrates Promotes healthy nervous system and skin	Skin disorders Diarrhea	Niacin has been used to lower high cholesterol levels in persons with a disorder that does not respond to dietary change.
B_6	Infants 0.4 mg Children 0.7 mg Adults 2 mg	Whole grain cereals, red meats, liver, legumes	Aids in protein, fat, and carbohydrate metabolism Aids in formation of blood cells	Anemia Nervous disturbances Skin disorders Kidney stone formation	B_6 has been used to relieve premenstrual depression and acne. B_6 is given to persons who repeatedly form kidney stones.
F Folic Acid	Infants 0.1 mg Children 0.2 mg Adults 0.4 mg	Whole grain bread, lean beef, leafy green vegetables, broccoli	Aids in blood formation Aids with enzyme function	Anemia	Incomplete British studies show 4 milligrams of F during pregnancy may prevent spina bifida, a congenital defect.
C Ascorbic Acid	Infants 35 mg Children 40 mg Adults 60 mg	Broccoli, oranges, grapefruit, strawberries, tomatoes	Forms a cement that holds cells together Strengthens blood vessels Helps resist infection Aids in the body's use of iron	Scurvy Frequent bruising Loose teeth Gum disease	Vitamin C may reduce the severity of the common cold. Vitamin C may help lower blood cholesterol. Vitamin C may lower risk of cancer of the stomach and esophagus. Vitamin C may prevent gum disease.
D Calciferol	Infants 400 I.U. Children 400 I.U. Adults 400 I.U.	Fortified dairy products, fish liver oils, egg yolk, salmon, tuna, exposure to sunlight	Aids use of calcium and phosphorus for healthy bones and teeth	Rickets—bowed legs, poor teeth Soft bones in adults	Vitamin D helps prevent osteoporosis or bone thinning. The use of vitamin D may aid in the body's production of insulin (University of California).
E Tocopherols	Infants 5 I.U. Children 10 I.U. Adults 12 I.U.	Corn oil, vegetable oil, egg yolks, wheat germ, green leafy vegetables	Aids in preventing oxygen from destroying vitamin A and tissue fats	Breakdown of red blood cells	A diet high in vitamin E may reduce bacterial and viral infections and tumor growths (Purdue University). Vitamin E relieves 70 percent of the cases of cystic mastitis or lumps in the breast.

several vitamins. Study the chart carefully, and make a plan to eat the foods that supply the vitamins you need. Be careful to prepare fruits and vegetables in a way that does not destroy their vitamin content.

Some persons decide to take vitamin pills to supplement their diet. They may take a **megadose**, an unusually large amount of a vitamin, greater than the U.S. RDA. Before taking a vitamin megadose, discuss the benefits or effects with a nutritionist and/or your family physician. Taking a megadose of some vitamins may produce harmful side effects. Taking vitamin pills is never a substitute for eating foods that contain those vitamins. Remember, one function of vitamins is to help you use the nutrients you ingest.

A vitamin megadose should be taken only with the advice of a nutritionist or physician.

12:7 Minerals

Five percent of your body weight is made up of minerals. **Minerals** are nutrients that regulate many of the chemical reactions in your body. The seven minerals found in the largest amounts are calcium, chlorine, magnesium, phosphorus, potassium, sodium, and sulfur. The Mineral Chart (Table 12–3) lists facts, U.S. RDA, sources, functions, and effects of a deficiency for these seven minerals plus iodine, iron, and zinc. Some food sources, such as leafy green vegetables, are excellent sources of both vitamins and the minerals calcium and iron.

Seven minerals direct many of the chemical reactions in the body.

FIGURE 12-3. Most nutrition authorities agree that the average person can get enough of the essential minerals by eating a variety of foods. Examples of foods rich in minerals are pictured here.

Table 12-3 Mineral Chart

MINERAL	FACTS	U.S. RDA FOR ADULTS	SOURCES	FUNCTIONS	EFFECTS OF DEFICIENCY
Calcium	Calcium is the most abundant mineral in the body. Calcium works with phosphorus to maintain healthy bones and teeth. Calcium works with magnesium for a healthy heart. To be absorbed, the body also needs vitamin D.	800–1200 mg	Milk, milk products, cheese, sardines, salmon, peanuts, dried beans	Maintains strong bones and teeth Aids regular heartbeat Aids in iron metabolism Aids nervous system	Rickets—bowed legs Osteoporosis—thin bones
Chlorine	Chlorine helps the liver function in waste removal.	No U.S. RDA	Table salt, kelp, olives	May keep you limber May aid in digestion	Loss of teeth and hair
Iodine	Two-thirds of the body's iodine is in the thyroid gland.	80–150 mg	Seafood, iodized table salt, vegetables grown in iron-rich soil, kelp	Aids in the manufacture of thyroid hormone Gives you energy Improves mental alertness Promotes growth Promotes healthy teeth, hair, skin, nails	Goiter Hypothyroidism
Iron	Iron is necessary for the body's use of the B vitamins. Women lose twice as much iron as men each month. Calcium and iron are two major deficiencies in women's diet.	10–18 mg	Liver, kidney, pork, clams, red meat, egg yolk, oatmeal	Needed to form red blood cells Prevents fatigue Aids growth Promotes resistance to disease	Anemia—too few red blood cells Fatigue
Magnesium	Magnesium helps relieve the effects of stress. Alcoholics usually lack this mineral. Magnesium is needed to convert blood sugar to energy.	300–400 mg	Grapefruit, lemons, nuts, seeds, apples, dark green vegetables	May help fight depression May aid in preventing heart attacks Prevents calcium deposits and gallstones Promotes healthy teeth	Nervousness Depression Unable to sleep Sensitive to noise
Phosphorus	Phosphorus is involved in all physiological chemical reactions. This mineral aids in maintaining regular heart rate. This mineral is present in all cells.	800–1200 mg	Eggs, nuts, fish, poultry, meat, whole grains	Promotes growth and repair of cells Aids in starch metabolism Promotes healthy gums and teeth	Rickets
Potassium	Potassium aids in regulating body's water balance and heartbeat. Physical and mental stress can cause a deficiency. Diarrhea and water pills cause a deficiency.	No U.S. RDA	Orange juice, citrus fruits, green leafy vegetables, bananas	Aids in reducing blood pressure Sends oxygen to brain to aid in clear thinking Aids in elimination of wastes from the body	Low blood sugar Edema—retaining water
Sodium	High intake is associated with high blood pressure. High intake causes potassium deficiency.	No U.S. RDA	Salt, shellfish, kidney, bacon, carrots, beets	Prevents heat prostration Aids in proper nerve and muscle function	Difficulty in digestion of carbohydrates
Sulfur	Sulfur creams have been used to treat skin problems.	No U.S. RDA	Fish, eggs, cabbage, lean beef	Fights bacterial infections Needed for healthy hair, skin, nails Works with B vitamins in metabolism	Not known
Zinc	Most zinc in foods is lost in processing. Recent studies show its usefulness in treating brain disorders.	15 mg	Lamb chops, wheat germ, round steak, eggs, pork loin	Promotes growth and mental alertness Aids in decrease of cholesterol deposits	Hardening of the arteries

FIGURE 12–4. Foods containing water are a main source of the large quantity of water needed each day by the human body. Lettuce is about 96 percent water, eggs about 75 percent, and white bread about 30 percent.

Your body needs two liters of water each day.

12:8   Water

Although water is not a food, it is considered a nutrient. Water makes up about 60 percent of your body mass and is involved in all body processes. As a basic part of blood, water carries nutrients to all body cells and waste products to the kidneys. Water is needed for each of the chemical reactions in the digestive process. Your body temperature is affected by water.

Water is excreted from the body as perspiration and urine. Your body needs two liters of water each day. You obtain this amount by drinking water and other liquids and from the water in foods. Your body's water balance is maintained with the intake of water and the output of urine and perspiration.

 Review and Reflect

1. What is the difference between a complete protein and an incomplete protein?
2. How can a vegetarian obtain all the essential amino acids that are needed for a healthful diet?
3. What is healthful about fruits that contain cellulose?
4. Why do you need to have a source of vitamin C each day?
5. How can taking a vitamin megadose of fat-soluble vitamins be harmful?
6. Why is it important to have a source of calcium in your daily diet?

PLANNING A HEALTHFUL DIET

It is important to use what you have learned about nutrients to plan a healthful diet. As you plan your diet, there are guidelines you can follow to obtain the nutrients you need and to reduce your likelihood of disease. Practicing a good plan for healthful eating is a wellness behavior.

12:9 Seven Diet Goals

To assist you in planning a healthful diet, the United States Department of Agriculture and the Department of Health and Human Services have prepared a list of seven diet goals for Americans. Examine each of the seven goals, make a plan to reach each goal, and use self-discipline to stick to your plan.

Plan to reach the seven diet goals to reduce your likelihood of premature disease.

Goal 1: Eat a Variety of Foods You need about 50 different nutrients each day to stay healthy. Foods that contain the same nutrients belong to a **food group.** There are four healthful food groups: milk, meat, fruit–vegetable, and grain. A fifth group, the combination group, contains ingredients from more than one food group and supplies the same nutrients as the foods they contain. Another group, the others food group, contains foods that are high in Calories and low in nutrients. A **Calorie** is a measure of the energy value of foods. Usually high-calorie foods contain processed sugars and saturated fats.

The healthful food groups are the milk, fruit, vegetable, grain, and combination groups.

The food groups and the number of servings you need each day from each of the four healthful food groups are shown in Table 12–4. A **balanced diet** is a daily diet that contains the correct number of servings from the four healthful food groups and the combination food group (Table 12–4).

Goal 2: Maintain Your Desirable (Ideal) Weight Your **ideal weight** is the weight and body composition that is recommended for your age, sex, height, and body build. Your body is made of two kinds of tissue—fat and lean. The percentage of fat tissue and lean tissue is known as body composition. When you maintain your ideal weight, your body is more likely to be lean, and you are more likely to have firm muscle mass. Consequently, you have a low percentage of body fat. Most persons now believe that it is more important to know your percentage of body fat than it is to know how much you weigh. Percentage of body fat will be discussed in detail in Chapter 15. Remember, ideal weight includes not only your weight but what proportion of your weight

The percentage of body fat is a better indication of health than actual weight.

Table 12–4 Food Groups and Suggested Servings for Teenagers

MILK	MEAT	FRUIT-VEGETABLE	GRAIN	COMBINATION
Supplies these key nutrients: ■ calcium ■ riboflavin (vitamin B$_2$) ■ protein for strong bones and teeth, healthy skin and good vision	Supplies these key nutrients: ■ protein ■ niacin ■ iron ■ thiamin (vitamin B$_1$) for muscle, bone, and blood cells and healthy skin and nerves	Supplies these key nutrients: ■ vitamin A ■ vitamin C for night vision and to help resist infections and heal wounds	Supplies these key nutrients: ■ carbohydrate ■ thiamin (vitamin B$_1$) ■ iron ■ niacin for energy and a healthy nervous system	Combination foods contain ingredients from more than one food group, and supply the same nutrients as the foods they contain.
A serving is: 1 cup Milk 1 cup Yogurt 1½ oz Cheese (1½ slices) 1 cup Pudding 2 cups Cottage cheese 1¾ cups Ice cream	A serving is: 2 oz Cooked, lean meat, fish, poultry 2 Eggs 2 oz Cheese 1 cup Dried peas or beans 4 tbsp Peanut butter	A serving is: ½ cup Juice ½ cup Cooked vegetable or fruit 1 cup Raw vegetable or fruit Medium Apple, banana, or orange ½ Grapefruit ¼ Cantaloupe	A serving is: 1 slice Bread 1 cup Ready-to-eat-cereal ½ cup Cooked cereal ½ cup Pasta ½ cup Rice ½ cup Grits	A serving is: 1 cup Soup 1 cup Pasta dish (macaroni and cheese, lasagna)** 1 cup Main course (stew, chili, casseroles) ¼ 14" Pizza (thin crust) 1 Taco, sandwich
Number of Servings 4	Number of Servings 2	Number of Servings 4	Number of Servings 4	These count as servings (or partial servings) from the food groups from which they are made.

is lean or fat tissue. When you maintain your ideal weight and have a low percentage of body fat, your statistical chances of a long, healthy life increase.

Over 40 million Americans have too much body fat. These persons are more likely to suffer from high blood pressure, diabetes, heart attack, and stroke. Consider the following. There is (1) a 13 percent increase in death rate for persons who have a high percentage of body fat and are 10 percent overweight, (2) a 25 percent increase for those who have a high percentage of body fat and are 20 percent overweight, and (3) a 40 percent increase for those who have a high percentage of body fat and are 30 percent overweight.

Too much body fat increases the likelihood of cardiovascular diseases and diabetes.

There are also immediate consequences for teens who have too much body fat. Having a high percentage of body fat will mean that you may not be involved in the activities that your friends are. You may not be involved in enough physical activity to improve your muscle tone and give you a healthful appearance. You may have low self-esteem. If you have too much body fat, you can reduce your percentage of body fat by selecting foods containing fewer Calories and by increasing your physical activity. Weight control will be discussed in Chapter 13.

Goal 3: Avoid Eating Too Much Fat, Saturated Fat, and Cholesterol Americans eat more meat per person, 100 pounds of beef per year, than do persons who live in any of the European countries. A heavy meat/fat diet is related to an increased incidence of breast, bowel, and colon cancers. A heavy meat/fat diet is high in Calories and may cause weight gain.

A diet high in saturated fats increases the likelihood of heart disease and cancer.

In an attempt to avoid the above problems, the amount of fat ingested should be reduced. In addition, the type of fat eaten should be carefully selected. In Section 12:5 of this chapter, you learned about saturated and unsaturated fats. The unsaturated fats come from foods of fish, bird, and plant origin. Unsaturated fats keep your blood cholesterol lower than do the saturated fats. Because of this fact, many researchers believe that a diet high in saturated fats contributes to heart disease.

Goal 4: Eat Foods With Adequate Starch and Fiber If you limit the amount of fat you eat, you will need to eat more carbohydrates to supply your body's need for energy. Increasing carbohydrates and reducing fats will help you maintain your ideal weight. The best way to increase carbohydrates is to eat more starch and fiber. Good sources of starch and fiber are whole grain breads and cereals, fruits and vegetables, beans, peas, and nuts. A report by the National Research Council of the National Academy of Sciences indicates that a high-fiber diet reduces the risk of colon and rectal cancers.

A high-fiber diet may reduce the risk of colon and rectal cancer.

FIGURE 12–5. Foods that supply adequate starch and fiber.

A high-sugar diet increases the likelihood of tooth decay and heart disease.

Too much sodium increases the incidence of heart disease, high blood pressure, and migraine headaches.

Goal 5: Avoid Too Much Sugar In Section 12:4 of this chapter, you learned about the different kinds of carbohydrates. To have a healthful diet, it is best to eat starches and avoid sugars. Too much sugar in the diet may cause tooth decay. A high sugar diet increases the fatty acid levels in the blood and increases the likelihood of heart disease. A plan to reduce sugar might include (1) avoiding soft drinks, candy, donuts, pies, and cakes, (2) eating more fresh fruits, and (3) reading food labels to become more aware of sugar content. Glucose, maltose, dextrose, lactose, and fructose are other types of sugar.

Goal 6: Avoid Too Much Sodium Most Americans consume six or more grams of sodium per day. Eating too much sodium is related to an increase in heart disease and high blood pressure. This is especially true for persons who have inherited a tendency for those diseases. There is also a relationship between sodium intake and having migraine headaches. Sodium increases blood pressure, which constricts blood vessels. A migraine headache results from constricted blood vessels in the head. You can limit your sodium intake to 5 grams (1 teaspoon) per day by (1) learning to enjoy the unsalted flavors of foods, (2) cooking with small amounts of added salt, (3) limiting intake of salty foods such as potato chips, salted pretzels, salted nuts, and popcorn, and (4) reading food labels carefully to determine the amounts and different sources of sodium in processed foods and snack items.

Goal 7: Avoid Alcohol Alcohol is high in Calories and low in nutrients. When someone drinks alcohol, vitamins in the body can be depleted. For example, persons who drink alcohol daily may not have enough vitamin B in their bodies. Vitamin B is needed for a healthful nervous system. Alcohol is a harmful drug that destroys brain cells and harms the liver, kidneys, heart, esophagus, stomach, and blood vessels. While some persons think that adults' drinking in moderation is not harmful, evidence proves the contrary. The best choice for optimum health is to avoid alcohol at any age.

Alcohol has no health benefits.

 ## Activity: **Planning Menus**

It is important to use the seven diet goals when planning daily food menus. Divide into groups of four. With your group, plan menus for a breakfast, lunch, and dinner. The menus should contain the correct number of servings from the healthful food groups and the combination group. Your menus should meet the seven diet goals. Be ready to explain why your group chose the foods on your menus. Share your menus with classmates.

12:10 Breakfast Choices

When you arise in the morning, usually it has been 12 to 14 hours since your last meal. Your body needs nutrients to supply energy for your day's activities. You need nutrients to feel

FIGURE 12–6. A healthful breakfast will provide a uniform level of energy during the morning.

mentally alert in school. Do you eat a healthful breakfast? Recent research indicates that 30 to 50 percent of Americans regularly skip breakfast. Of those who do eat breakfast, most do not select foods from the four healthful food groups and the combination group. A good breakfast would supply at least one-fourth of your daily nutrients and Calories.

A healthful breakfast is needed to provide a uniform level of energy throughout the morning. Foods that contain protein and starch provide a uniform level of energy. They are the best choices for breakfast. A healthful breakfast might also include a source of fiber. To follow diet goals, breakfast choices should be low in salt, fat, saturated fat, and cholesterol and contain servings from each of the healthful food groups.

12:11   Snacks and Convenience Foods

Snacks are foods and beverages that are consumed between meals. A nutritious snack is a food or beverage that belongs to one of the four healthful food groups or the combination group and follows the seven dietary goals. An apple is a healthful snack. It belongs to the fruit and vegetable group. An apple contains complex carbohydrates and naturally-occurring sugars. It is not high in Calories, saturated fat, or salt.

Some snacks are empty-calorie foods. An **empty-calorie food** lacks nutrients and is high in Calories. An empty-calorie food belongs to the others food group. These snacks are usually high in sugar, salt, and saturated fats. They may cause you to gain unnecessary weight. Some examples of these snacks are candy bars, cakes, soft drinks, and salted pretzels. These snacks are not healthful choices.

Fast foods are popular mass-produced foods that can be served quickly. Fast foods are sold at many popular restaurant chains. Some of the fast foods sold at restaurant chains are deep fried and heavily salted. Other fast foods, such as salads and yogurt, are low in fat, salt, and Calories. Fast food chains were asked to provide nutritional information about some of their foods. This information was included in the report by the Senate Select Committee on Nutrition and Human Needs. Table 12–5 shows a comparison of some popular fast foods. Consider their nutritional value when you choose to eat some of these foods.

Convenience foods are foods that are easily prepared at home. A TV dinner is an example of a convenience food. Some convenience foods are nutritious while the benefit of others is only the convenience. Many contain too much sodium, and most are very expensive.

Table 12–5   Nutrition in Fast Foods

ITEM	CALORIES	PROTEIN (g)	CARBOHYDRATES (g)	FATS (g)	SODIUM (mg)
McDonald's Big Mac	541	26	39	31	962
Burger King Whopper	606	29	51	32	909
Burger Chef Hamburger	258	11	24	13	393
Dairy Queen Cheese Dog	330	15	24	19	N.A.*
Taco Bell Taco	186	15	14	8	79
Pizza Hut Thin 'N Crispy Cheese Pizza (1/2 of 10-in. pie)	450	25	54	15	N.A.*
Pizza Hut Thick 'N Chewy Pepperoni Pizza (1/2 of 10-in. pie)	560	31	68	18	N.A.*
Arthur Treacher's Fish Sandwich	440	16	68	18	836
Burger King Whaler	486	18	64	46	735
McDonald's Filet-O-Fish	402	15	34	23	709
Long John Silver's Fish (2 pieces)	318	19	19	19	N.A.*
Kentucky Fried Chicken Original Recipe Dinner (3 pieces chicken)	830	52	56	46	2285
Kentucky Fried Chicken Extra Crispy Dinner (3 pieces chicken)	950	52	63	54	1915
McDonald's Egg McMuffin	352	18	26	20	914
Burger King French Fries	214	3	28	10	5
Arthur Treacher's Coleslaw	123	1	11	8	266
Dairy Queen Onion Rings	300	6	33	17	N.A.*
McDonald's Apple Pie	300	2	31	19	414
Burger King Vanilla Shake	332	11	50	11	159
McDonald's Chocolate Shake	364	11	60	9	329
Dairy Queen Banana Split	540	10	91	15	N.A.*

Data supplied by the companies to the Senate Select Committee on Nutrition and Human Needs. *N.A. = not available

Review and Reflect

7. How do you know if you are eating a balanced diet?
8. Why is someone who is overweight and who has a high percentage of body fat decreasing their projected life span?
9. What is the relationship between a high-fiber diet and the possible prevention of certain cancers?
10. How can you reduce the amount of sugar in your diet?
11. Why is it best to avoid drinking alcohol?
12. How do you know if your breakfast is healthful?
13. What is the difference between a healthful snack and an empty-calorie food?
14. How are fast food chains altering their menus to provide healthful alternatives for customers?

Health
ADVANCES

Extensive research is being done to evaluate and clarify the role of diet in the development of cancer. Currently, there is no proven cause-and-effect relationship. However, some things you eat may increase or decrease your chances of certain types of cancer.

12:12   Diet and Cancer

The American Cancer Society suggests that following certain guidelines for diet may prove helpful in avoiding cancer. You will notice that some of these guidelines are similar to the seven diet goals. Based on current evidence, you might lessen your chances of getting cancer by following these simple guidelines.*

The American Cancer Society has identified ways to reduce the risk of cancer.

Avoid obesity. Sensible eating habits and regular exercise will help you avoid excessive weight gain. Your physician can work with you to determine your best body weight since it depends on your present medical condition and body build and an appropriate diet to maintain this weight. If you are 40 percent overweight, your risk increases for colon, breast, and uterine cancers.

The intake of alcohol, fatty foods, smoked foods, salt-cured and nitrite-cured foods increases the risk of cancer.

Cut down on total fat intake. A diet high in fat may be a factor in the development of certain cancers like breast, colon, and prostate. If you avoid fatty foods, you will be able to control your body weight more easily.

Eat more high-fiber foods. Regular consumption of cereals, fresh fruits, and vegetables is recommended. Studies suggest that diets high in fiber may help to reduce the risk of colon cancer. Regardless, foods containing large amounts of fiber are a wholesome substitute for foods high in fat.

Including fiber foods, vitamins A and C, and cruciferous vegetables in your diet helps reduce the risk of cancer.

Include foods rich in vitamins A and C in your daily diet. Choose dark green and deep yellow fresh vegetables and fruits as sources of vitamin A, such as carrots, spinach, yams, peaches, and apricots. Good sources of vitamin C are oranges, grapefruit, strawberries, and green and red peppers. These foods may help lower the risk for cancers of the larynx, esophagus, and the lung.

Include cruciferous vegetables in your diet. Cruciferous vegetables include cabbage, broccoli, brussels sprouts, and cauliflow-
*The American Cancer Society, 1984

er, and may help reduce the risk of cancer. Research is in progress to determine the composition of these foods that may protect against cancer.

Eat limited amounts of salt-cured, smoked, and nitrite-cured foods. In areas of the world where salt-cured and smoked foods are eaten frequently, there is a greater incidence of cancer of the esophagus and stomach. The American food industry is developing new processes to avoid possible cancer-causing by-products.

Avoid alcohol. The heavy use of alcohol, especially when accompanied by cigarette smoking or chewing tobacco, increases the risk of cancers of the mouth, larynx, throat, esophagus, and stomach.

 Review and Reflect

15. What are some examples of cruciferous vegetables that may reduce the likelihood of cancer?
16. What types of cancers are related to alcohol consumption?

Focus on
Life Management Skills

- Eat a balanced daily diet that includes the correct number of servings from the four healthful food groups and from the combination group.
- Drink at least six to eight glasses of water each day.
- Maintain your ideal weight with a low percentage of body fat.
- Avoid eating too much fat, saturated fat, and cholesterol.
- Eat foods with adequate starch and fiber.
- Avoid eating or drinking foods and beverages that are high in sugar.
- Avoid too much sodium.
- Avoid consuming alcohol.
- Eat a healthful balanced breakfast.
- Select healthful snacks that contain nutrients.
- Reduce your risk of cancer by avoiding obesity, cutting down on total fat intake, eating more high-fiber foods, including foods rich in vitamins A and C, eating cruciferous vegetables, eating limited amounts of salt-cured, smoked, and nitrite-cured foods, and avoiding alcohol.

CHAPTER REVIEW 12

Summary

1. Nutrition is important to your health and well-being. **12:1**
2. There are six main kinds of nutrients in foods. **12:2**
3. Proteins are essential for growth and development, provide building material, are parts of some hormones and enzymes, and help regulate water balance. **12:3**
4. Carbohydrates are the main source of energy for your body. **12:4**
5. Fats provide energy, help your body store vitamins A, D, E, and K, help absorb vitamin D, and form tissue to protect the internal organs. **12:5**
6. Vitamins help other chemical reactions take place in the body. **12:6**
7. Minerals regulate many of the chemical activities in your body. **12:7**
8. Water is needed for all body processes, for digestion, for forming blood, for carrying nutrients to cells and waste to the kidneys, and for temperature regulation. **12:8**
9. The seven diet goals are eat a variety of foods, maintain your ideal weight, avoid eating too much fat, saturated fat, and cholesterol, eat foods with adequate starch and fiber, avoid too much sugar, avoid too much sodium, and avoid alcohol. **12:9**
10. A balanced breakfast provides a uniform level of energy all morning. **12:10**
11. The nutrient benefits of foods should be considered when choosing snacks, fast foods, and convenience foods. **12:11**
12. You might lower your chances of getting cancer by avoiding obesity, cutting down on total fat intake, eating more high-fiber foods, including foods rich in vitamins A and C in your daily diet, eating cruciferous vegetables, eating limited amounts of salt-cured, smoked and nitrite-cured foods, and avoiding alcohol. **12:12**

Vocabulary

Below is a list of vocabulary words used in this chapter. Use each word only once to complete the sentences. Do not write in this book.

cholesterol
complementary proteins
empty-calorie food
essential amino acids
fat-soluble vitamins
incomplete proteins
megadose
nutrition
saturated fats
water-soluble vitamins

1. There are eight _____ that must be obtained from the foods you eat.
2. Vitamins C and B complex are _____.
3. Macaroni with cheese is an example of a(n) _____.
4. When proteins lack one or more of the essential amino acids, they are _____.
5. Steak, whole milk, and cheese contain _____ that are solid at room temperature.
6. The liver is the main storage organ for _____, such as vitamin A.
7. A candy bar is a(n) _____.
8. Taking 400 percent of the U.S. RDA of a certain vitamin is a(n) _____.
9. You are studying _____ when you read about nutrients and their effects on your health.
10. A substance found in the brain, nerves, and skin is _____.

Review

1. What might happen to a child and to an adult if their diets are protein deficient?
2. How is eating cellulose healthful?
3. How do saturated fats differ from unsaturated fats?
4. Identify the functions of the following vitamins: retinol, thiamin, riboflavin, niacin, pyridoxine, folic acid, ascorbic acid, calciferol, and tocopherol.
5. What are the main functions of calcium, chlorine, iodine, iron, magnesium, phosphorus, potassium, sodium, sulfur, zinc?
6. Why is water considered a key nutrient?
7. What are the seven diet goals established by the United States Department of Agriculture and the Department of Health and Human Services?
8. Why do you need to eat a healthful, balanced breakfast each morning?
9. What is an empty-calorie food, and what is an example of an empty-calorie food that you might refrain from eating?
10. What are seven diet guidelines that might lessen your chances of getting cancer?

Application

1. A friend of yours is a vegetarian. Your friend is going to stay at your house for a day. What might be a source of complete protein your friend could eat for breakfast, lunch, and dinner?
2. Suppose your physician told you that you were anemic and suggested improving your diet. What mineral might you be lacking? What foods provide sources of this mineral?
3. A friend of yours has a donut and hot chocolate each morning for breakfast. The friend says it's healthful because carbohydrates are sources of energy. How would you respond to your friend?

Individual Research

1. List all the foods you eat for three days and evaluate your diet. (a) Did you obtain the correct number of servings from each of the healthful food groups each day? (b) If not, what changes do you need to make? (c) Does your diet follow the seven diet goals? (d) If not, what changes do you need to make?
2. Make a list of the following vitamins and minerals: (a) calcium, (b) iodine, (c) magnesium, (d) iron, (e) potassium, (f) retinol, (g) riboflavin, (h) folic acid, (i) calciferol, and (j) tocopherol. Identify two foods or beverages that contain this nutrient and state the main function of each.

Readings

Haas, Robert, *Eat to Win.* New York, NY: Rawson Associates, 1983.

Silverman, Harold Ph.D.; Romano, Joseph A.; and Elmer, Gary Ph.D., *The Vitamin Book.* New York, NY: Bantam Books, Inc., 1985.

Choices—How do you make decisions when you eat at a restaurant? Do you make sure you include the necessary nutrients each day? Your health is affected by your choices.

Prepare Your Own Salad With Dinner

FROM OUR
All You Care To Eat
Fresh Soup'n Salad Bar

If you order only our Soup'n Salad Bar 3.15

Chapter 13

Making Decisions About Foods

OBJECTIVES: You will be able to
- **use information on food labels to make consumer choices.**
- **make a plan to maintain ideal weight.**
- **identify eating disorders.**
- **identify healthful foods from other countries.**

Five teenagers—Celia, Mark, Carmen, Beth, and Rick—decide to have a picnic. Each person will provide part of the meal. Celia is going to bring canned soup. She reads the label to find the sodium content. Mark wants to bring a salad because it is low in Calories. Carmen, Beth, and Rick bring other luncheon foods. At the meal, Carmen did not eat at all. She has eaten almost nothing for weeks. Beth stuffed herself and then excused herself. Mark was careful about what he ate because he wants to balance his caloric intake with his caloric expenditure.

Who is concerned about maintaining his or her ideal weight? Who uses food labels to help make intelligent choices? Who might be bulimic? Who might be anorexic? Who might be overweight? As you read this chapter, you will gain information that will help you make decisions about foods. You will learn how your decisions about foods influence your health. You will be able to answer the questions about the five teenagers.

NUTRITION AND CONSUMER ISSUES

Imagine that you are going to make a grocery list. Which foods will you buy? How will your choices meet the seven diet goals? How will you obtain the best nutrition for your money?

13:1 Information on Food Labels

The information on food labels helps you decide what to buy and eat.

In the United States, federal law requires that the following information be included on food labels.

The label must identify the name of the product. The description of the variety, style, and method of packing may also be included.

The net quantity must appear. The net quantity is the total amount of the food, not including the container. The weight and/or mass is given in ounces or pounds and/or grams or kilograms. To compare the cost of similar products, compare the price per unit, which is the price per ounce or gram.

The unit price helps you compare the cost of foods.

The name, address, and zip code of the manufacturer, packer, or distributor must be identified. The ingredients in the food should be stated. The ingredients appear in order of decreasing amounts. For some foods, there is a standard of identity rather than listed ingredients. These foods do not require ingredients because there are set standards for them. Ketchup is an example because a certain number of tomatoes are required. If the product falls below government standards, you will see words such as Below Standard or Below Quality or Imitation.

Ingredients in food are listed on the packaging label in order of decreasing amounts.

Special diet foods must be labeled. A food labeled **low Calorie** cannot contain more than 0.4 Calories per gram. A **reduced-Calorie** food is not limited in Calories per serving but must be at least one-third lower in Calorie content than similar foods. Foods that are salt free or artificially sweetened must be labeled as such. The label of sugar-free or sugarless food that is not reduced in Calories must indicate that.

Salt-free and artificially-sweetened foods must be labeled as such.

FIGURE 13–1. Many people are on special diets and must rely on information stated on labels to make appropriate choices.

Additives or preservatives in food must be labeled except in ice cream, butter, or cheese. Chemicals that are added to foods are called **additives.** Additives may be used to help foods taste better, to change the color of a food, or to replace or add vitamins. An additive may also act as a preservative. A **preservative** is used to keep foods from spoiling. When a preservative is used, a food can be stored for longer periods of time. An **enriched food** has vitamins added to replace those lost during food processing. A **fortified food** has vitamins added in extra measure.

Additives may add taste or color to foods, or act as preservatives.

Federal law requires that manufacturers test for the safety of food additives. Some additives are required to have a warning label. **Saccharin** is an artificial sweetener that was found to cause a higher than normal incidence of bladder cancer in laboratory animals. The warning label on saccharin says, "Use of this product may be hazardous to your health. This product contains saccharin, which has been determined to cause cancer in laboratory animals." **Aspartame** is an artificial sweetener used in cereals, milkshake mixers, and diet colas. It is 180 times sweeter than sugar and lacks the bitter aftertaste of saccharin. At this time, aspartame is considered safe for use. However, research continues regarding its effects on health.

Manufacturers must test the safety of additives.

13:2 Health Foods and Organic Foods

Health foods claim to benefit a person's health in a special way. However, there is no evidence to support health food claims. Most foods are healthful when eaten in moderation, and many healthful foods are harmful when eaten in excessive amounts. Examples of health foods include alfalfa, bee pollen, carob, granola, honey, kelp, bean sprouts, and wheat germ. These foods, or foods containing similar nutrients, are usually less expensive if purchased in supermarkets rather than health food stores.

There is no evidence to support claims that health foods or organic foods benefit health.

Organic foods are foods grown without pesticides and chemical fertilizers. People who advocate the use of organically grown foods claim they contain more natural vitamins and minerals. There is no scientific evidence that these claims are true.

 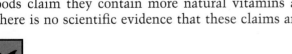 ## Review and Reflect

1. What is the best way to compare the price of two cans of fruit?
2. What does it mean when sugar is the first ingredient listed on a package of cereal?
3. How is a low-Calorie food different from a reduced-Calorie food?
4. How is an enriched food different from a fortified food?

IDEAL WEIGHT AND BODY COMPOSITION

For optimum health, you must maintain ideal weight and ideal body composition.

Your ideal weight is the weight and body composition that is recommended for your age, sex, height, and body build (Chapter 12). An ideal body composition is one in which your percentage of body fat is no greater than 18 percent for women and no greater than 15 percent for men. Your ideal weight and body composition are those measurements at which your statistical chances for a long life increase.

13:3 Maintaining Ideal Weight and Body Composition

Regularly assess your weight and percentage of body fat.

Have you stepped on a scale recently to weigh yourself? How much did you weigh? Did you weigh the correct amount for your sex and body build? Have you had your percentage of body fat calculated recently? This can be accomplished by using skin-fold calipers. For optimum health, it is important to know your ideal weight and ideal body composition and to maintain them by correctly eating, exercising, and relaxing.

Life insurance companies have devised tables to help you find your ideal weight (Table 13–1). These tables are helpful as guidelines. If your weight varies ten percent more or less from that shown on the tables for your ideal weight, you are within a healthful range.

Table 13–1   Desirable Weights for Men and Women*

MEN

Height Feet Inches		Small Frame	Medium Frame	Large Frame
5	2	128-134	131-141	138-150
5	3	130-136	133-143	140-153
5	4	132-138	135-145	142-156
5	5	134-140	137-148	144-160
5	6	136-142	139-151	146-164
5	7	138-145	142-154	149-168
5	8	140-148	145-157	152-172
5	9	142-151	148-160	155-176
5	10	144-154	151-163	158-180
5	11	146-157	154-166	161-184
6	0	149-160	157-170	164-188
6	1	152-164	160-174	168-192
6	2	155-168	164-178	172-197
6	3	158-172	167-182	176-202
6	4	162-176	171-187	181-207

WOMEN

Height Feet Inches		Small Frame	Medium Frame	Large Frame
4	10	102-111	109-121	118-131
4	11	103-113	111-123	120-134
5	0	104-115	113-126	122-137
5	1	106-118	115-129	125-140
5	2	108-121	118-132	128-143
5	3	111-124	121-135	131-147
5	4	114-127	124-138	134-151
5	5	117-130	127-141	137-156
5	6	120-133	130-144	140-159
5	7	123-136	133-147	143-163
5	8	126-139	136-150	146-167
5	9	129-142	139-153	149-170
5	10	132-145	142-156	152-173
5	11	135-148	145-159	155-176
6	0	138-151	148-162	158-179

*Metropolitan Life Insurance Company, New York

To reach or maintain ideal weight and body composition, you will need to understand the relationship between caloric intake, caloric expenditure or output, and body composition. Caloric intake is the total number of Calories you eat each day. Caloric expenditure or output is the total number of Calories you expend or use each day. Your body uses Calories to maintain body systems such as circulation, respiration, and digestion. You also expend Calories when you move. The more vigorous the movement, the more Calories are used. For example, you would use more Calories while walking than while watching TV.

As your body uses the food you eat, the Calories in the food provide energy for your daily activities. The number of Calories you need depends on your age, sex, body build, and amount of physical activity. When you eat more than the number of Calories you need, the excess Calories are stored in fat cells. One pound of fat is equal to 3500 Calories.

Your caloric intake and expenditure influence your body weight.

A pound of fat is equal to 3500 Calories.

13:4 Being Overfat, Overweight, or Obese

You are **overfat** if you are in excess of your recommended percentage of body fat. You are **overweight** if your weight is 15 percent above your recommended weight and you are also overfat. A high school football player who is muscular may weigh 15 percent more than recommended in the insurance table, yet the player may have a very low percentage of body fat. Thus, this person is not considered overweight.

You are not overweight if your weight is higher than the charts recommend and your percentage of body fat is low.

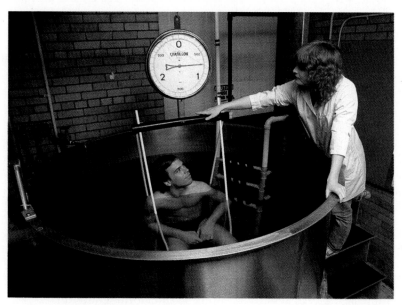

FIGURE 13–2. Hydrostatic weighing (weighing a person under water) is one way to determine the amount of body fat. The underwater weight is compared to scale weight to calculate the volume of a person's body and its density.

Many diseases are linked to excess weight and body fat.

Weight gain may be caused by overeating.

Heredity and environment may influence your body weight and composition.

Lack of exercise is a major cause of overweight during adolescence.

The setpoint theory is based on a natural weight that your body tries to maintain.

Increased physical activity and decreased caloric intake lowers your setpoint.

You are **obese** if your weight is 20 to 30 percent above your recommended weight and you are also overfat. Being overweight or obese increases the likelihood of heart disease, high blood pressure, stroke, diabetes, accidents, and cancer. For this reason, it is important to maintain ideal weight. If you are overweight, obese, or overfat, you will need a plan to reduce your weight and percentage of body fat.

You become overweight when you consume more Calories than you expend or use. In other words, your caloric intake exceeds your caloric expenditure. If you eat high-caloric foods, eat between meals, and eat excessive amounts at mealtimes, you will have a high caloric intake. People who do any or all of these will in all likelihood gain weight and increase their percentage of body fat. It is difficult to increase physical activity enough to counterbalance the effect of excessive caloric intake.

Heredity and environment are two factors that increase the likelihood that you will eat too many Calories. If one or both of your parents are overweight or obese, there is evidence to suggest that you are more likely to be overweight or obese.

Your exercise habits and your age also influence your weight and percentage of body fat. Exercise burns up Calories during a workout and increases your metabolic rate for an additional six hours. **Metabolic rate** is the rate at which your body burns Calories. Lack of exercise is a major contributing factor for weight gain and increased body fat. At your age, many experts feel that it is the most likely cause of being overweight. Metabolic rate slows down with age. This change may begin about age 28 and decrease three percent by age 35. As you age, you need fewer Calories to maintain your daily activities. If you continue to eat the same amount of food without increasing your activity, you will gain weight and increase your percentage of body fat.

Another factor may influence your weight and body composition. Some nutritionists believe that each of us has a setpoint. The **setpoint theory** states that you have a natural given weight range that your body attempts to maintain. Those who believe in the setpoint theory think that your body is able to change its metabolic rate to keep your weight at its setpoint.

The setpoint theory has implications for weight control and percentage of body fat. Suppose you starve yourself to lose weight. According to this theory, your body will respond by slowing the metabolic rate. At first, you may lose weight, but you will not continue to do so. You will not decrease your percentage of body fat. If the setpoint theory is true, the only way to lose weight and decrease your percentage of body fat is to accommodate to the lower setpoint. This can only be accomplished with increased physical activity along with caloric reduction.

FIGURE 13–3. Being active and increasing the amount of daily exercise are important factors in reducing weight and body fat.

13:5 Reducing Weight and Body Fat

Healthful weight reduction and reduction of body fat involves cutting down the number of Calories you eat and expending more Calories by exercising. These changes must become permanent in one's lifestyle to keep weight off and the percentage of body fat low. A weight loss of two pounds per week is recommended. A weight loss greater than two pounds per week should be supervised by a physician.

To lose weight and decrease percentage of body fat by caloric reduction, decrease the number of Calories eaten each day. Eating 500 less Calories per day for one week (500 × 7) is equal to 3500 Calories, or losing one pound of body fat. A healthful way to reduce Calories is to eat less meat and dairy products, fats, oils, flour products, and sugar. However, you cannot cut these important foods out entirely. Substitute these foods with fruits, vegetables, and grains.

To lose weight and decrease your percentage of body fat, expend more Calories by increasing your daily activity without increasing your caloric intake. Refer to Table 13–2 for examples of caloric expenditure through exercise. Suppose you went for a one-hour walk each day (250 Calories) and also golfed or bowled for an hour (250 Calories). You would expend 500 Calories a day or 3500 Calories each week. In one week, you would lose one pound of fat. Exercise would also help tone your body muscles and improve your appearance.

Weight loss strategies must become a permanent part of your lifestyle.

A weight loss of two pounds per week is healthful.

Table 13-2 Examples of Caloric Expenditure

CALORIES USED PER HOUR							
120-150	150-240	240-300	300-360	360-420	420-480	480-600	600-660
Strolling 1 mph Light housework Walking 2 mph	Typing, manual Riding lawn mower Golf, using power cart	Cleaning windows Mopping floors Vacuuming Pushing light power mower Bowling Walking 3 mph Cycling 6 mph Golf, pulling cart Horseback (sitting to trot)	Scrubbing floors Walking 3.5 mph Cycling 8 mph Table tennis Badminton Volleyball Golf, carrying clubs Tennis, doubles Calisthenics (many) Ballet exercises Dancing (fox trot)	Walking 4 mph Cycling 10 mph Ice Skating Roller skating Horseback ("posting" to trot)	Hand lawn mowing Walking 5 mph Cycling 11 mph Tennis, singles Water skiing Folk (square) dancing	Sawing hardwood Jogging 5 mph Cycling 12 mph Downhill skiing Paddleball Horseback (gallop) Basketball Mountain climbing	Running 5.5 mph Cycling 13 mph **Above 660** Running 6 or more mph Handball Squash Ski touring (5+ mph)

Fad diets are usually ineffective in decreasing weight and percentage of body fat.

Use of diuretics and rubberized sweat suits may rob the body of potassium.

The use of amphetamines may cause dangerous side effects.

Unfortunately, it is popular to try to lose weight and decrease percentage of body fat by using a fad diet. A **fad diet** suggests losing weight and decreasing the percentage of body fat by altering what you eat rather than by choosing the correct number of servings from the healthful food groups. Fad diets usually involve extremes. They are not realistic or healthful. Several fad diets suggest eating a high-fat, low-carbohydrate diet, or a high-protein, low-fat carbohydrate diet. A diet without carbohydrates or very low in carbohydrates results in fatigue. Carbohydrates are needed for energy.

Diuretics and the use of rubberized sweat suits are methods of losing weight by water loss. A **diuretic** is a drug that causes the kidneys to produce more urine. A rubberized sweat suit is worn while exercising to cause excess perspiration. The water loss from these two methods is not accompanied by a decrease in the percentage of body fat. Too much water loss is harmful to health. With water loss there is also a loss of potassium. Potassium is a mineral necessary for the healthful functioning of the heart. Excessive use of diuretics may harm your kidneys. Wearing a rubberized suit while exercising can be extremely dangerous because body temperature and water loss may be excessive.

An amphetamine is a drug that speeds body activities and suppresses appetite. At one time, physicians prescribed amphetamines for overfat and overweight persons. Now, most physicians agree that this is a dangerous way to lose weight and that it does not decrease body fat. Amphetamines are physically and psychologically addicting. People soon develop a tolerance to them, and a higher dosage is needed to produce the same effect. Side effects from amphetamines include nervousness, irritability, insomnia, and fatigue.

Activity: Finding Caloric Needs

You can make an estimate of the number of Calories you need each day by multiplying your ideal body weight (Table 13–1) by one of the behavior codes below.

Behavior		Code
Sedentary	Most of each day is spent doing school-work or watching TV with little or no leg or arm movement.	13
Light	Most of your time is spent walking slowly or doing light household chores that require standing or light arm movement.	14
Moderate	Most of your time is spent in activities requiring standing and moderate arm work, such as cleaning your room or walking moderately fast.	15
Active	Most of your time is spent performing heavy work, vigorous movement, lifting, or walking quickly.	16
Strenuous	Most of your time is spent in physically demanding activities, such as running, walking hard, or in vigorous sports.	17

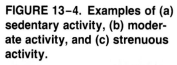

The intensity of activity is related to caloric expenditure.

Caloric Formula

_____ × _____ = _____
ideal body weight   activity code   caloric needs

Plan a one-day menu for yourself that contains the correct number of servings from the four healthful food groups and the total number of Calories equal to your caloric needs.

FIGURE 13–4. Examples of (a) sedentary activity, (b) moderate activity, and (c) strenuous activity.

a

b

c

13:6   Being Underweight

You are considered **underweight** if your weight is 15 percent below that recommended in Table 13–1. Many people believe that being underweight is not as serious a threat to health as being overweight. Being underweight is not usually linked to an increased incidence of heart disease, high blood pressure, accidents, diabetes, or strokes. However, underweight may be a symptom of poor health.

Underweight may be caused by poor eating habits or from being malnourished. A person who is **malnourished** is not eating the recommended amounts of nutrients from the healthful food groups. A malnourished person may lack energy, be more likely to get infections, and be prone to kidney problems. Underweight can be a symptom of disease or too much stress. Underweight accompanied by rapid weight loss should always be checked by a physician.

If you are underweight and want to gain weight, there are at least three healthful ways to do so—exercise, reduce stress, and increase caloric intake. Exercise helps build muscle mass, which contributes to body weight and a healthful appearance. Reducing stress will reduce muscle tension. Increasing Calories provides more energy and more nutrients. To increase Calories, find the number of Calories needed to maintain your ideal weight. Add extra Calories for weight gain. Remember, an extra 500 Calories per day equals one pound of weight gain per week. An extra 1000 Calories per day equals two pounds of weight gain per week. The healthful way to gain weight is to increase the number of Calories from carbohydrates, such as pasta, potatoes, bread, corn, and rice. At the same time, continue to eat servings from the healthful food groups and eat smaller meals more often.

Sometimes, persons who want to gain weight and increase muscle mass do so by engaging in poor eating habits. Avoid increasing your intake of sugars, saturated fats, and snacks with salt. Remember, these foods increase the likelihood of other health risks.

Being underweight may be related to being malnourished.

You can exercise, reduce stress, and increase Calories to gain weight.

Increase the intake of complex carbohydrates to gain weight.

Avoid empty-Calorie foods for weight gain.

 Review and Reflect

5. What happens when your caloric intake is greater than your caloric expenditure?
6. Why do setpoint theorists argue against starvation as a method of weight reduction?
7. Why do you need to eat fewer Calories at age 40 than at age 16 if your physical activity remains the same or decreases?

FIGURE 13-5. The pressure to be thin is evident in many places.

EATING DISORDERS

Think about the message you receive about body weight and appearance when you watch television, read a magazine, or go to a movie. The message that THIN IS IN is very prevalent. This message influences many adolescents to be overly concerned about their weight and their attractiveness. As a result, there has been a dramatic increase in eating disorders.

The media stress the idea of staying thin.

13:7 Anorexia Nervosa

Anorexia nervosa is an emotional disorder in which a lack of self-esteem and an intense fear of being overweight result in starvation. One out of 200 adolescent females are anorexic; males are rarely anorexic. These girls are frequently perfectionists and over achievers. At puberty, they are usually about five to ten pounds overweight. They may be concerned about the physical changes in their bodies, such as breast and hip development and menstruation. They may use dieting as a way to solve emotional problems. They begin to diet and set very unrealistic goals. Soon they begin to starve themselves and do not eat at all. Sometimes starvation is not the only method of weight reduction. These persons may take laxatives or diuretics to try to lose even more weight through water loss. For these reasons, anorexia nervosa is sometimes described as dieting gone wild.

Anorexia nervosa is an eating disorder most common among adolescent girls.

Anorexia nervosa may include the use of laxatives and diuretics as well as starvation.

The disorder is accompanied by harmful psychological and physiological changes. Psychological problems precede the disorder. As the disorder becomes more severe, the psychological problems worsen. These persons may become even more depressed and apathetic. Their self-esteem lowers. All body organs can become affected. There is a marked loss in muscle mass and a decrease in body fat. There is a decrease in blood pressure, heart rate, respiratory rate, and body temperature. Thyroid function decreases and breast development diminishes. Menstrual periods may change or stop.

If the person with anorexia uses laxatives, diuretics, and methods to induce vomiting for additional weight loss, other complications may occur. The kidneys may be affected. If the person frequently induces vomiting, there may be tearing and bleeding in the esophagus. Too much potassium may be lost causing abnormal heart rhythm.

The person with anorexia needs psychological and medical treatment. In extreme cases, the person may need to be hospitalized, fed through tubes, and placed on a well-balanced high-calorie diet. The goal of counseling is to help the person with anorexia accept his or her body and sexuality. The person with anorexia needs to build more positive self-esteem. As with any diet, changes must be part of a life-long process. Recovery may be a long process.

The counseling goal for persons with anorexia focuses on building self-esteem.

13:8 Bulimia

Bulimia is an emotional disorder in which an intense fear of being overweight and a lack of self-esteem result in secret binge eating followed by starvation, self-induced vomiting, and the use of laxatives or diuretics. Bulimia is not usually a means of dieting but rather of controlling weight.

Bulimia includes binge eating, vomiting, and the use of laxatives and diuretics.

Whereas anorexia nervosa is described as dieting gone wild, bulimia is sometimes described as eating gone wild. During an eating binge, a person may consume thousands of Calories in one to two hours. A binge usually follows stress at home, work, or school and is done in private. The binge stops when the person feels abdominal pain. The person then purges or gets rid of the food that was eaten by inducing vomiting or by using laxatives or diuretics.

The binge–purge pattern may be followed by normal eating. During this time, the person with bulimia is very depressed. The person feels angry because of inability to control eating. Consequently, he or she may abuse alcohol or other drugs and think about suicide.

Persons with bulimia may abuse alcohol and/or contemplate suicide.

Bulimia is usually a disease of females. It has severe physical and psychological results. The purging pattern causes a loss of potassium in the body. This may result in abnormal heart rhythm and/or cardiac arrest. There may be damage to the kidneys from the use of the diuretic. Frequent vomiting causes tearing and bleeding of the gums, stomach, and esophagus. Stomach acid passing through the mouth promotes tooth decay. The parotid gland may swell giving the person an appearance similar to a chipmunk. The person with bulimia may have muscle spasms, a dry mouth, and brittle hair. They are also more susceptible to urinary tract infections and ulcers. The person with bulimia suffers from depression. Without psychological help, this depression worsens.

Harmful changes may occur in the body organs of persons with bulimia.

The death rate from bulimia is difficult to estimate. Most persons with bulimia die from damage to body organs (the heart and kidneys) or suicide. Consequently, bulimia is seldom listed as a cause of death.

Treatment of bulimia involves medical and psychological help. As with anorexia nervosa, lifetime changes in self-acceptance and positive self-image must be made. If not, the person with bulimia will slip back into the harmful binge—purge pattern.

A person with bulimia must make changes in lifestyle for recovery.

✔ Review and Reflect

8. Why is anorexia nervosa described as dieting gone wild?
9. Why is bulimia described as eating gone wild?
10. Why are abnormal heart rhythm and cardiac arrest the most frequent causes of physical death from anorexia nervosa and bulimia?

Health
ADVANCES

In this chapter, you have been learning how to make responsible decisions about foods. You have learned tips for buying groceries and for maintaining your ideal weight. You also make decisions when you decide to eat out.

13:9   Nutritious Restaurant Foods

When planning to eat out, select AHA-approved restaurants.

The AHA makes suggestions for menus that promote a healthy heart.

The American Heart Association (AHA) is interested in decisions made about foods when people eat at a restaurant rather than at home. Recently, the AHA has become involved in making suggestions to restaurants that are in keeping with the seven diet goals and with maintaining a healthy heart. The AHA approves meals in some restaurants, hotels, and even on airlines. If this is the case, the AHA name will appear on the menu.

The AHA also produces dining-out guides in several localities. These guides list restaurants that will prepare foods according to AHA guidelines at your request.

The AHA suggests calling ahead to make a reservation so that you can obtain the following information. Find out if the restaurant would be willing to

- serve margarine rather than butter with the meal.
- serve skimmed milk rather than whole milk.
- prepare food using vegetable oil (corn, soy, sunflower, safflower) or margarine made with vegetable oil rather than butter.
- trim visible fat off meat or skin off poultry.
- broil, bake, steam, or poach meat, fish, or poultry rather than sauté or deep fry.
- limit portion size to four to six ounces of cooked meat, fish, or poultry.
- leave all butter, gravy, or sauce off an entree or side dish.
- serve fresh fruit or fruit in light syrup for dessert.
- prepare a dish without added salt or monosodium glutamate (MSG).
- accommodate special requests if made in advance by telephone or in person.
- have a special seating area for nonsmokers.

When you eat out, you may want to sample foods from different countries. Following are some suggestions to help you choose healthful foods from other countries.

Greek
- Tzatziki, an appetizer with yogurt and cucumber is nutritious.
- Pita bread is very low in fat.
- Plaki, fish cooked with tomatoes, onions, and garlic is a healthful entrée.
- Rice provides a serving from the grain group to complement entrées.

Indian
- Vegetables are an important part of an Indian meal. Lentils, or deal, are high in protein and fiber and low in fat.
- Indian foods are generally low in saturated fat, cholesterol, and Calories; spices add to the taste.
- Tanduri chicken and fish dishes that are marinated in spices and roasted in a clay pot are authentic and nutritious.

Italian
- Pasta is an excellent choice for people on low-fat diets. Order the appetizer portion as an entrée.
- Choose linguine with white or red clam sauce.
- Pasta primavera, with a small amount of oil, and fresh vegetables, is low in salt.

Japanese
- Japanese food is usually low in fat.
- Pickled vegetables are low in cholesterol, saturated fat, and Calories.
- Entrées that are described as Yakimono are broiled and low in fat.

Mexican
- Whole grains are staples of Mexican dishes.
- Salsa and guacamole are nutritious appetizers.
- Choose rice and beans instead of beef. They are high in fiber, low in fat, and complete vegetable proteins.

Suggestions for eating foods from other countries are AHA approved.

FIGURE 13-6. (a) A Japanese meal, and (b) a Mexican meal

a

b

FIGURE 13-7. A Chinese meal

Middle Eastern
- Healthful appetizers include midya dolma, mussels stuffed with rice, pine nuts and currants; yalanji yaprak, grape leaves filled with a similar mixture; and imam bayildi, baked eggplant stuffed with a variety of vegetables.

Chinese
- Choose from a variety of healthful entrees that are boiled, steamed, or lightly stir-fried in vegetable oil.
- Steamed rice is a healthful serving from the grain group.

Adapted from American Heart Association, *Dining Out: A Guide to Restaurant Dining*

Focus on
Life Management Skills

- Read food labels to make nutritious decisions about what you eat and what you buy.
- Avoid additives that carry a warning label.
- Maintain your ideal weight by eating the correct amount of nutritious foods, exercising, and relaxing.
- Should you need to lose weight, cut down on the number of Calories you eat, choose healthful foods, and increase your caloric expenditure by exercising.
- Should you need to gain weight, reduce stress, exercise to build muscle mass, and increase your Caloric intake of healthful foods, such as pasta, potatoes, and bread.
- Should you suspect an eating disorder, seek professional counseling and medical help.
- Check restaurant menus for American Heart Association approved meals to reduce your risks of overweight and of heart disease.

Health
CAREERS

Registered Dietitian (R.D.)

Jennie James Nicol, a registered dietitian (R.D.) at a children's hospital, develops diets for children with cancer. She talks with the children and their families about their usual eating habits. She weighs and measures the children to determine their growth rates. Jennie discusses nutrition and the side effects of chemotherapy with the children and their parents.

To become a registered dietitian, Jennie majored in nutrition and science in college and obtained a four-year bachelor's degree and a two-year master's degree. She served in an internship program for one year and then took a written exam on all aspects of nutrition and food management. To continue her education, Jennie regularly enrolls in classes approved by the American Dietetic Association.

If you are interested in dietetics as a career, other job opportunities are also available. You might work at a senior citizens' home, a day care center, an alcoholic rehabilitation clinic, a student health center on a college campus, or establish a private practice. Your patients may have heart, kidney, or diabetic conditions. The field offers many career possibilities.

Summary

1. Food labels provide information about the product, the manufacturer, and the ingredients, as well as special diets and food additives and their safety. **13:1**

2. There is no scientific evidence to support claims that organic foods or health foods are more nutritious than other foods you eat. **13:2**

3. Ideal weight and body composition is based on age, sex, and body build and is maintained by eating correctly, exercising, and relaxing. **13:3**

4. Being overfat, overweight, or obese increases the likelihood of heart disease, high blood pressure, stroke, diabetes, accidents, and cancer. **13:4**

5. Healthful weight loss involves decreasing the number of Calories eaten and increas-ing the number of Calories expended. Potentially harmful weight loss procedures include the use of fad diets, diuretics, and amphetamines. **13:5**

6. Healthful weight gain includes increasing the caloric intake of healthful foods, exercising to build muscle mass, and reducing stress. **13:6**

7. Anorexia nervosa is an eating disorder in which starvation results in harmful damage to body organs. **13:7**

8. Bulimia is an eating disorder involving binge eating and purging that results in harmful changes to body organs. **13:8**

9. The American Heart Association has identified ways to reduce fat and salt in your diet when choosing to eat at a restaurant. **13:9**

Vocabulary

Below is a list of vocabulary words used in this chapter. Use each word only once to complete the sentences. Do not write in this book.

anorexia nervosa
additives
bulimia
diuretic
fad diet

fortified food
malnourished
metabolic rate
preservative
setpoint theory

1. Using a(n) _____ for weight loss may cause kidney damage.

2. The _____ involves your body's attempt to maintain weight within a given range.

3. A(n) _____ does not contain recommended amounts of the healthful food groups.

4. Chemicals added to help foods taste better or to add vitamins are examples of _____.

5. A(n) _____ is added to food to keep it from spoiling.

6. A person who does not eat the recommended amounts of nutrients from the healthful food groups is _____.

7. Some cereals are a(n) _____ because extra vitamins are added.

8. An adolescent with _____ may binge eat, and then vomit, or use laxatives to control weight.

9. Your _____ determines how fast your body burns Calories.

10. An adolescent with _____ has an intense fear of being overweight that results in starvation.

Review

1. What are seven different types of information found on a food label?
2. What false claims are made about health foods and organic foods?
3. According to life insurance tables, what is considered a healthful range for your ideal weight?
4. What factors increase the likelihood that a person will become overweight?
5. What is the setpoint theory of weight maintenance?
6. What are three ways to lose weight that may have harmful results?
7. What types of healthful foods might be eaten in order to gain weight?
8. What harmful physiological changes might occur when someone has anorexia?
9. What harmful physiological changes might occur when someone has bulimia?
10. What are eleven questions you might ask when you call ahead at a restaurant to make reservations?

Application

1. Write a label for a healthful food that lists (a) a description of the product, (b) the net quantity, (c) information about the manufacturer, (d) the ingredients, (e) a special diet claim, and (f) one additive.
2. Locate your ideal weight on Table 13–1. What range is considered ideal for you? At what weight would you be overweight? obese? underweight?
3. In magazines or newspapers, locate three advertisements for harmful ways to lose weight. Discuss the method used in each advertisement using the information in your textbook.
4. Locate five advertisements that influence adolescents to be thin. How would you change each advertisement to be more realistic?

Individual Research

1. Learn about places to eat in your community. Visit local restaurants to examine their menus. Do any of the restaurants have the American Heart Association approval? Are they aware of the AHA program? Share findings with classmates.
2. Study the diets of Greece, China, Japan, India, Italy, Mexico, or a middle eastern country. Plan a healthful, balanced meal for a dinner. You may refer to the pamphlet *Dining Out*, which is available from the American Heart Association.

Readings

Cauwels, Janice, *Bulimia: The Binge-Purge Compulsion.* Garden City, NY: Doubleday & Co., Inc., 1983.

O'Neill, Cherry, *Starving for Attention.* New York, NY: Continuum Publishing Company, 1982.

UNIT 6

Exercise and Fitness

EXERCISE AND FITNESS

The runners try to do their best. They show courage and desire. They have chosen a healthful goal, made a plan to reach their goal, and are following through on this plan. In this unit, you will learn about physical fitness. You will learn about the components of physical fitness, different types of exercises, and how to design a physical fitness plan.

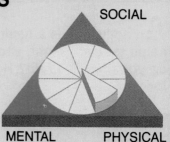

SOCIAL

MENTAL PHYSICAL

An active life is a healthy life. Exercise helps keep the heart muscle strong, helps reduce weight, and gives a psychological lift. What kinds of exercise do you choose to do? How can you know what types of exercise are best for you?

Chapter 14

Benefits of Physical Fitness

OBJECTIVES: You will be able to
- **identify the components and health benefits of physical fitness.**
- **identify types of exercises that promote physical fitness.**
- **explain the role of diet, exercise, and sleep in physical fitness.**

The following adolescents are involved in regular exercise. How much do you know about the types of exercises they chose and their health benefits?

Dave rides his bicycle 30 minutes to and from school each day. He rides at a fast and steady pace. Kara is on the soccer team at school. She practices four days a week for two hours each day. She has a game each Saturday. Mike belongs to a health club. Three days a week he works out by using weight machines. Candy takes gymnastics lessons twice a week. Each day she does stretching exercises for twenty minutes.

Which of these persons is most likely to have flexibility? Which one does exercises for the heart and lungs? Which one does isokinetic exercise? Which one is most likely to be physically fit? How does each exercise program contribute to physical fitness? As you read this chapter, you will study the answers to these questions.

Engage in many types of sports activities to promote physical fitness.

PHYSICAL FITNESS

Make a list of the exercises you enjoy. How does each of these exercises promote your health? Are the health benefits the same for each exercise you listed? There are many exercises from which you can choose to develop a well-balanced plan for physical fitness. Before you develop a plan, you need to know more about physical fitness.

273

14:1   What Is Physical Fitness?

Muscular strength and endurance, flexibility, cardiovascular endurance, and a lean body composition make up physical fitness.

Physical fitness is a level of health in which you have muscular endurance, muscular strength, flexibility, cardiovascular endurance, and a lean body composition. Physical fitness is achieved by the regular movement of muscles through a variety of exercises. Maintaining physical fitness is a life-long process and should always be part of your lifestyle. People with disabilities can also reach a measure of physical fitness by doing exercises appropriate for their conditions. When you are physically fit, you

- are more likely to be at your ideal weight.
- have more energy and work without fatigue.
- are better able to cope with stress.
- are less likely to be depressed and anxious.
- are less likely to have psychosomatic diseases and disorders.
- are less likely to have chronic diseases such as high blood pressure, coronary heart disease, and obesity-related diabetes.
- will develop muscle tone.
- have stronger bones.
- are better able to relax and sleep well.
- have better digestion and less constipation.
- have increased lung capacity.
- have a strong heart muscle.
- are more apt to be socially active.
- feel better about yourself and your appearance.
- are more likely to decelerate the aging process.
- are less likely to have accidents and injuries.

There are mental, physical, and social benefits gained from physical fitness.

14:2   Muscular Strength

Muscular strength helps you exert force against resistance.

Muscular strength is the amount of force that your muscles can exert against resistance. When you use your muscles regularly, they become strong. They help you lift, push, pull, jump, twist, turn, and bend. Having muscular strength can keep you from being easily fatigued. It can keep your muscles from becoming sore or injured when you do things like shovel snow or mow the lawn. Strong muscles also help you stand, sit, and walk easily. When you have strong abdominal and back muscles, you are less likely to have lower back pain. You are more likely to have correct posture.

Muscular strength improves performance in sports. You are able to throw a softball farther and hit a tennis ball harder and with more control when your muscles are strong. There is a difference in muscle size in males and females. Even if size, weight, and activity were equal, females would not develop as much muscle mass as males. The endocrine system, not physical activity, helps determine muscle size.

Males usually develop more muscle mass than females.

14:3 Muscular Endurance

Muscular endurance is the ability to continue using muscular strength. When you have muscular endurance, your muscles are able to perform repeated movements for long periods of time without becoming tired. Many daily activities as well as many sports activities require muscular endurance. Suppose you have a heavy load of books to carry home from school today. You use muscular strength to lift the books from your desk. If you walk home from school and continue to carry the books, you use muscular endurance to hold the books. Muscular endurance also helps you maintain correct posture.

Muscular endurance enables you to perform repeated movements.

Muscular endurance is important in many sports. To repeatedly hit a tennis ball, swing a golf club, or roll a bowling ball, you need muscular endurance. This is the reason your arm and shoulder muscles may become tired when you first begin practicing these sports. Muscular endurance is also needed to hike, ride a bicycle, or swim long distances.

Your muscles do not tire as easily when you have muscular endurance.

FIGURE 14-1. Endurance exercises require careful regulation. You have to work harder than you might ordinarily do, but be careful to not overtax your heart.

FIGURE 14–2. Ballet dancers acquire great flexibility in learning basic ballet movements.

14:4 Flexibility

Flexibility is the ability to move the body through a full range of possible motion. When you are flexible, your body does not get stiff easily. You are less likely to injure your muscles or to have lower back pain.

Inactive persons are less flexible than persons who enjoy a variety of activities in which movement is required. Active persons stretch their muscles more than inactive persons. If you spend most of your day sitting, muscles connected to your knee, hip, and elbow joints begin to shorten. To remain flexible, the muscles must be stretched. Many fitness experts claim that stretching for 20 minutes a day helps prevent the stiffness that accompanies aging.

Flexibility is important in many sports. A gymnast shows flexibility as he or she moves through a range of motion. A drum major shows flexibility twirling a baton, reaching, and bending.

14:5 Cardiovascular Endurance

Cardiovascular endurance is the ability to sustain vigorous activity that requires increased oxygen intake for extended periods of time. For example, you might take a long bike trip or swim several laps in a pool. You might help someone move to a new home. With cardiovascular endurance, you are able to walk up and down stairs for an extended length of time.

Flexibility enables you to move your muscles through a full range of motion.

Inactive persons are less flexible than those who enjoy various activities.

With cardiovascular endurance, you can engage in activities that require oxygen over an extended time period.

The ability to gain cardiovascular endurance depends on the frequency, intensity, and length of time spent in training. It also depends on the condition of your body and on your heredity.

Cardiovascular endurance has many health benefits. Cardiovascular endurance keeps the heart muscle, blood vessels, blood, and lungs in excellent condition. When you take part in exercises that promote cardiovascular endurance, your heart muscle and other body muscles need more oxygen. For example, when you rest, your heart pumps five to six quarts of blood per minute. When exercising, your heart pumps 20 to 25 quarts per minute. Like any muscle, the heart must be exercised to strengthen and increase its performance.

> Cardiovascular endurance strengthens the heart, blood vessels, and diaphragm muscle.

Cardiac output is the amount of blood pumped by the heart each minute. Cardiac output is equal to the heart rate multiplied by the stroke volume. **Stroke volume** is the amount of blood the heart pumps with each beat. Cardiovascular endurance strengthens the heart muscle increasing stroke volume. With a greater stroke volume, the heart will beat fewer times to supply oxygen to body cells. Consequently, the resting heart rate is lowered allowing the heart more rest between beats. Athletes generally have lower heart rates because they have strengthened their heart muscles.

> Cardiac output is determined by heart rate and stroke volume.

Cardiovascular endurance also increases oxygen capacity. Lungs function with the help of the diaphragm. Cardiovascular endurance strengthens the diaphragm, which helps the lungs expand and contract. This increases the volume of exchanged air. Consequently, the heart does not have to beat as often to supply the body with oxygen.

> When your stroke volume increases, your resting heart rate will become lower.

Cardiovascular endurance has healthful benefits to the arteries and blood. Even as an adolescent, you may already have some symptoms of atherosclerosis. **Atherosclerosis** (ath uh roh skluh ROH sus) is the accumulation of fat deposits on arterial walls. Because these fat deposits narrow the passageway, the heart has to work harder to pump blood through an artery. Cardiovascular endurance is helpful in preventing the buildup of these deposits.

> Cardiovascular endurance helps prevent the development of atherosclerosis.

Cardiovascular endurance also results in changing the ratio of HDLs to LDLs in the blood. A **high-density lipoprotein (HDL)** is a substance in blood that prevents the formation of fatty deposits in arterial walls. HDLs transport the extra fat in the blood to the liver to be removed from the body. A **low-density lipoprotein (LDL)** is a substance in blood that is a factor in the formation of fatty deposits in arterial walls. You can help prevent atherosclerosis by increasing HDLs and lowering LDLs in your blood.

> A healthy person has a high ratio of HDLs to LDLs.

Research indicates that exercises that promote cardiovascular endurance can change the ratio of HDLs to LDLs. Exercises done for 30 to 40 minutes a day three times a week for seven to ten weeks will increase HDLs and lower LDLs. These exercises will be discussed in Chapter 15.

14:6 Body Composition

Your body is made up of two types of tissues—fat tissue and lean tissue. Your **body composition** is the percentage of fat tissue and lean tissue in your body. As you become physically fit, the ratio changes. The percentage of fat tissue decreases and the percentage of lean tissue increases.

The body uses fat tissue every day. Fat is used as the body stores and uses nutrients. Everyone has stored fat beneath the skin and around the internal organs. The number of fat cells a person has is determined at a very young age. Fat cells can become smaller, but they cannot be lost. Females have more stored fat in their bodies than males. The total percentage of body weight that is fat is usually 16 to 19 percent for males and 22 to 25 percent for females.

Muscles, bones, cartilage, connective tissue, nerves, skin, and internal organs are lean tissue. The percentage of your body weight that is lean tissue varies. The amount of muscle and size of your bones are the factors that most greatly influence the percentage of your body that is lean tissue. As many people age, their level of physical activity decreases. By using less energy, muscle tissue decreases and a larger percentage of their body weight becomes fat.

Your heredity influences your body composition, the size of your bones, and your muscle structure. Generally, you inherit a

Body composition is a measure of the ratio of fat tissue to lean tissue.

Males usually have 16 to 19 percent body fat; females have 22 to 25 percent.

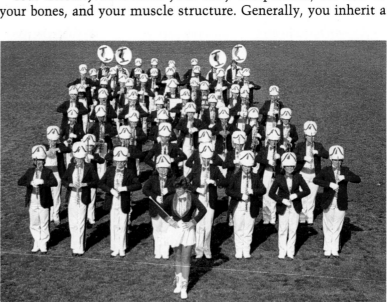

FIGURE 14–3. In most groups of people, there are examples of different body types.

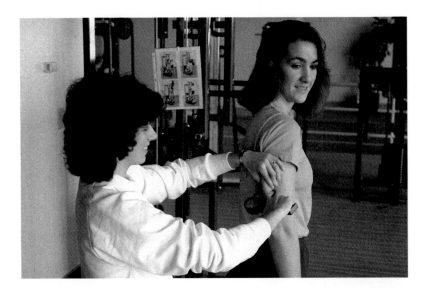

FIGURE 14–4. One method of measuring fat thicknesses at parts of the body involves using calipers.

tendency toward one of three body builds. An **ectomorph** is a person who is long-boned and has a lean body build. A **meso-morph** is a person who has a muscular body build. An **endomorph** is a person who has a greater percentage of fat tissues and a flabby appearance.

You inherit a tendency toward being an endomorph, ectomorph, or mesomorph.

The type and frequency of exercise in which you engage also influences body composition. When you exercise to develop cardiovascular endurance and become physically fit, the ratio of fat tissue to lean tissue changes. As mentioned earlier, your percentage of fat tissue decreases and the percentage of lean tissue increases. For example, marathon runners may have only eight to ten percent fat tissue.

Research indicates a relationship between susceptibility to heart disease and the area where fat accumulates. If you are wider in the abdomen than in the hips, you are more susceptible to heart disease than if the opposite is true.

If you tend to gain weight easily in your abdominal area, you may be more susceptible to heart disease.

 ## Review and Reflect

1. What are three ways that physical fitness will benefit you?
2. How do strong muscles help you?
3. How are muscular strength and muscular endurance different?
4. Why are persons who are older less likely to be flexible than persons your age?
5. How does having cardiovascular endurance affect the formula for cardiac output?
6. How are HDLs different from LDLs?
7. How can you decrease your percentage of body fat?

TYPES OF EXERCISES

A personal exercise plan should include a variety of exercises.

There are several types of exercises that will help you develop muscular strength, muscular endurance, flexibility, cardiovascular endurance, lowered percentage of body fat, and increased lean tissue. It is important to understand the benefits of each type of exercise. Then you will be better able to plan your personal exercise plan.

14:7 Isometric Exercise

Isometric exercises involve tightening muscles for five to ten seconds without moving body parts.

An **isometric exercise** is an exercise in which your muscles are tightened for about five to ten seconds without any movement of body parts. You may tighten your muscles or you may try to push or pull an immovable object. Pushing against the wall is an example of an isometric exercise. Tightening the abdomen while lying on your back with your knees bent is another isometric example. You might stand on a jump rope and pull the rope ends as hard as possible. Do not hold your breath while you do these isometric exercises.

Isometric exercises increase muscular strength.

Isometric exercises develop muscular strength. They help make the muscles attached to your bones larger and stronger. However, they are of limited value in building flexibility and muscular endurance and are of little value in promoting cardiovascular endurance. Isometric exercises may cause a sudden increase in blood pressure and should not be selected by persons with heart problems.

FIGURE 14–5. Standing on a jump rope and pulling on the ends help strengthen your biceps.

FIGURE 14–6. By properly performing the curl-up, you contract and strengthen your abdominal muscles. Press the small of your back against the floor. With bent legs, hip width apart, lift your shoulders off the floor. Repeat.

14:8   Isotonic Exercise

An **isotonic exercise** is an exercise in which there is contraction of a muscle causing movement. Swimming, walking, running, bicycling, and sports activities are isotonic exercises. Push-ups, curl-ups, and jumping jacks are all isotonic. Weight lifting is another example of isotonic exercise.

When beginning to do isotonic exercise, it is important to increase the amount of exercise gradually. Muscles need to be strengthened in order to build endurance. You may choose to begin with ten curl-ups and five push-ups and gradually increase the number of each. When beginning a weight-lifting program, you may begin with a certain weight and then gradually increase the amount of weight and the number of times you lift it.

Isotonic exercises help build muscular strength and improve flexibility. Some isotonic exercises may improve your cardiovascular endurance if you perform them at a certain intensity for a specified amount of time.

Isotonic exercises involve contraction and movement of muscles.

Isotonic exercises increase muscular strength and flexibility.

Activity: Isotonic Exercise

Divide into groups of five or six. Develop an isotonic exercise routine that includes two exercises for strengthening arm muscles, two exercises for strengthening leg muscles, and two exercises for strengthening abdominal muscles. Your group may want to obtain exercise and fitness books from the library to complete this project. Demonstrate the six exercises in your routine for the rest of your classmates.

FIGURE 14–7. Pneumatic equipment will enable you to move through an entire range of motion.

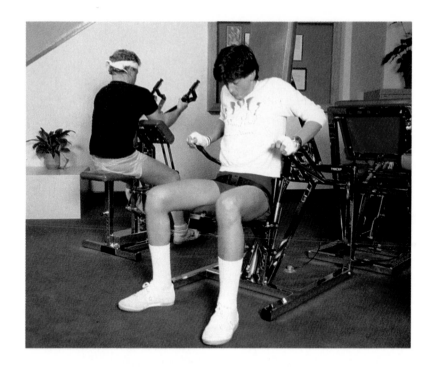

14:9   Isokinetic Exercise

Isokinetic exercises involve the movement of weight through an entire range of motion.

An **isokinetic exercise** is an exercise in which a weight, or resistance, is moved through an entire range of motion. Machines with weight plates, popular at exercise clubs, utilize isokinetic exercise that promotes flexibility, strength, and muscular endurance. An extra feature of machines with weight plates is that resistance can be varied. While resisting the weight plates, heart rate increases. Maintaining this heart rate level promotes cardiovascular fitness.

Some isokinetic exercises utilize weight plates; others involve pressurized air.

Another type of isokinetic strength training equipment is a pneumatic system. Pneumatic equipment uses pressurized air for resistance instead of weight plates. Resistance can easily be varied at any time during range of motion with the adjustment of a knob. Because weight plates are not used for resistance, injury is less likely to occur. The easy adjustment of resistance allows a smoother workout. This type of equipment also promotes flexibility, strength, and muscular endurance.

Learn the correct procedure for using weight machines.

To receive maximum benefit and prevent injury, you should learn correct ways to use exercise equipment. Have someone help you determine
(1) how much weight you should lift at each station,
(2) when to increase resistance, and
(3) how many repetitions you should perform at each station.

14:10   Aerobic Exercise

Aerobic means with air. An **aerobic exercise** is a form of exercise that requires a continuous use of oxygen over an extended period of time. This usually means at least 15 to 30 minutes of continuous exercise. Aerobic exercises help you develop cardiovascular endurance, some flexibility and muscular strength. Some examples include aerobic dancing, bicycling at a steady pace, distance swimming, distance running, and speed walking.

The American College of Sports Medicine (ACSM) recommends that aerobic exercise always be performed at your target heart rate for cardiovascular benefit. The **target heart rate** is between 60 and 90 percent of the difference between your resting heart rate and your maximum heart rate. This figure is added to your resting heart rate. **Maximum heart rate** is 220 minus your age. An average resting heart rate is about 70. An example will illustrate how to determine target heart rate.

Example:

Suppose you are 15 years old. Your maximum heart rate would be 220 minus 15 or 205. Your resting heart rate is 70. Target heart rate is between 60 to 90 percent of the difference between your resting heart rate and your maximum heart rate.

205 (maximum heart rate) − 70 (resting heart rate) = 135
.60 × 135 =   81 + 70 = 151 lowest target heart rate
.90 × 135 = 122 + 70 = 192 highest target heart rate
Target heart rate = 151 to 192 beats per minute

If you choose running as an aerobic exercise, you would need to run at a steady pace to maintain your target heart rate of 151 to 192 beats per minute. There is quite a difference between the lowest and the highest heart rates. Most healthy persons your age use 75 percent to determine the target heart rate at which they will exercise.

Example:
205 (maximum heart rate) − (resting heartbeat rate) = 135
.75 × 135 = 101 + 70 = 171 beats per minute

To achieve and maintain cardiovascular endurance, the ACSM recommends exercising three to five days per week. The exercise sessions should include 15 to 60 minutes of continuous aerobic activity. The number of minutes depends on the intensity of the activity. During exercise, you can take your pulse to see if you are maintaining your target heart rate. The ACSM tends to favor aerobic activity of longer duration and less intensity. When this plan is followed, there is more likely to be a total fitness effect and less likely to be any health hazards.

Aerobic exercises include those in which oxygen is used for at least 15 to 30 minutes.

Aerobic exercise benefits you most when performed at your target heart rate.

To calculate target heart rate, use 60 to 90 percent of the difference between your resting and maximum heart rate, and add that figure to your resting heart rate.

FIGURE 14–8. Shortness of breath occurs after anaerobic exercise.

14:11   Anaerobic Exercise

Anaerobic means without air. An **anaerobic exercise** is a form of exercise in which the body's demand for oxygen exceeds the supply. An anaerobic exercise is usually done in short, fast bursts of energy. This results in a condition known as oxygen debt. One sign of oxygen debt is shortness of breath. If the person slows or stops the exercise, recovery begins. You have seen this effect if you have watched someone out of breath after running the 100-meter dash.

Some isotonic exercises can also be anaerobic. For example, if you repeat exercises using weights, you would be doing an isotonic and anaerobic exercise. The exercise is isotonic because muscles are contracted with movement. The exercise is anaerobic because you would experience oxygen debt. Anaerobic exercises may improve muscular strength, muscular endurance, and flexibility. They also help increase speed. However, they are usually not beneficial to cardiovascular endurance.

Anaerobic exercises improve muscular strength and endurance and flexibility.

 Review and Reflect

8. Why should persons with high blood pressure avoid isometric exercises?
9. How do isokinetic weight exercises differ from isotonic weight exercises?
10. How do you know if you are doing an anaerobic or an aerobic exercise when you are running?

OTHER COMPONENTS OF PHYSICAL FITNESS

To achieve and maintain physical fitness, you need to do more than participate in a regular exercise program. You need to eat balanced, healthful meals and get the right amount of rest and sleep. Physical fitness is the result of a blend of healthful behaviors.

14:12 Nutrition and Physical Fitness

Which of the following statements do you believe is true?

- People engaged in physical fitness programs have special needs for nutrients.
- People engaged in physical fitness programs have similar needs for nutrients as those persons who are not engaged in physical fitness programs.

Physically fit persons need the same nutrients as those persons who are inactive.

Many people would support the first statement; however, it is false. All healthy persons have similiar needs for nutrients. The most healthful diet for all persons is to (1) eat the correct number of servings from the healthful food groups, (2) follow the seven diet goals identified in Chapter 12, (3) consume the correct number of Calories to maintain ideal weight, and (4) drink six to eight glasses of water a day.

Your diet contributes to your level of physical fitness.

Some people choose exercise programs that require prolonged activity, such as marathon running. Such persons might engage in a practice known as carbohydrate loading. Carbohydrate loading involves the increased consumption of complex carbohydrates, such as bread and pasta, for about one week prior to a strenuous event. The additional complex carbohydrates are to help increase the stored energy in the body. Many sports physicians do not find this practice beneficial.

14:13 Rest and Sleep

You have been learning about the importance of regular activity. It is also important to have periods of inactivity. Rest and sleep help your body rebuild itself and reenergize. While you sleep, several changes occur in your body. Your heart rate slows by about 10 to 15 beats per minute, your blood pressure decreases, and you take fewer breaths per minute. Your muscles lose tension during sleep. Growth hormone is released into the blood. You are actually growing while you sleep and rest!

A physically fit person needs to balance exercise with rest and sleep.

When planning your activities, keep your biorhythm in mind.

Regular exercise promotes healthful sleep.

Your need for sleep is influenced by your activity level.

Your need for sleep and the times at which you go to sleep and awaken are individual. Each person has a natural inborn energy cycle or **biorhythm.** Your biorhythm determines when your highest peaks of energy occur and when you feel most sluggish. Sometimes it is helpful to plan your activities around this energy cycle. When you feel sluggish, you will also want to check your diet to see if it is well-balanced.

Most adolescents sleep seven to nine hours each night. You may need more sleep if you feel fatigued, or overly tired. You may feel fatigued if you have exercised strenuously or if you are under stress. Fatigue may also result from a starvation diet, lack of sleep, or illness.

Sometimes you cannot get to sleep. This is normal. But when your inability to get to sleep becomes a pattern, you have **insomnia.** Insomnia has several causes—stress being the leading one. Insomnia is one of the most frequent symptoms of depression. Eating or drinking foods and beverages high in caffeine or sugar tends to stimulate you and may cause insomnia. Eating late, consuming spicy foods, and drinking alcoholic beverages are also causes. Following are some tips for getting a good night's sleep. Select a medium-hard mattress for your bed. This type of mattress will support your back. Try to keep your environment quiet or play soft, restful music. If you have difficulty sleeping, try some relaxation exercises. The relaxation exercises in Chapter 7 can also be used. You might drink a glass of milk. Milk contains tryptophan, which acts as a natural sedative. Examine your lifestyle. What are sources of stress that you might change?

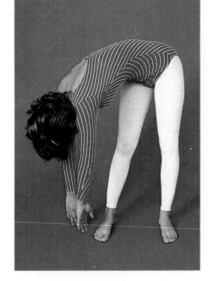

FIGURE 14–9. For relaxation, stand with your feet about a foot apart; let your torso droop forward, slightly stretching your lower back and thigh muscles; keep your knees straight. Bob slowly and gently from one side to the other.

Review and Reflect

11. How are your nutritional needs similar to those of an Olympic athlete?
12. Why do you need seven to nine hours of sleep a night to remain healthy?
13. What would you do if you could not get to sleep?

Health
ADVANCES

You have learned about the components of physical fitness. You have also learned how being physically fit and exercising regularly can benefit you. Perhaps you are thinking that the benefits of regular exercise are limited to people who are in good health. This is not the case.

14:14 Exercise and Cancer

Researchers have studied the physical and mental effects of exercise in helping cancer patients tolerate their treatment and have feelings of well-being. Exercise was found to help 93 percent of the 251 patients studied. Most of the patients had had surgery. About half had received chemotherapy or drug treatment. Some had been given radiation.

The patients derived better physical health and a more positive mental outlook after exercise. Forty-eight percent of the patients said the exercise helped them fight their cancer. Exercise helped in many cases to restore strength to muscles weakened by surgery. Exercising in groups often helped emotionally as people shared experiences and encouraged each other. The most popular exercises were running, swimming, bicycling, and weightlifting.

Researchers felt that this study should change the image of the cancer patient. A person can have cancer and still be active and involved with life.

Regular aerobic exercise helps many cancer patients experience better physical and mental health.

Review and Reflect

14. How do some cancer patients benefit from exercise?

FIGURE 14–10 Regular exercise is a must for everyone.

Focus on
Life Management Skills

- Enjoy the many health benefits of physical fitness.
- Improve muscular strength in order to lift, push, pull, jump, twist, turn, and bend.
- Improve muscular endurance in order to continue playing sports activities for extended lengths of time.
- Stretch 20 minutes each day to remain flexible.
- Increase high-density lipoproteins and decrease low-density lipoproteins by regularly engaging in exercises that promote cardiovascular endurance.
- Exercise regularly to increase your percentage of lean tissue and decrease your percentage of fat tissue.
- Engage in isometric exercises to increase muscular strength.
- Engage in sports activities, calisthenics, and other isotonic exercises to build muscular strength and improve flexibility.
- Before engaging in isokinetic exercises, consult with a trained fitness supervisor to learn about the weight training machines and your capabilities.
- Engage in aerobic exercise three to five days a week for 15 to 60 minutes at your target heart rate.
- Eat a balanced diet from the healthful food groups that follows the seven diet goals and helps you maintain your ideal weight.
- Get at least seven to nine hours of sleep each night.

Health
CAREERS

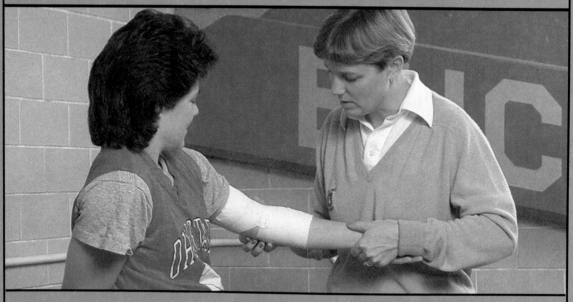

Athletic Trainer

Linda Daniel is the head athletic trainer at a major university. An athletic trainer is a health professional who carries out programs to prevent injury and gives immediate treatment and rehabilitation procedures for the injured athlete as directed by a physician. A university, college, or high school trainer's responsibilities might also include the physical education, recreation, and intramural programs.

You can begin preparing for this career in high school by studying science courses and by being a student trainer or manager. You can read about athletic training and attend clinics to become more knowledgeable in this field.

While in college, you can enroll in courses to complete the athletic training curriculum in addition to your major course work. If you choose a health-related major, many of these classes will be the same.

Linda Daniel received her undergraduate and graduate degrees in physical therapy. To become an athletic trainer, Linda had to fulfill certification requirements. These include (1) a degree from a four-year accredited college or university, (2) current American Red Cross Standard First-Aid certification, (3) current Basic Cardiopulmonary Resuscitation certificate, (4) completion of 1800 hours clinical experience, and (5) a passing score on the National Athletic Trainer Association Examination.

Currently, Linda is in charge of all athletic trainers at her university. She also travels with the women's basketball team and teaches physical education classes.

Summary

1. You must have muscular endurance, muscular strength, flexibility, cardiovascular endurance, and a lean body composition to be physically fit. 14:1

2. Muscular strength helps you lift, push, pull, and jump and prevents you from being easily fatigued. 14:2

3. Muscular endurance involves using muscles for long periods of time without becoming tired. 14:3

4. Flexibility enables you to move your joints and muscles without being stiff. 14:4

5. Cardiovascular endurance enables you to do activities such as running and bicycling in which you increase your oxygen intake for extended lengths of time. 14:5

6. When you regularly exercise to promote cardiovascular endurance, you change the ratio of lean tissue and fat tissue. 14:6

7. Isometric exercises help you develop muscular strength but are of little value in promoting cardiovascular endurance. 14:7

8. Isotonic exercises help build muscular strength, improve flexibility, and may improve cardiovascular endurance. 14:8

9. Isokinetic exercises promote muscular strength and endurance. 14:9

10. Aerobic exercises, such as running, build cardiovascular endurance. 14:10

11. Anaerobic exercises may improve muscular strength and endurance, and flexibility and speed. 14:11

12. Everyone has the same nutritional needs. 14:12

13. Rest and sleep help your body rebuild itself and help prevent fatigue. 14:13

14. Regular physical exercise helps some cancer patients tolerate their treatment. 14:14

Vocabulary

Below is a list of vocabulary words used in this chapter. Use each word only once to complete the sentences. Do not write in this book.

aerobic exercise   insomnia
biorhythm   LDL
body composition   mesomorph
cardiac output   muscular strength
flexibility   stroke volume

1. Cardiovascular endurance increases cardiac output because _____ is increased.

2. A person who can move through a full range of motion is exhibiting _____.

3. A muscular, heavy-boned wrestler most likely has a(n) _____ body build.

4. Speed walking is an example of a(n) _____.

5. The amount of force you can exert against resistance is a measure of your _____.

6. A person who likes to sleep late may have a different _____ than a person who likes to get up early.

7. The percentages of fat tissue and lean tissue in a person's body are known as _____.

8. A pattern of not being able to get to sleep is _____.

9. _____ can be increased by an increase in heart rate or the amount of blood pumped with each beat.

10. Exercises that promote cardiovascular endurance decrease the amounts of _____ in the blood.

Review

1. What are 6 health benefits derived from being physically fit?
2. What are two benefits of having muscular strength?
3. How does muscular endurance improve performance in sports?
4. Why should someone stretch twenty minutes each day?
5. How does cardiovascular endurance improve the condition of the heart, blood, blood vessels, and lungs?
6. Describe three types of body builds.
7. What are two benefits of isometric exercise?
8. What are two benefits of isotonic exercise?
9. What are safety precautions to follow when using machines for isokinetic exercise?
10. According to the American College of Sports Medicine, how should you exercise to achieve and maintain cardiovascular endurance?
11. What are four possible benefits of anaerobic exercise?
12. What are four nutritional guidelines that should be followed by persons engaged in a physical fitness program?
13. What are three ways to improve your chances of getting a good night's sleep?

Application

1. What type of exercise would you do if you wanted to improve your posture?
2. What type of exercise would you do if you wanted to lower your resting heart rate?
3. If your legs felt stiff, what type of exercise would you do to relieve the stiffness?
4. What is your maximum heart rate?

Individual Research

1. Visit a health and exercise facility that has machines for isokinetic exercise. Interview the physical fitness person in charge of the weight room. What programs are conducted at this facility? Describe the benefits of some of the machines. What safety precautions are observed? Prepare an oral report.
2. Learn about three places in your community that provide aerobic exercise or aerobic dance programs. When are these programs offered? Who attends the programs? How much do the programs cost? If possible, interview some people who use the programs. Prepare an oral report for classmates.

Readings

Todd, Jan, and Todd, Terry, *Lift Your Way to Youthful Fitness*. Boston, MA: Little, Brown & Company, 1985.

Wolf, Michael, *The Complete Book of Nautilus Training*. Chicago, IL: Contemporary Books, Inc., 1984.

Physical fitness does not just happen. It is accomplished as the result of setting a goal, making plans to reach the goal, and using self-discipline. Why does a basketball team warm up before a game? How can you make a plan to achieve physical fitness?

Chapter 15

Designing Your Physical Fitness Plan

OBJECTIVES: You will be able to
- **identify guidelines, principles, and lifetime sports to include in a physical fitness plan.**
- **identify ways to stay healthy and safe during exercise.**
- **describe the health hazards of anabolic steroids.**

What Is A Workout? A workout is 25 percent perspiration and 75 percent determination. Stated another way, it is one part physical exertion and three parts self-discipline. Doing it is easy, once you get started.

A workout makes you better today than you were yesterday. It strengthens the body, relaxes the mind, and toughens the spirit. When you work out regularly, your problems diminish and your confidence grows.

A workout is a personal triumph over laziness and procrastination. It is the badge of a winner—the mark of an organized, goal-oriented person who has taken charge of his or her destiny.

A workout requires self-discipline.

A workout is a wise use of time and an investment in excellence. It is a way of preparing for life's challenges and proving to yourself that you have what it takes to do what is necessary.

A workout is the key that helps unlock the door to opportunity and success. Hidden within each of us is an extraordinary force. Physical and mental fitness are the triggers that can release it.

A workout is a form of rebirth. When you finish a good workout, you don't simply feel better,
You feel better about yourself.

A workout helps promote self-esteem.

George Allen,
The President's Council on Physical Fitness and Sports

YOUR INDIVIDUALIZED PHYSICAL FITNESS PLAN

What message did you receive as you read the quote on page 293? This quote and the information in Chapter 14 focus on the need to work out regularly to obtain benefits of physical fitness. To obtain the maximum benefits, there are certain guidelines and training principles to follow.

15:1 Guidelines for Physical Fitness Plans

There are ten guidelines to use in designing your physical fitness plan.

Certain guidelines and training principles will help you obtain the maximum benefits of physical fitness.

- *Before you begin, determine your current level of physical fitness for each of the five components—muscular strength, muscular endurance, flexibility, cardiovascular endurance, and body composition.* You may obtain the help of your physical education teacher or a fitness instructor at a "Y" or health club. It is advisable to have a medical checkup, and to inform your physician that you would like to begin a fitness program. Your physician may have suggestions for your plan based on the results of your checkup.

Your physical education teacher can help you determine your current fitness level.

- *Identify the physical fitness goals you want to achieve in each of the five fitness areas.* Each person needs an individual plan. For example, if you are flexible but lack cardiovascular endurance, you will design a plan to maintain flexibility. You will focus on exercises such as distance walking to develop cardiovascular endurance.

Set goals for each component of fitness.

- *Select exercises appropriate for your age and current level of physical fitness.* Your plans need to include exercises you will be able to do. Do not begin with unreasonable expectations.
- *Plan a program that provides social activity.* Exercise can and should be enjoyable. Many exercises are done alone and provide time by yourself to think and relax. Other exercises provide time to share with a friend or a group of friends. Physical activity could also satisfy your need to compete.

Make your fitness plan enjoyable.

- *Select appropriate equipment and clothing.* It is best to run in shoes made for running. It is usually more comfortable to wear leotards, shorts, or sweat pants for aerobics instead of tight-fitting jeans. Your exercise sessions will be more enjoyable when you are comfortable and your equipment is right for you.
- *Follow training principles.* To get the maximum benefit from your fitness program, you will need to follow the principles discussed in Section 15:2.

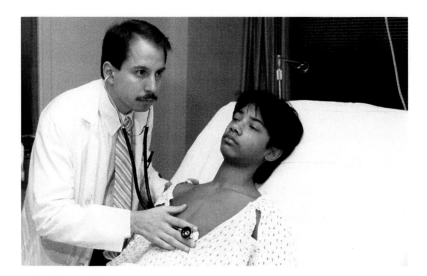

FIGURE 15-1. The first step in designing your fitness plan is to have a medical checkup. The types of exercise you choose should be based on your physical condition and ability.

- *Know and follow safety rules.* This chapter also includes a list of popular ways to exercise while staying safe.
- *Plan to prevent common injuries by understanding why and how they occur.* This chapter includes suggestions for prevention and treatment of common injuries.
- *Adjust exercise plans to weather conditions.* Extremely hot or cold weather and air pollution may alter your training plans and clothing needs. If you are allergic to ragweed, you may choose to exercise indoors during the ragweed season. When cold weather arrives, ice may accumulate on the sidewalks and streets. Running, walking, and biking may be hazardous.
- *Reevaluate your fitness level at regular intervals.* In order to maintain physical fitness, you need to establish new goals and make and follow new plans.

Planning ahead will help you avoid accidents and injuries.

You will need to revise your fitness plan at regular intervals.

15:2   Training Principles

Although your plan for physical fitness is individualized, all persons who exercise need to follow certain training principles. These training principles apply to all activities done to gain physical fitness.

The **principle of warming up** involves three to five minutes of activity where the joints and muscles of the body are made ready to do more exercise. You would do different warm-up exercises prior to participation in different exercises. For example, gymnasts may stretch for three to five minutes before their routine. They stretch the muscles they will be using in their activity. A marathon runner may run slowly or walk briskly before a race begins. This readies the heart and leg muscles for more work.

Warm-up exercises prepare your heart and other muscles for more intense activity.

FIGURE 15–2. Warming down is the opposite of warming up. Do not stop a strenuous exercise abruptly.

Cooling down helps return blood to your heart and other body parts.

Applying the principle of specificity helps you focus on a specific fitness goal.

The principle of overload helps you progress to higher fitness levels by increasing the body's capacity to work.

The principle of frequency involves engaging in exercise often enough to gain benefits.

The **principle of warming down** or **cooling down** involves at least three to five minutes of reduced exercise. During this time, heart rate slows and body temperature lowers. While cooling down, muscles help blood return to the heart more easily. Medical research shows that as much as 80 percent of blood volume may be in the legs after running or bicycling. If you abruptly stop exercising, the blood may remain pooled in the legs, and you may feel faint. Walking after running and slowing the pace of bicycling help blood return to the heart and the brain.

The **principle of specificity** involves choosing an exercise or activity that provides the desired benefit. For example, if you want to develop cardiovascular fitness, you would obtain more benefits from distance swimming than bowling. If you are a gymnast, you would want to increase flexibility. Exercise should be specific to help you reach your desired goal.

The **principle of overload** involves increasing the body's capacity to do more work than usual. Suppose you lift weights to strengthen your arms. If it is very easy for you to lift a certain weight, you will not be increasing muscular strength. You must gradually add more weights to improve your physical fitness.

The **principle of progression** involves gradually increasing the intensity and duration of exercise. Intensity is how hard you work while you exercise. Duration is the length of time you exercise.

The **principle of frequency** involves how often you engage in your exercise program. One day a week is not enough to develop physical fitness. You will remember that the American College of Sports Medicine (ACSM) recommends three to five days of exercise per week for cardiovascular endurance. This is true for other aspects of fitness also. Stretching exercises to obtain and maintain flexibility should be done daily or at least several times a week.

15:3   A Complete Workout for Physical Fitness

What is the best workout you can do to achieve and maintain physical fitness? The exercises you choose for your workout will depend upon your health status, your body build, your current level of physical fitness, and your preferences. A complete five-part workout is outlined for you in Table 15–1. Exercises that promote cardiovascular endurance also change the percentage of fat tissue and lean tissue. Your complete workout can be individualized. You can choose exercises that meet your needs and preferences.

A complete workout involves warming up, exercises to promote all five kinds of fitness, and a cool-down.

Table 15–1   A Complete Workout for Physical Fitness

1. **Exercises for Warming Up**	Plan three to five minutes of exercises that prepare the joints and muscles for more strenuous activity. Stretching exercises and aerobic exercises done at a reduced level should be included.
2. **Exercises for Flexibility**	Include stretching exercises to improve and maintain the range of movement in muscles and joints.
3. **Exercises for Cardiovascular Endurance and Body Composition**	The ACSM recommends 15 to 60 minutes of continuous aerobic activity at your target heart rate. The number of minutes depends on the intensity of the activity and your fitness level.
4. **Exercises for Muscular Strength and Endurance**	Choose exercises to strengthen and tone your muscles. Isotonic, isometric, and isokinetic exercises accomplish this purpose. Include exercises for all major muscle groups and joints.
5. **Exercises for Cooling Down or Warming Down**	Include three to five minutes of reduced exercise. During this time, the heart rate slows, the body temperature lowers, and muscles help return blood to the heart and brain. Stretching exercises and aerobic exercises done at a reduced level should be included.

FIGURE 15–3. Your choice of a lifetime sport may be determined by the area of the country in which you live.

15:4 Choosing Lifetime Sports

In planning your complete workout for physical fitness, you may want to include one or more of your favorite sports. Much emphasis has been placed on choosing to engage in lifetime sports at a young age to develop habits and sport skills that you can use for a lifetime. **Lifetime sports** include sports activities that can be continued as you grow older provided you stay in good health. Some examples of lifetime sports are swimming, bicycling, and playing tennis.

Now is the time to develop the habit of engaging in lifetime sports.

In order to choose sports that meet your needs, you will want to examine the advantages and disadvantages of particular sports. You will also want to know how each sport contributes to your weight-management plan by burning Calories and reducing your percentage of body fat.

Running improves cardiovascular endurance, burns Calories, and reduces the percentage of body fat.

Running is one of the most efficient and inexpensive ways to achieve cardiovascular endurance, improve muscular endurance, reduce percentage of body fat, and strengthen the leg muscles. While you run, you burn approximately 575 to 700 Calories per hour. A disadvantage to running is that there are few benefits to the muscles in the upper body. Some persons will carry hand weights while running to obtain some benefits to arm and shoulder muscles. It is important to have an exercise program for flexibility in addition to running. Running may cause the muscles in the legs to shorten, but flexibility exercises will help prevent this.

Swimming is one of the best sports for cardiovascular endurance if target heart rate is maintained for 20 minutes. Swimming promotes muscular strength and endurance in the leg and arm muscles. The abdominal muscles are also strengthened. Because swimming is less harmful to the legs and the joints of ankles than running, it can be used for physical fitness by persons who are overweight and/or recovering from certain types of surgery. An active swimmer burns approximately 350 to 425 Calories per hour.

Swimming promotes cardiovascular endurance without the risk of joint injuries.

Bicycling promotes cardiovascular endurance, strengthens leg and back muscles, and decreases percentage of body fat. To obtain these benefits, pedal fast, ride up hills, and use a gear that offers resistance. Stretching exercises are important for the legs and back as a warm up and warm down. Bicycling burns approximately 350 to 500 Calories per hour. Disadvantages to this activity include the hazards of severe weather and heavy traffic.

Bicycling at a fast and steady pace increases cardiovascular endurance and builds lean muscle mass.

Walking is helpful in maintaining ideal weight, decreasing percentage of body fat, and building cardiovascular endurance. To accomplish this goal, walk a minimum of 30 minutes a day, four days a week, at your target heart rate. Try to walk 15-minute miles. While you walk, you and a walking partner should be able to maintain a conversation. By wearing proper clothing and shoes, the walk should be painless, and you should not be tired for more than an hour after you finish. Check Table 15–2 below to learn how many Calories you might expend by walking.

Walking at a fast, steady pace promotes cardiovascular endurance and decreases the percentage of body fat.

Other lifetime sports include bowling, golf, handball, racquet sports, roller skating, ice skating, skiing, and tennis (Table 15–3).

Table 15–2   Number of Calories Expended by Walking (per hour)

Speed (MPH)	100	120	140	160	180	200	220
2	130	160	185	210	240	265	290
2 1/2	155	185	220	250	280	310	345
3	180	215	250	285	325	360	395
3 1/2	205	248	290	330	375	415	455
4	235	280	325	375	420	470	515
4 1/2	310	370	435	495	550	620	680
5	385	460	540	615	690	770	845

WALKING — WEIGHT IN POUNDS

Table 15–3 Other Lifetime Sports

SPORT	ADVANTAGES	DISADVANTAGES	CALORIES BURNED/HR
Basketball	• Maintains physical fitness • Builds cardiovascular endurance	• Must be presently physically fit • Requires other players • Risk of injuries	600–750
Bowling	• Relaxing effect • Low physical activity	• No physical fitness benefits • Not recommended for anyone with back problems	150–200
Golf	• Promotes flexibility	• No benefits toward muscular strength and endurance or cardiovascular fitness • Does not decrease percentage of body fat	250–325 (walking) 185–225 (carting)
Racquet Sports (Handball, Squash, Racquetball)	• Promotes cardiovascular endurance • Builds muscular strength and endurance	• Injury with inadequate warm up • Requires safety glasses to prevent eye injury	650–750
Skating	• Promotes cardiovascular endurance • Strengthens muscles • Increases flexibility	• Sore muscles with inadequate warm up	300–350 (leisure) 525–625 (vigorous)
Skiing (downhill)	• Promotes cardiovascular endurance to some degree	• Need conditioning program 6–8 weeks prior to engaging in sport	500 (depending on length of run)
Tennis	• Develops flexibility • Promotes cardiovascular endurance (highly skilled players only)	• Injury with inadequate warm up	250–500 (depending on skill)

Engaging in a variety of lifetime sports provides many physical benefits.

It is important to make lifetime sports a habit.

 # Activity: ## Applying Lifetime Sports

Divide into groups with classmates. Select one of the lifetime sports about which you have just read. Discuss how you might warm up before this activity. Discuss how you would use this activity as part of a physical fitness workout. How would you cool down? Prepare an oral report and share your group's report with the other groups.

 ## Review and Reflect

1. Why is it important to warm up before you exercise?
2. How does cooling down keep you from becoming light-headed or faint?
3. Why should a physical fitness program meet your social needs?
4. Why do you need to reevaluate your fitness goals at regular intervals?
5. Why are intensity and duration important when planning a running program?

STAYING HEALTHY AND SAFE DURING EXERCISE

Todd and Mark decided to go running. Mark sprained his ankle during the run. Todd thought they should apply heat to the sprain. Mark thought they should apply ice. What was the best choice? What decision would you have made? What procedures do you follow to stay healthy and safe during exercise?

Practicing your knowlege about exercise can keep you healthy and safe.

15:5 Prevention and Treatment of Exercise Injuries

Many people your age participate in sports activities and active exercises. This participation has been accompanied by an increase in exercise-related injuries. An estimated ten million injuries occur each year to youth involved in sports. Here are pointers to help you prevent injury or reinjury.

Many persons your age experience injuries that might have been prevented.

- *Know Your Body Limitations.* Sophisticated testing can be done by sports scientists to identify which sports are best for certain body types and/or body conditions. **Physical profiling** is a method of testing your physical limits to determine the types of sports that are best for you. For example, the results of your physical profile may show that you have weak knees. Running would aggravate your problem. If you are obese, you might choose an activity where your weight is not constantly supported by your legs, ankles, and feet. Bicycling might be a good sport for you to choose.

Physical profiling helps you determine the sports for which you are best suited.

FIGURE 15–4. During a physical profile, body systems such as heart rate and blood pressure are monitored constantly.

Biomechanics can help you analyze your body's motion during sports.

Safety rules are designed to help prevent injuries.

Most exercise injuries can be avoided.

Six causes of injury are poor flexibility, muscle imbalance, overtraining, structural problems, poor training methods, and inadequate equipment.

- *Improve Your Skills.* **Biomechanics** is the study of how the body functions during movement. High-speed cameras are used to film body movement. The film can be played back in slow motion for analysis. By analyzing the motion in a pitcher's throw or a tennis player's serve, form can be corrected to prevent injury. For example, an inexperienced tennis player may grip the racquet incorrectly. This may cause unnecessary strain on the elbow. Using the correct grip may correct the motion and prevent elbow injury.
- *Follow Safety Rules.* Safety rules are designed to promote safe play. Follow the safety rules outlined in Section 15:6.
- *Know the Causes of Exercise Injuries.* Approximately seventy-five percent of all injuries to youth occur in five sports: bicycling, football, basketball, running, and roller skating. Table 15–4 includes six common causes of exercise injuries.
- *Be Familiar With the Ten Most Common Exercise Injuries or Conditions.* Table 15–5 identifies ten common exercise injuries or conditions. Study the description for each injury or condition and the tips for preventing them. Follow the suggestions for prevention.

Table 15–4   Six Causes Of Exercise Injuries

1. Poor Flexibility	Training increases muscular strength, but as muscles strengthen, they shorten. This shortening results in tight muscles, which increases the chance of injury.
2. Muscle Imbalance	When you concentrate on one type of exercise, you may overdevelop some muscles and underdevelop others.
3. Overtraining	You may overdo your workout and ignore pain.
4. Structural Problems	You may need to change technique or use special equipment if you have an anatomical abnormality or a physical disability.
5. Poor Training Methods	You may try to do too much too fast. Following a hard workout, your body needs time to rest. Remember to warm up and cool down.
6. Inadequate Equipment	Quality equipment is important for safety. The correct shoes for running, a properly sized racquet for tennis, and helmets for bicyclists help prevent injury.

Source: Adapted from Nick Gallo "The ABCs of Athletic Injuries," *Current Health 2,* Volume 12, No. 1, September, 1985.

Table 15–5 Prevention and Treatment of Ten Common Exercise Injuries or Conditions

INJURY OR CONDITION	PREVENTION	TREATMENT
Athlete's Foot—a fungal infection that occurs between the toes and causes itching	Keep feet dry, wear clean socks, and dry feet thoroughly after swimming or showering. Do not wear socks or shoes belonging to others. Wear slippers or thongs in locker room and shower.	Apply a cream or spray that kills the fungus.
Blisters—an accumulation of fluid between the dermis and the epidermis of the skin, usually caused by friction from equipment or poorly-fitting shoes	Apply petroleum jelly or bandages to areas where blisters usually develop. When you feel a blister forming, stop your exercise and apply ice to the area to prevent the blister.	Cover small blisters with first aid cream, gauze, tape, or adhesive bandages. A large painful blister should be lanced with a sterile needle by a physician or a parent. Cover the area with first aid cream, gauze, and tape.
Bruises—injuries to muscles or bones that are accompanied by hemorrhaging, swelling, and pain	Avoid blows to muscles and bones. Wear knee pads or elbow pads when necessary.	Apply ice and cold packs to reduce bleeding and swelling for the first 48 hours. Avoid heat for 48 hours.
Joint Injuries—injuries to tissues surrounding the joints	Wear properly fitting shoes. Jog on soft surfaces to prevent jarring of joints.	The joint must be rested or the injury will be aggravated. Ice may be used.
Muscle Cramps—sharp pains from involuntary muscle contractions	Stretch out properly before exercise.	Massage the muscle. Stretch the muscle through its full range of motion.
Muscle Soreness—	Warm up before exercise by stretching. Avoid too much overload.	Massage with ice for a half hour. Then take a 15-minute break to avoid numbness. Repeat this procedure for three hours. Do not apply heat for 48 hours. Rest the muscle. When exercising again, begin gradually.
Muscle Strain—an injury to muscle and tendons resulting in hemorrhaging and loss of muscle strength. It is called tendinitis when only the tendons are involved. Shin-splint is a type of muscle strain that begins with aching pain near the shin bone	Avoid running too fast or too far when beginning a running program. Run on grass or an all-weather track. Do warm-up exercises and wear proper shoes.	Rest—no jogging or weight lifting. Apply ice to the area; stretch out the muscles well. Use alternative exercises rather than just running or weight lifting.
Side Ache—a dull or sharp pain in the side	Warm up sufficiently. Avoid exercise beyond safe overload. Avoid strenuous exercise shortly after a meal.	Slow down your exercise and wait for the side ache to stop.
Sprains—injuries to ligaments, particularly those in the ankle and knee	Avoid twisting an ankle or a knee. Strengthen the muscles around the joints, which help to support them.	Apply ice for 20 minutes. Repeat every four hours (up to 48 hours). Rest the sprained ankle or knee. See a physician.
Stress Fracture—a minor injury to one of the bones of the foot	Avoid running too fast or on hard surfaces. Wear shoes designed for the activity.	Rest for three to six weeks. During this time, avoid running and select other exercises.

FIGURE 15–5. It is best to give immediate treatment to an injury.

The RICE treatment includes *Rest*, *Ice*, *Compression*, and *Elevation*.

- *Use the RICE treatment* (Figure 15—6). Most exercise injuries are musculoskeletal injuries. These injuries can take several days or weeks to heal. The **RICE treatment** is a technique for treating these injuries, in which you lessen pain, limit swelling, reduce tissue damage, and promote faster healing.

FIGURE 15–6.

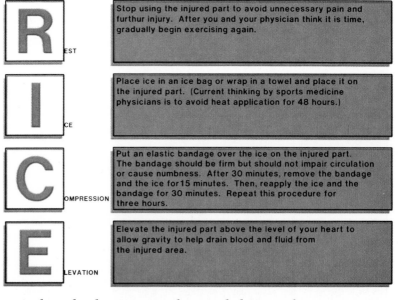

REST	Stop using the injured part to avoid unnecessary pain and furthur injury. After you and your physician think it is time, gradually begin exercising again.
ICE	Place ice in an ice bag or wrap in a towel and place it on the injured part. (Current thinking by sports medicine physicians is to avoid heat application for 48 hours.)
COMPRESSION	Put an elastic bandage over the ice on the injured part. The bandage should be firm but should not impair circulation or cause numbness. After 30 minutes, remove the bandage and the ice for 15 minutes. Then, reapply the ice and the bandage for 30 minutes. Repeat this procedure for three hours.
ELEVATION	Elevate the injured part above the level of your heart to allow gravity to help drain blood and fluid from the injured area.

Avoid heat on musculoskeletal injuries for the first 48 hours.

- *Seek medical treatment when needed.* You and your parents or coach may want to treat some minor injuries or conditions. However, medical treatment may be necessary at times. Consult a physician when an injury causes severe pain, joint problems, infection in or under the skin with accompanying pus or red streaks, swollen lymph nodes, or fever.

15:6   Safety Precautions for Exercise

Many of the ten common injuries about which you have learned could be avoided by knowing and following safety precautions and safety rules. Table 15–6 identifies popular exercises and ways to stay safe for each.

 Review and Reflect

6. How do sports scientists determine which sports are best for you?
7. Why do unskilled athletes have more injuries than those who are skilled?
8. How can you avoid getting athlete's foot if you shower at school each day?
9. Why is it better to run on a soft surface than a hard surface?
10. Why should you wear clothes that glow or have reflective tape if you walk or run at night?

Table 15–6   Safety Rules for Popular Ways to Exercise

BICYCLING	WALKING & RUNNING	SWIMMING & DIVING
• Ride in the same direction traffic is moving. • Obey all traffic signs. Use hand signals when turning. • Allow pedestrians to have the right-of-way. • Use lights on your bike at night. • Wear clothing that reflects or can be seen at dusk, dawn, or night. Use reflective tape on your bike. • Avoid bicycling on narrow, winding roads whenever possible. • Carry identification with you. • Know your route and destination. • Wear a safety helmet. • Check your bicycle to see that it functions properly.	• Walk or run in the opposite direction that traffic is moving. • Use designated paths and sidewalks as often as possible. • Avoid narrow, bending roads and highways. • Wear reflective clothing. • Obey all traffic signs. • Be defensive—watch for and anticipate what the drivers of cars are doing. • Avoid areas where you might slip on snow, ice, or rain. • Know your route and destination. • Carry identification and change for an emergency phone call.	• Do not swim too far from shore. • Always swim with another person. • Know the depth of the water before swimming or diving. • Do not dive into shallow water. • Swim only in supervised areas. • Call for help only when you need it. • Walk, do not run, around a pool. • Do not swim during an electrical storm.

Health
ADVANCES

Two teenage male athletes began to train for an important race. Each wanted to improve his performance. One of the young men had read something about anabolic steroids. He wondered if taking these drugs might help him become a champion. The other young man questioned this practice. "I'd rather be a true winner and use my body to the limit," he said. "Besides, I think there is recent evidence that this practice is dangerous." What are anabolic steroids? What is the recent research about their effectiveness and safety?

Exercise, diet, rest, and sleep are healthful ways to improve athletic performance.

15:7 Anabolic Steroids

Anabolic steroids are the synthetic derivatives of the male hormone testosterone. Anabolic steroids are injected or taken orally to stimulate increased muscle growth and strength gains. According to the ACSM, there is no conclusive scientific evidence that anabolic steroids aid or hinder athletic performance.

Anabolic steroids are synthetic male hormones that are dangerous to health.

However, there is scientific evidence that indicates anabolic steroids to be hazardous to health. When testosterone is taken at the onset of puberty, it stunts growth in both males and females.

When adult males take anabolic steroids, sperm are no longer produced and the male becomes sterile. In addition, the testes decrease in size, and the male shows signs of aggression. The male may begin to lose hair. These side effects may be reversible when the anabolic steroids are no longer taken.

Anabolic steroids may cause sterility and aggressiveness in males.

In females, the excess testosterone from anabolic steroids may cause masculine traits to appear. In extreme cases, behavior becomes more aggressive; the voice lowers; there is abnormal growth of hair on the face, breasts, and chest; the clitoris enlarges and menstruation stops. While these effects are sometimes reversible in the male, they are not in the female.

Anabolic steroid use may cause irreversible masculine traits to develop in females.

The long-term side effects of anabolic steroids in both males and females are even more serious. Increased use leads to hardening of the arteries, high blood pressure, and pulmonary arterial disease. There is a relationship between anabolic steroids and liver cancer. After long-term use, athletes experience withdrawal

The use of anabolic steroids may cause heart disease and liver cancer.

and severe depression when not taking them. These effects may begin when the athlete is in his or her late twenties or early thirties.

The hazards of anabolic steroids are some of the primary reasons for drug testing prior to athletic contests, including the Olympics. Another important reason involves ethics and competition. Athletes have traditionally measured the body's ability to perform within natural limits. The use of anabolic steroids changes the fairness of competition.

 ## Review and Reflect

11. Why are anabolic steroids dangerous?
12. Why is it unfair for some athletes to use anabolic steroids while others do not?

Focus on
Life Management Skills

- Follow guidelines when developing your individualized plan for physical fitness.
- Warm up before your workout and cool down afterward.
- Follow the principles of specificity, overload, progression, and frequency for all your exercise activity.
- Include exercises for cardiovascular endurance, percentage of body fat, muscular strength, muscular endurance, and flexibility in your workout.
- Know your body limitations for exercise.
- Work to improve the skills in the sports in which you participate.
- Avoid overtraining and using improper clothing and equipment.
- Keep your feet dry and wear clean socks and proper shoes.
- Remember the RICE treatment—rest, ice, compression, and elevation when you have a musculoskeletal injury.
- Seek medical treatment when an injury causes severe pain, joint problems, infection, swollen lymph nodes, or fever.
- Follow safety rules for sports.
- Avoid use of anabolic steroids.

Summary

1. There are ten guidelines to follow when you are designing your physical fitness plan. **15:1**

2. The training principles that apply to all activities for gaining physical fitness are warming up, warming down, specificity, overload, progression, and frequency. **15:2**

3. A complete workout for physical fitness includes exercises for (a) warming up, (b) cardiovascular endurance and body composition, (c) muscular strength and endurance, (d) flexibility, and (e) cooling down. **15:3**

4. Running, swimming, bicycling, and walking are four lifetime sports that develop cardiovascular endurance. **15:4**

5. You can help prevent injury and reinjury during exercise when you (a) know your body limitations, (b) improve your skills, (c) follow safety rules, (d) know the cause of injuries, (e) are familiar with the ten most common injuries and conditions, (f) use the RICE treatment, and (g) seek medical treatment when needed. **15:5**

6. There are safety rules for ways to exercise that should be followed to prevent injury. **15:6**

7. Anabolic steroids affect the cardiovascular and reproductive systems and are harmful to health. **15:7**

Vocabulary

Below is a list of vocabulary words used in this chapter. Use each word only once to complete the sentences. Do not write in this book.

anabolic steroids
biomechanics
lifetime sports
physical profiling
principle of
  cooling down
principle of
  frequency

principle of
  progression
principle of
  specificity
principle of
  warming up
RICE treatment

1. The _____ is used for musculoskeletal injuries.

2. An example of the _____ is stretching after a bicycle trip.

3. Walking, running, and swimming are examples of _____.

4. _____ is a method of testing your limits to determine the sports best for you.

5. An example of the _____ is running slowly for a few minutes before running sprints.

6. _____ are synthetic derivatives of the male hormone testosterone.

7. _____ may help tennis players improve their serves.

8. The _____ involves choosing an exercise activity that provides a desired benefit.

9. Increasing the intensity and duration of exercise is using the _____.

10. The _____ involves how often you participate in exercises to improve health.

Review

1. Identify ten guidelines to follow when developing an individualized plan for physical fitness.
2. Identify and describe six training principles to follow when participating in any exercise program.
3. What should be included in a complete workout for physical fitness?
4. What are five lifetime sports and the health benefits of each?
5. What are seven steps you can follow to prevent injury or reinjury?
6. What are six common causes of exercise injuries?
7. What are the ten most common exercise injuries or conditions?
8. When is a physician needed for an exercise injury?
9. What are the safety precautions for bicycling?
10. What are the dangerous side effects associated with the use of anabolic steroids?

Application

1. Why might it be dangerous to run at a fast pace without warming up?
2. Why would you not receive much benefit from a weight-training program in which you used weights that were easy for you to lift?
3. Why are walking and swimming considered to be two of the best lifetime sports?
4. Why is physical profiling helpful in the prevention of injuries?
5. How would you treat a musculoskeletal injury?

Individual Research

1. With classmates, prepare a community sports directory. Include a listing and description of any exercise, health, or sport facilities in your community.
2. Select one of the following topics and write a three-page research paper: arthroscopic surgery, sports medicine as a career, biomechanics, or stress testing. Present your report to the class.

Readings

Hoyt, Craig, and Hoyt, Julie, *Cycling.* Dubuque, IA: William C. Brown Publishers, 1984.

Cooper, Kenneth, *Running Without Fear.* New York, NY: M. Evans & Company, 1982.
Reeves, Steve, *Power Walking.* New York, NY: Bobbs-Merrill Company, 1982.

UNIT 7

Drugs

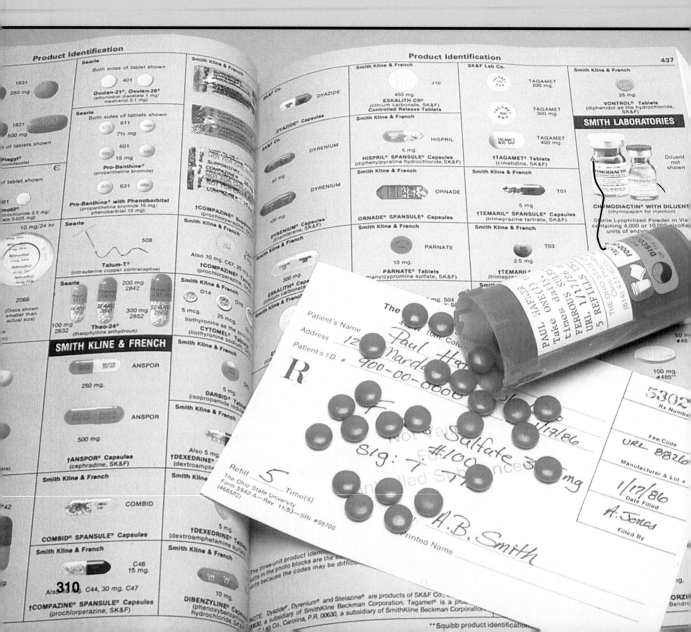

DRUGS

Your body systems maintain a unique chemical balance. This balance can be upset by many factors, such as microorganisms, food that is not preserved or processed correctly, or chemicals (drugs).

The purpose of this unit is to help you maintain your unique chemical balance. This unit focuses on the harmful effects of drugs and the behaviors you can follow to reach and maintain optimum health without drugs.

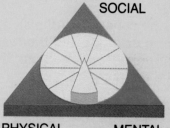

SOCIAL

PHYSICAL   MENTAL

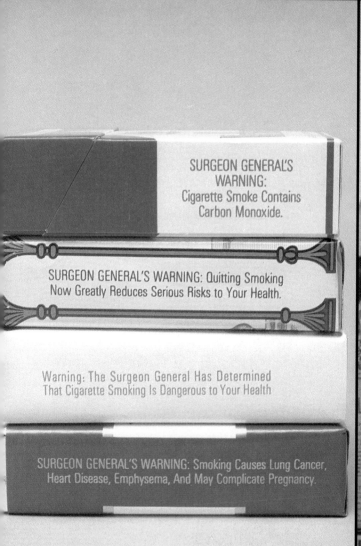

SURGEON GENERAL'S WARNING: Cigarette Smoke Contains Carbon Monoxide.

SURGEON GENERAL'S WARNING: Quitting Smoking Now Greatly Reduces Serious Risks to Your Health.

Warning: The Surgeon General Has Determined That Cigarette Smoking Is Dangerous to Your Health

SURGEON GENERAL'S WARNING: Smoking Causes Lung Cancer, Heart Disease, Emphysema, And May Complicate Pregnancy.

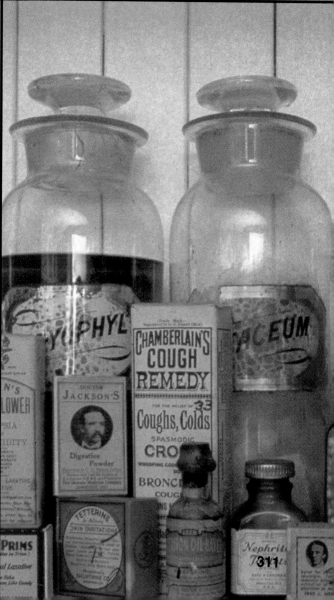

The capsules and pills form a "path." Where the path leads depends on the drug or drugs and the reason for use. If a prescription drug helps regulate a chronic health problem, the path leads to optimum health. Where else might the path lead?

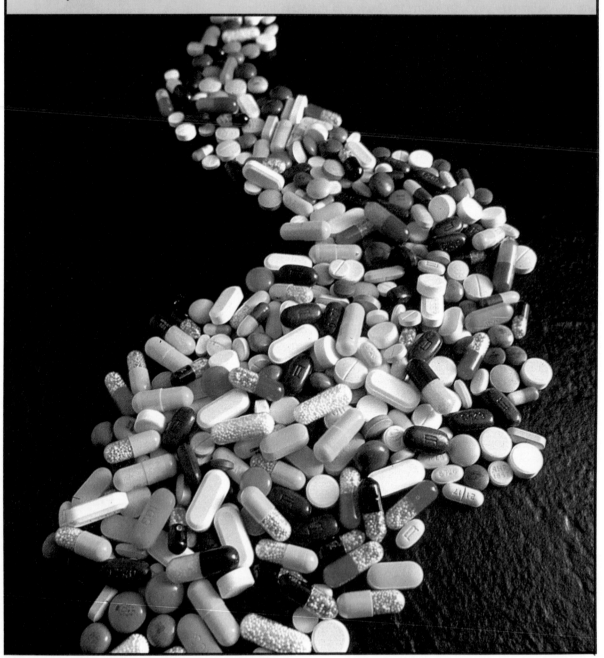

Chapter 16

A Lifestyle Free from Drug Misuse and Abuse

OBJECTIVES: You will be able to
- **describe how drugs affect the body.**
- **identify ways drugs can be helpful.**
- **identify various kinds of controlled substances.**
- **discuss ways that drugs that are not controlled substances can harm health.**
- **describe how a chemically-dependent person can be helped.**
- **develop skills to lead a productive life without abusing or misusing drugs.**

For millions of people, the discovery of certain drugs has improved the quality of their lives. Many drugs prevent and treat diseases that otherwise would interfere with physical, mental, and social health. Millions of other people await the discovery of new drugs that will prevent or treat diseases from which they now suffer. While the responsible use of drugs promotes optimum health for most persons, the misuse and abuse of drugs interfere with the achievement of optimum health for others. This chapter presents the facts about the responsible use of legal drugs. However, the main focus is to promote well-being by preventing the misuse and abuse of all types of drugs.

Drugs can be used to prevent and treat diseases.

Well-being is promoted by not abusing or misusing drugs.

UNDERSTANDING HOW DRUGS WORK

In Chapter 1, you learned that many aspects of living have a holistic effect upon you. The effects of a drug will depend on how the drug enters the body, when and how it is taken, and the person's health status and mood at that time.

16:1 Drugs: The Basic Facts

A drug is a substance other than food that changes the way the body works.

What is a drug? Most definitions of a drug indicate that it is a substance other than food that changes the way the body works. According to this definition, any number of substances to which you are exposed might be considered a drug. Suppose you were swimming in a pool and your eyes began to burn from the chlorine in the water. The chlorine might be considered a drug according to the definition. However, the term **drug,** as used in this text, is defined as any substance other than food that is purposely introduced into the body to change normal body functions.

Psychoactive drugs change a person's moods and behavior.

Most of the drugs emphasized in this chapter are psychoactive drugs. **Psychoactive drugs** are substances that act on the central nervous system and change one's moods and behaviors. These drugs can be misused or abused. **Drug misuse** is the unintentional or inappropriate use of a drug that interferes with physical, social, and mental well-being. **Drug abuse,** also known as substance or chemical abuse, is the intentional use of drugs for reasons other than their intended medical purpose. Drug abuse interferes with physical, social, and mental well-being.

16:2 How Drugs Enter the Body

There are three major ways drugs enter the body. Drugs can be taken orally, by injection, or inhalation. Drugs taken orally dissolve in the stomach or intestine and are absorbed into the bloodstream. Not all drugs can be taken orally.

Drugs can be injected directly into a vein, into muscle tissue, or just below the skin's surface. Drugs taken by injection are absorbed rapidly into the bloodstream.

Drugs administered by **inhalation** are absorbed into the bloodstream by passing through the lungs. Most drugs must be in a gaseous state to be inhaled. Some drugs can be sniffed. A drug is absorbed into the bloodstream through the mucous membranes of the nasal passages when it is sniffed.

FIGURE 16–1. Drugs are usually taken in measured amounts.

16:3 Drug Actions

Have you ever wondered why certain drugs are successful in relieving specific problems? Why might a certain drug relieve the pain of a headache while another clears up an infection? The answer lies with the concept of receptor sites. A **receptor site** is a specific part within a cell anywhere in the body where the chemical substance of a drug fits (Figure 16–2). Receptor actions are specific. The drug molecule acts only on the specific cell part, not the whole cell. Suppose Drug A is used to treat a toothache and Drug B is used to treat an infection. If you took Drug B, your toothache would not be relieved since the molecule for Drug B would not fit the receptor site. However, Drug A would relieve the toothache since it would fit the receptor site.

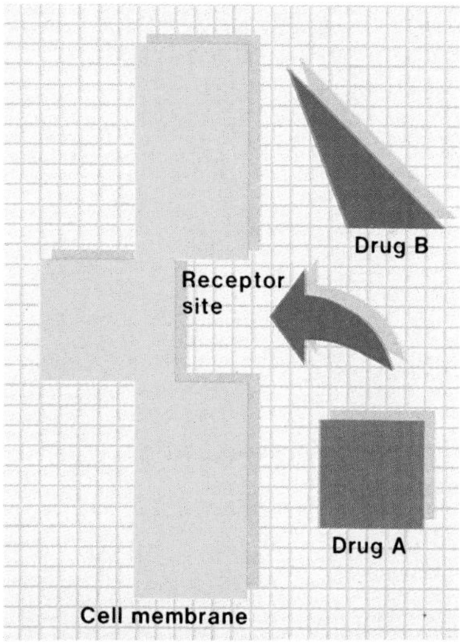

Unfortunately, many drugs do not act on only one specific receptor site. Suppose you had a headache. You might take aspirin to relieve your headache. However, the aspirin may not act only on the receptor sites for the headache. It also may act on the receptor sites of other cells, such as those in the stomach. This may result in an upset stomach. An upset stomach is an example of a side effect of aspirin. A **side effect** is an unwanted result not related to the major purpose of the drug. Thus, a major problem of drugs is the possibility that they can produce dangerous side effects because they act on many receptor sites throughout the body. For this reason, it is important that the correct drug be taken for specific results.

FIGURE 16–2. Drug receptor sites are very specific.

16:4   Factors Influencing Drug Effects

In addition to knowing how drugs are introduced into the body, it is important to be aware of the factors or combination of factors that may determine the effects of drugs.

Dose is the quantity or amount of a drug that is taken at any given time. Usually, the greater the dose, the greater will be the drug effect until the maximum effect is achieved.

Lightweight people usually experience a greater drug effect than heavier people who are given the same dose. This occurs because a heavier individual has more blood and body fluids to absorb the dissolved drug. The result is that the concentration is reduced.

Solubility is the ability of a drug to be dissolved. Water-soluble drugs dissolve only in water and do not penetrate cell membranes. Thus, they cannot reach cells of the nervous system. (Alcohol is a drug that is an exception and its effects will be discussed in Chapter 17.) Most psychoactive drugs are fat-soluble. Because they dissolve in the fat tissue of the body, they stay in the body longer than water-soluble drugs and affect the central nervous system. Fat-soluble drugs can remain in the body for days or even weeks until they are chemically broken down and eliminated.

A person's weight can determine a drug's effect on the body.

A person's emotional state can determine the effects of drugs on the body.

One's emotional state or mind set has an impact on drug effects. Taking a psychoactive drug can exaggerate a condition. For example, a person who has a great desire to feel high from smoking marijuana may act high even if the marijuana smoked was of low potency. Some studies show that a person who is given a cigarette with a substance substituted for marijuana will act high even though the substitute is not a psychoactive drug.

The environmental setting in which a psychoactive drug is taken can determine its effect. For example, a person may feel a greater effect from the drug alcohol at a party than at a quiet dinner.

Drugs may interact with other drugs in the body.

The effect of a drug may also be dependent upon its interaction with other drugs. Refer to Table 16–1.

16:5 Drug Dependence

Chemical dependence is the psychological and/or physical need for a drug.

Drug dependence is the state of psychological and/or physical need that can occur in a person who uses drugs. The term **chemical dependence** as a synonym for drug dependence is widely accepted. Anyone who uses almost any kind of psychoactive drug has the potential to develop chemical dependence.

Table 16–1   Drug Interactions

INDEPENDENT
Drugs taken together work independently of each other. Neither one affects the action of the other.

ANTAGONISTIC
Drugs taken together interact. The effect of either or both is blocked or reduced. This interaction can be seen in the "equation" 2 + 2 = 0, or 2 + 2 = 2.

ADDITIVE
Drugs taken together interact. The net effect is the sum of the effects. This interaction can be seen in the "equation" 2 + 2 = 4.

SYNERGISTIC
Drugs taken together may produce an effect that is greater than additive. That is, one drug increases the effects of the other by changing its chemical effects on the body. This interaction can be seen in the "equation" 2 + 2 = 5.

Source: National Institute on Alcohol Abuse and Alcoholism, Department of Health and Human Services

Chemical dependence is characterized by psychological dependence, physical dependence, tolerance, and withdrawal.

Psychological dependence is a strong desire to repeat the use of a drug for emotional reasons. People who are psychologically dependent on a drug think they need the drug. They are sure that they can control their use of the drug and that they are not harming themselves or others by using it. However, this is not true. They are constantly risking danger because they have an irrational concept of what they are doing not only to themselves but also to others.

Physical dependence is a condition in which the presence of a drug becomes "normal" and necessary. That is, the drug must be present for cells to continue functioning in the same way they functioned before the drug was first introduced into the body. It often is considered the most hazardous aspect of drug abuse because it drastically alters the normal functioning of the body. Another serious risk involves the use of needles for injecting a drug. If a drug user uses another person's needle, he or she runs the risk of getting AIDS. Physical dependence makes it difficult for a user to discontinue using a drug.

Physical dependence on a drug is harmful to the body.

Psychoactive drugs produce tolerance. **Tolerance** is a physical adaptation to a drug so that larger and larger doses are needed to produce the original desired effect. This also increases the risks of undesired side effects the drug may have. The development of tolerance can be rapid or gradual. It can accompany psychological and physical dependence.

Tolerance can result from the use of psychoactive drugs.

Withdrawal is a condition that occurs when the use of a drug to which one is physically addicted is discontinued. Common signs and symptoms of withdrawal may include loss of appetite, inability to sleep, nausea, vomiting, irritability, convulsions, anxiety, and depression. Not all of these changes are experienced by all withdrawal victims. The severity of these changes is determined by the type of drug and length of time it is used. Withdrawal permits the nerve cells to return to their normal state. In time, it also reduces the level of tolerance. Today, there are people who are physically dependent on several drugs. If they discontinue the use of any one of the drugs on which they are dependent, these people must undergo withdrawal for each drug.

A person who is physically addicted to a drug may suffer from withdrawal sickness if the use of the drug is discontinued.

 Review and Reflect

1. Why can a psychoactive drug taken by injection be more dangerous than one taken orally?
2. Why is any psychoactive drug dangerous?

DRUGS THAT PROMOTE HEALTH

Think about the last time you were ill. Perhaps you recovered by resting and drinking fluids. However, rest and fluids are not always enough. Your body may require additional resources to help fight germs.

16:6 Prescription Drugs

Certain drugs can only be obtained with a prescription.

Prescription drugs are drugs that can be obtained only by written permission from a physician. Other health professionals who can write prescriptions are dentists and psychiatrists. The written permission is called a **prescription.** It is illegal to obtain a prescription drug without a valid prescription.

There are many important facts to know about prescription drugs.

Prescription drugs can be sold only by licensed pharmacists. These drugs are used in treating specific disease conditions and can be quite powerful. For this reason, there are basic facts you should know about the safe use of prescription drugs (Table 16–2).

Table 16–2 Basic Facts About Prescription Drugs

- What is the name of the medicine? Write it down or have your physician write it clearly.

- When and how often should the medicine be taken? If it is to be taken three times per day, is it to be taken before or after meals?

- What is the medicine supposed to do? Does it relieve a symptom? Does it get rid of the disease?

- Can the medicine be taken along with others? Mixing medicines can be dangerous. Inform your physician if you presently take medication.

- What are possible side effects? Some drugs may have unwanted side effects. Contact your physician if these occur.

- Should certain foods be avoided? Some antibiotics may lose their effectiveness when taken with milk or food.

- Are precautions needed? If a medicine produces drowsiness, you should not participate in certain activities after taking it.

- What if you miss a dose? The effectiveness of a drug might be lowered. Doubling up might be dangerous. Ask your physician for advice.

- How long should the drug be used? Generally, the medicine should be taken until it is used up. If you stop taking the medicine too soon, the condition may remain.

16:7   Over-the-Counter Drugs

Over-the-counter drugs, or **OTC drugs,** are medications that can be purchased without a physician's prescription. There are thousands of different chemicals in OTC drugs. The major purpose of OTC drugs is to relieve minor symptoms of illness. Rarely do they cure illnesses. Many OTC drugs cover up signs and symptoms. Therefore, a person may require professional medical attention but does not seek help because he or she thinks the condition is cured.

No prescription is needed to purchase OTC drugs.

OTC drugs may cover up signs and symptoms.

Before taking any OTC medication, read its label. All OTC labels contain the following information.

All OTC drug labels contain certain information.

- Product name; manufacturer's name and address
- The net contents, such as the number of tablets
- The ingredients in the medicine
- The directions for safe use, including the frequency with which the drug may be taken, the total dose for one day, and the number of days for which it can be used
- Cautions or warnings such as, "See a physician if symptoms persist more than two days"
- Side effects such as drowsiness
- Date of expiration

Because OTC drugs can be harmful if misused, it is important that you follow safety precautions (Table 16–3).

 Review and Reflect

3. In what way can a prescription drug be harmful?
4. Why is it important to read the label of an OTC drug?

Table 16–3   Using OTC Drugs Safely

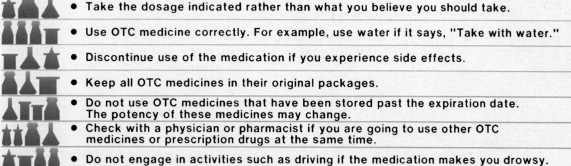

	• Take the dosage indicated rather than what you believe you should take.
	• Use OTC medicine correctly. For example, use water if it says, "Take with water."
	• Discontinue use of the medication if you experience side effects.
	• Keep all OTC medicines in their original packages.
	• Do not use OTC medicines that have been stored past the expiration date. The potency of these medicines may change.
	• Check with a physician or pharmacist if you are going to use other OTC medicines or prescription drugs at the same time.
	• Do not engage in activities such as driving if the medication makes you drowsy.
	• Do not take OTC medicines with alcohol.
	• Do not purchase an OTC medicine if its tamper-resistant seal is broken.

a

b

FIGURE 16–3. (a) Unripe poppy capsule, (b) ripe, incised poppy capsule

Physical dependence on opiates can result in withdrawal if a certain level of the drug is not maintained in the blood.

CONTROLLED DRUGS

The misuse or abuse of some drugs threatens the health of the user and may cause behaviors that threaten the health and safety of others. These drugs are called controlled drugs because their possession, distribution, manufacture, and sale are controlled by law.

16:8 Opiates

Opiates are psychoactive drugs derived from the opium poppy plant or made synthetically. They induce sleep and reduce pain. Morphine, codeine, heroin, and methadone are examples of opiates. Some opiates, such as morphine, are used short-term as medications to help relieve pain. Codeine can be used medically to control coughs. Nonmedical use of opiates is illegal and dangerous.

All opiates have a high potential for producing psychological and physical dependency as well as tolerance. It is easy to become addicted to opiates with only small doses. Once a person is physically dependent on opiates, withdrawal symptoms may occur. If a certain level of the drug is not maintained in the blood, flulike symptoms may result. These symptoms become worse as the opiate level in the blood drops. The result is weakness, nausea, vomiting, and stomach pains. The back muscles and limbs may ache severely.

Most methods of treatment for opiate dependency have not worked well. Methadone has been used to treat heroin dependency. Methadone maintenance eliminates the withdrawal reaction and the craving for heroin so an individual can function normally in personal, social, and employment environments. But methadone treatment must be viewed with caution since it is a substitution of one drug dependency for another. More about treatment procedures for drug dependency will be discussed later in this chapter.

16:9 Depressants

Depressants slow the function of the central nervous system.

Drugs that slow down the functions of the central nervous system (CNS) are classified generally as **depressants.** The psychoactive drugs discussed in Section 16:8 are depressants. Depressants that produce a calming effect, relax muscles, or relieve tension are called **sedatives.**

Large doses of sedatives induce drowsiness and eventually sleep. Drugs that have sleep-inducing effects are called hypnotics. The combination term of sedative-hypnotic describes the drugs in this section.

One major group of sedative-hypnotics are barbiturates. **Barbiturates** are sedative-hypnotic drugs that at one time were frequently prescribed to treat insomnia. Their effects can be short-acting, lasting less than six hours, or long-acting, lasting up to twenty-four hours. Most physicians now prescribe drugs that are safer than barbiturates to treat insomnia.

Antianxiety drugs are sedative-hypnotic drugs used to reduce fears of uneasiness and anxiety. Tranquilizers are antianxiety drugs.

Sedative-hypnotic drugs produce a variety of side effects when they are misused or abused. These drugs can produce nausea, headaches, dizziness, and drowsiness. A person using these drugs is at risk to serious injury from accidents. A person using a sedative-hypnotic drug should not drive or engage in other activities that require concentration.

Sedative-hypnotic drugs produce physical dependence as well as tolerance. A particular danger associated with these drugs is their use with other drugs. Any unintentional or deliberate combining of a sedative-hypnotic drug with another depressant, especially alcohol, will produce a synergistic effect (Table 16–1). Taking these drugs in combination can cause serious consequences, including death.

Another serious problem associated with sedative-hypnotic drugs is withdrawal. Withdrawal symptoms produced by those dependent on barbiturates and other sedative-hypnotic drugs are much more severe than those produced by opiates. Withdrawal symptoms from these drugs begin with nervousness and weakness. If untreated, these symptoms can result in seizures, hallucinations, and loss of consciousness. After about four days without treatment, withdrawal can result in death. Any person withdrawing from sedative-hypnotics drugs should do so under medical care.

> Barbiturates are examples of sedative-hypnotics.

> Physical dependence and tolerance may result with the use of sedative-hypnotics.

> Nervousness and weakness are withdrawal symptoms that result from the use of sedative-hypnotics.

16:10   Stimulants

Stimulants are drugs that increase the functions of those organs controlled by the central nervous system. Amphetamines and cocaine are stimulants discussed in this section. Nicotine, another stimulant, will be discussed in Chapter 18.

> Stimulants increase the function of organs controlled by the central nervous system.

FIGURE 16–4. Leaves of the coca shrub

Both short-term and long-term use of cocaine is dangerous.

Amphetamines are a group of synthetic chemicals that affect the areas of the brain that control blood pressure, the heart, breathing rate, and metabolism.

Short-term use of amphetamines can result in nervousness, elevated blood pressure, and headaches. These side effects can be dangerous, especially when driving or using dangerous tools.

Long-term use of amphetamines can result in sleeplessness, irritability, confusion, and dizziness. It may also result in elevated blood pressure, which in turn may result in a burst blood vessel. Amphetamine use results in tolerance and psychological dependence. Withdrawal symptoms of amphetamines include depression and a need to sleep more than usual.

Cocaine is an illegal stimulant drug that is obtained from the leaves of coca shrubs that grow in the Andes Mountains in South America. In almost all cases, cocaine is used illegally.

Cocaine enters the bloodstream when it is sniffed. It can also be taken into the body by injection. One use of cocaine that is extremely dangerous is freebasing. **Freebasing** is a chemical process in which cocaine powder is changed into a smokable solution. Cocaine used in any form can result in restlessness, irritability, and depression.

Short-term use of cocaine can be dangerous. It elevates blood pressure and can cause heart damage. Many suicides have been linked to cocaine use because a person who "crashes," or comes off the effects of cocaine, can become severely depressed. Often, this depression leads to suicide.

Long-term use of cocaine can permanently damage the mucous membrane of the nose. Thus, chronic cocaine users have runny noses and often appear to have a cold. Other effects of long-term cocaine use are disruption of eating and sleeping habits and weight loss. Users may also become irritable and anxious. Cocaine psychosis may also result. This condition is characterized by paranoia and hallucinations.

16:11 Psychedelic Drugs

Psychedelic drugs create illusions and distort the user's senses. Psychedelic drugs also are called hallucinogens. Although psychedelic drugs do not produce physical dependence, they may cause psychological dependence and produce tolerance. Several psychedelic drugs will be discussed in this section.

LSD is the most potent of the psychedelic drugs. It is usually sold in the form of tablets, capsules, or small pieces of paper with drops of the drug spotted on them. Sometimes, LSD is carried in sugar cubes, chewing gum, or hard candy.

LSD causes a blending of senses. That is, the user "sees" sounds or "hears" colors. It produces a rapid change in mood and a feeling that the body is distorted. The LSD user can experience "bad trips" in which paranoia and panic may set in. LSD users may also experience flashbacks. **Flashbacks** are brief, sudden distortions that are similar to those experienced when using LSD. Flashbacks may occur months or years after taking LSD. In addition, numerous fatal accidents and suicides have been known to result from LSD use.

LSD is an illegal and dangerous psychedelic drug.

PCP, also known as "angel dust," is an illegal psychedelic drug that at one time was used as a veterinary anesthetic. PCP may come in the form of powder, liquid, or tablets. This illegal and dangerous drug can act in any number of ways—stimulant, depressant, and hallucinogen. Its use results in numbness, disorientation, staggering, slurred speech, and aggressive and bizarre behavior. With increased dosage, it can result in vomiting, fever, loss of muscle control, rise in blood pressure, convulsions, and coma.

PCP can act as a stimulant, depressant, and hallucinogen.

Peyote is an illegal psychedelic drug produced from cactus tips. This drug has been used by Mexican Indians for thousands of years during religious rituals. This drug is harmful and illegal when used as a "street drug." It produces stomach disorders as well as perceptual distortions.

Peyote can produce stomach disorders and perceptive distortions.

Mescaline is an illegal psychedelic drug that produces LSD-like effects. It is the major psychoactive ingredient of the peyote cactus.

Jimsonweed is an illegal psychedelic derived from the jimson-weed plant. It is also known as jamestown weed, stinkweed, and loco weed. This drug is extremely dangerous, producing more toxic effects than LSD.

Psilocybin (si luh SI bun) is an illegal and dangerous hallucinogen derived from a type of Mexican mushroom.

FIGURE 16–5. The peyote cactus

16:12 Marijuana

Marijuana is an illegal drug that is a prepared mixture of the crushed leaves, flowers, stems, and seeds of the hemp plant, *Cannabis sativa.* In some cases, marijuana has been approved by the federal government in the treatment of specific medical conditions. The National Cancer Institute has approved a program whereby selected physicians can prescribe marijuana for cancer patients. Marijuana, in some cases, relieves the side effects of chemotherapy. Marijuana use has also been approved for the experimental treatment of glaucoma.

Marijuana and hashish are derived from the *Cannabis* plant.

Hashish is an illegal drug that is derived from the cannabis plant. It is much more concentrated and, therefore, more potent than marijuana. Over 150 chemical compounds have been identified in cannabis. The most powerful of these ingredients is THC. The amount of THC in marijuana determines its effect on the user.

Marijuana is illegal and dangerous.

Marijuana impairs judgment and coordination.

Several important facts must be noted about marijuana. It is a dangerous and illegal drug. The effects of marijuana are both short-term and long-term. Marijuana use impairs motor coordination. It causes a loss of steadiness in the hands and body movements so that a person becomes clumsy. It increases reaction time so that response to a stimulus is slowed. Visual perception, such as the ability to react to a flash of light, is altered. Marijuana diminishes short-term memory so that even small doses of this drug make it difficult to remember even simple things. Marijuana distorts one's sense of time so its users consistently overestimate the amount of time that has elapsed. Marijuana use also impairs the user's ability to conduct a logical conversation.

FIGURE 16–6. A marijuana plant

Consider some of these effects and their relationship to driving an automobile. How quickly can you hit your brakes? What happens when a flashing light is difficult to detect? Much research now indicates that marijuana is involved in a large number of traffic accidents. What is particularly dangerous is mixing marijuana and alcohol. This mixture impairs judgment and coordination with much greater significance.

It is also important to remember that the effects of marijuana can last up to eight hours. Thus, a marijuana user should not get behind the wheel of a car for at least this period of time.

The long-term effects of marijuana are serious. Tolerance can develop rather quickly, and physical and psychological dependence may result. There are other chronic concerns of long-term marijuana use.

Chronic use of marijuana may result in amotivational syndrome. **Amotivational syndrome** is a pattern of personality changes characterized by apathy, a lack of concern for the future, loss of ambition, and a decline in school and work performance.

Amotivational syndrome is associated with marijuana use.

Another major concern about marijuana is its potential harm to the lungs. A marijuana cigarette, or "joint," contains many more cancer-causing hydrocarbons than tobacco cigarettes. Smoke from marijuana also contains many more cancer-causing agents than cigarette smoke. The presence of these ingredients, added to the fact that marijuana smoke is held deep inside the lungs for long periods of time, causes increased damage to the lungs. Examination of the lungs of chronic marijuana users indicate abnormal cell changes. These changes may be precancerous conditions.

Marijuana contains cancer-causing hydrocarbons.

Research shows that marijuana increases blood pressure and forces the heart to work much harder. This can be extremely dangerous for people who may have heart problems or other cardiovascular diseases.

Marijuana increases blood pressure and forces the heart to work harder than it normally should.

The possible effects of marijuana on the reproductive system of males is a major concern to many researchers. Some researchers have noted a reduction in testosterone level of marijuana users. This reduction may interfere with endocrine functioning. Other studies have shown reduced sperm counts in marijuana users. Although these studies are not conclusive, these possible effects do exist.

There are also possible dangerous effects of marijuana use on females. Some studies indicate that long-term marijuana use may cause abnormal menstrual periods, including failure to ovulate. Other studies show that women who use marijuana have shortened periods of fertility. Female animal studies show that prolonged use of marijuana harms the functioning of the ovaries, thereby stopping ovulation and menstruation.

Pregnant women should refrain from smoking marijuana.

Because THC in marijuana can cross the placenta of a pregnant female, there is concern that there is a higher than normal risk of birth defects. One recent study found that pregnant females who smoked marijuana during pregnancy gave birth to babies with low birth weights and had a higher than normal rate of birth defects. While this evidence cannot be generalized as cause and effect, one fact is known for sure. Medical researchers and physicians feel strongly that pregnant women should not smoke marijuana.

Some experiments indicate that marijuana interferes with the functioning of the immune system. Many researchers believe that marijuana users will have higher than normal risk of infection and illness than nonusers.

The short-term effects of marijuana on the brain were discussed at the beginning of this section in terms of its effects on behavior and coordination. Studies using monkeys have shown significant changes in the cells of their brains. However, these changes have not been documented in humans. But since marijuana is fat-soluble, it can remain in the body, including the brain, for eight days after use.

Marijuana is a fat-soluble drug.

Knowledge of the effects of marijuana gives reason to be concerned. Suspicions about the possible effects of marijuana justify serious national attention. This is especially applicable to high school students who have not yet matured emotionally or physically. It is generally felt that marijuana may have the greatest detrimental effects on this age group.

Marijuana can be particularly harmful to adolescents.

 Review and Reflect

5. What causes a person who is physically dependent on a drug to go through withdrawal?

OTHER DRUG THREATS TO OPTIMUM HEALTH

There are other drugs that may threaten physical, mental, and social health. At this time, these drugs are not controlled by law. In some cases, warning labels have been proposed to inform you and others of their possible dangers. Suppose you were a member of an advisory panel. After you read the following information, decide if you would control any of these drugs or require them to have warning labels.

16:13 Inhalants

Inhalants are a group of chemicals that produce vapors that have psychoactive effects when inhaled. Among the household substances that can produce psychoactive effects when inhaled are furniture polish, paint thinner, insecticides, and gasoline. All of these products are extremely dangerous. They can damage the lungs, liver, kidneys, and brain and can cause death.

Nitrous oxide is a gas that is sometimes used by dentists as an anesthetic. Nitrous oxide is also found in aerosol cans as a propellant. Contrary to what may be believed, nitrous oxide is dangerous. Repeated long-term use of this drug can result in nerve damage, muscle weakness, anemia, and difficulty in maintaining a full-term pregnancy. If it is inhaled without enough oxygen, nitrous oxide can cause death.

Amyl nitrite is a drug that is sometimes prescribed for the treatment of angina. **Butyl nitrite** is a drug that is similar to amyl nitrite but it has little, if any, medical use. Both drugs can produce headaches, dizziness, increased heart rate, nausea, vomiting, and fainting. These drugs also produce tolerance. When used over a long period, they damage hemoglobin and cause heart and blood-vessel damage.

Many household substances can produce psychoactive effects when inhaled.

Repeated use of nitrous oxide can result in nerve damage, muscle weakness, and anemia.

16:14 Caffeine

Caffeine is a stimulant drug found in tea, chocolate candy, cocoa, and many brands of coffee and cola drinks. Suppose you drink a cup of coffee now. In less than five minutes, the caffeine will travel to every part of your body. Your heart rate, stomach acid, and metabolism will increase. Perhaps you might think of this as being advantageous. However, caffeine might make you feel uneasy and jittery.

Can large amounts of caffeine be harmful? Research indicates that the answer to this question is yes. If three or four cups of coffee are consumed at one time, the result can be irritability, headaches, nervousness, and possibly irregular heart rate.

Many researchers are studying the relationship between caffeine use and fibrocystic breast disease, certain types of cancer, and birth defects. Fibrocystic breast disease is a disease in which small cysts, small sacs of fluid surrounded by fibrous tissue, are present in a woman's breasts. These cysts make it more difficult to do an accurate breast self-examination.

No clear association has yet been made between the amount of caffeine consumed and the incidence of cancer and birth defects.

FIGURE 16–7.

CAFFEINE CONTENT OF SOME BEVERAGES	
Beverages and Chocolate	Caffeine (milligrams)
coffee (5-oz cup) brewed, drip method	110-150
tea (5-oz cup) brewed, major U.S. brands	20-46
cocoa (5-oz cup)	6
chocolate milk (8 oz)	5
milk chocolate (1 oz)	6
dark chocolate, semisweet (1 oz)	20
baker's chocolate (1 oz)	26
chocolate-flavored syrup (1 oz)	4
colas, regular diet caffeine-free	30-46 2-58 0-trace

However, according to a research study, two or more cups of coffee a day increases the likelihood of cancer of the bladder and pancreas. Many physicians recommend reducing the amount of caffeine or avoiding it altogether until studies are conclusive. It is especially important for pregnant women to avoid caffeine as well as other drugs.

Use of caffeine can result in physical dependence.

Caffeine can produce physical dependence. People who drink at least five cups of coffee per day can suffer withdrawal when they stop drinking coffee. They may have nausea, headaches, and be irritable. These symptoms can interfere with daily activities.

To reduce dependence on caffeine, drink beverages that are caffeine free. If you must drink coffee, drink half a cup or drink decaffeinated coffee. Decaffeinated coffee contains some caffeine. So it is not a good idea to drink large quantities of decaffeinated coffee. Drinking herbal tea instead of coffee will reduce the intake of caffeine.

16:15   Designer Drugs

Designer drugs are among the most dangerous of the psychoactive drugs.

Designer drugs are drugs produced in home-made labs by individuals who often have little, if any, knowledge about drug chemistry. These dangerous drugs are formed by altering the molecular structure of chemicals so as to produce effects similar to those produced by other drugs. Unfortunately, the problems created by designer drugs can be more dangerous than the original imitated drugs.

Designer drugs do not undergo quality controls. Thus, a designer drug can be as much as 3000 times more potent than the real drug it imitates. For example, designer drugs that are supposed to act like heroin may be much more deadly than heroin.

Humans are used as "guinea pigs" for testing designer drugs.

Parkinson's disease has been linked with the use of designer drugs.

Designer drugs, unlike other drugs, are not tested on animals by the government. The "guinea pigs" are humans and the results have been disastrous. Their use has been known to result in the immediate development of Parkinson's disease. Parkinson's disease is a disorder that usually affects people over 60 years of age. It results in trembling of the arms and legs and stiffness of the muscles. Thus, any kind of action is difficult to perform. There is no cure for this disease. For some users of designer drugs, getting Parkinson's disease is one result. For others, the result may be death.

 Review and Reflect

6. What is the real danger in using a designer drug?

TREATMENT FOR DRUG MISUSE AND ABUSE

You have learned about the effects of controlled and other drugs that may endanger health. You should also learn what to do if someone you know takes an overdose, and how to help chemically dependent persons. With this knowledge, you will be able to help promote a community free from drug misuse and abuse.

16:16 Emergency Treatment of a Drug Overdose

Drug abuse can lead to life-threatening situations unless quick and proper action is taken. Any kind of opiate can produce serious problems when too large a dose is taken. A person who overdoses on opiates may fall into a deep sleep and have slow or shallow breathing, look blue around the lips and skin, and have constricted pupils. First aid would involve keeping the person awake. If he or she is unconscious, place the victim on his or her side. If breathing stops, begin mouth-to-mouth resuscitation (see Chapter 25).

A person who has overdosed on PCP should be given special attention since this person may harm himself or herself or others. This person may be in a state of panic and become violent. Reassure the individual that the "trip" is temporary even though it may last several hours.

Regardless of the situation, any person who has taken an overdose of opiates or had a bad "trip" should receive medical attention at once. Call a medical emergency squad or take the person to the nearest hospital. Hospitals have personnel trained to help a person experiencing a drug reaction.

16:17 Treating the Person Who Is Chemically Dependent

Another emphasis of treatment focuses on long-term psychological help. Many therapeutic communities exist to help chemically-dependent people. A **therapeutic community** consists of trained professionals and former chemically-dependent individuals who help counsel the individual who has a drug problem. The individual seeking treatment often will live in a restricted environment and receive professional counseling as well as psychological support.

A person who has overdosed on an opiate drug needs immediate first aid.

People under the influence of PCP can harm themselves and others.

FIGURE 16–8. Drug abusers usually need professional help before they can be free of the habit.

Sometimes, chemically-dependent persons will enter a detoxification program. In a **detoxification program,** people are helped to withdraw from psychoactive drugs by receiving medical treatment to prevent withdrawal symptoms. The detoxification process can be viewed as a first step for further treatment of the chemically-dependent person.

Certain drugs can be used to treat individuals who are dependent on opium. These drugs are known as narcotic antagonists. **Narcotic antagonists** are chemical compounds that selectively block the psychological and physiological effects of heroin or other opiates. These drugs are safe to use only under medical supervision.

Narcotic antagonists block the effects of opiates.

 Review and Reflect

7. Why does a person who has taken an overdose of a drug need immediate medical treatment?

PROMOTING A HEALTHFUL LIFESTYLE

In this chapter, you have learned many facts about drugs and their misuse and abuse. Drug misuse and abuse threatens the health and safety of you and others as well as the quality of the environment in which you live. You are an important person in your community. Obeying the laws, working with your family, and keeping yourself and others free from drug misuse and abuse are worthwhile goals to set.

Drug abuse prevention is everyone's responsibility.

16:18 The Role of the Family

The family plays a very important role in drug prevention.

The individual, the family, the school, the community, and law enforcement agencies all play a role in drug abuse prevention. Each individual person is ultimately responsible for his or her decisions regarding drug use. Despite the many influences of the peer group, role modeling by parents is considered the most important factor in keeping children and teenagers drug-free. Many studies indicate that the majority of high school students support their parents' values. Parents who lead a healthful lifestyle transfer these values to their children.

FIGURE 16–9. Parents have a great influence on their children. Parental influence can be positive or negative.

These studies show that the need for chemical dependency will be decreased if certain characteristics are present. These characteristics are exhibited by parents who

- teach their children self-discipline and self-control.
- have clear values and a religious commitment.
- participate in activities with their children.
- promote supportive behaviors in their children.
- set boundaries for their children regarding actions that are healthful, safe, legal, and respectful.
- give love, understanding, appreciation, and respect.
- provide open channels of communication with their children.
- do not abuse or misuse chemicals.
- play an active role in their children's education.
- follow through on their commitments.
- teach their children about trust.

It is apparent that one of the most important keys in promoting a drug-free life is for parents to spend time with their children. Some day you may be a parent and play a role in helping your children remain drug-free. What values would you like to pass to your children? What behaviors will you follow to help reduce your children's risk of becoming involved with drugs?

Many parental characteristics serve to reduce a child's risk for chemical dependency.

Parental love and understanding can help reduce the risk of becoming involved with drugs.

16:19 Drugs and the Law

In 1970, the United States Congress redesigned and updated older drug-control laws so that the quantity of drugs that were available to drug users would be minimized. The update resulted in a law called the Comprehensive Drug Abuse Prevention and Control Act. It was changed again in 1973 to the Controlled Substances Act. The Controlled Substances Act places psychoactive drugs (except alcohol, nicotine, and caffeine) into one of five schedules or categories according to their degree of medical usefulness and abuse potential. According to the Controlled Substances Act, these drugs are illegal to manufacture, distribute, possess, or sell without government controls. Placing a drug in a particular schedule is determined by the United States Attorney General. Drugs may be moved up or down the schedule or new drugs may be added to the schedule.

Schedule I Substances with a high potential for abuse with no medical use. These drugs may be used for research purposes only. Among these are nonmedical opium derivatives, *Cannabis* and hallucinogens.

Schedule II Substances with a high potential for abuse with accepted medicinal uses, often with severe restriction. Abuse of these substances may lead to severe psychological or physical dependence. They are available by written prescription only and cannot be refilled. Among these are medically-used narcotics and injectable amphetamines.

Schedule III Substances that have potential for abuse less than those in Schedules I and II. These substances have accepted medical use. Abuse may lead to moderate or low physical or high psychological dependence. They are available by prescription. Five refills are allowed in six months. Among these substances are noninjectable amphetamines, barbiturates, and tranquilizers.

Schedule IV Substances with a low potential for abuse as compared to drugs in Schedule III. These drugs have accepted medical uses. Abuse may lead to limited physical or psychological dependence compared to drugs in Schedule III. They are available by prescription. Five refills are allowed in six months. Among these substances are mild sedatives, hypnotics, and some stimulants.

Schedule V Substances with a low potential for abuse compared to drugs in Schedule IV. These drugs have accepted medical uses. They may lead to limited physical dependence or psychological dependence when compared to drugs in Schedule IV. Their availability without prescription depends on laws established by individual states. Among these drugs are controlled over-the-counter mixtures of narcotics, sedatives, hypnotics, and amphetamines.

Psychoactive drugs are placed in one of five schedules or categories.

Drug schedules are determined by the United States Attorney General.

Schedule I drugs consist of nonmedical opium derivatives, *Cannabis*, and hallucinogens.

Controlled OTC drug mixtures belong to Schedule V drugs.

16:20 Choosing a Lifestyle Free from Drug Misuse and Abuse

Suppose you are at a party and a friend offers you a marijuana cigarette. To make a responsible decision about this offer, you should ask yourself some questions. Will my decision to smoke marijuana result in a behavior that is healthful? safe? legal? respectful of myself and others? within my parents' guidelines? If your answer to one or more or these questions is no, then you should think twice about accepting your friend's offer. Saying no to something you do not wish to do is an indication of strength, not weakness. Saying no is an indication of self-confidence.

Another way to avoid the dangers of chemical dependency is to choose activities that are drug-free. Often, people in the drug education field use the term alternatives to drug use rather than drug-free. In this text, drug-free is the term of choice. The term alternatives to drug use indicates that using drugs is the norm and that other activities are an alternative. The philosophy in this text is that engaging in healthful activities is the norm and that using drugs is a harmful alternative to healthful living.

One way to choose drug-free activities is to identify your needs. Perhaps you may have the need to engage in excitement, reduce stress, grow mentally, or be accepted by your peers. If you closely examine these needs, you will find that there are people your age who try to satisfy these needs by using drugs. Drugs are neither a permanent solution nor are they healthful ways to satisfy needs. Satisfy your need for excitement and reduce stress by participating in organized sports. Promote your mental growth by reading. Generate peer acceptance by getting involved in organized activities in your school. These are healthful ways to meet your needs and follow a drug-free lifestyle.

Another way to remain drug-free is to focus on activities that give you a sense of satisfaction. Here are some pointers to follow that will promote self-satisfaction.

Focus on being a finisher. Focus on a particular task you found difficult but still managed to complete. Everyone feels a sense of accomplishment when a goal is reached. When you set goals and work toward their successful completion, you feel good about yourself. Drug misuse or abuse changes potential finishers and leaves them in a state of incompleteness. Finishers avoid drugs.

Focus on priorities. Everyone feels overwhelmed at times. Perhaps you have days when responsibilities pile up and you ask yourself, "How am I going to do everything?" Soon you begin to spend more time thinking about the responsibilities and less time trying to accomplish them. If you feel this way, it is best to set up

FIGURE 16–10. Choose activities that will stimulate your mind.

When choosing drug-free activities, you should first identify your needs.

Focus on participating in activities that promote self-satisfaction.

Focus on your priorities.

People who value their health are least likely to harm themselves by using drugs.

a priority system. Select the responsibility with the highest priority and complete it first. When you do, you will feel a sense of accomplishment. Your good feelings will provide the incentive to move on to the next priority. While this may sound simple, it works! You begin to feel good about yourself and you tackle life's responsibilities in a healthful way. Self-satisfaction is promoted.

Focus on your health as being extremely important. Research shows that people who are concerned about their well-being are least likely to harm themselves by using drugs. Feeling good about yourself has a holistic effect.

 Activity: **Thoughts for the Future**

Think about your life ten years from now. Ask yourself the following questions: What work might I be doing? What will I need to do to reach my goals? How will I deal with setbacks? What can I do to be a "finisher"? How will I achieve self-satisfaction? Pretend your school invites you back ten years from now to speak to the high school classes. Using the above questions as a springboard, write a speech. In your speech, motivate these students of the future about the rewards of avoiding drug misuse and abuse.

Review and Reflect

8. Why is immediate medical treatment important for a person who overdoses with opiates?
9. What is the role of parents in preventing chemical dependence?

Focus on
Life Management Skills

- Avoid the misuse of any drug.
- Seek immediate medical help for anyone you suspect has taken an overdose of any drug.
- Apply the five criteria in the decision-making model when you need to make a decision about the use of drugs.
- Identify and engage in healthful activities that help avoid drug misuse and abuse.
- Establish your life's priorities, and identify ways to meet them.
- Obey all drug laws.

Health
CAREERS

Health Education Teacher

Deborah Horwitz is a high school health education teacher. Deborah promotes health education by exemplifying and instructing about healthful behaviors.

A health educator must be knowledgeable in many areas of health. These areas include nutrition, first aid, drugs, fitness, disease, and environmental, personal, and family health.

To become a health educator, Deborah needed to earn a college degree with a major or minor in health education. Deborah took specialized classes that focused on different health areas, such as nutrition, first aid, community and personal health, sexuality, alcohol, drugs, and school health services. Other courses dealing with psychology and educational theory provided

her with knowledge about student behavior. Toward the end of her college experience, Deborah was assigned to a high school where she completed student teaching. The student teaching experience provided her with an opportunity to practice skills needed in the teaching profession. After completing these requirements, Deborah graduated with a teaching degree in health education.

Health educators do not work only in schools. Many colleges and universities have now expanded their health education programs so that graduates can also gain employment within the community. Many health educators are employed by health and social service agencies, hospitals, and corporations.

CHAPTER
REVIEW 16

Summary

1. Drugs are substances that are purposely introduced into the body to change the way the body functions.　16:1
2. Drugs can be taken into the body orally, by injection, or by inhalation.　16:2
3. Drugs react in the body by working on specific receptor sites.　16:3
4. Among the factors that influence drug effects are dose, solubility, emotional state, and environmental setting.　16:4
5. Chemical dependence can be physical and/or psychological.　16:5
6. Prescription drugs are sold only by licensed pharmacists.　16:6
7. Over-the-counter drugs can relieve minor symptoms of illness, but they must be used only according to directions.　16:7
8. Morphine, heroin, and methadone are common types of opiates.　16:8
9. Barbiturates, sedative-hypnotic drugs, and antianxiety drugs are depressants.　16:9
10. Amphetamines and cocaine are controlled substances that stimulate the central nervous system.　16:10
11. Psychedelic drugs are dangerous drugs that cause users to hallucinate.　16:11
12. Marijuana is an illegal drug that affects physical and psychological health.　16:12
13. Household products, such as paint thinners, can harm a person if they are inhaled.　16:13
14. Caffeine is a stimulant that is found in tea, chocolate candy, cocoa, and many brands of coffee and cola drinks.　16:14
15. Designer drugs are dangerous.　16:15
16. It is important to provide immediate care and get medical help quickly for the victim of a drug overdose.　16:16
17. People who are chemically dependent can receive help in a therapeutic community or detoxification program, or be given narcotic antagonists.　16:17
18. Research indicates that parents play an important role in preventing drug abuse in their families.　16:18
19. Controlled substances are classified into five categories.　16:19
20. A person can avoid the dangers of chemical dependency by being drug-free.　16:20

Vocabulary

Below is a list of vocabulary words used in this chapter. Use each word only once to complete the sentences. Do not write in this book.

barbiturate　marijuana　receptor site
dose　OTC drug　side effect
drug abuse　psychedelics　solubility
flashbacks

1. The specific part in a cell in which the molecule of a drug fits is called the _____.

2. LSD can produce _____ as long as a month or year after the drug is taken.
3. The term _____ describes the taking of a drug for reasons other than intended medical purposes.
4. Aspirin is an example of a(n) _____ that can be purchased in a drugstore.

5. Drugs such as LSD and PCP are _____ because they change how the senses work.
6. The ability of drugs to dissolve is called _____.
7. THC is found in _____ and is responsible for its harmful effects.

8. The quantity of a drug that is taken at a specific time is also called the _____.
9. Drowsiness might be considered a(n) _____ of a barbiturate.
10. A drug that is used medically to relieve anxiety and tension is a(n) _____.

Review

1. What are the different ways drugs can be taken into the body?
2. Describe the factors that influence how drugs will affect a person.
3. Why are opiates dangerous?
4. Describe the difference between psychological and physical dependence.
5. Why should a person who might be using amphetamines avoid driving a car?
6. How can inhalants found inside the home pose serious dangers to the body?
7. What are the purposes of OTC drugs?
8. How would you know if a person overdosed on opiates?
9. How does the Controlled Substances Act categorize drugs?
10. How do people know when they have made a responsible decision about drugs?

Application

1. How might a person know if he or she is physically dependent on a drug?
2. Why can cocaine be dangerous even if taken only once?
3. How can the use of marijuana affect schoolwork?

Individual Research

1. All medicines must undergo strict testing before they are approved for use by the FDA. Research the criteria that must be met before a drug is approved.
2. Refer to Table 16–1 on page 316. Researching the drug literature, write the names of different drug combinations that would fall within each category—independent, antagonistic, additive, and potentiating or synergistic.
3. Research the drug laws in your state and prepare a chart that summarizes these laws.

Readings

Carroll, Charles R., *Drugs in Modern Society*. Dubuque, IA: William C. Brown Publishers, 1985.

Hammer, Signi, and Hazleton, Lesley, "Cocaine and the Chemical Brain," *Science Digest*, October, 1984, pp. 58-61, 100, 101, 103.

Approximately 50 percent of all traffic accidents involve the use of alcohol. Many local governments are making an effort to locate drivers who have been drinking alcohol before they cause an accident. How can you tell if a driver has been drinking? What else should be done to protect other people on the highway from alcoholic drivers?

A Lifestyle Without Alcohol Use

OBJECTIVES: You will be able to
- **describe the properties of alcohol.**
- **describe the holistic effects of alcohol on health.**
- **describe the stages in progressive drinking behaviors and their outcomes.**
- **explain alcoholism as a family disease.**
- **use the decision making model to make decisions about alcohol use.**

Suppose it is election day. On the ballot is an issue regarding the sale of alcohol in your community. Some people argue that alcohol helps people celebrate and feel jovial. Others state that over 50 percent of all traffic deaths involve the use of alcohol. Over 83 percent of persons arrested for crime and 74 percent of persons arrested for murder have been drinking. More than 3 million young people between 14 and 17 years of age have a serious drinking problem. Alcoholism affects more than 20 million people. How would you vote? Would you want alcohol to be sold in your community?

ALCOHOL

You have personal decisions to make about alcohol. Will you drink alcohol? Will you ride in an automobile driven by someone who has been drinking? What position will you take as laws are introduced to change the legal age for alcohol consumption? What will you do if a family member or close friend abuses alcohol? Do you know how to help such a person?

You will have many personal decisions to make about alcohol.

17:1   What Is Alcohol?

Alcohol is a psychoactive drug that depresses the central nervous system. It depresses the activity of the nerve cells of the brain. There are two types of alcohol. **Ethyl alcohol** or **ethanol** is the type of alcohol found in beverages. **Methyl alcohol** or **methanol** is the form of alcohol found in paint thinner or shellac. Methyl alcohol is unsafe to drink. It is poisonous. When ethanol and methanol are mixed, they form denatured alcohol. **Denatured alcohol** is a poisonous substance that is used for industrial purposes. The focus in this chapter is on ethanol—the alcohol in beverages.

Ethanol is the type of alcohol found in beverages.

The basis for the formation of all alcoholic beverages is fermentation. **Fermentation** occurs when yeast cells act on sugar in the presence of water producing a chemical change. The yeast recombines the carbon, hydrogen, and oxygen of sugar and water into ethyl alcohol and carbon dioxide. Wines are made from the fermentation of grapes or other fruits. Other alcoholic beverages are made from the fermentation of grains such as barley, corn, or rye.

Alcoholic beverages are formed by the process of fermentation.

Distilled spirits are alcoholic beverages that have concentrations of alcohol higher than those reached by fermentation. To get these high alcohol concentrations, a process called distillation is used. The solution that contains alcohol is heated. The ethyl alcohol in the solution boils first since alcohol has a lower boiling point than water. The vapors of alcohol are collected and condensed into liquid form again. The result is a higher concentration of alcohol in the distillate than there was in the original solution. Distilled spirits have the highest alcohol content of any alcoholic beverage. They usually are between 40 and 60 percent alcohol by volume.

Distilled spirits have the highest concentration of alcohol.

The amount of alcohol in any alcoholic beverage is indicated by its proof. **Proof** is double the percent of alcohol content in a beverage. Therefore, if an alcoholic beverage label indicates 80 proof, the beverage contains 40 percent alcohol by volume. Table 17–1 shows the types of alcoholic beverages and the percents of alcohol in each.

The percent of alcohol in a beverage is one-half the proof.

Table 17–1
Percents of Alcohol

Beverage	Percent of Alcohol
Table Wine	9-12
Fortified Wine	12-18
Wine Cooler	6
Beer	3-6
Light Beer	2.5-3.5
Distilled Spirits	40-60

17:2   Absorption and Oxidation of Alcohol

Alcohol is directly and quickly absorbed into the bloodstream. A small amount is absorbed through the tongue, 20 percent is absorbed through the stomach walls, and the balance is absorbed through the walls of the small intestine.

Once alcohol enters the bloodstream, it goes to all body tissues before being excreted. Five percent of the absorbed alcohol is excreted through the lungs and urine. The remaining ninety-five percent must be oxidized by the liver. Oxidation of alcohol is the process in which alcohol is changed to carbon dioxide and water in the liver. The liver can oxidize about a half ounce of alcohol per hour. Thus, it would take about one hour for the liver to oxidize the alcohol in an average drink.

Blood alcohol level (BAL) refers to the amount of alcohol in a person's blood. BAL is expressed as a percentage. Table 17–2 shows BAL according to number of drinks and approximate body weight. In general, the greater the BAL, the more harmful the effects on the body. Table 17–3 shows the changes that occur as BAL increases.

The liver can oxidize about one-half ounce of alcohol per hour.

The amount of alcohol in a person's blood is the blood alcohol level (BAL).

Body weight and number of drinks consumed influence blood alcohol level.

Table 17–2 Approximate Blood Alcohol Levels (BAL)

BODY WEIGHT IN KILOGRAMS AND POUNDS

| Number of Drinks in One Hour | (kg) | 45 | 54 | 63 | 72 | 81 | 90 | 100 | 109 |
	(lb)	100	120	140	160	180	200	220	240
1		0.04	0.03	0.03	0.02	0.02	0.02	0.02	0.02
2		0.08	0.06	0.05	0.05	0.04	0.04	0.03	0.03
3		0.11	0.09	0.08	0.07	0.06	0.06	0.05	0.05
4		0.15	0.12	0.11	0.09	0.08	0.08	0.07	0.06
5		0.19	0.16	0.13	0.12	0.11	0.09	0.09	0.08
6		0.23	0.19	0.16	0.14	0.13	0.11	0.10	0.09
7		0.26	0.22	0.19	0.15	0.15	0.13	0.12	0.11
8		0.30	0.25	0.21	0.19	0.17	0.15	0.14	0.13
9		0.34	0.28	0.24	0.21	0.19	0.17	0.15	0.14
10		0.38	0.31	0.27	0.23	0.21	0.19	0.17	0.16

Source: Ohio Department of Highway Safety, Columbus, Ohio

Table 17–3   Blood Alcohol Levels

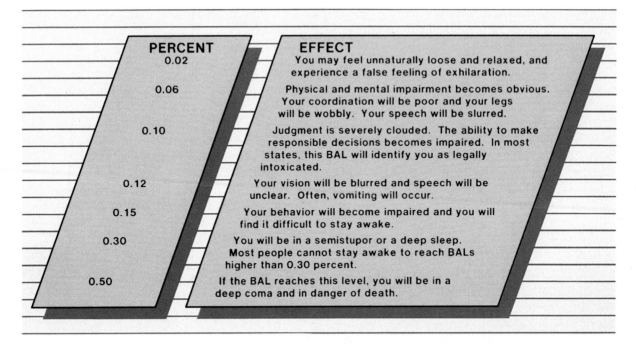

PERCENT	EFFECT
0.02	You may feel unnaturally loose and relaxed, and experience a false feeling of exhilaration.
0.06	Physical and mental impairment becomes obvious. Your coordination will be poor and your legs will be wobbly. Your speech will be slurred.
0.10	Judgment is severely clouded. The ability to make responsible decisions becomes impaired. In most states, this BAL will identify you as legally intoxicated.
0.12	Your vision will be blurred and speech will be unclear. Often, vomiting will occur.
0.15	Your behavior will become impaired and you will find it difficult to stay awake.
0.30	You will be in a semistupor or a deep sleep. Most people cannot stay awake to reach BALs higher than 0.30 percent.
0.50	If the BAL reaches this level, you will be in a deep coma and in danger of death.

As BAL increases, so do the physiological effects that are harmful to health.

Several factors determine how alcohol affects someone physically and psychologically.

Gulping drinks increases BAL quickly, thereby increasing the harmful effects.

Alcohol absorption is slowed after a meal.

17:3   Factors That Determine the Effects of Alcohol

Drinking the same amount of alcohol has different effects on different people. Even when the same person drinks the same amount on two separate occasions, the effects of alcohol can be different. There are several factors that determine how alcohol will affect a person.

Amount Consumed The greater the amount consumed, the stronger the effects. The kind of alcoholic beverage a person drinks is not as important as the amount of alcohol consumed.

Rate of Consumption The rate, or speed, at which alcohol is consumed also determines its effects. Suppose a person gulps a drink that he or she normally sips. The liver oxidizes the alcohol at the normal rate. The result is a high blood alcohol level.

Rate of Absorption Have you ever heard the saying, "Don't drink on an empty stomach"? Food slows down the passage of alcohol from the stomach to the small intestine. Most of the alcohol is absorbed by the small intestine. Thus, alcohol that is consumed after a heavy meal will be absorbed into the bloodstream more slowly.

Rate of Oxidation Most persons oxidize about a half ounce of alcohol per hour. However, for some persons, the rate of oxidation is much slower. This appears to be a hereditary factor. Persons with liver disease also oxidize alcohol more slowly. For these persons, alcohol has a more lasting effect.

Physical Condition The greater a person's weight, the longer it will take for alcohol to have an effect. A heavy person has more body fluids to dilute the alcohol. Fatigue also plays a role in determining the effects of alcohol. A tired person is apt to be affected by alcohol more quickly than a person who is not tired.

Expectations Some drinkers expect a certain effect from alcohol. Suppose a person thinks that alcohol will make him or her act silly. Most likely, this person will act silly regardless of the alcohol consumed. In one study, researchers gave alcoholic beverages to several people. Several other people were given similar tasting beverages without alcohol. All were told they were given alcohol. Their behavior was observed. Those who did not have alcohol acted the same as those who did.

Mood and Setting A person's mood when drinking influences the effects the person experiences. Someone who is unhappy may become very depressed. The setting is also a factor. A person who drinks alone is more likely to feel depressed.

Tolerance For many people, frequent or everyday use of alcohol may result in tolerance. They may need to drink more and more to experience the same effects they once obtained from smaller amounts.

> Heredity and liver disease may alter the usual rate of oxidation of alcohol.

> How persons believe alcohol will affect them will actually influence its effect.

> Unhappy persons usually become more depressed when they drink alcohol.

> Frequent alcohol consumption may result in tolerance.

 Review and Reflect

1. How much alcohol can the liver oxidize in one hour?
2. What is the relationship between BAL and the effects of alcohol on the mind and body?

EFFECTS OF ALCOHOL

Suppose you are invited to a party Friday night. A friend calls to tell you that alcoholic beverages are going to be served. You tell your friend that you will not go to the party unless it is alcohol-free. You can use the information in this section to explain to your friend how alcohol may affect a person's mental, social, physical, and economic health.

> Alcohol affects a person's mental, social, physical, and economic health.

FIGURE 17–1. Alcohol is a depressant drug and would affect a person's normal ability to have fun.

Alcohol is an "antisocial" drug because it interferes with learning healthful social skills.

Alcohol appears to be a major factor in most crimes and suicides.

Drinking alcohol impairs athletic performance.

17:4 Alcohol and Mental and Social Health

Drinking alcohol may influence mental and social health in a variety of ways.

Goal Achievement Many of the activities you perform each day prepare you for the future. Perhaps your long-term goal is to attend a technical school or a college. To prepare, you set a short-term goal of achieving the best grades you can in your high school classes. Drinking alcohol would interfere with your ability to study and concentrate. Drinking alcohol would affect your ability to reach your long-term goals.

Problem Solving As an adolescent, you also are learning to solve problems. You may be facing many situations for the very first time—becoming independent from parents, establishing relationships with the oppposite sex, working at a paying job, or saving to purchase a car. Each of these situations may be a source of stress for you. Drinking alcohol will not be helpful. Rather than relieving stress, alcohol increases stress.

Peer Relationships In most cases, alcohol is consumed in a social situation. What effect does drinking alcohol actually have on enhancing one's sociability? Most people who drink alcohol have the expectation that drinking will produce a pleasurable social environment. Some have the mistaken belief that alcohol is a "social" drug. However, a more realistic viewpoint is to classify alcohol as an "antisocial" drug. Adolescents or others who use alcohol are experiencing a social crutch rather than learning healthful ways to interact with peers and how to handle social situations successfully. Social poise and confidence can be gained by learning to talk with others in social situations without the use of alcohol. Your self-confidence will improve with the development of your social skills.

Crime and Suicide There is truth to the saying, alcohol brings out the worst in people. While under the influence of alcohol, physical and mental impairment occur (Table 17–3). Judgment and coping skills are affected. Crimes are more likely to happen when feelings are intensified and coping skills decreased.

17:5 Alcohol and Physical Health

Alcohol consumption may affect the body in several ways. The more alcohol a person drinks, the more difficulty he or she will have performing physical tasks, such as walking, running, and driving. Consequently, the loss of physical control increases one's chances of injury.

Alcohol causes blood vessels to dilate. Although a drinker feels warmer, body heat is being lost. Lowered body temperature may threaten health in cold weather since the person may be unaware of conditions that might cause frostbite, for example.

Alcohol use can affect body organs, increasing the likelihood of diseases, disability, and premature death. Alcohol consumption causes the stomach to increase the flow of gastric juices. With no food in the stomach, gastric juices may irritate the inner lining and cause ulcers.

Alcohol consumption increases urine production. As a result, a person must urinate frequently. Frequent urination disrupts the body's water balance causing a feeling of thirst. Body fluids need to be replaced.

Alcohol consumption causes damage to brain tissue. This results in a loss of ability to think and speak clearly. It also results in decreased muscle coordination. Heavy drinking over a period of years can reduce a person's ability to learn.

You learned that the liver oxidizes alcohol. Oxidation of large amounts of alcohol interferes with other liver functions. A disease known as cirrhosis of the liver can lead to liver failure and death.

Alcohol consumption increases the amount of sugar circulating in the bloodstream. Persons who drink frequently are more likely to have atherosclerosis.

Alcohol consumption causes changes in the cells that line the mouth, pharynx, larynx, and esophagus. Cancers of these organs are much more common in persons who drink alcohol excessively than in persons who do not drink.

Nutritional deficiencies are linked to excessive alcohol consumption. Alcohol ingestion interferes with appetite, digestion, and the absorption of vitamins.

Women who drink alcohol during pregnancy risk having babies born with fetal alcohol syndrome (FAS). FAS is characterized by mental retardation, slow growth, and physical defects.

In addition to these specific physical effects, alcohol can cause serious aftereffects. A **hangover** is a feeling of nausea, tiredness, extreme thirst, and headache that a person experiences after drinking too much. A hangover occurs after alcohol has left the body. No one knows exactly what causes a hangover. A hangover does not follow a certain number of drinks. A person may get a hangover from only one drink or from many drinks. There are no cures for a hangover.

A **blackout** is the period of time when someone who has been drinking cannot remember what has happened even though he or she is conscious. A person may black out after several drinks or after only one.

Drinking alcohol may prevent someone from feeling the true effects of cold weather.

Alcohol consumption may damage the stomach lining, the kidneys, and brain cells.

Cirrhosis of the liver is a serious disease caused by alcohol consumption.

Alcohol consumption increases the likelihood of heart disease and cancer.

FIGURE 17–2.

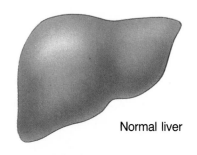

Normal liver

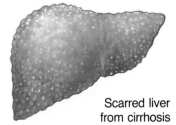

Scarred liver from cirrhosis

A person may have delirium tremens when he or she stops drinking alcohol after developing physical dependence.

Some people who use alcohol develop psychological dependence. They have an emotional need to keep drinking. Physical dependence can also result from alcohol consumption. Without alcohol, a person may experience symptoms of withdrawal. One symptom of withdrawal from alcohol is delirium tremens. **Delirium tremens (DTs)** is a condition characterized by hallucinations, shaking, and nausea.

Alcohol is a depressant. The greater the BAL, the greater the depressant effect on the brain (Table 17–3). Very large amounts consumed in a short time period may depress the brain centers that control heart rate and respiration.

Alcohol is particularly dangerous when taken with antihistamines, barbiturates, tranquilizers, aspirin, or narcotics.

Alcohol is particularly dangerous when combined with other drugs.

- Alcohol taken before or after cold medicine or antihistamines makes people sleepy.

- Alcohol taken with phenobarbital or other barbiturates below the lethal level can cause death.

- Alcohol taken with a tranquilizer causes dizziness and clumsiness.

- Alcohol and aspirin combine to destroy stomach tissues.

- Alcohol and narcotics depress the brain and respiration center and may cause a coma or death.

17:6   Alcohol and Economic Health

It is difficult to calculate all the costs of alcohol-related problems. However, some facts are well known. Many types of accidents occur as a result of alcohol use. The accidents, in turn, may result in injuries and lost days on the job. An auto accident may cause property damage, not only to the person who drinks, but also to another person. Insurance companies may raise the cost of insurance to a driver who is involved in an accident.

Many accidents are attributed to alcohol use.

Alcohol-related illnesses, whether physical or psychological, are a leading cause of absenteeism at work. If the absent person has used up sick days, pay may be deducted. Absenteeism results in lower productivity on the job, which is always costly to an employer. School absenteeism also has a financial cost although that cost may be more long range than immediate. The skills you learn in school enable you to prepare to earn a living in the future and to attain your long-range goals.

Persons who abuse alcohol miss more days from work and school than those who do not.

Alcohol abuse is disruptive to family life and often contributes to divorce. Families who experience divorce often must change their standards of living.

Alcohol abuse causes stress and disruption within the family.

FIGURE 17–3. Many communities are making an effort to find drivers who have been drinking alcohol before they cause an accident.

Alcohol consumption increases the likelihood of cancer, heart disease, cirrhosis of the liver, and other diseases. The treatment and rehabilitation for each of these illnesses may be very expensive.

The treatment for alcohol-related diseases is expensive.

Alcoholic beverages—beer, wine, liquor—can also be an expensive item in a person's budget. Often there are hidden expenses associated with drinking alcohol. The expense of getting into a bar (cover charge) or of buying drinks for others adds to the cost. Purchasing alcoholic beverages often replaces other essential purchases such as food and clothing.

Money used to purchase alcoholic beverages might be used for other necessary items.

Taxpayers must support many agencies and institutions that help alcoholics and their families. Many hospitals and other facilities have services and counseling programs available to treat alcoholism.

Alcohol rehabilitation programs are expensive to taxpayers.

17:7   Alcohol and Holistic Health

Drinking alcohol affects every area of a person's lifestyle. This single behavior not only influences a person's lifestyle but also has a negative effect on health. The effect is holistic. Study Table 17–4 and observe that every possible effect listed is a risk to optimum health.

Drinking alcohol has a holistic effect on all ten areas of a person's health.

 Review and Reflect

3. Why might alcohol be described as an antisocial drug?

Table 17–4   Holistic Effects of Drinking Alcohol

HEALTH COMPONENT	POSSIBLE EFFECT
Mental Health	• Interferes with learning and school performance • Intensifies moods • Interferes with problem-solving skills • Increases stress • Causes organic mental disorder • Produces psychological dependence • Causes various brain disorders
Family and Social Health	• Increases number of family arguments • Gives a false sense of effective communication • Increases violent interactions • Causes FAS
Growth and Development	• Destroys brain cells • Impairs physical skills • Affects and dulls all senses • Lowers body temperature • Increases heart rate and blood pressure
Nutrition	• Interferes with appetite and vitamin absorption • Causes niacin and thiamine deficiency
Exercise and Fitness	• Interferes with coordination and muscle movement • Decreases physical performance
Drugs	• Produces serious side effects when used with other drugs • Depresses brain and respiration center and may cause coma or death when used with narcotics • Causes dizziness or clumsiness when used with tranquilizers
Diseases and Disorders	• Causes cirrhosis of the liver • Increases the likelihood of heart disease • Increases the likelihood of cancer of the mouth, esophagus, larynx, and pharynx when combined with smoking cigarettes • Causes kidneys to overwork
Consumer and Personal Health	• Has an offensive odor to others • Increases perspiration • Is an expensive habit • Causes feelings of nausea, tiredness, thirst, and headache
Safety and First Aid	• Increases drownings, falls, fires • Is responsible for most auto accidents and traffic deaths • Is involved in most crimes and murders
Community and Environmental Health	• Adds costs to industry, law enforcement, health, and family life • Adds to environmental pollution

DRINKING PROBLEMS

One out of ten persons who drinks is an alcoholic. The disease known as alcoholism affects people of all social and economic backgrounds. Alcoholism can happen to anyone who drinks.

17:8 Progression of Drinking Behavior

People who are alcoholics did not plan to become addicted to alcohol. Their involvement with the drug may have progressed over a period of time. Their drinking behavior may have developed through four progressive stages: experimentation, mood change, intoxication, and harmful dependence.

Experimentation Why does anyone take that first drink of alcohol? In most cases the answer is simple—curiosity and the desire to be accepted. The advertising media portray the message that drinking alcohol is a means to being popular and adult. These implications, accompanied by pressure from friends, may encourage some teenagers to drink. This experimentation may occur when a teenager is dealing with other aspects of becoming adult. However, an increasing number of teenagers are choosing not to experiment with alcohol. A current trend in regard to alcohol is to choose healthful behaviors that promote a high-quality and productive life.

Curiosity and the advertising media encourage some teenagers to drink.

Most teenagers are emphasizing healthful behaviors rather than experimenting with alcohol.

Mood Change Those who do experiment with alcohol and continue to drink move to the second stage. They may not like the taste of alcohol, but eventually, they become used to it. They may experience a pleasant mood change and decide that they can change their moods by the amount of alcohol consumed. They progress from having one drink to two drinks in hopes that there will be an even greater effect. They consider themselves to be moderate drinkers.

Drinking in moderation may falsely be described as responsible drinking.

Intoxication Those persons who continue to drink to alter their moods will eventually consume larger and larger quantities of alcohol. Or, they may start using drinks with a higher percentage of alcohol. Consequently, they may become intoxicated. For many people, intoxication is used as a means of dealing with problems. Unfortunately, the effects of intoxication add to a person's stress. Symptoms of intoxication include a hangover, nausea, vomiting, or diarrhea. Because alcohol is a depressant, the drinker may feel sad and unhappy and have low self-esteem. This person may return to drinking to deal with these problems. The cycle continues.

Drinking to the point of intoxication has harmful physiological and psychological effects.

Persons who are physically or psychologically dependent on alcohol are alcoholics.

Harmful Dependence In the final stage, the drinker is physically and psychologically dependent on alcohol and has the disease known as alcoholism. At this stage, it does not matter how much or how often the person drinks. He or she will always be an alcoholic from this point on.

17:9   What Is Alcoholism?

The American Medical Association (AMA) and the British Medical Association (BMA) classify alcoholism as a disease. **Alcoholism** is a progressive disease that is characterized by physical and psychological dependence on alcohol. Alcoholism causes harmful body changes as well as changes in personality and behavior.

Alcoholism is a disease that affects 20 million people and their families.

The Department of Health and Human Services describes alcoholism as a neglected disease because more should be done in the way of prevention. There are more than 20 million alcoholics, and the number is growing.

Some people inherit a tendency toward a slower rate of alcohol oxidation.

Some people may inherit a body chemistry that affects their reaction to alcohol. Just as you may have a tendency for heart disease and diabetes if your parents had these diseases, you may also inherit a body chemistry that makes you prone to alcoholism. If you have one or more alcoholic members in your family, you need not become an alcoholic. Remember that you will never be an alcoholic if you never take a drink of alcohol.

FIGURE 17–4. Everyone faces stressful situations, such as traffic jams, every day. Some people use alcohol as a means of coping with stress.

In some families, children are exposed constantly to the use of alcohol as a means of solving problems. These children may begin to copy self-destructive behaviors that increase the likelihood of alcoholism.

Some people choose to drink for pleasure or to be sociable. Some people use alcohol to relieve everyday stress and tension. They drink to change their moods. As people continue to drink, they develop psychological and physical dependence on alcohol. This self-destructive behavior may lead to alcoholism.

Alcoholism is incurable—once an alcoholic, always an alcoholic. However, alcoholism can be treated. This is why prompt diagnosis is important. Methods of diagnosis include recognizing one or more of the following ten signs and symptoms. The alcoholic

- is preoccupied with the effects produced by alcohol and looks forward to drinking.

- consumes alcohol quickly to get the desired effect.

- does not distinguish between drinking alone or with others.

- cannot control drinking. The alcoholic almost always drinks more than intended.

- almost always makes sure there is a supply of alcohol to drink. The alcoholic rationalizes that the supply is needed for friends.

- uses alcohol in all situations when he or she feels depressed, uptight, anxious, frightened, angry, or happy.

- increases the amount of alcohol consumed to get the same effect.

  An alcoholic will use alcohol to cope with most situations.

- has difficulty remembering, the day after drinking, anything he or she said or did the day before.

- swears off drinking or cuts down, but returns to drinking again and again.

  An alcoholic may start and stop drinking, but will begin again.

- experiences a continuous series of problems before, during, or after drinking. The result is an internal and persistent conflict between values and behavior.

  An alcoholic experiences a conflict between values and behavior.

 Review and Reflect

4. Why does the Department of Health and Human Services describe alcoholism as a neglected disease?
5. How might body chemistry increase the likelihood of alcoholism in some families?

ALCOHOL AND THE FAMILY

Alcoholism affects not only the person who drinks but also his or her family. Each family member is affected. Family members recognize when drinking is out of control and try to do something about it. They often are ashamed and embarrassed. Their behavior often becomes self-destructive in the process. This is the reason alcoholism is sometimes called a family disease.

Alcoholism is a family disease—the alcoholic and other family members are affected.

17:10 An Alcoholic Family Member

When the alcoholic is a parent, the children may lose their feeling of security. They cannot count on the parent. The parent may be inconsistent or even violent with discipline. Children may not want to bring friends home for fear of embarrassment.

Children of alcoholics are often insecure.

Teenage alcoholics are often hostile and have poor peer relationships.

Family members of alcoholics are often obsessed with the alcoholic's behavior.

Family members of alcoholics experience anxiety.

Family members of alcoholics eventually become angry about the alcoholic's behavior.

Family members of alcoholics often deny the problem.

Family members of alcoholics often feel that they have caused the problem.

When the alcoholic is a teenager, parents may become distrustful. Teenage alcoholics usually have problems at school and suffer low self-esteem. They usually have poor peer relationships. They may be argumentative and hostile. Parents often do not know how to cope with these problems as well as with the drinking. Whether it is a parent or teenager, there are some typical ways that family members respond to the alcoholic.

Obsession Obsession is having something on your mind most of the time. Family members may become obsessed with what the alcoholic is doing or not doing. They want the alcoholic to stop drinking. They begin to count how many drinks the alcoholic consumes. They may search the house for hidden bottles of liquor and pour the liquor down the drain. They may follow the alcoholic to watch his or her behavior.

Anxiety Family members also become anxious as they observe the changes in the alcoholic's lifestyle. They notice that certain responsibilities are not met. An alcoholic parent may have difficulty on the job or doing household chores. An alcoholic adolescent may not be concerned about schoolwork or other responsibilities. However, family members are concerned. They often make the mistake of covering up and making excuses for the alcoholic. They may tell lies to help mend damaged relationships at home, school, or work.

Anger Eventually, family members get tired of the alcoholic's behavior. They are tired of doing his or her work and telling lies or covering up in other ways. Family members begin to feel used and unloved because of the alcoholic's behavior. They want to strike back and punish the alcoholic. It is not uncommon for adolescents who have alcoholic parents to act in hostile ways at school to express their anger and frustration. It is not uncommon for parents of alcoholic teenagers to constantly argue as a means of venting their anger.

Denial Often family members begin to pretend that there is no problem or that the problem is going away. They accept promises from the alcoholic. For example, the alcoholic might have a period of being sober, and the family believes that the alcoholic will stop drinking.

Guilt Most family members experience guilt because they think they are to blame for the problem. They think the alcoholism was caused by something they did or did not do. Family members often try to overcome their guilt by trying to please the alcoholic. Their self-worth suffers because nothing they do changes the alcoholic's behavior.

Because alcoholism is a family disease, family members need help in coping. Family members may choose individual or group counseling. Possible sources of help are a family physician, rabbi, minister, priest, school counselor, teacher, or other trusted adult.

Alateen is a treatment organization for teenage children of alcoholic parents. **Al-Anon** is a treatment organization for husbands, wives, other family members, and friends of alcoholics. Members of Alateen and Al-Anon learn how to help the alcoholic take responsibility for his or her behavior. Members also get help in regaining inner strength and stability.

17:11 Responding to the Alcoholic

Eventually, family members realize that something must be done about the alcoholic. They try to persuade the alcoholic to quit drinking and to get treatment. In only a small percentage of cases are family members successful without outside help. In most cases the alcoholic refuses help, denies the problem, and becomes very angry. Outside help usually becomes necessary.

Family members may seek outside help from many sources. They may consult their family physician, their religious leader, a drug rehabilitation center, an alcohol treatment center at a hospital or clinic, or a mental health center. Costs for services vary. In most communities, the community mental health center or drug rehabilitation center assists families without financial resources. Persons trained to help alcoholics and their families meet with family members to discuss the alcoholic. Each family member makes a list of all the events that have happened because of the alcoholic's drinking. Family members may even have pictures or movies of the alcoholic's behavior. Other persons who are close to the alcoholic are included. An employee, close friend, school teacher, or athletic coach may be asked to share what he or she has observed.

The counselor and family plan a confrontation. A **confrontation** is a meeting with the alcoholic to present the facts about his or her drinking and the results of this behavior. The alcoholic usually wants to deny that he or she has the disease. However, the facts are difficult to deny when they are presented in detail. The confrontation also includes a discussion of how treatment will be approached.

Usually, the alcoholic is aware that the family has planned a confrontation. However, the alcoholic is sometimes caught off guard by the gathering of family members and others. When forced to listen to documented facts during a confrontation, most alcoholics agree to treatment. Usually the alcoholic goes from the confrontation to a treatment facility.

FIGURE 17–5.

It is important for family members of alcoholics to be able to describe the alcoholic's behavior.

During a confrontation with the alcoholic, family members present facts concerning the alcoholic's behavior.

The terms confrontation and intervention are often used interchangeably.

An alcoholic usually is taken from a confrontation to a treatment facility.

Many alcoholics must begin treatment with detoxification.

Treatment usually begins with detoxification. **Detoxification** is the process of getting alcohol out of the alcoholic's system, breaking the physical and psychological dependence, and treating any health problems that exist. Special attention is given to the nutritional needs of the alcoholic.

Psychological help is needed to help the alcoholic examine behavior and find a healthful way of living. Alcoholism is a progressive disease. This means it continues even when the person no longer drinks alcohol. If the alcoholic does not drink for even ten years and then has an alcoholic beverage, the alcohol will be a problem. Thus, the alcoholic should never drink again. For this reason, many alcoholics continue individual counseling or join support groups.

An alcoholic should never drink alcohol again.

Alcoholics Anonymous (AA) is a treatment organization that consists of alcoholics who share their experiences to help one another resist the urge to drink again. To receive support from this group, alcoholics must

Alcoholics Anonymous is a support group that treats a group of alcoholics.

- accept the fact that alcohol is ruining their lives and admit that they cannot stop drinking without help.
- ask AA members for help and attend regular AA meetings.
- depend on others for help.
- help others.

 Review and Reflect

6. How are Alateen and Alcoholics Anonymous different?
7. Why do family members usually have to confront the alcoholic with specific facts about drinking behavior?

MAKING RESPONSIBLE DECISIONS

Think about the many situations in which your peers try to influence your actions. Think about the situations in which you try to influence the actions of your peers. Peer pressure can be healthful or harmful depending on whether or not it leads to actions that are responsible.

Peers may exert pressure to encourage or prevent friends from drinking alcohol.

You may experience peer pressure to drink alcohol. Your response to this pressure is critical. If you choose to drink alcohol because others do, you have allowed others to influence you in behaviors that are not healthful.

FIGURE 17-6. You will work better and feel better if you choose a lifestyle that does not include alcohol.

17:12   Choosing a Lifestyle Without Alcohol

You have learned that a responsible decision results in actions that are healthful, safe, and legal. Responsible decisions result in actions that promote self-respect and show respect and concern for others. They result in actions that your parents would approve. It is important to make responsible decisions regarding the use of alcohol. It is best to do this by examining the possible results before you are in the position of being offered a drink. Consider the following.

Would the results of my decision be healthful? We have previously discussed the effects of alcohol on several body organs. Continued use of alcohol increases the likelihood of disease, disability, and premature death.

Would the results of my decision be safe? Earlier in this chapter, you learned that drinking alcohol depresses your central nervous system. The alcohol begins its effects by making you feel unnaturally relaxed. Eventually, alcohol affects the parts of the brain that control judgment. You may say or do things that you would not normally say or do.

If you drink and drive, your chances of being involved in an automobile accident are increased. This may cause injury to you as well as to others. It is well known that half of all traffic-related accidents and deaths are a result of persons drinking and driving.

Would the results of my decision be legal? At a BAL of 0.06, there is an impairment of muscle control and motor skills. Unfortunately, it is not illegal in many states to drive with a BAL of 0.04 to 0.05 percent. In other states, driving while intoxicated (DWI) is stated as driving with a BAL of 0.10 percent. Some states are

Alcohol consumption is not healthful because it increases the likelihood of disease, disability, and premature death.

Alcohol consumption is not safe because it increases the likelihood of accidents.

Drunk driving is illegal because it increases the likelihood of fatal automobile accidents.

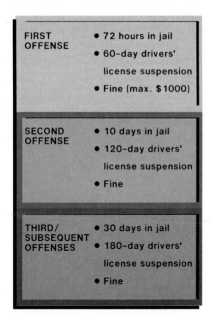

FIRST OFFENSE	• 72 hours in jail • 60-day drivers' license suspension • Fine (max. $1000)
SECOND OFFENSE	• 10 days in jail • 120-day drivers' license suspension • Fine
THIRD/ SUBSEQUENT OFFENSES	• 30 days in jail • 180-day drivers' license suspension • Fine

FIGURE 17–7. The penalties for driving while intoxicated have become more strict in many localities.

Drinking alcohol may cause you to change your sexual behavior, endangering your self-respect and the respect of others.

Drinking alcohol usually violates parental guidelines.

Saying "No" to drinking alcohol is a responsible decision that gains you the respect of others.

currently changing their laws to protect you and others from intoxicated drivers.

The penalties for driving while intoxicated are becoming more and more strict (Figure 17–7). One reason is the influence of different interest groups who are exerting organized campaigns to increase the penalties for those arrested for drunk driving. One of these groups is Mothers Against Drunk Driving (**MADD**). Begun by a mother whose child was killed by a drunk driver, MADD has actively sought the passage of DWI laws that have stiffer penalties than present laws.

As an offshoot of MADD, Fathers Against Drunk Driving (**FADD**) and Students Against Drunk Driving (**SADD**) were formed. Through groups like these, many states have now passed legislation that increases the penalties for those guilty of DWI.

Another change involves the legal drinking age. In the 1970s, many states lowered the drinking age to 18, 19, and 20 from age 21. This was accompanied by an alarming increase in alcohol-related traffic deaths. All of the 19 states that lowered the age have increased it again.

Would the results of my decision show respect for myself and others? Drinking alcohol may change your perceptions and feelings about your sexuality. Even small amounts of alcohol may lower your inhibitions and cause you to be more physically affectionate than you would normally be on a date. While drinking alcohol, you may engage in activities that would cause you to lose self respect and the respect of others.

Would the results of my decision follow my parents' guidelines? Most parents have guidelines that prefer teenagers not drink alcoholic beverages. Disregarding your parents' guidelines will cause stress in your relationships with them.

Choosing not to drink alcohol is a responsible decision. Choose friends who will reinforce your decision to not drink. Attend only drug-free activities. Many communities now sponsor alcohol-free parties on New Year's Eve and other occasions for high school students.

Saying no to drinking alcohol influences your peers in healthful ways. When your friends know that you do not drink and that others cannot influence you, it makes it easier for your friends to say no. An increasing number of teenagers and young adults are choosing not to drink alcohol. There are many reasons.

• the physical effects of long-term alcohol use
• the emotional and social costs
• the significant number of deaths of young people caused by drunk drivers
• reluctance to waste efforts to attain optimum health

Remember, you are responsible for your own actions. Consider the results of your decision and the effects on your health and your future well being. Say no to drinking alcohol.

 Activity: _____ **Alcohol-Free Party**

Divide into groups of five with classmates. Each group is to plan an alcohol-free party. Give the party a clever name. Plan healthful activities and a healthful menu. Design an invitation on a sheet of poster board. Share your invitation with the class. Discuss the specifics of the party you planned.

Reflect and Review

8. Why do many people want to change the BAL for which a driver can be charged with DWI?
9. How might drinking alcohol influence decisions about sexual behavior?
10. Why is it important to tell peers you do not want to drink or to attend parties where alcoholic beverages are served?

Focus on
Life Management Skills

- Know the factors that determine the effects of alcohol.
- Develop social poise and confidence without the use of alcohol.
- Spend your money on healthful products and services rather than alcohol.
- Participate in healthful activities that promote self-satisfaction.
- Plan healthful ways to celebrate and have fun with others.
- Recognize the symptoms of alcoholism, and encourage problem drinkers and alcoholics to get treatment.
- Do not drive or ride with someone who has been drinking.
- Be aware of the dangers of FAS.
- Attend only drug-free parties.

Summary

1. Ethyl alcohol is a depressant drug found in alcoholic beverages. 17:1
2. The greater the BAL, the more harmful the effects on the body and mind. 17:2
3. The effects of alcohol are determined by the amount of alcohol consumed, the rates of consumption, absorption, and oxidation, physical condition, expectations, mood and setting, and tolerance. 17:3
4. Drinking alcohol may influence goal achievement, problem solving, peer relationships, and criminal behaviors. 17:4
5. Drinking alcohol may decrease performance, lower body temperature, cause disease, and induce hangovers, blackouts, delirium tremens, and death. 17:5
6. Economic costs of drinking alcohol may result from injuries, accidents, work and school absenteeism, family disruption, disease, and social programs. 17:6
7. Drinking alcohol has a holistic effect on a person's lifestyle. 17:7
8. Four progressive stages of drinking include experimentation, mood change, intoxication, and harmful dependence. 17:8
9. The American Medical Association and the British Medical Association classify alcoholism as a disease that causes harmful physical and psychological dependence on alcohol. 17:9
10. Family members of an alcoholic usually experience obsession, anxiety, anger, denial, and guilt. 17:10
11. Alcoholics can be helped through confrontation, detoxification, counseling, and support groups such as Alcoholics Anonymous. 17:11
12. It is easier to say no to drinking alcohol when you choose friends who do not drink. 17:12

Vocabulary

Below is a list of vocabulary words used in this chapter. Use each word only once to complete the sentences. Do not write in this book.

Alateen	detoxification
alcoholism	fermentation
blood alcohol level	hangover
confrontation	MADD
delirium tremens	proof

1. An alcoholic may have to go through _____ when treatment begins.
2. The process in which yeast reacts with sugar is _____.
3. Teenage children of alcoholics might attend _____ to learn to cope with family problems.
4. _____ is an organization that has actively sought the passage of stiff DWI laws.
5. The _____ of distilled spirits is greater than that for table wine.
6. A(n) _____ of 0.50 percent might result in a deep coma and/or death.
7. An alcoholic is forced to listen to documented facts during a(n) _____.
8. When an alcoholic stops drinking, he or she may experience _____.
9. The feeling of nausea, thirst, and headache that follow drinking is called a(n) _____.
10. _____ is an incurable disease that affects a person's total health.

Review

1. Identify eight factors that influence the affects of alcohol on the mind and body.
2. What are two possible social effects from increased alcohol consumption?
3. How does alcohol consumption affect the body's senses?
4. What are four stages through which drinking behavior progresses?
5. What are ten symptoms of alcoholism?
6. What are five behaviors usually displayed by family members of alcoholics?
7. What is the purpose of a family confrontation of an alcoholic?
8. What organizations exist to help the alcoholic and other family members?
9. What are the purposes of MADD, FADD, and SADD?
10. What is detoxification?

Application

1. Why do many people support the lowering of the blood alcohol level needed to convict someone for driving while intoxicated?
2. Why is drinking alcohol often associated with unwanted teenage pregnancy?
3. If there were a warning label on a liquor bottle about fetal alcohol syndrome (FAS), what might it say?
4. What would you do if you were offered a ride by an intoxicated friend?
5. Why do you think it is against the law for a police officer or an airplane pilot to drink alcohol while on duty?

Individual Research

1. Some Alcoholics Anonymous, Alateen, and Al-Anon meetings are open to the public. Attend an open meeting and write a report.
2. Call your local police department to ask about the current drinking and driving laws in your community and state. Write a report about these laws to share with class members.

Readings

Gross, Leonard, *How Much Is Too Much?* New York, NY: Ballantine Books, 1983.

Johnson, Vernon, *I'll Quit Tomorrow: A Practical Guide to Alcoholism Treatment.* San Francisco, CA: Harper & Row Publishers, Inc., 1980.

Ryerson, Eric, *When Your Parent Drinks Too Much.* New York, NY: Facts On File Publications, 1985.

Cigarette smoking is as potentially dangerous as a loaded gun. A smoker is aiming a "gun" at himself or herself with every smoked cigarette. What are the holistic effects of smoking? When is a good time to stop if you are presently a smoker?

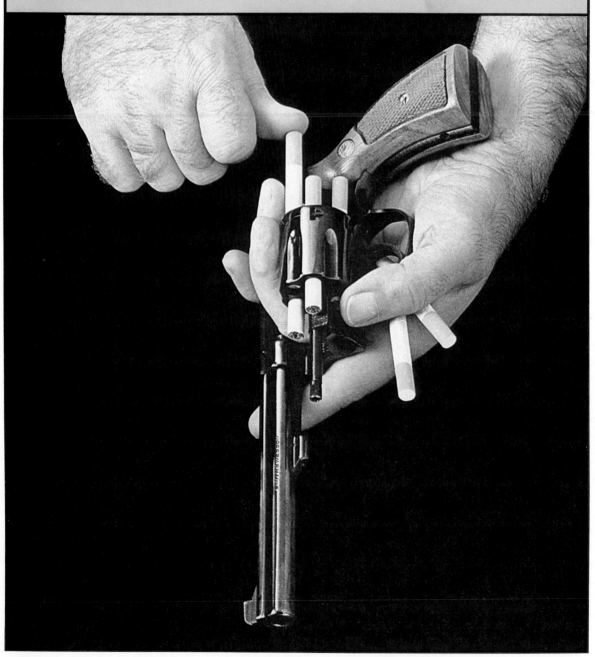

Chapter 18

A Tobacco-Free Lifestyle

OBJECTIVES: You will be able to
- **identify the factors involved in tobacco use.**
- **describe how smoking harms a person's health.**
- **describe why lower-yield cigarettes and smokeless tobacco are harmful.**
- **discuss what can be done to avoid passive smoke.**
- **promote a tobacco-free lifestyle for yourself and others.**

Cigarette smoking is the single most preventable cause of death in the United States today. Some research indicates that nearly one out of every five deaths and one out of every three cancer deaths in the United States are related to smoking. With these figures in mind, why do smokers choose to risk shortening their lives? What can be done to move toward a smokeless society? What can you do to have a smoke-free life?

CIGARETTE SMOKING: THE BASIC FACTS

According to a 1985 national high school survey conducted for the National Institute on Drug Abuse, 82 percent of the high school senior class did not smoke cigarettes. Almost three-fourths of this class expressed strong disapproval of daily smoking because of its harmful health effects. These effects have an impact on all areas of health. Referring to the ten components of the Health Behavior Wheel in Chapter 1, consider the holistic effects of cigarette smoking (Figure 18–1). There are many other ways that cigarette smoking harms health. To understand how this occurs, we will review the basic facts about smoking.

The majority of high school seniors do not smoke cigarettes.

Cigarette smoking has a holistic effect on the body.

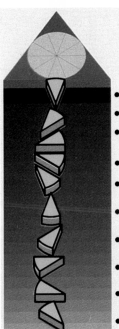

- Mental Health – Smoking impairs the ability to concentrate and relax.
- Family and Social Health – Smoke from a cigarette can harm those in the same room.
- Growth and Development – Pregnant women who smoke have babies of lower birth weight than pregnant women who do not smoke.
- Nutrition – Smoking harms the taste buds on the tongue and impairs the sense of taste.
- Exercise and Fitness – Smoking decreases cardiovascular endurance.
- Drugs – Smoking produces physical and psychological dependence.
- Diseases and Disorders – Smoking increases the risk of lung and heart diseases.
- Consumer and Personal Health – Cigarette smoking causes teeth to yellow and breath to smell.
- Safety and First Aid – Cigarette smoking, especially in bed, is a major cause of home fires.
- Community and Environmental Health – Cigarette smoking is a major source of indoor pollution.

FIGURE 18–1. The holistic effects of smoking cigarettes.

18:1 Why People Choose Not to Smoke

Consider the following response of a student your age who was asked to give a reason for not smoking. "I don't smoke because I feel good now, and I want to keep feeling that way. I want to do everything I can to stay feeling good." When ads in publications focus on cigarette smoking, the emphasis appears to be on the reasons people smoke. Since most adults and people your age do not smoke, the emphasis in this textbook will focus on healthful behaviors related to not smoking rather than the risk behaviors related to smoking. Here are some reasons people your age choose not to smoke.

Parental Influence Parents play a crucial role in the smoking behavior of their children. If both parents do not smoke, chances are that their children will not become smokers. These parents may have a no smoking policy in their home. In most cases, parents who smoke take steps to discourage their children from smoking. Maybe these parents smoke because of the physical and psychological dependence created by tobacco. Yet, they know that smoking is harmful to health, and they do not want their children to choose a behavior that will harm them now and in the future. Parental guidelines play an important role in guiding people your age to choose a tobacco-free lifestyle.

There are many reasons people have for not smoking.

Parents play an important role in a child's decision to smoke or not to smoke.

Peer Pressure Studies show that peer groups play an important role in the decision to smoke or not to smoke. If your close friends do not smoke, chances are that you will not smoke. Young people have a strong desire to be accepted by their peers. This is the reason peer pressure plays such an important role. Since most people your age do not smoke, your chances to remain tobacco-free are increased. Although some adolescents think it is adult to smoke, most realize that it takes a mature person to say no.

Stimulation and Gratification Smokers often argue that smoking gives them a lift and a feeling of satisfaction. However, the lift is achieved by the action of many harmful chemicals in tobacco and smoke. Nonsmokers get their lifts and gratification by participating in healthful activities such as athletics or other organized or individual activities.

Stress There are healthful and harmful ways to deal with stressful situations. Many people choose not to smoke because they realize that smoking is a harmful way to deal with stress. The ingredients in tobacco act as stimulants, which may increase the physical effects of stress. Dealing with stress by healthful means, such as exercising or discussing concerns with another person, will relieve the physical effects of stress.

Health The facts about cigarette smoking are clear. Most people your age realize that cigarette smoking is a threat to health—both

Peer pressure can serve to promote or discourage cigarette smoking.

Smoking is a harmful way to deal with stress.

FIGURE 18–2. Cigarette smoking is a major cause of grass and forest fires.

Most adolescents realize that cigarette smoking is a health threat.

now and in later years. Smokers have discolored teeth and bad breath. They may experience shortness of breath in ordinary activities such as walking up a flight of stairs. After many years of smoking, the risks of heart and lung diseases increase sharply. Perhaps, these are the major reasons that most of your peers choose not to smoke.

18:2   Smoking and Dependency

Smoking can result in physical dependence.

Cigarette smoke contains drugs. These drugs have the ability to create physical as well as psychological dependence. **Nicotine** is a colorless, oily chemical in tobacco that produces physical dependence and a stimulating effect on the central nervous system. Tolerance develops with nicotine. This means smokers must smoke more and more to get the same effects.

Nicotine is a stimulant that is harmful to a person's health.

When smoke is inhaled, nicotine goes directly to the lungs where it enters the bloodstream. It takes about seven and one-half seconds for nicotine to reach the brain after it is inhaled. Once in the brain, nicotine causes stimulation of the cardiovascular system. But nicotine affects other parts of the body also. These are discussed later in this chapter.

Some studies show that nicotine produces physical dependence because it causes the brain to adapt to a state of stimulation. When the smoker does not use tobacco for a period of time, the brain is less stimulated. Smokers must then light up again to get the level of activity in the brain back to a stimulated state.

Smokers will go through withdrawal when denied cigarettes. Withdrawal symptoms from smoking include irritability, inability to sleep, muscle pains, headaches, and nausea. Many smokers find it difficult to quit smoking because they cannot tolerate the withdrawal symptoms.

Psychological factors often are involved in a person's dependence on tobacco.

People may continue to smoke because of psychological factors. They may think that smoking relieves boredom or gives them self-confidence. Often, the psychological factors combine with the physical factors to promote smoking. For example, people may smoke every time they drink coffee or when they awake in the morning. Particular activities become associated with a desire to smoke. Such activities help keep people dependent on tobacco.

 ## Review and Reflect

1. What healthful actions can you follow to relieve stress?
2. Why is it difficult to break the cigarette smoking habit?

He Watches His Weight and He Doesn't Smoke.

He's Dr. Michael DeBakey, one of the world's great heart surgeons.
He should know what's good for a healthy heart.

Take a walk instead of a smoke.
Have thinner dinners.
Cut fat from meat.

A good health message from the National Heart, Lung, and Blood Institute.

FIGURE 18–3.

TOBACCO AND HEALTH

If you are a smoker now, it may be difficult for you to think seriously about the future risks of continuing to smoke. After all, you are young and feel healthy. You may not be able to relate to your health status 25 or more years from now. However, there are many symptoms that gradually affect a smoker's health over a long period of time. These symptoms may affect a person's lifestyle. People who are now 40 or 50 years old who have a lung disease were once your age and most likely were smokers. They did not plan to get a smoking-related disease. If you are a smoker and quit now, you will avoid many harmful effects of tobacco. If you are not a smoker, the latest information about smoking and health should assure you that your decision not to smoke is a responsible one.

The harm produced by smoking begins when a person first starts smoking.

18:3 Smoking and the Cardiovascular System

Place your index finger on the artery in your neck and count your pulse rate. Most likely, your pulse is between 60 and 80 beats per minute at rest. Suppose you smoked a cigarette and took your pulse rate again. It would increase to between 80 and 100 beats per minute at rest. This means your heart is working about 25 percent harder after smoking. This excess work causes undue

Cigarette smoke increases heartbeat rate.

stress on the heart. After years of smoking, this stress increases the risk of developing coronary heart disease (CHD). CHD can begin to develop at your age.

The ways in which cigarette smoking increases the risk of CHD are not fully understood. Nicotine causes an unnecessary increase in heart rate, blood pressure, and cardiac output. When the heart works harder than normal, it requires more oxygen. At the same time, another substance in cigarette smoke comes into play. This substance is carbon monoxide. **Carbon monoxide** is an odorless, colorless gas. Carbon monoxide displaces oxygen from hemoglobin in the blood. Thus, the heart is deprived of the oxygen it needs. It is also thought that carbon monoxide injures the walls of the arteries. As a result, many researchers believe the combination of carbon monoxide and nicotine is responsible for a large number of smoking-related deaths.

Carbon monoxide is a colorless, odorless gas in cigarette smoke.

18:4 Smoking and the Respiratory System

The health risks of smoking to the respiratory system are numerous and alarming. Smoking causes shortness of breath during mild physical exertion. The so-called smoker's cough can develop. This cough occurs because the cilia in the throat do not function to remove foreign particles from the air passage. Studies

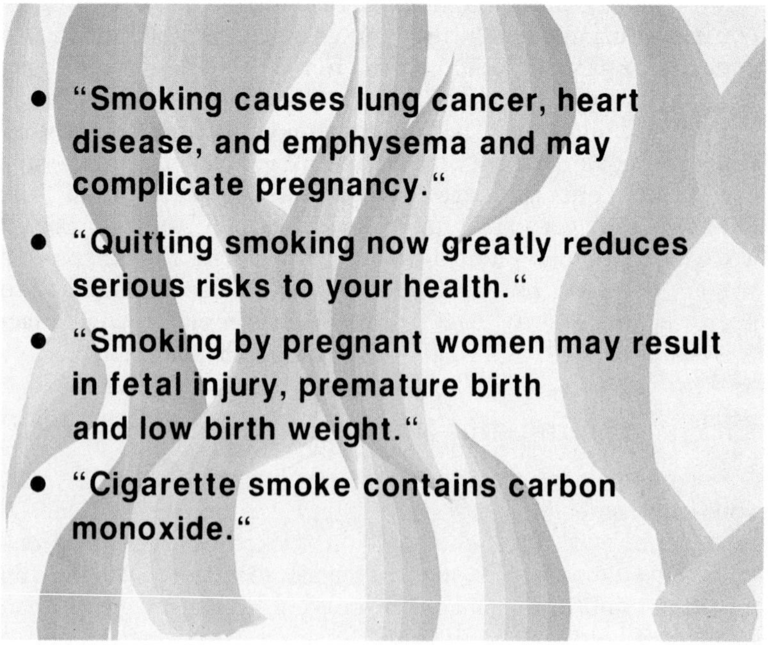

- "Smoking causes lung cancer, heart disease, and emphysema and may complicate pregnancy."

- "Quitting smoking now greatly reduces serious risks to your health."

- "Smoking by pregnant women may result in fetal injury, premature birth and low birth weight."

- "Cigarette smoke contains carbon monoxide."

FIGURE 18–4. One of these warnings appears on every package of cigarettes to warn a smoker of the potential dangers to health.

indicate that smoking for 20 years presents a great risk of developing lung cancer. It is a proven fact that smoking is the major cause of lung cancer in both men and women. It is also a fact that 90 percent of all lung cancer victims die within five years after the cancer is diagnosed.

Cigarette smoking increases the risk of developing lung cancer.

The greatest contributing factor to lung cancer is the tar found in cigarette smoke. **Tar** is a thick, sticky fluid produced when tobacco burns. Over 200 different chemicals make up tar. Tar is also a carcinogen.

Tar is a carcinogen produced when tobacco burns.

Other factors influence the possible development of cancer. The deeper a person inhales, the greater the harm to the lungs. Choosing to smoke cigarettes with high levels of tar increases the risk of developing lung cancer. Finally, the greater the number of years a person smokes, the greater the risks of developing lung cancer.

If you smoke, it pays to quit now. If a 15-year-old cigarette smoker stops smoking today, the risks of developing lung cancer will be the same as those of a 25-to-30 year old nonsmoker by the time he or she is 25 to 30. In addition, this smoker will decrease the risk of two other diseases that are reaching epidemic proportions among smokers. These diseases are pulmonary emphysema and chronic bronchitis.

Pulmonary emphysema is a disease in which the alveoli in the lungs lose the ability to expand and contract. Eventually, they rupture. As this disease progresses, the passage of oxygen into the bloodstream is impaired. The victim develops shortness of breath and an overworked heart. Thus, the person with pulmonary emphysema is highly susceptible to heart disease.

Smoking damages the alveoli in the lungs.

Chronic bronchitis is the recurring inflammation of the bronchial tubes. The bronchial tubes become filled with excessive mucus and a cough develops to dislodge it. The coughing and mucus interfere with normal breathing and normal lung function.

Pulmonary emphysema and chronic bronchitis are lung diseases associated with smoking.

Constant smoking irritates the alveoli and bronchial tubes. In time, the cilia in the respiratory tract also lose their ability to function. Foreign matter cannot be removed from the air passages. As a result, smokers with pulmonary emphysema and chronic bronchitis are more susceptible to respiratory infections than nonsmokers. Many people with pulmonary emphysema and chronic bronchitis are permanently bedridden.

18:5 Smoking and Pregnancy

The facts about smoking and pregnancy are clear. There is an established relationship between smoking during pregnancy and harmful effects to the developing baby.

Now that you're pregnant, you're not just *eating* for two...

...you're *breathing* for two.

QUITSMOKING

...for *both* of you.

AMERICAN LUNG ASSOCIATION

FIGURE 18–5. A pregnant woman who smokes adversely affects the developing fetus.

It is believed that nicotine may constrict the arteries, causing reduced blood flow across the placenta.

A pregnant woman should quit smoking when she first finds out that she is pregnant.

Pregnant women who smoke are more likely to have miscarriages or stillborn babies than nonsmoking women. In addition, other complications of pregnancy can result including excessive bleeding during delivery and premature birth. As many as 14 percent of all premature births in the United States are attributed to smoking. Research also indicates that smoking by a woman during pregnancy may interfere with a baby's long-term physical growth as well as intellectual development. In addition, there appears to be a relationship between smoking during pregnancy and disorders of the placenta. A disorder of the placenta can interfere with the healthful development of the baby.

The weight of a newborn baby is a crucial factor in a baby's health status. The lower the weight of a newborn, the greater the risk of death. Babies born to women who smoke weigh an average of seven ounces less than babies born to women who do not smoke. Consider also that babies born to teenagers generally weigh less than babies born to mothers who are past their teens. Thus, a pregnant teenager who smokes poses even greater dangers to the health of her unborn child.

How much a woman smokes during pregnancy is also a factor in infant birth weight. The more cigarettes smoked, the greater the reduction in birth weight. However, if a woman quits smoking early during pregnancy, her risk of having a low birth weight infant decreases.

How tobacco smoking affects the fetus is not fully known. Researchers believe that carbon monoxide from the cigarette smoke reduces the amount of oxygen the fetus gets. Studies show that fetuses of women who smoke have large concentrations of carbon monoxide in their blood. Also, the higher the level of carbon monoxide, the smaller the baby. Researchers also believe that nicotine may constrict the arteries, thereby reducing blood flow across the placenta.

Lowered birth weight is not a problem that ends after the child is born. There is some evidence that fetal growth that is affected by a woman's smoking during pregnancy may affect long-term growth. This includes physical, mental, and intellectual development. For these reasons, many adolescent women say no to a habit that endangers their health and the health of their children in the future.

 Review and Reflect

3. How does smoking affect the cardiovascular system?
4. Why is it important for a pregnant woman not to smoke?

OTHER HARMFUL FORMS OF TOBACCO

Is there such a thing as a safe cigarette? Can cigarettes with reduced amounts of tar be safe for consumption? Are cigarettes with lower amounts of nicotine a safe alternative? Is the use of smokeless tobacco a healthful alternative to cigarette smoking? Does using smokeless tobacco eliminate the risks of getting cancer? Does using smokeless tobacco pose any dangers to oral health?

18:6 Lower-Yield Cigarettes: Are They Safe?

By the 1980s, about half of all cigarettes smoked were lower-yield cigarettes. **Lower-yield cigarettes** are made with tobaccos that yield reduced amounts of tar and nicotine. The movement to lower-yield cigarettes came about due to people's concerns about the dangers of smoking.

> Lower-yield cigarettes have reduced amounts of tar and nicotine.

Is smoking lower-yield cigarettes safe? Many people consider this to be a positive move. After all, the dangers of smoking are related to the amount of inhaled tar, nicotine, and other ingredients. If so-called safer cigarettes are consumed, it follows that the risks to one's health should be reduced. However, there is a lack of evidence indicating that lower-yield cigarettes are any safer than high-yield cigarettes. There is no research to indicate that lower-yield cigarettes reduce the incidence of cancer, heart disease, bronchitis, emphysema, and other diseases associated with smoking. In fact, the Surgeon General of the United States has stated that lower-yield cigarettes definitely increase a person's health risk.

The above statement may appear as a contradiction. But take into account the smoking behavior of those who use lower-yield cigarettes. Users of these cigarettes tend to compensate for the decreased intake of nicotine. They smoke more cigarettes, take shorter intervals between puffs, and smoke more of the cigarette. Thus, the change to lower-yield cigarettes may increase the overall amount of harmful chemicals consumed.

> Lower-yield cigarettes are harmful to health.

Another concern of lower-yield cigarettes is related to the use of tobacco additives that are used for processing or flavor. Some of these additives are carcinogenic or they produce carcinogens when they are burned. These additives offset any possible advantage of the lower-yield cigarettes. Perhaps the only cigarette that will ever be a safe cigarette is one that is not lighted.

> Some lower-yield cigarettes contain additives that are carcinogens.

18:7 Smokeless Tobacco

Have you seen healthy looking people promoting the merits of smokeless tobacco? The message tries to persuade you that you can use tobacco without smoking it. You can, but is it safe? The answer is definitely "No"!

One form of smokeless tobacco is chewing tobacco. **Chewing tobacco** is leaf or plug tobacco that is placed between the cheeks and gum. The other form of smokeless tobacco is snuff. **Snuff** is a flavored powder made from ground tobacco leaves and stems. The placing of a pinch of snuff between the cheek and gum is called snuff dipping.

Smokeless tobacco in either form contains the same harmful substances found in cigarette tobacco. Nicotine in chewing tobacco reaches the blood through capillaries in the mouth. This triggers increased heart rate and blood pressure. With prolonged use, physical as well as psychological dependence occurs.

Smokeless tobacco is particularly dangerous to oral health. When held in place in the mouth for a period of time, the tobacco often produces leukoplakia. **Leukoplakia** is either a smooth white patch or a thick hardened sore on the inside of the mouth that has the potential to become cancer.

Studies also show that smokeless tobacco has high levels of carcinogens that may increase the risk of cancer of the mouth and throat. When smokeless tobacco is used for a long period of time, the tobacco juices cause the gums to pull away from the teeth. This exposes the roots of the teeth and makes them more sensitive to heat and cold. Smokeless tobacco also produces gum disease. Gum disease can cause the loss of gum and bone support for the teeth.

Smokeless tobacco contains high levels of grit and sand. The grit and sand rub against the surface of the teeth and wear them away. Also, sugar is added to smokeless tobacco during processing. The sugar promotes dental caries.

Finally, users of smokeless tobacco have traits that are generally considered to be socially unacceptable. They have bad breath, discolored teeth, and a constant need to spit.

 Review and Reflect

5. What are some of the dangers related to the use of lower-yield cigarettes?
6. Describe the two forms of smokeless tobacco.
7. Why might people think that the use of smokeless tobacco is a healthful alternative to cigarette smoking?

Chewing tobacco and snuff are forms of smokeless tobacco.

Use of smokeless tobacco can result in the development of leukoplakia.

Smokeless tobacco contains sand, which wears away the surface of the teeth.

THE SOCIAL ASPECTS OF SMOKING

Think about a situation in which you have been in a room with smokers. You probably were able to see clouds of smoke or smell burning cigarettes. How do you think you and others in the room were affected by the smoke?

Nonsmokers are affected by the cigarette smoke from others.

18:8   Sidestream and Mainstream Smoke

The smoking behavior of others can affect you whether you are a smoker or a nonsmoker. When you are around smokers, you may inhale the smoke from their cigarettes. The smoke you inhale from these cigarettes is called **sidestream smoke.** Sidestream smoke is also referred to as passive smoking. The smoke that a smoker inhales and exhales from his or her own cigarette is called **mainstream smoke.**

Some studies show that sidestream smoke can be harmful to the nonsmoker. The Surgeon General's report on the consequences of smoking indicates that sidestream smoke contains harmful chemicals that are much higher in concentration than those found in mainstream smoke. This occurs because the smoke burned from the cigarette is released directly into the air rather than being trapped in the smoker's lungs. As a result, if you

Sidestream smoke contains harmful chemicals in greater concentrations than mainstream smoke.

FIGURE 18-6. The Nonsmoker's Bill of Rights

FIGURE 18–7. Many business offices are designating areas where smoking is not allowed.

FOR YOUR HEALTH
THIS IS A
**NON-SMOKING
AREA**

compared sidestream smoke to mainstream smoke, you would find that sidestream smoke contains twice as much tar and nicotine, five times as much carbon monoxide, and even higher levels of other harmful chemicals.

Many nonsmokers are annoyed by sidestream smoke. They may experience watery eyes and headaches. Certain individuals may be allergic to smoke and suffer upper respiratory congestion. Others, such as those with heart or asthma problems or those who wear contact lenses, may be especially sensitive to sidestream smoke. Sidestream smoke threatens their health.

There is evidence that parents who smoke may be endangering their children's health.

There is growing evidence that parental cigarette smoking may be harmful to children's health. Babies of parents who smoke have been shown to have higher than normal incidents of bronchitis and pneumonia than children of nonsmoking parents. In addition, respiratory and ear infections may be more common among children of parents who smoke.

Many laws are being passed to protect the nonsmoker.

Many steps are being taken to protect the nonsmoker. Many restaurants have no smoking sections. Commuter trains in many cities have reserved cars for nonsmokers. Many cities are passing laws that forbid smoking in certain public areas as well as in certain work settings.

18:9   The Antismoking Groups

There exists a debate between the antismoking groups (such as the American Lung Association and the American Cancer Society) and the supporters of smoking (most notably, tobacco companies). Many of the antismoking groups such as ASH (Action on Smoking and Health) and GASP (Group Against Smoker's Pollution) have succeeded in getting laws passed for nonsmokers' rights. More than half the states have passed clean indoor air laws that restrict smoking in public places as well as in hospitals.

The American Medical Association is on record to support laws that will

- prohibit smoking on public transportation.

- oppose free distribution of tobacco products.

- prohibit smoking in any indoor place where children or non-smokers might inhale smoke.

The American Medical Association supports laws that protect the nonsmoker.

Yet, the debate continues. Those on the medical and scientific fronts indicate that premature death from heart and lung disease is statistically related to cigarette smoking. Members of the tobacco industry point out that the relationship between smoking and premature death is entirely statistical. They argue that the statistics might also be coincidental. However, this argument ignores the fact that smoking is harmful and thousands of studies have proven this over and over.

There is no doubt concerning the harmful effects of cigarette smoking.

The tobacco industry states that the increase in cases of lung cancer is due to improved diagnosis and not to smoking. In response, those in the medical field agree that detecting lung cancer has improved. But techniques for detecting other types of cancer also have improved. The fact remains that cases of lung cancer increased dramatically during the twentieth century when large numbers of people began to smoke. Furthermore, the cases of cancer found among nonsmoking groups are low in number.

While the debate continues between those on both sides of the smoking issue, the tobacco industry spends hundreds of millions of dollars to promote its products and recruit new smokers. When cigarette advertisements were banned from radio and television in 1970, the tobacco companies increased their advertising in other areas. In addition to placing magazine ads, tobacco companies began to sponsor events such as tennis tournaments and rock concerts. They began to distribute free samples of their cigarettes at events that young people attend. To combat these media campaigns, antismoking groups put forth their own media campaign. Hundreds of messages about the health consequences of smoking are placed in the media each year.

Cigarette advertisements are banned from radio and television.

Who is winning the cigarette war? If the answer is statistical, then the constant decrease in the number of smokers in all age groups each year indicates that those opposed to smoking are winning the battle.

Review and Reflect

8. What can you do to avoid sidestream smoke?
9. Why do you think tobacco companies can continue to promote cigarette smoking?
10. What role does the American Medical Association play in protecting people from sidestream smoke?
11. How does the tobacco industry encourage people to smoke?

 Activity: Toward a Smokeless Society

In *Healthy People: The Surgeon General's Report on Health Promotion and Disease Prevention*, the following objectives for the nation were developed regarding smoking and health.

1. By 1990, at least 85 percent of the adult population should be aware that smoking is one of the major risk factors for heart disease.
2. By 1990, at least 90 percent of the adult population should be aware that smoking is a major cause of lung cancer as well as many other cancers.
3. By 1990, at least 85 percent of the adult population should be aware of the special risk among smokers of developing worsening lung diseases.
4. By 1990, at least 85 percent of women should be aware of the special health risks for women who smoke.
5. By 1990, at least 65 percent of 12 year olds should be able to associate the smoking of cigarettes with increased risk of serious diseases of the heart and lungs.

Working in small groups, design strategies that you would use to reach each of these objectives.

PROMOTING A TOBACCO-FREE LIFESTYLE

Most adolescents strongly disapprove of cigarette smoking.

In a recent survey, three fourths of the people your age expressed strong disapproval of daily smoking because of its harmful effects. These harmful effects occur to the smoker, to those around the smoker, and in the environment. You and others can choose health for yourselves and the environment by promoting a tobacco-free lifestyle.

18:10 Methods of Quitting Smoking

There are many ways to break the cigarette smoking habit. Some are structured and require class attendance. Some are guidelines a smoker can perform at home. Regardless of the approach, it is safe to say that different methods work for different people. Programs can be successful only if the smoker is committed to changing behavior.

The first ingredient needed in breaking the cigarette smoking habit is an awareness that smoking is harmful to health. Fortunately, most smokers already are aware of this fact. However, knowing about the dangers is not always enough to persuade a person to quit. When a smoker has a desire to quit, there are many programs and methods that can be used to help a person stop smoking.

Many organizations, such as the American Lung Association, sponsor smoking cessation programs. A smoking cessation program consists of specific activities that encourage giving up smoking. These programs may consist of classes that teach steps to take to avoid lighting up a cigarette when the urge is present. These classes are conducted by leaders who have been trained to help people stop smoking. Many leaders are health professionals. It is important to determine the costs of these programs as well as their success rates.

Hypnosis can be done by qualified individuals for one person or a group. The smoker is placed in a trance and told about the harmful effects of smoking as well as how to stop.

Aversion therapy is a technique in which a person's habit is made to be unpleasant. In the case of smoking, a smoker may be asked to chain-smoke as many cigarettes as possible with puffs taken every several seconds. Treatment sessions may last several months after which time the person may find smoking disgusting. As a result, he or she may quit. It should be noted that while undergoing this program, the hazards of smoking are concentrated. The success rate of this procedure has not been good.

Behavior modification is a technique in which one behavior is substituted with another more beneficial behavior. Suppose a person lights up a cigarette every time a meal is over. The next time a person finishes eating, a walk may be substituted for a cigarette. Behavior modification is an individual approach to change a behavior like smoking.

Regardless of the type of program, studies show that the most successful way to stop smoking is to quit cold turkey and do it on your own. Cold turkey means giving up cigarettes completely, all at once. Every smoker has the ability to quit regardless of the number of years he or she has smoked.

There are many ways to quit smoking.

Many organizations sponsor smoking cessation programs.

Hypnosis and aversion therapy are sometimes used to help people stop smoking.

FIGURE 18–8. People quit smoking for many reasons.

18:11   Health Benefits of Quitting

There are many health benefits to be gained for a person who quits smoking.

When a person gives up smoking, many health benefits become clearly evident. The senses of taste and smell are improved so that food becomes more enjoyable. This should not be interpreted to mean that ex-smokers always gain weight. Often, ex-smokers substitute smoking with healthful behaviors, such as exercise. This helps maintain or even reduce weight.

Quitting smoking has an important effect on the cardiovascular system. Resting heart rate decreases, blood pressure drops, and the heart works more efficiently during exercise as well as at periods of rest.

The respiratory system improves when cigarette smoking is given up. Breathing capacity increases and the rate of breathing decreases, so that the lungs work more efficiently. A reduction occurs in the number and severity of upper respiratory infections as well as a reduced risk of having chronic lung diseases.

The younger people are when they quit smoking, the more obvious are the health improvements. These improvements continue as one leads a nonsmoking lifestyle.

 Review and Reflect

12. Why might a smoker try to quit smoking by joining a smoking cessation program?

FIGURE 18–9.

Health
ADVANCES

Tobacco comes in different forms. Each form is dangerous. One such form of tobacco is clove cigarettes.

All forms of cigarette smoking are dangerous.

18:12 Clove Cigarettes

Clove cigarettes are made from tobacco, ground cloves, and clove oil. They usually are imported from Indonesia and have a strong, sweet smell.

Clove cigarettes are usually imported.

Research shows that smoking clove cigarettes can be dangerous. It is believed that clove oil builds up in the lungs. This causes an allergic reaction that can paralyze the cells that fight infection in the lungs. A 1985 report from the Centers for Disease Control indicates that clove has been related to a buildup of blood and fluids in the lungs, constriction of air passageways, and coughing up of blood.

A major study by the American Health Foundation in New York shows that eugenol, the major component of clove, can be lethal to animals. When eugenol is placed in the lungs of rats, they die. While more research is needed about the effects of clove, several lawmakers feel the evidence so far warrants action. Discussions are taking place to pass laws that will forbid the sale and smoking of clove cigarettes. Already, a number of states have implemented laws that ban the sale of clove cigarettes.

Eugenol is the major component of clove cigarettes.

Focus on
Life Management Skills

- Reinforce your decision not to smoke by engaging in healthful behaviors, such as exercising when under stress.
- Do not use lower-yield cigarettes or smokeless tobacco as they are not healthful or safe alternatives to smoking cigarettes that contain high amounts of tar.
- Exert your rights politely to others if you find their smoking bothers you.
- Choose nonsmoking sections when available to avoid sidestream smoke.

Summary

1. Most people your age choose not to smoke because of the positive influences of their family and peers. **18:1**

2. Cigarette smoke contains drugs that produce physical and psychological dependence. **18:2**

3. Cigarette smoking is a risk factor in CHD by causing an increase in heart rate, blood pressure, and cardiac output. **18:3**

4. Cigarette smoking causes smoker's cough and shortness of breath, and is responsible for most cases of lung cancer, emphysema, and chronic bronchitis. **18:4**

5. Pregnant women who smoke increase risks to their unborn babies. **18:5**

6. Smoking lower-yield cigarettes is not safe for a person's health. **18:6**

7. The use of smokeless tobacco is harmful to the teeth and gums and increases the risks of oral cancer. **18:7**

8. Sidestream smoke, or passive smoking, causes health hazards. **18:8**

9. Antismoking groups have been successful in influencing states and cities to pass laws that protect the nonsmoker. **18:9**

10. A person who wishes to quit smoking can get help from many sources. **18:10**

11. People who quit smoking will improve the functioning of their cardiovascular and respiratory systems. **18:11**

12. Clove cigarettes pose significant dangers to health and have been banned in a number of states. **18:12**

Vocabulary

Below is a list of vocabulary words used in this chapter. Use each word only once to complete the sentences. Do not write in this book.

aversion therapy	lower-yield cigarettes
carbon monoxide	mainstream smoke
chronic bronchitis	nicotine
clove cigarettes	snuff
leukoplakia	tar

1. The smoke a person inhales and exhales from his or her own cigarette is ____.

2. The harmful ingredient eugenol is found in ____.

3. A harmful ingredient in cigarette smoke that is made up of over 200 different chemicals is ____.

4. A chemical in tobacco that stimulates the nervous system is ____.

5. Excessive mucus and coughing are symptoms of ____.

6. People who smoke ____ will not reduce their intake of harmful products because they usually smoke more and take shorter intervals between puffs.

7. A white precancerous patch in the mouth associated with the use of smokeless tobacco is ____.

8. A person undergoing ____ may be made to think that smoking is unpleasant.

9. Smokeless tobacco in the form of ground tobacco leaves and stems is called ____.

10. A hazardous gas that displaces oxygen from hemoglobin and is found in cigarette smoke is called ____.

Review

1. List and briefly describe four reasons people choose not to smoke.
2. What are some withdrawal symptoms associated with cigarette smoking?
3. What is the relationship between nicotine and CHD?
4. How is cigarette smoking harmful to people your age?
5. In what ways can smoking affect the unborn child of a pregnant woman?
6. Describe why lower-yield cigarettes are not considered to be safe.
7. What are the dangers to oral health of using smokeless tobacco?
8. Why is sidestream smoke more dangerous to the nonsmoker than mainstream smoke is to the smoker?
9. What steps are being taken to protect the nonsmoker from the smoker's cigarette?
10. How can quitting smoking improve a person's health?

Application

1. Describe how you can influence your peer group to avoid smoking.
2. Describe how dependency created by smoking is similar to dependency created by other drugs described in Chapter 17.
3. Why is it important for a woman to make a plan for quitting smoking before she becomes pregnant?
4. Describe why using smokeless tobacco is not a safe alternative to smoking.

Individual Research

1. Cigarette companies are making greater profits now than ever before and yet the number of Americans who smoke has been decreasing. One reason this has occurred is the increased use of cigarettes by people in Third World Countries. Go to the library and look up ways companies market their cigarettes in other countries.
2. Write to your local chapter of the American Heart Association, American Lung Association, or American Cancer Society for information about ways to quit smoking. Share the information with your class.
3. Write a research report about the reasons the number of teenage smokers is declining.

Readings

Langway, Lynn, et al., "Showdown on Smoking," *Newsweek*, June 6, 1983, pp. 60-67.

Shepard, Roy, *The Risks of Passive Smoking.* New York, NY: Oxford University Press, Inc., 1982.

Diseases and Disorders

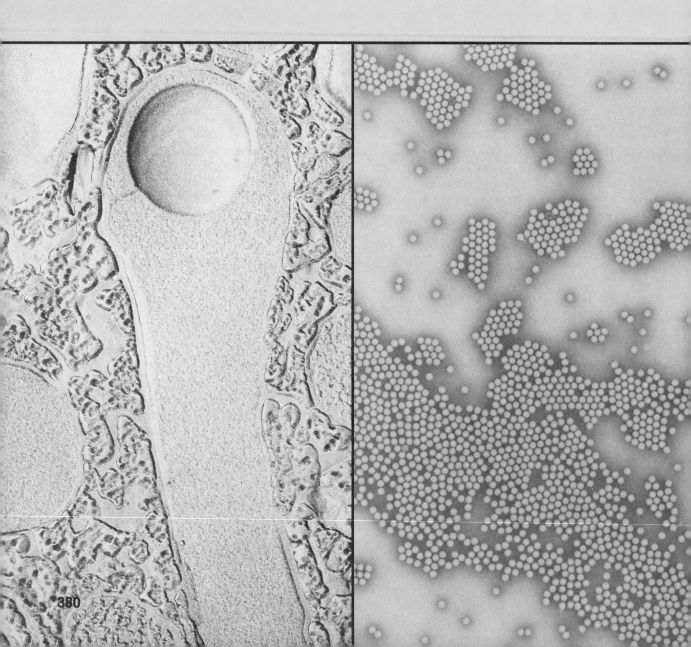

DISEASES AND DISORDERS

In 1900, the three leading causes of death in the United States were influenza, tuberculosis, and diarrhea. In the 1980s, heart disease was the number one cause of death followed by cancer and stroke. What do you think accounted for these changes? How does the incidence of heart disease, cancer, and stroke parallel changes in our society?

This unit identifies the major kinds of diseases that affect people of all ages. Health promotion activities are identified for the purpose of disease prevention and control. By following a healthful lifestyle, you can decrease your chances of being affected by these diseases.

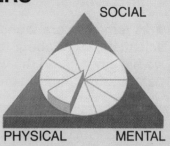

SOCIAL

PHYSICAL   MENTAL

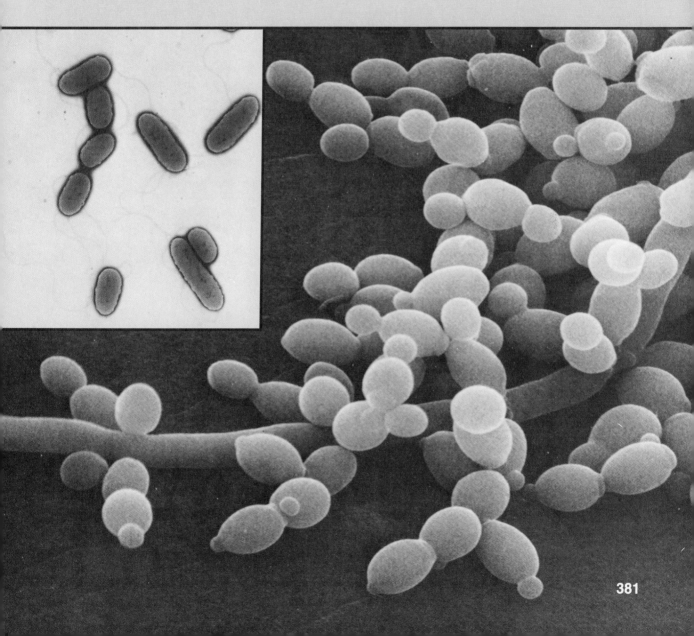

As remedies are found for some diseases, other diseases seem to puzzle scientists. What about the common cold? We can relieve the symptoms, but we have not found the way to prevent having a cold. The answer to the puzzle will be found someday in a research laboratory.

Chapter 19

Communicable Diseases

OBJECTIVES: You will be able to
- **describe how communicable diseases are caused, spread, and prevented.**
- **identify the causes, treatments, and methods of prevention of the common cold, influenza, pneumonia, hepatitis, and mononucleosis.**
- **identify the causes, methods of prevention, and treatments of common STDs.**

You have often heard the expression "I've caught a cold." Have you ever heard anyone say, "I've caught heart disease"? Most likely, you associate the word "caught" with a cold and not with heart disease. There is a reason for this association. A cold can be "caught" because it is a communicable disease.

This chapter focuses on communicable diseases. What are some of these diseases? How are they caused? How can you recognize the signs and symptoms of these diseases? What health behaviors should you practice to help prevent these diseases from affecting you?

The common cold is a communicable disease.

PRINCIPLES OF COMMUNICABLE DISEASES

Communicable diseases have plagued humankind throughout history. However, the Great Plague of 1665 began to change the way people viewed the causes of communicable diseases. During this period, people came to realize that these diseases were infectious.

19:1 Understanding Disease

A **communicable disease**, also called an **infectious disease,** is an illness that is caused by pathogens that enter the body through direct or indirect contact. **Pathogens** are disease-causing organisms that affect plants and animals. Thus, you catch a cold when pathogens that cause the common cold enter your body. Heart disease is a noncommunicable disease. A **noncommunicable disease,** also called a **noninfectious disease,** is an illness that is not caused by direct or indirect contact with a pathogen. Heart disease may result from hereditary factors, improper diet, smoking, and other risk behaviors.

An understanding of communicable diseases became clearer with the development of the microscope during the 1680s. This invention enabled scientists to isolate specific pathogens and study their growth. Today, epidemiologists provide information that helps control the spread of communicable diseases. An **epidemiologist** is a scientist who studies disease patterns. The work of epidemiologists and other scientists has led to our present knowledge of communicable diseases.

As you are reading this book, millions of microorganisms are living in your body. **Microorganisms** are small living organisms that are invisible to the unaided eye. They exist in your mouth, nose, intestines, and in many other parts of your body. These microorganisms may be helpful or harmful. Helpful ones assist in carrying out the body's normal functions. Harmful ones are pathogens.

When pathogens enter the body, they can disrupt normal body functions and cause disease. Pathogens produce poisonous chemicals called **toxins.** Toxins travel to body organs through the bloodstream and disrupt the function of these organs. Some pathogens destroy body tissues while using them for food. Rapid

Communicable diseases are also called infectious diseases.

Pathogens are organisms that cause disease.

Epidemiologists study disease patterns.

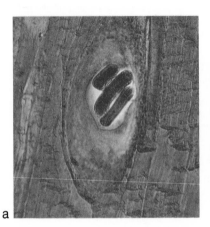 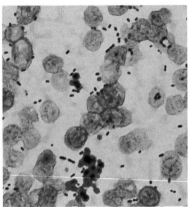

FIGURE 19–1. (a) *Trichinella spiralis*, (b) *Streptococcus pneumonia*

a

b

FIGURE 19–2. Local water supplies may be contaminated during a flood.

pathogen reproduction may alter the body's metabolism. There are six basic kinds of pathogens: bacteria, viruses, fungi, protozoa, rickettsia, and parasitic worms. See Appendix A for general information on pathogens.

There are six basic kinds of pathogens.

19:2 How Diseases Are Spread

Communicable diseases are spread as pathogens enter a person's body. Sometimes, the number of cases of a communicable disease can reach epidemic proportions. An **epidemic** is a greater-than-average increase in new cases of a disease in a specific geographic area. This affected area may be a community, city, state, or an entire country.

Communicable diseases are spread through direct or indirect contact. An infected person can spread pathogens to others through direct physical contact. Kissing and touching are two major ways communicable diseases are spread from person-to-person by direct contact.

Communicable diseases can be spread through direct or indirect contact.

Indirect contact occurs when pathogens are spread in ways other than direct contact. An example is being near someone who sneezes. Germ-laden mists can result from a sneeze. **Droplet infection** is the spread of pathogens through a mist.

Indirect contact also involves association with anything that has been touched by an infected person. You can contract a communicable disease by using an infected person's toothbrush, eating utensils, clothes, or food.

Pathogens can also be found in water. Diseases such as typhoid fever and dysentery are spread through water that is polluted by

Some diseases may be spread through contaminated water.

FIGURE 19–3. Insects can transfer pathogens from one place to another.

sewage. Since drinking water in the United States is treated, these diseases are no longer a problem. However, in many parts of the world, typhoid fever and dysentery are common because of a lack of proper water treatment procedures.

Typhoid fever and dysentery can also be spread by eating contaminated food. The process of freezing foods and improved packaging have reduced the chances of contamination. Fresh milk is a source of pathogens. These pathogens are destroyed by pasteurization. Pasteurization is a process in which milk is heated, immediately cooled, and placed in bottles or cartons. The heat kills all pathogens.

Finally, insects serve as an indirect source of spreading disease by transferring pathogens. For example, an insect may land on sewage and then land on food. If this food is eaten, a disease may be transmitted.

19:3 The Body's Defenses Against Disease

You have just played your best soccer game ever. As the goalie, you made many spectacular shot blocks. Your team won by a score of 2−0. Your defensive plays prevented penetration of your team's goal.

Think of your body as the goal that pathogens can penetrate. But unlike the single goal cage in a soccer game, your body is protected by several defenders or "goalies." Unlike the goalie in a soccer game who must think about strategies to defend the goal, the body's defenders are not under your voluntary control. What are the major defenses your body has for fighting pathogens?

Your body has defenses to help fight pathogens.

Skin is considered the first line of defense against pathogens. As long as the skin remains unbroken, it is more difficult for pathogens to penetrate. Many of the pathogens that contact the skin are killed by perspiration or body oils.

Pathogens can enter the body through body openings.

Body openings also have ways of stopping pathogens from penetrating. Hairs in the nose catch foreign objects. Short, fine hairlike structures in the throat, called **cilia,** trap pathogens that travel toward the lungs. Pathogens that can enter through the eyes are trapped by eyelashes or washed away by tears.

Antibodies are proteins in the blood that neutralize or destroy pathogens. Antibodies are produced when pathogens are present in the body. These pathogens produce poisons called **antigens.** Antibodies neutralize or destroy pathogens by attaching to the antigens. After they attach, some antibodies remain in the body and continue to react to specific pathogens and their antigens. When antibodies destroy a pathogen, some antibodies remain in the body and provide immunity for a specific disease. **Immunity** is the body's resistance to disease.

Antibodies help protect the body from disease.

Immunity can be acquired in different ways. (1) When you were an infant, you were given a vaccine to acquire immunity from a disease. A **vaccine** contains weakened or dead pathogens, which are introduced orally or by injection into a person's body. The vaccine causes specific antibodies to be produced. (2) If pathogens enter your body, your immune system produces antibodies and you acquire immunity. Both of these ways of gaining immunity result in **active immunity.** In other words, your body was active in producing antibodies. Active immunity results in long-lasting or permanent protection from a disease.

On the other hand, you may receive short-term protection from a disease by being given antibodies produced by an animal. This is known as **passive immunity.** For example, you may receive a puncture wound from a rusty nail that is contaminated. To prevent tetanus, you will be given a shot that contains the preformed antibodies. This will protect you for several years.

White blood cells surround and kill pathogens that enter the body. Suppose you fall and scrape your knee. Infection and inflammation may occur. Inflammation is pain, swelling, and redness in an infected area. Inflammation is a sign that your body's white blood cells are at work. The white blood cells attack the pathogens and destroy them. Sometimes a higher-than-normal body temperature, or fever, accompanies an infection. The fever acts as a body defense because it destroys pathogens.

Interferon was discovered in the late 1950s. It is now being studied as a protection from disease. **Interferon** is a protein that inhibits viral reproduction. Suppose you are developing a cold. Infected cells will produce interferon. The interferon then makes contact with healthy cells nearby. These cells will produce special chemicals that stop the virus from rapidly spreading. Eventually, the pathogens weaken and lose their effectiveness to attack other cells.

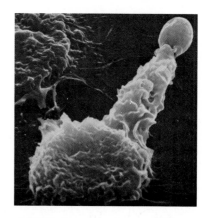

FIGURE 19–4. A kind of white blood cell, called a macrophage, engulfs a yeast cell.

Interferon is a protein that can inhibit viral reproduction.

19:4   Stages of Diseases

Unfortunately, the body's defense systems cannot always stop the spread of diseases. Once a disease develops, it goes through certain stages.

The incubation stage is the period from the time the pathogen enters the body until the first symptoms appear. This period varies with the type of disease.

In the prodromal stage, the victim first appears sick. Because the symptoms are general, it is difficult to form a diagnosis. The person may experience fatigue, fever, or irritability.

In the illness or acute stage, the symptoms that characterize the specific disease begin to occur. The person who has chicken pox will have pox marks over the body.

The first symptoms of a disease appear during the incubation stage.

The last stage of a disease is the recovery stage.

During the recovery stage, the body's defense system begins to overtake the disease, many times with the aid of medicine prescribed in an earlier stage. Symptoms begin to disappear. It should be emphasized that diseases are communicable in any of these four stages.

 ## Review and Reflect

1. How can pasteurization help keep you healthy?
2. How can a disease be spread through direct contact?
3. Why could a break in the skin be harmful?

COMMON COMMUNICABLE DISEASES

Think about the last time you were ill. Most likely you had a communicable disease. The sections that follow describe some of the more common communicable diseases.

19:5 Common Cold

Consider yourself fortunate if you do not "catch" at least one cold a year. Most people have as many as three colds each year.

The common cold can be caused by any of hundreds of different viruses.

The common cold is not caused by just one virus. Hundreds of different viruses can produce the discomforts that we associate with a cold. These include a runny nose, coughing, sneezing, sore throat, watery eyes, and headache.

Colds are spread from person-to-person.

Viruses that cause colds can be transmitted through direct or indirect contact. Immunity against a cold is not possible. Thus, the only way to prevent getting a cold is to avoid contact with a cold sufferer. Realistically, this may be difficult since cold viruses can be spread in so many ways. It would also be wise to avoid contact with a person who has symptoms of a cold. The first 24 hours a person has a cold is the most communicable period. Coldlike symptoms can sometimes be a signal of a more serious disorder. The early stages of measles and strep throat start out with cold symptoms.

Medications can help relieve the symptoms of the common cold.

There is no cure for the common cold. Some people believe that large doses of vitamin C will prevent colds or reduce the seriousness of the symptoms. Many others do not believe this to be true. There are medications available that relieve the symptoms of a cold but not the cause. Cough syrups may suppress coughs, and decongestants may clear nasal passages.

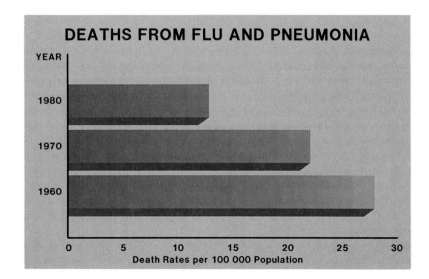

FIGURE 19–5.

19:6 Influenza and Pneumonia

Influenza, or **flu**, is a disease that affects the respiratory system and is caused by different viruses. Symptoms of flu include fever, chills, muscle pains, headaches, coughing, sore throat, and runny nose.

There are three main types of flu, which are labeled A, B, and C. Each type is caused by many strains or kinds of viruses. Because of these different strains, it is difficult to find one vaccine that would prevent all types of flu. When a certain strain is identified, a specific vaccine can be given to help prevent it. Often, older adults are given vaccines to prevent flu because they might not be strong enough to cope with its possible complications.

Flu-causing viruses can be easily spread by coughing or sneezing. People with flu can affect others before their own symptoms appear.

Since the initial symptoms of flu are similar to those of a cold, people tend to treat them the same. For many people, this means taking aspirin. Caution must be taken when using aspirin. Parents should carefully consider possible side effects before giving aspirin or aspirin-containing products to their children or teenagers for either flu or chicken pox. There appears to be an association between taking products containing aspirin to relieve symptoms of flu and chicken pox and the onset of Reye (RI) syndrome. **Reye syndrome** is a disease of children that produces vomiting, damage to the central nervous system, and/or liver damage. Reye syndrome develops in young people just when they appear to be recovering from flu or chicken pox. Many victims of Reye syndrome suffer permanent brain damage or die.

There are three main types of flu.

The symptoms of flu and the common cold are similar during the early stages.

Pneumonia is an inflammation of the lungs accompanied by fever, shortness of breath, headache, chest pain, and coughing. Flu complications often lead to pneumonia. Laboratory tests, X rays, and a physical examination are used to diagnose pneumonia.

Pneumonia can be caused by viruses, bacteria, or other organisms. If caused by bacteria, pneumonia can be treated with prescribed antibiotics. **Antibiotics**, produced by living organisms, are special drugs that kill some pathogens. The symptoms of viral-caused pneumonia may be treated by other drugs.

Pneumonia may be caused by any of several different organisms.

19:7 Hepatitis

Hepatitis is a viral liver infection. As the virus destroys liver cells, bile enters the bloodstream and causes a yellowing, or jaundice, of the skin. Hepatitis is most common in children, young adults, and the elderly. Signs of this disease are pain in the upper right part of the abdomen, fever, chills, loss of appetite, headache, nausea, and muscle pains.

Hepatitis is an infection of the liver.

There are two types of hepatitis. Hepatitis A, or **infectious hepatitis**, is usually transmitted through contaminated food and water. Bed rest and a high-carbohydrate and protein diet is the treatment for infectious hepatitis.

Hepatitis B, or **serum hepatitis**, is transmitted through transfusions of whole blood or blood products. Often it is transmitted through contaminated needles and syringes shared by drug users.

19:8 Mononucleosis

Mononucleosis, or **mono,** is a viral infection that occurs most frequently to those in the 15-to-19-year-old age group. It is called the "kissing disease" because it is transmitted primarily by oral contact with exchange of saliva.

Mononucleosis is a viral infection.

Symptoms of mono are swollen glands, fever, sore throat, enlargement of lymph nodes (especially in the neck), chills, headache, and extreme fatigue. Mono can affect body organs such as the liver and spleen and is diagnosed through blood tests.

Recuperation from mono usually requires a few weeks of bed rest. Antibiotics are effective in treating secondary bacterial throat infections, but they do not treat mono itself.

Bed rest is important in the treatment of mono.

 Review and Reflect

4. Why is there no vaccine to prevent the common cold?
5. Why might it be dangerous to use aspirin products to treat children who have flu?
6. Why are antibiotics ineffective in treating mono?

SEXUALLY TRANSMITTED DISEASES

Sexually transmitted diseases are a major health concern because of their increase among teenagers and adults. Sexually transmitted diseases, or STDs, are infections spread by sexual contact with an infected person. Sexual contact includes sexual intercourse or other intimate body contact. You undoubtedly have heard the term venereal disease, or VD. VD and STD mean the same. However, the term STD is more commonly used when referring to diseases transmitted through sexual contact.

Like other diseases described in this chapter, STDs are communicable. But unlike the other diseases, STDs are almost always preventable. See Appendix B for general information on several STDs.

STDs are spread through sexual contact.

19:9 Gonorrhea

Gonorrhea is the oldest known STD. It is among the most frequent infectious diseases in America today. More than one million cases are reported each year. Researchers think that this number represents only 25 percent of the cases that occur each year.

Gonorrhea is transmitted by any form of sexual contact. The pathogens that cause gonorrhea survive in the mucous membranes of the body where it is moist, dark, and warm. These conditions are necessary for survival of the pathogen. For this reason, it is difficult to contract gonorrhea in ways other than sexual contact.

Symptoms of gonorrhea in the male can occur within two to seven days after contact with an infected person. It may take as long as 30 days for symptoms to occur. Inflammation of the urethra results in heat, redness, swelling, and painful urination. At first, discharge from the tip of the penis is watery; later it has a white to greenish-yellow color. Frequent and painful urination is another symptom. If left untreated, gonorrhea in men may result in the spread of infection to the other internal reproductive organs. Sterility can result. **Sterility** is the inability to reproduce.

Women who get gonorrhea are at a greater disadvantage than men. Almost half of all women who have gonorrhea do not have symptoms. This leads to an increased chance of complications as well as the possibility of unknowingly infecting sexual partners. When they occur, the symptoms of gonorrhea in women include increased vaginal discharge, irritation of the outside of the vaginal area, and a pain or burning with urination. Untreated gonorrhea

Gonorrhea is among the most frequent STDs in the United States.

FIGURE 19–6. The arrow points to the pathogens that cause gonorrhea.

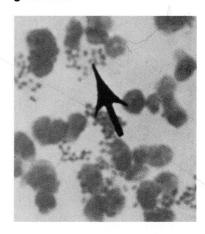

FIGURE 19–7. The gonorrhea pathogens grow in a special nutrient in petri dishes.

Syphilis is a very serious STD.

Syphilis can be passed by a pregnant woman to her unborn child.

FIGURE 19–8. Electron micrograph of the pathogen that causes syphilis.

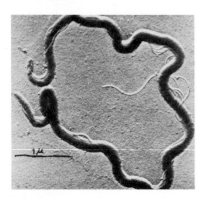

in women may result in pelvic inflammatory disease (PID). Although not always caused by gonorrhea, PID is the most common cause of female sterility.

Gonorrhea in men is detected by examining a discharge from the urethra under a microscope. This method is 90 percent accurate. It may also be necessary to grow the pathogens in a culture.

Gonorrhea in women is detected in culture tests. Swabs are taken from the infected area and grown on a culture.

The most effective treatment for gonorrhea is a large dose of penicillin. People allergic to penicillin can be given an antibiotic called tetracycline.

19:10   Syphilis

Syphilis is far less common than gonorrhea but is much more serious. It is usually transmitted through sexual activity. It can also be passed from a pregnant mother to her fetus.

The earliest sign of syphilis in its primary stage is a sore called a **chancre** (SHANG kur). In males and females, the chancre appears two-to-four weeks after infection. Most chancres appear around the genital area, but they can appear on any part of the body through which the organism entered. The chancre begins as a dull, red spot. It develops into a painless open sore surrounded by a red rim. In four-to-six weeks, the chancre will heal, but syphilis is still present in the body.

Secondary syphilis will begin one week to six months after a chancre disappears. The disease is spread throughout the body by the blood. Symptoms during this period include a pale red or pink rash on the palms and soles, fever, sore throat, muscle pains, and weight and hair loss. These symptoms may last from three-to-six months before disappearing.

The next stage of syphilis is the latent stage. During this stage, the pathogens work their way into different body parts including the brain. Syphilis remains in this stage for most people for the rest of their lives. But for some people, syphilis enters the tertiary stage, or late syphilis. Symptoms in this stage include heart, brain, and spinal cord damage. This stage can lead to paralysis and death.

A pregnant female can infect her unborn child since the pathogens can cross the placenta. The result is congenital syphilis. Congenital syphilis produces bone and teeth deformities as well as kidney damage and other problems in the baby. Congenital syphilis may be prevented if a pregnant woman with syphilis is treated before the 16th week of pregnancy.

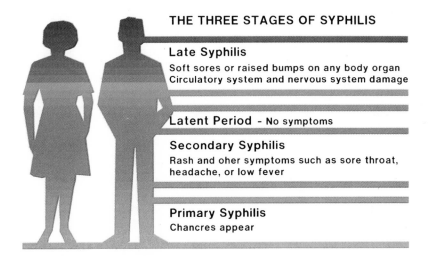

THE THREE STAGES OF SYPHILIS

Late Syphilis
Soft sores or raised bumps on any body organ
Circulatory system and nervous system damage

Latent Period - No symptoms

Secondary Syphilis
Rash and oher symptoms such as sore throat,
headache, or low fever

Primary Syphilis
Chancres appear

FIGURE 19–9.

Syphilis can be diagnosed in a blood test. It can usually be cured with penicillin or another type of antibiotic in its primary or secondary stages. In the late stages, one may need larger doses of medications over longer periods of time.

19:11   Genital Herpes

Genital herpes is an STD that is caused by two different but related forms of a virus known as herpes virus type I and herpes virus type II. At one time, herpes virus type I was almost always a cause of cold sores and fever blisters. Genital herpes was almost always caused by the type II virus. Today this is not true. About 20 percent of genital herpes cases are caused by the type I virus. The reasons for this are not fully understood.

Genital herpes has reached epidemic proportions in the United States. It affects about 20 million Americans with about a half-million new cases occurring each year. Genital herpes is usually transmitted through sexual intercourse with an infected person. However, in some cases, genital herpes can be transmitted by kissing or through a cut, rash, or sore on the skin.

Signs and symptoms of genital herpes occur within a week after contact. Generally, clusters of small, painful blisters will appear on the genitals. After a few days, these blisters break and leave small ulcers. A person is highly contagious at this time. Fever, headache, and muscle soreness may appear. Other symptoms may be a burning during urination, a discharge from the urethra or vagina, and swollen lymph nodes in the groin area. All of these symptoms will disappear, but the virus stays in the body for the rest of the person's life. Some people have recurrences of the

Genital herpes can be caused by herpes virus types I or II.

Genital herpes is usually transmitted through sexual intercourse.

The herpes virus remains in a person's body throughout his or her life.

FIGURE 19–10.

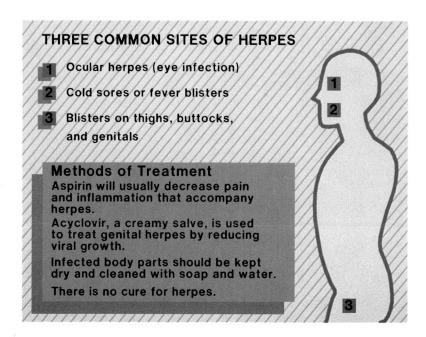

THREE COMMON SITES OF HERPES

1 Ocular herpes (eye infection)

2 Cold sores or fever blisters

3 Blisters on thighs, buttocks, and genitals

Methods of Treatment
Aspirin will usually decrease pain and inflammation that accompany herpes.
Acyclovir, a creamy salve, is used to treat genital herpes by reducing viral growth.
Infected body parts should be kept dry and cleaned with soap and water.
There is no cure for herpes.

There is no cure for genital herpes.

FIGURE 19–11. Electron micrograph of the herpes type II virus.

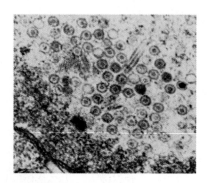

symptoms while others never have further signs or symptoms. Recurring symptoms may be brought on by stress or illness. Scientists are puzzled that some people have recurrences while others do not.

Genital herpes causes two major problems. First, it can cause a birth defect in the developing baby of a pregnant woman. The virus can pass to the baby through the placenta. Second, there appears to be a link between genital herpes and cancer of the cervix and vulva. Thus, it is advisable for women who have genital herpes to have a Pap smear and pelvic exam every six months.

It is more difficult for a physician to diagnose genital herpes than other STDs because genital herpes has the same symptoms as other STDs. Among the various laboratory tests used to diagnose genital herpes are Pap smears in women, blood tests, and cultures.

It is important to remember that there is no cure for genital herpes. There are medications that treat symptoms of genital herpes, but the disease always remains in the body. Genital herpes remains contagious from the time symptoms appear until ten days after symptoms disappear in the first episode. For recurrent episodes, the contagious period is decreased until two days after symptoms heal. But this does not mean genital herpes is not contagious at other times. Symptoms may appear, and the infected person may not be aware of their presence.

19:12   Other STDs

Trichomoniasis (trihk uh muh NI uh sus) is an infection caused by protozoa that most often affects women. Ordinarily, the pathogens that cause trichomoniasis are present in small numbers in the vagina. They can multiply rapidly or be transmitted by sexual contact. Signs and symptoms of trichomoniasis in women are a thin greenish white or yellowish brown discharge from the vagina. The vagina and vulva may burn and itch. Most men do not show symptoms of trichomoniasis even though they can carry this disease.

Diagnosis of trichomoniasis is made by examining a discharge under a microscope. Prescription drugs are available to cure this disease. It is recommended that both the woman and her partner receive treatment because the pathogens can be passed back and forth to each other.

Nongonococcal urethretis (NGU), or nonspecific urethritis (NSU), is any inflammation of the urethra that is not caused by a gonorrheal infection. The main symptoms of NGU are similar to those of gonorrhea. However, the NGU symptoms are somewhat milder. Diagnosis for NGU is made by doing a culture for gonorrhea. If the pathogen that causes gonorrhea is not present, then the disease is NGU. **Chlamydia** are pathogens that are known to cause NGU, although many others have also been identified. Chlamydia infection is the most common STD and is a primary cause of PID. PID is the leading cause of acquired female sterility.

Regardless of the cause, more is known about the diagnosis, treatment, and complications of NGU. NGU is treated with tetracycline or other antibiotics. It is not treated with penicillin.

Trichomoniasis is caused by a protozoan.

Trichomoniasis can be cured with the use of prescription drugs.

Chlamydia infection is the most common STD.

FIGURE 19–12. Pathogens that cause (a) trichomoniasis, (b) chlamydia

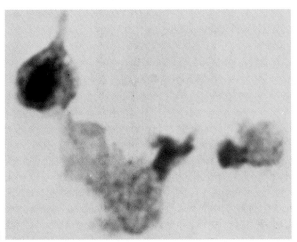
a

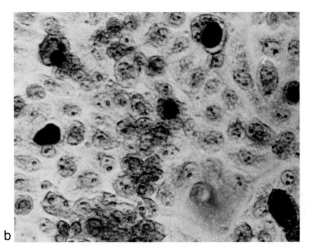
b

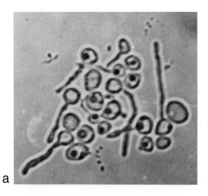

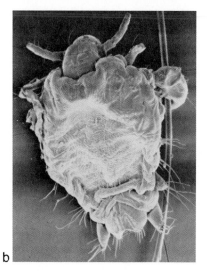

FIGURE 19–13. Germ tubes of (a) *Candida albicans*, the cause of moniliasis, (b) a pubic louse

Finding ways to control the spread of STDs is a top federal, state, and local priority.

Education about STDs is the first step in prevention.

If not treated in males, it can lead to complications of the male internal reproductive organs. In women, untreated NGU may cause PID and lead to sterility. A baby born to an infected mother may develop pneumonia.

Moniliasis (moh nuh LI uh sus) is a fungus or yeast infection caused by the overgrowth of a specific pathogen normally found in the vagina. It can be transmitted by sexual contact. The symptoms of moniliasis are a thick, white, cheesy discharge. Women who are diabetic or pregnant have an increased incidence of this infection.

Men can develop moniliasis from sexual contact with an infected woman. Symptoms are irritation and redness of the head of the penis. Treatment consists of medications such as creams that are applied to the infected area.

Genital warts, or **venereal warts**, are warts that usually are caused by a sexually transmitted virus. The warts are greyish-white and look like a small cauliflower. They can be treated by special ointments or liquids.

Pediculosis (pih dihk yuh LOH sus) is caused by pubic lice, or crab lice, tiny insects that invade the pubic area. They are usually transmitted by sexual contact although they can be picked up from sheets, towels, and clothing used by an infected person. The lice attach themselves to the base of the pubic hair and suck blood from the victim. This causes itching and possibly a rash. Pubic lice can be killed by using any of a number of special medications.

19:13 Controlling and Preventing the Spread of STDs

There are no vaccines that can be given to prevent contracting an STD. Therefore, many different approaches have been undertaken to attack this serious health problem.

Federal, state, and local health agencies have been working to find ways to reduce the incidence of STDs. Epidemiologists have been looking for disease patterns that may provide insights to specific prevention techniques. Health officers have been tracking down possible carriers of STDs and encouraging them to receive treatment. Clinics in local health departments have been providing treatment to STD patients. Patients are also encouraged to change their risk behaviors.

The first step in preventing STDs is knowing the important facts about them. Health programs in schools have been educating young people about the dangers of STDs. Community health agencies have taken a positive role by educating the public about

FIGURE 19–14. There are many sources of information about STDs.

STDs. It is hoped that knowledge of STDs will lead to prevention. More accurate diagnostic procedures have been developed to enable physicians to effectively recognize and treat STDs. Research is continually being conducted to find cures for many kinds of STDs. Parent groups have been influential in getting STD education placed in the curriculum in many school districts.

In addition to these efforts, individuals must take responsibility for their own health.

People who have STDs need medical treatment.

1. Clearly, STDs can be prevented if sexual contact is avoided. Sexual contact with only one infected partner can transmit an STD.

2. Condoms used during sexual intercourse are somewhat effective in preventing STDs from being transmitted. However, they are not successful all the time. Washing the genital area with soap and water immediately after sexual intercourse also reduces the chances of an STD occurring.

3. Persons who suspect that they have an STD should seek immediate medical treatment. These persons could enlist the aid of family members, a private physician, or the local health department. Physicians and health department workers will keep all information confidential. An infected person's sexual contacts will also need medical attention.

Reduction of the incidence of STDs is a main objective of *Healthy People*.

 Review and Reflect

7. In what way is genital herpes unlike other STDs?
8. How can some STDs affect an unborn fetus?

Activity: Fulfilling an Objective

Healthy People: The Surgeon General's Report on Health Promotion and Disease Prevention was released with the following central theme. The health of this nation's citizens can be significantly improved through individual action. Decision makers in the public and private sectors can also promote a safer and healthier environment at home, work, or play. One of the objectives of this report is to drastically reduce the incidence of STDs. Suppose you were the Surgeon General of the United States. Describe five rules you would develop to fulfill this objective. Assume that you have an unlimited budget to meet your objectives.

Health ADVANCES

Perhaps the newest and most frightening disease is **Acquired Immune Deficiency Syndrome** or **AIDS.** AIDS is a breakdown of the functioning of the immune system that protects the body against infections.

19:14 The Problem of AIDS

No cure has yet been found for AIDS.

AIDS is most often transmitted by sexual contact between homosexual men.

The symptoms of AIDS can vary from person-to-person.

AIDS was first identified in the United States in 1981. Research continues for a cure. AIDS is caused by the HTLV-III virus. AIDS can be spread through intimate sexual contact. For this reason, AIDS is considered to be an STD. AIDS can also be transmitted by means other than sexual contact. An increasing number of AIDS patients are intravenous drug users. The disease is spread when an infected needle is injected into the bloodstream. AIDS is being diagnosed in persons (even young children) who have received blood transfusions. If a person who has AIDS donates blood, pathogens can be transferred to the recipient. Fortunately, a new blood test can screen out potential blood donors who are carriers of the HTLV-III virus.

Not all persons who come in contact with the AIDS virus become ill. Some become carriers. In those who do become ill, the symptoms vary. Patients may feel as if they have the flu. They may lose weight, have a persistent fever, and have reddish-purple, coin-sized spots on the skin. These spots often turn out to be a rare form of cancer called Kaposi's sarcoma.

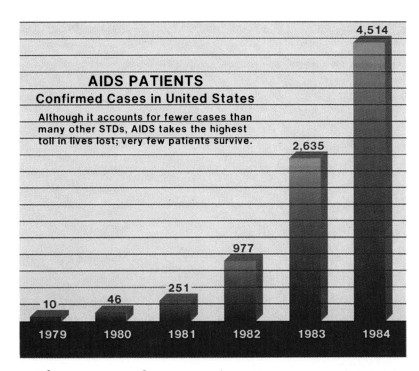

AIDS PATIENTS

Confirmed Cases in United States

Although it accounts for fewer cases than many other STDs, AIDS takes the highest toll in lives lost; very few patients survive.

4,514

2,635

977

251

46

10

1979 1980 1981 1982 1983 1984

FIGURE 19–15.

When symptoms first appear, they may remain unchanged for several months. Although many of these symptoms can be treated, the person's immune system is destroyed. The person becomes susceptible to many infections, including pneumonia and Kaposi's sarcoma. In most cases, AIDS is not cured and the victim dies.

At the present time, the battle against AIDS is geared on prevention. Physicians and researchers must work together to develop a vaccine that will wipe out this disease. We also need public education about the transmission of the AIDS virus and the risk behaviors that are associated with AIDS.

Having AIDS almost always results in death.

Focus on
Life Management Skills

- Recognize that many different pathogens can be present in your environment.
- Identify the different pathogens that cause communicable diseases.
- Identify risk factors associated with different communicable diseases.
- Seek medical attention immediately if the presence of an STD is suspected.

CHAPTER REVIEW 19

Summary

1. The six basic kinds of disease-causing organisms are bacteria, viruses, fungi, protozoa, rickettsia, and parasitic worms. **19:1**

2. Communicable diseases can be spread by direct and indirect contact. **19:2**

3. Among the body's defenses against disease are skin, small hairs in the nose, tears, antibodies, and white blood cells. **19:3**

4. The stages of diseases are incubation, prodromal, illness or acute, and recovery. **19:4**

5. The common cold has no cure and is caused by viruses. **19:5**

6. Flu and pneumonia are two common respiratory infections. **19:6**

7. The two types of hepatitis are infectious and serum. **19:7**

8. Mononucleosis is a viral infection that commonly occurs in the 15-to-19-year-old age group. **19:8**

9. Gonorrhea is one of the most frequent infectious diseases in America. **19:9**

10. Untreated syphilis may lead to complications in the infected person and in an unborn fetus. **19:10**

11. Genital herpes is an STD for which there is no known cure. **19:11**

12. Among other more common STDs are trichomoniasis, NGU, moniliasis, genital warts, and pubic lice. **19:12**

13. Federal, state, and local agencies work together to control and prevent the spread of STDs. **19:13**

14. AIDS is an incurable disease. **19:14**

Vocabulary

Below is a list of vocabulary words used in this chapter. Use each word only once to complete the sentences. Do not write in this book.

antibodies	pneumonia
communicable	Reye syndrome
disease	toxins
interferon	trichomoniasis
moniliasis	vaccine
NGU	

1. A(n) _____ is an illness that is caused by pathogens.

2. A disease whose symptoms include a thin greenish white or yellowish brown discharge from the vagina is _____.

3. Proteins in the blood that destroy pathogens are _____.

4. A(n) _____ contains weakened or dead pathogens that can be injected into the body.

5. The symptoms of _____ are similar to those of gonorrhea.

6. Poisonous chemicals produced by athogens are called _____.

7. _____ is associated with aspirin products used to treat flu or chicken pox in young people.

8. _____ is an inflammation of the lungs and often results from flu complications.

9. A protein that inhibits the production of viruses is _____.

10. A yeast infection found in the vagina is _____.

Review

1. Differentiate between a communicable and a noncommunicable disease.
2. Describe three ways diseases are spread.
3. How does your body protect you from disease?
4. How do antibodies help keep you healthy?
5. Identify the stages of diseases and their symptoms.
6. How are flu viruses spread?
7. How do infectious and serum hepatitus differ?
8. What are some dangers that can result from untreated gonorrhea?
9. Describe two major problems related to genital herpes.
10. What are several ways to control and prevent the spread of STDs?

Application

1. Why might a person who exercises, eats healthful foods, and gets enough rest reduce the chances of getting a communicable or noncommunicable disease?
2. Why might a person traveling to a foreign country with poor living conditions be at an increased risk of getting a disease?
3. Why might a person who has mono avoid heavy physical exercise?
4. Why do blood donors receive special screening tests before donating blood?

Individual Research

1. Look at the chart, *Six Types of Pathogens*, on page 574. Select a disease caused by one of the pathogens. Describe the signs and symptoms of the disease as well as its treatment and cure.
2. Write a one-page report that describes the latest information about the use of inteferon in treating cancer.
3. Use your school or public library to gather information about AIDS. Write a report about the latest research findings concerning this disease.

Readings

Bennet, Hal, *Cold Comfort*. New York, NY: Clarkson N. Potter, 1979.

Kolata, Gina, "Vaccines: Six Shots You May Need Now," *American Health*, December, 1985, pp. 27-30.

Mizel, Steven B., and Jaret, Peter, *In Self-Defense*. New York, NY: Harcourt Brace Jovanovich, Inc., 1985.

Many heart problems can be corrected by surgery. Skilled surgeons can repair or bypass or replace damaged heart tissue. How does a heart implant differ from a heart transplant? How can you protect your cardiovascular system?

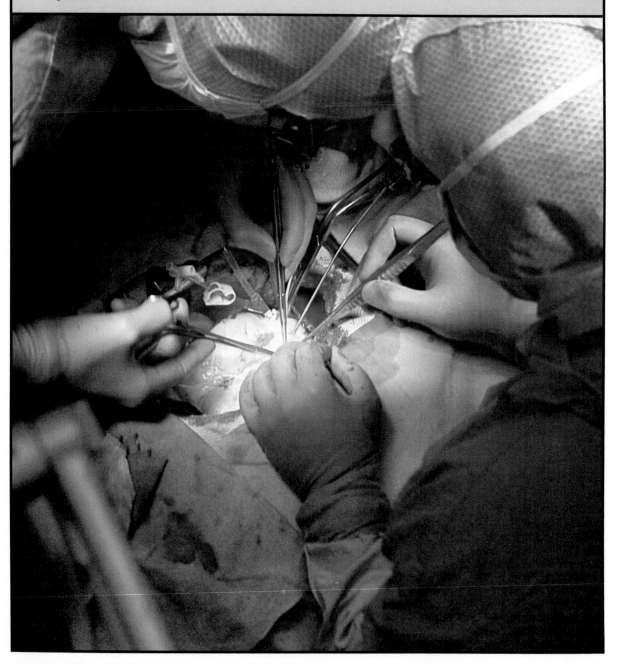

Chapter 20

Cardiovascular Diseases and Cancer

OBJECTIVES: You will be able to

- **explain the causes, treatments, and methods of prevention of cardiovascular diseases.**
- **identify the causes of cancer and describe lifestyle choices that reduce the risks of cancer.**

Think about the last time you saw a major sports event. Perhaps there were 10 000 spectators in the stands. Think of these people as representatives of the general population. A startling fact would be evident. Of these 10 000 people, 7500 will die from a chronic disease. A chronic disease is an illness that develops and lasts over a long period of time and is most often disabling. Chronic diseases usually are not communicable diseases. This chapter focuses on the chronic diseases responsible for most deaths in the United States—cardiovascular diseases and cancer.

Chronic diseases last over a long period of time.

CARDIOVASCULAR DISEASES

Cardiovascular diseases account for approximately half of all deaths in the United States today. **Cardiovascular diseases** are illnesses or disorders that affect the heart and blood vessels. Almost one in five Americans has some form of heart or blood vessel disease. Research has shown that people can reduce their risks of developing these diseases both now and later in life. You can help promote your cardiovascular health.

Cardiovascular diseases affect the heart and blood vessels.

- Become aware of diseases that affect your heart and blood vessels.
- Become aware of risk factors associated with these diseases.
- Choose behaviors that promote the health of your heart.

403

20:1   Atherosclerosis

Look around your classroom and notice your friends. They may have the appearance of good health. However, you cannot tell what is happening inside their bodies. The beginning symptoms of cardiovascular diseases may not be obvious. However, for many Americans, cardiovascular diseases begin at your age and even earlier.

Atherosclerosis is commonly referred to as clogged arteries.

One major form of cardiovascular disease is atherosclerosis (ath uh roh skluh ROH sus). **Atherosclerosis** is a medical term for clogged arteries. Over a period of time, an artery may be narrowed because of a buildup of fatty deposits called **plaque** (PLAK). Plaque causes the once-smooth lining of an artery to become thick and rough. The opening to the artery narrows and its elasticity is reduced. The artery cannot expand and contract as it should. As a result, blood flow is affected. The heart must pump harder to force blood through the artery. Thus, blood pressure is increased. If too much plaque builds up in a blood vessel, it forms a **thrombus,** or clot, that shuts off the flow of blood.

Increased plaque in a blood vessel results in increased blood pressure.

Sometimes plaque breaks away within an artery and forms a moving clot, or **embolism,** in a blood vessel of a major body organ. Blood flow in that organ may become blocked. This can result in permanent damage to the organ and possible death to the person. For example, a blood clot in a blood vessel in the heart muscle results in a heart attack. The term heart attack is a general term that refers to the death of any heart muscle cells due to a blockage. Later in this chapter, you will read about healthful behaviors you can follow to reduce your risks of cardiovascular disease caused by atherosclerosis.

A heart attack results from a blood clot in a blood vessel in the heart.

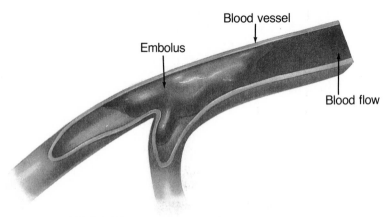

Blood vessel

Embolus

Blood flow

EMBOLISM

FIGURE 20–1. Diagram of an embolism

RISK OF HAVING A HEART ATTACK OR STROKE

Risk Factor		Score	Risk Factor		Score
Smoking	0	Nonsmoker	Cholesterol	0	Less than 150
	2	Less than 20 cigarettes a day	Level	2	150 to 250
	4	20 cigarettes or more a day		4	Over 250
Weight	0	Desirable	Physical Activity	0	Regular vigorous exercise
	2	Up to 10 percent		2	Moderate exercise
	4	More than 10 percent over		4	Sedentary
Systolic Blood Pressure	0	Less than 120	Stress and Tension	0	Rarely tense or anxious
	2	120 to 140		2	Feel tense two or three times a day
	4	Over 140		4	Extremely tense

Total Risk	0-4 Low	15-20 High
	5-9 Below average	21-24 Very high
	10-14 Average	

FIGURE 20–2. To rate yourself, find the number on the chart that fits your lifestyle or characteristics in each level. (You may not know your cholesterol level.) Total the figures to know your risk factor.

20:2 Hypertension

Hypertension is chronic high blood pressure. It affects more than one in five adults in the United States. What is most alarming about hypertension is that over 25 percent of its victims are unaware of their problem. They do not know they need treatment that would relieve the condition.

Hypertension creates several conditions that can severely damage the cardiovascular system. It can cause the heart to work harder to pump blood, thus weakening it. It can cause a speedier buildup of plaque on the walls of arteries. This increases the chances of a clot forming. Hypertension may cause pressure severe enough to burst an artery wall.

Hypertension can cause an artery wall to burst.

In many cases, the causes of hypertension are not known. Yet certain risk factors have been linked to its cause. The following risk factors are unchangeable.

Some risk factors of hypertension cannot be changed.

- Genetic traits—Those with a family history of hypertension are at greater risk of developing hypertension.
- Age—Risk of hypertension increases with age.
- Race—Almost half of black Americans between the ages of 55 and 64 have hypertension compared to 25 percent of white Americans in the same age group.
- Sex—Generally, men are at a greater risk of developing high blood pressure earlier in life than women.

The above risk factors cannot be changed. However, other risk factors can be changed to reduce the chances of getting hypertension. These include cigarette smoking, unbalanced diet, lack of exercise, stress, and drug use (Section 20:8).

FIGURE 20–3. A typical blood pressure reading for healthy young adults is about 130/70. The bar in the center reflects a seriously high reading. The bar on the right reflects an abnormally low reading.

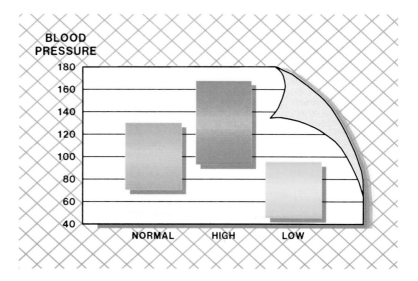

While hypertension cannot be cured, it can be controlled. Physicians usually recommend that overweight people with hypertension lose weight. People with hypertension should decrease their use of salty foods. Salt is associated with increased blood pressure. Hypertension can also be treated with the use of medications. Most importantly, people with hypertension who smoke are encouraged to quit. Smoking contributes to cardiovascular disease.

20:3 Angina Pectoris

The heart is just like any other muscle in the body in that it requires a constant supply of blood. The arteries that supply the heart muscle with blood are the **coronary arteries.** Sometimes, atherosclerosis causes the coronary arteries to become narrow. This can result in angina pectoris. **Angina pectoris**, also known as angina, is pain in the chest or arm caused by these narrowed coronary arteries. Pain results when the heart muscle cells do not receive enough oxygen. Angina does not damage heart tissue, but it can be a warning signal of a future heart attack.

Angina pectoris may occur during extreme physical activity, emotional stress, or excitement. The extent of pain can range from a mild ache to a severe pressing sensation under the breastbone. Generally the pain is momentary, and it can be relieved by medications. A person with angina pectoris should be under a physician's care.

Coronary arteries can narrow due to atherosclerosis.

Several conditions may cause angina pectoris.

20:4   Coronary Thrombosis

Cells in the muscle tissue of the heart can die as a result of a coronary thrombosis. A **coronary thrombosis** is an obstruction caused by plaque deposits in a coronary artery. An obstruction can prevent circulation in the heart muscle. Therefore, nutrients and oxygen are not supplied to the muscle cells. This causes a heart attack.

Think about a time you saw a movie or a TV program in which a person experienced a heart attack. You probably saw the victim clutching his or her chest. Some heart attack victims react this way. But most victims are not aware that they are having a heart attack. They can mistake chest pain for indigestion and not seek treatment.

The best way to survive a heart attack is to be aware of its warning signals and seek immediate help. The common signals of a heart attack are

- uncomfortable pressure, fullness, squeezing, or pain in the center of the chest that lasts for more than two minutes.
- pain that spreads to the shoulders, neck, jaw, or arms.
- paleness, dizziness, sweating, fainting, nausea, or shortness of breath.

Remember that these signals are not always present. Heart attack victims who get to the hospital within an hour greatly increase their chances of survival.

20:5   Rheumatic Heart Disease

Sometimes unrelated health problems if left untreated can result in damage to the heart. One such problem is strep throat. Untreated strep throat can be followed by rheumatic fever. **Rheumatic fever** is an acute disease characterized by inflammation, swelling, and soreness of joints. A possible serious danger of rheumatic fever is the damage of valves in the heart. When the valves become inflamed, scar tissue can form and cause permanent damage. **Rheumatic heart disease** is the resulting condition in which the heart valves are so scarred they cannot open or close completely. This condition causes the heart to work harder than it should. Over a period of years, the heart can become less efficient and eventually fail.

Fortunately, rheumatic heart disease can be prevented. A sudden case of sore throat accompanied by fever, swollen neck glands, or nausea should be treated by a physician. Antibiotics can be prescribed to treat the strep throat. This will lessen the risk of rheumatic heart disease.

A coronary thrombosis can result in death.

Knowing the signals of a heart attack can result in survival.

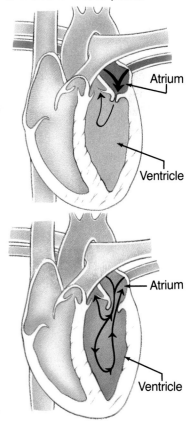

FIGURE 20–4. Two problems associated with heart valves. In each case, blood circulation is affected.

Valve stuck in closed position

Atrium

Ventricle

Atrium

Ventricle

Valve stuck in open position

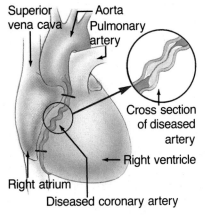

Superior vena cava — Aorta — Pulmonary artery

Cross section of diseased artery

Right ventricle

Right atrium

Diseased coronary artery

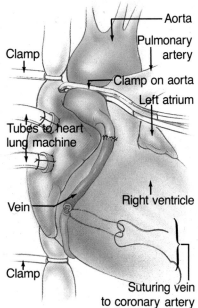

Aorta

Pulmonary artery

Clamp

Clamp on aorta

Left atrium

Tubes to heart lung machine

Vein

Right ventricle

Clamp

Suturing vein to coronary artery

FIGURE 20–5. Note the segment of a blocked coronary artery (upper view). The portion within the circle will be cut and removed and then replaced. During bypass surgery, the patient is attached to a heart–lung machine so that blood will not circulate through the heart during surgery.

20:6 Treating Heart Disease

Heart disease can be difficult to detect. It may take several tests to determine if a heart attack has occurred. A definite diagnosis can be made through blood tests and an electrocardiogram. An **electrocardiogram,** or **ECG** (some people use the term EKG), is a test that records the electrical impulses of the heart muscle. By reading the ECG printout, a physician usually can determine if damage has occurred and the extent of damage.

Sometimes, heart abnormalities can be diagnosed during a stress test. A **stress test** involves an ECG administered while a person walks or runs on a treadmill. A stress test can be more accurate than a resting ECG because it shows how the heart performs under stress or work.

Potential heart problems may be detected by angiography. **Angiography** is a process in which a special dye is injected into an artery or heart chamber. This dye passes through the coronary arteries and can be seen on a special X-ray machine. Any blockage of coronary arteries will be detected.

If a blocked coronary artery is detected, a physician may use one of several options. One option is to administer special drugs to help dissolve the blood clot. Another option is to insert a small tube that carries a balloonlike object into an artery in the arm. The tube is moved to the coronary artery where the blockage has occurred. Then the balloon is inflated, and the blockage is pushed against the artery wall. This opens the coronary artery so that blood can pass through more freely. Another procedure used by physicians is coronary bypass surgery. **Coronary bypass surgery** is the rerouting of blood flow around a clogged coronary artery. The clogged artery is replaced by a vein removed from the patient's leg. Blood flow to the heart continues as the blocked artery is bypassed. Often two or more arteries are bypassed during a surgical procedure.

Heart transplants have been successful for some patients. In a heart transplant, a patient's diseased heart is removed and replaced with the heart of a person who has died recently. In many cases, a patient's immune system rejects tissue from another person's body. Many new drugs have been developed to help keep this from happening (Section 11:13).

The latest efforts in heart research have centered around the use of heart implants. A heart implant is the substitution of the patient's diseased heart with a mechanical heart. There are several different models of mechanical hearts. For a person needing a heart transplant, a mechanical heart can be used temporarily until a human heart is available.

Some people have irregular heartbeats or **arrhythmia** (ay RITH mee uh). To help regulate arrhythmia, a pacemaker may be inserted. **A pacemaker** is an electronic device that stimulates the heart to beat at regular intervals. Wires from the pacemaker are attached to the heart muscle.

A pacemaker helps regulate heartbeat.

20:7 Stroke

A **stroke** is a condition caused by the sudden interference of blood flow through the brain. This usually results in a loss of brain function. Strokes can result from the following causes.

Strokes may result from any of several causes.

- A **cerebral embolism** occurs when a clot travels through the bloodstream and lodges in the brain.

- A **cerebral thrombosis** occurs when a clot forms inside one of the arteries in the brain. Blood flow to parts of the brain is blocked.

- A **cerebral hemorrhage** occurs when an artery inside the brain bursts. This presents two problems. One, blood flow to a part of the brain is cut off. Two, accumulated blood from the burst artery causes pressure in the surrounding brain tissue.

- An **aneurysm** (AN yuh rihz um) is a blood-filled pouch that balloons out from a weak spot in an artery wall. A stroke occurs when the aneurysm bursts in the brain.

- A **brain tumor** can press on an artery and cut off circulation.

ANEURYSM

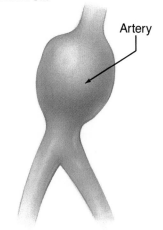
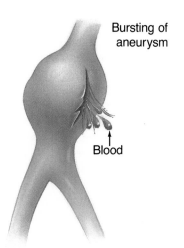

Artery

Bursting of aneurysm

Blood

FIGURE 20–6.

High blood pressure increases the risk of stroke.

A stroke can occur at any time or place. People who have high blood pressure are frequently at risk of having a stroke.

As with heart disease, the warning signals of a stroke should be identified early so that treatment can be given quickly. These warning signals are

- a sudden, temporary weakness or numbness on the face, arm, leg, or one side of the body.

- temporary loss of speech or trouble in speaking.

- dimness or loss of vision, especially in one eye.

- unexplained dizziness or unsteadiness.

Strokes may cause paralysis.

Effects of a stroke may range from a temporary loss of vision or speech to sudden death. The effects depend on how many brain cells are damaged and in what part of the brain those cells are. A person who suffers a severe stroke may suffer paralysis from which recovery is difficult. These people may need physical therapy for a long time before they can recover even minimal use of the affected body part.

Strokes can be diagnosed by use of a CAT scan or EEG. The earlier the diagnosis and treatment of a stroke, the better the chances for recovery. Treatment for stroke consists of surgery to remove the blockage or the administration of clot-dissolving drugs.

20:8 Promoting Cardiovascular Health

Throughout this chapter, the term risk factor has been used relative to cardiovascular diseases. You have learned that certain risk factors such as a person's age, sex, race, and genetic makeup cannot be changed. However, certain risk factors of cardiovascular disease may be changed.

Smokers have a much higher chance of heart disease and stroke than nonsmokers. Smoking also increases the amount of damage of atherosclerosis. If you smoke, quitting now will decrease your chances of suffering cardiovascular disease in the future.

Being overweight is linked to high blood pressure, high levels of cholesterol, and diabetes. Being overweight also causes the heart to work harder than it should. Being careful about the amount of food you eat, as well as the kinds of foods consumed, can help reduce the buildup of plaque and thus reduce your risk of cardiovascular disease.

Studies have revealed a link between heart disease and consumption of saturated fats and cholesterol. These substances are mainly found in eggs, red meats, butter, and cream. Reducing the

FIGURE 20–7. Fruits and vegetables are low in saturated fat; cheese is high in saturated fat.

intake of these foods and removing fat from meat can help reduce the saturated fats and cholesterol consumed.

At one time, it was thought that there was no definite link between cholesterol levels and the development of cardiovascular disease. This thinking has now changed. When physicians talk about cholesterol, they also talk about lipoproteins. Lipoproteins are molecular compounds that consist of cholesterol and triglycerides that link up with proteins. There are three kinds of lipoproteins—low-density lipoproteins (LDLs), very-low-density lipoproteins (VLDLs), and high-density lipoproteins (HDLs). Research links LDLs and VLDLs with the development of atherosclerosis. HDLs are associated with a decrease in cardiovascular disease and thus are called good lipoproteins. They are good lipoproteins because they help clear the cardiovascular system. HDLs travel through the arteries and collect cholesterol deposits. The deposits are carried to the liver where they are broken down and excreted from the body.

Salty foods promote a high level of salt in the blood. This increases blood volume and puts more pressure on artery walls. The heart then must work harder to pump extra fluid. Increased blood pressure increases the risks of cardiovascular disease. It is important to be aware of hidden sources of salt. Hidden salt is present in fast foods and in canned foods, such as tomatoes and soups. Foods that are cured, such as ham, also contain salt. It is important that the intake of salt and salt products be limited.

Exercise can reduce the risk of developing cardiovascular disease (Chapter 15). Regular participation in aerobic exercises increases the amount of HDLs in the body.

Research shows a link between stress and cardiovascular disease. If you feel under stress, it is important to have your blood pressure checked frequently. The sooner high blood pressure is diagnosed and treated, the greater your chances of preventing serious damage to the cardiovascular system.

FIGURE 20–8. Labels give information about ingredients.

Salt increases the risk of having high blood pressure.

Exercise increases the amount of HDLs in the body.

 ## Review and Reflect

1. Why is hypertension sometimes called the "silent killer"?
2. Why is it important to know the warning signals of a heart attack?
3. Why would it be difficult for a physician to detect a heart attack by listening to the heartbeat with a stethoscope?
4. What is the relationship between swimming 20 minutes each day and HDLs in the body?

CANCER

Cancer is the second leading cause of death in the United States. It affects people of all ages but usually those over 40 years of age. This disease causes more deaths to people your age than any other disease. Cancer is most often treatable if detected in its early stages.

Early detection is the best treatment for cancer.

20:9 What Is Cancer?

Cancer refers to any diseases that are characterized by the uncontrolled growth and spread of useless abnormal cells. A normal cell reproduces itself by dividing into replicas of itself. However, cancer cells reproduce differently. They may have defective nuclei with too little or too many chromosomes. They may have defective membranes and reproduce more frequently.

When abnormal cells in the body build up in one place, they create a lump called a **tumor.** Most tumors found in the body are **benign tumors,** harmless, noncancerous tumors. However, some tumors are cancerous or **malignant tumors.** Benign tumors remain in one place in the body. Malignant tumors grow and spread when not treated. It is the spread of cancer cells from malignant tumors that makes cancer a fatal disease.

Most tumors found in the body are benign.

The cancer cells spread in the body from the original site and affect other organs. The spread of cancer cells in the body to other sites is called **metastasis** (muh TAS tuh sus). Metastasis usually occurs through the lymph system. However, it can also occur through the bloodstream. Metastasis of some cancers, such as lung cancer and breast cancer, can happen through both the lymph system and the bloodstream.

FIGURE 20–9. A cancerous skin growth

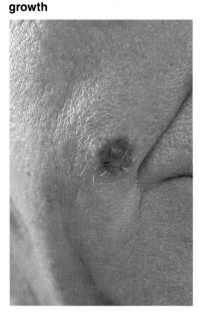

20:10 Causes of Cancer

The basic causes of cancer remain unknown. While scientists know the causes of some kinds of cancer, many others remain a mystery.

Research shows that certain substances called carcinogens play an important role in causing cancer. **Carcinogens** are substances in the environment that are thought to cause cancer. For example, working with or being in an environment with asbestos fibers can produce cancer. Other examples of carcinogens are cigarette tars and automobile pollutants.

Many other factors have been examined as possible causes of cancer. Some kinds of cancers run in families. Cancers of the breast, colon, and rectum are more prevalent in families with a history of these diseases. A study released in 1985 conducted by the Centers for Disease Control has revealed that women whose mothers or sisters had breast cancer were more than twice as likely to develop the disease as women with no family history of breast cancer.

There is no doubt that tobacco use causes cancer. While not a carcinogen, alcohol is linked to cancers. The combination of drinking and smoking increases the risk of developing cancers of the tongue, throat, and lungs. Chronic use of marijuana is also linked to lung cancer.

People who eat foods high in cholesterol and fats and low in fiber may increase their chances of developing cancer of the colon, rectum, and breast. Certain foods and food additives have been identified as possible carcinogens. Preservatives, which may be found in hot dogs or cured ham, also have been linked to cancer. Controversy presently exists about the use of certain artificial sweeteners and their relationship to cancer.

Research indicates a link between exposure to radiation and cancer. Overexposure to the sun's rays is known to cause skin cancer. However, it may take years for skin cancer to develop.

Scientists have debated whether or not certain viruses cause cancer. Some studies show that certain viruses cause cancer in animals. However, a link between viruses and cancer in humans has not been established.

20:11   Types of Cancer

Cancer can strike any part of the body. However, certain cancers seem to occur more frequently. Breast cancer is the most common form of cancer in women. About one of every 11 women will develop breast cancer in her lifetime. Women most likely to develop breast cancer are over age 50, have a family history of breast cancer, have never had children, or had a first child after age 30. Signs of breast cancer are a lump, thickening, swelling, or dimpling of the breast. A discharge may appear from the nipple. Any of these signs should be checked by a physician. If the physician believes any chance of cancer exists, a biopsy may be taken. A biopsy is the removal of cells from the body for analysis. Most abnormalities found in the breast are not malignant. It should be noted that men also get breast cancer although the incidence is much lower than that of women.

Some kinds of cancers run in families.

Some preservatives have been linked to cancer.

FIGURE 20–10.

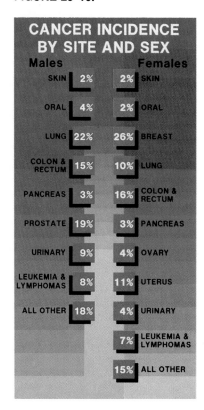

Lung cancer is the leading cause of cancer deaths in women.

Avoiding the sun's harmful rays between 10:00 A.M. and 3:00 P.M. can help reduce the risk of skin cancer.

Colon and rectal cancers can be detected by special tests.

At one time, uterine cancer was one of the most frequent causes of deaths from cancer in women. However, the use of the Pap test has enabled uterine cancer to be detected and treated early. Women with the greatest risk of developing uterine cancer are those who have multiple sex partners, fail to ovulate, or are obese.

In 1986, lung cancer overtook breast cancer as the leading cause of cancer deaths in women. Lung cancer is the most common cancer in men. Research clearly shows that cigarette smoking is the main cause of lung cancer. Unfortunately, over 90 percent of people who get lung cancer survive less than five years after it is diagnosed.

Skin cancer is a common form of cancer. It is often related to exposure to the sun. Fortunately, it is almost always curable when detected early. The warning signs of skin cancer are a sore that does not heal, a change in the size or color of a wart or mole, and the development of an unusual pigmented area. The best prevention of skin cancer is avoiding the sun's harmful rays between 10:00 AM and 3:00 PM. Sunscreen lotions with high levels of a chemical called PABA should be used as protection from the sun's rays.

Colon and rectal cancers are leading causes of cancer deaths in men and women. Symptoms include bleeding from the rectum, blood in the stool, or a change in bowel habits. Early detection of this type of cancer can be made by a rectal examination given by a physician. A special stool blood slide test can be used at home. The person then sends this test to a laboratory for analysis.

Several different types of cancer affect children. These cancers most often are found in the blood, brain, nervous system, and kidneys. Remember these warning signals by thinking of the word CHILDREN.

C ontinued unexplained weight loss

H eadaches with morning vomiting

I ncreased swelling or persistent pain in bones or joints

L ump or mass in abdomen, neck, or elsewhere

D evelopment of a whitish appearance in the pupil of the eye

R ecurrent fevers not due to infections

E xcessive bruising or bleeding

N oticeable paleness or prolonged tiredness

FIGURE 20–11.

Source: Susan Kranstuber: *Know the Eight Warning Signals of Possible Childhood Cancer.* Franklin County Unit, American Cancer Society, 1985.

Leukemia is cancer of the blood-forming tissues and is the most common form of cancer in children. The symptoms are similar to those of a cold. Other symptoms may be fatigue, paleness, weight loss, repeated infections, easy bruising, and nosebleeds. While new treatment methods for leukemia have met with some success, the five-year survival rate for its victims is only 15 percent.

Leukemia is a common form of cancer in children.

Activity: The Cost of Smoking

A famous cancer surgeon once stated, "You can buy cancer over a period of 20 years for approximately $7200." This is the approximate cost of smoking one pack of cigarettes per day for 20 years at an average cost of one dollar per pack.

Suppose someone offered you $360 per year for 20 years if you did not smoke. In what ways would not smoking improve your health? If you were to spend this amount only for health products or services, what health changes could occur? How would you spend your money the first year? Because of this decision not to smoke, what healthful qualities might you have 20 years from now?

20:12 Treating Cancer

The best way to deal with cancer is to detect it early. Ways to detect cancer are to have regular medical examinations and perform breast or testicular self-examinations. Another way to detect cancer is to be aware of its warning signals. Remember the warning signals by thinking of the word CAUTION.

It is important for cancer to be detected early.

C hange in bowel or bladder habits

A sore that does not heal

U nusual bleeding or discharge

T hickening or lump in breast or elsewhere

I ndigestion or difficulty in swallowing

O bvious change in the size of a mole or wart

N agging cough or hoarseness

PLUS TWO
- weakness or fatigue
  (may be caused by an anemia resulting from cancer-causing bleeding)
- unexplained weight loss

Courtesy of American Cancer Society

FIGURE 20–12.

There are several treatments available to cancer patients.

If cancer is detected, there are several treatments available. A person who has cancer should learn all the options available for treatment of the cancer. Most cancers consist of tumors. Often, the most effective way to fight cancer is to have the tumor surgically removed. The surgeon may also remove apparently healthy tissue around the tumor to be sure all of the cancer cells are removed. The major surgical procedures for breast cancer include

- lumpectomy—removal of only the tumor and a small area of surrounding tissue.
- simple or total mastectomy—removal of the entire breast.
- radical mastectomy—removal of the breast, underlying muscles, and nearby lymph nodes.

Women are advised to get an opinion from a second surgeon when breast cancer surgery is recommended. The woman may be required to make a choice of what kind of surgery will be performed when medical opinions vary. Surgery is not always the only option.

Radiation may be used to destroy cancer cells.

Sometimes, tumors cannot be surgically removed. Radiation therapy then becomes an option. Doses of radiation are directed to the cancerous area to help destroy the rapidly growing cells. Consequently, the cancer cells cannot reproduce. At other times, radiation therapy is administered after a tumor is removed. There are limitations in the use of radiation therapy. Radiation itself can cause cancer. For this reason, it cannot be used for long periods on healthy tissue.

Chemotherapy is often used to treat cancer when metastasis has occurred.

Chemotherapy, or the use of drugs, is the main method of treatment for certain kinds of cancers. A surgeon may recommend chemotherapy when there is reason to believe that metastasis may occur after a tumor is surgically removed. Chemotherapy can create side effects, such as nausea and vomiting or loss of hair. However, the possibility of cure generally outweighs the negative effects. When cancer patients are receiving chemotherapy, other forms of therapy, such as group therapy, may also be recommended.

20:13 Preventing Cancer

Healthful behaviors can reduce the risk of developing cancer.

There are many healthful behaviors people can follow to reduce their risks of developing cancer. Knowing the risks of certain types of cancers can help serve as a guide to cancer prevention. Know the risk factors for several types of cancer (Table 20–1) and have regular health checkups. Remember, some risk factors can be controlled while others cannot.

Table 20–1 Some Risk Factors and Preventions for Specific Cancers

TYPE OF CANCER	RISK FACTORS (Not in Your Control)	POSSIBLE PREVENTION FACTORS (In Your Control)
Breast	• over age 50 • personal or family history	• practice a monthly breast self-examination
Colon and Rectum	• personal or family history of polyps in the colon or rectum	• maintain a diet low in beef and high in fiber • have a regular examination especially after age 40
Leukemia	• possible inherited susceptibility	• avoid exposure to radiation and certain chemicals such as benzene
Lung		• avoid smoking • avoid exposure to industrial substances such as asbestos
Oral		• avoid smoking and drinking • avoid use of chewing tobacco
Skin	• having a fair complexion	• avoid excessive exposure to the sun, coal tar, pitch, arsenic compounds, and radium
Testicular		• practice monthly testicular self-examination
Uterine (cervical neck of the uterus) endometrial (lining of the uterus	• history of infertility • failure to ovulate	• avoid prolonged estrogen therapy • avoid obesity • avoid having first intercourse at an early age • avoid having multiple sex partners • have a regular pelvic examination and pap smear

 Review and Reflect

5. Why should a person who finds a tumor on any part of the body see a physician?
6. Why is it important to know if someone in your family has had breast cancer?
7. Explain why delaying treatment for cancer reduces the chances of survival.

Health
ADVANCES

Finding the causes of cancer as well as searching for new ways to diagnose the early stages of cancer are the focus of numerous research efforts. Significant findings have sparked hope that a cure for this disease will soon be found.

20:14   Major Breakthroughs in Cancer Research

Scientists have been studying oncogenes to find a cure for cancer.

Why do normal body cells turn into rapidly growing cancer cells? The answer to this question may help scientists find a cure for cancer. According to many scientists, the discovery of oncogenes (AHN koh jeenz) may be the greatest single breakthrough in cancer research. **Oncogenes** are small, cancer-causing parts of genetic material. They are thought to be activated by both viruses and chemicals. When activated, oncogenes cause changes in the structure and function of normal cells. These changed cells continue to multiply as cancer cells. Scientists have now been able to isolate certain oncogenes, and they have identified certain types of cancers caused by them. They have also concluded that at least two oncogenes must cooperate for cancer to arise in normal cells. Each oncogene must fulfill a different requirement in the cancer process. By understanding how oncogenes work, scientists hope to discover the mystery of the cancer cell and find ways to halt its destructive nature.

Special blood tests can be used to detect the recurrence of cancer of the colon.

Another discovery focuses on the use of a special blood test that can indicate the recurrence of cancer of the colon and rectum (colorectal cancer). This blood test is given to patients on a monthly basis after they have had surgery to remove colorectal cancer. By using this test, physicians can detect the recurrence of cancer as early as two-and-a-half months before symptoms would be noticed by previous standard examinations.

Another type of cancer therapy involves a technique called adoptive immunotherapy. This type of therapy uses the body's immune system to react against cancer cells. The procedure involves using a natural hormone called interleukin-2. This hormone is used to treat white blood cells that have been removed from a cancer patient's blood. After treatment, these cells are injected back into the patient's body.

Focus on
Life Management Skills

- Avoid foods high in fats and cholesterol.
- Reduce intake of salt.
- Exercise regularly for cardiovascular health.
- Identify the risk factors of cardiovascular diseases and cancer.
- Follow healthful behaviors, such as exercising and eating healthful foods, to prevent these diseases.

Health
CAREERS

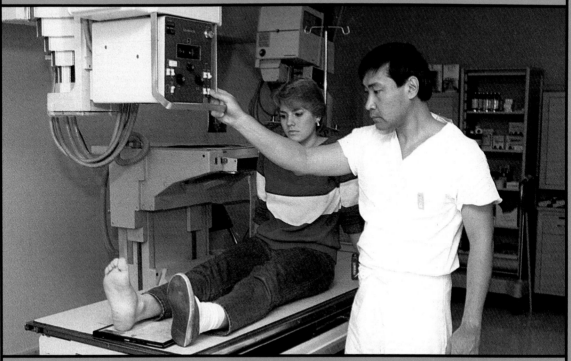

Radiologic Technologist

A patient has complained of stomach pains. His physician has ordered X rays and other tests to be taken in an effort to determine the cause of the pain.

A **radiologic technologist,** or X-ray technologist, is a person who is trained to operate X-ray equipment. He or she may prepare chemical mixtures that a patient swallows to make specific body parts appear more clearly on the X rays. The radiologic technologist determines the correct voltage and desired exposure time needed for particular X rays. These X rays are then interpreted by a physician.

Some radiologic technologists may perform radiation therapy. This involves administering prescribed doses of X rays or other forms of radiation in the treatment of various conditions in which radiation is believed to be helpful.

Radiologic technologists may receive formal training in a hospital, technical school, or college. Programs take from two to four years to complete. Students take courses in anatomy, physiology, nursing procedure, physics, radiation, principles of radiographic exposure, and equipment operation. With experience, competence, and knowledge, a radiologic technologist may become an instructor in X-ray techniques or advance to chief of X-ray technology.

Summary

1. Atherosclerosis is a major form of cardio-vascular disease.   20:1
2. Hypertension plays a role in the development of cardiovascular disease.   20:2
3. Narrowed coronary arteries can lead to angina pectoris, which results in chest pain.   20:3
4. An obstruction of the coronary arteries can result in coronary thrombosis and cause death.   20:4
5. Untreated health problems, such as strep throat, can result in rheumatic heart disease.   20:5
6. Heart disease can be detected by an ECG, stress test, or angiography and may be treated in various ways.   20:6
7. Five causes of strokes are cerebral thrombosis, hemorrhages, embolisms, aneurysms, or tumors.   20:7

8. Cigarette smoking, poor diet, lack of exercise, and stress are risk factors of cardiovascular disease.   20:8
9. Cancer is a disease in which abnormal cells in the body have uncontrolled growth.   20:9
10. Possible causes of cancer are related to heredity, tobacco, alcohol, diet, radiation, and viruses.   20:10
11. There are many types of cancer each of which has a different cure rate and treatment.   20:11
12. Early recognition of the signs of cancer will lead to increased rates of cure.   20:12
13. The chances of developing certain types of cancers can be reduced if risk factors are identified.   20:13
14. The discovery of oncogenes may be a clue to the cause of cancer.   20:14

Vocabulary

Below is a list of vocabulary words used in this chapter. Use each word only once to complete the sentences. Do not write in this book.

aneurysm
angina pectoris
arrhythmia
benign tumor
chemotherapy

hypertension
metastasis
plaque
stress test
thrombus

1. A buildup of noncancerous cells is called a(n) ⎯⎯.
2. The movement of cancer cells from one site of the body to the other is called ⎯⎯.
3. Pains in the chest caused by a narrowing of coronary blood vessels is known as ⎯⎯.

4. A clot in a blood vessel is known as a(n) ⎯⎯.
5. If metastasis of cancer cells occurs, ⎯⎯ can be used as treatment.
6. The buildup of fatty deposits in the artery walls is known as ⎯⎯.
7. Another term for an irregular heartbeat is ⎯⎯.
8. Chronic high blood pressure is known as ⎯⎯.
9. An ECG that a person takes on a treadmill is called a(n) ⎯⎯.
10. The ballooning out of a weak spot in a blood vessel is called a(n) ⎯⎯.

Review

1. Why is a buildup of plaque in the blood vessels dangerous?
2. Why is hypertension considered a "silent killer"?
3. What genetic factors linked to hypertension cannot be changed?
4. What behaviors can people change to control hypertension?
5. Under what conditions may angina occur?
6. What are the warning signals of a heart attack?
7. How can rheumatic heart disease be prevented?
8. What is the difference between a stress test and a resting ECG?
9. What are four causes of stroke?
10. What risk factors of cardiovascular disease can be changed?

Application

1. Why is it important to control hypertension?
2. Why should a person who experiences severe chest pains seek medical care?
3. Why might a stress test be more efficient than a resting ECG in diagnosing heart disease?
4. In what way might following a high-fiber diet be a preventive behavior?

Individual Research

1. Find information in your school or public library that identifies the death rates for cardiovascular disease over the past 10 years. Draw a graph that indicates the death rates over this period and describe the trends you notice.
2. Develop a "Healthy Heart Diet" menu for one day. Describe the foods you would select for the three meals in a day that would promote your heart health.
3. Write a paper that examines the controversies concerning the different kinds of surgery for breast cancer.

Readings

Cranton, Elmer, *Bypassing Bypass.* Briarcliff Manor, NY: Stein & Day, 1984.

Foley, Conn, and Piger, H.F., *The Stroke Fact Book.* New York, NY: Bantam Books, 1985.

Margolies, Cynthia P., and McGredie, Kenneth B., *Understanding Leukemia.* New York, NY: Charles Scribner's Sons, 1983.

Some health problems are chronic; they cannot be cured. Some chronic illnesses cause a person to have a handicap; some do not. What about inherited diseases? How can you tell if a person has a chronic health problem?

Chapter 21

Chronic Health Problems

OBJECTIVES: You will be able to
- describe the relationship between heredity and disease.
- identify the causes, signs and symptoms, and treatment of common chronic diseases.
- differentiate between a physical disability and a handicap.

Do you know that in one way cystic fibrosis, epilepsy, and arthritis are alike? Each is a chronic noncommunicable disease. Some chronic diseases may be inherited; some may be acquired during a person's life. This chapter focuses on some different kinds of chronic diseases.

Some chronic diseases may be inherited; others may be acquired during a person's lifetime.

HEREDITY AND DISEASE

People from the same biological family share common physical characteristics, such as eye color, skin tone, or body structure. These characteristics are passed by genes from generation to generation in a family. Genes not only influence physical makeup but also can contain the codes that result in genetic disorders.

Genes influence a person's physical makeup.

21:1 Genes and Chromosomes

Genes are special structures that transmit hereditary characteristics. Genes also contain the code for the reproduction and development of body cells. The scientific study of genes and how they determine and control development is known as **genetics.** Genes are part of a larger structure known as a chromosome. A chromosome is a distinct body in a cell nucleus that becomes apparent during cell division.

Genes are parts of a chromosome.

423

FIGURE 21–1. The color of a person's hair is determined by genes.

Humans normally have 46 chromosomes in each body cell. These 46 chromosomes are arranged in 23 pairs. One chromosome of each pair comes from each parent. One of the 23 pairs contains the genes that determine the sex of an individual.

Each pair of chromosomes has a pair of genes that determine a particular trait, such as eye color. Some genes are dominant. A **dominant gene** prevents another gene from expressing itself. The gene that is not expressed is a **recessive gene.** For example, the gene for brown eyes is dominant over the gene for blue eyes. If one gene for blue eyes and one gene for brown eyes are inherited, the dominant brown gene will prevail and the person will have brown eyes. However, this person could pass a blue-eye color gene to the next generation. A person can have blue eyes only if two genes for blue eye color are inherited.

21:2 Mutation

Mutations can occur in many ways.

Sometimes, cells fail to divide in a normal way. This results in a **mutation** or a change in the genetic makeup of an organism. Mutations can occur in many ways. For example, part of a chromosome may fall off and be lost. This lost part may attach onto a different chromosome. These changes can result in abnormal information in the genetic code. Some mutations may have little effect or even be helpful for the survival of a species. However, most mutations are harmful.

Overexposure to some forms of radiation is thought to cause changes in the genetic code. Some types of cancer cells are thought to begin as mutations. These abnormal cells then reproduce and cause serious illness or death unless their ability to reproduce is altered.

Mutations can cause inherited genetic disorders. Each year, thousands of babies are born with genetic diseases. These diseases may appear more often in one sex. However, it takes both parents with a defective gene to produce an offspring with a genetic disease. The chance of having offspring with a genetic abnormality increases when two people marry who are closely related. This is one reason that marriage between close relatives is forbidden by law in some places.

Mutations can cause genetic disorders.

21:3 Sex-Linked Inherited Disorders

If a mutation occurs in the genes that determine sex, then a sex-linked disorder may occur. Examples of sex-linked disorders are muscular dystrophy, hemophilia, and color blindness.

Muscular dystrophy is a disease that is characterized by weakness due to the deterioration of muscle fibers. Although this disease is sex-linked, identification of carriers is not currently possible. One form of muscular dystrophy affects boys and involves weakness around the pelvic area. The disease becomes evident when the child begins to walk. He waddles, walks on his toes, falls frequently, and has difficulty standing up for a child of his age. The disease worsens as time goes on and the victim is usually confined to a wheelchair. Another form of muscular dystrophy affects both sexes. This form may often begin during adolescence. The symptoms appear slowly and may vary from person-to-person. Since there is no known cure for muscular dystrophy, treatment focuses on physical therapy.

Hemophilia is a sex-linked disease characterized by the absence of a protein factor necessary for the clotting of blood. Thus, a minor injury can result in severe blood loss. Fortunately, persons with hemophilia may be treated with blood transfusions. This method of treatment is only a temporary measure. There is no cure.

Color blindness is a sex-linked disorder in which the person cannot distinguish one or more colors. The term color blindness may be misleading. It is very rare for a person to totally lack the ability to see any colors. The most common type of color blindness is red-green. Persons with this disorder cannot see the colors red or green. Rather, these colors appear as shades of gray.

Muscular dystrophy is a sex-linked disease.

FIGURE 21–2. A patient with muscular dystrophy has to learn to cope with handicaps caused by the disease.

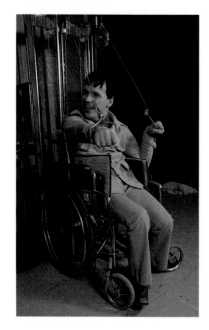

FIGURE 21–3. Normal red cells appear as red discs; sickle cells are elongated and curved and resemble a sickle.

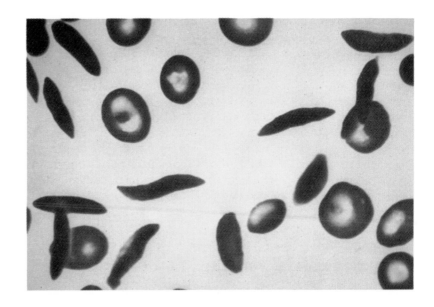

21:4   Recessive Inherited Diseases

Sickle-cell disease, cystic fibrosis, and Tay-Sachs are recessive inherited diseases. This means that two defective genes are needed to cause the disease. These diseases result when a person inherits a recessive gene from each parent.

Sickle-cell anemia is a blood disease that gets its name from the shape of the abnormal red blood cell. This cell is elongated and sickle-shaped rather than being disc-shaped. It is also rigid and brittle. The sickle-shaped cell has difficulty passing through small blood vessels in the body. Consequently, these cells clump together and prevent oxygen from reaching parts of the body.

Sickle-cell anemia results from an inherited abnormality in hemoglobin. Hemoglobin has a specific biochemical structure. The structure of the usual hemoglobin gene is called Hemoglobin A. The recessive hemoglobin gene that can cause sickle-cell anemia is called Hemoglobin S.

People with sickle-cell anemia may experience severe pain and possible tissue damage. Other complications may include frequent infections and damage to the body organs. Physical activity may be extremely limited, and the person's life span may be shortened. However, the effects of sickle-cell anemia vary for any number of reasons. This results in some patients being very ill while other patients rarely experience difficulties. Being aware of the symptoms of sickle-cell anemia will enable patients to promote their own good health.

Recessive inherited diseases are caused by two defective genes.

Sickle-cell anemia is caused by a recessive hemoglobin gene.

There are several misconceptions about sickle-cell disease. One misconception is that sickle-cell trait and sickle-cell anemia are the same. These two conditions are different. A person with the sickle-cell trait is a carrier of the sickle-cell gene. A person with the sickle-cell trait has inherited a sickle S gene from one parent and a normal A gene from the other parent (forming Hemoglobin AS). This person does not have sickle-cell anemia. Yet, this person is capable of passing on the sickle-cell gene trait. This contrasts with the Hemoglobin SS of a person with sickle-cell anemia. A person with Hemoglobin AS, or trait, usually has no illness because of the structure of the hemoglobin.

Another misconception about sickle-cell disease is that it affects only blacks. It is a fact that sickle-cell disease is most prevalent among people of African descent. However, sickle-cell disease is found among ethnic groups of African, Mediterranean, and Asian ancestry.

An important fact about sickle-cell anemia is that it cannot be cured. Several promising treatments of sickle-cell anemia are being used. Different chemicals are being used that, among other things, help hemoglobin to hold more oxygen. Many sickled red cells will return to their normal shape when carrying a lot of oxygen. People who are concerned that they might have the sickle-cell trait should be tested for its presence. After testing, these individuals may be counseled about their status. Counseling gives people of childbearing age options about reproduction, based upon accurate medical information.

Cystic fibrosis is a disease that affects the mucous and sweat glands. It is the most common genetic disease that affects the white population in the United States. A person with cystic fibrosis secretes a thick and sticky mucus rather than a thinner and more free-flowing mucus. This mucus blocks the passageways of different parts of the body, including the air passages. As a result, the person has difficulty breathing. Cystic fibrosis can be detected by checking the salt content of a person's perspiration. However, tests to accurately check for carriers of this disease are lacking. A person with cystic fibrosis has a 50 percent chance of living to adulthood if the disease is detected and treated early.

Tay-Sachs is a disease caused by the absence of a key enzyme needed to break down fats in the body. The result is an accumulation of fatty materials in the brain that leads to mental retardation, blindness, and death by age three or four. Most patients of Tay-Sachs disease are from Jewish families of eastern European descent. Carriers of Tay-Sachs disease can be identified by blood tests and may choose to undergo genetic counseling for help in making decisions about childbearing.

Sickle-cell trait is not the same as sickle-cell anemia.

Sickle-cell disease is most prevalent among people of African descent.

Cystic fibrosis is a disease in which the mucous and sweat glands are affected.

Blood tests can be used to detect Tay-Sachs disease.

FIGURE 21–4. The Special Olympic's program is especially designed for persons with handicaps. These persons have the same needs as others to have friends and to share.

21:5 Extra- or Missing-Chromosome Inherited Diseases

Sometimes genes fail to segregate properly during cell division. The result is a disease caused by an extra or missing chromosome. Down syndrome, Klinefelter syndrome, and Turner syndrome are examples of these genetic diseases.

Down syndrome is a genetic disease that is the result of an extra chromosome. A child born with Down syndrome has 47 instead of 46 chromosomes. Characteristics of a child with this disease are folds around the eyes that make the eyes appear slanted; a broad, flat nose; mental retardation; and sometimes a heart defect. Many individuals with Down syndrome live into the adult years. Down syndrome is much more likely to occur in children born of mothers over the age of 35. At this age, one pregnant woman in 365 will give birth to a Down syndrome baby. At age 38, the odds double. And at age 41, it nearly doubles again. By age 45, the chance of a pregnant woman giving birth to a Down syndrome baby is one in 45. Down syndrome can be diagnosed by amniocentesis.

A Down syndrome child has 47 chromosomes.

Klinefelter syndrome occurs when a male has an extra X chromosome. This results in abnormal structure of the testes and the production of few sperm. Testosterone production is also usually reduced. Men with Klinefelter syndrome tend to be tall and have poor muscular development.

An extra X chromosome in a male can result in Klinefelter syndrome.

Turner syndrome occurs when a female is missing an X chromosome. This results in the improper development of the ovaries. Girls with Turner syndrome may have a variety of abnormalities that involve facial appearance as well as internal organs, such as the heart and kidneys. Girls with Turner syndrome who do not have physical limitations usually develop normally as children. However, when other girls their age begin to menstruate and develop other secondary sex characteristics, these girls do not because of their nonfunctioning ovaries. Through hormone therapy, these characteristics can be induced.

Hormone therapy is used to treat females who have Turner syndrome.

 ## Review and Reflect

1. Describe the relationship that might exist between mutations and certain diseases like cancer.
2. Why might married couples with a family history of birth defects seek counseling before deciding to bear children?
3. Why should a person with hemophilia try to avoid handling tools with sharp edges?

CHRONIC DISEASES

Many chronic diseases and disorders affect people at birth or at some later point in their lives. Each of these diseases has unique characteristics. Some of these diseases are more damaging than others. Yet, most of these diseases can be controlled so that the victims can lead healthy and productive lives.

Chronic diseases and disorders can affect individuals throughout life.

21:6 Epilepsy

Epilepsy is a disturbance of impulses in the brain that causes temporary loss of control of the mind and body. The periods during which the loss of control occurs are called seizures.

There are two classifications of seizures, partial and generalized. Partial seizures occur in a specific area of the brain and may not involve a loss of consciousness. Generalized seizures occur in both halves of the brain at the same time and always involve a loss of consciousness.

Partial and generalized seizures are broken down further into categories depending on the exact nature of the seizures. Partial seizures may include twitching on one side of the body. Other partial seizures may be preceded by an aura. An **aura** is a dreamlike state in which the body experiences a strange sensation. A generalized seizure is not preceded by an aura. It comes on

Epileptic seizures are classified as partial and generalized.

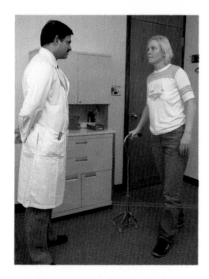

FIGURE 21–5. A person with multiple sclerosis needs regular checkups by a physician.

The causes of MS are not known.

The signs and symptoms of MS vary from person to person.

Diabetes may be either insulin-dependent or noninsulin-dependent.

with little warning. A person who has this kind of seizure will drop to the ground and suddenly become rigid, or experience twitches and shakes.

Epileptic seizures can be mild or serious. However, with medical treatment, most people who have epilepsy can lead nearly normal lives. Early diagnosis of epilepsy is important. First, mild seizures can develop into more serious seizures if they go untreated. Second, a seizure can be fatal if the victim is engaged in an activity, such as swimming or gymnastics, when it occurs. Once epilepsy is diagnosed, physicians can prescribe one of several drugs to reduce the frequency and severity of seizures. In some cases, the cause of the seizures can be treated and eliminated.

21:7   Multiple Sclerosis

Multiple sclerosis, or **MS**, is a disease characterized by a breakdown of the outer covering of the nerve fibers in the brain and spinal cord causing scar tissue to form. About 300 000 people in the United States, most of them young adults, have this disease. Its cause is not known, and it has no cure. Patients are counseled to learn how to manage life skills.

The signs and symptoms of MS vary from person to person depending on which nerve fibers are affected. An early symptom of MS in some people may be blurred vision or a numbness or tingling in a part of the body. Others may experience a loss of balance or paralysis. Speech and hearing difficulties may also develop. At other times, the signs and symptoms may disappear and suddenly reappear after a period of time. MS is a progressive disease; its signs and symptoms get worse.

21:8   Diabetes

Diabetes is a disease in which the body is unable to process the sugar in foods in normal ways. It occurs when the pancreas does not produce enough insulin, or it produces insulin that does not help the cells break down sugar. This results in too much sugar or glucose in the bloodstream. Diabetes cannot be cured, but it can be controlled.

There are two types of diabetes. One type is insulin-dependent diabetes, formerly called juvenile diabetes because it most often appears in young persons. **Insulin-dependent diabetes** is characterized by little or no insulin produced by the pancreas. People with this type of diabetes must have daily injections of insulin to stay alive.

The second type of diabetes is noninsulin-dependent diabetes, formerly called maturity-onset diabetes. **Noninsulin-dependent diabetes** is characterized by the pancreas producing some insulin, but the body cells are not able to properly use it. This type of diabetes is most likely to affect people who are over age 40, inactive, and overweight. This type of diabetes can be controlled with oral medication. Many people control this type of diabetes through a program of diet and exercise.

Both forms of diabetes have obvious symptoms. Among them are frequent urination, abnormal thirst, weakness, fatigue, drowsiness, blurred vision, tingling and numbness in the hands and feet, and slow healing of cuts. Not all of these symptoms appear at the same time.

People with diabetes must realize that they need a life-long commitment to control this disease. Diabetes kills approximately 34 000 Americans yearly and is the seventh leading cause of death in the United States. Complications of diabetes are blindness and poor circulation, which can lead to gangrene and amputation of the extremities.

What is of particular concern about diabetes is that an estimated five million Americans have this disease and are unaware of it. Thus, it continues to cause irreversible damage inside the body. Once the symptoms are recognized, healthful behaviors can be followed to prevent its harmful effects.

Diabetes is a disease that can be controlled.

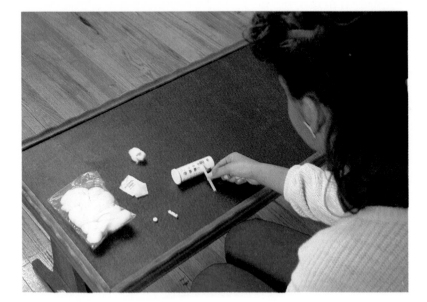

FIGURE 21–6. A person with diabetes can learn to check blood sugar level by using special, chemically treated strips of paper. Blood sugar levels are indicated by changing colors on the strips of paper.

FIGURE 21–7. A plastic implant shows up on an X ray of a hip joint. Many persons who have been unable to walk because of arthritis are able to walk again after hip relacement surgery.

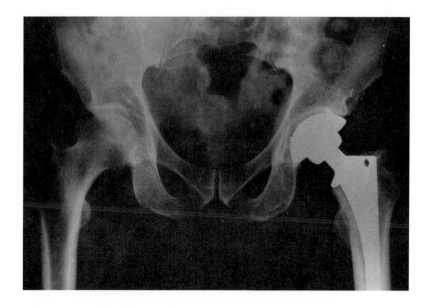

21:9   Arthritis

Arthritis is an inflammation of the joints.

Arthritis is a general term that includes over 100 diseases, all of which involve inflammation. Out of the millions of people who have this disease, most suffer from one of two kinds.

The first kind of arthritis is osteoarthritis. **Osteoarthritis** is a wearing down of the moving parts of a joint. It usually occurs due to wear and tear. Some cases of osteoarthritis appear to be hereditary. Other cases are caused by physical damage, such as sports injuries. Being overweight can be a factor in the disease since it is believed that extra weight adds stress on a joint.

Exercise may be used to improve joint movement for a person who has osteoarthritis.

Treatment for osteoarthritis often consists of aspirin and other pain relievers. Exercise can sometimes improve movement in a joint area. In some cases, surgery is needed to implant new joints. These joints are usually made of plastic and are joined to the bone with special cements.

The second kind of arthritis is rheumatoid arthritis. **Rheumatoid arthritis** is a serious disease in which joint deformity and loss of joint function occurs. This type of arthritis most often affects people between the ages of 20 and 55, but it can also affect children.

Rheumatoid arthritis may result in joint deformity.

It is important for people with this kind of arthritis to carefully follow a prescribed plan of exercise. Once movement in a joint is lost, it is difficult to regain. Certain medications, including aspirin, can be used to treat rheumatoid arthritis. At other times, cortisone is prescribed to reduce swelling and ease pain. However, cortisone has strong side effects and often cannot be used on a regular basis. Sometimes, surgery is needed to relieve pain and improve movement in the joint.

21:10 Allergies

About one out of seven people in the United States today has an allergy. An **allergy** is a reaction of the body to a certain substance. Among the many reactions that may occur are asthma, hives, and hay fever. The substances that cause allergic reactions are called allergens.

Allergens affect specific parts of the body in susceptible people. For example, allergens that are blown through the air and collect on the mucous membranes of the nose and eyes cause hay fever. Other allergies may affect the skin. Eczema is a skin allergy in which the skin becomes red, swollen, crusty, and scaly.

Allergies may develop gradually. An allergic reaction may not occur upon first exposure to an allergen. With repeated exposure, the body becomes more sensitive. To reduce the effects of allergens, two treatment objectives are usually implemented. One treatment objective is removal of the allergen. This is possible with the removal of certain foods. However, avoidance is sometimes impossible, such as from pollen that is in the air.

Changing the sensitivity to allergens is another treatment objective. This is done by injecting an extract of the allergen to which the person is reacting. Increased amounts of the specific allergen is injected until a maximum tolerance dose is reached. This results in lessening of sensitivity. It takes several years of this type of therapy before sensitivity is lost.

FIGURE 21–8. A medic–alert tag alerts other people to a person's allergy. In an emergency, this person could receive immediate and appropriate help.

Allergies can be treated by removing specific allergens.

21:11 Cerebral Palsy

Cerebral palsy is a nervous system disorder that involves nerve and muscle coordination. The exact cause of this disorder is unknown although some factors have been isolated. Brain damage from an injury may cause cerebral palsy. It may also be caused by pressure on a baby's head during birth. The pressure may restrict the flow of oxygen to the brain.

If a person has cerebral palsy, the following symptoms may occur.
- poor muscle coordination
- an awkward way of walking
- loss of balance
- problems standing or walking
- difficulty in speaking, hearing, or seeing

Cerebral palsy is a nervous system disorder.

FIGURE 21–9. Geri Jewell has cerebral palsy. As a professional entertainer, she wants to help others understand the needs of people with disabilities and to share a positive attitude concerning her disability.

These symptoms remain with a person throughout life. While physical abilities may be affected, mental abilities may not.

Treatment for cerebral palsy focuses on having a person live as normal a life as possible. Physical, speech, and hearing therapy may be needed. Braces may be used for support and walking.

 ## Review and Reflect

4. Why can a person with epilepsy be given a license to drive a car?
5. Why should a person with diabetes limit sugar intake?
6. What is the relationship of early detection of diabetes to life span?

PHYSICAL DISABILITIES AND HANDICAPS

Persons with disabilities can achieve optimum health.

Franklin Roosevelt, Beethoven, and Helen Keller were famous and successful people at meeting their goals. They also were able to overcome particular obstacles that would prevent many people from being at their best.

21:12 Defining Disabilities and Handicaps

Franklin Roosevelt was confined to a wheelchair because of polio. Beethoven, a musical genius, could not hear. Helen Keller could not see or hear, but she realized her potential by helping others to realize theirs. Each of these individuals had a disability. A **disability** is a physical or a mental impairment. It may result from a birth defect, an accident, illness, or disease.

People with disabilities may be limited in what they can do. The limit that is set by a disability is called a **handicap.** Some people with disabilities have handicaps while others do not. However, a handicap does not need to limit what a person wants to be. Homer, a great poet, could not see. He wrote poetry that is read and studied in high school and university classes throughout the world. His handicap did not prevent him from expressing his creative talent.

Physical disabilities affect many people in all walks of life. Among these are being unable to see, hear, or walk. Mental disabilities were discussed in Chapter 6. Many people are disabled and handicapped because they have a disease that has been described in this chapter.

One area of concern today focuses on the rights of persons with handicaps. People with and without handicaps have worked hard for the passage of laws and changes in policy to accommodate the needs of persons with handicaps. This has resulted in many constructive changes.

There are many types of physical disabilities.

Special accommodations have been made to help people who have handicaps.

FIGURE 21–10. Many people with handicaps are able to learn difficult and precise skills.

Many television shows have made special accommodations for the hearing impaired. Libraries have increased the number of books in braille that are available to people who are sight impaired or sightless. Office buildings, schools, and other public buildings must follow government mandates to have physical facilities that are accessible to persons in wheelchairs.

 ## Activity: <u>Being Without Sight</u>

This activity will simulate what it is like for people who cannot see. Select a partner to lead you around your classroom while your eyes are closed. Then switch positions so that you can lead your partner whose eyes are now closed. Discuss the following questions: What was it like to be guided while you could not see? What fears did you have? What did your partner do that was most helpful to you? How can you be helpful to someone who cannot see? Describe how a person who cannot see could experience optimum health.

▶ Review and Reflect

7. Describe why an event such as the Wheelchair Olympics has many benefits to its participants.
8. What is the difference between a disability and a handicap?

Health
ADVANCES

Imagine how difficult it must be for people with arthritis to perform tasks such as twisting a cap off a bottle or getting out of bed in the morning. When unable to perform these simple tasks, many people begin to feel desperate. They try just about anything to cure their arthritis. They may go to foreign countries for special treatments, or pay large sums of money for the relief of arthritic pain. Yet, the fact remains that there are no cures for arthritis. However, certain procedures are being used on an experimental basis and hold some hope for millions of arthritis sufferers.

21:13 Laser Beams for Arthritis

Dr. Robert Willner is a pain specialist who practices medicine in Miami, Florida. He sees many patients suffering from arthritic pain. Dr. Willner has been experimenting with a laser light to treat osteoarthritis in patients. A laser is a concentrated beam of light. A laser can be used to produce changes in the body.

Soft lasers have been used in Europe for 15 years to help heal burns, wounds, and scars due to surgery. Light has been known to have an effect on tissue metabolism in the body. Light is now being experimentally used to treat patients with osteoarthritis. The pain associated with osteoarthritis is due to blood clots in the capillaries that surround the joint. This prevents oxygen from getting to the joint, and the arthritis does not heal. Dr. Willner found that by beaming a laser on arthritic joints for a few minutes, the blood unclots in the capillaries and flows to the tissue surrounding the joints. The inflammation decreases, pain is relieved, and the injury heals.

The United States Food and Drug Administration has approved laser therapy for treating osteoarthritis on an experimental basis for study purposes only. Such studies are necessary to determine whether harmful side effects occur. It is felt that this procedure will provide one alternative to anti-inflammatory drugs, such as aspirin, which many arthritis sufferers regularly take. Aspirin and other similar drugs can produce harmful effects to the body, particularly the stomach, when used for an extended period of time. Dr. Willner has reported that he has had excellent results with laser therapy.

There is no cure for arthritis.

Experimental laser therapy is being used to treat arthritic patients.

Laser therapy helps reduce joint inflammation.

Focus on
Life Management Skills

- Take steps to become aware of genetic diseases that may exist in your family.
- Learn about the first-aid procedures needed to help a person who might have an epileptic seizure.
- Get regular medical examinations for early detection of diseases or disorders that may affect you.

CHAPTER REVIEW 21

Summary

1. Genes can be dominant or recessive and are responsible for transmitting hereditary characteristics. 21:1
2. Cells that fail to divide in a normal way cause mutations. 21:2
3. Hemophilia and muscular dystrophy are sex-linked inherited diseases. 21:3
4. Sickle-cell anemia and cystic fibrosis are recessive inherited disorders. 21:4
5. An extra or missing chromosome can cause Down syndrome, Klinefelter syndrome, or Turner syndrome. 21:5
6. Epilepsy is characterized by partial or generalized seizures. 21:6
7. MS is a progressive disease in which there is a breakdown of the nerve fiber coverings in the brain and spinal cord. 21:7
8. A person who has diabetes has an inability to process sugar in foods. 21:8
9. Arthritis is a general term for a number of diseases characterized by inflammation of the joints. 21:9
10. Any number of substances can produce reactions in the body called allergies. 21:10
11. Cerebral palsy is a nervous system disorder that affects people throughout their lives. 21:11
12. People with disabilities or handicaps can learn to function at their best. 21:12
13. Laser beams are being used experimentally to help treat arthritis. 21:13

Vocabulary

Below is a list of vocabulary words used in this chapter. Use each word only once to complete the sentences. Do not write in this book.

cystic fibrosis
diabetes
Down syndrome
hemophilia
multiple sclerosis
mutation
osteoarthritis
recessive gene
Tay-Sachs
Turner syndrome

1. A(n) _____ results when a cell fails to divide in a normal way.
2. A person with _____ has difficulty producing insulin.
3. _____ results when a female is missing an X chromosome.
4. Some cases of _____ may be hereditary, while others may be caused by sports injuries.
5. A gene that is not expressed is called a(n) _____.
6. A person whose blood fails to clot has _____.
7. A breakdown of nerve fibers in the brain results in a disease called _____.
8. _____ is a disease that affects the mucous and sweat glands.
9. A person with _____ disease has an inability to break down fats in the body.
10. A child with _____ has 47 chromosomes instead of the usual 46.

Review

1. How does a recessive gene differ from a dominant gene?
2. Describe how mutations can occur.
3. Why do sex-linked inherited disorders appear more often in one sex?
4. Why can a minor injury be dangerous to a person with hemophilia?
5. How does sickle-cell trait differ from sickle-cell anemia?
6. What are the effects of Tay-Sachs disease?
7. How do the causes of Klinefelter syndrome and Turner syndrome differ?
8. Why is early diagnosis of epilepsy important?
9. How might you know if a person has MS?
10. Differentiate between a disability and a handicap.

Application

1. What can you do to reduce the risks of mutations that result from radiation?
2. What can you do to be sure a person in your class with hemophilia is kept safe from injury?
3. What can you do to assist a person with arthritis?

Individual Research

1. Select a chronic disease not discussed in this chapter and describe the latest research attempts to treat or cure this disease. Resources in your school or public library will be helpful.
2. Write to a health organization that focuses on a specific chronic disease and ask for brochures and pamphlets related to this disease. A librarian may help you locate an appropriate agency.
3. Select any handicap and describe what is being done to help people with this handicap lead healthful and productive lives.

Readings

Hart, Frank D., *Overcoming Arthritis.* New York, NY: Arco Publishing, Inc., 1981.

Kahn, Ada P., *Help Yourself to Health: Diabetes.* Chicago, IL: Contemporary Books, Inc., 1983.

Soll, Robert W., and Grenoble, Penelope B., *M.S.: Something Can be Done and You Can Do It.* Chicago, IL: Contemporary Books, Inc., 1984.

Consumer and Personal Health

CONSUMER AND PERSONAL HEALTH

The theme of this textbook is making responsible decisions about your health and well-being. You are learning that this involves the development of skills that will assist you in becoming autonomous. These skills involve the wise use of your money and time as well as managing your personal health. In this unit, you will study about making intelligent consumer choices, what agencies protect you, and what to do when you suspect fraud. You will also study about personal health management and the health-care delivery system.

SOCIAL

MENTAL

PHYSICAL

Time and money. Everyone spends both. Learning to spend time and money wisely is a skill. Who influences the way you spend time? How do you spend your money?

Chapter 22

Consumer Health

OBJECTIVES: You will be able to

- identify and describe the components of consumer health.
- describe how consumers are influenced and protected.
- identify procedures for making a consumer complaint.

In earlier chapters, you have considered the importance of self-responsibility and the factors that play a role in the quality of your life. You are learning that your choices are very important. Many of your choices are made as a consumer.

BEING A RESPONSIBLE CONSUMER

A **consumer** is a person who buys or uses products and services and who makes choices about how to spend time. Suppose you had to buy shampoo for your hair. You go into the drugstore and notice over a dozen different kinds of shampoo. Some of these products contain different ingredients. Others have different instructions for use. Some come in tubes while others are in plastic bottles. The prices may vary several dollars from the least expensive to the most expensive. Which shampoo should you buy? What factors would need to be considered before you make your choice?

A consumer makes choices about the use of money and time.

22:1 What Is Consumer Health?

Two key words were introduced in the definition of a consumer—products and services. Products are material goods, such as food and clothing, that are made for consumers to purchase. Services are activities that are provided for people.

443

Consumer health emphasizes the wise expenditure of money and time on health products and services.

Medical care and garbage pickup are examples of services. In this chapter, you are going to focus on one aspect of the consumer—that of health. Thus, the term consumer health is used in this chapter title. **Consumer health** is the study of products and services that have an effect on health. Emphasis is placed on making responsible decisions about spending money and time.

Think back to the chapter opening example about shampoo. Shampoo is an example of a product concerned with health. To make a decision about which shampoo to buy, certain factors have to be considered. One of these factors centers around the kinds and amounts of ingredients in the shampoo. Another factor to consider is the price of the shampoo.

Price and quality are important factors to consider when choosing a health product.

Now, think about the health services you might use. Suppose you visit a physician for an illness. To make a decision about this health service, you will need information about the physician's qualifications. You will also want to know what the physician charges for the service you need. Unless you make a responsible decision, you may waste money. You may also waste time. Consumer health involves having knowledge about health products and services as well as understanding the economics and use of your time. Consumer health involves decisions about whether or not health products and services are worth your money and time.

The qualifications of persons involved is important when choosing health services.

22:2 Budgeting Money

Learning to manage your money is one of the skills needed to become an autonomous adult. One way to manage your money is to have a budget. A **budget** is a plan for spending and saving the money you have. Your budget involves planning your income, your expenses, and your savings. Your **income** is the money you receive from different sources. You may receive an allowance for mowing the grass, washing the dishes, or helping with other household chores. You may have a part-time job. Perhaps you received money for your birthday. Your **expenses** are the items you need and want to buy. Perhaps some of the money you earn is used to help with family expenses. If you are old enough to drive, you may need to purchase gasoline and insurance. You need money to spend on dates. You may set money aside to give to a religious or charitable organization.

A carefully planned budget includes income, expenses, and savings.

Your **savings** is the money you set aside for future use. You may be saving to buy a new pair of running shoes in the near future. You may be saving to help pay for technical school or college expenses or to buy a car sometime in the future. You may be saving for the future and the time when you will be living on your own. It is important to consider savings for use in the near future and distant future.

Research indicates that people who have a budget are less likely to purchase unnecessary items and more likely to have savings. Your ability to make a budget and follow it closely today will be helpful in the future. Your understanding of your family's budget will also help you to budget money as an adult. You will be developing some skills of a responsible consumer.

Most family budgets include expenses for groceries, medical care, clothing, cosmetics, and entertainment. Table 22–1 identifies helpful suggestions for the consumer when purchasing these items.

Persons with a budget are usually less wasteful than those without one.

Adolescents can help parents by following guidelines for the family budget.

Table 22–1 Some Helpful Suggestions for a Consumer

CLOTHING

- Compare prices at several stores.
- Learn the store's policy on returned goods.
- Find out when the clothing sales are during the year.
- Read the labels and tags before you purchase clothes.
- Select clothes that will fit for a long time.
- Try to buy color-coordinated outfits to mix and match.
- Take care of your clothes so they will last as long as possible.

COSMETICS

- Read labels to check ingredients.
- Compare unit prices of different brands.
- Write the manufacturers when you have questions.
- Read the directions to learn the safe way to use cosmetics.
- Observe the warnings and check for side effects.
- Test products by trying a small amount first.

MEDICAL & DENTAL CARE

- Have regular checkups to avoid serious health problems.
- Keep all your appointments or call at least one day ahead if you must cancel.
- Ask the physician or dentist questions and follow directions.
- Practice preventive health habits between visits.

GROCERIES

- Read labels and compare unit prices.
- Avoid shopping when you are hungry.
- Make a grocery list and purchase only those items.
- Use coupons only for things on your grocery list.
- Do not buy foods that are in opened, bent, or bulging cans.
- Do not buy frozen foods that are soft or that show signs of leaking.

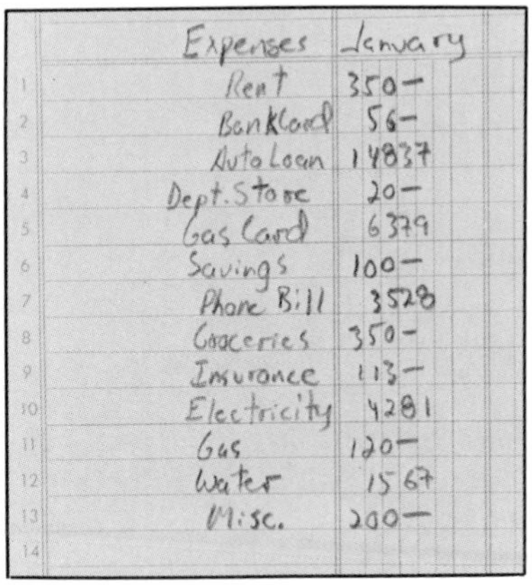

Expenses	January
1	Rent	350—
2	BankCard	56—
3	Auto Loan	14837
4	Dept. Store	20—
5	Gas Card	6379
6	Savings	100—
7	Phone Bill	3528
8	Groceries	350—
9	Insurance	113—
10	Electricity	4281
11	Gas	120—
12	Water	1567
13	Misc.	200—
14		

FIGURE 22–1. It is important to keep a record of all income and expenses.

A time management plan should include time for healthful activities.

When making a time management plan, you must plan first for necessary activities.

Other important items to include in a budget are housing, utilities, household furnishings, child care, insurance, and transportation expenses. Your family also budgets for savings. Perhaps your family has savings that will cover future educational expenses for you and your brothers or sisters. Discuss the importance of a family budget with your parents or guardian. Ask them how you can help maintain the family's budget.

22:3 Budgeting Time

Often people think of consumer health only in terms of spending money on products and services. Their concern is to avoid wasting money. It is just as important to avoid wasting time. Suppose you have a major school project due in two weeks. Will you start working on it now? Will you plan your time so that you will not have to do a frantic job at the last minute? Or, perhaps you have two hours between your last class and the start of basketball practice. How will you use the two hours? Will you accomplish something or will you waste the time?

As a consumer, you need to be careful about the use of your time. You are more likely to achieve balanced physical, mental, and social health when you value your time and use it wisely. Just as you need a budget to plan wisely for spending and saving, you also need a time management plan. A **time management plan** is a plan that shows the time you will allocate for activities you do regularly and for leisure activities. Persons who have a budget spend less money on unnecessary items. They do not waste money. It is also true that persons who make a time management plan accomplish more. They do not waste time. They plan their time to include activities that should be done to promote health.

To make a time management plan, you must first identify the daily activities for which you are responsible. The list below includes some examples. Next to each activity is the area of health that is promoted when you plan time to complete the activity.

Talking with Family Members	• Family and Social Health
Attending School	• Mental Health
Cleaning Room	• Environmental Health
Household Chores	• Family Health
Eating Balanced Meals	• Nutritional Health
Exercising	• Exercise and Fitness
Attending to Grooming Needs	• Personal Health

FIGURE 22–2. Time management plan list

After you have completed a time management plan, it is important to evaluate the effectiveness of your plan. Do you complete the activities you must do? Do you make time for the activities that promote mental, social, and physical health? Is some of your time spent improving your critical thinking (mental health)? Is some of your time spent improving your relationships with family and friends (social health)? Is some of your time spent improving your fitness level (physical health)?

Regularly evaluate the effectiveness of your time management plan.

 ## Review and Reflect

1. Why are you a consumer when you buy a book about skin care?
2. Why are you a consumer when you have a tooth cavity filled by a dentist?
3. How will having a budget now help you in the future?
4. Why is it important to have a time management plan?

MAKING RESPONSIBLE CONSUMER CHOICES

By planning a budget and making a time management plan, you are developing skills to become a responsible consumer. However, others will try to influence how you spend your money and time. You will need to be aware of these influences when you make decisions about your money and time.

There are many influences on consumer choices.

22:4 Influence of Family and Friends

Your family and their values probably have the greatest influence on how you spend your money and time. For example, if your family values sports activities, you may spend time and money participating in various sports. If your family values eating a healthful diet, you may read food labels before purchasing food. You may be selective about restaurants you choose when you eat out. Suppose your family lacks knowledge about the healthful food groups, caloric intake, and caloric expenditure. Your family might try a fad diet that would not be healthful. This is an important reason for you to study health in school. You are gaining knowledge about many subjects so that you will make responsible choices.

Your family's values influence how you spend your time and money.

FIGURE 22–3. Peer pressure is a factor when a teenager shops for clothes.

Your family's income influences priorities for consumer expenditures.

Your peers may try to influence how you spend your time and money.

The amount of family income influences consumer choices too. Families must set priorities. A family member may wish to purchase a pair of designer jeans. However, the available money may be needed for repair of the family car instead. Suppose you would like to go to a movie tonight. However, your parents need you to babysit for a younger brother or sister to avoid paying someone else to babysit. Sometimes it is difficult to give up what you would like to buy or do with your time. Because there are limits on the money and time a family has, responsible choices must be made for the benefit of the whole family.

In earlier chapters, you learned about peer pressure. Peer pressure can lead to healthful or harmful consumer choices. For example, if your peers influence you to study harder, their pressure is healthful because you derive positive benefits. If your peers try to influence you to spend money on cigarettes, their pressure is harmful because the money is spent on a product that will harm you.

Think about the clothes you wear, the records you buy, the way you have your hair cut, and the leisure activities you choose. How much influence do your peers have on the choices you make? Are you able to examine the physical, mental, and social benefits of how you spend your time as well as the choices you make? Remember that learning to be an autonomous adult means learning to make responsible decisions without being swayed by peers.

22:5 Advertisements

The advertisements in magazines and newspapers and the commercials on television are all designed to influence you. Think about a product you saw advertised for the first time on television or in a magazine. **Advertising** is a form of selling in which you are informed of products and services. An **advertisement** or **ad** is a paid announcement. An ad on television or radio is called a commercial.

Sellers pay money for their advertisements so they can tell you about their products and/or services. Different products and services are advertised on television and radio and in magazines and newspapers. The ads appear in places to be seen or heard by the consumer who is most likely to desire the product. For example, toys and games are shown during commercials in children's television shows. Clothes for teens are advertised in a teen magazine.

Sellers use a variety of techniques in their ads to try to make their products and services appeal to you more than those from their competitors. Be familiar with the following common advertising techniques so that you can analyze ads.

- A *bandwagon appeal* approach tries to convince you that everyone wants this product or service and you should too. "Three out of four physicians recommend this product."
- When advertisements tell you that one brand is best, it is *brand loyalty appeal*. "This product is the original one that has been around for 50 years."
- In *false image appeal*, you are encouraged to see yourself in a certain way if you use a product. The image is false because it is not the way you are. "Wouldn't you like to see your hair color like this?"

FIGURE 22–4. Advertising on television is a major source of consumer information.

FIGURE 22–5. Advertisers use many kinds of slogans in their ads.

- A *glittering generality* is a general statement that is exaggerated. If you do not pay attention to details, you will believe the statement. "Brand X contains greater pain fighters than Brand Y."

A seller may use humor to catch your attention about a product or service.

- *Humor appeal* is the use of a slogan, jingle, or cartoon to catch your attention. "Grow muscle with Hustle—the muscle strength medicine."
- *Just plain folks appeal* tells you that there are no surprises or gimmicks because this product is for the common person. "Just ask for Joe."
- When *progress appeal* is used, you are told that an old product has become much better than before. Sometimes just the package has changed. "Now 20 percent more effective"

A seller may promise you a reward if you purchase a product.

- In *reward appeal* you are told that if you buy one product or service you get something else. You may get coupons or stamps as a free enclosure. "Free sticker in each box of Sweet Cinnamon Tiger Cereal"
- When *scientific evidence appeal* is used, you are given the results of surveys or laboratory tests to give you confidence in your purchase. "A noted researcher claims our product prevents aging."

A seller may promise that you will be better than others with a certain product.

- An ad using *snob appeal* tells you that you deserve the best. By buying the best, you are better than others. "You'll be the talk of the neighborhood in our robot shoes."
- *Testimony appeal* is an appeal by a well-known person who says a product is the best one for you. "I use Snow Suds because it makes my wash whiter."

Activity: Advertisement Appeal

Divide into groups of four. Collect several old magazines. Refer to the list of advertising techniques. Find one ad for each of the 11 techniques described. Examine the ads for hidden messages. Tell how each ad fits each technique. As a group, make a list of at least five reasons why it is important to analyze ads. Share your list with the other groups in your class.

22:6 Quacks and Quackery

Your choices are influenced by family, friends, and advertising. Choices may also be influenced by other factors. Fear of illness, aging, death, and pain may strongly influence a consumer's choice. The fear of being unattractive and unpopular is also a powerful influence. Unfortunately, these fears may prompt a consumer to select an ineffective or harmful health product or service that wastes both money and time. Each year more than ten billion dollars is wasted on quackery. **Quackery** is the promotion and selling of ineffective or harmful products and services. A **quack** is a person who promotes or sells ineffective or harmful health products and/or services.

Why is quackery profitable? Why are quacks so successful? Illness, aging, death, and pain are uncomfortable experiences for many persons. Many fear being unattractive or unpopular. A quack uses these fears to make sales. As you might imagine, persons with diseases such as arthritis or cancer are the target of much quackery. Persons who have these diseases want to live longer and more healthful lives without pain. The quack promises results that appeal to their needs. Unfortunately, much money and time is wasted. The wasted time may delay getting effective care from a competent physician.

The fountain-of-youth concept is another motivator that entices many consumers to fall prey to quackery. The promise of beautiful skin without wrinkles may motivate a consumer to buy an ineffective product. The quack works on a person's emotions to make a sale.

A particular concern for teenagers involves not being attractive and popular. Quacks capitalize on these fears and try to persuade teens to buy products guaranteed to help lose weight or to clear up acne. Other devices include products that claim to develop a larger bust or make you grow taller. Remember, these concerns should be discussed with your parents or guardian and your family physician.

Consumer choices may be influenced by fears of illness, aging, death, or pain.

A quack uses quackery to promote harmful products and services.

Persons with arthritis or cancer may delay effective care if they are influenced by quackery.

Teenagers may be influenced by quacks if they are overly concerned about popularity.

There are ten questions you can ask to help recognize quackery.

Table 22–2 How To Recognize Quackery

- Does the seller of the product or service claim that the medical profession does not recognize this product or service?
- Does the seller claim that the product or service is unknown to the medical profession?
- Does the seller claim that the traditional medical treatment such as X rays and surgery is more harmful than healthful?
- Is the product or service sold door-to-door rather than at a reliable place?
- Is the product or service advertised in a publication that gives only a post office box number for an address?
- Is the product or service promoted by a person or a group of persons about whom you know very little?
- Is the product or service claimed to be useful in the treatment and cure of several diseases or ailments?
- Does the seller use testimonials or before-and-after pictures from satisfied customers?
- Does the seller use scare tactics that play on fears?
- Does the seller guarantee a quick cure or a cure for an incurable disease?

You can avoid quackery if you are aware of your fears and know how to recognize quackery.

How can you avoid quackery? First, understand your emotions. Be aware of your fears if you have any. Know what you would like to change about yourself. Second, recognize signals that can alert you that quackery is being used (Table 22–2). Refer to each question in the table. If one or more of the answers to these questions is yes, you should suspect quackery.

22:7 Consumer Protectors

Consumers are protected by governmental agencies and public, private, and professional associations.

As a consumer, you are protected from individuals and organizations that are deceptive by governmental agencies and public, private, and professional associations. You have the greatest protection when you know how each of these agencies and associations operate and how you can use them.

Governmental Agencies

The **Food and Drug Administration** (FDA) is a federal agency within the Department of Health and Human Services that checks the safety and effectiveness of drugs and medical devices and the purity and safety of foods and cosmetics.

The **Federal Trade Commission** (FTC) is an independent agency of the United States. It deals with advertising for foods, drugs, cosmetics, devices, and all advertising on national television. It fosters effective consumer protection at state and local levels.

The **United States Postal Service** protects the public against the use of mail fraud to promote products, devices, or services.

The **Office of Consumer Affairs** represents the interests of the consumer to the President of the United States and represents the President to the consumer. This agency investigates consumer problems, coordinates research, conducts seminars on consumer issues, and assists state and local governments in protecting consumer interests.

The **Consumer Product Safety Commission** develops and enforces safety standards for household products.

State and Local Agencies and Associations

State health departments usually have a consumer affairs office that takes action when harmful products are sold within the state.

Local or city health departments often have a consumer affairs department that takes action when there is consumer fraud at the city or local level; the Legal Aid Department may assist in consumer cases.

Professional Associations

The **American Medical Association** (AMA) is a professional association for medical physicians. It sets standards for the education and conduct of medical physicians who are members. AMA has a Department of Investigation and a Department of Health Education to assist the consumer and the medical profession.

The **American Dental Association** (ADA) is a professional association for dentists. It sets standards and rules of conduct for its members and assists in public education for consumers.

Private and Consumer Agencies

The **Better Business Bureau** is a nonprofit, voluntary, self-regulating organization supported by private firms for their protection against unfair competition and misleading advertising. This agency works closely with businesses to resolve problems with consumers. The agency has no legal power but encourages businesses to maintain a favorable reputation and distributes educational materials for consumers.

The FDA checks the safety and effectiveness of drugs and medical devices and the purity and safety of foods and cosmetics.

The FTC protects the consumer against faulty advertising.

The President works closely with the Office of Consumer Affairs.

State, local, and city health departments have consumer affairs offices to stop fraud.

The AMA and the ADA are examples of professional associations that protect consumers by setting standards for their members.

The BBB works closely with businesses to resolve problems with consumers.

The **Consumers' Research** and **Consumers' Union** are private groups that test and rate products on an impartial basis. They are supported by donations and by the sales of their publications. These publications compare prices, performance, and safety of a variety of brand name products.

22:8   The National Consumers' League

No government, public, private, or professional agency or association can give you complete consumer protection. You have an individual responsibility as a consumer to be informed and to take action when appropriate.

Consumers are joining together to take necessary action to stop faulty advertising and selling. Consumers want products and services to be safe and healthful and to be a wise expenditure of time and money. One such group of consumers is the National Consumers' League. The National Consumers' League suggests these steps to follow when there is a valid complaint.

1. Keep records including sales slips, receipts, and canceled checks.
2. Start the complaint where the purchase was made.
3. If unsuccessful, put the complaint in writing and send it to the president of the company. Type the letter, date it, and keep a file copy. If necessary, send the letter by certified mail with a return receipt requested.
4. If the initial letter brings no satisfaction, make photocopies of the letter and send it to city, county, or state voluntary consumer groups, the state's attorney general, the local Better Business Bureau, the state's consumer affairs office, a senator, or a member of congress.
5. If the company is involved in interstate commerce, bring the problem to the FTC or the FDA.
6. Be sure to advise the original company that these additional steps are being taken. This is most important.
7. If the company has a misleading or deceptive ad in a local news media, tell the station or newspaper involved and encourage them to stop running the ad.
8. If these steps prove ineffective, contact a local voluntary consumer organization. Some voluntary groups will write letters and make visits to the offending business on your behalf. Government agencies often send out investigators and will take action if it is justified.

Your original complaint should be made to the source, then to the company president.

When you are not satisfied after making a consumer complaint, you might contact a voluntary consumer organization or a governmental agency.

9. Finally, you may sue the business in a small claims court. This court will process suits to recover moderate amounts of money; the limit is usually $750. No lawyers are used, and the fee to the consumer is kept to a minimum.

 ## Review and Reflect

5. In what ways can peers influence consumer choices?
6. Why are advertisements on prime time TV expensive?
7. Why do athletes often appear in commercials?
8. Why is quackery profitable?
9. Why might someone with arthritis send away for an expensive product that claims to cure arthritis?
10. Whom would you contact if you purchased a useless product through the mail?

Focus on Life Management Skills

- Make a budget to plan for your income, expenses, and savings.
- Shop wisely when making decisions about groceries, medical care, clothing, cosmetics, and entertainment.
- Make a time management plan that includes activities that promote physical, mental, and social health.
- Examine personal and family values and budget before making choices about how to spend time or money on products and services.
- Learn to be autonomous in your consumer choices rather than being swayed by peers.
- Analyze advertisements to learn why they appeal to you before purchasing the product or service that was advertised.
- Know the clues for recognizing quackery.
- Be familiar with the various governmental agencies, professional associations, and private associations that promote and protect consumer health.
- Follow the guidelines from the National Consumers' League for taking action when you have a complaint.

Summary

1. A responsible consumer uses or purchases health products and services that are worth the time and money spent. **22:1**
2. A responsible consumer makes and follows a budget that promotes optimum health. **22:2**
3. A responsible consumer makes and follows a time management plan that promotes optimum health. **22:3**
4. Family values, income, and knowledge, as well as the attitudes of peers, may influence consumer choices. **22:4**
5. Advertisements in magazines and newspapers and commercials on television are designed to influence consumer choices. **22:5**
6. Fear of pain, illness, aging, and death has led many consumers to waste money and time on products and services sold by quacks. **22:6**
7. There are several government, state, local, professional, and private agencies and associations that protect and promote consumer health. **22:7**
8. The National Consumers' League is a group of consumers who want products and services to be safe and healthful and worth the time and money used for them. **22:8**

Vocabulary

Below is a list of vocabulary words used in this chapter. Use each word only once to complete the sentences. Do not write in this book.

advertisement
budget
consumer health
Federal Trade
  Commission
Food and Drug
  Administration
Office of
  Consumer Affairs
quack
quackery
time management
  plan
United States
  Postal Service

1. A(n) _____ is a person who promotes the sale of useless health products or services.
2. The study of _____ includes learning information that will help you choose products and services that are worth your time and money.
3. If you make and follow a(n) _____, you are less likely to purchase unnecessary items.
4. The public is protected from the use of mail fraud by the _____.
5. Your _____ should allow specific times for activities that promote physical, mental, and social health.
6. Each year consumers spend money purchasing useless health care products that were promoted by _____.
7. A(n) _____ promotes a product by appealing to you as a consumer.
8. The _____ checks the purity and safety of foods and cosmetics.
9. Regulation of all advertisements on national television is the responsibility of the _____.
10. The _____ investigates consumer problems, coordinates research, and conducts seminars on consumer issues.

Review

1. What is the emphasis of consumer health?
2. What are two different kinds of savings?
3. What does research show about persons who make and follow a budget?
4. What questions might you ask to evaluate the effectiveness of your time management plan?
5. What are three ways that your family influences your consumer choices?
6. What are 11 types of appeals used in advertisements and commercials to influence consumers?
7. What are four types of fears that make it easier for quacks to sell health products and services?
8. What are ten ways to recognize quackery?
9. List the (a) governmental agencies, (b) state and local agencies and associations, (c) professional associations, and (d) private consumer agencies that protect and promote health.
10. List the nine steps to follow for a consumer complaint that are suggested by the National Consumers' League.

Application

1. Peers may have a healthful or harmful influence on consumer choices. Identify two ways you might influence your peers in a healthful way.
2. Someone you know has athlete's foot. This person sees an ad in a magazine for a new cure that is advertised to be 100 percent foolproof. Your friend wants to send a check for $10.00 to the post office box address given in the ad. What would you advise your friend to do? Why?

Individual Research

1. Write a sample letter to the FDA that describes a skin rash that you developed from the use of a skin lotion.
2. Interview someone at the local chapter of the Arthritis Foundation or the American Cancer Society to learn about possible quackery at the local level. Write a two-page report.
3. Locate a magazine article that compares two similar health products or services. Discuss the comparisons. Which product or service would you choose? Why?

Readings

Braverman, Jordan, *The Consumer's Book of Health*. Philadelphia, PA: W. B. Saunders Company, 1982.

Cornacchia, Harold J., and Barrett, Stephen, *Consumer Health*. St. Louis, MO: C. V. Mosby, Co., 1985.

Many people put off planning for health care until they have an illness. Others plan to maintain optimum health. They are informed about the status of their own health and the health care they may need someday. They make responsible decisions for their present and future needs. What plans do you have for your health needs?

Chapter 23

Planning for Health Care

OBJECTIVES: You will be able to
- **describe the components of personal health management and outline responsibilities for self-care.**
- **identify and describe the services of health-care providers.**
- **identify and describe health-care facilities.**
- **identify and describe three broad areas of health insurance.**

Achieving and maintaining optimum health should be a top priority for you throughout your entire life. There are several means by which you can achieve optimum health. You can follow self-care practices that promote your well-being. You will need to gain knowledge to follow these practices. You may read health magazines or books. You may watch health-related programs on television. You can develop an awareness of the health-care delivery system that is available to you. The health-care delivery system is made up of the people, places, and plans that assist you in meeting your health-care needs.

Optimum health can be achieved by several means.

MANAGING YOUR HEALTH

In today's health environment, there is a trend toward becoming an informed health consumer. An informed health consumer is a person who can take responsibility for deciding when professional health care is needed and when health problems can be treated without professional care. Many physicians have welcomed this new awareness. They believe that an informed patient is a more responsible patient. An informed patient who understands the basic principles of self-care is a valuable partner in the health-care team.

People are assuming more responsibility for their health care.

459

23:1 Personal Health Management

An autonomous adult is responsible for personal health management.

Personal health management, or planning for your health care, is a major step in becoming an autonomous adult. **Personal health management** involves
- self-care that promotes your well-being.
- keeping your own personal health-care records.
- choosing and visiting a physician for regular physical examinations.
- getting medical care for injuries and illnesses.
- choosing and visiting a dentist for regular dental examinations and preventive dental care.
- choosing health-care facilities when necessary.
- arranging for payment of health-care services.

Your parents or guardian have been taking care of you. They have provided medical and dental care as you have needed it. They have kept records of your health and the care you have received. Someday, you will assume the responsibility of keeping your own records. A personal health record is a history of your personal health, of the health care that you have had, the health facilities you have used, and the health insurance policies that you own. Some of the items that might be included in a personal health record appear in Table 23–1.

A personal health record describes how you have managed your health.

Table 23–1 Personal Health Record

PERSONAL HEALTH RECORD

I Personal Health History
A. record of growth and development
B. record of habits

II Family Health History
A. record of parents' habits
B. blood relatives' medical history

III Health Care
A. dates and results of previous physicals
B. eye examination
C. hearing examination
D. immunization history
E. childhood diseases
F. other diseases

IV Health Facilities Used
A. hospitalization record
B. emergency care record

V Health Insurance Policies

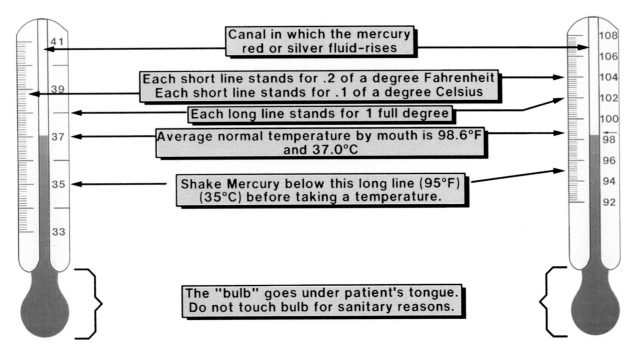

Canal in which the mercury red or silver fluid-rises

Each short line stands for .2 of a degree Fahrenheit
Each short line stands for .1 of a degree Celsius

Each long line stands for 1 full degree

Average normal temperature by mouth is 98.6°F and 37.0°C

Shake Mercury below this long line (95°F) (35°C) before taking a temperature.

The "bulb" goes under patient's tongue. Do not touch bulb for sanitary reasons.

FIGURE 23–1. The thermometer on the left is Celsius and the thermometer on the right is Fahrenheit.

23:2 Understanding Your Normal Health Signs

To begin to take responsibility for your own health, it is important to understand the normal indicators of your own health. These indicators relate to your body temperature, respiration, pulse, and blood pressure.

Body temperature For most people, normal temperature is 98.6° Fahrenheit (37° Celsius). This is an average figure. Your normal body temperature may vary as much as a degree or more—usually below the 98.6° mark on the thermometer. See Figure 23–1 for ways to use and read a thermometer. A body temperature above 98.6° often indicates an infection somewhere in the body. Temperature may also vary temporarily with the amount of physical activity performed. In women, it may vary during the menstrual cycle. Physical symptoms that accompany a change in your normal body temperature may require professional help. Sometimes a telephone call to the physician's office is all that is needed to determine how to proceed if your body temperature is not normal. You and your parents should make a decision to seek professional care when in doubt about the seriousness of any condition.

Respiration Respiration is another important factor to consider when determining your health-care needs. A person your age

The normal body temperature averages about 98.6° Fahrenheit (37° Celsius).

FIGURE 23–2. Pulse rate is an indicator of a person's health.

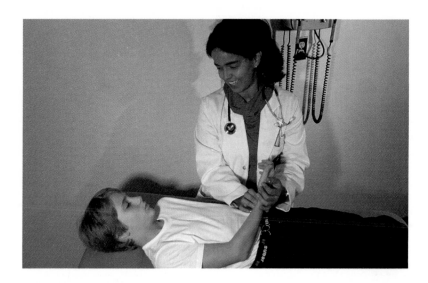

Normal respiration is 12 to 15 breaths per minute.

has a normal respiration rate of 12 to 15 breaths a minute. To measure your respiration, count the number of your breaths for three minutes. Divide the total number of breaths by three. This will give your average breathing rate for one minute. In addition to your breathing rate, you should become aware of other aspects of your breathing. Do you hear any abnormal sounds? Is your breathing too shallow or too deep? This kind of information about your normal breathing habits is important for both you and your physician in determining a diagnosis in case you become ill.

Pulse Being aware of your average pulse rate can also help you make decisions about your health care. The average resting pulse rate for a person your age is 60 to 90 beats a minute. A well-conditioned athlete may have a resting pulse rate as low as 40 beats a minute. When taking your pulse rate, be sure you are completely at rest. See Figure 23–2 for the correct procedure for taking your pulse rate. To determine your pulse rate for one minute, count the number of beats for 30 seconds and multiply by two. Do this several times to obtain an average. Any abnormally high or low rate should be reported to your physician.

Being aware of your average pulse rate can assist in making decisions about your health.

Blood pressure Any of the above changes might result in an abnormal blood pressure. Be aware of your normal blood pressure. Refer back to Chapter 3, Section 3:7. An abnormal blood pressure might indicate a very serious condition, and your physician should be contacted at once.

Abnormal blood pressure can result in serious physical effects.

23:3 Products that Promote Self-Care

An important and responsible aspect of self-care is knowing about products usually found in the home that can be used to treat an illness or injury. Among these products are over-the-counter drugs. OTC drugs can be dangerous when they are not used responsibly. However, there are situations in which using OTC drugs are appropriate for your self-care and health promotion. It is important that you act in consultation with a responsible adult in your home before using these products. Responsible self-care can improve your health status, but a mistake in self treatment can have lifelong effects.

OTC drugs should always be used responsibly.

What are some OTC drugs and supplies that are recommended for the home first-aid cabinet? The following items are suggested as being helpful for basic home-care needs. Remember, all medicines are to be kept out of the reach of small children. Expiration dates should be checked and medicines should be discarded when the expiration date has passed.

- adhesive tapes and bandages
- antacid
- antifungal preparations
- antihistamines, nose drops and sprays
- aspirin
- baking soda
- cold pack
- cold tablets, cough syrup
- elastic bandages
- eye drops
- heating pad
- hydrogen peroxide
- milk of magnesia
- sprays
- sunscreens
- topical dressings or ointments

23:4 Managing Your Grooming Needs

An important part of promoting your well being is to care for your grooming needs. Good grooming consists of following practices that keep your body healthy. Good grooming also helps you look and feel your best.

When you are well-groomed, you look and feel good.

Skin is one part of your body that needs daily attention. It is important to bathe and wash with soap every day. Soap breaks down oil on the skin and removes dirt that may clog pores and cause infection. There are detergent and nondetergent soaps. Detergent soaps may be more effective for removing dirt. Some soaps may be scented, but this does not make them more effective than unscented soaps.

The use of deodorants and antiperspirants is not only a personal choice but a healthful choice. A deodorant is a product used to control body odor. A deodorant may have a fragrance that disguises the odor. An antiperspirant performs the same as a deodorant, but it also helps reduce the amount of perspiration produced. It is important to understand that deodorants and antiperspirants are not substitutes for bathing. In fact, they are only effective when used following a bath or shower.

Deodorants and antiperspirants help fight body odor.

In addition to skin care, hair care is another important grooming need. Dirt and oils should be removed frequently for a

Hair care consists of brushing daily and washing with shampoo.

healthful, shiny appearance. Washing your hair at least twice a week with a shampoo will remove dirt and oil. If you are active, perspire heavily, or have an oily scalp, you may need to shampoo daily. Using a shampoo also helps control dandruff. You may need to experiment to find the type of shampoo best suited for your hair.

Combs and brushes must be kept clean and clear of accumulated hair. Brushing your hair daily helps keep it neat and clean. Brushing not only removes loose dirt but also gives your hair a natural shine. Brushing wet hair may damage the hair shaft. Use a comb on wet hair, instead of a brush. Special care should be taken when blow drying or using heat on your hair. If you blow dry your hair, use a low temperature setting. Too much heat can cause hair to become dry, brittle, and to have split ends. Split ends may also be caused by the overuse or improper use of chemicals, such as hair sprays or hair colorings, on the hair.

Special care is important when using cosmetics.

Cosmetics may be used to enhance your appearance. You may need to try several brands before finding cosmetics that are best for you. If cosmetics irritate your skin, you might try some of the nonallergenic brands. These brands are especially designed for persons with sensitive skin. Do not use cosmetics belonging to other people. Bacteria that cause eye and skin infections may be transferred this way. All cosmetics should be removed from the skin each day by using soap and water or special cleansing creams.

Contact lenses can improve sight, and in some cases, appearance.

Over the past few years, many people with vision problems have switched from wearing eyeglasses to contact lenses. Contact lenses are placed over the cornea of the eye on the surface of the eyeball. Contact lenses have several advantages over eyeglasses. They are not affected by environmental changes. They also do not reduce the rate of vision change, and they enable a wider peripheral (side) vision. Clean your contact lenses according to your physician's instructions and follow his or her advice regarding wearing time and scheduled eye examinations.

Another part of correct grooming is having clean, trimmed fingernails. Nails that are dirty and broken are unattractive and unhealthy. Fingernails can collect dirt and bacteria. They should be cleaned and trimmed often.

Poor care of the feet can cause many problems.

Finally, follow practices that promote the health of your feet. Wear comfortable shoes of the right size, wash your feet daily, and keep toenails cut straight across. If feet are not cared for, problems such as blisters, calluses, corns, and ingrown toenails may result. A blister may be caused by irritation due to the foot rubbing against the shoe. When a blister develops, cover with an adhesive bandage or a light coating of petroleum jelly. If the blister breaks and releases fluid, clean the area with an antiseptic and cover with a sterile bandage.

Some common foot problems are blisters, ingrown toenails, calluses, and corns.

Sometimes, excess rubbing on the foot causes extra layers of skin to form. This condition is called a callus. When the source of rubbing is removed, a callus will generally heal itself.

Excess rubbing of the shoe against the foot can also cause a hard, painful growth called a corn to form. Special pads may be used to relieve pain, and OTC medications often remove corns. If a corn persists, consult a physician.

An ingrown toenail results if pressure forces the nail to grow into the skin. If swelling or infection occurs, seek medical help.

23:5   Your Posture and Health

Correct posture promotes optimum functioning of your internal body organs. Practicing correct posture also adds to your appearance. Correct posture may indicate a positive attitude about yourself. Suppose you were being interviewed for a job. Using correct posture may positively influence a prospective employer. Incorrect posture may be interpreted as being unenthusiastic and having low self-esteem. Incorrect posture may also result in physical problems, such as backaches, poor circulation, and cramped internal organs. Some of these problems may not become apparent until you are much older than you are now.

The most common cause of incorrect posture is weak, inflexible muscles. The best way to maintain correct posture is to engage in a regular exercise program that strengthens the abdominal muscles. Curl-ups and other abdominal exercises will strengthen the abdominal muscles and prevent them from sagging outward. Outward sagging causes the spine to move out of line and may be why many adults suffer from severe backache. They may have overlooked the importance of doing abdominal exercises when they were your age.

Start forming habits now to promote correct posture. Stand so that you can draw an imaginary straight line through your neck, shoulders, lower back, pelvis and hip, knee, and ankle joints. Sit so that the hips and back of your thighs support your weight. Keep your feet flat on the floor. If you cross your legs, cross them at the ankles. Sit in chairs that give support to the lower part of your back.

FIGURE 23–3. A wall-sit helps a person get a feel for a proper body alignment.

Having strong abdominal muscles helps maintain correct posture.

Correct posture can improve your health.

Review and Reflect

1. Why should you be aware of your normals, such as body temperature, respiration, pulse, and blood pressure?
2. Why should a responsible adult in your home be consulted if you wish to take an OTC drug?
3. Why is it important to practice correct posture?

There are a variety of health providers on your health-care team.

Your physician and dentist are key health-care providers.

Knowing how to locate a competent dentist and physician will be helpful to you someday.

FIGURE 23–4. Medical centers provide a variety of health-care services.

HEALTH-CARE PROVIDERS

You have learned that sometimes you and your parents make choices to manage your health. At other times, you need the help of trained professionals. Physicians, dentists, nurses, and pharmacists are some of the professionals involved in the health-care delivery system. These health-care providers work closely as a team to provide you with health care. You and your parents choose who will be members of your health-care team. You need to know what kind of health care each team member can provide.

23:6 Choosing Health-Care Providers

When you think of health-care providers, you probably name your family physician and family dentist first. You may or may not use the same physician and dentist as you grow older. You may move, or your physician or dentist may retire. Therefore, it is important to know how to locate a physician or dentist. Here are some suggestions.

- Call the local society of the American Medical Association or the American Dental Association.
- Call a local, accredited hospital.
- Call a medical school or dental school closest to your community.
- Ask another trusted health-care provider, such as a pharmacist, for a reference.
- Ask a physician or a dentist from the community where you previously lived.
- Ask a friend or a neighbor who is satisfied with the services of his or her physician and dentist.

Pretend that you are now in charge of your health and the health of your family. You need to call a new physician or dentist for the first time. How will you evaluate this physician or dentist? You might seek answers to these questions.

- Does this person promote preventive health care?
- How long do you usually have to wait to get an appointment for a problem or an examination?
- What arrangements can be made for weekend or after hour health care?
- Are phone calls promptly returned?
- Is there an association with a good hospital?
- What are the procedures for paying fees? Are the fees reasonable?

23:7 Your Physician and Medical Care

Your physician assists when you are ill and when you are well. When you are ill, you may have symptoms that persist. A **symptom** is a change in a body function from a normal pattern. A symptom may be an indication of a health problem. Some symptoms, such as constant headaches, interfere with usual daily routines. You may not feel like eating or exercising properly. The headaches may interfere with your sleep. In such cases, a person seeks help from a physician to relieve the symptoms and/or the health problem that is causing the symptoms. Some symptoms that require medical attention are listed in Table 23–2. Remember, prompt medical care means early diagnosis and treatment.

When you have certain symptoms, you should seek prompt medical care.

When you are well, you should make a plan to prevent illness. Your physician has an important role in your preventive health-care plan by giving you a routine physical examination. A physical examination includes gathering information about you and your family and checking your body.

You and your physician need to make a plan for your wellness.

Your first visit to a physician would include completing a health history. A health history consists of gathering information about you and your family. It is usually in the form of a questionnaire.

Table 23–2   Some Symptoms that Require Medical Attention

- Shortness of breath after mild activity
- Loss of appetite for no obvious reason
- Cold symptoms that last more than a week
- Blood in urine or bowel movement
- Blood coughed up
- A constant cough
- Fever of 100°F (37.7°C) or higher for more than one day
- Swelling, stiffness, or aching in the joints
- Severe pain in any body part
- Frequent or painful urination
- Sudden weight gain or loss
- Dizziness or fainting
- Any warning signs of cancer (Chapter 20)
- Any warning signs of heart attack or stroke (Chapter 20)

Your personal health record will provide information for your health history.

You should ask questions when your physician discusses treatment.

You can choose behaviors that promote health.

You will be asked questions concerning your lifestyle, your health in the past, and your family's health. It is helpful to have your personal health record with you as you complete this questionnaire. The health history is an important tool the physician uses to provide the best possible health care. With every appointment, you may be asked to update your health history.

The extent of a physical examination can vary. Some of the usual components of a physical examination and laboratory tests are listed in Table 23–3.

After the physical examination, your physician will discuss the results of the tests with you. If the tests reveal health problems, the physician will recommend appropriate treatments. This is an important part of your health care. You need to feel free to ask questions. Together, you and your physician will make a plan to achieve and maintain optimum health.

Your role in your preventive health plan is to choose behaviors that will promote your optimum health. Some of these behaviors include

- eating healthful foods.
- exercising regularly.
- maintaining your ideal weight.
- learning to cope with stress.
- getting enough sleep.
- refraining from the use of illegal drugs, alcohol, and tobacco.
- scheduling regular physical examinations.

Table 23–3   The Physical Examination

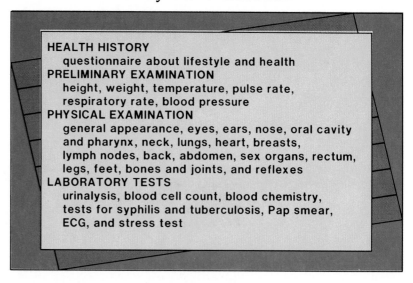

HEALTH HISTORY
   questionnaire about lifestyle and health
PRELIMINARY EXAMINATION
   height, weight, temperature, pulse rate,
   respiratory rate, blood pressure
PHYSICAL EXAMINATION
   general appearance, eyes, ears, nose, oral cavity
   and pharynx, neck, lungs, heart, breasts,
   lymph nodes, back, abdomen, sex organs, rectum,
   legs, feet, bones and joints, and reflexes
LABORATORY TESTS
   urinalysis, blood cell count, blood chemistry,
   tests for syphilis and tuberculosis, Pap smear,
   ECG, and stress test

23:8   Your Dentist and Dental Care

If you have ever had a toothache, you wanted relief from the pain as soon as possible. You might avoid such dental problems by working with your dentist to make a preventive dental health plan. Such a plan includes a health history and having your teeth cleaned and examined every six months.

A sticky substance called plaque is always forming on your teeth especially near the gum line. Plaque contains bacteria that can combine with sugar to produce acid, which causes tooth decay. Daily toothbrushing and flossing help remove plaque. If plaque is not removed, it becomes hard and forms calculus. Calculus cannot be removed with normal toothbrushing and flossing. A dentist or dental hygienist removes plaque and calculus using special instruments.

Prior to the dental examination and cleaning, X rays are taken. The X rays show the inside of the teeth and the supporting bone. The dentist can see the alignment of your teeth, bone changes, and any cavities that were not detected by a visual examination. The visual examination also detects any gum diseases. Some common dental problems include tooth decay, periodontal disease, and malocclusion.

Tooth decay results in cavities. A cavity in a tooth is an area of progressive decay caused by bacteria. The bacteria produce acid that destroys the enamel and dentin of the tooth. A **filling** is a material used to repair the cavity in a tooth.

You and your dentist can make a preventive dental health plan.

Toothbrushing, flossing, and dental cleaning help prevent plaque buildup.

STRUCTURE OF A TOOTH

- Enamel
- Dentin
- Blood vessels
- Pulp
- Gum
- Nerve
- Jawbone

FIGURE 23–5. X ray of a tooth

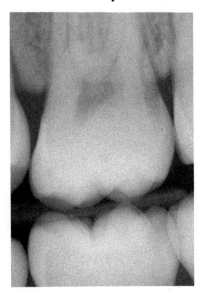

Sometimes tooth decay progresses into the pulp of the tooth. The pulp contains nerves and blood vessels. If the pulp becomes damaged irreversibly or dies, it must be removed and replaced with a material to keep the bacteria out. This procedure is called a **root canal.** Without a root canal, the tooth will soon have to be removed.

The main cause of tooth loss in adults, however, is periodontal disease. **Periodontal disease** is a disease of the gums and other tissues that support the teeth. Nine out of ten people over the age of forty have some periodontal disease. The disease often begins in persons your age or younger with plaque or calculus buildup when brushing and flossing are neglected. The bacteria associated with the plaque or calculus causes **gingivitis,** a condition in which the gums are red, swollen, and bleed easily.

If gingivitis is not treated, the disease usually progresses. The gums pull away from the teeth, forming pockets between the teeth and gums. Plaque, calculus, and pus collect in the pockets causing bad breath and infection. Food particles get trapped in the pockets and begin to decay. The supporting bones and ligaments that connect the root of the tooth to the bone are destroyed. The teeth loosen and may fall out. If this occurs, a bridge may be needed. A **bridge** is a partial denture or replacement that is used to take the place of one or more teeth. The natural teeth that surround the bridge support it. A complete denture is a full set of false teeth.

A **periodontist** is a dentist who specializes in the treatment of periodontal disease. The periodontist removes the calculus and may cut away the diseased parts of the gum and bone. When the bones are severely damaged, the periodontist sometimes does a bone graft procedure.

Malocclusion is the abnormal fitting together of teeth when the jaws are closed. Malocclusion may be caused by heredity, by jaw size, from early loss of primary teeth, or from injury to the teeth. When teeth do not fit together properly, extra stress is placed on the jaw. The teeth grind together unnecessarily. Plaque is more likely to collect and cause cavities.

An **orthodontist** is a dentist who treats malocclusion. The orthodontist may need to remove teeth or apply braces. Braces are cemented or bonded to the teeth and wired together to bring the teeth into correct alignment. Children wear braces from 18 to 24 months. Adolescents and adults usually wear them longer. After the braces are removed, a retainer usually is worn. A **retainer** is a plastic device with wires that keeps the teeth from moving back to their original places.

You have a role in your preventive dental health plan.

Periodontal disease is the leading cause of tooth loss.

Gingivitis that is not treated progresses to periodontitis.

A periodontist may need to cut away part of the gum or perform a bone transplant.

- Brush your teeth after every meal.
- Floss your teeth every day.
- Plan a diet that includes sources of calcium, phosphorus, and vitamins C and D.
- Limit the amount of sugar you eat.
- Include fluorides in your dental care.
- Choose safe practices to protect your teeth from injury.
- Avoid risks, such as smokeless tobacco, cigarettes, and alcohol, that may cause oral cancer.
- Know the signs of oral cancer.

You should follow a dental health plan to help keep your teeth and gums healthy.

 Review and Reflect

4. Why is it important to keep personal health records?
5. How might you locate a prospective physician or dentist?
6. Why is a routine physical examination important?
7. How can periodontal disease be prevented?

HEALTH-CARE FACILITIES

You and your family use a variety of health-care facilities.

There are many places that provide health-care services. Where do your physician and dentist practice? Where do you go when you need emergency medical service? What other kinds of health-care facilities might other members of your family use?

23:9 Individual and Group Practices

Some physicians and dentists have individual practices. They provide their services at a private office. When you make an appointment with such a physician or dentist, you always see the same person unless he or she is ill or on vacation. During those times, you may be referred to another physician or dentist to receive temporary services.

Other physicians and dentists have group practices. They share office facilities. You may see one or more of the physicians or dentists depending on the arrangement they have for scheduling patients. Each physician provides the same kind of service.

Another type of group practice involves several physicians, each specializing in a different medical area. In this type of arrangement, you can receive several types of care at the same facility. For example, an eye doctor, an allergy doctor, and a family doctor might be in the same group practice.

FIGURE 23–6. In a clinic, several physicians may work together in a group practice.

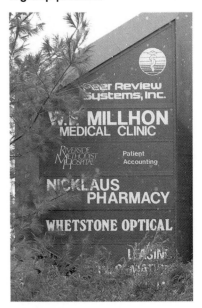

FIGURE 23–7. St. Jude Children's Hospital is a specialty hospital. Danny Thomas, a well-known entertainer, founded St. Jude in 1962 to conduct research on catastrophic diseases in children.

A group practice has many benefits for holistic care.

Other persons might also be in this practice besides physicians. There might be a nutritionist or a physical therapist. Some people think this arrangement is advantageous to holistic health care. Many areas of health can be examined and treated simultaneously. Suppose you had diabetes. You might see a specialist about treating the disease and a nutritionist to help you plan an appropriate diet to help control the disease.

23:10 Hospitals

General medical-surgical and specialty are two types of hospitals.

A **hospital** is a health-care facility where you can receive medical care, diagnosis, and treatment on an inpatient or outpatient basis. An **inpatient** is a patient who stays at the hospital while receiving health care. An **outpatient** is a patient who comes to the hospital to receive health care without having to stay at the hospital overnight.

A hospital provides services on an inpatient and outpatient basis.

There are two types of hospitals: (1) general medical-surgical, and (2) specialty. A general medical-surgical hospital provides a variety of services. One floor may have patients who have had orthopedic surgery while another floor might have patients who have cancer. A specialty hospital limits admissions to persons who have a particular health problem or condition. For example, a specialty hospital may be for cancer patients only or for children only, or for women only.

Hospital standards in the United States are determined by the Joint Commission on Accreditation of Hospitals (JCAH). Representatives from the American College of Physicians, the American College of Surgeons, and the American Hospital Association set standards for accreditation for the JCAH. The standards include the credentials of the staff, the cleanliness of the facility, and the quality of services rendered. When a hospital is accredited, you can feel confident that high standards have been met.

As a consumer, there are certain questions you and your family might ask to determine whether or not you want to be a patient at a specific hospital.

- Does the hospital have a wide range of diagnostic and treatment facilities?
- Does the hospital follow the American Hospital Association Patient's Bill of Rights (Figure 23–8)?
- Does the hospital have a wide range of specialists on its staff?
- Does the hospital have peer review and frequent up-to-date staff training?
- Does the hospital review the work of physicians and prevent incompetent physicians from continuing to practice at the hospital?
- Is the hospital accredited by the JCAH and listed in the *American Hospital Association Guide to the Health-Care Field*?
- Are the fees and insurance coverage estimates clear to you?
- Are you able to obtain the type of room and room service you can afford during your stay?

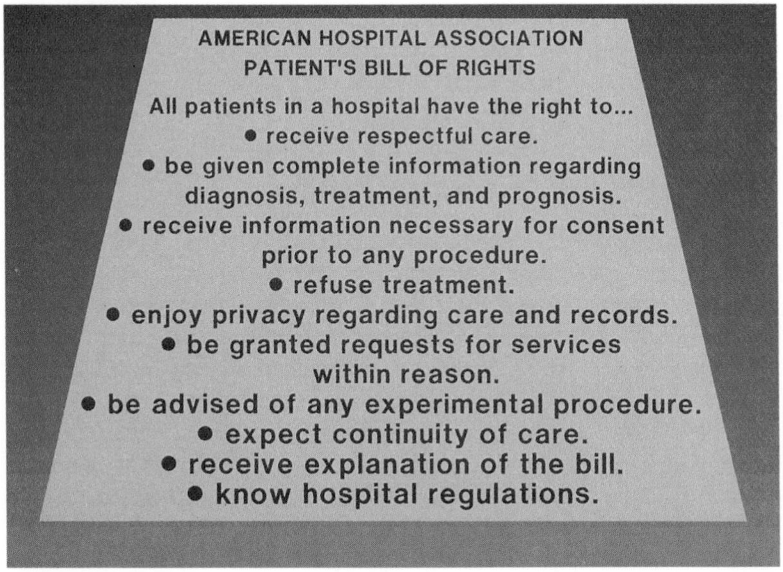

The JCAH determines hospital standards in the United States.

Answers to specific questions can help you decide about a hospital.

AMERICAN HOSPITAL ASSOCIATION PATIENT'S BILL OF RIGHTS

All patients in a hospital have the right to...
- receive respectful care.
- be given complete information regarding diagnosis, treatment, and prognosis.
- receive information necessary for consent prior to any procedure.
- refuse treatment.
- enjoy privacy regarding care and records.
- be granted requests for services within reason.
- be advised of any experimental procedure.
- expect continuity of care.
- receive explanation of the bill.
- know hospital regulations.

FIGURE 23–8

23:11 Urgent-Care Centers

Urgent-care centers provide emergency care 24 hours a day.

Urgent-care centers are in convenient locations.

It is helpful to visit an urgent-care facility before needing emergency care.

Another type of medical care facility is the urgent-care center. An **urgent-care center** is a facility separate from a hospital that offers immediate care. Urgent-care centers are conveniently located. Some have physicians on call 24 hours a day. They may charge fees somewhat higher than individual physicians but lower than those charged at hospital emergency rooms.

Many people like the concept of the urgent-care center. They do not want to pay the higher cost of the hospital or wait for services. They find the urgent-care center easy to get to and open during hours when it might be difficult to see a private physician.

It is best to become informed about an available urgent-care center before your family has an emergency. Visit the center to become an informed consumer. Here are some important questions you might ask.

- Does your family physician recommend this emergency care center?

- Is the head physician certified by the American College of Emergency Physicians?

- Will you always see a licensed physician or are some procedures handled by a support staff?

- Does the center have life-support equipment and rapid transport to a hospital?

- How will follow-up care and consultation with your physician be done?

- What are some typical fees, and how do they compare to the charges at a hospital?

23:12 Extended-Care Facilities

Extended-care facilities are becoming more popular.

Extended-care facilities provide nursing, personal, and residential care.

With life expectancy increasing, the number of people reaching age 65 has increased dramatically. Although the majority of persons over 65 are not ill or disabled, some elderly persons need assistance in daily living. Other persons who are not elderly may need assistance in daily living because of an injury, crippling disease, or disability. An **extended-care facility** is a facility that provides nursing, personal, and residential care. These facilities are equipped to care for persons who are elderly, for those with an injury or illness, for those with chronic physical disabilities, and for those who need other assistance in daily living.

FIGURE 23–9. Many extended-care facilities offer complete personal and nursing care.

The nursing care provided consists of services such as administering medicine, giving injections, monitoring diet, and providing physical therapy. Personal care includes services such as grooming, walking, and feeding assistance. Residential care provides a safe, healthful environment in which to live.

Many extended-care facilities are part of a larger complex that provides independent living facilities. Persons who live independently are close to the nursing and personal care services should they need assistance. In addition, some persons may elect to live in the independent living facility and not require care. These persons select this living arrangement as part of a plan for the future when they may need assistance.

Persons living in these kinds of extended-care facilities enjoy the freedom they have. They are free to take part in different kinds of activities. Transportation to such activities and to banks and shopping malls is usually provided on a regular basis as part of the service of the facility's program.

All extended-care facilities must be licensed by the state. To get a license, an extended-care facility must meet minimum standards. Those facilities that barely meet the minimum standards would not be desirable to consider. As a consumer, it is very important for you and your family to evaluate any potential extended-care facility you might use. Visit the extended-care facility at mid-morning when most activities are likely to be occurring.

Extended-care facilities must meet minimum standards to obtain a state license.

FIGURE 23–10. Residents of extended-care facilities can take part in social events and programs.

Some extended-care facilities provide much better care than others.

The following questions may be useful as you and your family make a careful evaluation.

• Is the extended-care facility licensed by the state?
• Is there a warm, friendly atmosphere generated by the administrators and staff?
• Is someone on call 24 hours a day for problems or emergencies?
• Is the location convenient for your physician and family and close to an accredited hospital?
• Is the physical environment attractive, clean, and free of safety hazards?
• Are the social needs of patients given a priority?
• What is the ratio of the staff members to the residents?
• Are appropriate medical services provided?
• Are the meals appealing and nutritious, and do they meet individual needs of the patients?
• Are the charges for services clear?

 ## Activity: Extended-Care Facility

Divide into groups of five. Each group is responsible for designing an extended-care facility for persons who are elderly. The facility should provide nursing, personal, and residential care. It should also meet the physical, mental, and social needs of the patients. Think about rooms that will be needed other than patient rooms. Make an extensive list of the services available at your facility. Then obtain a large sheet of poster paper. Design the facility and draw it on the poster. Give your facility an appropriate name. With your group, write a two-page brochure that describes your extended-care facility and its services. Present your project to the class.

Review and Reflect

8. How does an individual practice differ from a group practice?
9. Why do people become patients in hospitals?
10. What is the difference between a general medical-surgical hospital and a specialty hospital?
11. How do fees at an urgent-care center usually differ from those at emergency rooms in hospitals?
12. How might you evaluate the services provided at an extended-care facility?

HEALTH INSURANCE PLANS

A part of the health-care delivery system is based on the fee-for-service concept. That is, when a person receives health-care services, he or she must pay for them. Because health care can be unexpected and quite expensive, many consumers have health insurance. There are three broad types of health insurance plans: private prepaid, group prepaid, and public.

Health insurance plans cover fee-for-service in various ways.

A wise consumer needs to understand the three varieties of health insurance coverage before making a choice. Most likely you are currently covered under your parents' or guardian's insurance plan. You may have some type of health insurance coverage with a job that you have. In the future, you will need to know what questions to ask about health insurance coverage. You will then be able to make intelligent choices about health insurance coverage for yourself and for a family you might have in the future.

Someday you will have to choose some type of health insurance for yourself.

23:13 Private Prepaid Plans

Private prepaid plans are individual or group health insurance plans that may cover fees for the physician, hospital, and clinic based on predetermined fee schedules. These health insurance plans are provided by private insurance companies and nonprofit agencies. Premiums or payments are paid yearly or quarterly.

Fees for the physician, hospital, and clinic are provided for in private prepaid plans.

People who are self-employed usually have individual plans and make the premium payments themselves. Group plans are usually provided by organizations to which you belong or by the

Private prepaid plans can be for individuals or groups.

Private prepaid plans cover basic health insurance, major medical, and disability.

Comprehensive major medical combines basic health insurance with major medical coverage.

employer for whom you work. Group plans are often less expensive than individual plans. Because a large number of people are covered, premiums are lower.

Private prepaid plans offer different types of coverage, such as basic health insurance, major medical, and disability. **Basic health insurance** includes payments for part of physicians' fees, prescriptions, hospital, and surgical expenses. The insured person may have to pay a deductible. A **deductible** is a specific dollar amount that must be paid by the individual. The insurance company pays the balance. In other policies, there may be a deductible that must be paid by the individual. Then, the individual and the insurance company each pay a percentage of the remaining expenses. For example, an individual may have to pay the first $100 of medical expenses. After this payment, the insurance company pays 80 percent of all covered expenses and the individual pays 20 percent. Since policies differ, it is important to read a policy carefully to learn about what is covered, the percentages covered, the deductibles, and the exclusions.

Most persons who have basic health insurance also have major medical coverage to cover catastrophic situations. If you have a plan that combines basic health insurance and major medical coverage, your plan is called **comprehensive major medical insur-**

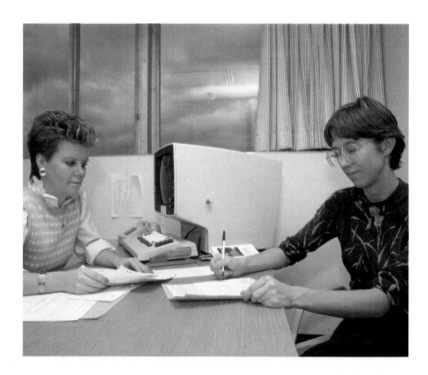

FIGURE 23–11. When a person is admitted to a hospital as a patient, he or she must fill out forms with vital information for the hospital's records.

ance. **Major medical coverage** includes payment of fees for prolonged injury or serious illness. Major medical coverage usually picks up where basic health insurance leaves off. The coverage is usually quite extensive.

Disability insurance provides income when you are absent from work for illness or injury. The definition of disability is carefully defined in the policy. Many policies have a waiting period before payments are made for an illness. Most policies begin payments immediately when an accident causes a disability. The payments are either a specific percentage of the salary you would receive if you were working or a flat dollar amount. Other types of insurance may be included in private prepaid plans, such as vision or dental insurance.

> Disability insurance coverage depends on the definition of disability and the waiting period.

As a consumer, it is important for you to carefully assess your need for health insurance and to make decisions that will provide you with the best possible way to take care of your expenses. Your individual and family needs may differ from the needs of others. Read and examine several policies before making a decision. Ask questions to be certain you understand a policy before paying premiums. If your employer has obtained a policy for you, read it carefully to learn what is covered. Decide if you need additional health insurance for you and your family.

> It is important to read a health insurance policy carefully before purchasing it.

23:14 Group Prepaid Plan

A **group prepaid plan** is an insurance plan in which the fees for the services of a group of physicians are paid for in advance. The group of physicians may include general practitioners, internists, pediatricians, allergists, gynecologists, and so on. The group may also include other health-care personnel, such as nutritionists or physical therapists.

> Services for physicians are prepaid in a community prepaid group practice plan.

One example of a group that offers this type of plan is a Health Maintenance Organization. A **Health Maintenance Organization (HMO)** is a group that provides comprehensive health services for a monthly fee. You may decide to join an HMO as an individual or through a group plan. Once the fee has been paid, the health services of the HMO are available to all persons enrolled in the plan regardless of the frequency or duration of the services. The main idea behind an HMO is that people will have basic services and facilities at a minimum cost that allows for preventive health care. They are encouraged to visit a physician before they are sick. It is hoped that this will limit long-term hospital care due to major illness. HMOs also try to provide more care and treatment out of the hospital.

> HMOs hold the cost of medical services down by operating on a preventive health plan.

> Persons with HMOs are sick less often than those with fee-for-service insurance plans.

HMOs have been growing in popularity since the passage of the Health Maintenance Organization Act. The **Health Maintenance Organization Act** requires employers with 25 or more workers to allow these workers to join an HMO if one exists in the area. Many believe HMOs will cut health-care costs by providing early services to keep people well. One study showed that when 1000 persons enrolled in an HMO were compared to a comparable number who had fee-for-service insurance, those in the HMO spent less than half the number of days in the hospital than the other group.

23:15 Public Plans

Medicare is a public health insurance plan for persons who are 65 or disabled.

There are two major public health insurance plans in the United States—Medicare and Medicaid. **Medicare** is a federal government program that provides health insurance benefits for persons age 65 and older and for certain persons under age 65 who are disabled. Medicare is divided into two parts. Part I is paid for by taxes collected from employees, employers, and the self-employed. Medicare provides compulsory hospital insurance. Part II is a voluntary program that is paid in monthly payments by eligible persons. It pays for physician's services and other medical costs.

Medicaid is a public health insurance plan where HHS and individual states share expenses for low-income and needy persons.

Medicaid is a federal government program in which each state enters an agreement with the Department of Health and Human Services to cover the cost of health care for low-income persons and persons with special medical needs. Persons with special medical needs include people who have disabilities, the elderly, and low-income, single parent families with dependent children. The definition of low-income family differs from state to state. A formula is used to determine how much each state pays and how much the federal government pays.

 Review and Reflect

13. Why do you need to learn about health insurance plans?
14. What is the difference between basic health insurance and major medical coverage?
15. Why might persons who belong to an HMO spend less time in the hospital than those who have a fee-for-service insurance plan?
16. Medicare is divided into two parts. How do these two parts differ?

Health
ADVANCES

An important part of personal health management involves care of your teeth. The toothbrush is the basic investment used in this care. However, changes in toothbrush design are occurring. Some people are replacing the traditional toothbrush with differently shaped toothbrushes. An important concern is the effectiveness of these modified toothbrushes.

Effectiveness is the basic concern of high-technology toothbrushes.

23:16   High-Technology Toothbrushes

Is the traditional toothbrush a thing of the past? Some manufacturers have developed toothbrushes that they claim have advantages over traditional toothbrushes.

One toothbrush has two outer rows of long, soft bristles that curve around an inner row of short, stiff ones. The outer bristles curve around to clean the sides of the teeth while the inner bristles clean the top of the teeth. The developer of this toothbrush claims that it reduces plaque with less gum damage than the straight bristles of traditional toothbrushes.

Another toothbrush design has two heads with bristles angled to help clean gums while cleaning teeth. The brush is wide and oval so that it reaches both sides of the teeth and gum line in one stroke.

FIGURE 23–12. One model of a high-technology toothbrush.

Tests are being performed to determine if these toothbrushes are more effective than traditional ones. The results are not conclusive. Some users feel these toothbrushes save time because they cover more area than the traditional toothbrushes. Other users feel that the traditional toothbrushes are still the best.

What is the best kind of toothbrush to use? The American Dental Association usually recommends certain toothbrushes. Check with your dentist for this recommendation.

Focus on
Life Management Skills

- Learn how to take your body temperature, respiration rate, and pulse.
- Have your blood pressure checked regularly.
- Carefully select products for your home pharmacy and use these products according to directions.
- Bathe each day using soap to break down oil and dirt on the skin.
- Use a deodorant or antiperspirant to control body odor.
- Shampoo your hair at least twice a week. If you use a dryer, use a low heat setting.
- Use cosmetics carefully. Avoid using cosmetics belonging to others.
- Follow correct procedures for wearing and cleaning contact lenses.
- Keep your fingernails clean and neatly trimmed.
- Wear comfortable shoes, wash your feet daily, and keep toenails trimmed.
- Use the correct posture technique for standing, sitting, bending, and lifting.
- Follow guidelines for choosing competent, qualified health-care providers, such as physicians and dentists.
- Visit a physician for diagnosis and treatment of symptoms and for regular physical examinations.
- Visit a dentist for routine dental examinations and preventive dental care, including fluoride treatment.
- Brush and floss teeth daily and plan a diet that includes calcium, phosphorus, vitamins C and D, and reduced sugar.
- Avoid risk behaviors that cause oral cancer.
- Learn about the health-care facilities in your community.
- Evaluate a hospital and urgent-care center before becoming a patient.
- Carefully evaluate extended-care facilities that might be used for a family member.
- Read and evaluate policies for the varieties of health insurance coverage before you make choices.

Health
CAREERS

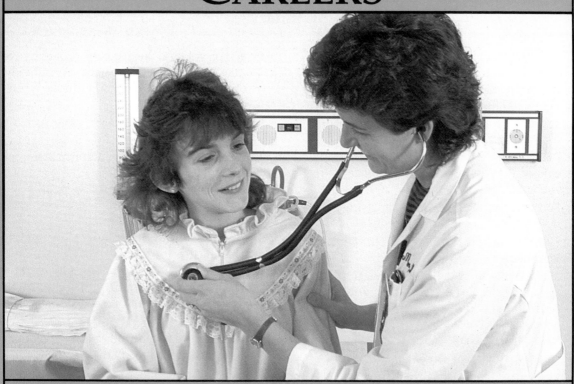

Physician

The health-care delivery system offers opportunities for many health-related careers. One career you might consider within this system is that of a physician. Dr. Leslie Mihalov considered becoming a physician from the time she was very young. She has always had a keen interest in the relationship between the mind and the body.

To prove to herself just how well she could maximize her body's performance, she began to swim competitively when she was six years old. She took part in national competitions as well as international games in Canada and Mexico.

To prepare academically for her career, Leslie selected science courses in high school and majored in biology in college. During her four years of medical school, she became interested in children's disease, particularly diseases of the lungs. Dr. Mihalov has completed a one-year internship and is at present completing a two-year residency at a children's hospital. She plans further study in pulmonology, a medical specialty in lung diseases, such as asthma and cystic fibrosis.

Dr. Mihalov enjoys an energetic lifestyle, which includes her husband, her daughter, and her career.

Summary

1. Personal health management involves self-care management to help you become an autonomous adult.   23:1

2. Understanding your normal health signs can help you assume more responsibility for your health.   23:2

3. OTC drugs found in the home medicine cabinet can be an important asset in responsible self-care.   23:3

4. Self-care involves selecting and using products to promote good grooming.   23:4

5. Correct posture promotes your physical well-being.   23:5

6. The American Medical Association and the American Dental Association are sources to check when first selecting a physician or dentist.   23:6

7. Your physician assists you with your personal health management.   23:7

8. Preventive dental health includes health practices that promote dental health.   23:8

9. When you use health-care providers, you may obtain their services at individual offices or group practice facilities.   23:9

10. There are two main types of hospitals: general medical-surgical and specialty.   23:10

11. Urgent-care centers offer immediate care.   23:11

12. An extended-care facility is equipped to provide nursing, personal, and residential care.   23:12

13. Private prepaid insurance plans provide basic health insurance.   23:13

14. A Health Maintenance Organization (HMO) is an example of a community group prepaid plan in which fees cover preventive health care.   23:14

15. Medicare and Medicaid are two major public health insurance plans.   23:15

16. High technology toothbrushes promote optimal dental health care.   23:16

Vocabulary

Below is a list of vocabulary words used in this chapter. Use each word only once to complete the sentences. Do not write in this book.

basic health insurance
deductible
extended-care
 facility
group prepaid plan
hospital
Medicare
orthodontist
periodontist
personal health
 management
symptom

1. An effective plan for _____ includes regular physical examinations.

2. _____ includes payment for physician's fees, hospital expenses, and prescriptions.

3. A Health Maintenance Organization is an example of a(n) _____.

4. In a(n) _____ patients with physical disabilities or injuries might receive nursing, personal, or residential care.

5. A(n) _____ is a health-care provider who specializes in gum disease.

6. A(n) _____ provides diagnosis and treatment on an inpatient or outpatient basis.

7. _____ is a public health insurance plan that provides for persons who are older and disabled.

8. A(n) _____ is a change in a body function from a normal pattern.

9. If you suffer from malocclusion, you need treatment from a(n) _____.

10. Before purchasing a health insurance policy, read it carefully to learn the _____ you must pay before the insurance company pays the balance.

Review

1. What does personal health management involve?

2. What is included in a physical examination?

3. What are five ways you can assume responsibility for your dental health?

4. What are two types of group practices?

5. What are four questions you might ask when evaluating a hospital?

6. What are three questions you might ask to evaluate an urgent-care center?

7. What are three questions you might ask to evaluate an extended-care facility?

8. What costs does basic health insurance usually cover?

9. What is the Health Maintenance Organization Act?

10. Describe two federal public health insurance programs for specialized populations.

Application

1. Suppose your family is buying individual comprehensive major medical insurance. What two types of policies would this include? List what you would look for when evaluating each type of policy.

2. Suppose you work for a large corporation. You can choose between a private prepaid plan or a group prepaid plan. Although you do not know the specifics of each policy, which appeals more to you? Why?

Individual Research

1. Select a health career. Interview someone in this career and write a report of the interview.

2. Many countries, including Canada and Great Britain, offer some type of national health insurance program. The possibility of national health insurance in the United States is a current issue. Write a paper about the implications for national health insurance after researching the pros and cons.

Readings

Ferm, Max, and Ferm, Betty, *How to Save Dollars With Generic Drugs.* New York, NY: Quill, 1985.

Nierenberg, Judith, R.N., M.A., and Janovic, Florence, *The Hospital Experience.* New York, NY: Berkley Publishing Corp., 1985.

Safety and First Aid

Photo Teaching Tip: Safety is a daily priority. Use each photo to identify safety precautions everyone should observe.

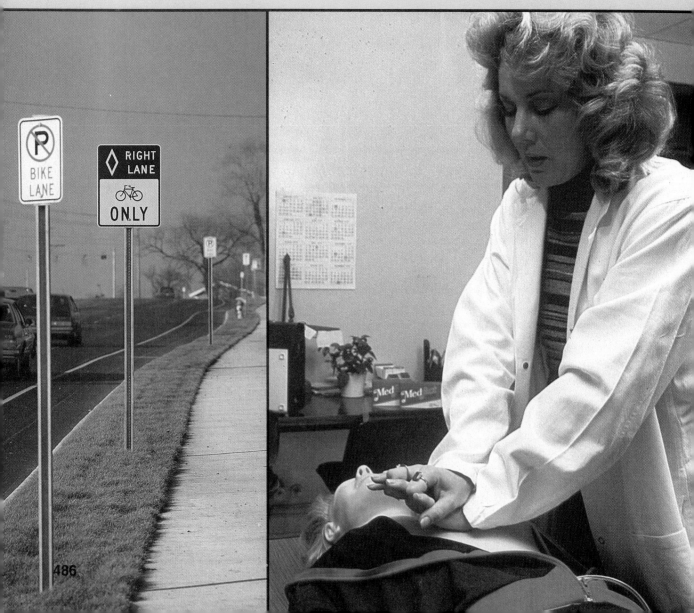

486

SAFETY AND FIRST AID

Major strides have been made to make your environment a safer place in which to live. Efforts have been increased in schools and communities to teach you how to protect yourself from harm inflicted by others. The products you use have been designed to minimize and reduce injuries due to accidents. Safety rules in the workplace have been implemented and updated.

What skills do you need to maximize your safety? If you or someone else suffers a serious injury or illness, what first-aid procedures will you follow? The information in this unit will help promote your health and safety as well as the health and safety of others.

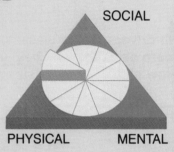

SOCIAL

PHYSICAL   MENTAL

In driver training classes, you learn how to drive defensively and safely. You learn skills that will help you prevent having an accident when you drive. How else can you ensure your personal safety?

Chapter 24

Personal Safety

OBJECTIVES: You will be able to
- **identify ways to reduce your risk of becoming a victim of a violent crime.**
- **describe steps you can take to avoid accidents.**

There is a great emphasis on the importance of being as safe as possible. In some situations, other people endanger your safety. However, in other areas, you have some control over your safety in the products you choose and the care that you use.

SELF-PROTECTION

You have many rights. These rights have been granted to you by the written laws of society. Among your rights is the right to keep safe from illegal and harmful behaviors of other people. This section of the chapter focuses on how you can protect your right to be safe and move toward optimum health.

Everyone has the right to be protected.

24:1 Protecting Yourself from Crime

Crime is one of the major health problems facing Americans because of the physical and mental effects on the victim. Some violent crimes are those crimes in which a person receives physical harm. These are often domestic crimes. Domestic crimes occur within families. Some aspects of violent crime were covered in Chapter 9. This section focuses on crimes that may occur in a home or community. Among these crimes are homicide and robbery.

Homicide is the killing of a human being by another. Homicide is one of the leading causes of death in adolescents. In many cases, homicide occurs after an intense emotional argument.

Violent crime has become a major health problem.

Domestic homicide is homicide that takes place within a family. Domestic homicide might be prevented if family members use a cooling off period during stressful situations. Families might also seek counseling on how to deal with anger. Homicides that involve people who are not related are often the result of arguments.

Many homicides involve the use of alcohol. It is important to avoid persons who are argumentative and under the influence of alcohol. In addition, homicide may occur because someone has a disturbed personality.

Robberies can be prevented. At school, keep your purse or wallet with you. If you drive to school, always keep your car locked. Robberies are more likely to occur in homes in which people do not take proper precautions. Here are some tips you can follow to deter robbers from entering your home.

- Keep doors and windows locked at all times.
- Open doors only when you know who is knocking. Use the peephole, if there is one. When babysitting, never open a door unless you have been told to expect someone at a specific time.
- Know how to make an emergency telephone call. If someone tries to enter your home forcefully, call the police and give your name, address, and a description of what is happening. Even if you suspect someone might be attempting to enter your home but you are not sure, call the police anyway.
- Do not give information to a stranger over the telephone. Be polite, but avoid giving information to a person who might possibly be thinking of using the information to plan a robbery.

Always follow certain rules to protect yourself from crime.

FIGURE 24–1. Be ready in case of an emergency. If you have a list of important numbers near your phone, you can get help without delay.

24:2 Sexual Assault

Any kind of sexual activity that occurs using physical force or the threat of physical force is referred to as **sexual assault.** Rape is one type of sexual assault. According to a legal definition, **rape** is an act of sexual intercourse against a person's will through the use of violence or force. When a person is younger than a legally defined age of consent, and agrees to have sexual intercourse, the act is considered corruption of a minor. The legally defined age of consent varies but usually ranges between 12 and 16 years of age.

Rape can be defined in broader terms. For example, some states have enacted laws that make it possible for a husband to be legally tried for raping his wife. Rape has also been defined as any kind of sexual invasion of the body by force or threat of force. This includes homosexual rape in which one male sexually assaults another male. Very rarely will homosexual rape occur between two females. Legally, a female can be accused of raping a male but this occurs very infrequently. The most common form of rape is heterosexual rape or the act of rape committed by a male against a female.

There are three important facts to consider about rape.

- First, rape is an act of violence. It is often a desire by a male to express hostility and to show power over a female.

- Second, any female can become a rape victim. Age is not a factor.

- Third, rape is not necessarily committed against females by males who are strangers to them. Rather, many females who are raped know their attackers. If a female does not trust a male, it is best for her not to be alone with him. Many rapes occur when a man is under the influence of alcohol.

Of particular importance is the high incidence of acquaintance rape, sometimes called date rape, that occurs to people your age. That is, a male may refuse to stop his unwanted sexual advances toward his date. To avoid the possibility of acquaintance rape, it is best for the female to know the male she is dating. Double dating may be appropriate, especially if going on a blind date. It might also be wise to avoid being alone with a date when first beginning to date that person. However, it should be noted that acquaintance rape can occur after dating a person several times or even after several months. It is important to understand that knowing a person for a long time does not guarantee safety. The avoidance of any kind of sexual aggression is an individual right that is protected by law.

Rape is a type of sexual assault.

Rape has been defined as any kind of sexual invasion of the body by force or threat of force.

Rape is an act of violence.

Rape often is committed by a person who is known to the victim.

24:3 Rape Prevention and Treatment

Unfortunately, knowledge about rape may not stop it from occurring. What should a female do in an actual rape encounter? There is no single right answer that applies to all rape encounters. Every female must judge for herself what the best course of action should be. The National Center for the Prevention and Control of Rape recommends the following.

- Run away if possible. If running away is not possible, decide whether or not screaming, arguing, biting, and fighting may be of help. Repulsive tactics such as vomiting or acting crazy can disgust and confuse an attacker.
- Verbal assertiveness and aggression may turn off an attacker since rapists like to feel in control.
- Self-defense tactics learned in a class may overwhelm the attacker allowing the victim to escape.
- If an attacker has a gun or knife, think clearly about what action to follow. Perhaps talking to the attacker and waiting for an appropriate time to escape might be the best course of action to follow.

Many police sexual assault units and local rape centers have general safety tips about rape. Some groups are opposed to these suggestions because they encourage a woman to live in fear. They would rather see changes that encourage more severe penalties for rapists and greater sensitivities toward the treatment of women in the media and movies. If a rape does occur, it is important that certain procedures be followed.

- Always report the attack to the police. Even an unsuccessful attack should be reported. Provide as much information about the attacker as possible—physical characteristics, personal habits, clothes, car, and so on. This information can help others from becoming innocent victims of violence.
- Call the police immediately; do not shower, bathe, or change clothes. Many hospitals have trained personnel who can obtain evidence from the victim's body that can be used to help catch and convict the rapist.

Remember, you have a right to be healthy, safe, and respected by others. After a rape, victims are usually angry because their rights have been violated. Rape victims may need counseling to learn to express their anger and to cope with their fears.

There are many steps to follow for rape prevention.

If rape occurs, certain procedures should be followed.

The police should be informed of all cases of rape.

Rape victims may need counseling.

 Review and Reflect

1. What steps can you follow to help protect yourself from violent crime?

ACCIDENT PREVENTION

Almost all accidents can be prevented. The best way to prevent accidents is to be aware of their causes so that you can follow preventive behaviors. Accidents do not simply happen. People cause them to happen. Think back to a time you fell. Were you running too fast? Was the ground wet and slippery? Did you fail to see an object in your path? If you examined all the factors involved in your fall, you probably would discover that certain changes in your behavior could have prevented the accident.

24:4 Causes of Accidents

Stress is a major cause of all kinds of accidents. Research shows that people who are not coping with stress do not concentrate fully, and thus, they increase their risks of having accidents. People who are extremely upset often become careless and are not aware of changing conditions.

Stress can create problems other than losing the ability to concentrate. Stress can produce fatigue. When you are fatigued, you are less alert. You do not react or respond as quickly as usual. A delay in reaction time may create a dangerous situation.

A person's age plays an important role in accidents. Young people may be influenced by peers to be daring and to take chances they would not ordinarily take. Young people may lack the experience necessary to anticipate the potential danger in a situation.

Elderly people may experience changes in muscular strength and coordination. They may take medicines that interfere with the ability to think clearly and respond quickly. This may result in a person's taking unwise risks. Refer to Table 24–1 for the leading causes of accidental deaths in different age groups.

Drugs, especially alcohol, play a significant role in motor vehicle accidents, as well as other kinds of accidents. Generally, drugs impair reflexes, perception, balance, coordination, concentration, and judgment. Drugs are implicated in injuries and deaths due to fires, falls, drownings, and accidents involving the use of tools, machines, and firearms. Drugs are also involved in over half of all fire fatalities and drownings and in almost half of all deaths in the workplace.

A number of research studies have focused on the relationship between marijuana use and accidents. These studies show that marijuana increases a person's risk of having an accident.

Stress can be a major factor in the cause of accidents.

Age can play a role in the cause of accidents.

Many accidents result from drug and alcohol use.

Table 24–1   Leading Causes of Accidental Deaths

UNDER 1 YEAR	1 TO 4 YEARS	5 TO 14 YEARS	15 TO 24 YEARS
• choking • motor vehicle accidents • suffocation • fire, burns • drowning	• motor vehicle accidents • fire, burns • drowning • choking • falls	• motor vehicle accidents • drowning • fire, burns • firearms • falls	• motor vehicle accidents • drowning • firearms • poison • fire, burns
24 TO 44 YEARS	**45 TO 64 YEARS**	**65 TO 74 YEARS**	**75 YEARS AND OLDER**
• motor vehicle accidents • drowning • poison • fire, burns • falls	• motor vehicle accidents • falls • fire, burns • drowning • choking, poisoning	• motor vehicle accidents • falls • fire, burns • choking • surgical or medical complications	• falls • motor vehicle accidents • surgical or medical complications • fire • choking

Source: *Accident Facts: 1985 Edition*, National Safety Council, 1985.

People who are ill increase their risk of having an accident.

One's attitude can be a cause of accidents.

Accidents occur more frequently at certain times of the day and during certain days of the week. Some accidents occur at night with greater frequency than during the day because of reduced visibility. Other kinds of accidents have a tendency to occur during weekends rather than during the week because they may be related to leisure activities. Yet, other accidents may occur with greater frequency during the week because they are related to environmental factors in the workplace. The incidence of accidents also increases during holidays. More people travel or experience stress during such times.

Illnesses cause changes in the body that result in an inability to perform tasks optimally. Thus, the risks of having an accident increase.

Some people are considered to be more susceptible to accidents than other people. This may be due to their attitudes. For example, a person may have a know-it-all attitude and not be concerned about specific hazards. Others may get into accidents because they like the excitement of a challenge, regardless of the risks involved. Have you ever played "I dare you" as a young child? Did you do something dangerous that resulted in injury? Probably, you outgrew this behavior. Unfortunately, some people do not.

Activity: Analyzing Accidents

Six causes of accidents include stress, age, drugs, time of day or day of the week, illness, and attitude. Collect ten articles about accidents from magazines or newspapers. Analyze each article by defining the cause(s) of the accident and what actions might have prevented the accident. The articles you choose should include examples from each of the six causes of accidents.

24:5   Preventing Vehicle Accidents

Efforts are being made toward preventing motor vehicle accidents and reducing the risks of injury and death to people involved in accidents. These efforts focus on factors involving vehicles, highways, drivers, and laws.

Vehicle factors relate to the design and maintenance of the automobile. Injuries and fatalities are reduced when automobile bumpers, front ends, and steering columns are designed to absorb the impact from a crash. Passenger compartments that have recessed knobs and heavy padding are important for safety.

Airbags are an option on some vehicles. One advantage of air bags is that drivers do not have to make a conscious effort to use them. In most cases, a safety belt must be hooked up by the driver. Even though their effectiveness has been proven, safety belts are not used by the majority of drivers. Many vehicles are made with crush zones. Shocks can be absorbed in a head-on crash with less resulting injury to a driver or passenger. Antilock braking systems (ABS) are now recognized as aids in accident prevention. These systems help cars stop in a straight line when the brakes are suddenly applied. The brakes do not lock the wheels in a sudden stop.

Highway factors play a role in automobile safety. Studies show that certain road features promote automobile accidents. Among these are sharp curves, steep grades, potholes, and a lack of a physical median that separates opposing traffic. On city streets, shielded signs, missing signs, and poor lighting increase accident rates. Highway and street engineers are now more aware than ever before of the importance of designing safe automobile routes.

The most important factor in motor vehicle accidents is the driver. Table 24–2 lists several ways that drivers of motor vehicles can promote safety.

Alcohol is responsible for half of all automobile-related accidents. Many groups that are against drunk driving, such as MADD (Mothers Against Drunk Driving) and SADD (Students

Every 12 minutes someone is killed in an automobile-related accident.

Many safety features are now being placed in cars.

FIGURE 24–2. Air bags and other features of vehicles are tested for safety. These tests are conducted regularly to help prevent accidents and injuries.

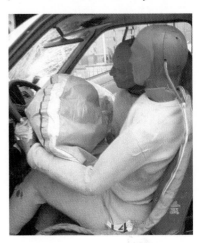

Table 24–2 Tips for Promoting Vehicle Safety

- Do not use alcohol or other drugs, especially prior to and when operating a motor vehicle.
- Always wear seat restraints even near your home.
- Drive according to the speed limit and weather and road conditions.
- Drive defensively; anticipate what others will do.
- Have enough stopping distance between your vehicle and the one in front of you.
- Be sure your motor vehicle is in good mechanical condition, especially the brakes and tires.
- Be sure your car doors are locked to prevent you from being thrown out of the car in an accident.
- Wear a helmet when driving a moped or motorcycle since many deaths result from head injuries. Also, follow local laws regarding the safe operation of these kinds of vehicles.

Against Drunk Driving), have pressured lawmakers to enact stricter laws concerning those who fail to follow the laws related to alcohol and driving. Through the pressure of these and other groups, many states are considering reducing the blood-alcohol level that indicates when one is legally intoxicated. Other laws are being changed with stricter penalties for those who are caught drinking and driving.

The use of drugs such as barbiturates, amphetamines, and marijuana is suspected in many motor vehicle accidents. The effects of these drugs can be dangerous to both the driver and others.

Groups such as SADD and MADD are against drunk driving.

FIGURE 24–3. Many groups are active in programs that seek to reduce the number of drunk drivers.

Each year, more states implement laws mandating the use of safety belts. Research shows that 10 000 to 16 000 lives would be saved each year if drivers and their passengers would use safety belts. Laws mandating the use of child-restraint systems in automobiles have been implemented in many states. Under these laws, children under a certain weight (often under 40 lb) and/or under a certain age must be properly secured in a child-restraint system. Some hospitals, health departments, and other organizations provide families with young children the use of child-restraint systems for a minimal fee or free of charge. Many hospitals have rules that require newborn babies to be fastened in a child-restraint seat when leaving the hospital to go home for the first time.

In addition to automobiles, other motor vehicles are also responsible for many injuries and deaths. Drivers of motorcycles greatly increase their risks of dying in an accident. Motorcycle drivers need to drive defensively. They must regard every car as a potential hazard. Wearing a helmet is essential. Some motorcycle drivers argue that laws mandating helmets infringe on their personal liberties. They maintain that other people are not endangered by their choice not to wear a helmet. However, family members and society must pay the medical costs of those drivers who have accidents.

Many young people drive mopeds. Moped drivers must follow the same rules as other drivers. Communities usually determine local laws regarding moped use.

All terrain vehicles (ATVs) are often driven on dirt roads. Unfortunately, ATVs overturn easily and, at times, fall on the driver. The following safety tips should be followed when operating an ATV (Table 24–3).

With an increase in bicycling, there has been an increase in injuries. To keep safe while riding a bicycle, follow the tips listed in Table 24–4.

Many states have mandatory seat belt laws.

Wearing a helmet while on a motorcycle will reduce the risk of head injury.

Safety rules should be followed when driving an all terrain vehicle.

There are many ways bicycle accidents can be prevented.

Table 24–3   Tips for Promoting ATV Safety

- Always wear an approved protective helmet and other protective gear.
- Always read the instruction manual that comes with the ATV and follow the manufacturer's directions for use, maintenance, and pre-use checks.
- Do not use ATVs on paved roads or streets.
- Do not operate ATVs when using alcoholic beverages.
- Observe local laws.
- Never ride double.

Table 24–4   Tips for Promoting Bicycle Safety

- Use a bicycle that is the correct size, durable enough for your needs, comfortable, and structurally sound.
- Follow the same traffic rules that automobile drivers follow. Observe all traffic signs and signals.
- Ride in the same direction as automobile traffic.
- Stay close to the right edge of the road and ride single file.
- Be sure that your bicycle and all safety equipment, such as brakes, tires, lights, and reflectors, are in good operating condition.
- Use hand signals when turning or stopping.
- Walk your bicycle across busy intersections.
- Dress appropriately. Wear light clothing or reflectorized clothing or tape at night. Prevent long pants or other clothing from becoming tangled in bicycle chains. Always wear a helmet when traveling unusually far distances or in traffic.
- Be aware of road conditions and hazards, such as ice, or oil slicks, or potholes.
- Ride your bicycle defensively: anticipate what automobile drivers or other cyclists may do.
- Use headlights and reflectors for evening and night safety.
- Yield right-of-way to pedestrians.
- Keep off interstate highways and other highways where bicycles are prohibited.

24:6   Preventing Water Accidents

Drinking alcohol and swimming is a dangerous combination.

You can follow many actions to keep safe in water.

Drowning is the second leading cause of accidental death to people your age. Unfortunately, a large number of drownings occur because of alcohol use. Drinking alcohol and swimming do not mix. A person who drinks and swims may have a tendency to take unnecessary risks. In addition, alcohol deprives the body of energy and interferes with coordination. There are many tips for keeping safe in water (Table 24–5).

A drowning victim can panic and pull a rescuer under water.

You should also know what to do if you notice a person drowning. Always call for a lifeguard. If there is no lifeguard nearby, do not jump into the water to save a drowning victim. A drowning victim may panic and pull you under. Rather, throw a life buoy to the victim and pull the person to safety. If a life buoy is not available, throw a rope or something else that will float, such as an empty or partially-filled plastic milk jug or a tire. If the drowning victim is near the edge of a pool, lie flat on your stomach and pull the person in. If possible, form a human chain with other people who are nearby for additional strength and support in the rescue.

Table 24–5 Tips for Keeping Safe In and On the Water

- Learn to swim. You are never too old to learn.
- If you cannot swim well, stay in shallow water.
- If you are babysitting, watch the child closely. Always stay in the water with a young child.
- Always swim, skin-dive, or scuba-dive with a companion.
- Before diving, be sure the water is deep enough and free of obstructions.
- When swimming in an ocean, swim parallel to the shore and not away from it. Remember, you always have to be strong enough to return.
- Learn the safety rules for boating or canoeing before using a boat or canoe.
- Wear a life jacket when on a boat. Stay with the boat should it overturn by hanging on to the side of it.
- Only an expert swimmer should water ski, skin-dive, or scuba-dive. You should have adequate instruction before attempting any of these.
- Enroll in a class for basic water safety.
- Stay out of the water during threatening weather conditions.

24:7 Preventing Accidents with Firearms

Each year close to 2000 Americans are killed because of firearm accidents. Of this number, approximately 500 are children. While many of these accidents happen while hunting, the majority occur in the home. If guns are left where children can reach them, guns may be used as toys. About one in five American households possesses a handgun. Many of these handguns are kept loaded as protection from intruders. Loaded handguns often are invitations to accidents. To reduce the number of firearm accidents, there are certain rules that should be followed (Table 24–6).

Many people die each year from firearm accidents.

There are many ways to avoid firearm accidents.

Table 24–6 Tips for Preventing Firearm Accidents

- Receive instructions before handling any weapon. Only the licensed owner of a gun should use it.
- Always assume that a gun is loaded. Never point a gun at a person. Never lay it down pointed at a person.
- Store guns unloaded in locked cabinets. Ammunition should be locked in a separate place.
- Before handling a gun, check to make sure it is not loaded.
- Keep a safety lock on a gun until it is ready to be fired.
- When hunting, stay with a group. Most hunters who get shot are those who stray from the group.
- Wear bright orange vests and hats when hunting so you can be seen easily by other hunters.

24:8   Preventing Home Accidents

Falls, fires, burns, and poisonings are major causes of accidental deaths in the home.

About 24 million Americans become injured each year in their homes. The National Safety Council lists falls, fires, burns, and poisonings as the leading causes of accidental deaths in the home for all ages.

The greatest number of injuries and deaths in the home are caused by falls. Be sure you and others in your home are protected from falls. Be sure walking surfaces are clear and well-lighted. Furniture and other objects should be placed so that they are not where people least expect them. If you must climb to reach an object, use a secure ladder rather than a chair that may be less secure or have a tendency to tip over.

Most fires in the home are caused by improper use and disposal of cigarettes.

The second leading cause of accidental death and injury in the home is fire. More than half of all fires in a home are caused by improper use and disposal of cigarettes. Other causes are improper storage of gasoline and cleaners, overheated cooking oils, and children playing with matches. Overloaded electrical wiring can also result in fire, especially in older homes with original wiring. Modern electrical appliances may overload the electrical circuits. This can result in a buildup of heat in the wires, which can cause nearby dry wood to burst into flames. People who move into older homes should have the electrical wiring checked by a professional. Damaged or dangerous wiring should always be replaced.

Fires can result from faulty electrical wiring.

There are many ways to reduce the risk of burns due to fire.

The number of deaths and injuries from fires could be prevented or reduced if proper steps were taken. What would you do if you were in a home or building that caught on fire? See Table 24–7 for important tips you should know.

Table 24–7   Tips for Reducing Risks of Burns Due to Fire

- Be sure your place of residence is equipped with smoke detectors to warn you of fire.
- Be sure your home is equipped with a fire extinguisher that is in good working condition.
- Keep rope ladders in rooms that are on the second floor.
- Keep the telephone number of your fire department near all phones.
- Have a fire escape plan from your home and practice it.
- Be sure your family has a meeting place outside your home in case of fire.
- Practice crawling as if there were smoke. Smoke rises, so it is important to keep low to the floor.
- If your home is on fire, test the door of the room you are in. Do not open a warm door. If you can leave the room, close the door behind you to prevent the fire from spreading.
- If you cannot get out by the door exit, keep the door closed and stuff the cracks so that smoke will keep out of the room. Stand by the window and signal or scream for help.
- If you must leave through a window without a rope or ladder, drop to the ground feet first.

Most cases of poisoning in a home occur to children. Substances most commonly associated with poisoning are medicines and pesticides. If there are young children in your family, place Mr. Yuk stickers on all poisons. Tell young children the meaning of these stickers. All medicines and poisons should be kept out of the reach of young children. If someone you know takes a poison, call the poison control center in your community. If at all possible, give information about the type of poison. Often the poison will be near the victim or you can ask the victim to show you what was taken. In Chapter 26, you will learn about first-aid procedures you can follow for different types of poisoning.

Medicines and pesticides are substances most commonly associated with poisoning.

24:9 Preventing Accidents in the Workplace

Perhaps you have had a part-time job. If you have not held a job as yet, eventually you will. It is important that the time you spend in a workplace is as safe as possible. Naturally, some occupations are going to be safer than others. For example, firefighters are more likely to become injured than people who sit at desks in an office.

Many accidents can occur in the workplace.

Today, people are safer at work than ever before. This has occurred because steps have been taken by employers and lawmakers to enforce healthful working conditions. One significant law that helped reduce occupational accidents was the 1970 Occupational Safety and Health Act (OSHA). **OSHA** is a series of minimum safety and health standards that all employers must meet. OSHA requires that each employer furnish employees with a safe working environment. Recognized health hazards that are causing or may cause serious physical harm or death must be eliminated. New employees should be trained and made aware of hazards. They must also receive periodic review of safety regulations. Supervisors must be alert to factors that can cause accidents. Employers who do not meet these standards can be fined.

OSHA is a series of safety and health standards that employers must meet.

Farm work presents unique dangers because of the size and type of equipment used. A person working on a farm should be thoroughly trained in the safe operation of every piece of machinery or equipment. OSHA has current safety regulations and practices for working on farms also.

Be aware of safety rules in the workplace.

Wherever you work, you should be trained in all safety aspects of the job. Your supervisor should keep you aware of potential occupational hazards and inform you of any new safety rules. When any new equipment is added to your workplace, make sure that you learn how to properly operate it before you use it. Take the responsibility to follow safety rules on the job, and promote a safer working environment for yourself and others.

24:10 Preventing Accidents During Dangerous Conditions

One of the more common weather-related accidents results from lightning. A person who is struck directly or indirectly by a lightning bolt can be killed.

Tornadoes occur most often in flat, open areas. A **tornado** is a funnel-shaped, rotating cloud with high winds. You may have heard of tornado watches and warnings. A **tornado watch** means that weather conditions are favorable for a tornado to develop. A **tornado warning** means that a tornado has been sighted.

Hurricanes are violent, tropical storms with high winds and heavy rains that usually occur between June and November along the Gulf and Atlantic coasts. Hurricanes have been known to

Lightning, tornadoes, hurricanes, and earthquakes pose great threats to a person's safety.

Table 24–8 Protecting Yourself During Dangerous Weather and Earthquakes

LIGHTNING	TORNADO
• Seek shelter indoors if possible. • Get inside a car; rubber tires act as a ground for lightning. • If in an open field, curl up in a ball to prevent yourself from being a target; lightning strikes objects that stand out. • Keep away from metal objects, such as golf clubs or fences. • If swimming or boating, get out of the water. • Move away from trees. • Do not hold hands with another person as lightning can pass from one person to another.	• If at home, go to a basement. • If at floor level, hide under heavy furniture. • If outdoors, get into an open ditch. • Get out of an automobile and take shelter. • Get out of a mobile home or trailer and take shelter. • In a public building, stay inside the hallway. • In school, get under desk or follow other instructions. • Do not stand near windows or heavy objects.
HURRICANE	**EARTHQUAKE**
• Listen to emergency broadcasts on the radio. • Stay away from large windows. • Do not leave a building until absolutely sure the storm is over; often the wind returns after the quiet. • Move to a higher elevation if flooding is expected. • Evacuate your home if advised to do so and go to identified shelters. • If advised, shut off water, gas, and electricity. • Follow advised preparation procedures.	• Stay calm — do not panic. • Stay clear of any objects that can fall on you, whether indoors or outdoors. • Move to an open space. • In a building, get under a desk or table. • In school, get under a desk; watch out for broken glass. • If outdoors, avoid broken power lines. • In an automobile, stop as soon as possible and get out. If on a bridge, get off as soon as possible.

cause thousands of deaths when people were not alerted in time to escape their paths.

Earthquakes are violent shakings of the earth. Movements in the earth cause the foundations of buildings to give way. This may cause parts of buildings or even entire buildings to collapse. The greatest number of injuries from earthquakes occurs from falling debris.

What should you do if you are in a dangerous weather situation or an earthquake? See Table 24–8 for important safety tips.

 ## Review and Reflect

2. Why is it important for parents to use child-restraint seats for their children?
3. Name two ways to prevent bicycle accidents.
4. Why should people who own weapons enroll in a firearms safety course?
5. Why is it important to know where the exit signs are in a hotel?
6. Why should you roll along the floor if your clothes catch on fire?
7. Why should you avoid standing near a tall structure during an earthquake?

Focus on
Life Management Skills

- Know and follow guidelines to help prevent violent crimes.
- Report to a trusted adult or a law enforcement officer any kind of sexual assault or other crime.
- Be aware of the conditions that can increase your risks of having an accident.
- Avoid being a show-off when driving a bicycle or any motor vehicle.
- Have smoke detectors in your home.
- Know how to escape from your home if a fire should occur.
- Make a fire escape plan for your home.
- Keep the telephone number of the nearest poison-control center near your telephone.
- Be aware of and follow the rules for safe swimming.
- If you work, be aware of the safety rules in your workplace.
- Be aware of safety rules to follow in cases of extreme weather conditions.

CHAPTER REVIEW 24

Summary

1. You can follow rules to help keep yourself safe from criminals. **24:1**
2. Sexual assault can sometimes be avoided through appropriate actions. **24:2**
3. Treatment and preventive measures for rape are available. **24:3**
4. Stress, age, alcohol use, drug use, illness, and attitudes can cause people to have accidents. **24:4**
5. Efforts to prevent and reduce vehicle accidents focus on the vehicle, highways, drivers, and the law. **24:5**
6. Call for a lifeguard and follow safety rules for rescuing a drowning victim. **24:6**
7. Firearm accidents can be prevented by understanding the proper use of guns. **24:7**
8. Taking steps to reduce falls in the home can greatly reduce the risk of injury. **24:8**
9. It is important to learn safety rules around the workplace to reduce the risk of injury. **24:9**
10. Tornadoes, hurricanes, and earthquakes can cause serious injury and death unless precautions are taken. **24:10**

Vocabulary

Below is a list of vocabulary words used in this chapter. Use each word only once to complete the sentences. Do not write in this book.

earthquake
homicide
hurricane
OSHA

rape
sexual assault
tornado warning
tornado watch

1. When weather conditions are right for a funnel-shaped cloud to develop, a(n) _____ is said to be in effect.
2. High winds and heavy rains that strike coastal areas are called a(n) _____.
3. _____ is a crime in which a person is forced or threatened by force to engage in sexual intercourse.
4. An employer who does not meet safety standards set by _____ can be fined.
5. When a funnel cloud has been spotted, a(n) _____ is in effect.
6. A person who tries to engage in any form of sexual activity without consent is committing _____.
7. A person who intentionally kills another person has committed _____.
8. A violent shaking of the earth that may cause buildings to collapse is called a(n) _____.

Review

1. Why can stress cause accidents?
2. How can a person's attitude influence the chances of having an accident?
3. Identify ways that automobiles are being made safer.
4. Describe safety tips you can follow when you are riding a bicycle in the street.
5. Identify ways you can design your home to reduce the risk of falling.
6. Why is it important to identify containers in your home that contain poisons?
7. What can you do to rescue a person who is drowning?
8. How does OSHA help protect workers throughout the country?
9. Describe rules to follow to prevent injuries due to firearms.
10. Describe the advantages of driving a car that has an air bag system.

Application

1. How can your frame of mind play a role in your ability to avoid having an accident?
2. Describe how the use of safety belts can reduce automobile-related deaths.
3. What can you do to keep your home safe from a robber?
4. Why should any form of sexual assault be reported?

Individual Research

1. Obtain a new car brochure from an automobile dealer in your community. Read this brochure and describe the safety features built into the automobile. Compare these safety features with those on other automobiles studied by your classmates.
2. Obtain materials from your local law enforcement agency that deals with sexual assault. Summarize the steps you should follow if you or someone you know is sexually assaulted.
3. Interview someone you know who has a job. Write a report in which you describe this person's job and the safety rules this person must follow to protect his or her health while at work. You may also describe how this person's employer promotes health in the working environment.

Readings

Castleman, Michael, *Crime Free*. New York, NY: Simon and Shuster, 1984.

Gibilisco, Stan, *Violent Weather: Hurricanes, Tornadoes, and Storms*. Blue Ridge Summit, PA: TAB Books, Inc., 1984.

Schwarz, Ted, *Protect Your Home & Family: A Common Sense Guide to Personal Safety*. New York, NY: Arco Publishing, Inc., 1984.

When timing is crucial, some hospitals use helicopters as a rapid means of transportation in life-threatening situations. With advanced life-support equipment, the in-flight medical team becomes an extension of the emergency room.

Chapter 25

Emergency Care

OBJECTIVES: You will be able to
- **describe the importance of first aid.**
- **identify the priorities of giving first aid.**
- **describe first-aid procedures for environmental hazards.**

You and your friend are on your bikes when suddenly you hear a car's tires screeching behind you. You turn around and see that your friend has been hit by the car, and is lying unconscious in the street. Your friend is bleeding severely from one leg and is not breathing. What is the first step you need to take? Do you know how to stop bleeding from a wound? Do you know how to help a person who has stopped breathing?

The information in this chapter will help you answer questions like these and many more. You will learn how to provide emergency care for others as well as yourself.

FIRST AID

Have you ever been in a situation in which someone around you became injured or suddenly ill? Perhaps you were afraid and felt confused. You may have wondered whether or not you should take certain actions. There are many rules to follow to provide emergency care. The right emergency care can save lives.

25:1 The Importance of First Aid

First aid is the immediate and temporary care given to a person who has been injured or suddenly becomes ill. It also includes self-help and home care when medical assistance is delayed or is not available.

Having knowledge of proper first-aid procedures may help you to save yourself and others.

Knowing first-aid procedures may enable you to save yourself and others from possible permanent disability or death. Thousands of lives are saved each year because people like you knew what to do as well as what not to do in emergency situations.

Knowing how to perform first aid also promotes safety awareness in the home, at work and play, and on the road in a motor vehicle or on a bicycle. As a result, you become more cautious in your behavior and take steps to eliminate hazards that can increase the risks of having an accident.

PRIORITIES OF FIRST AID

Suppose you came across a person who became suddenly injured or seriously ill. You would need to think quickly and clearly to make a plan of action.

25:2 General Directions for Giving First Aid

Have a plan of action to follow before giving first aid.

The plan of action you would follow in giving first aid would depend on the circumstances surrounding the accident or illness. Sometimes, prompt action is needed to save a life. In other situations, reassurance and prevention of further injury may be more of a priority than haste.

Know how to summon help in a first-aid situation.

Assuming that someone needs medical care quickly, it is important to know how to summon help. You can dial the emergency assistance telephone number in your community. Many areas in the United States use the 911 telephone number. Other areas have their own local emergency telephone number. Once an emergency telephone connection is made, give the following information.

- Identify the exact location at which you may be found. This means a building address, a floor in the building, and an area on the floor. If help is needed on a street, provide the closest nearby address.

- If possible, leave a telephone number at which you or a rescuer can be reached.

- Give the name of the rescuer.

- Provide as much specific information about the illness or injury as possible so that appropriate emergency equipment can be sent. If you as a rescuer cannot make the call, ask someone else to summon help.

After help has been called, further evaluate the situation. Standard first-aid priorities to help a victim of an accident or illness include

- prompt rescue, if necessary.
- checking for open airway.
- controlling severe bleeding.
- checking for signs of poison.

When life-threatening situations have been controlled, the victim's condition should be assessed. Check for a Medic Alert tag. A **Medic Alert tag** is a medical identification that provides important information about the person wearing it. These are usually worn as a necklace or bracelet. Be sure no other serious conditions exist, such as bleeding from the ears, bone fractures, or serious bruises.

It is important to give an ill or injured person psychological first aid. **Psychological first aid** is the process of helping people deal with the emotional aspects related to physical injury or illness. This kind of aid can be administered at the same time as physical first aid. An example of psychological first aid would be to tell a victim who is suffering severe pain that medical help is on the way and that steps will be taken as soon as possible to relieve the pain. Be truthful to the victim. Explain the situation, and let the victim know your plan of action.

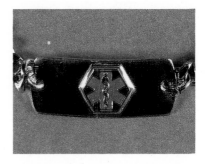

FIGURE 25–1. A Medic-Alert tag

Psychological first aid helps victims adjust mentally to a life-threatening situation.

25:3 Respiratory Emergencies

There are many situations under which breathing may stop or be limited. Among these are drowning, heart failure, electric shock, drug overdose, and carbon monoxide poisoning. This stoppage or limit of breathing is called **asphyxiation.** When a person is asphyxiated, it is important that breathing be restored quickly through artificial respiration. **Artificial respiration** is a term that includes many techniques that are used by one person to another to restore breathing. In mouth-to-mouth or mouth-to-nose respiration, the rescuer inflates the victim's lungs by forcing air into them. Use the following steps in deciding whether or not to give artificial respiration.

Asphyxiation occurs when a person stops breathing.

- Determine if the victim is responsive. Tap the victim on the shoulder and ask, "Are you OK?" If there is no response, place the victim on his or her back.
- If a spinal injury is suspected, do not move the victim.
- Check for breathing by looking for chest movement and listening for air movement.
- Follow the steps outlined in Figure 25–2.

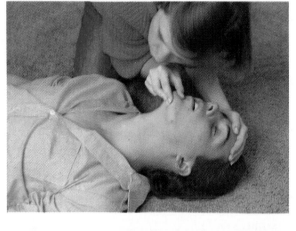
a

b

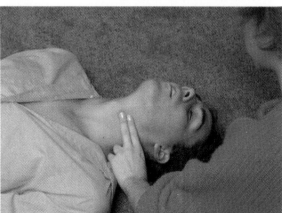
c

d

FIGURE 25–2. Mouth-to-mouth breathing: (a) open the airway by the head-tilt/chin-lift maneuver; check for breathing; (b) if the victim is not breathing, pinch the victim's nose, seal the victim's mouth with yours and give two full breaths; (c) check the victim's pulse on the side of the neck near you; check for breathing; (d) if you find a pulse but no breathing, administer one breath every five seconds (for an older child or adult).

The abdominal thrust is also known as the Heimlich maneuver.

Respiratory obstruction or choking is the sixth leading cause of accidental death among adults in the United States. Choking occurs most often because a piece of food becomes stuck in the throat and air cannot enter the lungs.

Immediate action must be taken if someone is choking. The "signal" for choking is to place one hand to the throat. If the victim can cough, speak, or breathe, do not do anything. He or she may free the blockage. If the victim cannot cough, speak, or breathe, begin action.

- Perform the abdominal thrust. Standing behind the victim, wrap your arms around his or her waist. Place the thumb side of the fist against the victim's abdomen just below the tip of the breastbone and slightly above the navel. Grasp your fist with your other hand and press into the victim's abdomen with four quick, upward thrusts. Hopefully, the matter that is lodged in the airway will be forced out of the body.
- If the above steps are not successful, repeat them.

If you experience an obstructed airway yourself and no one is around, you can perform this technique on yourself. Press your own fist into your upper abdomen and give a quick, upward thrust. Or, lean forward over a chair and press your abdomen quickly on the edge of the chair.

Suppose an infant or child has an obstructed airway. Place the victim faceup with the face lower than the rest of the body. Perform four chest thrusts. For an infant, apply pressure on the chest by using two fingers on the sternum between the nipples.

The abdominal thrust helps remove objects lodged in the throat.

25:4 Cardiopulmonary Resuscitation

Cardiopulmonary resuscitation, or **CPR**, is an emergency procedure that is used with mouth-to-mouth resuscitation when the heart has stopped beating. CPR should never be done on a conscious person or on someone who has a heartbeat. Only persons trained in CPR should administer these techniques.

The ABCs of CPR are general procedures you should know.

A–Airway—Always be sure the victim's airway is open. The tongue is the most common cause of airway obstruction in an unconscious victim.

B–Breathing—After making sure the airway is open, check to see if the person is breathing. CPR should not be performed if the person is breathing.

C–Circulation—Always check the victim's pulse to determine if chest compressions will be necessary.

If necessary, CPR is performed by placing the victim on his or her back. If an adult victim or large child has no pulse or is not breathing, a trained person will perform CPR. The trained person will

- find the lower part of the breastbone (xiphoid process) and measure up the width of two fingers from that point (Figure 25–3, step a).

- place the heel of his or her other hand on the sternum next to the fingers. He or she will then place the hand used to find the xyphoid process on top of the hand on the sternum. By interlocking the fingers of the two hands, the trained person keeps his or her fingers off the chest of the victim (Figure 25–3, step b).

- lock his or her elbows and bring the shoulders directly over the hands so that pressure is forced straight down (Figure 25–3, step c). This person will exert enough pressure to depress the breastbone one and one-half to two inches. Each compression forces blood from the heart to other parts of the body.

FIGURE 25–3.

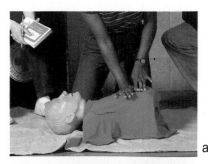
a

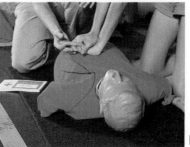
b

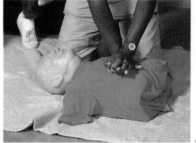
c

Give compression at a rate of 80 per minute. After every 15 compressions, the person trained in CPR will give two full breaths. This cycle is to be repeated until respiration and circulation are restored or until medical help arrives.

Become trained in CPR. Contact your local chapter of the American Red Cross, the American Heart Association, or other organizations that teach CPR, and enroll in a class.

25:5 Controlling Bleeding

Any break in the skin is called a wound.

A **wound** is any break in the continuity of the body's tissues. An open wound is one in which the skin is broken, and there is injury to underlying tissues. A closed wound is one in which the skin is not broken. This section will focus upon treatment for open wounds since they usually are associated with bleeding.

An open wound presents unique problems. The first is the possibility of infection. Even the smallest break in the skin can permit the entrance of bacteria into the body. The second problem is the loss of blood. The type of wound and its severity will determine the extent of bleeding. See Table 25–1 for the different types of wounds.

Table 25–1 Types of Wounds

There are five main types of wounds.

NAME OF WOUND	DESCRIPTION
Abrasion	Caused by scraping or rubbing. The skin's surface is raw; bleeding is limited. Danger of infection exists.
Avulsion	Tissue is separated or torn from the body; bleeding is heavy. These occur in motor vehicle accidents and animal bites.
Incision	Caused by a sharp cut, such as from a knife; bleeding may be heavy.
Laceration	A jagged or irregular tearing of the skin; bleeding is heavy. Danger of infection is great because foreign matter is forced deep into the wound.
Puncture	Produced by pointed instruments, such as needles or nails. They can be very deep; bleeding is limited. Tetanus may develop unless the patient has a tetanus injection. Danger of infection is high.

PRESSURE POINTS

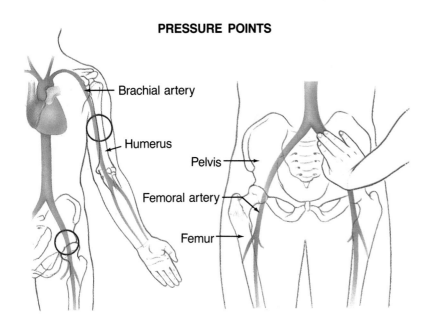

Brachial artery

Humerus

Pelvis

Femoral artery

Femur

FIGURE 25–4. The pressure points involve two main arteries—the brachial artery and the femoral artery.

The first priority in any wound is to stop severe bleeding and prevent germs from entering the wound. A person with a wound may bleed to death in a matter of minutes.

The application of direct pressure is one way to stop bleeding. Apply direct pressure by pressing the palm of the hand on a clean dressing directly over the wound. In most cases, this step will be enough to stop bleeding. If blood soaks through the dressing, do not remove it. Removing the dressing can promote more bleeding by pulling away clots that may be forming. Instead, add more layers of dressing. In addition to direct pressure, also elevate the wounded body part above the level of the heart. This helps reduce blood flow to the area. If a foreign object is lodged deep in the tissue of the wound, do not remove it. This can cause further bleeding and serious damage.

A second method of stopping bleeding is the use of pressure on a supplying artery. If direct pressure and elevation do not stop bleeding, the pressure-point technique may be required. The pressure point technique compresses the main artery that supplies blood to the affected body part. This technique stops circulation within the limb. The two pressure points recommended by the American Red Cross are under the arm (the brachial artery) and inside the groin area (the femoral artery). It is important to remember that if the use of pressure points is necessary, it should be used with direct pressure and elevation. Using pressure points to stop bleeding is not a substitute for direct pressure.

Stopping blood flow through a wound is a priority.

Direct pressure can be used to stop bleeding.

Using pressure on a supplying artery can help stop bleeding.

A tourniquet should be used only as a last resort.

Guard against shock in all cases of bleeding.

Poisons introduced into the body can cause illness or death.

An unconscious victim should not be forced to vomit.

A third method of stopping bleeding is the use of a tourniquet. A **tourniquet** is a band that is applied to stop blood flow to a wound. Using a tourniquet is dangerous because severe tissue damage may result from lack of blood and oxygen if the tourniquet is left on too long. A tourniquet is a last resort and should be used only for severe, life-threatening bleeding that cannot be controlled by other means.

If a tourniquet is applied, it should not be loosened. A note showing the location and time of application of the tourniquet should be attached to the victim's clothing in a visible location. The tourniquet should be visible at all times. A physician should be seen immediately.

25:6 Poisoning

A **poison** is any substance that can cause illness or death when introduced into the body. Poisons can enter the body through ingestion (swallowing), inhalation, injection, or absorption through the skin or mucous membranes.

The first step in the treatment of a poison victim is to determine immediately the poison ingested. If a container is nearby, follow the first-aid directions on the label. Get additional clues by asking others what they think occurred. Call your local Poison Control Center or physician for further information. Seek medical help for the victim.

What should be done if there are no first aid directions on the container or there is no container? Dilute the ingested poison by having the victim drink milk or water. Seek immediate medical attention.

Never force an unconscious victim to vomit. Also, never force a victim to vomit who has swallowed a corrosive substance such as lye, bleach, or a petroleum product such as gasoline or kerosene. Vomiting these products can cause further damage to the digestive tract. Rather, have the victim swallow milk or eat raw eggs or mashed potatoes so that the stomach can be coated and the poison neutralized.

25:7 Shock

Any serious injury or illness can result in shock. **Shock** is a condition in which the rate of the functions of the vital organs of the body slows.

A person who goes into shock will have certain signs and symptoms. In the early stages of shock, blood flow to the skin is reduced resulting in a lowered body temperature. The skin may appear bluish and feel cold and clammy to the touch. The pulse may be too weak to detect at the wrist. Breathing rate may

FIGURE 25–5. Labels of all poisonous materials contain instructions to follow in case the material is swallowed or inhaled.

increase and nausea may occur. These early stages of shock may last for a period of time after which the signs and symptoms of the late stages of shock appear.

During the late stages of shock, the victim may not be responsive. The eyes may be sunken and the pupils dilated. Body temperature and blood pressure may continue to fall to a low level. The victim may lose consciousness and perhaps die if treatment does not begin immediately.

It is important to improve the circulation of a shock victim. This means keeping the airway open or administering artificial respiration or CPR. It is also important to maintain body temperature. To accomplish this, keep the person lying down. The head should be level with the body and the lower extremities raised about 8 to 12 inches above the level of the heart. However, do not raise the victim's feet if there is a head injury or fracture in one or both legs. If the victim is having difficulty breathing, raise the head and shoulders. Allow the victim to get adequate oxygen and keep him or her warm with a blanket. Do not add heat, but maintain body temperature. Unless medical assistance will be delayed more than six hours, do not give anything by mouth.

It is important to maintain body temperature and blood circulation in a shock victim.

 ## Review and Reflect

1. How could knowing about first aid help you?
2. What four priorities should you check when coming upon an accident victim?
3. How does the abdominal thrust help clear a blocked air passage?
4. Why is it important for you to learn CPR?
5. Why are open wounds subject to infection?
6. Why is it important to administer first aid immediately for a victim who is poisoned?
7. Why should a victim who has swallowed a corrosive substance not be forced to vomit?

SUDDEN ILLNESS OR INJURY

When a person becomes suddenly injured or ill, the function and possibly the structure of the body changes. The objective of first aid is to prevent these changes from causing further harm to the body.

25:8 Heart Attack and Stroke

First aid should be administered to victims of heart attack and stroke.

Heart attack and stroke are leading causes of death in the United States today. However, many victims of these conditions might be saved each year if first aid techniques were administered. Before giving first aid for a heart attack victim, it is important that certain signs and symptoms be recognized.

It is important to recognize the signs and symptoms of a heart attack.

A person having a heart attack may experience uncomfortable pressure, squeezing, fullness, tightness, or pain in the center of the chest and/or in the left arm. The pain may spread to the shoulders, arms, neck, or jaw. Pain may be accompanied by sweating, nausea, weakness, and shortness of breath.

If a heart attack victim is conscious, place him or her in a semireclining position and loosen any tight clothing. Provide reassurance and call for help immediately. If the victim is not breathing, begin artificial respiration. Be sure to get medical help immediately.

A stroke victim may be conscious or unconscious. Breathing rate may be slow and pupils in the eyes may be unequal in size. The victim may have slurred speech and paralysis on one side of the body.

A stroke victim should be kept lying down with the head and shoulders raised.

First aid for a stroke victim consists of keeping the person lying down with the head and shoulders raised to relieve the force of blood on the brain. The victim's air passage should be kept open. Keep the victim calm, and summon medical help immediately.

25:9 Fractures, Dislocations, Sprains, and Strains

Injuries to muscles, joints, and bones include fractures, dislocations, sprains, and strains.

Injuries involving bones, joints, and muscles are common to people your age. A **fracture** is a break or a crack in a bone. Sometimes, a fracture is not easy to detect because its signs and symptoms may be similar to those of a sprain. A **sprain** is an injury to the ligaments, tendons, and soft tissue around a joint caused by undue stretching. If you are not sure whether a fracture or sprain exists, always treat the injury as if it were a fracture (Table 25–2).

Dislocations are common sports injuries.

People who are involved in sports involving physical contact often suffer dislocations. A **dislocation** is the movement of a bone from its joint. Dislocations often are accompanied by stretched ligaments.

Muscle strain is another common injury. **Strain** is an overstretching of muscles and/or tendons. One of the most common strains involves the muscles of the back.

Table 25–2   First Aid for Fractures, Dislocations, Sprains, and Strains

	SIGNS AND SYMPTOMS	FIRST AID
FRACTURES	pain, swelling, loss of movement, and deformity. Fracture of the skull may be seen by bleeding from head and/or ears; drowsiness; headache.	• Treat for bleeding and shock if necessary. • Prevent injured part from moving. • For head injury, keep victim still. • Apply ice to prevent swelling. • Get medical help immediately.
DISLOCATIONS	pain, swelling upon movement, loss of movement, an obvious deformity.	• Apply cold compresses, and keep the body part still. • Do not pull a dislocated finger - it may be fractured.
SPRAINS	pain that increases with movement or weight bearing; tenderness, swelling.	• Apply cold compresses and elevate. • Get medical help if a fracture is suspected.
STRAINS	pain, swelling, stiffness, and firmness to the area.	• Apply moist heat if injury is in lower back; apply cold compresses to other injured areas. • Severe strain should be seen by a physician.

25:10   Burns

Each year, over two million burn accidents occur in the United States. Burns may result from contact with various sources: touching fire, a hot stove, an exposed electrical wire, chemicals, and/or exposure to the sun.

Burns produce significant problems. They produce pain since nerve endings in the skin are harmed. The burned area may become swollen. In severe burns, there may be a loss of body fluids as well as severe infection caused by the destruction of skin tissue. Severely burned victims who initially survive their accident most often die because of infection that results from their burns.

There are three different types of burns. See Table 25–3 for a description of each type as well as their treatments and outcomes.

Burns produce pain by harming the nerve endings in the skin.

Table 25-3   Types of Burns and Their Treatment

TYPE OF BURN AND SIGNS	TREATMENT	OUTCOME
First Degree - outer skin reddened; slight swelling; pain.	Cool area with cold tap water or cool compresses.	Heals without scarring in about six days.
Second Degree - blisters form, skin may have a wet, shiny appearance; may be discharge of fluid.	Apply cool water or cold cloths; apply sterile dressing over blisters; if burns over large part of body, treat for shock and get medical attention. Do not break blisters or remove tissue.	Heals in about two weeks with slight scarring.
Third Degree - skin is white, brown, or charred; painless at first due to nerve damage.	Apply sterile dressing immediately; treat for shock and get medical attention.	Can take months or years to treat; may require skin grafting; often permanent scars.

25:11   Nosebleeds

Nosebleeds often occur easily because fragile blood vessels lie near the surface of the nose. Nosebleeds can result from injury, vigorous nose blowing, or dry, nasal membranes. In many cases, you can stop your nose from bleeding. Stand up or sit on a chair and lean forward. Pinch your nose with the thumb and forefinger just below the cartilage or hard part of the nose for ten minutes. If bleeding does not stop within a reasonable time, insert a small, clean pad of gauze into one or both nostrils and again apply pressure.

Usually, nosebleeds can be treated by the affected individual.

Prevent nosebleeds by keeping nasal membranes moist. To do this, apply petroleum jelly inside your nose daily. You may also choose to use a vaporizer to increase the humidity in the air you breathe. Try to protect your nose from injury. If you do have a nosebleed, refrain from blowing your nose until several hours after the bleeding has stopped.

A person who has frequent nosebleeds should see a physician.

If you experience regular nosebleeds or ones that persist, see a physician. Recurrent nosebleeds may indicate a health problem that requires further medical attention.

Review and Reflect

8. Describe first-aid measures for heart attack.

9. What are ways that you might prevent a nosebleed?

ENVIRONMENTAL HAZARDS

Exposure to environmental hazards can result in serious physical harm. Some of these environmental hazards include snake bites, poisoning from plants and animals, particles in the air that are blown into the eyes, and overexposure to heat and cold.

25:12 Snakebites

About 45 000 people are bitten each year by snakes in the United States. Of these, 20 percent are bitten by poisonous snakes. Over half of all snakebites occur in Texas, North Carolina, Florida, Georgia, Louisiana, and Arkansas.

Among the poisonous snakes in the United States are the coral snakes and the pit vipers, such as rattlesnakes, water moccasins, and copperheads. Coral snakes have a black nose and alternating red, yellow, and black rings around the body. Pit vipers have a pit between the eye and nostril and one to six fangs.

Symptoms of snakebite can be mild, moderate, or severe. Mild to moderate symptoms include mild swelling and pain or discoloration at the site of the wound. Rapid pulse, dimmed vision, nausea, vomiting, and shortness of breath are also mild to moderate symptoms. Severe symptoms may include rapid swelling and numbness followed by severe pain at the wound site. The victim may also have constricted pupils, slurred speech, shock, and paralysis. This may be followed by difficulty in breathing and unconsciousness.

The victim of a snakebite should be taken to a hospital immediately. Meanwhile, the following first-aid procedures should be performed.

1. Keep the victim still and as calm as possible. This will help reduce the speed with which toxins will circulate in the body.

2. Keep the bitten extremity at or below the level of the heart. If the victim will be in a hospital within four or five hours and no further symptoms develop, no further first-aid measures need be applied.

3. For victims who develop mild to moderate symptoms, apply a constricting band two-to-four inches (five-to-ten cm) above the bite but not around a joint or the head, neck, or trunk. The band should be three-fourths to one and one-half inches (2 to 4 cm) wide yet loose enough for a finger to be slipped underneath.

Coral snakes and pit vipers are two kinds of poisonous snakes.

FIGURE 25–6. (a) Coral snake (b) copperhead

a

b

FIGURE 25–7. (a) Fang marks of a poisonous snake (b) fang marks of a nonpoisonous snake

PATTERNS OF FANG MARKS

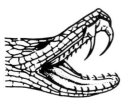
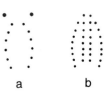
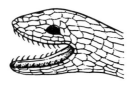

Poisonous snake

a   b

Nonpoisonous snake

4. For victims who develop severe symptoms and stop breathing, apply mouth-to-mouth resuscitation. If there is no pulse or heartbeat and you are trained, perform CPR.

Remember, a person who has been bitten by a snake needs medical attention as soon as possible. To prevent being bitten by a snake, take the following precautions.

- Do not disturb snakes.

- Avoid areas where snakes are found.

- If you enter an area infested with snakes, wear heavy midcalf boots and long trousers.

Poison ivy, poison oak, and poison sumac are some examples of poisonous plants.

25:13   Poisons from Plants

Among the plants that may cause severe irritation if touched or contacted are poison ivy, poison oak, and poison sumac. Learn to recognize these plants so that contact with them can be avoided. These plants are even hazardous in the winter when they have dropped their leaves.

If you contact a poisonous plant, you may develop a skin reaction accompanied by redness, swelling, itching, or burning. Blisters may form and seep or ooze a watery substance. A reaction may be prevented if you remove contaminated clothing, wash the exposed area with soap and water, and apply alcohol and calamine lotion.

Rashes from poisonous plants can be treated with over-the-counter gels and liquids. If the rash is spread over large parts of the body, applications of cool, saltwater compresses (two teaspoons per quart) will be helpful in relieving itching. Apply the compresses for ten minutes, four times daily. Do not scratch the affected areas because infection may occur and delay healing. Itching may be relieved through medication or cold compresses, but a skin reaction may continue for as long as two weeks. You may need to see a physician if the affected area covers a large part of the body.

FIGURE 25–8. Poison ivy leaves

25:14   Stings and Bites

Among the more common insects that sting people are bees, hornets, wasps, and yellow jackets. Hornets, wasps, and yellow jackets can sting repeatedly. They inject venom with each thrust of their tails. A bee stings once and usually leaves its stinger with its sac of venom in the victim's skin. For most people, insect stings are not a problem. A sting will usually produce a burning sensation followed by reddening and itching at the site. Swelling and pain may also occur. For people who are allergic to insect bites, a sting from an insect poses a serious problem that may result in death. A person who is sensitive to these stings may develop headaches, nausea, stomach pains, go into shock, and have swollen vocal cords. This may result in respiratory failure. These individuals can be given special medications to fight the effects of stings.

Preventive measures can be taken to reduce being stung. If you will be in an area where there are bees, avoid wearing bright colors, strong perfumes and lotions, and scented soap. All of these products attract bees. Other safeguards against bee stings range from wearing shoes when outdoors to covering food at a picnic.

For a bee sting, first flick out the stinger with a nail file or other similar object. Do not squeeze the sac as venom can be forced into the body. Apply an ice bag or cold compress to the sting for 15 minutes. This procedure can be followed for all stings. Unless a person is sensitive to the sting, no further medical treatment is needed.

Spiders are also known to bite people. Spiders are found in attics, basements, and outdoor woodpiles. Some spiders, such as the black widow spider and the brown recluse spider, are poisonous. The black widow spider has a glossy black body with red or yellowish markings on the abdomen. The sign of a black widow spider bite is the appearance of a small pinprick that is followed by a dull, numbing pain. Headache, muscular weakness, vomiting, and sweating may develop.

When first bitten by a black widow spider, clean the area with soap and water, and apply ice to relieve pain. See a physician immediately for appropriate medication.

The brown recluse spider has a violin-shaped marking on its back. A stinging sensation occurs when it bites. The bitten area will become red, swollen, and tender after a number of hours. The area will be encircled with a red ring and look somewhat like a bull's-eye on a target. Chills, nausea, and vomiting may follow. Treatment for a brown recluse spider bite is the same as that outlined for a bite from the black widow spider. It is essential to get immediate medical attention.

FIGURE 25–9. Honeybee

The first procedure to follow for a bee sting is to remove the stinger.

FIGURE 25–10. Black widow spider

FIGURE 25-11. Removing a particle from an eye

REMOVING A PARTICLE FROM THE EYE

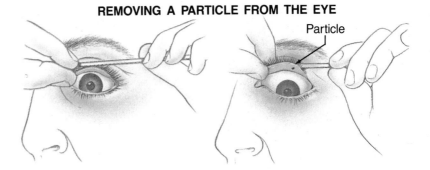

Particle

25:15   Objects in the Eye

Most eye problems resulting from small dirt particles can be treated at home.

Foreign bodies, such as dust or small dirt particles, often lodge in your eyes, especially on windy days. This eye problem can usually be treated at home. Generally, these dust particles are found under the upper lid and can be irritating. Never rub the eye because further injury can result. Get assistance from someone to help you lift the upper lid. If the pain is not relieved, the object is probably sticking to the inside of the eyelid.

The object may be removed by pulling the upper lid over the lower lid. When the object is seen, remove it with a clean, moist, cotton swab. If the object is seen on the clear surface of the eye, it can be dislodged by blinking or by flushing the eye very carefully with water.

Careful attention should be given to a speck of dirt on the cornea of the eye.

Pay particular attention to an object lodged on the cornea. The object can scratch the cornea and cause vision damage. If a speck of dirt or dust does not leave the cornea through rinsing, seek medical attention.

25:16   Overexposure to Heat

Heat stroke, heat exhaustion, and heat cramps are examples of heat-related problems.

Heat-related problems affect many individuals. These include heat stroke, heat exhaustion, and heat cramps. **Heat stroke** is a sudden attack of illness from exposure to high temperatures. Often, physical exertion is a contributing factor. Signs and symptoms of heat stroke are flushed, hot, and dry skin; no perspiration; strong, rapid pulse; high body temperature; and possible convulsions.

A heat-stroke victim should be taken to a cool area and receive cold applications. If possible, the victim should be placed in a tub filled with cold water. Do not overchill. A heat-stroke victim should always receive medical care.

Heat exhaustion is a health condition caused by extreme physical exertion and excessive sweating over a long period of time. A person suffering from heat exhaustion will feel tired; have pale, cool, and clammy skin; have heavy perspiration; experience weakness or dizziness; and suffer from a headache.

A victim who suffers from heat exhaustion should receive the following treatment.

A person who suffers heat exhaustion needs special care.

- Move the victim to a cool place, but do not allow the person to become chilled.

- Loosen the victim's clothing, and lay him or her down, raising the feet 8 to 12 inches.

- If the victim is conscious, administer sips of cool water. Do not administer fluids to a victim who vomits or is unconscious.

- Treat the victim for shock.

Heat cramps are painful muscles caused by overexertion during hot, humid conditions. Signs of heat cramps are painful muscles, especially in the legs and stomach. Faintness and dizziness may occur.

Heat cramps occur most often during hot, humid conditions.

First aid for heat cramps includes rest, muscle massage, and fluid replacement. To prevent heat-related illnesses, be aware of the onset of the specific signs and symptoms. Go to a cool area and rest.

25:17 Overexposure to Cold

The major cold weather hazards are frostbite and hypothermia. **Frostbite** is the damage to tissue caused by exposure to severe cold. It most often occurs to the extremities such as the fingers, toes, and ears. The blood supply to these parts decreases because the blood vessels constrict. For this reason, the tissues do not get the warmth they need.

The signs of frostbite appear in stages. At first, the skin feels cold and becomes red. Then, it turns grayish and numb. Eventually, the exposed body part can be damaged beyond its ability to repair itself.

First-aid procedures include going indoors and keeping the body part warm and dry. Remove all cold and wet clothing. Frostbitten body parts should be placed in warm water—102° to 108°F (39° to 42°C). Be sure the water remains warm. Drink hot fluids. If the frostbite appears serious, medical attention is needed.

First aid should be given to victims of frostbite.

FIGURE 25–12. Exposure to low temperatures requires proper clothing and equipment if a person is to avoid frostbite or hypothermia.

A person suffering from hypothermia has a lowered body temperature.

A victim of hypothermia needs a warm, dry environment.

Hypothermia is a lowering of the body temperature to a level where body functions are affected. Hypothermia is a leading cause of death among people who are active in the outdoors.

Hypothermia can occur in temperatures between 30° and 50°F (−1° to 10°C). The combination of wind, moisture, and low air are enough to cause body temperature to drop to dangerously low levels.

When exposed to these conditions, a person's first reaction is to shiver and keep active in order to stay warm. However, the body soon becomes fatigued as body temperature drops. The victim may feel lightheaded and dizzy. Muscular coordination may become impaired and speech slurred. Eventually, the victim may suffer complete exhaustion, which may lead to death.

First aid for hypothermia consists of getting the victim into a warm, dry environment. Remove all wet clothing, and wrap the victim in a blanket. Add additional sources of heat. This can mean direct body contact, such as the victim being hugged by the first aider. Be sure to keep the victim awake, and get medical attention. Hypothermia is dangerous and life-threatening.

 Review and Reflect

10. What should you do if you are jogging and begin to suffer from heat exhaustion?

11. How can you suffer from hypothermia on a day that the temperature is 50°F (0°C)?

Activity: Preparing for Heat and Cold

You are preparing to take a five-mile hike. You will be exposed to a temperature that is 40°F (4°C) for two hours. Drizzle and strong winds may occur. Describe the precautions you should follow in planning your hike. Emphasize and describe the kinds of clothing you will take with you. What kinds of clothing would best protect your extremities? You may need to gather information from publications that discuss safety.

Health ADVANCES

About 8000 people die each year in drowning accidents. Recent medical research indicates that victims, who in the past have been considered beyond help, may be saved despite being submerged in water for a long period of time.

New research shows drowning victims submerged in cold water for long periods of time can be revived.

25:18   The Cold Water Drowning Syndrome

Several years ago, a high school senior in Michigan accidentally drove his car into what he thought was a snow-covered field. However, this student found that instead of a snow-covered field, he had driven into a pond. He was thrown out of his car and was rescued after being submerged under water for 38 minutes. You might think that normally under this condition this person would be dead. However, today he is alive and suffers no brain damage.

A victim may survive a near drowning when submerged in water 70°F (21°C) and under for extended periods of time. This phenomenon is called the mammalian diving reflex. Scientists have observed this reflex in sea mammals, such as whales, since the 1930s. However, only recently has a human application been made.

When submerged in water below 70°F (21°C), the body mobilizes defenses to protect the heart, brain, and lungs. Changes occur so that heart rate and metabolism come to a near stop, thereby decreasing the need for oxygen. A person under these conditions pulled from the water may appear dead.

FIGURE 25–13. In January 1984, four-year-old Jimmy Tontlewicz was pulled from 32°F water below an icy covering on Lake Michigan along Chicago's lakefront. The boy was submerged for twenty minutes. Special procedures were followed to save him. He survived the experience, and after a lengthy hospital stay, continues to show steady improvement.

Special techniques can be used to save victims of cold water drowning.

Such recoveries are no longer considered miraculous. More and more they are becoming a matter of standard emergency medicine. With the administration of CPR and some special techniques, many people who were once considered dead are being saved. In these cases, the rapid onset of hypothermia helped.

Focus on
Life Management Skills

- When someone requires immediate medical attention, check for breathing, circulatory failure, severe bleeding, and poisoning.
- Know how to summon help if a medical emergency arises.
- Always apply direct pressure first to a person who is bleeding.
- Always treat a severely injured or ill person for shock.
- Administer mouth-to-mouth artificial respiration to a person whose heart may be beating but who is not breathing.
- Become trained to administer CPR.
- Poison victims who have not ingested an acid should be forced to vomit if they are conscious.
- Learn to recognize poisonous plants so you can avoid contact with them.
- Use caution in removing an object from the eye.
- Place frostbitten body parts in warm water.
- A person undergoing hypothermia should be placed in a warm environment and given warm fluids.

Health
CAREERS

Emergency Medical Technician

There has been a bad accident on the highway. Two cars collided, and a few people have been injured. One man has had a heart attack, and a young girl has gone into shock. You can hear sirens from the distance. An emergency medical vehicle is on the way. Mike Jones is in the vehicle.

Mike is an emergency medical technician (EMT). EMTs are trained to provide emergency care to ill or injured persons until they can be transported to a hospital or receive a physician's care.

To become an EMT, federal guidelines recommend that you be a high school graduate, 18 years of age, proficient in reading, writing, and speaking English, be physically fit, have a driver's license, and have no drug dependency. You must then complete a basic EMT training course through an accredited institution. You will learn how to administer first aid and CPR.

Eighty percent of EMTs have full-time jobs and work as volunteers for emergency rescue squads. So, after completing the basic EMT course, you might want to take additional courses if you have interest in doing this full time. These extra courses would train you to begin IVs, use a defibrillator, which restores heart rhythm, and administer the hormone epinephrine, which is a heart stimulant in cases of shock.

The most advanced course is for EMT paramedic. The EMT paramedic can begin IVs, perform ECGs, use the defibrillator, and administer prescribed drugs. These people generally work full time as EMT paramedics.

Summary

1. Learning first aid promotes safety awareness for yourself and others. **25:1**

2. General first-aid directions include evaluating the situation and making and following a plan of action. **25:2**

3. A person who suffers respiratory failure may need artificial respiration. **25:3**

4. The ABCs of CPR are airway, breathing, and circulation. **25:4**

5. Bleeding can often be controlled by applying direct pressure. **25:5**

6. Poisons can enter a person's body through ingestion, inhalation, injection, or absorption through the skin or mucous membranes. **25:6**

7. All victims of serious injury or illness should be treated for shock. **25:7**

8. Heart attack and stroke victims should receive first aid. **25:8**

9. All fractures and dislocations as well as severe sprains and strains should receive medical attention. **25:9**

10. Second- and third-degree burns should receive medical attention. **25:10**

11. Prevent nosebleeds by keeping nasal membranes moist and protecting the nose from injury. **25:11**

12. Victims of poisonous snakebites need immediate medical attention. **25:12**

13. Poison ivy, poison oak, and poison sumac can result in skin irritations. **25:13**

14. Insect stings and bites from certain poisonous spiders may be harmful and even fatal if not treated. **25:14**

15. Careful procedures must be followed for removing objects from the eye. **25:15**

16. Among the conditions that can occur from overexposure to heat are heat stroke, heat exhaustion, and heat cramps. **25:16**

17. A person who suffers from frostbite or hypothermia needs first aid. **25:17**

18. With improved emergency medical care, the survival rate has increased for persons submerged under cold water for long periods of time. **25:18**

Vocabulary

Below is a list of vocabulary words used in this chapter. Use each word only once to complete the sentences. Do not write in this book.

asphyxiation   hypothermia
CPR   shock
dislocation   sprain
fracture   strain
heat exhaustion   wound

1. _____ is a technique that can be used on a heart attack victim whose heart stops beating.

2. Always apply ice to a(n) _____ rather than heat.

3. A general term that describes any break in the skin is a(n) _____.

4. Another name for a broken bone is a(n) _____.

5. In _____, the body temperature may drop so low that death may result.

6. _____ occurs when a person has trouble breathing.

7. In a(n) _____, the bone moves away from its joint.
8. Always apply heat if you suspect a person has suffered a(n) _____.
9. A person who suffers from _____ may feel tired and have cool, clammy skin.
10. A person with serious injuries, such as fractures or severe bleeding, should be treated for _____.

Review

1. What steps should you follow in making an emergency telephone call?
2. What are the life-threatening situations that require first aid?
3. What are the ABCs of CPR?
4. Why are wounds particularly dangerous?
5. How does the use of pressure points stop bleeding?
6. Why is psychological first aid important to administer?
7. What are the different kinds of wounds that a person can suffer?
8. Why should a person who swallows a corrosive not be forced to vomit?
9. What characteristics would identify certain snakes as being poisonous?
10. What signs and symptoms might indicate that a person is having a heart attack?

Application

1. Why should an unconscious person whom you suspect has ingested poison not be forced to vomit?
2. Why should you suspect a fracture if a person suffers a severe sprain?
3. Why is it important to take immediate action upon the onset of hypothermia?

Individual Research

1. Many hospitals have set up special burn units so that unique procedures can be used in grafting skin. Research these advancements and write a one-page report about your discoveries.
2. Enroll in a CPR course given by your local American Red Cross chapter, American Heart Association, or other local agency. Obtain CPR certification. Share your learning experience with your classmates.

Readings

Rosenberg, Stephen, *The Johnson and Johnson First Aid Book.* New York; NY: Warner Books, Inc., 1985.

Seymour, Rogers J., *The Heart Attack Survival Manual.* Terrytown, NY: Prentice-Hall Media, 1981.

Community and Environmental Health

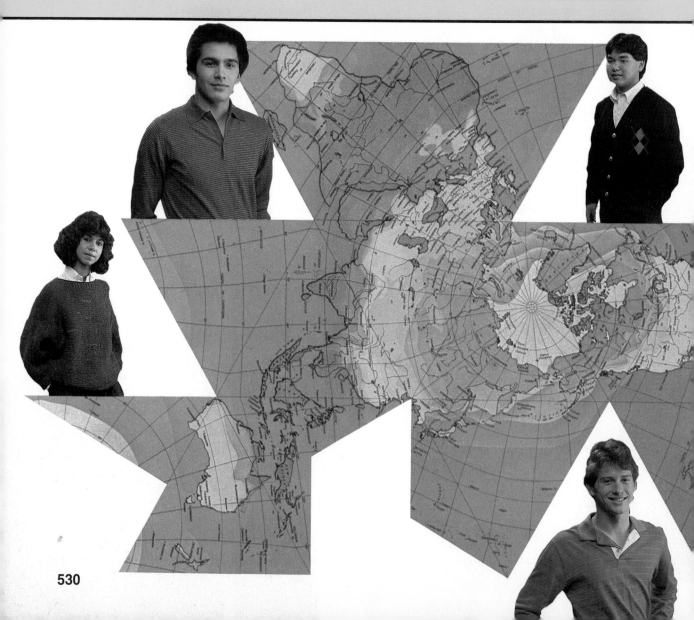

COMMUNITY AND ENVIRONMENTAL HEALTH

"We Are the World" was the title of a recording produced in 1985 by many artists who wanted to help raise money for hungry and starving people in the world. Millions of dollars were collected. Since then, concerts and other benefits have been planned to raise money for research and to promote health programs all over the world. When you take actions to keep your environment healthful and safe, you show concern for others. This unit focuses on the actions you can take to improve the environment for yourself and others.

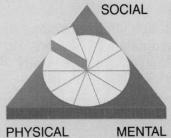

SOCIAL

PHYSICAL   MENTAL

Each kind of community has ways to take care of health needs of the people who live there. Do you know what agencies help protect your health? How is your community like other communities all over the world?

Chapter 26

Community and World Health

OBJECTIVES: You will be able to
- describe the characteristics and responsibilities of a healthful community.
- describe the services of voluntary health organizations, private foundations, professional associations, and corporate health programs.
- describe the services of local and state health departments.
- describe the services of federal health organizations.
- describe the health promotion activities of international organizations.

You have studied about healthful and responsible relationships. When you think about relationships, you most likely think about the persons you know well or see often. Their physical presence or contact with you keeps you informed of what is going on in their lives and what health needs they have. As a responsible person, you learn to make decisions about the health needs of persons with whom you are close.

There are many other persons with whom you do not have close association. Some live nearby in your community; others live in your state, country, or in foreign nations. Regardless of locality, all people have health needs. To meet these needs, government and private organizations have been formed to make decisions about how the health needs of people can and must be met. This is a difficult and expensive task. In this chapter, you will learn about the organizations that try to meet the health needs of persons in your community, nation, and world.

People in your community, nation, and world have various health needs.

COMMUNITY HEALTH

A community is a group of people living together in a particular location. People living in a community make decisions that influence their individual health, the health of others, and the quality of the environment.

People in communities make decisions that affect their health, the health of others, and the environment.

26:1 Characteristics of a Healthful Community

You live in a community. As an individual, you have certain rights and responsibilities with regard to health. For example, you have the right to live safely within your home, to eat healthful foods in clean restaurants, and to exercise in a public park.

You have many rights and responsibilities that influence community health.

You also have many responsibilities in your community. You obey traffic signs. You do not litter, and you dispose of trash properly. You may work with others to promote a positive health program in your community. You may volunteer to work at a community agency on a health promotion project or donate money for a healthful cause.

As a responsible person in your community, you understand the relationship between public health laws and community health. You know that public health laws protect the health and safety of everyone in your community. For example, there are NO SMOKING signs in public buildings because smoking is a fire hazard. There are laws about the cleanliness of employees at restaurants to protect you from unnecessary exposure to harmful microorganisms and disease. Many states have passed laws making the wearing of seat belts mandatory to keep persons safe and to lower automobile insurance rates. There are many laws that control the amount of air and water pollution from factory wastes. These laws protect the quality of your community.

Public health laws protect the health and safety of you and others.

In order to be a responsible citizen, respect and follow public health laws and encourage others to do so. Stay informed on issues that arise regarding public health laws and act upon them. Prepare for the time when you will be able to vote on many public health issues.

Knowing and following public health laws is your responsibility.

 Review and Reflect

1. How does your behavior influence community health?
2. Why are public health laws necessary?

FIGURE 26–1. In every community, there are laws to protect the people who live and work there.

HEALTH IN THE PRIVATE SECTOR

There are many organizations that engage in health promotion activities in your community. Some of these organizations are supported by taxes. Others are not tax supported. Voluntary health organizations, private foundations, professional associations, and corporate health programs are not tax supported. You will study how each of these organizations promotes health in your community. You will also study ways that you might become involved.

Many organizations engage in health promotion activities.

26:2 Voluntary Health Organizations

Voluntary health organizations focus on a specific disease, a health problem affecting certain body organs, or a problem that is related to a large part of the population. The National Anorexia Association would be an example of a voluntary association that centers upon a specific disease. The National Kidney Foundation is a voluntary association that deals with a particular body organ. The focus of the National Safety Council is the safe behavior of the entire population.

A voluntary organization usually has programs and activities that exist at the national, state, and local levels. Voluntary

Voluntary health organizations may provide money for research, direct services, educational programs, or political lobbying.

You can be a volunteer at most voluntary health agencies.

A school health fair can educate the community about voluntary health organizations.

organizations may receive funding from the United Way, United Appeal, and Community Chest as well as their own fund-raising events. Private contributions and bequests (gifts from wills) are also sources of income. The money may be used for research, services, educational programs, political lobbying, and operational expenses.

Most voluntary organizations rely on many volunteers to help with fund raising and health promotion activities. Volunteers help agencies meet their goals. There are many ways that you can volunteer to help. Learn how by calling an agency that interests you (Table 26–1).

Activity: Health Fair

Divide into groups with your classmates to plan a school health fair. Each group will have a booth at the fair to hand out literature and other information on one of the voluntary organizations. Your group should select one of the voluntary organizations listed below. Visit this voluntary organization to gather information. Design a pamphlet to describe its purpose, funding, services, and volunteer opportunities. Gather other materials to use as a display or handouts. Ask resource personnel to assist at the fair with health appraisal such as blood pressure readings.

Table 26–1   Some Voluntary Health Organizations

American Cancer Society	National Association for Mental Health
American Diabetes Association	National Council on Alcoholism
American Foundation for the Blind	National Foundation — March of Dimes
American Heart Association	National Kidney Foundation
American Lung Association	National Multiple Sclerosis Society
American Red Cross	
Arthritis Foundation	National Safety Council
National Society to Prevent Blindness	National Anorexia Association

26:3 Private Health Foundations

Private health foundations are organizations formed to support nonprofit health and social service programs. These foundations are formed by individuals within the community who have a vision for the future. They provide education, donate money for medical research, or have their own research laboratory.

There are several notable private health foundations. The Rockefeller Foundation is one of the largest. The purpose of the Rockefeller Foundation is to establish programs to reduce human suffering. The Henry Kaiser Foundation encourages the expansion of health maintenance organizations. The W. K. Kellogg Foundation's philosophy is to enable people to help themselves. It provides money for health promotion. The Metropolitan Life Foundation provides money for health education, health care planning, health cost containment, and research as well as for programs on illness prevention, and safety. The foundation has also actively supported (1) minority students seeking education in the medical field and (2) various wellness programs conducted in colleges and universities.

> Private health foundations provide education and donate money for research.

26:4 Professional Health Associations

A **professional health association** is an organization formed to meet the needs of a group of health-related professionals and to promote education in the health field. Usually, the professional

> Professional health associations promote education in the health field.

FIGURE 26–2. The American Association of Health, Physical Education, Recreation, and Dance is a professional organization that sponsors Jump Rope for Heart programs.

association exists at the national level with state and local affiliates. The association may produce a professional publication and hold a convention. Membership fees provide financial support needed for the activities. Examples of professional associations include the following.

There are many professional health associations that health-related professionals may join.

- American Association for Health, Physical Education, Recreation, and Dance (AAHPERD)
- American Dental Association (ADA)
- American Hospital Association (AHA)
- American Medical Association (AMA)
- American Nurses Association (ANA)
- American Public Health Association (APHA)
- American School Health Association (ASHA)
- American College of Sports Medicine (ACSM)

How might you become involved with a professional association? Perhaps you need information about an aspect of health or about a health career. You might read the organization's publication or contact the association for information. Perhaps a professional association has a convention in your city. You might want to attend to learn more about the health field. Later, if you choose a college major or career in the health field, you may want to join a professional association.

26:5   Corporate Health Programs

Corporate health programs benefit and promote the health and well-being of employees and their families. Businesses may assist in a variety of ways. A major benefit is employee health insurance for workers and their families. A nurse or physician may be on staff at the workplace to counsel employees regarding their health concerns. These medical professionals may conduct regular tests for glaucoma and hypertension. In addition, they may conduct classes on ways to stop smoking, lose weight, use effective communication, or manage stress constructively. There may be employee incentives for positive behavioral change, such as rewards for not smoking.

Many businesses provide corporate health programs for employees and their families.

Many corporate health programs offer employee assistance programs. These programs are designed to help employees who have drug abuse problems. There may be counseling, treatment, and 24-hour hotlines.

Some businesses have their own physical fitness facilities and hire fitness experts to design and implement individual physical fitness programs. The accomplishments of these corporate health programs have been successfully proven. Research shows that

FIGURE 26–3. The Corporate Challenge is one way companies encourage their employees to be physically fit.

employees who do not smoke are more physically fit, communicate better with their families, manage their sources of stress effectively, and are ill less often. They are also more productive on their jobs.

When you are hired for a job, ask what health programs are available for employees. Ask your parents what health programs and benefits are available for employees and families at their places of employment.

Those involved in corporate health programs are usually ill less often.

 ## Review and Reflect

3. How can individuals play a vital role in the promotion of health?
4. Why would someone join a professional health association?
5. Why do businesses have corporate health programs?

LOCAL AND STATE HEALTH DEPARTMENTS

Your state and local health departments provide statistical records of birth and death. These departments also help to control disease through early detection, screening, treatment, and education.

FIGURE 26–4. The local health department has the responsibility of examining restaurants and the foods they serve.

26:6   The Local Health Department

The local health department is officially responsible for the health of citizens in your community.

The **local health department** is the official government agency that has responsibility by law for the health and well-being of persons who reside in your community. This area may include your city, county, or township. The local health officer or commissioner directs the activities of the local health department. The local board of health consists of persons who determine policy for the local health department. The funding is derived from federal, state, and local taxes.

As the health care provider for your community, the local health department assumes various responsibilities. These services include nutrition, ambulatory care, sexually transmitted disease clinics, home care, chronic disease prevention, tuberculosis control, environmental protection, immunization, family planning, and maternal and child health care. The local health department may run various clinics and provide medical services. There is a charge for some of these services; however, arrangements are made for those who cannot afford to pay. The local health department may also test water quality in the water supply, certify food preparers, and inspect restaurants, school cafeterias, and other public eating establishments.

26:7   The State Health Department

The state health department is officially responsible for the health of citizens in your state.

The **state health department** is the official governmental agency that by law has responsibility for the health and well-being of the persons who reside in your state. The state health director or commissioner directs the activities of the state health department. The director or commissioner is usually a physician who is appointed by the governor or by the state board of health. The state board of health is made up of a variety of health professionals.

The administrative structure of state health departments varies. All states have a vital statistics department, assume a role in preventing communicable diseases, maintain environmental protection, and have a public health laboratory. In addition, there are usually family planning, nutritional, and public health nursing services. The state health department has the responsibility for inspecting hospitals, nursing homes, restaurants, and controlling the production and sale of drugs. The state health department may award licenses for certain health professionals. It also works closely with the local health department.

The funding for the state health department is derived mostly from taxes. Fees are collected for permits, registrations, and licenses. The federal government or a private organization may provide money for specific programs.

> The state and local health departments work closely together.

 ## Review and Reflect

6. What is the relationship between the local and state health departments?
7. Why are the local and state health departments considered governmental agencies?

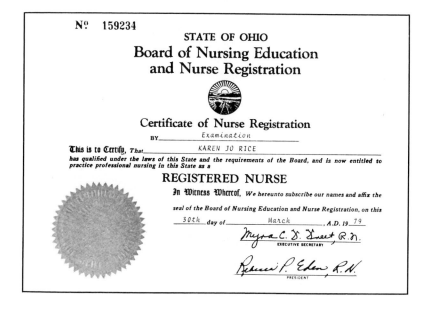

N⁰ 159234

STATE OF OHIO

**Board of Nursing Education
and Nurse Registration**

Certificate of Nurse Registration

BY _____ *Examination* _____

This is to Certify, That _____ KAREN JO RICE _____

has qualified under the laws of this State and the requirements of the Board, and is now entitled to practice professional nursing in this State as a

REGISTERED NURSE

In Witness Whereof, We hereunto subscribe our names and affix the

seal of the Board of Nursing Education and Nurse Registration, on this

__30th__ day of _____ March _____ , A.D. 19__79__

Myra C. S. Sweet R.N.
EXECUTIVE SECRETARY

Reamer P. Eden R.N.
PRESIDENT

FIGURE 26–5. The state health department issues certificates to qualified health professionals.

FEDERAL HEALTH ORGANIZATIONS

Federal taxes support services provided by national health organizations.

Besides organizations that promote health at the local and state level, there are also organizations at the national level. These services are provided by federal taxes.

Not everyone agrees where the primary responsibility for the administration and services associated with health care should be. Some taxpayers prefer that more individual responsibility be assumed by the private sector and less by those at the federal level. Some prefer more state and local responsibility and less by the federal government. This section focuses on the structure and purposes of federal health organizations.

Not everyone agrees where the primary responsibility for paying for health services should be.

26:8 Department of Health and Human Services

HHS is the department of the federal government that is responsible for health.

The **Department of Health and Human Services** (HHS) is the department of the federal government that is responsible for the administration and planning for health. HHS is divided into four governmental offices. These offices and their responsibilities are listed below.

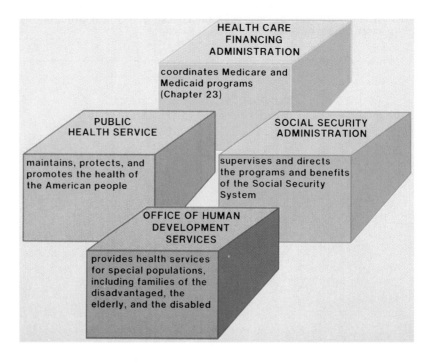

HEALTH CARE FINANCING ADMINISTRATION

coordinates Medicare and Medicaid programs (Chapter 23)

PUBLIC HEALTH SERVICE

maintains, protects, and promotes the health of the American people

SOCIAL SECURITY ADMINISTRATION

supervises and directs the programs and benefits of the Social Security System

OFFICE OF HUMAN DEVELOPMENT SERVICES

provides health services for special populations, including families of the disadvantaged, the elderly, and the disabled

26:9 The Public Health Service

The United States Public Health Service is directed by the **Surgeon General,** who is a physician appointed by the President. The Public Health Service is like other governmental organizations in that it is controlled by the current political administration. The Public Health Service is divided into agencies. These agencies reflect the structure that the current administration finds most effective. Presently, there are five agencies.

The Surgeon General is the head of the Public Health Service.

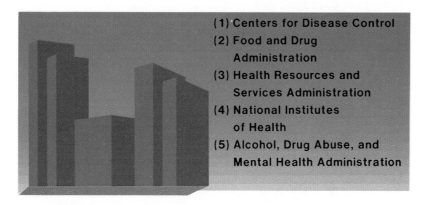

(1) Centers for Disease Control
(2) Food and Drug Administration
(3) Health Resources and Services Administration
(4) National Institutes of Health
(5) Alcohol, Drug Abuse, and Mental Health Administration

The **Centers for Disease Control** (CDC) is the agency of the Public Health Service of HHS that is responsible for preventing, controlling, and eradicating disease. The headquarters for CDC are in Atlanta, Georgia. Six different bureaus have specific functions related to the overall purpose of CDC.

The CDC is responsible for preventing, controlling, and eradicating disease.

- The Center for Infectious Diseases coordinates the program to control infectious disease.

- The Center for Environmental Health coordinates the efforts to control environmentally related diseases.

- The National Institute for Occupational Safety and Health (NIOSH) promotes a safe and healthful work environment.

- The Center for Preventive Services coordinates efforts with state and local health departments to prevent diseases.

- The Center for Health Promotion and Education designs, implements, and evaluates health promotion and risk reduction programs in schools, work settings, community settings, and health-care facilities.

- The Center for Professional Development and Training updates the instruction and professional skills of health professionals.

The FDA is responsible for checking the safety and effectiveness of foods, drugs, and cosmetics.

The **Food and Drug Administration** (FDA) is the agency within the Public Health Service of HHS that checks the safety and effectiveness of foods, drugs and cosmetics (Chapter 22). There are 10 regional offices and 25 district offices. The FDA is headed by a commissioner who directs six main bureaus.

- Center for Food Safety and Applied Nutrition
- Center for Drugs and Biologics
- Veterinary Medicine
- Center for Devices and Radiological Health
- Toxicological Research
- Regional Operations

The Health Resources and Services Administration works closely with health-care providers.

The **Health Resources and Services Administration** is the agency within the Public Health Service of HHS that assists various agencies in improving health resources and administering health services. This agency works closely with health-care providers and recommends ways to improve the health-care delivery system. There are four bureaus that carry out these functions.

- The Indian Health Service is the federal agency that provides for the health care needs of native Americans (Indians).
- The Bureau of Health Maintenance Organizations and Resources Development coordinates federal programs for the development of Health Maintenance Organizations (Chapter 23).
- The Bureau of Health Professions coordinates the efforts to maintain the quality of professional training of professionals.

FIGURE 26–6. The Indian Health Service provides medical help.

In the past, this has included financial support for certain types of training, such as medical school.

- The Bureau of Health-Care Delivery and Assistance helps with programs that serve specific health problems or populations. Genetic counseling for a specific group would be an example of programs for a specific population. The inner city might be an example of a locality with specific problems.

The **National Institutes of Health** (NIH) is an agency within the Public Health Service that conducts and supports biomedical research at eleven research institutes, a research hospital, the National Library of Medicine, and the Fogarty International Center. The eleven institutes are the

The NIH supports biomedical research at eleven research institutes.

- National Institute on Aging
- National Institute on Allergy and Infectious Diseases
- National Institute of Arthritis, Diabetes, and Digestive and Kidney Diseases
- National Cancer Institute
- National Institute of Child Health and Human Development
- National Institute of Dental Research
- National Institute of Environmental Health Sciences
- National Eye Institute
- National Institute of General Medical Sciences
- National Heart, Lung, and Blood Institute
- National Institute of Neurological and Communicative Disorders and Stroke

The Clinic Center is the research hospital of NIH. People who are admitted to this hospital are studied by one of the eleven institutes in order to further health knowledge about disease control and prevention. The National Library of Medicine is the largest medical reference facility in the world. The Fogarty International Center conducts health research on the international level and provides seminars that bring nations together to control and prevent diseases.

The National Library of Medicine of NIH is the largest medical reference facility in the world.

The **Alcohol, Drug Abuse, and Mental Health Administration** is the agency within the Public Health Service of HHS that coordinates efforts to prevent and treat alcohol abuse and alcoholism, drug abuse, and mental and emotional illness. This agency provides money to groups to design research programs to accomplish these efforts.

Review and Reflect

8. How does the Surgeon General influence the nation's health?

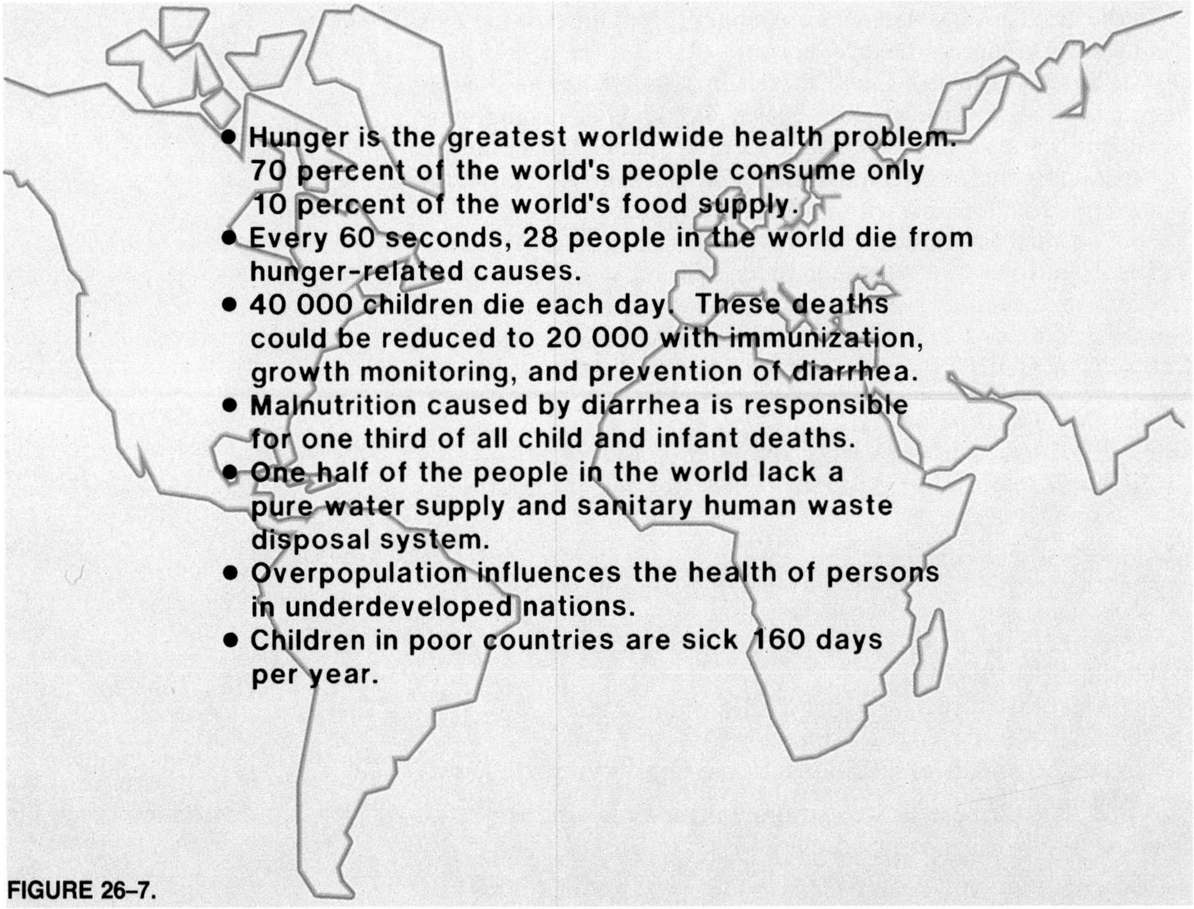

- Hunger is the greatest worldwide health problem. 70 percent of the world's people consume only 10 percent of the world's food supply.
- Every 60 seconds, 28 people in the world die from hunger-related causes.
- 40 000 children die each day. These deaths could be reduced to 20 000 with immunization, growth monitoring, and prevention of diarrhea.
- Malnutrition caused by diarrhea is responsible for one third of all child and infant deaths.
- One half of the people in the world lack a pure water supply and sanitary human waste disposal system.
- Overpopulation influences the health of persons in underdeveloped nations.
- Children in poor countries are sick 160 days per year.

FIGURE 26–7.

INTERNATIONAL HEALTH ORGANIZATIONS

Hunger is the greatest factor affecting worldwide health.

Lack of pure water and sanitary human waste disposal create many world health problems.

The purpose of WHO is to improve the quality of health worldwide.

The most critical issues in international health involve world hunger, basic health care, lack of a pure water supply, sanitary human waste disposal, and overpopulation. The following discussion includes some of the organizations that work to remedy the issues highlighted in Figure 26–7.

26:10 World Health Organizations

The **World Health Organization** (WHO) is an agency of the United Nations. Its purpose is to improve the quality of health and well-being throughout the world. The headquarters for WHO are located in Geneva, Switzerland.

WHO has six regional offices in different areas of the world: Africa, the Americas, Europe, Eastern Mediterranean, Southeast Asia, and Western Pacific. Although an agency of the United Nations (UN), member nations of WHO do not have to belong to the UN. For this reason, WHO has been controversial.

Member nations of WHO do not need to belong to the UN.

WHO is divided into a governing and an executive body. The governing body is known as the World Health Assembly. The World Health Assembly meets every year to formulate policy, develop a program, and establish a budget. Each member nation sends three delegates to the World Health Assembly. Each nation has one vote.

The Executive Board of WHO consists of representatives of 30 member nations. The nations take turns having a representative on the Executive Board. The purpose of the Executive Board is to conduct and direct the work outlined by the World Health Assembly.

WHO helps nations plan and provide health services, particularly in the area of basic health care. WHO has worked with the United Nations International Children's Emergency Fund (UNICEF) to reach this goal. UNICEF is a program to promote health in children in the developing nations by controlling communicable diseases and meeting nutritional needs. Voluntary contributions from governments and private citizens support UNICEF.

Primary health care is the main focus of WHO.

UNICEF and WHO sponsored a conference in Alma-Ata, U.S.S.R. The purpose was to promote primary health care in all nations. At this conference, the Declaration of the Alma-Ata included the following recommendations for primary health care throughout the world.

UNICEF and WHO sponsored the Alma-Ata Conference, which focused on primary health care.

FIGURE 26–8. UNICEF helps children all over the world.

- Education concerning prevailing health problems and the methods of identifying, preventing, and controlling them
- Promotion of a food supply and proper nutrition, an adequate supply of safe water, and basic sanitation
- Maternal and child health care, including family planning
- Immunization against major infectious diseases
- Prevention and control of locally epidemic diseases
- Appropriate treatment of common diseases and injuries
- Promotion of mental health
- Provision of essential drugs

FAO coordinates programs to alleviate world hunger.

Other organizations also emphasize some of these recommendations for primary health care. The Food and Agriculture Organization (FAO) coordinates programs to alleviate world hunger and malnutrition. FAO promotes research, designs school lunch programs, and assists with education. The United States Agency for International Development (AID) provides funds for nutrition and health programs in third world countries.

AID provides funds for nutrition in third world countries.

 ## Review and Reflect

9. What was the purpose of the Alma-Ata Conference?
10. How has WHO worked with UNICEF?
11. How are FAO and AID similar in purpose?

Focus on
Life Management Skills

- Select behaviors that keep your community a healthful and safe place to live.
- Select behaviors that promote the health of those who reside in your community.
- Know and follow public health laws.
- Be familiar with the purposes of the various voluntary organizations and become a volunteer.
- Know the professional associations that are available for health-related professionals.
- Encourage health promotion activities at your place of employment.
- Be aware of the services you can receive from your state and local health departments.
- Know the structure of federal agencies that promote health and the services provided by each.
- Be aware of the health needs of people worldwide and decide how you can help to solve them.

Health
CAREERS

Community Health Educator

Donna Moore is planning her current heart health project. She is the program coordinator for the local chapter of the American Heart Association. The new project will consist of the promotion of a new heart health menu and education program for people in her community.

Donna Moore is a community health educator. A community health educator can be employed in a voluntary health organization, private foundation, or local or state health department. These responsibilities include the planning, implementation, and evaluation of health promotion programs in a particular community. Community health educators may give speeches, organize programs, such as smoking-cessation clinics, or conduct health fairs.

To become a community health educator, one must graduate from a four-year college with a degree in health education or social work. Training consists of specialized courses stressing disease prevention and control, epidemiology, health program planning, and communications. A strong background in the sciences is also emphasized. The student must also complete an internship. During an internship, the student gains experience by working in a community health agency.

Many community health educators continue their education by regularly attending health-related seminars or taking additional course work. Being a community health educator can be a rewarding experience through helping others.

Summary

1. You have a responsibility to promote health in your community. **26:1**

2. Voluntary health organizations focus on a specific disease, certain health problems, or problems that are related to a large part of the population. **26:2**

3. Private health foundations support health and social service programs by providing education for health, donating money for medical research, or having their own research laboratory. **26:3**

4. Professional health associations promote education in the health field to meet the needs of health professionals. **26:4**

5. Corporate health programs promote the health and well-being of employees and their families. **26:5**

6. A local health department is the official agency that by law has responsibility for the health and well-being of persons who reside in a community. **26:6**

7. The state health department is the official health agency that by law has responsibility for the health and well-being of the persons who reside in your state. **26:7**

8. The cabinet-level department of the federal government responsible for planning for health is the Department of Health and Human Services. **26:8**

9. The Public Health Service is responsible for maintaining, protecting, and promoting the health of the American people. **26:9**

10. The World Health Organization helps nations plan and provide health services in the area of primary health care. **26:10**

Vocabulary

Below is a list of vocabulary words used in this chapter. Use each word only once to complete the sentences. Do not write in this book.

corporate health programs
Department of HHS
FDA
local health department
private health foundations
professional health association
state health department
Surgeon General
voluntary health organization
World Health Organization

1. The health programs and benefits that exist in the workplace are _____.

2. The _____ checks the safety of foods, drugs, and cosmetics.

3. The American Medical Association is a(n) _____ that provides services for members and promotes public education.

4. The _____ helps member nations plan and provide health services.

5. The American Heart Association is a(n) _____ that supports cardiovascular research and develops educational programs.

6. The _____ is a physician appointed by the President to direct the Public Health Service.

7. A(n) _____ has a vital statistics department, plays a role in preventing communicable diseases, maintains environmental protection, and has a public health laboratory.

8. The Social Security Administration is an office within the _____.

9. A(n) _____ has responsibility for the health of individuals within a community.

10. _____ are organizations that support non-profit health and social service programs.

Review

1. What are the qualities of a healthful community?
2. Where do voluntary organizations get their funds and how is the money used?
3. What are private foundations and how do they contribute to community health?
4. What are the purposes of professional associations?
5. What are some of the benefits of corporate health programs?
6. What services are provided by most state health departments?
7. What services are usually provided at local health departments?
8. What are the five agencies within the Public Health Service?
9. What recommendations were made at the conference in Alma-Ata?
10. What is UNICEF?

Application

1. Why do voluntary organizations usually use many volunteers?
2. How can a professional association help you?
3. Why is the Public Health Service influenced by the current political administration?
4. Where would you write to learn about the latest biomedical research being conducted by the government?
5. How are the health problems in the United States different from those of other nations?

Individual Research

1. Research three public health laws that protect your community. What are the consequences if any of these laws is broken?
2. Visit the local health department nearest you and write a short paper describing its services.
3. Obtain a copy of one of the reports or books directed by the Surgeon General. Write a short report about what you learn.
4. Suppose you want to work with a voluntary health organization. Which agency might you choose? Why?

Readings

Miller, Dean F., *Dimensions of Community Health*. Dubuque, IA: William C. Brown Publishers, 1984.

Sherriffs, Janet H., *Community Health*. Englewood Cliffs, NY: Prentice-Hall Media, 1982.

Litter not only can spoil the appearance of an area, but also can affect the health of people who live there. What can you do to improve the quality of your environment? What factors in your environment threaten your health?

Chapter 27

Environmental Health

OBJECTIVES: You will be able to
- **identify ways air and water pollution can be controlled.**
- **describe how you can keep safe from hazardous wastes.**
- **identify sources of radiation pollution.**
- **describe how to reduce exposure to excessive noise.**

A quality environment is important for the promotion of your well-being. Throughout this text, you have been exposed to information that if practiced will help you be at your best. To be at your best and to achieve optimum health, your environment must be in a healthful state. When it is, it enhances the quality of your life. It allows you to achieve your highest levels of mental, physical, and social health.

AIR AND WATER POLLUTION

Every day you breathe in and out about 35 pounds of air. This is over six tons of air per year. Unpolluted air is needed for your body to function at optimum capacity. Unfortunately, pollutants are often in the air that you breathe and thus, they are health hazards.

27:1 Types of Air Pollutants

Pollution is a major environmental health hazard today. **Pollution** is the introduction of harmful substances into the environment. These harmful substances are called **pollutants.** Pollutants

FIGURE 27–1. Restoration of the Statue of Liberty was necessary to repair damage caused by pollution and other factors.

There are many pollutants that promote poor health.

Particulates can irritate many parts of the body.

Sulfur oxides irritate the eyes, throat, and lungs.

can alter the quality of our lives by affecting the products we use. Among the air pollutants that affect health are particulates, carbon monoxide, sulfur oxides, nitrogen oxides, and hydrocarbons.

Particulates are matter in air such as dust, ash, and fumes that are by-products or wastes of fuels or other substances. These products may settle on the ground, on objects, or they may remain suspended in the air. Particulates can come from automobiles, industrial plants, and farms. Particulates irritate the eyes, throat, and lungs.

In Chapter 18, you learned that carbon monoxide is a dangerous gas produced from burning tobacco products. However, most of the carbon monoxide in the environment is produced by automobile exhaust. Carbon monoxide levels are highest in dense traffic, at busy intersections, and in enclosed areas such as garages. Exposure to large doses of carbon monoxide can produce headaches, impair hearing and vision, damage the respiratory system, and be fatal.

Sulfur oxides are gases produced mainly from the burning of fossil fuels such as natural gas, coal, and oil. Sulfur forms acids that can cause metal to pit and concrete buildings to erode. These gases irritate the eyes, throat, and lungs.

Nitrogen oxides are harmful by-products of automobile exhaust. They impair the function of the lungs and the oxygen-carrying capacity of blood cells. Nitrogen oxides help produce the brown haze often visible over polluted cities.

Hydrocarbons are harmful pollutants. Automobile exhaust is responsible for a significant amount of hydrocarbons in most large cities. Hydrocarbons irritate the eyes and harm the respiratory system. Some hydrocarbons are known to cause cancer.

27:2 Environmental Problems Created by Air Pollutants

Smog is a combination of smoke and fog. Cities that are crowded with many automobiles have an increased tendency to be covered with photochemical smog. Photochemical smog results from the interaction of sunlight with exhaust from automobiles. This type of smog occurs in areas where there is little air movement, as in valleys. It also occurs when there is sunny weather and low humidity.

As an area or city becomes covered with a layer of warm air, the cooler air underneath becomes trapped. This trapping of cooler air under warm air is called a **temperature inversion.** At such times, the exhaust from automobiles cannot penetrate the warm cover of air blanketing the area. As a result, the amount of pollutants in the air increases. A hazy, brownish layer of pollutants may form. These pollutants irritate the eyes and lungs. People with respiratory problems are likely to have complications from lung diseases, such as emphysema and bronchitis. In severe temperature inversions, many deaths can result. Temperature inversions vanish with air movement.

Another problem related to temperature inversions is the production of ozone. **Ozone** is another harmful substance formed from the interaction of sunlight on pollutants. This ozone should not be confused with the layer of ozone in the upper atmosphere that screens 99 percent of the sun's ultraviolet rays. The ozone associated with photochemical smog is poisonous. It irritates the mucous membranes, causes coughing, and harms the lungs.

Unfortunately, the ozone layer of the upper atmosphere has been threatened by the use of fluorocarbons. **Fluorocarbons** are chemicals that contain the elements fluorine and carbon. One type of fluorocarbon is used in aerosol-spray cans to propel ingredients out of the can. Some scientists believe that these propellant chemicals float up through the different layers of the atmosphere where they set off reactions that weaken the ozone layer. If the ozone layer is damaged, the sun's ultraviolet rays cannot be absorbed. This allows more rays to reach the earth's surface. The consequences may be an increase in the number of cases of skin cancer.

Automobiles play an important role in contributing to air pollution.

A temperature inversion may cause complications in people with respiratory problems.

The ozone layer filters the sun's ultraviolet rays.

FIGURE 27–2. Many lakes in the northeastern United States and Canada are affected by acid rain.

Acid rain can destroy fish life.

Sulfur dioxide is produced when coal is burned.

Air pollution is also involved in the production of acid rain. **Acid rain** is rain that results from the mixture of moisture, nitrogen oxides, and sulfur oxides. This mixture results in nitric and sulfuric acids, which eventually fall as rain and/or snow.

Acid rain can harm the environment. Most notable is the destruction of fish when lakes become so acidic that they cannot support aquatic life. Acid rain can also cause plants to die. Even buildings and statues experience erosion.

Solutions to the problems of acid rain are difficult to determine. One reason is that acid rain can fall thousands of miles from its source. Consequently, the source may be difficult to pinpoint.

Consider the political and economic decisions that must be made regarding this problem within different countries and regions. For example, some large factories in midwest United States burn coal as an inexpensive source for electric power. When the coal is burned, sulfur dioxide is produced. This produces sulfuric acid when mixed with moisture. When winds blow the moisture northeast, Canada and other parts of the United States become recipients of acid rain. People in these regions object that they suffer possible effects of acid rain because these factories choose to use this cheaper way to produce electricity. On the other hand, politicians do not want to make voters in their districts pay increased rates for other forms of electricity. In addition, politicians representing states that rely heavily on coal mining do not want to have coal miners out of work because of a decreased demand for coal. The solution to the acid rain question is a complex one.

27:3 Controlling Air Pollution

Cleaning the air is a complex task. It takes cooperation from many different sources to create positive changes. The first major step to control and reduce air pollution occurred in the early 1970s. At this time, the United States government established the **Environmental Protection Agency (EPA)** to implement and enforce laws to improve air and water quality and other environmental concerns. Among these laws were the Clean Air Amendments, which set strict guidelines for automobile emission standards. These guidelines dramatically improved air quality throughout the United States. Laws were also passed to govern the amount of chemicals that industries could emit into the air.

While steps have been taken to improve air quality, manufacturers and environmental groups often disagree. Some manufacturers claim that pollution control guidelines are too expensive to follow and result in higher prices that are passed on to the consumer. On the other hand, environmental groups contend that increased costs are offset by a decrease in pollution-related illnesses such as upper-respiratory infections, emphysema, bronchitis, and lung cancer. While the battles continue, studies show that the overwhelming majority of people favor laws that promote pollution controls.

Individuals have also taken steps to help improve air quality. These steps include car pools, use of mass transit, and increased use of bicycles for transportation. Many individuals and groups of individuals have been instrumental in promoting the passage of laws that reduce indoor pollution caused by cigarette smoking. Thus, many cities now have rigid guidelines that prohibit smoking in many areas, such as restaurants and other places where large numbers of people meet.

FIGURE 27–3. Car pooling has proved to be an effective way to reduce air pollution and conserve energy.

You can take actions to improve air quality.

27:4 Water Pollution and the Environment

After air, water is the most essential requirement for the human body. A person can live without water for only a few days. Drinking clean water is essential to maintaining good health.

Water used for drinking, as well as for recreation, can be subject to pollution. Water pollution can result from many sources. Industrial wastes can enter water and create a high percentage of

Water can become polluted from many sources.

FIGURE 27–4. Environmental efforts have restored many lakes that were once polluted.

Private industry has developed innovations to reduce water pollution.

Water may become polluted by chemicals filtering into underground water sources.

toxic materials that kill fish. Litter may be disposed or dumped in lakes and oceans. Groundwater that contains high levels of chemicals can enter lakes, rivers, and streams from farmlands.

Thermal pollution can produce harmful changes in the water. **Thermal pollution** is excessive heat that is added to a natural water supply. This may occur after water is used as a coolant in the operation of an electric power plant. The heated water is often dumped into a nearby river or lake. Consequently, the water temperature of the river or lake is increased. Heated water holds less dissolved oxygen than cooler water. This can result in the destruction of water plants that are used as food by fish. Consequently, these waters can no longer sustain a fish population.

27:5 Controlling Water Pollution

Steps have been taken to control or reduce water pollution. The Federal Water Pollution Control Act of 1972 resulted in efforts to upgrade municipal sewage-treatment facilities. Thus, sewage released into rivers and lakes is treated so that both the fish population and recreational facilities are being revived and recovered. An example of this revival is Lake Erie, which now has an active fish population and is used by thousands of people for recreational purposes.

New methods by private industry have helped promote a reduction in water pollution. For example, one chemical company uses special bacteria that turn specific chemical wastes into harmless end products.

Laws enacted by governmental agencies help prevent water pollution. However, you can take several steps to help keep water clean. Perhaps you live in an area in which well water is used. Well water comes from water deep underground. To avoid contaminating underground water, avoid spilling harmful chemicals on the ground. Avoid using salt to melt ice or snow. These substances can filter into groundwater.

About half the United States population gets its drinking water from surface water in rivers, lakes, streams, and creeks. Avoid dumping garbage or any kinds of chemicals in surface water.

 Review and Reflect

1. How might smog interfere with some of your activities?
2. How does a temperature inversion form?
3. Why is it important to protect the earth's ozone layer?

HAZARDOUS AND SOLID WASTES

Along with the many advantages of being industrialized, there is the responsibility of safely getting rid of wastes produced in the industrial process. What are some of these wastes? What is being done to minimize their potential harm?

27:6 Hazardous Wastes

As industry has become more complex, it has relied more and more on chemicals. Greater use of these substances has led to an increase in hazardous wastes. A **hazardous waste** is a harmful by-product that is difficult to discard safely.

Many kinds of hazardous wastes are not biodegradable. A substance is **biodegradable** if it decomposes through biological processes into harmless materials. Other hazardous wastes that may be biodegradable may not break down for many years. This has led to many health concerns. The toxic waste disaster of Love Canal, a community near Niagara Falls, New York, is one such incident. A chemical and plastics company had dumped wastes around Love Canal between 1947 and 1952 and then covered it with dirt to form a landfill. Soon, a new community was developed on the landfill. But in 1978, heavy rains caused the buried contents to surface. The result was an increase in the number of cases of cancer and birth defects in people living around the canal. Many other physical disabilities were discovered. Over 200 families had to be evacuated while the Federal government worked to make the area safe for living again.

Today, the EPA is extremely concerned about the dumping of wastes that are toxic, or poisonous. When buried underground, toxic wastes may leak from their containers and threaten groundwater supplies. Even those chemicals that were once thought to be harmless are becoming suspect. One such chemical is dioxin. **Dioxin** is a chemical that is formed in some chemical processes and is now considered one of the most toxic wastes in the environment. Dioxin is the chemical that Vietnam veterans blame for the host of illnesses and disorders produced by Agent Orange. Conditions thought to be produced by Agent Orange are cancer, depression, liver damage, and miscarriages. Agent Orange is a substance that contains dioxin. It was sprayed to kill plant life in Vietnam during the Vietnam war.

Hazardous wastes must be discarded safely.

Improper disposal of toxic wastes can become a health hazard.

FIGURE 27–5. The disposal of hazardous chemicals affects everyone.

The EPA has enacted several laws to safeguard the public from exposure to hazardous wastes. These laws place regulations on the transport, burying, and packaging of toxic wastes.

27:7 Solid Wastes

Solid wastes are substances such as trash, junk, and litter that pose threats to the environment. The threats produced by solid wastes are two-fold. First, they fill beautiful land with litter. The second threat involves the needless disposing of substances that may be recycled.

The first problem can be handled by proper disposal of trash and junk. This includes dumping wastes in sanitary landfills and incineration. It also includes persuading individuals not to litter.

The best method of handling the second problem is through recycling. **Recycling** is the breaking down of products to their basic components so that they can be used again. For example, aluminum cans can be heated and melted so they can be reused to make more aluminum cans or other products.

Consider the fact that more than half the trash in the United States is paper. If this paper were brought to a recycling center, it could be reorganized and reused. Many paper products you use each day are made of recycled paper. Among these products may be greeting cards and cardboard boxes.

Solid wastes can harm the environment if not disposed of properly.

Many products can be reused by recycling.

FIGURE 27–6. Many communities have recycling centers.

FIGURE 27-7. Compost can be used as fertilizer.

There are many ways you can help reduce problems associated with solid wastes.

- Return bottles for deposit refunds where applicable.
- Save aluminum cans and take them to a recycling center.
- Build a compost pile. Compost is the black, crumbly residue that comes from vegetable wastes that have decomposed over a period of time. Compost is a valuable soil additive for plants or gardens. To make a compost pile, mix vegetable wastes, such as coffee grounds, lettuce leaves, or grass clippings with dry material, such as straw. This mixture is arranged in such a way that soil organisms can thrive and multiply by using the vegetable wastes as nutrients.

Some household products are toxic or can become toxic. Some materials deteriorate with age; some may deteriorate if not stored properly. Labels should give information about proper storage and usage. Following are some tips on how to dispose of toxic household products.

- Always read labels when you want to dispose of a product.
- Wear gloves and protective clothing to prevent skin contact.
- Handle the substance gently, especially if you do not know what it is.
- Thoroughly dilute any liquid you are going to wash down a drain.
- When disposing of liquids, always put the original container into a second container and fill the space in between with an absorbent material.
- Keep toxic substances out of the reach of children and pets.

27:8 Pesticides

A **pesticide** is any substance used to kill or control the growth of unwanted organisms, such as plants or insects. Pesticides can be used on farms or in homes.

Pesticides play an important role in farming because they destroy insects that kill crops. Pesticides can also create health problems. A widely used pesticide, DDT, was banned from use a few years ago because it was found in food products after harvest. DDT is dangerous because it can accumulate in the fat tissues of humans and act as a carcinogen. Pesticides are also known to kill wildlife when they feed on crops. Wildlife may also die when they eat fish from bodies of water that have been contaminated from runoff into lakes and rivers.

Numerous steps are being taken to control these unwanted organisms more safely. (1) Predators, insects that eat other insects, have been introduced in certain areas. (2) Sterilized males of insect species that mate only once have been released in high pest-infested areas. If the female mates with a sterilized male, fertilization will not occur. (3) Special sexual attractants have been used to trap or confuse male insects. This also hinders their ability to reproduce. These methods, along with the development of safer pesticides, are being used to control the pest problem in a safe way.

However, accidents with pesticides still occur. In 1985, a pesticide was found in watermelons grown in California. People who ate these watermelons became nauseous, had diarrhea and abdominal pains, and perspired excessively. Fortunately, no deaths occurred.

Pesticides used in the home can pose serious problems. According to the EPA, about 20 000 people are rushed to emergency rooms each year because of accidental pesticide poisoning. To avoid pesticide poisoning in your home, the American Council on Science and Health offers these tips.

- Read labels and directions on pesticide containers thoroughly.

- Keep pesticides locked up and out of children's reach.

- Do not mix or measure chemicals with utensils used to prepare food.

- Do not mix chemicals with each other unless the label says to do so.

- Wear rubber gloves when handling pesticides.

- Store pesticides in their original containers.

Leaded

Federal law prohibits
the introduction of any
gasoline containing lead
or phosphorus into any
motor vehicle labeled
"unleaded gasoline only"

PRICES BEING
CHARGED FOR
GASOLINE
DO NOT EXCEED
MAXIMUM
ALLOWABLE PRICE

FIGURE 27–8. The EPA has proposed a ban on all leaded gasoline by the year 1988.

27:9 Lead, Mercury, and Asbestos

At one time, lead that was produced from the combustion of leaded gasoline was a major harmful element in the air. But today, the amount of lead in the air caused by leaded gasoline has been reduced drastically with EPA regulations that now promote the use of unleaded gasoline.

Until its dangers became evident, lead was used in many products, such as glassware, ceramics, and paint. The basic danger was lead poisoning. Children got lead poisoning when they ingested paint chips that fell from ceilings and walls. Among the symptoms of lead poisoning are weakness, loss of appetite, and anemia. Studies also indicate that lead poisoning is related to the development of learning disabilities in children.

Lead found in many substances can harm health.

The element mercury and most of its compounds are toxic. In the early 1970s, a factory in Japan released industrial wastes containing mercury compounds into the Pacific Ocean. The mercury passed along the food chain to humans. People in a small fishing village ate the fish that contained mercury. The results were mental retardation, numbness of body parts, loss of vision and hearing, emotional disturbances, and 52 deaths. As a result of this and similar occurrences, most industrialized nations have taken steps to prevent mercury dumping.

Ingested mercury can cause serious mental and physical problems.

FIGURE 27–9. An asbestos mine

Exposure to asbestos can increase the risk of cancer.

Asbestos is a mineral that can be processed to form almost indestructible fibers. These fibers have been used in manufacturing insulation, water pipes, and brake linings. Research shows that people who are exposed to asbestos run an increased risk of cancer of the lungs and intestinal tract. Since this concern, many steps have been taken to eliminate the use of asbestos. For example, asbestos insulation used in buildings, including schools, is being removed and replaced with asbestos-free insulation.

 Review and Reflect

4. Why is it best to use products that are biodegradable?
5. What can you do to help prevent the buildup of solid wastes in your community?

RADIATION POLLUTION

Radiation in the environment poses a health hazard.

Radiation is a natural part of the environment. Radioactive substances can be found in the soil, air, and water. Cosmic rays are also radioactive. Radiation from these sources is sometimes called natural background radiation. However, many medical researchers are concerned about possible health hazards of artificial radiation that is added to the environment.

mutations may result
idue exposure to
n.

The parts of the body most susceptible to radiation are those that reproduce the fastest. This includes the tissues in the digestive tract, blood cells, and sperm and egg cells. Exposure to high doses of radiation is known to cause infertility, birth defects, and miscarriage. A pregnant woman should avoid X rays. There is widespread belief that any undue exposure to radiation, either natural or artificial, may have harmful effects.

There is a growing belief that people are being exposed to excessive amounts of X rays. Some recent studies indicate there may be no safe level of radiation. That is, any exposure to radiation may increase a person's risk of developing leukemia or bone cancer. X rays are an important diagnostic tool used to help maintain optimum health. However, to avoid unnecessary X rays, request that X rays taken previously be sent to a new physician when you move or change physicians.

 Review and Reflect

6. What are some sources of artificial radiation?

NOISE POLLUTION

bise is a form of
n.

Exposure to loud noise is a form of pollution that is hazardous to health. It can affect not only the ears but all parts of the body.

27:12 Health Hazards of Noise

In some ways, people are developing a tolerance to noise in a way that a chemically dependent person develops a tolerance to drugs. That is, the intensity of sound must be increased so that it can sound normal. According to recent estimates, the intensity of noise in the environment doubles every ten years.

dness of sound is
ed in decibels.

The intensity of sound is measured in **decibels.** The smallest difference in sound intensity detectable by the human ear is one decibel. A whisper may be 20 decibels while a jet plane at takeoff may be 150 decibels. Continuous exposure to any sound above 85 decibels can result in hearing loss (Table 27–1).

Exposure to loud noise also affects mental health. Noise can cause stress, which causes blood pressure to rise and increases the

27:10   Sources of Artificial Radiation

There are several major sources of artificial radiation. One of these is radiation used in medicine. X rays and other forms of radiation are used to detect and treat diseases. However, they are also known to cause cancer in otherwise healthy cells. For this reason, it is felt that X rays should be used only when necessary.

Radiation is also used in industry. In this circumstance, X rays are used to detect hidden flaws in welds, castings, and other products. Nuclear power plants also can emit radiation into the atmosphere under normal operation. Rigid governmental controls help regulate the amount of radiation that enters the environment.

Some radiation enters the environment through inappropriate disposal of radioactive wastes. The major problem here is that there is no way to destroy radioactivity other than letting it break down. This process can take thousands of years. Presently, scientists are searching for a way to dispose of radioactive wastes.

27:11   Radiation and Health

Although radiation can enter the body through the skin, it is usually inhaled or ingested. Whether or not radiation becomes a health problem depends upon how much enters the body, how long the person is exposed, and individual sensitivity.

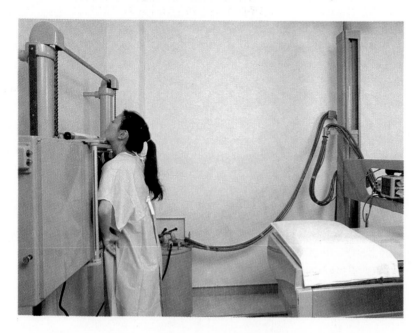

Gene
from
radia

Radiation m
environment
plants.

The effects
determined

Loud
pollut

The lo
measu

FIGURE 2
to detect

Table 27–1 Decibel Levels of Common Sounds

Decibel	Sound
180	rocket engine
160	fuel dragster
150	jet plane at takeoff
140	air-raid siren
120	loud rock music
110	motorcycle
100	snowmobile
90	heavy street traffic
80	garbage disposal
70	average automobile
60	conversation
50	average home
40	library
30	quiet auditorium
20	quiet whisper
10	leaves rustling

production of acid in the intestines. This can result in ulcers. Studies show that exposure to loud noise causes people to become irritable and aggressive. It also causes a lack of concentration. It will take a much longer period of time to absorb information while studying with loud noises in the background than if one were studying in a quiet room.

Exposure to loud noises increases the risks of being involved in an accident. Many joggers have had accidents when running while listening to music on headsets. Often, they do not hear the sound of approaching motor vehicles or bicycles.

Loud noise can result in an increase in accidents.

Activity: Creating a Decibel Graph

Using Table 27–1, make a bar graph in intervals of 20 decibels ranging from 20 to 180 decibels. Next to each bar on the graph, write the name of an everyday sound you hear that is most appropriate for that bar. Use Table 27–1 as a guide, but do not use any of the items listed in the table. Select one item above 80 decibels and describe how you can adapt your lifestyle to avoid undue exposure to that sound.

27:13   Controlling Noise Pollution

Unlike other forms of pollution discussed in this chapter, noise pollution can be controlled more easily through individual efforts and technology. Sound-reducing devices are available to control noises produced by engines. There is no reason that mufflers cannot be standard equipment on lawn mowers. In fact, lawn mowers produced in the past were quieter and just as powerful as the current ones. Unfortunately, consumers associated power lawn mowers with loud sounds—the louder, the better. With the declining sales of quieter lawn mowers, manufacturers increased the production of louder ones and saw an increase in sales. A similar trend has occurred with motorcycles. However, the EPA has mandated that all motorcycles manufactured after 1986 are to have a noise level of 80 decibels or below.

Many communities have noise control laws. Some of these laws govern the hours in which loud noises, such as the playing of stereos, can occur. Other laws may govern when and where automobile horns can be blown.

A great deal has been accomplished in business and industry to reduce noise pollution. Workers in high-noise occupations are outfitted with special headgear to absorb sound. Soundproofing walls and installing proper architectural structures also minimize undue sounds to which workers are exposed.

What can you do to reduce your exposure to the harmful effects of noise? Following are some tips.

- If you listen to music through headphones, keep the music low enough so that you can hear someone speaking clearly in a normal conversation.

Most forms of noise pollution can be easily controlled.

Many communities have noise control laws.

There are steps you can take to reduce exposure to loud noise.

FIGURE 27–11. Protection against noise is needed in some workplaces.

FIGURE 27–12. Everyone needs quiet at times.

- If you attend concerts, do not sit close to the performers.
- If you use a lawn mower or are around other loud noises for a prolonged period of time, wear earplugs.

It is important to have your hearing checked during periodic medical checkups. Having your hearing checked will enable you to determine a hearing loss. Exposure to prolonged, loud noise can cause hearing loss.

It is important to have your hearing checked during regular medical checkups.

 ## Review and Reflect

7. How can exposure to loud noise affect mental health?
8. List two ways you can help reduce noise pollution.

Focus on
Life Management Skills

- Save recyclable products and turn them into the appropriate recycling center.
- Use pesticides according to directions.
- Keep a record of all medical X rays so you can have them forwarded to a new physician if you move.
- Avoid hazards of noise pollution by avoiding areas where there are loud noises and by playing your stereo at a low volume.
- Support legislation to reduce air and water pollution and to safely dispose of hazardous wastes.

Summary

1. Particulates, carbon monoxide, sulfur oxides, nitrogen oxides, and hydrocarbons are types of air pollutants.   27:1

2. Temperature inversions trap polluted air that can harm a person's health.   27:2

3. The EPA has taken measures to control air pollution.   27:3

4. Water pollution can result from litter, industrial wastes, chemicals that seep underground, and thermal pollution.   27:4

5. Federal laws help control and prevent water pollution.   27:5

6. The EPA has enacted many laws to reduce the risks associated with the removal of hazardous wastes.   27:6

7. Recycling is a major way that items can be reused so that the amount of solid wastes can be reduced.   27:7

8. Pesticides must be disposed of carefully so that risks to health are minimized.   27:8

9. Lead, mercury, and asbestos are dangerous substances that have been controlled by the passage of laws.   27:9

10. Artificial radiation can enter the environment from X rays, industry, and the disposal of radioactive wastes.   27:10

11. Undue exposure to radiation can harm cells in the body and cause birth defects.   27:11

12. Excessive exposure to loud noise can harm a person's hearing and alter many of the body's normal functions.   27:12

13. Noise pollution in business and industry, as well as in the community, can be controlled through passage of laws as well as healthful actions by people.   27:13

Vocabulary

Below is a list of vocabulary words used in this chapter. Use each word only once to complete the sentences. Do not write in this book.

acid rain   particulates
asbestos   pesticide
decibels   recycling
fluorocarbons   smog
ozone   thermal pollution

1. DDT is an example of a(n) _____ banned several years ago.

2. The higher the level of _____, the greater the risk to hearing.

3. The interaction of sunlight on pollutants can result in _____.

4. Falling moisture that is high in nitric acid and sulfuric acid is called _____.

5. Smoke and fog can combine and form _____.

6. _____ is used in insulation because its fibers are strong.

7. Dumping warm water into a stream can result in _____.

8. _____ are used in aerosol spray cans to propel the ingredients of the cans.

9. Another term for reusing materials is _____.

10. Ash, dust, and fumes in the air are called _____.

Review

1. How do particulates form and enter the air?
2. What causes photochemical smog?
3. How does the EPA work to improve air quality?
4. Why is it important for hazardous wastes to be biodegradable?
5. What are some appropriate ways you can dispose of solid wastes?
6. What are some items that can be recycled?
7. How can pesticides be helpful in farming?
8. Identify three ways to avoid pesticide poisoning.
9. Why has the use of asbestos been eliminated?
10. What are the major sources of artificial radiation?

Application

1. Why is it healthful to listen to music at a level of 60 decibels or below?
2. Why is a temperature inversion particularly dangerous to a person who has lung problems?
3. How could acid rain be a problem to people who live in a community with no industry?

Individual Research

1. Research the problem of acid rain, and write a report about steps that are being taken to control this problem.
2. Visit a water-treatment facility in your community. Observe how your water supply is made usable.
3. Write a report about steps you can follow to avoid undue exposure to radiation from the sun.

Readings

King, Jonathan, "Is Your Water Safe to Drink?" *Self-Care,* November-December, 1985, pp. 44-47.

Laws, Priscilla W., *The X-Ray Information Book.* New York, NY: Farrar, Straus, Gerous, Inc., 1983.

Lillyquist, Michael J., *Sunlight and Health.* New York, NY: Dodd, Mead & Co., 1985.

APPENDIX

GLOSSARY

INDEX

APPENDIX A

SIX TYPES OF PATHOGENS

Name	Characteristics	Methods of Spreading	Some Diseases They Cause	Prevention
Bacteria	• one-celled organisms found in air, water, soil, and in other living organisms	• having direct contact with an infected person or with droplets from sneezing or coughing • consuming contaminated water, milk, or food	• tuberculosis • typhoid fever	• pasteurizing milk • taking a TB test for detection • having properly protected sewers and water systems • adding chlorine to public water supplies • pasteurizing milk • refrigerating food
Viruses	• no cellular organization • smallest known pathogen	• having direct contact with an infected person or their excretions	• measles • mumps • common cold	• being vaccinated at the prescribed age • being vaccinated at the prescribed age • avoiding others with colds • getting enough sleep
Fungi	• plantlike organisms grow on skin cells on the body's surface	• having direct contact with an infected person or the surfaces or articles they have contaminated	• ringworm • athlete's foot	• bathing daily • drying thoroughly • keeping feet dry • wearing shoes that allow room for air • using a fungicidal powder daily • visiting only those pools and locker rooms that are disinfected each day
Protozoa	• one-celled animallike organisms usually thrive in tropical areas	• ingesting contaminated food and water • getting bitten by an infected mosquito	• amoebic dysentery • malaria	• disposing properly of human wastes • ensuring cleanliness of food preparation • controlling mosquitoes by treating ponds where they gather with chemicals • draining or filling in ponds • spraying
Rickettsia	• nearly spherical cells survive by living in other cells	• receiving bites from infected lice, fleas, mites, and ticks	• many kinds of typhus fever • Rocky Mountain spotted fever	• practicing personal care • checking your body, clothing, and pets when possibly exposed to these insects
Parasitic Worms	• many-celled animals live on or in other organisms by sucking blood from body tissues or eating the digested food in a person's body	• entering the body through broken skin on the feet • eating pork or beef that is not cooked thoroughly	• hookworm disease • tapeworm infections • trichinosis	• disposing properly of human wastes • wearing shoes • avoiding stepping in feces • cooking meat thoroughly • cooking meat thoroughly

APPENDIX B

SEXUALLY TRANSMITTED DISEASES

Disease	Organisms Responsible for the Disease	Signs and Symptoms		Diagnosis	Treatment	Complications
		Male	Female			
Gonorrhea	*Neisseria gonorrhoeae*	Painful urination, discharge or dripping from penis	Lower abdominal pain especially after menstrual period, possible burning during urination, discharge from vagina	**Women:** bacteria grown in culture **Men:** smear, or bacteria grown in culture	Ampicillin, penicillin, tetracycline	Sterility, painful joints, circulatory and nervous system damage, perithepatitis **Women:** internal abdominal infection **Men:** urethral blockage **Newborn:** blindness
Syphilis	*Treponema pallidum*	**Primary syphilis:** Chancres on penis **Secondary syphilis:** Rash anywhere on body, sore throat, muscle pain, headache, raised bumps, spotty hair loss **Late syphilis:** Soft sores, heart and nervous system disease	**Primary syphilis:** Chancres inside vagina **Secondary syphilis:** Same as male **Late syphilis:** Same as male	Examination of bacteria under a microscope or by blood test	Penicillin, erythromycin, tetracycline	If untreated by late stage, heart disease and nervous system damage such as brain damage, insanity, paralysis and death **Fetus and Newborn:** damage to skin, bones, teeth, eyes, and liver
Genital Herpes	*Herpes simplex virus II*	Minor rash and blisters in genital area, swollen glands, fever, muscle aches, sores on penis and painful urination	Minor rash and blisters in genital area, swollen glands, fever, muscle aches, sores in vagina or on cervix, painful urination	**Women:** Pap smear **Men and Women:** herpes cells examined under microscope	**No cure:** treatment consists of ointment on blisters and warm baths	Recurring symptoms, possible higher incidence of cervical cancer in women, severe damage to central nervous system or death to newborn infected during birth process
Nongonococcal Urethritis (NGU)	*Chlamydia trachomatis* and several others	Burning and itching in penis, burning during urination	Pain, burning or itching in vagina, discharge from vagina, painful urination	Smear, bacteria grown on culture	Tetracycline, erythromycin	**Women:** internal abdominal infection, possible sterility **Men:** testicular infection, possible sterility **Newborn:** eye and lung infections
Trichomoniasis	*Trichomonas vaginalis*	Usually no signs, sometimes a white discharge from urethra	Thin greenish-white discharge from vagina, burning and itching in vagina	Smear of protozoans under microscope	Special antibiotic	
Moniliasis	*Candida albicans*	Red, itching rash in groin	Thick, white discharge from vagina, genital itching	Smear of yeast, grown on culture	Vaginal suppositories	**Women:** secondary infections from bacteria
Pediculosis Pubis	*Phithirus pubis* (louse)	Black spots on pubic area or possibly other hairy areas of body, itching, tiny blood spots on underwear	Same as male	Observation	Special shampoo or lotion	Secondary infections resulting from scratching

GLOSSARY

acid rain: rain that results from the mixture of moisture, nitrogen oxides and sulfur oxides

acne: a skin infection that occurs when sebum blocks ducts and pores

acquired immune deficiency syndrome: AIDS; a breakdown of the functioning of the immune system that protects the body against infections

active immunity: a type of immunity that results from the action of your body producing antibodies; long-lasting or permanent protection from a disease

active listening: a process in which you reassure the other person that you heard both the facts and the feelings behind them

additives: chemicals that are added to foods

adolescence: the period from childhood to adulthood

adulthood: the period from adolescence through old age

advertisement: ad; a paid announcement

advertising: a form of selling in which you are informed of products and services

aerobic exercise: a form of exercise that requires a continuous use of oxygen over an extended period of time

ageism: discrimination against a person based on age

aggressive behavior: the use of words and/or actions that communicate disrespect toward others

AIDS: acquired immune deficiency syndrome; a breakdown of the functioning of the immune system that protects the body against infections

Al-Anon: a treatment organization for husbands, wives, and friends of alcoholics

alarm stage: the body's initial response to a physical, mental, or social stressor

Alateen: a treatment organization for teenage children of alcoholic parents

alcohol: a psychoactive drug that depresses the central nervous system

Alcohol, Drug Abuse, and Mental Health Administration: agency within the Public Health Service of HHS; coordinates efforts to prevent and treat alcohol abuse, drug abuse, and mental illness

Alcoholics Anonymous: AA; a treatment organization that consists of alcoholics who share their experiences to help one another resist the urge to drink again

alcoholism: a disease that progresses to uncontrolled drinking of alcoholic beverages and physical and psychological dependence on alcohol

allergy: a reaction of the body to a certain substance

Alzheimer's disease: a condition in which there is progressive deterioration of mental functions

American Dental Association (ADA): a professional association for dentists

American Medical Association (AMA): a professional association for medical physicians

amino acids: small units or building blocks of proteins

amnesia: the inability to recall past experiences

amniocentesis: a technique that can detect fetal disorders

amotivational syndrome: a pattern of personality changes characterized by apathy, a lack of concern for the future, loss of ambition, and a decline in performance

amphetamines: a group of synthetic chemicals that affect the areas of the brain that control blood pressure, the heart, breathing rate, and metabolism; drugs that speed body activities and suppress appetite

amyl nitrite: a prescription drug that is sometimes prescribed for the treatment of angina

anabolic steroids: the synthetic derivatives of the male hormone testosterone

anaerobic exercise: a form of exercise in which the body's demand for oxygen exceeds the supply

aneurysm: a blood-filled pouch that balloons out from a weak spot in an artery wall

anger: the feeling of being irritated, annoyed, and furious

angina pectoris: pain in the chest or arm caused by narrowed coronary arteries

angiography: a process in which a special dye is injected into an artery or heart chamber

anorexia nervosa: an emotional disorder in which a lack of self-esteem and an intense fear of being overweight result in starvation

antianxiety drugs: drugs used to reduce fears of anxiety

antibiotics: products of living organisms used to treat bacterial diseases

antibodies: proteins in the blood that neutralize or destroy pathogens

antigens: specific poisons produced by pathogens that enter the body

anxiety: the feeling of worry or fear over what might happen

anxiety disorders: disorders in which real or imagined fears occur so often that they prevent a person from enjoying life

Apgar score: a rating of the physical characteristics of an infant one to five minutes after birth

arrhythmia (ay RIHTH mee uh): irregular heartbeats

arthritis: a general term that includes over 100 diseases, all of which involve inflammation of the joints

artificial respiration: the many techniques that are used by one person to another to restore breathing

aspartame: an artificial sweetener

asphyxiation: stoppage or limit of breathing

assertive behavior: expression of thoughts and feelings without experiencing anxiety or threatening others

astringent: a substance that contains alcohol and can dry the skin

atherosclerosis (ath uh roh skluh ROH sus): a medical term for clogged arteries; the accumulation of fat deposits on arterial walls

athlete's foot: an itching, redness, and cracking of the skin between the toes that is caused by a fungus

athletic trainer: a health professional who carries out programs to prevent injury and gives immediate treatment and rehabilitation procedures for the injured athlete as directed by a physician

aura: a dreamlike state

autogenic training: a technique in which a series of exercises are used to increase muscle relaxation

autonomic nervous system: that part of the nervous system that controls a person's internal environment

autonomous: independent

aversion therapy: a technique in which a person's habit is made to be unpleasant

avoidant personality: one who prefers to avoid all social contact because of low self-esteem and fear of rejection

balanced diet: a daily diet that contains the correct number of servings from the four healthful food groups and the combination food group

barbiturates: drugs that are used medically in the treatment of insomnia

basic health insurance: health insurance that includes payments for part of physicians' fees, prescriptions, hospital, and surgical expenses

basic needs: requirements for sustaining life and promoting physical and mental growth

battered spouse: a person who is physically abused by a marriage partner

behavior modification: a form of therapy in which the therapist teaches the patient new behavioral patterns to use when responding to difficult life situations

benign tumors: noncancerous tumors that remain in one place in the body

bereavement: the state of suffering the death of a loved one

beta-endorphins: substances produced in the brain that relieve pain and create a feeling of well-being

Better Business Bureau: a nonprofit, voluntary, self-regulating organization supported by private firms for their protection against unfair competition and misleading advertising

biodegradable: to break down naturally or decompose through biological processes into harmless materials

biofeedback: a technique in which you are fed back information about what is occurring in your body so that you can alter psychological function

biomechanics: the study of how the body functions during movement

biorhythm: a natural inborn energy cycle

bipolar disorder: manic depressive disorder; a mood disorder in which a person's moods vary from being very high to being very depressed

blackout: the period of time when someone who has been drinking cannot remember what has happened even though he or she is conscious

blood: the fluid by which essential substances are transported to cells throughout the body

blood alcohol level: BAL; the amount of alcohol in a person's blood

blood pressure: the force exerted by the flowing blood against the walls of the arteries

body composition: the percentage of fat tissue and lean tissue in your body

boil: a skin infection that invades all the layers of the skin

bone marrow: a special kind of tissue in the hollow center of some bones where red blood cells are produced

brain tumor: a lump of abnormal cells in the brain

bridge: a partial denture or replacement that is used to take the place of one or more teeth

budget: a plan for spending and saving your money

bulimia: an emotional disorder in which an intense fear of being overweight and a lack of self-esteem result in secret binge eating, followed by starvation, self-induced vomiting, and the use of laxatives or diuretics

caffeine: a stimulant drug that is found in tea, cocoa, and many brands of coffee and cola drinks

Calorie: a measure of the energy value of foods

cancer: any large group of diseases characterized by uncontrolled growth and spread of useless abnormal cells

carbohydrates: chemical substances that are the main source of energy for your body

carcinogens: substances in the environment that are thought to cause cancer

cardiac cycle: series of events in each heartbeat

cardiac muscle: a kind of muscle found only in the heart

cardiac output: the amount of blood pumped by the heart each minute

cardiopulmonary resuscitation: CPR; an emergency procedure that is used with mouth-to-mouth resuscitation when the heart has stopped beating

cardiovascular diseases: illnesses or disorders that affect the heart and blood vessels

cardiovascular endurance: ability to do exercises that require increased oxygen intake for extended time periods

cartilage: a rigid type of connective tissue that is softer than bone

CAT scan: a combination computer and X-ray machine that can produce pictures of internal body parts

Centers for Disease Control (CDC): the agency of the Public Health Service of HHS that is responsible for preventing, controlling, and eradicating disease

central nervous system: that part of the nervous system consisting of the brain and spinal cord

cerebral embolism: a clot that travels through the bloodstream and lodges in the brain

cerebral hemorrhage: bursting of an artery in the brain

cerebral palsy: a nervous system disorder that involves nerve and muscular coordination

cerebral thrombosis: a clot that forms inside one of the arteries in the brain blocking blood flow to parts of the brain

cesarean section: the surgical removal of the baby through the mother's abdomen

chancre (SHANG kur): a sore that appears as the earliest sign of syphilis in its primary stage

chemical dependence: a synonym for drug dependence

chemotherapy: the use of drugs as the main method of treatment for certain kinds of cancers

chewing tobacco: leaf or plug tobacco that is placed in between the cheeks and gum

child abuse: the maltreatment of children

childhood: the period of time between the end of infancy and the beginning of puberty

chlamydia: pathogens that are known to cause nongonococcal urethritis (NGU)

cholesterol: a saturated fat that is normally found in the brain, nerves, and skin

chronic bronchitis: the recurring inflammation of the bronchial tubes

chronic disease: an illness that lasts over a long period of time, recurs frequently, and is often disabling

chyme (KIME): food in the form of a thick paste, resulting from the action of peristalsis and digestive juices

cilia: short, fine, hairlike structures in the trachea that trap pathogens traveling toward the lungs

client-centered therapy: a form of treatment in which the client understands his or her present behavior and choices and decides what the goal of the treatment should be; nondirective therapy

clinical psychologist: one who has a Ph.D. degree and has had an internship in a psychiatric setting

clove cigarettes: cigarettes made from tobacco and ground cloves and clove oil

cocaine: an illegal drug obtained from the leaves of coca shrubs

color blindness: a sex-linked disorder in which the person cannot distinguish one or more colors.

colostrum: a watery substance that is believed to provide a baby with immunity to diseases

columbarium: a compartment in a special building that holds the ashes of the deceased

commitment: a promise to yourself that you will schedule your time so that your priorities can be realized

communicable disease: an illness caused by pathogens that enter the body through direct or indirect contact; an infectious disease

communication: the verbal and nonverbal sharing of ideas, information, and feelings

community mental health centers: a type of mental health service that provides crisis intervention, emergency services, and short-term inpatient or outpatient services

complementary proteins: proteins that are combined to provide the eight essential amino acids

complete proteins: proteins that contain all eight of the essential amino acids

comprehensive major medical insurance: insurance plan that combines basic health insurance and major medical coverage

conception: fertilization; the union of an egg and sperm

cones: receptor neurons in the retina of the eye that register color in bright light

confrontation: a meeting with an alcoholic to present the facts about his or her drinking and behavior

consumer: a person who buys or uses products and services and who makes choices about how to spend time

consumer health: the study of products and services that have an effect on health

Consumer Product Safety Commission: develops and enforces safety standards for household products

Consumers' Research: a private group that tests and rates products on an impartial basis

Consumers' Union: a private group that tests and rates products on an impartial basis

controlling reinforcements: a technique used in which a person is given a reward for a desirable behavior and a punishment or lack of attention for undesirable behavior

convenience foods: foods that are easily prepared at home

conversion disorder: a disorder involving sudden changes in a person's body that, to some extent, provide a solution to a problem

cooling down: a training principle of physical fitness that involves at least 3 to 5 minutes of reduced exercise

coronary arteries: arteries that supply the heart muscle with blood

coronary bypass surgery: the rerouting of blood flow around a clogged coronary artery

coronary thrombosis: an obstruction caused by plaque deposits in a coronary artery

corporate health programs: programs to promote the health and well being of employees and their families

corpus luteum: part of the follicle left in the ovary following ovulation that forms a temporary endocrine gland

crab lice: pubic lice; tiny insects that invade the pubic area

cremation: the complete reduction of the deceased's body to ashes by intense heat

crematory: the place in which a person's body is cremated

crisis intervention services: a 24-hour service to help a person who experiences a crisis such as a suicide attempt, child abuse, or drug use

culture: a blend of the influence of people in your home, city, state and nation

cyclosporine: a fungal compound that blocks the production of white blood cells that fight organ rejection, but not those that fight infection

cystic fibrosis: a genetic disease that affects the mucous and sweat glands

dandruff: dead cells on the scalp

dating: the sharing of social activities and time with members of the opposite sex

decibels: a measurement of the intensity of sound

deductible: a specific dollar amount that must be paid by the individual in an insurance claim

defense mechanism: a behavior that you use to cope with uncomfortable situations or emotions

dehydrate: to lose too much water from the body

delirium tremens: DTs; symptoms a person has when he or she stops drinking alcohol

dementia: a condition of impaired thinking processes

denatured alcohol: a poisonous substance that is used for industrial purposes

Department of Health and Human Services (HHS): the department of the federal government that is responsible for the administration and planning for health

dependent personality: one that is very insecure and leans on others for advice and support

depressants: drugs that slow down the functions of the central nervous system

depression: a feeling of being sad, unhappy, or discouraged

dermatologist: a physician who specializes in diseases and disorders of the skin

desensitization: a technique used to help patients overcome fear and anxiety by gradually learning to cope with increasingly stressful situations

designer drugs: substances produced by individuals with little, if any knowledge about drug chemistry

detoxification: the process of getting alcohol out of an alcoholic's system and breaking the physical and psychological dependence

detoxification program: a program in which people are helped to withdraw from opiates

diabetes: a disease in which the body is unable to process the sugar in foods in normal ways

diabetes mellitus: a disorder in which the blood sugar level is abnormally high

dialysis: a process in which a person's blood is filtered by a special machine

digestion: the process in which food is chemically changed to a form that can pass through cell membranes

dioxin: a hazardous chemical now considered one of the most toxic wastes in the environment

disability: a physical or a mental impairment

disability insurance: provides income when you are absent from work for illness or injury

dislocation: the movement of a bone from its joint

dissociative disorders: disorders involving behaviors in which persons separate themselves and their memories from their real personality

dissolution: a legal way to end a marriage; the marriage partners decide conditions for settlement

distilled spirits: beverages with alcoholic concentrations higher than those reached by fermentation

distress: unsuccessful coping or a harmful response to a stressor

diuretic: a drug that causes the kidneys to produce excess urine

divorce: a legal way to end a marriage in which a judge decides the conditions for the settlement

dominant gene: prevents another gene from expressing itself

dose: the quantity or amount of a drug taken

Down syndrome: a genetic disease that is the result of an extra chromosome usually causing mental retardation

droplet infection: the spread of pathogens through a mist

drug: any substance other than food purposely introduced into the body to change normal body functions

drug abuse: substance or chemical abuse; the intentional use of drugs for reasons other than their intended medical purpose

drug dependence: the state of psychological and/or physical need that can occur in a person who uses drugs

drug misuse: the unintentional or inappropriate use of a drug

earthquakes: violent shakings of the earth

ectomorph: a person who is long-boned and has a lean body build

ectopic pregnancy: the growth of a fertilized egg in a part of the body other than the uterus

edema: a buildup of fluid in the body

EEG: electroencephalogram; a record of the electrical activity of the brain

ejaculation: the discharge of semen from the urethra

electrocardiogram: ECG; a test that graphs the electrical impulses of the heart muscle

embalming: the replacing of a dead person's blood with a special fluid that helps preserve the body

embryo: a developing cluster of cells

emotional maltreatment: type of action that involves mistreatment by a destructive way of relating

emotions: feelings used to respond to life situations

empty-Calorie food: a food that lacks nutrients and is high in Calories

endocrine system: glands that control many of the body's activities by producing hormones

endometrium: a soft, spongy tissue that forms the inner lining of the uterus

endomorph: a person who has a greater percentage of fat tissues and a flabby appearance

engagement: the time period between announcing marriage plans and making the marriage commitment

enriched food: a food that has vitamins added to replace those lost during food processing

environment: everything that is around you

Environmental Protection Agency (EPA): an agency established to implement and enforce laws to improve air, land, and water quality

environmental stress: the physical or mental demands associated with your surroundings

enzyme: a chemical that speeds up a chemical reaction

epidemic: a greater than average increase in new cases of a disease in a specific geographic area

epidemiologist: a scientist who studies disease patterns

epilepsy: a disturbance of impulses in the brain that causes seizures

erection: the expanding and stiffening of the penis

essential amino acids: those amino acids that must be obtained from the foods you eat

ethyl alcohol: type of alcohol in beverages; ethanol

eulogy: a speech given in which the deceased is praised

eustress: a healthful response to a stressor

euthanasia: the intentional ending of life for reasons of mercy

exhaustion stage: the stage of GAS that results in wear and tear on the body, lowered resistance to disease, and/or death

expenses: the items you need and want to buy

expiration: the process of forcing air out of the lungs

extended care facility: a facility that provides nursing, personal, and residential care

external respiration: the exchange of oxygen and carbon dioxide between the blood and the air in the lungs

fad diet: any diet plan suggesting quick weight loss without use of the healthful food groups

FADD: Fathers Against Drunk Driving

family: persons with whom you are related by blood, marriage, or other legal action

family therapy: a form of group therapy where family members of the patient meet with a therapist to interact with one another and discuss new ways of behavior

fast foods: mass-produced foods that can be served quickly

fat-soluble vitamins: vitamins that the body can store

fats: chemical substances that provide additional energy and help your body store vitamins A, D, E, and K

feces: solid waste materials that must be expelled regularly from the body

Federal Trade Commission (FTC): an independent agency that deals with advertising for foods, drugs, cosmetics, devices, and all advertising on national television

fermentation: a process whereby yeast cells act on sugar in the presence of water

fertilization: conception; union of a sperm and ovum

fetal alcohol syndrome: FAS; a condition usually accompanied by birth defects caused by the mother's use of alcohol

filling: the material used to repair the cavity in a tooth

first aid: the immediate and temporary care given to a person who has been injured or suddenly becomes ill

flashbacks: brief, sudden, distortions that are similar to those experienced when using LSD

flexibility: the ability to move the joints and muscles through a full range of possible motion

flu: influenza; a disease that affects the respiratory system and is caused by different viruses

Food and Drug Administration (FDA): the agency within the Public Health Service of HHS that checks the safety and effectiveness of foods, drugs and cosmetics

food group: foods that contain the same nutrients

fortified food: a food with extra vitamins added

fracture: a break or a crack in a bone

fraternal twins: two babies that develop from two different eggs being fertilized by two different sperm

freebasing: a chemical process in which cocaine powder is changed into a smokeable solution

frostbite: the damage to tissue caused by exposure to severe cold

FSH: follicle-stimulating hormone; stimulates the growth and development of follicles in the ovaries

funeral: a ceremony in which family and friends pay respect to a person who has died

general adaptation syndrome: GAS; the body's response to stress during the alarm stage, the resistance stage, and the exhaustion stage

general anxiety disorder: a disorder in which a person may feel anxious, tense, fearful, and upset most of the time

genetic counseling: counseling in which a couple is advised about their chances of producing offspring with birth defects

genetics: the scientific study of genes and how they determine and control development

genital herpes: an STD that is caused by two different but related forms of a virus known as herpes virus type I and herpes virus type II

genital warts: venereal warts; warts that usually are caused by a sexually transmitted virus

gerontologists: people who study aging

gerontology (jer un TAHL uh jy): the study of aging

gingivitis: a condition in which the gums are red, swollen, and bleed easily

goal: a desired achievement toward which you work

goiter: an enlarged thyroid gland

gonads: male reproductive glands

gonorrhea: the oldest known STD; among the most frequent infectious diseases in America today

grief: the open expression of sorrow

group prepaid plan: an insurance plan in which the fees for the services of physicians are paid for in advance

group therapy: a type of therapy where a number of people meet together with a therapist to react to one another as they discuss new ways of behaving

guilt: the feeling of having done wrong or being at fault

handicap: the limit that is set by a disability

hangover: nausea, tiredness, extreme thirst, and headache experienced after drinking too much alcohol

hashish: a drug derived from the cannabis plant but more potent than marijuana

hazardous waste: a harmful substance that is difficult to discard safely

HCG: a hormone produced by the placenta

health: a quality of life that includes your physical, mental, and social well-being

health appraisal: an evaluation of healthful behaviors and risk behaviors

health awareness: the knowledge you gain about your own health behaviors

health behavior contract: a specific plan that is followed to reach a desired health goal

health foods: foods that are claimed to benefit a person's health in a special way

Health Maintenance Organization (HMO): a group that provides comprehensive health services

Health Maintenance Organization Act: an Act requiring employers with 25 or more workers to allow these workers to join an HMO if one exists in the area

health promotion: the informing and motivating of people to maintain or adopt wellness behaviors

Health Resources and Services Administration: agency within the Public Health Service that assists in improving health resources and services

health status: the combination of the healthful and risk behaviors you select

healthful behavior: an action that helps prevent illness and accidents, helps promote health for you and others, or improves the quality of the environment

Healthy People: the Surgeon General's report on health promotion and disease prevention

heat cramps: are painful muscles caused by overexertion during hot, humid conditions

heat exhaustion: a health condition caused by extreme physical exertion and excessive sweating

heat stroke: a sudden attack of illness from exposure to high temperatures

hemoglobin: a substance that combines with oxygen and gives blood its red color

hemophilia: a sex-linked disease characterized by the absence of a factor necessary for blood clotting

hepatitis: viral liver infection where bile enters the blood causing a yellowing or juandice of the skin

heredity: the transmission of features from one generation to the next

heterosexual: a person who has a sexual preference for someone of the opposite sex

high-density lipoprotein: HDL; a substance in blood that prevents the formation of fatty deposits in arteries

histrionic personality: one who constantly behaves in ways to draw attention to himself or herself

hives: small, itchy lumps on the skin

holistic effect: the influence of a wellness or risk behavior on any one or more of the ten components of health

homeostasis (hoh mee oh STAY sus): the state in which the body remains relatively constant

homicide: the killing of a human being by another

homosexual: a person who has a sexual preference for someone of the same sex

hormones: chemicals that act as messengers and regulate body activities

hospice: a facility or program of caring for terminally ill persons and of counseling their families

hospital: a health-care facility where you receive medical care, diagnosis, and treatment on an inpatient or outpatient basis

hurricanes: violent storms with high winds and rains

hurt: a feeling of being distressed and harmed

hyperglycemia: high blood sugar level

hyperopia: farsightedness; visual condition in which a person sees distant objects clearly

hypertension: chronic high blood pressure

hypochondria: a somatoform disorder in which there is constant anxiety about illness

hypochondriac: one constantly anxious about illness

hypoglycemia: an uncommon condition in where there is too little sugar in the blood

hypothermia: a lowering of the body temperature to a level where body functions are affected

I messages: statements that tell about you, your feelings and your needs

ideal self: your conscience that tells you how you ought to be or how you would like to be

ideal weight: the weight and body composition that is recommended for your age, sex, height, and body build

identical twins: two babies that develop from the same egg and sperm

immunity: the body's resistance to disease

incest: any form of sexual activity that occurs between blood relatives as well as stepparents and stepchildren

income: the money you receive from different sources

incomplete proteins: proteins that lack one or more essential amino acids

infancy: the period of development from birth to one year

infectious disease: an illness caused by pathogens by direct or indirect contact; communicable disease

infectious hepatitis: a type of hepatitis usually transmitted through contaminated food and water; hepatitus A

influenza: flu; a disease that affects the respiratory system and is caused by different viruses

inhalants: a group of chemicals that produce vapors that have psychoactive effects when inhaled

inhalation: the absorption of substances into the bloodstream by passing through the lungs

inpatient: a patient who stays at the hospital while receiving health care

insomnia: a condition in which the inability to sleep becomes a pattern

inspiration: the process of taking air into the lungs

insulin-dependent diabetes: a disease characterized by little or no insulin produced by the pancreas

interferon: a protein that inhibits viral reproduction

internal respiration: the exchange of oxygen and carbon dioxide between body cells and circulating blood

in-vitro fertilization: IVF; conception that occurs in a laboratory environment rather than in a woman's body

involuntary muscles: those muscles over which you have no control

islets of Langerhans: cells located within the pancreas that produce the hormone insulin

isokinetic exercise: an exercise in which a weight, or resistance, is moved through an entire range of motion

isometric exercise: an exercise in which muscles are tightened for five to ten seconds with no movement

isotonic exercise: an exercise in which there is contraction of a muscle causing movement

jimsonweed: a psychedelic drug

joint: a place where two bones meet

kidney transplant: the exchange of an unhealthy kidney that does not function for a healthy kidney

Klinefelter syndrome: a genetic disease that occurs when a male has an extra X chromosome

laxative: a medication that stimulates the digestive tract so that there is a bowel movement

leukemia: cancer of the blood-forming tissues

leukoplakia: either a smooth white patch or a thick hardened sore on the inside of the mouth that has the potential to turn into cancer

LH: luteinizing hormone; a hormone secreted by the pituitary gland that promotes ovulation

life crisis: a shocking experience that involves a high level of mental stress

lifestyle: the way you live

lifetime sports: sports activities that can be continued as you grow older, provided you stay in good health

ligaments: tough bands of connective tissue holding bones together

lithotripter: a machine that uses a focused shock wave to crumble kidney stones

living will: a written document of a preference for medical treatment in the event of serious illness or injury

local health department: has responsibility for the health of persons who reside in your community

love: a strong affection or liking for someone or something

low birth weight: a baby's weight when it is less than five and one-half pounds at birth

low Calorie: a food with 0.4 Calories per gram or less

low-density lipoprotein (LDL): blood substance that is a factor in the formation of fatty deposits in arteries

lower-yield cigarettes: cigarettes made with tobaccos that yield reduced amounts of tar and nicotine

LSD: the most potent of the psychedelic drugs

lymph: the clear liquid of the blood that collects into spaces between the body cells

lymph nodes: structures of the lymphatic system that filter harmful organisms in the body

lymphatic system: part of the circulatory system that filters harmful organisms in the body

MADD: Mothers Against Drunk Driving; an interest group exerting organized campaigns to increase the penalties for those arrested for drunk driving

mainstream smoke: the smoke that a smoker inhales and exhales from his or her own cigarette

major medical coverage: insurance plan including payment of fees for prolonged injury or serious illness

malignant tumors: cancerous tumors that spread and grow when not treated

malnourished: condition resulting from not eating sufficient nutrients from the healthful food groups

malocclusion: the abnormal fitting together of teeth when the jaws are closed

mammogram: an X-ray examination of the breast

manic depressive disorder: mood disorder in which a person's moods vary from very high to very depressed

marijuana: a prepared mixture of the crushed leaves, flowers, stems, and seeds of the hemp plant, *Cannabis sativa*

marriage: a loving relationship in which two people make a commitment or pledge to love and care for each other

mausoleum: a building with a compartment for the deceased

maximum heart rate: a heart rate that equals 220 minus your age

Medic Alert tag: a medical identification that provides important information about the person wearing it

Medicaid: a federal government program to cover the cost of health care for low income persons and persons with special medical needs

Medicare: a federal government program that provides health insurance benefits for persons age 65 and older and for certain persons under age 65 who are disabled

megadose: an unusually large amount of a vitamin

meninges: membranes that surround the brain

menstrual cycle: series of hormonally controlled changes that occur monthly in a woman's body

mental health: a state of mind that allows you to be comfortable with yourself feel good about your relationships, and meet the demands of life

mental health specialists: persons trained to help examine and change behaviors harmful to mental health

mental health status: the combination of your healthful and risk behaviors with regard to being comfortable with yourself, feeling good about your relationships with others, and being able to meet the demands of your life

mental illness: a low self-esteem and self-concept, being unable to relate to others, and being incapable of coping with personal problems

mescaline: psychoactive ingredient of the peyote cactus

mesomorph: a person who has a muscular body build

metabolic rate: the rate at which your body burns calories

metabolism: the body's use of food

metastasis (muh TAS tuh sus): the spread of cancer cells in the body to other sites

methyl alcohol: the form of alcohol found in paint thinner or shellac; methanol

microorganisms: small living organisms that are invisible to the unaided eye

minerals: nutrients that regulate many of the chemical reactions in your body

miscarriage: spontaneous abortion; the ending of a pregnancy by natural causes

modeling: a technique in which the patient learns to handle a situation by observing how someone else would respond to a similar situation

moniliasis (moh nuh LI uh sus): a fungus or yeast infection caused by the overgrowth of a specific pathogen normally found in the vagina

mononucleosis: mono; a viral infection that is transmitted primarily by oral contact with exchange of saliva

mood disorders: disorders involving moods that are extreme and interfere with daily living

MS: multiple sclerosis; a disease characterized by a breakdown of the outer covering of the nerve fibers in the brain and spinal cord causing scar tissue to form

multi-infarct dementia: a disorder in which a person suffers many small strokes

multiple personality: a mental disorder in which two or more personalities coexist within the same person

multiple sclerosis: MS; a disease characterized by a breakdown of the outer covering of the nerve fibers in the brain and spinal cord causing scar tissue to form

muscular dystrophy: a disease that is characterized by weakness due to deterioration of muscle fibers

muscular endurance: the ability to contunue using muscular strength

muscular strength: the amount of force that your muscles can exert against resistance

mutation: a change in the genetic makeup of an organism

myocardium: the muscular wall of the heart

myopia: nearsightedness; a visual condition in which a person sees close objects clearly

narcissistic personality: one who is vain, boastful, conceited, and inconsiderate of others

narcotic antagonists: chemical compounds that selectively block the psychological and physiological effects of heroin or other opioids

National Institutes of Health (NIH): an agency within the Public Health Service that conducts and supports biomedical research, a research hospital, the National Library of Medicine, and the Fogarty International Center

neglect: a type of action that involves inadequate or dangerous child-rearing practices

nervous system: the network of nerve cells that carries messages or impulses to and from the brain and spinal cord to all parts of the body

neurologist: physician who diagnoses and treats diseases and disorders of the nervous system

neuron: a nerve cell

nicotine: a colorless, oily chemical in tobacco that produces physical dependence and a stimulating effect on the central nervous system

nitrous oxide: gas used as a dental anesthetic

noncommunicable disease: an illness that is not caused by a pathogen; a noninfectious disease

nondirective therapy: a form of treatment in which the client understands his or her present behavior and choices and decides what the goal of the treatment should be; client-centered therapy

nongonococcal urethritis: NGU; nonspecific urethritis (NSU); any inflammation of the urethra that is not caused by a gonorrheal infection

noninfectious disease: an illness not caused by a pathogen; a noncommunicable disease

noninsulin dependent diabetes: a disease characterized by the pancreas ability to produce some insulin, but the body cells are unable to use it properly

nonverbal communication: the use of behavior rather than words to share feelings

nutrients: chemicals in food that provide energy and materials for the growth, maintenance, and repair of cells

nutrition: the relationship of the food you eat to your health and well-being

obese: a weight 20 to 30 percent above the recommended body weight when the person is also overfat

obsessive-compulsive behavior: behavior characterized by unreasonable thoughts and actions

obstetrician: a physician who specializes in the care and treatment of a pregnant woman and her developing baby

Office of Consumer Affairs: investigates consumer problems, coordinates research, conducts seminars, and assists state and local governments

olfactory receptors: receptors that are sensitive to chemicals in vapor form that enter the nose

oncogenes (AHN koh jeenz): small, cancer causing parts of genetic material thought to be activated by both viruses and chemicals

opiates: psychoactive drugs derived from the opium poppy plant or made synthetically

optimum health: the best health possible for you

organic foods: foods that are grown without pesticides and chemical fertilizers

organic mental disorder: a change in mental health status caused by a physical condition that affects the brain

orthodontist: a dentist who treats malocclusion

OSHA: Occupational Safety and Health Act; minimum safety and health standards all employers must meet

ossification: a process by which bone cells and minerals replace cartilage

osteoarthritis: eroding of the moving parts of a joint

osteoporosis: a bone disease in which bone tissue becomes brittle and porous due to a loss of bone calcium

outpatient: a person lives at home while receiving regular care at a hospital, clinic, or private office

over-the-counter-drugs: OTC drugs; medications that can be purchased without a physician's prescription

overfat: a condition where you are in excess of your recommended percentage of body fat

overweight: a weight 15 percent above the recommended body weight when the person is also overfat

ovulation: the rupturing of a follicle and the release of a mature egg cell from the ovary

ozone: a harmful substance formed from the interaction of sunlight on pollutants

pacemaker: an electronic device that stimulates the heart to beat at regular intervals

paranoid schizophrenia: a disorder in which a person has delusions of either persecution or grandeur

paraplegic: a person who is paralyzed in the lower part of the body, including both legs

passive behavior: the holding back of ideas, opinions, and feelings

passive immunity: a type of immunity that results from the injection of antibodies produced by an animal into a person's body; short-term protection from a disease

passive-aggressive personality: one who switches back and forth between being forceful and frightened

pathogens: disease-causing organisms

PCP: angel dust; a psychedelic drug that may come in the form of powder, liquid, or tablets

pediculosis (pih dihk yu LOH sus): an STD caused by pubic lice or crab lice

pericardium: the fluid-filled sac which encloses the heart

periodontal disease: a disease of the gums and other tissues that support the teeth

periodontist: a dentist who specializes in the treatment of periodontal disease

peripheral (puh RIHF rul) nervous system: a system of nerves that branch from the brain and spinal cord to the periphery, or outer edges of the body

peristalsis: a series of involuntary muscle contractions in the digestive tract

personal health management: a plan you make for your health care

personality: an individual's unique blend of physical, mental, and emotional traits

personality disorder: a pattern of thinking, feeling, and acting so unusual that it interferes with the person's happiness and daily living

pesticide: any substance used to kill or control the growth of unwanted plants, insects, or animals

peyote: a psychedelic drug produced from cactus tips

philosophy of life: an overall vision of life or an attitude toward life and the purpose of life

phobia: the excess fear of a situation, object, or person

physical abuse: maltreatment that harms the body

physical dependence: a condition in which the presence of a drug becomes "normal" and necessary

physical fitness: a level of health in which you have muscular endurance, muscular strength, flexibility, cardiovascular endurance, and a lean body composition

physical profiling: a method of testing your physical limits to determine the types of sports that are best for you

plan: detailed steps you will take to reach your goal

plantar wart: a wart that grows on the bottom of a foot

plaque (PLAK): fatty deposits in arteries

plasma: the liquid part of blood

platelets: blood cells that help form clots to prevent blood from leaking from injured vessels

PMS: premenstrual syndrome; symptoms a woman may experience for several days before menstruation

pneumonia: condition of the lungs with fever, shortness of breath, headache, chest pain, and coughing

poison: any substance that can cause illness or death when introduced into the body

pollutants: harmful substances in our environment

pollution: the introduction of harmful substances into the environment

postpartum period: time after a baby is born

premature birth: the birth of a child before it is fully developed

prenatal care: the health practices a woman follows during her pregnancy

prenatal development: the growth of a baby in the uterus from conception to birth

prescription: written consent from a physician for a drug

prescription drugs: drugs that can be obtained only by written permission from a physician

preservative: a substance added to foods to prevent spoilage

principle of frequency: a training principle of physical fitness that involves how often you engage in your exercise program

principle of overload: training principle that involves increasing the body's capacity to do more work than usual

principle of progression: a training principle of physical fitness that involves gradually increasing the intensity and duration of exercise

principle of specificity: a training principle of physical fitness that involves choosing an exercise or activity that provides the desired benefit

principle of warming down: a training principle that involves at least three to five minutes of reduced exercise

principle of warming up: training principle of exercise involving 3 to 5 minutes of activity where the joints and muscles of the body are made ready to do more exercise

priority: something you consider to be of great importance

private health foundations: foundations formed to support nonprofit health and social service programs

private prepaid plans: an individual or group health insurance plan that may cover fees for the physician, hospital, and clinic based on predetermined fee schedules

private self: the actual you

problem-solving approach: a series of steps you apply to a situation to help you make a responsible decision

professional health association: an organization formed to meet the needs of a group of health-related professionals and to promote education in the health field

progressive relaxation: a technique used to induce nerve-muscle relaxation

prolactin: a hormone that stimulates the breast to produce milk

proof: double the percent of alcohol content in a beverage

proteins: chemical substances that are essential for the growth, development, and repair of all body tissues

psilocybin (si luh SI bun): a psychoactive ingredient derived from a type of Mexican mushroom

psoriasis (suh RI uh sus): a skin disease in which the skin is red and raised with white scales

psychedelic drugs: drugs that create illusions and distort the user's senses

psychiatric nurse: one who is trained in the care of persons with mental disorders

psychiatric social worker: one who concentrates on mental health casework

psychiatrist: a physician who specializes in the treatment of mental disorders

psychoactive drugs: substances that act on the central nervous system and change one's moods and behaviors

psychoanalysis: a form of therapy in which a patient examines past experiences in order to understand how those experiences might affect his or her present thoughts, emotions, and actions

psychological dependence: a strong desire to repeat the use of a drug for emotional reasons

psychological first aid: the process of helping people deal with the emotional aspects of injury or illness

psychologist: one who does not have a medical degree but is trained to administer psychological tests and diagnose and treat human behavioral disorders

psychopharmacology: the use of drugs in treating mental disorders

puberty: the stage of sexual development; males and females become physically able to produce offspring

pubic lice: crab lice; insects that invade the pubic area

public self: the opinion you want others to have of you

pulmonary emphysema: a disease in which the alveoli in the lungs lose the ability to expand and contract

pulse: the rhythmic expansion of an artery

quack: a person who promotes or sells ineffective or harmful health products and/or services

quackery: the promotion and selling of ineffective or harmful products and services

rape: the act of sexual intercourse against a person's will, and through the use of violence or force

rate of oxidation: the rate in which most persons oxidize about a half ounce of alcohol per hour

receptor neurons: neurons that receive information that is transmitted to the spinal cord and brain

receptor site: a specific part within a cell anywhere in the body where the chemical substance of a drug fits

recessive gene: a gene that is not expressed

recycling: the breaking down of products to their basic components so that they can be reused

red blood cells: cells that contain hemoglobin and are responsible for carrying oxygen to body cells

reduced Calorie: a food not limited in Calories per serving but must be at least one-third lower in Calorie content than similar foods

reflex: an involuntary response to changes inside or outside the body

reflex arc: the path of an impulse along sensory neurons to the spinal cord to motor neurons

rejection: the feeling of being abandoned and unloved

relationships: the associations you have with people

relaxation response: changes that occur due to the slowing of the body's activities using self-induced techniques to help restore homeostasis

remarriage: the marriage of two persons in which at least one has been married before

repression: the act of removing an anxiety-producing thought or event from the consciousness

resistance stage: the stage of GAS in which the body attempts to regain homeostasis

respiration: the exchange of gases between a living organism and its environment

respiratory therapist: a person trained in the treatment of patients with respiratory problems

responsible decision: a choice that promotes optimum health for you, others, and the environment

retainer: a plastic device with wires that keeps the teeth from moving back to their original places

Reye syndrome: a disease of children damaging to the central nervous system, and/or liver

rheumatic fever: an acute disease characterized by inflammation, swelling, and soreness of joints

rheumatic heart disease: a condition resulting from rheumatic fever in which the heart valves are so scarred they cannot open or close completely

rheumatoid arthritis: a disease in which joint deformity and loss of joint function occurs

Rh factor: a harmless substance in blood unless an Rh negative woman is pregnant with an Rh positive fetus

RIA test: a special lab test that can detect the presence of HCG in the blood

RICE treatment: a technique for treating musculoskeletal injuries

risk behavior: an action that helps increase the likelihood of disease and accidents, threatens your health and the health of others, and helps destroy the environment

rods: receptor neurons in the eye that are sensitive to light

root canal: pulp is removed from a decayed tooth and replaced with a material to keep the bacteria out

saccharin: an artificial sweetener that was found to cause a higher than normal incidence of bladder cancer in laboratory animals

SADD: Students Against Drunk Driving

saliva: a secretion of the salivary glands

saturated fats: fats obtained from foods of animal origin and are usually solid at room temperature

savings: the money you set aside for future use

schizoid personality: one who has disturbing thought patterns, prefers social isolation, and does not enjoy life

schizophrenia: a mental disorder in which there is a split or breakdown in logical thought processes

sebum: an oily secretion from the oil glands

sedatives: depressants that produce a calming effect, relax muscles, or relieve tension

self-actualization: making full use of your ability; the highest level on Maslow's Hierarchy of Needs

self-concept: all the beliefs you have about yourself; your self-evaluation, such as your strengths and weaknesses

self-discipline: the effort or energy with which you follow your plan to achieve optimum health

self-disclosure: making yourself known to others

self-esteem: respect or worth you have about yourself

semen (SEE mun): the mixture of sperm and fluids from the male reproductive glands

separation: an agreement between a married couple to live apart but remain married

septum: a wall that separates the two sides of the heart

serum hepatitis: hepatitis transmitted by transfusions of whole blood or blood products; hepatitis B

setpoint theory: a theory that you have a natural weight range that your body attempts to maintain

sex role: the way you act as a result of your attitude about being male or female

sexual abuse: inappropriate sexual behavior between an adult and a child

sexual assault: sexual activity that occurs using physical force or the threat of physical force

sexual orientation: preference that involves sexual activity with someone of the same or opposite sex

sexuality: your sex role, your sexual orientation, and your feelings about yourself

sexually transmitted diseases: STDs; infectious diseases spread by sexual contact with an infected person

shock: a condition in which the function of the vital organs of the body become slowed

sickle-cell anemia: a blood disease that results when an S hemoglobin gene is inherited from both parents

sickle-cell trait: a genetic disease that is a blood disorder caused by an inherited abnormality in hemoglobin

side effect: an unwanted result not related to the major purpose of the drug

sidestream smoke: the smoke you inhale from cigarettes being smoked by those around you; passive smoking

skeletal muscles: muscles that move the bones of the skeleton

smog: a combination of smoke and fog

smooth muscles: those muscles that line internal organs

snacks: foods and beverages consumed between meals

snuff: a flavored powder made from ground tobacco parts

solid wastes: substances such as trash, junk, and litter that pose threats to the environment

solubility: the ability of a drug to be dissolved

somatic nervous system: that part of the nervous system concerned with a person's external environment

somatoform disorder: a group of disorders in which there are physical symptoms of illness from emotional causes but no physical explanation of illness

sphygmomanometer (sfihg moh muh NAHM ut ur): an instrument that measures blood pressure

spinal cord: nerve tissue that extends from the base of the brain about two-thirds of the way down the back

spinal tap: the insertion of a needle into the fluid in the spinal column

spleen: an organ of the lymphatic system that helps remove used red blood cells

spontaneous abortion: the ending of a pregnancy by natural causes

sprain: an injury to the ligaments, tendons, and soft tissue around a joint caused by undue stretching

state health department: has responsibility for the health and well-being of the persons who reside in your state; takes action when harmful products are sold within the state

STDs: sexually transmitted diseases; infectious diseases spread by sexual contact with an infected person

stereotype: an assumption that people in a particular group will think or act in a certain way

sterility: the inability to reproduce

stethoscope: instrument that enables a physician to hear sounds inside a person's body

stimulants: drugs that increase the functions of those organs controlled by the central nervous system

strain: an overstretching of muscles and/or tendons

stress: the nonspecific response of the body to any demand made upon it

stress management skills: techniques used to help you cope and to prevent or lessen the harmful effects produced by the stress response

stress test: an ECG administered while a person walks or runs on a treadmill

stressor: a demand made upon the body

stroke: a condition caused by the sudden interference of blood flow through the brain

stroke volume: the amount of blood the heart pumps with each beat

suicide: the intended taking of one's own life

suppression: the act of postponing emotional responses to allow yourself time to reason, plan, and think

Surgeon General: a physician appointed by the President to direct the United States Public Health Service

symptom: a change in a normal body function pattern

syphilis: a type of STD less common than gonorrhea but much more serious

tar: a thick, sticky fluid produced when tobacco burns

target heart rate: a heart rate between 60 and 90 percent of the difference between your resting heart rate and your maximum heart rate

taste buds: receptor neurons on the tongue that are sensitive to chemicals in foods

Tay-Sachs: a genetic disease caused by an absence of a key enzyme needed to break down fats in the body

temperature inversion: cool air trapped under warm air

tendons: bands of tissues that attach muscles to bones

terminal illness: an illness that is incurable and will eventually cause death

thanatologists: scientists who study death

therapeutic community: trained professionals and former chemically-dependent individuals who help counsel the individual who has a drug problem

thermal pollution: excessive heat that is added to natural water supply

thermography: a process used to detect heat in the body

thrombus: clot; too much plaque builds up in a blood vessel, forming a clot that shuts off the flow of blood

time management plan: a plan that shows the time you will allocate for activities you do regularly and for leisure activities

time perspective: the way you usually view time

tolerance: a physical adaptation to a drug so that larger doses are needed to produce the original effect

tornado warning: a tornado has been sighted

tornado watch: weather conditions are favorable for a tornado to develop

tourniquet: a band applied to stop blood flow to a wound

toxemia: a condition marked by the sudden rise of blood pressure and the presence of protein in the urine after the twentieth week of pregnancy

toxins: poisonous chemicals produced by pathogens

trichomoniasis (trihk uh muh NI uh sus): an infection caused by protozoa that most often affects women

tumor: a lump of abnormal cells

Turner syndrome: a genetic disease that occurs when a female is missing an X chromosome

ultrasound: high-frequency sound waves that produce an image of the fetus

umbilical cord: the structure that connects the embryo to the placenta

underweight: a body weight 15 percent below the recommended body weight

United States Postal Service: protects the public against the use of mail fraud to promote products, devices, or services

unsaturated fats: fats from foods of vegetable, nut, or seed origin; usually liquid at room temperature

ureters: tubes that extend from the kidneys to the urinary bladder

urethra: a narrow tube leading from the bladder through which urine passes out of the body

urgent care center: a facility separate from a hospital that offers immediate care

urinalysis: the chemical examination of a person's urine

urinary bladder: a structure of the urinary system that stores urine

vaccine: weakened or dead pathogens introduced orally or by injection into a person's body

value: anything that is desirable or important to you

venereal warts: genital warts; warts that usually are caused by a sexually transmitted virus

vitamins: substances in foods that help other chemical reactions in the body take place

voluntary health organization: non-tax supported organizations that focus on a specific disease, health problem affecting certain body organs, or problems that are related to a large part of the population

voluntary muscles: muscles that a person can control

warts: raised skin growths caused by a virus

water-soluble vitamins: vitamins that are easily dissolved and cannot be stored in the body

wellness: the quality of a lifestyle you choose in order to achieve your highest potential for well-being

white blood cells: blood cells that destroy germs or harmful substances that enter your body

will: a legal document that describes how a person's possessions are to be distributed

withdrawal: a condition that occurs when the use of a drug to which one is physically addicted is discontinued

World Health Organization (WHO): an agency of the United Nations that seeks to improve the quality of health and well-being throughout the world

wound: any break in the continuity of the body's tissues

zygote: a fertilized ovum

INDEX

PHOTO CREDITS

Introduction: **2,** Shostal Associates; **4,** Mark Antman/The Image Works; **5,** Mimi Forsyth/Monkmeyer Press; **10,** Cobalt Productions; **17,** Courtesy American Heart Association. **UNIT 1: 22–23, 24,** Courtesy Ford Motor Company/Design Center; **28,** Runk/Schoenberger from Grant Heilman; **31,** Courtesy American Podiatric Medical Association; **37** (tr) Pat Lanza Field/Bruce Coleman, Inc., (bl)Courtesy General Electric, (br)© 1982, Technicare Corporation; **39,** Courtesy Wright State University, Dayton, Ohio; **42,** Antique Automobile Club of America; **47,** Pictures Unlimited; **51,** Doug Martin; **52,** Alec Duncan/Taurus Photos; **58,** Ted Rice; **59,** First Image; **62,** Courtesy Ford Motor Company; **67,** Jim Theologos/Monkmeyer Press; **68** (t)Tim Courlas, (b)Edward Lettau/FPG; **71,** Gerard Photography. **UNIT 2: 78–79,** Tim Courlas; **80,** Mimi Forsyth/Monkmeyer Press; **83,** Mary Messenger; **85,** Image Workshop; **89,** Doug Martin; **90** (t)Tony Freeman Photographs, (b)Cincinnati Convention and Visitor's Bureau; **94,** Mary Elanz Tranter; **97,** E. Degginger/H. Armstrong Roberts; **100,** Tim Courlas; **103,** Michal Heron/Monkmeyer Press; **106,** Paul Conklin/Monkmeyer Press; **115, 117,** Cobalt Productions; **118,** Mark Antman/The Image Works; **120,** Allen Zak; **124,** Brian Parker/Tom Stack & Assoc.; **129,** Doug Martin; **130, 131, 133,** Cobalt Productions; **134,** R. Bruce Satterthwaite; **137,** Brent Jones; **139, 140,** Cobalt Productions. **UNIT 3: 144–145,** George Anderson; **146,** S. Field/H. Armstrong Roberts; **148,** Tom Meyers; **150,** Pictures Unlimited; **151, 152, 154, 156,** Cobalt Productions; **157,** Brent Jones; **158,** J. Moss/H. Armstrong Roberts; **162,** Seghers 2/H. Armstrong Roberts; **164,** Ted Rice; **165,** J. Zimmerman/FPG; **168,** Elaine Comer; **171,** Children's Hospital, Columbus, Ohio/Cobalt Productions; **175,** File Photo. **UNIT 4: 178–179,** Tim Courlas; **180,** Lennart Nilsson, *Behold Man,* Little, Brown and Co., Boston; **186,** Gerard Photography; **188,** March of Dimes Birth Defects

Foundation/Tim Courlas; **189**, Doug Martin; **192** (l)James Westwater, (r)Elaine Comer; **193** (l)Ruth Dixon, (r)Tom McGuire; **194**, Tom McGuire; **195**, Ruth Dixon; **196** (l)Anne Schullstrom, (c)Eric Hoffhines, (r)Frank Balthis; **197**, Cobalt Productions; **199**, Mt. Carmel Medical Center/Allen Zak; **202**, H. Armstrong Roberts; **204**, Cobalt Productions; **205**, Doug Martin; **206** (l)Strix Pix, (c)Steve Lissau, (r)Larry Hamill; **207**, Ira Wyman/Sygma; **208**, Ohio Department of Aging/Gerard Photography; **209**, Studio Ten; **210**, Cobalt Productions; **211**, Image Workshop; **212** (t)Kevin Fitzsimmons, (b)Cobalt Productions; **215**, Suzanne Karp Krebs; **217**, Elaine Comer; **218**, Forest Lawn Memorial Gardens, Columbus, Ohio; **219, 220**, Cobalt Productions; **223**, Gerard Photography. **UNIT 5: 226–227**, Gerard Photography, George Anderson; **228**, Allen Zak; **230, 233, 236, 238**, Cobalt Productions; **240** (l)(lc)(c)(rc)Courtesy National Dairy Council, (r)Cobalt Productions; **242, 243**, Cobalt Productions; **250, 252**, Allen Zak; **255**, Tim Courlas; **257**, Doug Martin; **259** (l)(c)Hickson-Bender Photography, (r)Brent Jones; **261, 265**, Cobalt Productions; **266**, Gerard Photography; **267**, George Anderson.**UNIT 6: 270–271**, Joseph DiChello, Roy Gumpel/Leo DeWys; **272**, Tim Courlas; **275**, David Brownell; **276**, Elaine Comer; **278**, Cobalt Productions; **279**, Allen Zak; **280, 281, 282**, Cobalt Productions; **284**, Steve Lissau; **286**, Cobalt Productions; **288**, Ted Rice; **289, 292**, Doug Martin; **295**, Mt. Carmel Medical Center/Allen Zak; **296**, Peter Kaplan/The Stock Shop; **298**, Craig Kramer; **301**, Doug Martin; **304**, Cobalt Productions. **UNIT 7: 310–311**, Doug Martin, Larry Hamill; **312**, Larry Hamill; **314**, Pictures Unlimited; **320**, Carolina Biological Supply Company; **322**, David L. Perry; **323**, Carolina Biological Supply Company; **324**, Rod Planck/Tom Stack & Assoc.; **329**, Larry Hamill; **331**, First Image; **333**, David R. Frazier; **335**, Carl Toleno/Schenley High School, Pittsburgh, PA; **338**, Billy Grimes/TIME Magazine; **344**, David R. Frazier; **347**, Jerry Rosen/TIME Magazine; **350**, David Falconer/Frazier Photo Library; **353**, Al-Anon Family Group Headquarters, Inc./Gerard Photography; **355**, Alan Benoit; **360**, Canadian Cancer Society/Gerard Photography; **363**, David R. Frazier; **365**, Courtesy National Heart, Lung, & Blood Institute/Cobalt Productions; **368**, American Lung Association/Gerard Photography; **371**, Courtesy National Interagency Council on Smoking and Health; **372**, Ted Rice; **375, 376**, Courtesy Central Ohio Lung Association. **UNIT 8: 380–381**, BPS/Tom Stack & Assoc.; **382**, Latent Image; **384** (l)Roger K. Burnard, (r)File Photo; **385**, File Photo; **386**, Elaine Comer; **387**, BPS/Tom Stack & Associates; **391**, Centers for Disease Control, Atlanta; **392** (t)Doug Martin, (b)Centers for Disease Control, Atlanta; **394, 395, 396**, Centers for Disease Control, Atlanta; **397**, Gerard Photography; **402**, D. C. Lowe/Medichrome; **410**, Pictures Unlimited; **411**, John Youger; **412**, Dianora Niccolini/Medichrome; **419**, Mt. Carmel Medical Center/Allen Zak; **422**, Norman Prince; **424**, Tom Stack/Tom Stack & Assoc.; **425**, Larry Hamill; **426**, ECCO Family Health Center, Columbus, Ohio; **428**, Steve Lissau; **430, 431**, Cobalt Productions; **432**, Mt. Sinai Medical Center/Nancy Heim; **433**, Gerard Photography; **434**, Courtesy Lippin & Grant, Inc; **435**, David Brownell. **UNIT 9: 440–441**, Allen Zak, Ted Rice; **442**, George Anderson; **446, 448**, Ted Rice; **449**, Dave Davidson/Tom Stack & Assoc.; **450**, Cliff Beaver; **458**, Cobalt Productions; **462**, Doug Martin; **465**, Ted Rice; **466, 469, 471**, Gerard Photography; **472**, Courtesy St. Jude Children's Research Hospital; **475, 476, 478**, Ted Rice; **481**, Gerard Photography; **483**, Cobalt Productions. **UNIT 10: 486–487**, Ted Rice, Allen Zak, USDA; **488**, Allen Zak; **490**, Ted Rice; **495**, Courtesy National Highway Traffic Safety Administration; **496**, File Photo/Gerard Photography; **506**, Cobalt Productions/Grant Hospital; **509**, Gerard Photography; **510**, Cobalt Productions; **511**, Doug Martin; **514**, Gerard Photography; **519** (t)David M. Dennis, (b)Roger K. Burnard; **520**, Paul Nesbit; **551** (t)Al Staffan, (b)Stephen J. Krasemann/DRK Photo; **524**, Spencer Swanger/Tom Stack & Assoc.; **526**, AP/Wide World Photos; **527**, D. C. Wetter/Medichrome. **UNIT 11:530–531**, George Anderson, Gerard Photography; **532**, David R. Frazier; **535**, Ted Rice; **537**, American Heart Association; **539**, File Photo; **540**, Allen Zak; **541**, Ted Rice; **544**, David R. Frazier; **547**, Columbus Committee for UNICEF; **549**, File Photo; **552**, H. Armstrong Roberts; **554**, Jim Rudnick/A-Stock Photo Finders; **556**, Larry Hamill; **557**, Ted Rice; **558**, Dave Spier/Tom Stack & Assoc.; **559**, Jeffrey D. Smith/Woodfin Camp; **560**, Ted Rice; **561**, USDA; **563**, Ted Rice; **564**, Clyde Smith/FPG; **565**, Ted Rice; **568**, Eric Kroll/Taurus Photos; **569**, Larry Hamill.